# WILDERNESS PARTNERS

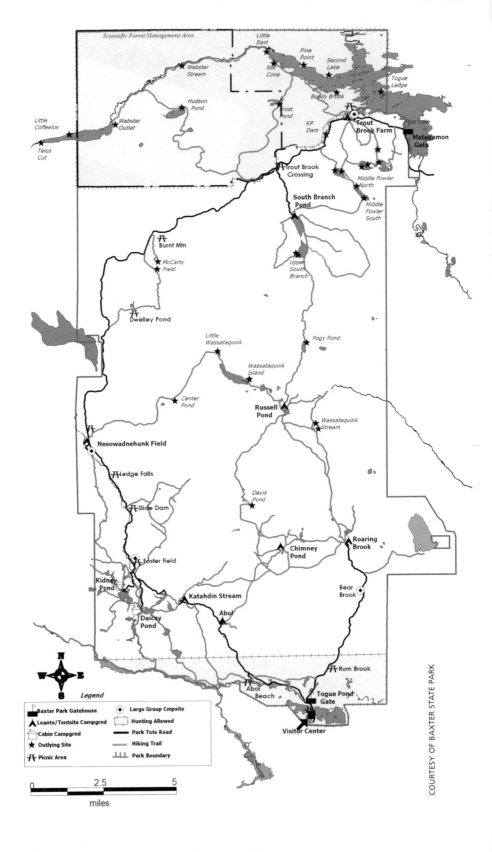

Scientific Forest Management Area

Little Coffelos

Telos Cut

Webster Outlet

Webster Stream

Hudson Pond

Little East

NW Cove

Pine Point

Second Lake

Frost Pond

Boody Brook

KP Dam

Togue Ledge

Trout Brook Farm

First Lake

Matagamon Gate

Trout Brook Crossing

South Branch Pond

Middle Fowler North

Middle Fowler South

Burnt Mtn

McCarty Field

Upper South Branch

Dwelley Pond

Little Wassataquoik

Pogy Pond

Wassataquoik Island

Center Pond

Russell Pond

Wassataquoik Stream

Nesowadnehunk Field

Ledge Falls

Davis Pond

Slide Dam

Chimney Pond

Roaring Brook

Foster Field

Kidney Pond

Katahdin Stream

Bear Brook

Daicey Pond

Abol

Rum Brook

Abol Beach

Togue Pond Gate

Visitor Center

Legend

Baxter Park Gatehouse

Leanto/Tentsite Campgrnd

Cabin Campgrnd

Outlying Site

Picnic Area

Large Group Cmpsite

Hunting Allowed

Park Tote Road

Hiking Trail

Park Boundary

N
W    E
S

0    2.5    5
miles

COURTESY OF BAXTER STATE PARK

▲▲▲▲▲▲▲▲

# WILDERNESS PARTNERS

*Buzz Caverly and Baxter State Park*

Phyllis Austin

TILBURY HOUSE, PUBLISHERS
Gardiner, Maine

TILBURY HOUSE, PUBLISHERS
103 Brunswick Avenue
Gardiner, Maine 04345
800–582–1899 • www.tilburyhouse.com

First paperback edition: December 2008
10 9 8 7 6 5 4 3 2 1

*Library of Congress Cataloging-in-Publication Data*
Austin, Phyllis, 1941-
 Wilderness partners : Buzz Caverly and Baxter State Park / Phyllis Austin. — 1st pbk. ed.
  p. cm.
 Includes bibliographical references and index.
 ISBN 978-0-88448-304-5 (pbk. : alk. paper)
 1. Caverly, Buzz, 1939- 2. Park rangers—Maine—Baxter—Biography. 3. Baxter State Park (Me.)—Management—History—20th century. 4. Wilderness areas—Maine—Baxter State Park—History—20th century. 5. Baxter State Park (Me.)—Biography. 6. Baxter State Park (Me.)—History—20th century. 7. Baxter State Park (Me.)—Environmental conditions. I. Title.
 SB481.6.C385A94 2008
 333.78′2160974125—dc22
 [B]
                                                                2008029574

Cover photograph of Katahdin from Kidney Pond by Kevin Shields
Cover photograph of Buzz Caverly by Joe Devenney
Designed by Geraldine Millham, Westport, Massachusetts
Copyediting: Genie Dailey, Fine Points Editorial Services, Jefferson, Maine
Printed and bound by Versa Press, East Peoria, Illinois

For everyone who cherishes and defends wilderness
and especially for
my beloved mother, Mabel S. Austin (1918–2007)

▲▲▲▲▲▲▲▲

## CONTENTS

## GLOSSARY OF ABBREVIATIONS

| | |
|---|---|
| ACF | Agriculture, Conservation and Forestry Committee |
| ADA | Americans with Disabilities Act |
| AMC | Appalachian Mountain Club |
| AT | Appalachian Trail |
| ATC | Appalachian Trail Conference |
| BLM | Bureau of Land Management |
| BSP | Baxter State Park |
| BSPA | Baxter State Park Authority |
| Bt | *Bacillus thuringiensis* |
| CCC | Civilian Conservation Corps |
| CETA | Comprehensive Employment and Training Act |
| CTC | Caribou Transplant Committee |
| DED | Department of Economic Development |
| DOC | Department of Conservation |
| DOT | Department of Transportation |
| FERC | Federal Energy Regulatory Commission |
| G-P | Georgia-Pacific |
| GNP | Great Northern Paper |
| IAT | International Appalachian Trail |
| IF&W | Inland Fisheries and Wildlife |
| KMPS | Katahdin Medical and Philosophical Society |
| LURC | Land Use Regulation Commission |
| MATC | Maine Appalachian Trail Club |
| NOLS | National Outdoor Leadership School |
| NPS | National Park Service |
| NRCM | National Resources Council of Maine |
| NWR | National Wildlife Refuge |
| SCA | Student Conservation Association |
| SFMA | Scientific Forest Management Area |
| TPS | Trust for Public Land |
| TWS | The Wilderness Society |
| UMO | University of Maine at Orono |
| USGS | United States Geological Survey |
| YCC | Youth Conservation Corps |

**PREFACE**

THERE SEEMED TO BE DESTINY in my writing this book, as there was in Buzz Caverly joining the Baxter State Park ranger crew in 1960. By the time Buzz left the park as director in 2005, I had been reporting on park politics and controversies for thirty-five years, first for the Associated Press and then for the statewide weekly, *Maine Times*. As the journalist who had followed such a seminal era in the park's history, I felt a responsibility to write about the storied character at the center of it all.

In 2000, anticipating Buzz's retirement, I started interviews with him, expecting that it would be a long research project. It turned out to take seven years. The research was stop-and-start because of the illnesses and deaths of all members of my immediate family. Writing the book became a source of comforting focus outside the sadness of such great loss.

There are two official park history books. *Legacy of a Lifetime: The Story of Baxter State Park* by Dr. John W. Hakola, has stood for twenty-seven years as the principal scholarly account. The sequel, *In the Deeds We Trust* by Dr. Trudy Irene Scee, covers a number of defining park issues of the period 1970 to 1994. Prior to publication, both books were subject to revision by park history committees.

*Wilderness Partners*, on the other hand, is an assessment of Buzz Caverly's career and the events he helped shape from 1960 to 2006. There is some unavoidable overlap with the Hakola and Scee books because of Buzz's role in the making of park history. However this book is an independent work.

From 1970 to 2005, I followed park issues as a journalist and have written this book from the fortuitous position of having known so many park leaders and employees and having attended Baxter State Park Authority meetings for decades. Throughout the book, I have called on my own knowledge and experience as a witness to the evolution of the park and its important controversies.

Buzz's early years in the park in the 1960s were the most interesting to research and the easiest to write about because the times were so experiential. His field reports were rich in detail of the life of a ranger in that bygone era. When Buzz entered the ranks of management in 1968, his story thinned out. He kept no personal diary and few letters.

As for official documents of his management years, Buzz's trail was difficult to follow because of the destruction of key park records. By the late 1980s, state laws and regulations dealing with agency archival files guided the elimination of records on a systematic basis, making the documents saved in earlier years all that more valuable. Some of the otherwise unavailable files that Buzz provided were his annual management reviews from the Authority chairs. The evaluations were evidence that every Authority over three decades rated Buzz an outstanding administrator, manager, and leader.

Interviewing 180 people associated with Buzz and the park filled in many blanks, and conversations with them was my reward in writing this book. I felt privileged to sit face to face with Helon Taylor's rangers from the 1950s and 1960s to hear their accounts of life in the park almost sixty years ago and their memories of Buzz. Their tales were so fascinating that each one deserves a monograph of his own.

Getting to know my primary subject was an adventure. I hiked and traveled with Buzz in the park and spent many days interviewing him at his home in East Corinth and at park headquarters in Millinocket. I probed sensitive subject matter. I unearthed his management weaknesses in the process of finding out why his tenure was peppered with controversy. He had shortcomings, as do we all. However, I concluded he was truly a larger-than-life individual. I found a depth of commitment and courage behind Buzz's park defender image that is realized by living one's beliefs. It took a long time studying Buzz's style of leadership, relationships, and the changing times to grasp just how important he was to the wilderness park that thrives today.

I couldn't have been in position to write Buzz's story without the influence of my family and Peter Cox, co-founder and editor of *Maine Times*. My parents figured prominently in my earliest interest in the outdoors in North Carolina's Piedmont country and the Pamlico shore; those southern forests and waters set my path to Maine and Baxter Park. After arriving in Maine in 1969 and first visiting the park in 1970, my own passion for wilderness developed quickly. The activist paper I joined in 1974 was a rare opportunity to concentrate on environmental journalism, and Peter gave me free rein to persistently write about Baxter Park.

My thanks extend to the Maine State Archives staff, notably Anne Small and Anthony Douin, and to Maine State Library reference librarians Melanie Mohney and Cathryn Wilson. All were wonderfully helpful in providing park records that reside in their care. Charlie Campo, chief librarian at the *Bangor Daily News*, was a gem in finding past park news stories, and I also received timely assistance from the staff in the Portland Room at the Portland Public Library. The Baxter Park staff offered unrestrained access to files at the Millinocket headquarters and were gracious with their time in searching for requested documents in their own personal files. Lester Kenway retained his trail files from 1979 to the time he resigned as trail leader in 2000, and those documents were a godsend. There were two confidantes who were critical to my understanding of Buzz's relationship with different Authorities over the years, and they will remain confidential but will know that I trusted their perspective and am greatly indebted to them for sharing it with me.

Editor and author Liz Pierson oversaw the initial review and editing of the book, providing indispensable guidance on how to elevate Buzz's story over that of park history. My friend Debora Price read parts of the manuscript with a critical eye, correcting my parochial accent and making many helpful suggestions.

Before I ever put pen to paper, author Bunny McBride challenged me to write this book and sustained me with enthusiasm to complete it when continuing was difficult. Publisher Jennifer Bunting at Tilbury House never doubted that I would deliver and kept the due date flexible in response to my family's needs. I wish my dear mother, father, sister, and Peter Cox were still living to celebrate with the rest of us the conclusion of this effort.

I discovered that writing a book about the controversial career of a living person carries its own particular responsibility for honesty, as best as that can be determined at the moment. Buzz and Jan Caverly invested a tremendous amount of time and faith in me, not knowing what the book would say about him or the kind of legacy I would conclude he left. They knew there would be some revealing material in the book. But they wanted the whole story told.

My hope is that the book, with the new details on important issues, will be a valuable addition to the historical record of the park, and that I have accurately portrayed the extraordinary role of Buzz Caverly in the Baxter Park we have to enjoy and explore today.

—Phyllis Austin
Brunswick, Maine

**INTRODUCTION**

WHAT WERE THE TWO OF THEM THINKING?

Percival P. Baxter, the wealthy philanthropist and former governor of Maine, surprised at mid-morning in his Portland office by a tenderfoot ranger from Baxter State Park.

Buzz Caverly, coltish, curious, and impulsive enough to seek out this larger-than-life figure in a strange city.

None of park supervisor Helon Taylor's rangers had ever appeared unannounced in Portland, 225 miles south of Governor Baxter's great wilderness preserve. Buzz drove around the Congress Street block of the Trelawny Building several times while gathering his courage. At the bottom of the polished mahogany stairway that led to Baxter's office, he hesitated momentarily. He felt the gaping differences between Percival Baxter's cultured world and his own rural Cornville roots, but he swallowed hard and walked up to the fifth floor.

Surprisingly, there was no awkwardness between the two men. Both loved nothing more than Baxter State Park, and they fell easily into talking about their favorite subject for almost an hour. They reminisced about their most memorable experiences, especially at Russell Pond and Chimney Pond. Baxter kept returning to his reasons for creating the park and the "forever wild" goals he hoped to accomplish.

Twenty-one-year-old Buzz was light-headed from excitement, mesmerized by the time alone with the man he considered a hero because of his gift to the people of Maine and the nation. Percival Baxter, now eighty-five and concerned about who would carry on his park mission, must surely have been struck by the unusual show of gusto and passion from his youngest ranger.

The Portland meeting on December 18, 1961, wasn't the first time the two had met. Baxter visited the park twice a year as long as his health allowed, and he first shook hands with Buzz at Abol Campground in 1960. It was there, at Buzz's first ranger post, that Baxter invited him to Portland during the off-season—an invitation the cordial former governor may have given to other "Helon's boys," not necessarily expecting any of them would take him up on it.

When Buzz returned to the park, he told Taylor about his meeting with Baxter. "He's a grand old man, isn't he?" Taylor commented. Yes, splendid he was and appreciated as such, in and out of Maine, for a long list of achievements before creating Baxter Park: reforming the state's educational system, establishing a school for the deaf, blocking the giveaway of Maine's water resources without compensation, supporting women's rights, fighting against abuse, and battling vivisectionists and the Ku Klux Klan.

▲ ▲ ▲ ▲ ▲

Baxter was a Yankee patrician, a scion of one of Portland's most cultured, influential, and rock-ribbed Republican families. As such, he had access to far-flung business and political circles. As far back as his state legislative days and gubernatorial years, when his idea of a park project took root, he was cultivating acquaintances and friendships with national political and conservation leaders. Among the luminaries were presidents Herbert Hoover, Warren G. Harding, Franklin D. Roosevelt, and Dwight D. Eisenhower; New York City's master builder Robert Moses; federal forest and parks notables Gifford Pinchot, Harold Albright, and Stephen Mather; and The Wilderness Society principals Robert Marshall, Robert Sterling Yard, and Howard Zahniser.[1] Hoover even offered Baxter an ambassadorship. When Baxter declined, the president offered him other high-profile possibilities, among them membership on a federal conservation commission.[2]

However by 1930, Baxter was self-assured that his "entire interest in politics and in life in general is right here in Maine, where I intend to remain and play my part."[3] He already knew his path. He would create a large state park around Katahdin, the tallest mountain in Maine—dramatized in the mid-1800s by writer/explorer Henry David Thoreau and exalted in the ensuing years by American landscape artists, notably Frederic Church and Marsden Hartley.[4] Protecting the remote mountain, regardless of its unmatched (in Maine) grandeur and allure, was an idea the legislature had previously rejected, even laughed at. But Baxter was undeterred. The once vast wilderness of the unsettled north had been felled by loggers, who had cut so hard that traditional lumbering was over and in its place was industrial-scale papermaking. Baxter was determined to save the Katahdin area from further exploitation.

The first of twenty-eight land gifts he made to the state over thirty-three years came in 1931 and secured part of the Katahdin township that included much of the 5,267-foot mountain. Five years later, when Baxter learned of Maine Congressman Ralph Owen Brewster's bill to allow the federal government to establish a national park around (and including) his beloved Katahdin, he turned to well-placed friends in Washington for help in defeating the plan.[5] When that battle was over in 1938, the victorious Baxter withdrew from the national scene and concentrated on knitting together the rest of the 200,000 acres he envisioned for his park.

But Washington didn't lose sight of Percival Baxter. In the 1960s, the last decade of his life, Baxter was still receiving appreciative letters from the White House and the Secretary of the Interior for accomplishing his remarkable goal.

Percival Baxter made Baxter State Park unique in the nation—and perhaps the world—by purchasing the lands with his own money, establishing trust funds for the park's financial support, creating an independent park authority to oversee it all, and mandating that the primary mission was to "preserve and protect" the natural resources, with recreation secondary. It was quite a feat for an early twentieth-century wildlands philanthropist, especially when the major opponents were powerful paper companies that owned most of the land needed for the park. The last parcel added by Baxter was in 1963, six years before his death at age ninety-three.

In his writings and in the deeds transferring the gifts from Baxter to the state, Percival Baxter called his park a "wilderness" and a "sanctuary for wild beasts and birds."[6] He never defined what he meant by wilderness, a term given a legal definition in the 1964 federal Wilderness Act. The park never met that strict meaning, because Baxter allowed roads, vehicle access, campgrounds, buildings, and motorized tools for rangers.

However, for almost eighty years, the amazing array of natural attributes of the park—forty-six mountains, fifty-five lakes and ponds, pockets of virgin forest, the almost impenetrable Klondike, outstanding alpine and subalpine "islands," and rare plants and animals—have been reason enough for Mainers and park lovers to consider it wilderness.

▲ ▲ ▲ ▲ ▲

By the time Buzz knocked on Baxter's door, Providence appeared to be helping Baxter find someone to whom he could pass his mantle. The same mysterious guidance seemed to be at work on Buzz, steering him to apply for a ranger's job to please his father instead of pursuing his own desire to become a state trooper.

Buzz's trip to Portland surely impressed Baxter. Later, when Buzz felt forced to leave his seasonal job for year-round work to support his growing family, Baxter responded by reaching into his own pocket to pay for Buzz's winter salary, making him a year-round employee and keeping him at the park.

When Buzz was first appointed supervisor in 1968, Baxter charged him with following Helon Taylor's example of setting "a high standard" of leadership. Baxter let Buzz know that he thought of him "often." Several months before Baxter died in 1969, he wrote Buzz another note, letting him know how much he was depending on him. *"We are partners in this project,"* said Baxter.7 Those words resounded in Buzz like a heartbeat for the rest of his life.

During Buzz's career, from 1960 to 2005, he was in charge of park operations for most of those forty-five years. Like a hero out of a Horatio Alger novel, he rose from humble beginnings and limited education to succeed through tireless work, grit, spirit, and courage.

Buzz Caverly became Baxter's "general," with an upbeat, infectious passion about keeping the governor's vision alive and protecting the resources, no matter what career risks he had to take. In an article on one of the "line in the sand" battles over motorized access to the park, the *Boston Herald* magazine described Buzz as "a grinning combination of [NBC weatherman] Willard Scott and [Gulf War] General Norman Schwarzkopf."8

Buzz had the strength of conviction to stand defiantly against all manner of park opponents and, at times, his own bosses, because he was captivated by Baxter—pure and simple. First, it was because of who Baxter was and all he did for the people of Maine. Then it was the direct conversations Buzz had with Baxter and the exchange of personal letters that gave him a feeling of credibility and "authority" he wouldn't have felt otherwise. The "glitter" that fell from Percival Baxter over Buzz transformed him into the most influential and enduring figure in park history other than Baxter himself.

How Buzz, the rangers, and the park's users interacted on that landscape over almost a half century is entertaining and intriguing, reflecting a rustic way of living and recreating that largely has passed. The period was peppered with controversy over Buzz's dominant (and, some said, domineering) and idiosyncratic style and over votes by the Baxter Park Authority that were politically motivated. Both behind the scenes and in public, the fight for the heart and soul of the park among insiders and outsiders was an ongoing battle.

Without Buzz—his management continuity, the values he held, and his reverence for Percival Baxter—decisions on both important and ordinary matters could have well turned out differently for Baxter State Park. Buzz was a minimalist, approaching issues with the philosophy that "less is more" and that the park's natural resources would evolve to a healthier state on their own if he could just keep people from interfering with them too much. He was convinced that a conservative, defensive position on everything from recreational use to finances was the way to keep faith with Percival Baxter.

For Buzz, Baxter Park was a magnificent obsession. His "preachering" about Baxter—the man and the park—was inspiring to generations of employees, generations of entire families, and many others who visited and loved the park. When all was said and done, the net effect of his lifelong leadership was to root in peoples' consciousness the fact that the park was a legal and sacred trust, and that its caretakers' foremost mission was to carry out the wishes of the donor, not those of political or special interests.

▲ ▲ ▲ ▲ ▲

Although tens of thousands of American and international visitors travel to Baxter Park each year, it is not known as much outside New England as the region's other wild jewels—the White Mountains and the Adirondack Park, with its million-acre wilderness preserve. Percival Baxter didn't want Baxter Park advertised and in 1959 had refused the White House a Christmas tree from the park to avoid the publicity.[9] Moreover, with the word "state" in the name, perhaps it has been easy for people to assume that Baxter is just another state park, and small and lacking in the natural features associated with wilderness.

Yet it doesn't take long for people entering the park gates to recognize what an extraordinary place it is. Even when early caretakers were struggling to clean up the park's dumps, stop poaching, and control overuse, national figures were singing its praises. Myron Avery, chairman of the Appalachian Trail Conservancy (ATC), penned many articles in the 1930s lauding the natural characteristics that he felt qualified the preserve for federal park status.[10] Writer Edmund Ware Smith achieved national fame partly because of the books and articles on his park experiences that he wrote for *Field & Stream* and other publications in the 1950s and 1960s.[11] U.S. Supreme Court Justice William O. Douglas and Secretary of the Interior Stewart Udall also glorified the park in books.

In 1961, Douglas wrote in *My Wilderness: East to Katahdin* that if the human species is to survive, "we must make Katahdin the symbol of our struggle for independence from the machine that promises to enslave us. We must multiply the Baxter Parks a thousandfold" to provide a "great school of the outdoors" for the increasing population so they will "discover the never-ending glories of God's wilderness."[12] Three years later, Udall, in *The Quiet Crisis,* called Baxter "the most majestic state park in the nation."[13]

American presidents continued to keep in touch with Percival Baxter. John F. Kennedy sent Baxter birthday greetings in 1962, and in 1967 Lyndon B. Johnson praised him for his "unmatched decades of selfless public service . . . and achievements for the beauty of America."[14]

▲ ▲ ▲ ▲ ▲

In addition to an abundance of kudos, Percival Baxter and Buzz Caverly received many prestigious national awards over the years. In 1948 Baxter was awarded the then-highest recognition for park achievements in the U.S.—the gold Pugsley Medal from the American Scenic and Historic Preservation Society. Interior Secretary Udall traveled to Baxter's hospital bedside in 1962 to present him with the department's Conservation Service Award in recognition of his pioneering efforts on behalf of wilderness.

In 1991 Buzz was presented the Olaus and Mardy Murie Award from The Wilderness Society for his "uncompromising commitment" and "tireless effort toward preserving one of the most spectacular places in the eastern United States." He has been honored with many other regional and state environment awards for his extraordinary park stewardship.

As a team, Percival Baxter created and Buzz Caverly sustained and strengthened Baxter State Park and its "forever wild" mandate to ensure its preservation for future generations. Their gift is beyond measure.

---

1. Percival P. Baxter Collection, Maine State Library, Augusta.
2. *The Baxters of Maine: Downeast Visionaries,* by Neil Rolde, Tilbury House, Publishers, Gardiner, Maine, 1997, p. 295.
3. Ibid, p. 295.
4. *Katahdin: An Historic Journey,* by John Neff, Appalachian Mountain Club Books, Boston, 2006, p. 130.
5. *The Baxters of Maine: Downeast Visionaries,* p. 253.
6. *Legacy of a Lifetime: The Story of Baxter State Park,* by John Hakola, TBW Books, Woolwich, Maine, 1981, pp. 101; 114–16.
7. Letter from Percival Baxter to Buzz Caverly, May 20, 1968.
8. *Boston Herald* Sunday magazine, August 18, 1991, pp. 6, 8, 13.
9. Letter from Percival Baxter to Al Nutting, August 18, 1958.
10. *Legacy of a Lifetime,* pp. 155–58.
11. Edmund Ware Smith, *Field & Stream:* April 1, 1959; July 1, 1959; May 1, 1960; April 1, 1962; December 1, 1965.
12. *My Wilderness: East to Katahdin,* by William O. Douglas, Doubleday & Co., Inc., Garden City, New York, 1961, p. 290.
13. *The Quiet Crisis,* by Stewart Udall, Avon Books, New York, 1964, p. 152.
14. *The Baxters of Maine,* p. 298.

Conversations and communications: Buzz Caverly, Neil Rolde, Doug Scott, Howard Whitcomb, George Wuerthner.

# PERCY BAXTER'S DREAM COME TRUE

PERCIVAL PROCTOR BAXTER (1876–1969) first sighted Katahdin in 1903 when he was twenty-seven years old. The occasion was a trout-fishing trip to Kidney Pond with his father. "We came to Kidney Pond by railroad, tote team, and on foot," according to Baxter. "It was an interesting experience. [Highway] Commissioner [David] Stevens had not put his magic touch on the rock and mud of that region."

Baxter's reference to his inaugural Katahdin experience was in a speech delivered for him by Maine Forest Commissioner Austin Wilkins at the opening ceremony for the Togue Pond gatehouse on August 10, 1967. Percy never wrote down how he *felt* upon seeing Katahdin sixty-four years earlier, only about the modes of transportation employed to reach Kidney Pond, where Irving O. Hunt had recently built a sporting camp. From most anywhere on the pond's shore, he would have had a dazzling view of the southwestern slope of Katahdin, the Gateway, and South Peak, and, northwest, some of the lower, splendid peaks of Nesowadnehunk Valley.

Despite Percy's silence about the moment he first laid eyes on the mountain, a later experience suggests it must have been electric, given his decision to dedicate his life to preserving what was Maine's grandest massif. His father, James Phinney Baxter, was dutiful in keeping a diary, but he doesn't mention the Kidney Pond trip in his 1903 journal. There is a ten-day interruption of his entries for September, and it's reasonable to believe that was the period the Baxters made the Kidney Pond trip.

It would be seventeen years before Percy Baxter would make his first climb of Katahdin, and by that time, he was an experienced politician and had initiated efforts in the legislature to have the state acquire the Katahdin area for preservation. In contrast to his first sighting of Katahdin, Percy's inaugural hike—up the steep Pamola Peak

Trail—was documented and publicized. He was part of a group of upstanding Mainers who also were interested in the state park idea. The lengthy account in the *Lewiston Journal Illustrated Magazine* on October 2, 1920, two months after the venture, was largely comical, reflecting the trials and tribulations of the transit to Katahdin and the physical demands of the climb itself. The article's author, *Journal* editor Arthur G. Staples, mentioned Percy several times. Whimsically, he pondered why blackflies didn't bite Percy. After summiting Katahdin, Percy declared he "wouldn't do it again for a million; I wouldn't have missed it for a million," Staples reported.[1]

A dozen years passed before Baxter's next climb up Katahdin over the arduous Hunt Trail in September 1932. His second hike, with two Baxter Park Authority members and two Great Northern Paper Company officials, was to place a bronze plaque on a boulder at the summit to commemorate the creation of the park in 1931. Percy repeated the hike over the Hunt route to the peak in September 1933, this time with twenty-one of Millinocket's prominent citizens for an "inspection" of the mountain.

There is no evidence that Baxter ever stood on Baxter Peak again. As much as he obviously loved the mountain and was dedicated to preserving the wilderness experience, he apparently spent little time in the north woods experiencing it for himself. When visiting the Katahdin area, he stayed for only brief periods, overnighting at tourist or hotel establishments or sporting camps rather than roughing it at primitive park facilities.

It would take Baxter more than three decades to acquire the twenty-eight parcels that would comprise the park by the early 1960s. His initial purchase from Great Northern in 1930 was the center-piece—5,960 acres, including most of Katahdin. Baxter's intention then was to amass 100,000 acres. However, as he progressed with his project, his success emboldened him to set higher goals, finally reaching 201,000 acres in 1962, when he was eighty-five years old. At the time, the park was the fourth largest in the U.S., and Baxter consented to future expansion after he was gone from the scene.

The land transfers from Baxter to the state, called the Deeds of Trust, provided the legal grounding, as well as inspiration, for the Authority in making policy decisions, for the attorney general in making basic rulings, and for justices or others seeking legal clarifications of policies or operations. Although Baxter relaxed restrictions in sequential trust provisions, he clarified for future generations that the park was to be "maintained primarily as a wilderness" and recreation could not "encroach upon the main objective . . . which is to be 'forever wild.'"[2]

As Baxter had given the state one tract after another, he became concerned about what would happen to his park after he died. In 1939 he said in a letter to Governor Lewis O. Barrows, "In conveying these lands to the State of Maine a definite Trust is created, and I have the utmost confidence that the word of this Sovereign State as given by the Chief Executive and by the representatives of the people never will be broken and that this State never will violate the Trust provisions in the Deeds it accepts from me."[3]

The challenges that Baxter faced in negotiating the land purchases were Herculean—upsetting land and hydropower owners, cultural traditions, personalities, and politics. But from early childhood, Baxter showed a resolute character and self-confidence that were essential in helping him achieve his strikingly ambitious ends. The most repeated story is how, at seven years of age, the boy managed to land by himself an eight-pound trout on Oquossoc Lake near Rangeley, collected the promised ten dollars a pound from his father, and invested the money, leaving it in a bank account for almost fifty years until the eighty dollars had grown to more than a thousand.

Frugality was a long-standing trait in the Baxter family, whose English immigrant ancestors started out as hand-to-mouth Connecticut Yankees in the late 1600s. The Baxters drifted with the flow of settlement into northern New England. In Maine, the family was restless, moving here and there before putting down roots in Portland, where they prospered.

Young Percy—"tall, blond, erect" and a sixth-generation American—was molded by a privileged upbringing in a stable, upper-middle-class family of eight children, exposed to fine culture at home and abroad, and provided an excellent education.[4] He was very close to his father, James Phinney Baxter, who put a lot of value on character building, service to community, charitable giving, creating visions for political reform, and cleaning up and beautifying Portland. Percy had a perfect role model in observing how his father handled difficult problems and personalities—most pointedly when James Phinney fought to create a green belt along Back Bay. "James Phinney's stubbornness and perseverance [in achieving his goals] had to be an inspiration to his son," said Neil Rolde, author of *The Baxters of Maine: Downeast Visionaries.*

A highlight of Percy's boyhood summers was adventures in the north woods. In the 1880s, his father introduced the brood to the wild, taking them on fishing trips to the Rangeley Lakes, and then, when they were older, to the Katahdin area.

Percy's first experience abroad came when he was nine years old. James Phinney, a noted historian, picked his three youngest ones—Percy and his two stepsisters (James Phinney's first wife had died shortly after childbirth)—to accompany him to Europe and Great Britain. They traveled to Ireland, Scotland, and Europe, and then they settled down in London. James Phinney set out to acquire original documents related to New England's colonial past, and the children were enrolled in English schools. Percy attended the day school connected to the famed Eton boarding institution.

Upon his return to Maine, Percy reentered public school. He was an adequate student at Portland High School but popular because he was also a varsity football athlete. After graduating in 1894, he was accepted at his family's alma mater, Bowdoin College in Brunswick. Three of his half-brothers had preceded him to the exclusive private school, and his father was an overseer of the institution and had received his first honorary degree from Bowdoin. Percy, who fell in love with Irish setters as a boy, felt enfranchised enough by his family standing at Bowdoin to have his dog live with him at his fraternity, DKE, and accompany him to classes.

Percy showed increasing intellectual and creative strength in college. A gifted orator in the eyes of his classmates, he co-founded and became editor of the *Quill*, a literary magazine, and was editor in chief of the student newspaper, the *Orient*. His high marks qualified him for membership in Phi Beta Kappa, the national society for academic achievers.

Percy's fun-loving nature at that time got him into trouble with the law. In his sophomore year, he joined a group of Bowdoin Republicans and disrupted a big Democratic political rally in Bath by singing a GOP "fight song." He became a hero to his Republican classmates by getting arrested and thrown into jail for a few hours before he was sprung by the mayor of Bath as a courtesy to Portland mayor James Phinney Baxter. James Phinney wasn't amused by the town's reaction and sued the municipality for wrongful arrest. A jury exonerated Percy, but awarded him one cent rather than the thousand dollars in damages being sought. The *Bath Record* suggested that the special treatment given Percy was due to the family's prominence, calling the Baxters "Portland princes."

Graduating from Bowdoin in 1898, Percy then entered Harvard Law School, where he earned his LLB degree in 1901. He returned to Portland to apprentice at a local law firm but soon left to work for his seventy-year-old father. James Phinney needed Percy to manage his hodge-podge financial, civic, and political affairs. In late 1903, Percy was initiated into politics when he agreed to manage his father's reelection campaign for mayor. He then ran himself for the Maine House of Representatives. In both endeavors, Percy Baxter was a winner.

Baxter's first term in the house was in 1905–06 when he was twenty-nine years old, and it was a motivating educational experience for him. ". . . I began to learn something of my native State, the people, the resources and its possibilities for the future." He didn't return to the legislature for the next term but was elected to the Maine State Senate for the 1909–10 session.

He dropped out of public life again from 1911 to 1916. By the time he was reelected to the house for the 1917–18 term, he was firming up his long-term goals. "[M]y plans began to crystallize and then and there I determined to have the State purchase what I consider the most spectacular and beautiful part of Maine, Mt. Katahdin and the surrounding mountainous territory," he said. Baxter described the landscape of New Hampshire's White Mountains as "tame and ordinary when compared with that of Mount Katahdin and the range beyond, and Katahdin is not unworthy of a place among the great mountains of the world." Katahdin was more rugged, he thought, than the "difficult passes of the Alps, or in some portions of the Rockies," where pitons and iron rungs had been hammered into the rock.

Katahdin as the nucleus of a park or preserve did not originate with Percy Baxter. The mountain was so inspiring that the idea of protecting it had been kicking around for more than a half century. The first concrete but unsuccessful attempt came in 1913 when Maine Congressman Frank Guernsey introduced a bill to establish a national park and national forest around Katahdin.

After another failed attempt by Guernsey, Baxter's efforts took center stage. Winning a seat in the Maine Senate in 1919, he proposed a bill for a Mount Katahdin Preserve of about 115,000 acres. The appro-

*Percy Baxter, with his dog Garry II*
BAXTER COLLECTION, MAINE STATE LIBRARY

priation requested was for $20,000, and lawmakers balked at the proposal. Baxter tried again during the 1921 senate session but was stymied again because the large pulp and paper companies, notably Great Northern Paper, had joined the anti-park opposition.

Baxter was elected president of the senate but abruptly had to relinquish that post when Governor Frederick Parkhurst died of a heart attack on January 31, 1921. Baxter's elevation to the governor's office still didn't give him enough power to get his park plan approved. But he was not defeated by a long shot.

Percy Baxter was a multi-millionaire. The family wealth had originated from patents for hermetically sealing canned foods, which James Phinney had purchased around the time of the Civil War. After Percy left office in 1925, he determined to use his inheritance to buy the

Katahdin area for the people of Maine. "Katahdin Park will be for Maine what Yosemite is for California," he declared.

Over the years, Great Northern Paper would be Baxter's most formidable opponent—and no wonder, because the Katahdin area that Baxter wanted to acquire was smack in the middle of the Northern's 2-million-acre ownership. In the face of resistance, Baxter showed time and again that he wouldn't be stopped by a "no" when he needed a "yes." His strategy was the art of unhurried, sugar-coated persuasion, and he relied on his family's history of longevity to outlast his antagonists and eventually acquire the lands he desired.

The initial land purchase of 5,960 acres, including most of Katahdin, was deeded to Baxter on November 18, 1930, as "common and undivided land." He paid $25,000 for the tract in Township 3, Range 9. The other owner of the township, Harry Ross, opposed Baxter's project and sued, but the court found in Baxter's favor. The legislature accepted the gift on April 2, 1931.

There was no "park opening" per se. No rangers. No fees, and no reservations. Vehicle access to the region was limited, and most of it in the shadow of Katahdin was over rough, potholed tote roads built by Great Northern and other timberland owners for logging purposes. Although difficult to access, people still flocked to the Katahdin area because of the thrilling opportunities for fishing, hiking, canoeing, hunting, and sightseeing. Sojourners found accommodations near the mountain at rustic sporting camps and at the state camp at Chimney Pond at the base of Katahdin's Great Basin.

There were myriad trails up Katahdin. The Hunt Trail, which became the Appalachian Trail (AT) in 1933, and the Abol Trail were primary routes from the south. The trails from Chimney Pond up the mountain's eastern flanks were easily reached from the sporting camp at Katahdin Lake, where Percy stayed during his 1920 hike.

More than half of the tracts that comprised the park up to Baxter's death were purchased by him in the 1930s, with the others in the 1940s and 1950s. He closed on just one parcel in the 1960s—a key tract that made possible a single road access from the south. The lack of control over visitation convinced him that one entry from Togue Pond was necessary to regulate the traffic.

Until the late 1940s, the legislature had accepted Baxter's land gifts quickly without public hearings or public opposition. But resentment in the north country had been building against the wealthy outsider as he acquired more land for his wildlife sanctuary and prohibited hunting and trapping. While those parcels had long been in the private hands of other wealthy outsiders—namely the major timberland/pulp and paper mill owners—that was different to locals. Corporate owners allowed residents free access to their lands and let them build simple camps for a nominal fee.

After sportsmen in Aroostook and Penobscot counties leaned on their legislators for help, state senator George Barnes of Houlton took the unprecedented action of holding up acceptance of a parcel, raising questions about whether Baxter Park, then at more than 150,000 acres, had expanded enough.

Baxter, then seventy years old, chose to compromise rather than fight. He amended the deeds to certain tracts to allow hunting and trapping to resume. The consequence of Baxter's change of mind was to complicate the mission and management of the park by establishing non-wildlife areas within the greater wildlife sanctuary, and, in the opinion of many park lovers in the years to come, this undermined his own original intent.

▲ ▲ ▲ ▲ ▲

The tracts Baxter acquired were noticeably not wilderness. They had been logged and burned, and the streams and rivers dammed. Sporting camps, inns, logging camps, and shacks were scattered throughout the region. Baxter wasn't worried about the less-than-pristine condition of the land. He knew that given time, most would revert to its former natural state.

Baxter talked and wrote about the park as "wilderness" and "forever wild." But he never intended for it to meet a strict definition of wilderness because he willingly sanctioned roads, motorized vehicles, campgrounds, and timber harvesting (in one area of the park). He called the park a wilderness, and so it was in the public mind, even after passage of the 1964 Wilderness Act. That law established a legal definition of wilderness that Baxter Park couldn't meet without severe alteration and political upheaval.

Historic use of the park was concentrated on Katahdin. From the early 1800s, adventurers, climbers, and scientists were drawn to the mountain, most of them from out-of-state. What was so compelling about Katahdin, which was small by western park standards? *Field &*

*Stream* magazine's answer was lyrical: "She is a loner, mysterious and profound in her secrets of the seasons. Her profile is aloof and magnificent, her history incomprehensible, her answers only for the stars."[5]

Despite the impacts of timber harvesting and fire into the first part of the 1900s, the area still looked and felt exciting, edgy to most people. Although New Hampshire's White Mountains and the Green Mountains of Vermont attracted more visitors, wild and woolly Katahdin was the prize for the hardy. All kinds of outdoors enthusiasts were willing to invest the time and strain it took to get there—usually by train, horse-and-buggy, boat, and/or foot.

From its founding in the late 1870s on, the Boston-based Appalachian Mountain Club (AMC), played a major role in promoting the Katahdin region, organizing member camping and mountaineering expeditions and writing alluring accounts for its annual bulletin, *Appalachia.* Also, the club began publishing mountain guides to the Katahdin area in 1917 for an increasingly enthusiastic and growing climbing and camping community. The 1930s development of the Maine section of the Georgia-to-Maine Appalachian Trail (AT), with its northern terminus on Katahdin, was a major boon to recreation in Baxter's expanding park.

The public was kept informed about Baxter's park project by newspapers, magazines, and tourist publications. The Bangor and Aroostook Railroad's promotional publication, *In the Maine Woods,* was widely read and carried articles on Katahdin in each annual issue in the 1920s and 1930s. Katahdin was featured in state tourist publications before and after Baxter began creating his park.

After World War II, Baxter made it clear that he didn't want the park advertised by state government agencies, but by then the cat was already out of the bag. Katahdin, home of the mythical storm god Pamola, was a nationally important recreation destination. William Clark Larrabee, an early climber, aptly named it "the Prince of eastern mountains."

Evidence of its national status were the ideas and plans that surfaced from the late 1800s to the late 1930s to create a national park in the Katahdin area. Notably in 1933–36, Democratic Governor Louis Brann began a campaign for a one-million-acre national park around Katahdin to help reverse the economic impacts of the Great Depression. His efforts merged into the last and most intense fight over a federal takeover of Baxter's park-in-the-making.

Baxter was understandably dead set against Congress upending his project and the National Park Service getting control of the region. Creating a "splendid park" for the people of Maine was now his chosen life's work, and he would not tolerate outside interference. He pulled every string he could with Washington politicians, lobbyists, and activists. Republican Baxter even deigned to seek the help of Democratic President Franklin D. Roosevelt, whose New Deal and other policies he had attacked.

Maine native Myron Avery of the ATC, a major proponent of a Katahdin National Park, fought fiercely with Baxter. He thought federal ownership was needed to stop the "despoliation" of the mountain area by overuse (especially Chimney Pond and its camping grounds) and to restore its wilderness characteristics. However Baxter garnered two important allies from the national wilderness movement to his side—U.S. forester Robert Marshall and Robert Sterling Yard, the first president of The Wilderness Society (TWS).

Baxter had been a member of the society since its beginnings. Marshall had climbed Katahdin in 1932, remembering "vividly the grand spectacle looking northwest" to the largest unroaded forest area in the U.S. In 1937 Yard visited Maine, but letters exchanged with Baxter do not indicate that they met.

Robert Marshall didn't meet Baxter either, although he wished he could. "It is a great thing when a man who has risen so high in public life as you gives in such a substantial manner to the preservation of the wilderness," wrote Marshall in a letter to Baxter on May 8, 1937. "Those of us who believe that is one of the most vital fights in the country today are all very much encouraged by your splendid actions."

▲ ▲ ▲ ▲ ▲

All the while, Baxter continued to propose, cajole, and wait in order to purchase additional tracts to knit together the large area he envisioned for the park. The national park battle was over toward the end of 1938, and Baxter won. Even before his victory, he was candid that the contest had been a "long and tiresome" one, fought "absolutely single-handed and in the face of abuse and bitterness that you would not believe possible where a man is merely trying to do something worthwhile for his native state."[6]

The controversy had surely helped advertise Katahdin and Baxter Park. More and more people wanted to have a look-see.

Katahdin attracted at least 10,000 hikers in 1940. They wrote their names in a notebook kept in a metal cylinder on Baxter Peak. World War II almost stopped visitation. Only 332 people were counted at Katahdin Stream in 1941, 111 of them nonresidents. The count of park visitors was limited to Katahdin Stream from 1942 to 1949.

The park's first supervisor, Harold Dyer, was just getting started in 1941 when the draft took him. After the war, he resumed his duties at a salary of $2,400 a year. Dyer had a degree in forestry and wildlife from the University of Maine at Orono and had written his thesis on managing Baxter Park. He showed unusual vision and foresight for his time, making proposals for changes that were ultimately implemented in the areas of campground and trail development, fire control, and park oversight.

After Baxter's victory over the federal park proponents, TWS's interest in Baxter Park's wilderness protection continued. In early 1948, executive secretary Howard Zahniser, a prolific national writer on conservation issues, contacted Percival Baxter about traveling to Maine to meet with him and visit the park. In his letter, Zahniser inquired about a Maine newspaper editorial on policy changes that Baxter had made to two land deeds to allow new roads that would pry open the north end of the park to vehicle traffic. Baxter's reply assured Zahniser that the amendments did not compromise the park's natural wild state—although it did just that from a wilderness perspective. It created a thru-way from one end of the park to the other that would cause problems with traffic and road maintenance from then on.7

Zahniser referred to unroaded Baxter Park and Katahdin as the model "of the possibilities for wilderness preservation under State auspices." Baxter welcomed the visit from Zahniser, who arrived in Maine in the fall of 1949 and not only saw Baxter and Hal Dyer but visited with members of the Authority.

Zahniser's diary provides intriguing impressions and tidbits about the early park personalities and issues. On September 23, 1949, he met with two of the three Authority members—forestry commissioner Al Nutting in Augusta and fish and game commissioner George Stobie.

> [Nutting] is concerned with maintenance problems and expenses and is eager to see the park pay its way . . . but after a thorough

exchange of our ideas he said that he agreed with us with regard to the wilderness values here and the need to safeguard them. I felt he was somewhat on the defensive at first but by the end of our conference was favorable. (He does not, I believe, want to see the park enlarged much further. He is thinking about some substantial yield of lumber program in this general area [on private lands], I believe, but did not say much about it. I saw Stobie but not the [attorney general, the third member of the Authority]. Stobie seemed much of our way of thinking about Katahdin. . . . Stobie said he had climbed Katahdin every month of the year. He was not concerned, he said, about the park's safety status. He didn't think there would be a deer problem here, said there were more moose than deer everywhere . . . (He volunteered without my even referring to the trail folks, on Myron Avery's efforts to get things done at the park. I remember that Avery is a Maine man, etc.). Mr. Nutting also though cautiously and indirectly seemed to me to indicate that they had quite a bit of correspondence. Stobie was outspoken, blunt.

The next day, Zahniser drove to Portland to see Governor Baxter at his downtown office. He termed the meeting "altogether favorable" and said how much he "liked and admired" Baxter.

He has made a grand enterprise of his park acquisition. I had to be tactful and was under some strain but was able to at least speak candidly about roads and wilderness and finally had the satisfaction of hearing him say that apparently he had gone too far in loosening restrictions. He said, though, he had done all he could and we would just have to trust those who came later. We then had quite an earnest discussion and I was able to speak fervently of wilderness values and their appreciation by the public, etc. Finally he said that perhaps he could at some later occasion modify somewhat his broad actions regarding roads and felt good at this. . . . He seemed like an earnest, patient, understanding noble gentleman to me and I felt the better for having talked with him.

After a visit to L. L. Bean's store in Freeport, Zahniser headed for Baxter Park, traveling to Matagamon Lake to see the park scenery from the north end before heading into the park at the southern entrance at

*Katahdin from Pockwockamus Hill in the early days*
JAKE DAY PHOTO, BAXTER STATE PARK PHOTO ARCHIVES

Togue Pond. He hiked to Chimney Pond and then met with Dyer at Roaring Brook Campground.

> [We] had a rich and satisfying discussion for about 3 solid hours. . . . Mr. Dyer seems personally much interested in the preservation of the park as wilderness and in avoiding the road-building that we are concerned about. He seems remarkably adept in his position in trying to exert an influence along these lines while scrupulously following a course to satisfy Baxter's wishes and faithfully carrying out the Authority's decisions. He is unbelievably busy. He spoke candidly and in detail. I believe now that the new road authorizing came partly as a result of conditions Baxter had to meet in acquiring the new lands just added in the north.

Zahniser speculated that Baxter's key reason for opposing the national park proposal was fear of a road-building program to open up the area to traffic far beyond what he intended. (The history of Baxter's fight against the national park is more complex than Zahniser suggests.)

On September 27 Dyer accompanied Zahniser on an early morning hike up Katahdin. They encountered mist and clouds but were able to see some of the classic views, such as The Owl and the Klondike. Near the obscured summit, they met two "elderly hikers" who had been dissuaded by the weather from going to the summit. Zahniser and Dyer went ahead, and at the peak they hunkered down out of the wind and ate a box of raisins, four small chocolate bars, and two packages of cheese crackers.

> Just as we were to turn downwards, concluding that the clouds would not go away, suddenly there was no cloud at all near us— on either side—and we saw away and away the marvelous views on all sides, walked out to the Knife Edge, [then] down toward the Saddle and took pictures. The trip down was wearying. . . . At the bottom, we hastily ate, said our appreciations and farewells, and "dashed" for Ripogenus to cross the dam before the [Great Northern] gate closed.

▲ ▲ ▲ ▲ ▲

In mid-1950, Dyer resigned to become director of the Maine Parks and Recreation Commission. The Authority hired Robert Dyer (no relation) from Mount Blue State Park, and he turned out to be an embarrassment. He was fired after just two months on the job, ostensibly because he didn't attend to his responsibilities and had poor relations with the staff. However, the real reason he was dismissed was that he was caught romancing a ranger's wife.

There is no record of whether Percival Baxter knew of Dyer's indiscretion. But the quick changeover in supervisors caused the governor and the Authority to look for someone who would not rock the boat further—someone above reproach. They found those traits in Helon Taylor.

By the time the respected state warden supervisor arrived in August 1950 to take the reins of Baxter Park, the park had its first data showing that annual visitation to the park had doubled since before the war, to about 20,000 people (campers and day users).

People from all over the country were interested in the park because of attention from popular national figures. The prolific American magazine writer and author Edmund Ware Smith sang the glories of the park to a national audience in the 1950s and 1960s.

Besides, Marshall, Yard, and Zahniser of TWS, U.S. Supreme Court Justice William O. Douglas was another prominent leader drawn to Katahdin and the park. So attracted, in fact, that he also sought out Percival Baxter and spent time in the preserve. Like Smith's writings, Douglas's books about Maine's north woods and waters carried the message of what a special place Percival Baxter was creating.

U.S. Interior Secretary Stewart Udall was enamored of Baxter too. In his 1963 book *,The Quiet Crisis,* Udall singled out Percival Baxter as one of the private conservation philanthropists who had made an "outstanding contribution to the legacy of wild things." He called Baxter Park "the most majestic state park in the nation."

The first Baxter Park campgrounds—Chimney Pond and Katahdin Stream—had been built and maintained by the state before Percival Baxter created the preserve. The forestry department built the cabin at Chimney Pond for Leroy Dudley, a legendary storyteller of the time. For their quarter fee per night, campers could count on enchanting tales from Dudley about Pamola. Richard Holmes manned the camping area at Katahdin Stream developed by the Civilian Conservation Corps (CCC) in 1935 and administered by the Maine Forest Service. Holmes was hired as the first ranger in 1939, when Katahdin Stream became part of Baxter Park, and he charged ten cents per person per night for a site. The state developed the Roaring Brook Campground in 1949.

With virtually no administrative oversight in the 1930s and the 1940s, campers in the new and expanding park could do about what they pleased. They drove their cars, trucks, and trailers into any spot they could access, blaring their radios and, later, televisions. They littered the campsites and roadsides, and polluted waterways with soap and garbage. Poachers had the run of the place. There was no prohibition against pets, which ran around harassing wildlife.

The only one calling attention to the problems and pollution in the park was Baxter's nemesis Myron Avery, who had hiked Katahdin since he was a teenager. He urged Baxter to attend to the environmental abuses, hire sufficient park staff, and develop a long-range management plan. Baxter ignored those problems, choosing to focus his energy, influence, and money on acquiring land for the park.

To have resolved the problems that Avery highlighted would have required a lot of money, and neither Baxter nor the legislature was willing to pay. Baxter had established trust funds to operate the park and keep it from dependency on the state's general fund, but those estate monies would not be available until the governor died.

Meanwhile, Helon Taylor would have to make do with small hand-outs from the legislature. In his first few years at Baxter Park, he was more hands-on ranger/clerk than supervisor because he was the only year-round park employee from 1950 to 1954. He personally answered all correspondence for accommodations and reservations. His regular reports to the Authority—mimeographed or typed—had a pleasant, laid-back tone in general, but Taylor also expressed his frustration with the shortage of money and manpower to meet park needs.

The park's season was from May 15 to October 15. The limited funds for seasonal employees restricted Taylor to hiring only five rangers until 1957, when a reservations clerk was employed. A Baxter ranger's job was tantamount to that of a campground custodian at the time. Most of the rangers had been raised on farms, had shoveled cow manure, cut wood, knew how to repair vehicles, and could handle most any handyman job. Despite the simple living conditions and low pay, "Helon's Boys," as the rangers came to be known, were loyal and kept returning for another season. The attraction largely was a satisfying way of life in the wild with unlimited fishing, hunting, paddling, and hiking. For some, it also was the closest they would come to realizing their dream of having a sporting camp.

After Taylor's tenure began, the first set of rules and regulations were put into place. They were straightforward, asking for general good behavior. Camping, bathing, and fires were prohibited anywhere except designated areas. Visitors weren't allowed to have guns or to land aircraft in the park. Motors on boats were prohibited, too, as was liquor. Those who chose to ignore the rules pretty much got away with it, since rangers were so few and far between.

In the park's nascent years, administrative matters were handled by the forest commissioner because the law designated him to handle those duties for all lands given to the state. The commissioner of fish and game was responsible for enforcing game statutes. The minimal expenses incurred were paid by those two agencies.

Baxter needed a policymaking entity that he trusted to follow his directives—those set forth in the Deeds of Trust and his personal wishes while he was still alive. Baxter was adamant that the park be insulated from politics as much as possible, and to achieve that goal, he felt the park had to be independent of the state parks system and the legislature. He struggled to come up with a governing board that would do.

In 1933 Baxter asked the legislature to create a five-member commission composed of the governor, commissioners of forestry and fish and wildlife, and two public members. They were to operate the park, handle the finances, oversee facilities and trails, and make rules and regulations for the protection and preservation of the park. The state highway commission was made responsible for making road maintenance equipment available to the park. The federal government actually paid most of the costs of building roads and improving and maintaining trails through the CCC. The scanty archival papers from that period confirm that despite the existence of the commission, the forest commissioner continued to be the one in charge of the park.

In 1939, after Baxter's fight with Congress over the proposed national park and his contemplation of political realities, he decided to ditch the commission in favor of a three-member structure called the Baxter Park Authority. The new board was composed of the commissioners of the forestry department and the fish and game department, and the attorney general. Baxter felt that their areas of expertise qualified them to make the best informed decisions. And he invested his hope and faith that they would keep politics from interfering with park matters. The power of the Authority was not spelled out in law until 1949, and it basically confirmed that the trustees could do as they saw fit—an astonishing show of confidence by Percival Baxter.

The Baxter Park Authority was a unique setup for a U.S. park. The park's financial support also set the preserve apart from all others once it came into being. In his desire to have an independent park, Baxter established a trust fund to pay for operations and another to acquire land—but only after his death. At times when the legislature declined the Authority's requests to fund projects, penny-pinching Baxter would dig into his own pocket, but those instances were infrequent.

When the trust funds were released after Baxter's death in 1969, the park truly began to develop in infrastructure, employees, and budget and acquire more land. That in itself was a gargantuan job beyond what Baxter or anyone else would have wanted to contemplate, given the obstacles. The park's maturation would take decades, spreading over generations of employees and managers. Eventually all state monies would be eliminated, and the park would achieve complete financial autonomy—thanks to the wise investment of Percival Baxter's wealth and the persistence of Buzz Caverly.

▲ ▲ ▲ ▲ ▲

Despite all the attention that Percival Baxter and Katahdin received and the ways the park was distinct from all other wilderness areas in America, its public notoriety ebbed and flowed. By the time that Percival Baxter died in 1969, Baxter Park had been eclipsed as a pioneering wilderness preserve by western wildernesses. "It simply appears that Baxter State Park and its unique private trust/State 'park' preservation arrangement has never been known widely among national wilderness [activists and leaders]," according to Doug Scott, a national wilderness history authority.

While the park wasn't celebrated as a national treasure like Yosemite or Yellowstone, its low profile was a plus when a national hiking and backpacking craze developed in the mid-1960s into the early 1970s, and Buzz Caverly would always see the park better off from a protection standpoint for being in the shadows.

---

1. Arthur G. Staples, "Katahdin—The Highest Mountain in the Wildest Part of New England—The Story of a Seventy-Five-Mile Trip to Its Summit, Told in Plain Prose with Many Adventures," *Lewiston Journal,* October 2, 1920, magazine section, Part I, pp. 1–9.
2. Public & Special Laws of the State of Maine, 1955, Ch. 2.
3. Letter from Percival Baxter to Governor Lewis O. Barrows, 1939 (no specific date).
4. The physical description of Percival Baxter was in a short memoir written by his nephew, John L. Baxter, Sr., and sent to park headquarters in October 1982.
5. Smith, Edmund Ware, "Mister Maine and the Mountain," *Field & Stream,* December 1, 1965, p. 11.
6. Letter from Percival Baxter to Dr. E. A. Pritchard, August, 15, 1936.
7. Howard Zahniser's diary of his Maine trip, from the personal file of Edward Zahniser.

Primary Sources: *Legacy of a Lifetime: The Story of Baxter State Park,* by John Hakola, TBW Books, Woolwich, Maine, 1981; *The Baxters of Maine: Downeast Visionaries* by Neil Rolde, Tilbury House, Publishers, Gardiner, Maine, 1997; *Percival P. Baxter's Vision for Baxter State Park, An Annotated Compilation of Original Sources,* compiled and annotated by Howard Whitcomb, Friends of Baxter State Park, Bangor, Maine, 2005.

Conversations and communications: Neil Rolde, Doug Scott, Howard Whitcomb.

**PART 1: THE EARLY YEARS**

▲▲▲▲▲▲▲▲

**CHAPTER 1**

# CORNVILLE

STRING BEANS WERE THE FIRST CONNECTION between Buzz Caverly and Percival Baxter.

In the 1940s, the Caverly family grew beans to supplement their income, and they trucked their crop from Cornville to the Portland Packing Company in Hartland. The plant was part of the Baxter canning business that financed Percival Baxter's political career and enabled him to purchase the 201,018 acres of mostly cutover land that became "forever wild" Baxter State Park.

When he was old enough to use a hoe, Buzz spent summer mornings in the garden weeding the beans and then picking them to take to Hartland, about twenty-five miles north of Waterville. Buzz was an outdoors boy, and he was at home no matter where he wandered around the community. Cornville was small enough that everyone knew and looked out for each other, and its woods and ridges were inviting for children with explorer instincts.

Agriculture once thrived in the hamlet spread over forty square miles of southern Somerset County. Dairying was the most important livelihood, but the town got its name because corn grew so well there— first grain corn, then sweet corn. Later, there were just as many, if not more, string beans in the fields. Both were major crops in the 1930s and 1940s, and the high production attracted processing canneries to the region.[1]

What passed for the "town" of Cornville were a few stores, blacksmith shops, saw- and gristmills, and a wood product factory. Serious commerce happened in Skowhegan, the county seat six miles south. Cornville was reliably Republican, even though the rest of Somerset was a swing county.

Like other country hamlets in the first half of the last century, Cornville required its residents to be self-sufficient. It took hard labor to hold together a family that relied on milk cows, hens, crops, and the woods. Cash was always in short supply, and a barter economy thrived. Electricity and running water were unavailable or unaffordable for most families until after World War II, when utilities expanded their lines and families' incomes improved.

Regardless of the hardships, life was good, not sacrificial, in Cornville—kind next-door neighbors, hunting and fishing out the back door, and fun-filled dancing, eating, and politicking at the local Grange, Ladies Aid Society, and town meetings. The economic stability of the community was partially due to the Baxters, who bought produce from many families in the area besides the Caverlys.

Cornville folk could only imagine the life of the wealthy Baxter clan in Portland, eighty-five miles south on the coast. Portland was Maine's center of commerce and social sophistication. Some of the landmark downtown buildings had been built by the Baxters, and James Phinney Baxter initiated beautification projects along the waterfront. The Baxters were one of the state's most prominent families, with all the luxuries that were usually associated with such high standing.

When Buzz was born, there were just over six hundred residents in Cornville, a third fewer than a generation earlier.[2] His family was well planted in the area, especially on his mother's side. The Stevenses, most of them grain and dairy farmers, went back five generations. In that respect, they had something in common with the Baxters, whose immigrant ancestors in Connecticut had also farmed to keep body and soul together.

Buzz's paternal grandfather, Irvin Christopher Caverly, Sr., owned a successful car dealership in West Somerville, Massachusetts. He married Edda Locke at the time women were beginning to march for suffrage, and they had a son, Irvin Jr., not long after the sinking of the *Titanic*. Edda suffered post-partum depression, and her mental state gradually worsened to the point where she would sometimes hide her son under the bed to protect him from "gremlins" she feared would snatch him. In 1921, when Buzz's father was eight years old, Irvin Sr. committed his wife to the Bangor Mental Health Institute and sent Irvin Jr. to Cornville to live with his maternal aunt and uncle, Emma and Chauncey Locke. Irvin Sr. traveled to Cornville now and then to visit, but for Irvin Jr., Cornville became home. For many years, his only significant absence from Cornville would be the four years he spent at New Hampton Prep School in Hampton, New Hampshire. Cornville's high school was long gone by then, but Irvin Sr. was determined that his son would be well educated.

On his return to Cornville, Irvin Jr. renewed his interest in an old school friend, Pauline Stevens, whose family owned a 200-acre farm not far from the Lockes. Friendship quickly turned to courtship, and on September 30, 1933, Irvin and Polly—both twenty years old—married at her parents' home in Cornville. Irvin worked at the A&P in Skowhegan for a short time and then shifted to a laborer's job at the American Woolen Company mill. Unable to afford a vehicle, he walked the five miles to work every day—a trek he could accomplish in about an hour—and then walked home. Year-round, he carried just a tin lunch pail with a thermos of hot coffee or soup and fresh biscuits or sandwiches for dinner.

Irvin and Polly started their family in 1935 with the birth of Steven Locke Caverly, who was followed four years later by Buzz. Jimmie was born in 1942 and died seven months later of leukemia. Tim, the future director of Maine's Allagash Waterway Wilderness, came along in 1948.

▲ ▲ ▲ ▲ ▲

Buzz was born on March 16, 1939—one of thirteen babies born in Cornville that year—and World War II was on the horizon. The *Waterville Sentinel,* the area's daily newspaper, was awash with news of Hitler's march into Czechoslovakia and Japan's bombing of China. Even with the somber world political situation, the knobby-kneed race-horse-that-could, Seabiscuit, beat out President Franklin D. Roosevelt, Hitler, and Italian dictator Mussolini as the number one story of the year.

On the homefront, headline news included legislative debate over a bill to outlaw buckshot for deer hunting. The *Independent-Reporter,* the Skowhegan weekly, focused more on bread-and-butter issues such as taxes and elections, relegating war news to the inside pages. People flocked to the Bijou Theater in Waterville to see the big hits, *The Wizard of Oz* and *Gone with the Wind.* Kate Smith belted out "God Bless America," stirring the public's patriotic sentiments.

Buzz Caverly was initially called Junior, although his legal name was Irvin Christopher Caverly III. His mother never liked Junior as a name. So when Steve started calling his kid brother "Buzzer" because he couldn't say "brother," the nickname stuck. After Irvin Sr. commit-

*The Caverly family: Polly, Steve, Irvin, and Irvin Jr. (Buzz), 1939*
COURTESY OF THE CAVERLY FAMILY

ted suicide in 1934 (a late victim of the Great Depression), his son took on the "Sr." Buzz officially became Irvin C. Caverly, Jr., when he got his first social security card at age fifteen.

Buzz was a sturdy child—all boy—with brown hair and eyes and a winsome smile. He enjoyed mischief, but overall he was "a traditional good kid," recalled a neighbor, Alyce Corson, whose three children grew up with the Caverly boys. Buzz relished being outdoors, exploring the woods, making lean-tos, playing cowboys and Indians with pets and farm animals.

Home was a nearly self-sufficient eighty-acre homestead. Working the late shift at the mill gave Buzz's father the daytime hours he needed to farm part-time, growing vegetables and apples, making maple syrup, and raising cows, pigs, and chickens. A growing family made homegrown food an important focus—cash was in short supply in the Caverly household. "We were all poverty cases money-wise, but we had plenty to eat," Buzz remembers.

The conservative way of life—producing food, mending clothes, recycling, hitchhiking—wasn't sacrificial. It was just how things were in Cornville, and the war enforced that kind of conservation across the nation. The war took several of the town's young men, but for the most part, everyday life in Cornville was affected by events in people's own backyards rather than overseas.

▲ ▲ ▲ ▲ ▲

When Buzz was just a few years old, his mother started taking in foster children to help supplement the family income. There were usually two or three state wards (all but one were boys) living with the family at any given time. The spacious upstairs of the house had four bedrooms, but that still left Buzz having to share a bed with two foster brothers until he started school. Snow blew in underneath the windows in winter, so Buzz didn't mind sleeping with other boys so he could stay warm. He didn't have a room of his own until he left home.

Even with a half dozen children around, Polly Caverly and Buzz had a close relationship. Both were outgoing. "They were easygoing with each other, and they teased each other a lot," recalls Buzz's brother Tim.

Polly Caverly had an entrepreneurial streak and loved to be busy. When she didn't have foster children, she worked at a shoe shop in Skowhegan, and she always made evergreen wreaths at Christmas to bring in extra money for presents. She established Bonnie Haven Kennels and raised registered collies for show and sale. The collie business made it easy for the boys to have their own dogs. Buzz had Bonnie and Tim had Solo. Like his mother, Buzz also enjoyed horses and for many years kept Flicka, a gentle, dark-coated filly he rode bareback or sitting on an old grain bag because he couldn't afford a saddle. Polly Caverly loved ponies, and there were always a few in the barn she boarded for friends. She trained one to pull a sleigh to take the kids on winter rides around the neighborhood.

Even with two incomes, new clothes for the boys weren't affordable, and Buzz made do with hand-me-downs until he was a teenager and earned his own money.

The security he felt at home was in stark contrast to the times he had to travel with his parents to visit grandmother Edda Caverly in the asylum at Bangor. Doors locked behind them as they went to her room, which was "dark and dingy" in Buzz's memory. It was all terrifying for him, and the visits depressed his father. But everyone cheered up afterward when they stopped at the Auto Rest Park outside Bangor to see the zoo animals, ride the merry-go-round, and eat hot dogs.

When Buzz started school at age seven, he walked. It was seven-tenths of a mile almost straight down the dirt Oxbow Road to the Revere School that his father had attended. After school, there were plenty of chores to expend youthful energy. The Caverly boys hauled water to the farm animals, cleaned the barn stalls, and stacked cordwood for the cookstove. There was one way to accomplish the work—the "right way" that Irvin Caverly required. Buzz was eager to please and adopted his father's values for neatness and efficiency.

Buzz's first favorite wildlife was the ruffed grouse that was common in the woods and fields around Cornville. He loved to hear the bird's thunderous wings in flight and watch the mother run and feign a broken wing to protect her chicks. Deer and porcupines were also in easy sight, and he enjoyed trailing after them.

In winter, Buzz used his sled to tote maple sap from the sugarbush to the house and cut pond ice to store. The ice was kept under sawdust in the icehouse and moved as needed to the oak ice chest in the house. It was used over the summer to preserve milk, cream, and other perishables, and some was sold to the Fairfield Creamery, which would make rounds of the farms to pick up ice. The Caverly boys tried to have a nickel each on hand for an ice cream sold by the truck driver.

After chores, supper, and homework, there was hardly time for anything else—except, perhaps, checkers and listening to a favorite radio program. Checkers was the whole family's favorite game, and each person played to beat the socks off his competitors. Polly Caverly enticed the boys to go quietly to bed by letting them listen to the battery-powered radio. Buzz's action heroes were cowboys, the Green Hornet, and Sargeant Preston of the Yukon. They were surely more interesting than books, he said.

Looking back on Mrs. Edna Parson's schoolroom, Buzz describes himself as "a terrible student. I did the minimum of work." Practical

*Steve Caverly (L) and Buzz, 1944*
COURTESY OF THE CAVERLY FAMILY

jokes were much more interesting. He loved to surprise his teacher with a turtle or frog in a May basket. A chase often ensued, with Mrs. Parsons chasing Buzz across the schoolyard. "Mrs. Parsons had been outdoors all her life, so that turtle or frog didn't really faze her in the slightest way," recalls Buzz. "She was just a good sport."

▲ ▲ ▲ ▲ ▲

The Caverlys were members of Skowhegan's big Congregational Church. "Mother was persistent that we would go on Sundays," says Buzz, "and she made Dad go, too. She'd get us all gussied up—us and the foster kids. She would sit us in chairs and say, 'Don't get up' because she worried we would get a smudge on us."

Polly Caverly was a generous provider of sweets for church occasions and known best for her graham-cracker pies. If her pies and cakes weren't perfect for suppers at the church, she would give them to the boys to eat. They discovered that if they stomped around the kitchen, the cake would fall, their mother would let them eat it, and then she would cook another one for the church.

Not much was made of the boys' birthdays because Irvin Caverly was away at work during most of their waking hours. (He had moved up to the position of night foreman.) There was usually a cake or a special dinner but no party or a lot of presents. A new baseball was present enough for Buzz, and a new glove was thrilling. A first baseman, he loved the game and whiled away many afternoons playing with his brothers and pals.

Thanksgiving and Christmas at the Caverlys were festive. The women in their extended family were all good cooks, and the children were allowed to eat as much dessert as their stomachs could hold. Before Christmas, relatives gave the boys a couple of dollars to spend on presents, and they were treated to a shopping trip to Waterville, in their minds "the big city."

The boys remember vividly their mother making Christmas wreaths with telephone wire and fir tips to earn money to buy presents for them. "She'd sit in her chair making the wreaths until her fingers bled," Buzz says, "but she always had money to spend on us."

Other than holidays, the only time that Irvin Jr. could be with his sons was on weekends. When he was a child, Buzz was content to just burn brush with his father and cherished any time they had together. Later, they hunted deer and gamebirds together. Buzz didn't harass songbirds. He was attracted to them and would lie on the grass for hours observing them. The exception was starlings, which he didn't like.

On rare occasions, Buzz's father would cram the family into the old Ford pickup and take them to Mount Chase in Canaan, where there was

*Buzz and Flicka, 1945*
COURTESY OF THE CAVERLY FAMILY

a fire tower. They would stop at a little country store and buy a box of soda crackers and a couple of cans of sardines. Such a simple lunch was considered a treat, and they'd take it to the top of the peak, sit on the rocks and eat, and visit with the tower man.

These trips were a way that Irvin Caverly, a quiet, disciplined man, expressed his love for his sons. "Dad wasn't an 'I love you' person but would say, 'Well, son, do you want to go with me to Mt. Chase?'" Buzz recalls. The most outward affection his parents showed toward each other was hugs. But there was no question about Irvin and Polly

Caverly's devotion to each other, and it made a strong impression on Buzz when he began to imagine having a family of his own.

▲▲▲▲▲

When he was eleven years old, Buzz joined the Boy Scouts. The weekly meetings of Troop 232 were in Skowhegan, so on Tuesday nights he would ride his bicycle, catch a ride with a teacher, or walk from Cornville to his aunt's house in town on Silver Street. Aunt Emma would have supper ready for Buzz, send him off to the meeting, and put him up for the night. There was a curfew for kids in 1950. Buzz had to be back on her porch by 9:00 P.M., before the fire department and shoe-shop whistles blew. Stopping at Three G's store to get a five-cent frosted root beer at the soda fountain made it a race against time. Buzz ran the last quarter mile to avoid getting in trouble with patrolling police. The next morning, he would catch a ride to school with Mrs. Parsons.

Being a Scout taught Buzz the value of "doing good" in the world, as evidenced in a speech he made to students at his old Revere School in 1955 when he was sixteen:

> I often feel that when the sun goes down, the world is hidden by a big blanket from the light of heaven. The stars are little holes pierced in that blanket by those who have done good deeds in the world. The stars are not all the same size. Some are big, and some are small. Some men have done small deeds but they have made their hole in the blanket by doing good before they went to heaven. Try and make your hole in the blanket by doing good. . . . It is important to *be* good, but it is far better to *do* good.

Buzz achieved his first public notice—a photo in the *Waterville Sentinel*—when he was fourteen and was the first in his troop to have a uniform. He achieved the rank of "Life," just short of Eagle, and belonged to the troop until 1957. (Later he became a scoutmaster in Enfield.) The skills he learned in the Scouts would come in handy later in Baxter Park. As a Scout, he learned how to paddle a canoe on Great Pond in the Belgrade Lakes and how to winter camp at Moose Pond in St. Albans, where he earned a cooking badge. It wasn't the baked beans and hot dogs he remembers about that badge work, but the fact he "smoked the food" because he was so inept at starting a fire.

As in most Maine households at the time, guns were as common as kitchen brooms, mostly for hunting rather than fending off intruders. From the time he was big enough to shoot a BB gun, Buzz had one of his own and got into trouble with it from time to time. Once, he and his cousin decided that the old milking cow in the pasture was too comfortable lying down, and they peppered her behind with BB shot to get her up. When Buzz's father went to milk her and found little bumps embedded in her hide, "my hide got tanned on a trip to the woodshed," Buzz says. There were other high-jinks with the BB guns between Buzz and Steve. Buzz shot his older brother in the thigh once, but Steve got even by shooting up Buzz's new Gene Autry cowboy hat.

Both brothers remember not being close growing up because of their age and personality differences. Steve viewed Buzz as a tattletale and a brat. As a result, he bullied Buzz. Buzz and Tim, however, were close, with Buzz enjoying his role of big brother. Tim was Buzz's first experience with "command and control"—over Tim. He was patient with Tim, letting Tim follow after him and teaching him how to do farm chores, drive a tractor, ride the pony, play games, and take care of himself in the woods. Buzz bought Tim his first train set and his first BB gun, and took him to his first movie (at the Strand Theater in Skowhegan). Buzz's inclination for keeping his things clean and in shipshape condition manifested itself early. He taught Tim to ride a bicycle using his cherished twenty-six-inch red Columbia, and made Tim learn on the lawn so he wouldn't scratch or muddy the bike if he fell.

▲ ▲ ▲ ▲ ▲

After grammar school, Buzz shifted to the junior high school in Skowhegan and then to the high school. His options were to walk the five miles or catch the school bus. Many mornings he missed the bus, and it was a cold trudge to school.

Buzz doesn't blame fatigue on his lack of interest in "book learning. I just couldn't sit still"—except to read *Boys' Life* magazine or his favorite cartoon strip, *Mark Trail*. When he was required to give a book report, he would only read the introduction, first and last chapters, and back cover, managing to slide by with a passing grade.

One book, however, he read with unsurpassed interest. Edward C.

James's *Wilderness Warden* recounted the adventures of a rookie state fish and game warden, Dan Hubbard, patrolling the northern Maine backcountry on foot and by canoe. The warden service, wrote James, "had brought law and order to the north country just as the rangers had cleaned up the old-time West."

The connection between Buzz's cowboy idols and wardens caused him to pore over the book cover to cover. Hubbard was stationed in Newport, a small community of a dozen families, most of whom worked for Baxter Lumber. He worked under warden Tom Grant, "the toughest man in the Allagash," who had been a colleague of Hubbard's father. An outlaw gang of poachers was killing deer and moose in the fictional Swift River Game Preserve, and it was Hubbard's job to root them out. The young warden saved the day, put the bad guys in jail, and won the heart of a young woman. The tale stirred Buzz's imagination for years to come, as well as thoughts about a career in law enforcement.

The significance of the book was noted by a handwritten note in it saying, "This story is the first book read in its entirety by Buzz Caverly for freshman class English."

Despite the deviltry Buzz showed as a boy, "We were sure he would grow up to be a good man," says Alyce Corson. Buzz's role model was his father. Irvin Caverly was "pretty disciplined," recalls Buzz, and he wanted his sons to be gentlemen. "Dad was real mannerly, and I think it came from his training at prep school."

It was in high school that Buzz had his first and only experience attempting to poach deer—and a near run-in with the law. Buzz worked part-time at White's Poultry Farm. Parkman White raised broilers and had lots of laying hens and a modern hatchery. It was a big business in a small town, with eight to ten full-time employees and two part-timers: Buzz and Jimmy White, Parkman's son. They were the same age and were cutups from the get-go.

One evening, Buzz and Jimmy were standing around the time clock in the hatchery building. It was getting dark outside, and Jimmy mentioned it might be fun to go jacking deer. Buzz agreed, and the two developed a plan. At 5:00 P.M., they would take a flashlight and Jimmy's .22 and go to Everett Cayford's field, next door to the Whites. What the boys didn't know was that Cayford and the hatchery crew were on the other side of some chicken crates overhearing everything.

Buzz and Jimmy tramped over to the field, readied the rifle, and

*Buzz's prom photo, 1956*
COURTESY OF THE CAVERLY FAMILY

turned on the flashlight. There were no deer around, but in a few min-utes a pickup truck with the headlights out raced across the field toward them. "We were scared and knew it must be the game warden," says Buzz. "I dropped the light and ran for the woods. Jim dropped the gun and did the same. After running for what seemed forever and being totally out of breath, I was hit hard, stunned, and fell to the ground. I had run smack into a big hardwood tree. When I got my senses back, a light was shining in my eyes. I could see this long set of legs and pair of boots. A gruff voice was on the other end and said, 'Have you learned your lesson, boy?' It was Everett Cayford, and I credit him for instill-ing in me a desire never to go night hunting again. In later years, I had the opportunity to work as a game warden's aide and found it a lot more exciting to *catch* a poacher than to be one."

▲ ▲ ▲ ▲ ▲

Although Buzz grew up in an out-of-the-way place, proximity to Skowhegan provided face-to-face encounters with a couple of heroes—Ike and the Lone Ranger.

The Caverlys were enthusiastic supporters of Maine Republican Senator Margaret Chase Smith of Skowhegan, who had been a close friend of Buzz's grandmother and had babysat the Caverly boys a few times. Former World War II hero Dwight D. Eisenhower was running for president on the GOP ticket and made a stop at the Skowhegan Fairgrounds in the fall of 1952. Smith was taking him around to meet voters, assuring friends and neighbors that Ike was the only candidate who could make good on a promise to avoid war in Korea.

Buzz was riding his bike down a back street to avoid the crowds when suddenly he was face to face with Ike. "Hiya, son. How are you today?" Ike asked. Buzz was speechless. The fairgrounds brought other famous people to town that made an indelible impression on Buzz, such as western cowboy icon Clayton Moore—the Lone Ranger. Those experiences helped imbue young Buzz with patriotic fervor and esteem for American heroes.

▲ ▲ ▲ ▲ ▲

In 1957 Buzz's father, now forty-three years old, actualized a dream. After eighteen years working in the woolen mill and then a short stint as a day laborer with Scott Paper Company in Madison, Irvin Caverly applied for a job with the Maine Forest Service. Irvin had long admired a cousin who was a fire patrolman for the service, and, at Polly Caverly's urging, he decided to apply for the same kind of job. He went to Augusta in the spring of 1957 and met with the deputy commissioner of the forest service, Austin Wilkins. Wilkins must have taken an immediate liking to Irvin because he hired him on the spot—a kindness that Irvin never forgot.

After an initial assignment to Greenbush, about eighty miles from Cornville, Irvin was transferred to a fire tower on Mt. Abraham, just outside Kingfield, to work as a forest watchman and, six months later, as a forest warden. He rarely got back home to Cornville, but both Buzz and Tim spent as much time with their father as they could. Polly Caverly saw him when she delivered food to him on weekends. Tim rode with him in the truck at every opportunity and acted out the part of junior ranger every minute he could. "My mother bought clothes to match his uniform and insisted I wear a green tie and brown shirt like Dad's," says Tim, who was eight years old at the time.

Buzz was older and stronger, so he helped his dad (who had suffered a heart attack in 1953) with the physical work. Every weekend he helped haul supplies from the warden's camp at the bottom of the mountain to the fire tower at 4,049 feet. The heaviest load was wooden shutters made to protect the tower windows from getting blown out by winter winds. The Mt. Abraham trail is straight up. Buzz, feeling his oats, strapped the shutters on a military packboard and pushed himself to the limit carrying those shutters to the tower. It was a helping hand his father always remembered.

The trips to Mt. Abraham were Buzz's first ventures into some of Maine's highest mountains. He spent many weekends bushwhacking in the mountains surrounding Abraham, such as 3,988-foot Spaulding and 4,237-foot Sugarloaf. "I'd go up with Dad, take off for the day, and meet him when the sun set. Why I never got lost in there and disappeared forever, I don't know. It was exciting."

▲ ▲ ▲ ▲ ▲

Buzz was driven by high energy, and from the age of fifteen he was pretty much self-supporting financially. Whether it was turning litter in a commercial henhouse, raking hay for a neighboring farmer, or working at the A&P, he loved being busy, helping with his parents' expenses, and having a small luxury for himself now and then.

Buzz's various after-school jobs made it impossible for him to play sports in high school. Leroy Jones, who was two years behind Buzz in school and later a ranger at Baxter Park, remembered Buzz as "a quiet student, kind of shy." Buzz marched to his own drum among his peers, partly because he was working so much outside school, but also because he wasn't interested in being popular. For instance, he didn't go along with his friends who were wild about Elvis Presley. Instead, Buzz loved country and cowboy music, and Hank Williams, Sr., was his favorite singer.

Dating came into the picture, despite Buzz's time constraints. His high school girlfriend, Marjorie Cossaboom, was the daughter of the owners of a local motel/restaurant. They both loved dancing and going to drive-in movies. Buzz was the Cossabooms' dream of a boyfriend for their daughter—he didn't smoke or drink, was well-behaved, and acted like a gentleman. But the prospect of a future together for Buzz and Marjorie ended when her family sold their business and moved away.

▲ ▲ ▲ ▲ ▲

During his teens, Buzz's idea for what he would do after graduation was law enforcement. His interest was first piqued during his Scout years. The troop's meeting place was in the recreation room in the Skowhegan police department, and he met a lot of town officers and state troopers there. Sometimes they invited him to ride around in their vehicles, and he was so wowed in particular by the troopers' stature—and the uniform—that he applied to enter their ranks at age seventeen.

State Police Colonel Robert Marks wrote Buzz that he was too young, and after Buzz tried again, Marks told him he was too short. Buzz's five feet nine inches was one inch under the minimum height for troopers. Showing unusual determination, Buzz tried to stretch himself physically with exercise. He refused to give up on his dream.

In 1958, when the forest service relocated Buzz's father farther north to Enfield and Polly Caverly decided to join him there, Buzz was crushed about the move. It was to be his senior year at Skowhegan High, and he felt "like it was the end of the world." His dad enrolled him at Lee Academy in Lee, about fifteen miles from Enfield, in 1958. Buzz struggled with English, hated typing, fought with his teachers, and spent time in detention. However, as things turned out, going to Lee was a positive change for Buzz.

Jefferson Mountain was across the road from his dormitory, and another hill, Rollins Mountain, was also close by, providing easy escapes from schoolwork and prep-school life. Buzz's first trip up Rollins was in winter on snowshoes, and it was from the fire tower there that he could see Katahdin any time he wanted to.

He had seen the mountain before from a distance. There was a clear view of it on the road from Enfield to Lincoln that he remembered. Also, when he drove with his father to Island Falls, he could see

Katahdin and wonder what it was like to climb.

But the first time Buzz really saw the mountain as more than a beautiful vista was from the Rollins tower. "I was inspired in my heart and soul," he said.

---

1. *Canning Gold: Northern New England's Sweet Corn Industry,* by Paul Frederic, University Press of America, Lanham, MD, 2002, p. 55.
2. *Register of Maine: State Year Book and Legislative Manual,* Fred L. Tower Companies, Portland, Maine, 1959, p. 569.

Conversations and communications: Laurence Amazaeen, Phil Beckwith, Buzz Caverly, Tim Caverly, Alyce Corson, Marjorie Cossaboom, Jere Cossaboom, Kathy Hopkins, Paul Frederic, Peter Mills.

▲▲▲▲▲▲▲▲

CHAPTER 2

# Helon's Boys

As Buzz approached his graduation from Lee Academy in June 1959, his mother pressed him to go to college. Without a higher education degree, she told him, he would never amount to anything.

He was spared from making a decision immediately when notified that his failure of English as a sophomore back at Skowhegan High meant that he couldn't receive his diploma. Unable to participate in graduation ceremonies, he returned to Lee for another term to take English. To pay his expenses, Buzz worked on the school farm, had janitorial duties, and stoked the school's furnace.

Once he had his diploma in hand, he had to fish or cut bait on the question of a career. A family friend had offered to provide him financial assistance to attend college, but the alternative of going directly into law enforcement was still on the table.

Irvin Caverly had reservations about Buzz's interest in the Maine State Police. He worried over how exceptionally sensitive Buzz might be affected if he had to investigate a child's death in a car accident or deal firsthand with other tragic circumstances. Irvin reasoned that a job as a warden or ranger would satisfy Buzz's interest in law enforcement and be less draining emotionally.

Irvin had met Baxter Park supervisor Helon Taylor in the spring of 1959 at the annual forest service meeting. Taylor mentioned there were three ranger openings for the summer of 1960. Irvin Caverly appealed to his son to consider a park ranger's career before pursuing a trooper job. Buzz was skeptical, but he wanted to please his parents, so he applied for the position. He was one of thirty-nine men who sought those three jobs.

Helon Taylor invited Buzz to an interview at Guilford, where he lived with his wife, Hilda, a schoolteacher, when he wasn't in the park. Buzz arrived filled with excitement knowing he was about to shake hands with a Maine woods legend. "For many visitors to the Park [during the fifties and sixties], Taylor was the park," wrote Dr. John Hakola, author of *Legacy of a Lifetime: The Story of Baxter State Park.*[1] The role model Taylor would become for Buzz would reverberate throughout the long course of his career.

▲ ▲ ▲ ▲ ▲

Taylor's roots were in the Eustis-Stratton area. Born on October 17, 1897, his rural, poor circumstances caused him to have to work as a boy to help supplement the family income. He dropped out of school in the ninth grade to trap bears for the fifteen-dollar bounty. After a stint with the U.S. Navy during World War I, Taylor returned home, took up bear trapping again, and delivered mail to remote sporting camps. His endurance on cross-country skis was almost Olympian in the long distances he covered.

In 1929 Taylor began working for the state fish and game department as a warden supervisor out of Eustis, patrolling his area on a Harley-Davidson motorcycle with a sidecar. He became a formidable enemy of night hunters, crediting his success to his own experience as a poacher before he became a state warden. After Taylor's warden years, he became superintendent of the private Megantic Fish and Game Club at Coburn Gore. In 1948, he was hired as the chief forest warden with the Maine Forest Service in the Dead River District, overseeing the clearing of the land to create the Flagstaff Lake impoundment.

As an active member of the fledging Maine Appalachian Trail Club (MATC), Taylor knew Myron Avery, a key figure in establishing the Appalachian Trail. Taylor's familiarity with the Bigelow range prompted Avery to ask him in 1932 to lay out about fifty miles of the trail over Bigelow and Sugarloaf mountains. Taylor accomplished the difficult task with an ax and bucksaw.[2]

When Buzz first met Taylor, he was surprised at how big the supervisor was. At six feet, two inches, Taylor stood a good six inches taller than Buzz, with broad shoulders and an impressive, clean-cut square jaw. His hands were oversized and strong. "When you shook hands with Helon, you wanted to have your feet braced," says Buzz. Taylor's accent was pure native Mainer, and his eyeglasses were as thick as bottle glass. He wore suspenders and a thick belt to hold up his trousers.

The interview with Taylor was the usual short once-over he gave all ranger candidates. "He asked me where I'd worked and if I knew the difference between a grub hoe and an ax," Buzz recalls. "I told him about my jobs at White's poultry farm and the A&P, and said I would have no problem using an ax. He asked me if I'd ever sharpened an ax, and I told him not much. The last question was whether I liked school. I told him the truth—no."

Taylor promised Buzz that he would hear from him but didn't say how soon. Their meeting had turned Buzz around on the subject of career, and he was gung-ho about joining Helon's rangers.

When Austin Wilkins was appointed to replace Al Nutting as commissioner of the Maine Forestry Department in 1958, he also took over chairmanship of the Baxter Park Authority and began to consult with Taylor when there were ranger vacancies in the ranks. Wilkins and Taylor met on April 25, 1960, to decide who they would hire to fill three posts available for the season. Buzz would go to Abol Campground; Ralph Heath of Sherman, to Chimney Pond; and Wilbur Smith of Brownville Junction, to Roaring Brook. For the first time, the park hired a roving ranger/carpenter, Owen Grant from Sherman Station. In a quirky twist of circumstances, Austin Wilkins offered Buzz's father, Irvin Caverly, Sr., the forest service job that Grant was leaving.

▲ ▲ ▲ ▲ ▲

The letter from Taylor welcoming Buzz to the Baxter family asked him to report to the Great Northern Hotel in Millinocket on May 1 for ranger training. Buzz was on cloud nine. He had no doubt he could handle the job. He knew how to work hard, and a ranger's job was mostly physical.

Buzz's father drove him to the Maine Forest Service office on Central Street to meet his new colleagues. The park had a small reservations office in a corner of the service's storeroom. The room was paneled in pine and had a linoleum floor. Visitors made reservations at a long wooden counter, and clerk Helen Gifford's gray metal desk sat behind it. Gifford had a hand-cranked phone that connected the office with multiple outposts to the north. The park's phone number was the same as the forest service and remained so for another two years, when the office got its own number.

Baxter Park was seventeen miles north of Millinocket, and Buzz had never stopped in town when he went through on camping trips as a teenager. The town was a little smaller than the Skowhegan that Buzz knew well. But with the flagship Great Northern Paper (GNP) mill in town, "the Magic City" was thriving, as was its adjoining sister town of East Millinocket, where GNP had a second mill. Those were the best of times for Great Northern, then the largest landowner in the state, with 2.25 million acres spread out in all directions of the compass and almost completely surrounding Baxter Park.

The town's population was 5,890 in 1960, with the majority aged sixty-five or older. It was a "company town" in every respect because of the mill's employment, economic, and political power. In those days, industrial domination was felt throughout the so-called "paper plantation" of rural Maine, and most people accepted it without resistance.

Paper mills were unionized, and on average, workers earned $5,647 a year—$1,624 more than the average wage for all manufacturing employees. The high pay supported a bustling downtown—restaurants, barber shops, druggists, clothing shops, and hardware and department stores. Indicative of the area's recreational wealth were a dozen nearby waterside sporting camps for tourists, hunters, and nature lovers.[3] Although it was relatively well-off, Millinocket was still in the boonies geographically and culturally. There was plenty of drinking and fighting at bars and poaching in the woods, regardless of who owned the land. "It was just like Jesse James's time—wild," remembers Donat Bisque, then owner of the Terrace Motel and Restaurant.

Park guidebook author Stephen Clark recalled "gagging like a maggot" when he drove through East Millinocket and Millinocket because of the paper mills' air pollution. The sulfite papermaking process emitted a stink similar to that of rotten eggs. The fumes were so strong they sometimes peeled the paint off houses. Buzz was accustomed to the awful odor from the paper mill in "stinkin' Lincoln," near Enfield, so he didn't particularly notice the smell in Millinocket.

From many points in Millinocket, residents could look out their windows and see Katahdin. The woods and ponds were considered the town's backyard. Generations of families were accustomed to roaming the land with gun and fishing pole, doing just about what they pleased and without anyone looking over their shoulders. When the park began to restrict locals' access with chains, they formed the Fin and Feather Club in 1951 to assert their traditional "rights."

▲ ▲ ▲ ▲ ▲

Taylor was on hand to greet Buzz, Heath, and Smith, as were veteran rangers Frank Darling and Myrle Scott, who was the park's unofficial deputy supervisor and Taylor's son-in-law.

After the introductions and handshakes, Taylor took Buzz to pick up a park vehicle and a Grumman aluminum canoe, and handed him a key to the front door of the Abol Campground ranger's cabin. Buzz was luckier than he knew at the time. He and Owen Grant were the only ones to receive new 1959 Ford trucks to drive; the other rangers made do with the old battered vehicles in the park's fleet.

Ranger training in 1960 was held at the Great Northern Hotel. Known as "the Palace in the Woods," the three-story shingled facility had a tower, bay windows, and long verandahs from which to view lofty Katahdin in the distance. Buzz had never been in such a big, fancy building, so he stood outside the entrance for a few minutes to gaze at the place. Inside, he surveyed the expansive foyer, the high ceilings, and the mahogany registration desk that almost stretched the length of the room.

The lobby featured polished brass spittoons, and it opened to a billiard room and a bar, writing rooms, a barbershop, and a baggage elevator. In the dining room, silverware and cut-glass carafes and flower vases graced the white linen-covered tables. There were two sittings for regular dinners, and people dressed in their finery.4

Ranger training was a three-day affair, and Buzz assumed he would sleep in a bunkhouse somewhere in town with the other new men. But he was given a key to second-floor quarters all his own in the hotel. The room had a double brass bed covered by a white spread. A red wool blanket lay at the foot just in case the night was cool. Buzz was so thrilled about all that was ahead of him that he could hardly sleep.

The agenda for the training sessions covered topics foreign to Buzz—finances and accounting, income, capital equipment, refund policy, forms, reservations, accountability, vacation, inventory, personnel liability insurance, first aid, park rules and regulations, and construction projects. When the training was over, Buzz was expected to know how to be a Baxter ranger, although his familiarity with the park itself was minimal. Compared to the requirements today, his three-day orientation was elementary. Even so, it was too much to absorb quickly.

While Buzz's official job description was "very, very vague," what was very clear was that he was supposed to do what he was told—not question authority. And he was required to sign a paper acknowledging that if he didn't pay his bills, he would be dismissed.

▲ ▲ ▲ ▲ ▲

Buzz was one of seven seasonal rangers and one roving ranger/carpenter hired for the 1960 season. A ranger's job was to oversee his assigned campground. The roving ranger/carpenter built picnic tables, lean-tos, and camps, and worked on other building projects until he was needed to fill in for a day or so for a campground ranger sick or off duty. The ranger season lasted from twenty-eight to thirty-two weeks, depending on how much money was available to keep some men on for several weeks after the end of the season.

Abol was the newest campground, having been built in 1958 by rangers Rodney Sargent and Myrle Scott. This was where Buzz was to go to replace Tom Sprague, who had resigned. Abol was like the other ranger facilities—a simple cabin, kerosene light, a water line to the kitchen sink, and a gas refrigerator. But Abol also had a special amenity. In 1958 Sargent, one of the handiest rangers, had rigged up a flush toilet with gravity-fed water, and soon rangers at Katahdin Stream and South Branch Pond were clamoring for them, too.

Chimney Pond was the park's oldest campground. In 1924 a cabin had been built at the remote site, a three-mile hike from Roaring Brook, and it quickly became the most popular camping spot for Katahdin-bound hikers. The area became part of Baxter Park when Percival Baxter made his original Katahdin land purchase in 1930.

Katahdin Stream Campground had opened in 1939; Roaring Brook and Russell Pond in 1950, South Branch Pond in 1951, and Nesowadnehunk in 1952. It was another eighteen years before the seventh and last campground was established—at Trout Brook Farm.

All of the campgrounds except those at Chimney and Russell Ponds were accessible by vehicle. Roaring Brook was the trailhead for Chimney and Russell Ponds. Chimney was a three-mile hike west, and Russell, a eight-mile backpack north. Rangers assigned to the remote campgrounds took all their supplies on their backs when there was no snow on the ground, or hired bush pilots to fly in goods ranging from groceries to lumber. In winter, sleds and snowmobiles were put into service.

Bush aircraft were necessary in the north woods because the road system then was very limited. Small float planes were the easiest, fastest way to get to a backwoods camp for hunting, fishing, or a vacation.

Elmer "Birdman" Wilson, Ray Porter, and Eugene "Chink" Legasse operated flying services outside the park and transported people and supplies from the late forties into the sixties. The little Piper Super Cub was used to take just one passenger. The larger Cessnas were put into service to haul groceries, lumber, woodstoves, refrigerators, boats, canoes, and just about anything else that could be shoved through the cab door or tied to the pontoons.

Wilson and Porter became legendary for their skills at dealing with difficult landing terrain, especially Russell Pond. The small size of the pond (twenty acres) and its boulder-strewn shoreline called for creative takeoffs in the two-seater Piper Super Cubs. The pilots ferried their planes into a small cove and, while making the turn into the way the wind was blowing, goosed the throttle, coming out of the turn at full speed. It looked like the craft lifted straight up into the sky not more than halfway down the pond. Legasse stuck with jobs that allowed him to land at larger Wassataquoik Lake in a four-seater Cessna 180.

The park land was much like most of the north woods at the time—stripped of the towering giants, riddled with stumps, and marred by hydro dams built to transport the wood down streams and rivers to markets. There were well over two hundred structures within park boundaries—double the number today. In addition to campground facilities (cabins, bunkhouses, garages, sheds, outhouses), there were quarters for the forest service and the warden's service, as well as private sporting camps, with their blacksmith shops and hovels for animals.

The pre-1950s buildings were mostly traditional low, round-log structures chinked with oakum, while the newer ones were half-round, tongue-and-groove logs or shiplap. After Helon Taylor became supervisor and had to begin replacing rangers' cabins and other structures, he didn't insist on replicating the original buildings of the day. The ranger staff didn't have time to cut and whittle logs for the old-style cabins, and the park didn't have the money to pay for the extra time.

In practice, rangering centered mostly around the campgrounds, and there was a seasonal rhythm to everything. In the spring, rangers spent April and May getting their sites ready for visitors, cutting firewood, and beginning construction projects.

After the park opened on May 15, the daily routine included cleaning the facilities and privies, taking garbage to the dumps, manning the office desk, collecting fees, keeping up with paperwork, and assisting campers. At dusk, the ranger made a sweep of the parking lot to make sure that all the day-use hikers had left. If a camper or day user was still out on the trail after dark, the ranger took a flashlight and went looking. Any emergency meant that the ranger's chores were put on the back burner, sometimes for weeks, and he might be working all night and start the next day without a wink of sleep. As for trail clearing or maintenance, it was hit or miss, depending on a ranger's ambition. The busiest months of July and August were usually so demanding that rangers often didn't get to sit down to a hot supper, or finish it, without answering knocks on the door from visitors. The crew was glad to see Labor Day come, when visitation dropped off and they could begin to relax a little.

After the park closed on October 15, tasks included putting the facilities to bed, surveying the park boundary, and checking hunters to make sure they were obeying park rules. During the winter for many years, there was little to be done by the few year-round employees except haul supplies to the backcountry campgrounds and watch over the few visitors who braved the harsh conditions to climb Katahdin.

It went without saying that rangers were to be as nice as possible to visitors, who came in all varieties. There were the experienced, uncomplaining ones and the novices and critics. The roadside rangers bore the brunt of the problem users who didn't know how to paddle a canoe, start a campfire, or what to take on a hike. Visitors' questions and demands were persistent, and some rangers became angry or sarcastic and ridiculed users. Visitors retaliated by complaining to Helon Taylor or Austin Wilkins, both of whom blamed the rangers' bad behavior on fatigue.

All rangers were authorized to enforce park rules. Only those who had been "commissioned" were empowered to enforce state fish and wildlife laws. They could arrest violators and physically take them to court. In fact, however, enforcement was pretty much left to state fish and game warden Elmer Knowlton, Jr., because rangers were too busy with campgrounds and gone in the winter.

Although there was no television provided for evening entertainment, the park had a nightly "show" for visitors: bears feeding on garbage. Rangers were happy to direct people to the dumps at dusk to watch the bruins paw through stinking leftovers and rubbish. The

*Great Basin headwall in winter*
COURTESY BAXTER STATE PARK PHOTO ARCHIVES

scene was a photo op that visitors relished.

The field crew felt like part of a close family for many years. A ranger driving from one end of the park to the other would be welcomed in any other ranger's camp and invited to a sit-down meal. Any couple having a baby was given a shower that included the husbands.

▲ ▲ ▲ ▲ ▲

Rangers reported directly to Helon Taylor. If there was a need or a problem, Taylor dealt with it. He had almost a free hand in running field operations the way he wanted because the park was 170 miles from Augusta and park overseers.

Governor Baxter made inspection trips to the park two or three times a year, but those were special occasions that invited pleasant conversation with the field crew he happened to see along the way. Baxter's predictable question to the rangers was, "Are the people enjoying their park?"

Members of the Authority visited the park even less than Percival Baxter. To the degree they were actively involved in park affairs, most of them chose to carry out those duties in Augusta. Most members were not interested in the park and largely deferred to Austin Wilkins during his tenure. Wilkins was a nationally respected forest commissioner who pioneered development of the Maine Forest Service. After the devastating Maine wildfires in 1947, he played a key role in establishing a forest fire compact among the six New England states, New York, New Brunswick, and Quebec to provide mutual help in times of fire emergencies.

Wilkins's view of the Maine woods was utilitarian. His close connection with industry—they paid part of his salary—was considered at the time to be in the public interest. One-third of his pay came from the general fund and two-thirds from taxes paid mostly by the large timberland owners for forest fire protection.

Eleven pulp and paper companies owned outright 5.8 million acres, or 25 percent, of the state, employed 17,000 workers, and were so powerful in Augusta that they could virtually defeat any legislation they didn't like. What was good for Great Northern Paper, International Paper, Scott Paper, St. Regis Paper, St. Croix Paper, Brown Paper, and their allies was deemed good for the state.

In a couple of townships that Great Northern sold to Baxter, cutting rights were retained for a period of time, and its ownership bordered the preserve on all sides. Thus, the Northern had more than a passing interest in park affairs.

The park supervisor reported directly to the trustees, and in Taylor's case, it was almost always only to Austin Wilkins. The two got along well enough. If Taylor got riled over a disagreement with Wilkins, he knew he could go to Percival Baxter, and Baxter usually saw things Taylor's way.

On occasion Taylor would visit Baxter at his Portland home for two or three days, and in an expression of his affection for the supervisor, Baxter had seven-foot-long specially built bed for Taylor so that he would be comfortable.

Taylor was touched, even humbled, by Baxter's friendship, as evidenced by his September 18, 1951, letter to the governor asking for a photograph of him. "I have hesitated to ask, for I did not know you too well, but it seems to me that the man who is responsible for all this should be in evidence at the headquarters camp," said Taylor. Baxter sent Taylor a photo, and later all campground ranger stations displayed a picture of the park donor. Taylor's affectionate name for Baxter was "Governor B."

Baxter's deep regard for Taylor was underscored later in an August 1, 1963, letter to Clarence LeBell, an international adventurer and frequent park visitor from Peabody, Massachusetts. LeBell asked about doing trail work in the park, and Baxter replied that anything Taylor approved "automatically receives my consent. Helon is a grand man, devoted to his important position in the Katahdin Park area, and with him to guide, you will do no harm."

A public declaration of Baxter's esteem for Taylor was naming a Katahdin trail for the supervisor. At the September 28, 1963, ceremony, Baxter praised "the good management" of the park under Taylor.[5]

Between them, Baxter and Taylor referred to the park as "our park." The expressions of ownership were understandable given the lifeblood that Baxter gave to the creation of the park. Baxter's territoriality was assumed by many rangers who stayed for any length of time, and it would color Buzz's approach to every park position he had.

▲ ▲ ▲ ▲ ▲

On May 13, 1960, Buzz received his ranger's badge and identification card from the Maine Parks and Recreation Bureau, making him a member of the Baxter Park staff. Employees of the park were under the state personnel board, but it was just a distant agency to the rangers.

Officially speaking, park employees had to meet the requirements of state employment—such as being a resident of Maine and eighteen years of age. But there were "personnel rules" and then there were Helon Taylor's rules. Rodney Sargent and Dalton Kirk were underage, for example, but Taylor found a way to hire them. Taylor also bent work conditions and dismissal rules to his liking.

There was a flap about Buzz's starting position and pay. Initially, Buzz was put in a Ranger II position at a salary of fifty-five dollars a week. The state forestry department's business manager, Bill Cross, who assisted the park with finances, reviewed the pay scale of all three new rangers and objected to Buzz's position level and salary. It wasn't fair, Cross concluded for "a kid out of high school" to make the same salary as Ralph Heath and Wilbur Smith, who were older and had more experience. Cross dropped Buzz back to a Ranger I level with a salary of thirty-nine dollars a week. Buzz showed gumption by questioning Taylor about the decision. Taylor told him that "the road that brought you in will take you out" if he didn't like the pay. Buzz conceded to the lower salary in order to keep the job. Taylor actually was on Buzz's side on the pay issue. In a letter to Wilkins, Taylor thought anyone in charge of a campground was automatically a Ranger II. He wrote, "[Buzz] is an exceptionally clean-cut young man and is very interested in the work. I think he will make a fine Ranger. He is not too disappointed that he was demoted to Ranger I just so long as he holds his job. He is proud of his calling and you can make something of boys like that."

There was no park uniform for rangers—just a Baxter State Park arm patch. Percival Baxter felt that uniforms would cause a distance between users and the park staff. In a June 18, 1952, letter to forestry commissioner Al Nutting, the governor said that since the season was short, an arm patch was "adequate to identify the rangers . . . we want everything in the Park to be friendly and simple as possible."

Buzz was told by Taylor to go to a local clothing store in Millinocket and buy some jeans and shirts at his own expense and sew the patch on his shirt. He spent about twelve dollars for the outfit of his choice. Not long after that, Governor Baxter finally relented to pressure from Wilkins, and the park paid for rangers to have "the issue"— two pairs of green cotton workpants, two khaki shirts, a green necktie, and green coveralls. Rangers still had to buy their own leather boots.

At the end of the training session in Millinocket, Buzz followed Myrle Scott on the old Great Northern logging road north to Millinocket Lake, and the tarred road stopped where the Trading Post store is now. There was a cement post on either side of the gravel road with a notice to travelers that passage could be closed by Great Northern if fire hazard necessitated it.

Although there was a telephone line and a major electrical line running along the road connecting the mill to the hydropower station at Ripogenus Dam, the dense woods provided an opportunity to settle into a backcountry frame of mind. The eight-mile approach road to the park was a rough dirt and gravel logging road built by Great Northern, and during a good rain, it turned into a muddy mess. Pockwockamus Rock, a huge roadside boulder from which there is a stunning view of Katahdin, hadn't yet been transformed into the wildlife mural it is today.

▲ ▲ ▲ ▲ ▲

Spring runoff was so great that the main access road up the west side of the park was flooded, forcing Buzz and Myrle to take an old horse-built tote road to Abol Stream deadwater. The stone-lined road was narrow, rough, and had no ditches. "We got to the steepest pitch," Buzz recalls. "Myrle stopped his truck, came back to me and said, 'Now I don't know what I'm going to find over this hill. So you sit here and when you hear me beep the horn, you come on down.'"

Buzz sat in the truck, wondering what he had gotten himself into so far away from home. He didn't have long to get too nervous because Scott blew his horn, signaling that everything was okay. As they proceeded, a wild cat leapt from a rock down onto the tote road and ran into the woods. It was a mountain lion, according to Scott, and the sighting gave Buzz the shivers.

At the western park boundary there were signs four feet by eight feet on posts with the words, "Entering Baxter State Park" in brown and cream-colored letters. Underneath, the park's area was given as 193,254 acres.

Helon Taylor's camp was on Togue Pond, some distance away from the "entrance." The lot, just past Bartlett's sporting camp, was leased from Great Northern Paper. The sign in front of the cabin said, "Togue Pond Office, Helon Taylor, supervisor." The thirteen-year-old camp was of shiplap siding. Slate steps led up an incline to Taylor's front porch, where many a ranger, woodsman, and camper received a warm welcome.

Taylor's living situation was enhanced by a generator that enabled him to have electric lights and running water for a bathroom and kitchen. There were other noisy, vaporous generators in the neighborhood at Daicey and Kidney Pond sporting camps. At the time, they weren't looked upon by park officials—or apparently by Percival Baxter—as out of place in the wilderness park. Neither were the gasoline tanks situated about every ten miles throughout the park to fuel park vehicles.

Road access into the park then was split. The way to Roaring Brook Campground went past Taylor's cabin. To reach the rest of the park required driving several miles back from Togue Pond to the Great Northern road and up to the Abol Stream deadwater, where Buzz had entered the park with Myrle Scott.

The road along the park's western border to the northern gate was known as the Tote Road because it had been built by previous landowners to haul logs. It was narrow, bumpy, potholed, and hazardous. Signs with red lettering on a white background were posted at Abol Hill and near Matagamon warning that the road was "winding and narrow and is to remain as a wild forest tote road. It is not a parkway or boulevard. Drive Slow. Sound horn on corners." Travelers obeyed—to avoid risking a broken axle or flat tire—blowing their horns at every curve and creating more and more of a racket as the number of visitors increased. It was usual for vehicles to have to back up to an occasional wide spot to let another one pass.

▲ ▲ ▲ ▲ ▲

After bumping along the Tote Road for a half-hour or so, Myrle Scott and Buzz reached the Abol camp, Scott jumped out and threw Buzz a bunch of keys, pointed to the ranger's quarters, and said, "Thar she is—she's all yours. I'll see you later." He got in his park pickup and drove away.

Suddenly Buzz was alone 165 miles from little Cornville in the middle of a vast, isolated territory. If he could have viewed the landscape from 1,000 feet up, the woods and lakes in every direction would have seemed to have no end. Great Northern's ownership had been intact since 1900. Other major north woods holdings had changed little, providing the region with a sense of job and cultural stability and security. Horses were still being used in harvesting and to transport pulpwood to the mills, and logging camps abounded on the edges of the preserve.

The park that Buzz encountered was 193,254 acres, or 16,247 acres smaller than today. Most of it was designated in law as wildlife sanctuary. Protecting the flora and fauna was essential, in Governor Baxter's mind, to providing park visitors a wilderness experience. However, in Township 6 Range 9 and Township 6 Range 10 (covering 28,594 acres), hunting and trapping were allowed by Baxter. Those two townships were also specially designated to eventually become a showcase for the practice of "scientific forestry." In order to acquire the land he wanted for the park, Baxter sometimes compromised and continued private leases or other rights, such as hunting and timber harvesting—at least for awhile. Some of those rights, such as logging, had official cutoff dates, and Baxter expected that he could resolve other contracts and arrangements in time.

Although loggers were still mostly using saws and horses in 1960, the cumulative impact of their activities over time was environmentally abusive. The north woods was high-graded for the best trees, leaving few virgin reserves. There was no state regulatory control over erosion, stream sedimentation, or impacts on wildlife habitat.

Public entry was helter-skelter because there were no control gates. The majority of visitors entered at Togue Pond, Nesowadnehunk Field, Telos, and Matagamon. But there were seven major logging roads and an untold number of old fire roads and illegal trails that led into the park.

Anyone trying to get in through Nesowadnehunk Lake via Harrington Lake in the spring, however, had tough going. The dirt road to Ripogenus Dam and to Frost Pond was usually passable, but from Frost to Harrington was often soupy with mud. Once inside the park, the forty miles of roads were primitive, and depending on weather and time of year, they too could be slippery with mud or ice. Anytime the roads were dry, dust was the bane of drivers.

Katahdin was the hub of activity in the park, since it was the highest peak and the one most hikers wanted to climb. There was a total of seventy-five miles of trail throughout the park, compared to 218 miles today. There was no "design" to footpaths. Mountain trails were the straight-to-the-top variety; lowland paths were mostly narrow old fishermen's tracks and tote roads built for loggers' access. There was no extra money then to build new trails, properly maintain the ones that were there, or manage their environmental impacts. The AMC and MATC shared the work of signing trails.

By the time of Buzz's arrival, chaos abounded in the park. There were conflicts between day-use picnickers and overnight campers at the roadside campgrounds, and difficulties keeping tabs on rock climbers, illegal camping, and littering. People with motor homes, TVs, and generators were taking up more and more campsites, and the number of campers' dogs was rising. Visitors were bringing in more alcohol and causing disturbances. Fishing limits were routinely violated, poachers were killing deer, beaver, and moose, and campers built cooking fires. The Authority began talking to Governor Baxter about installing control gates and limiting the number of campers.

Roaring Brook ranger Ed Werler, who resigned not long after Buzz came on board, was so exasperated with peoples' behavior that he wrote to Taylor and the Authority complaining of excessive traffic, speeding vehicles, the increase in camper accidents, oversized parties, damage to camping sites, uncontrolled waste, and too much paperwork for over-worked rangers to handle.

Myrle Scott, on behalf of all the rangers, dwelled on day-use problems largely created by local people, especially at Katahdin Stream:

> Day Users are causing a very bad public relations situation at every campground. These Day Use People enter onto the camp-ground and take over whatever facilities are not occupied at the moment, even though these sites may be reserved for campers expected momentarily. When the campers arrive at their assigned site, they find a number of people rejoicing with a picnic. The ranger has to sort out the problem and get these intruders to leave . . . even thought they may have a nice charcoal fire and steaks about half cooked.[6]

Vandalism was not a serious issue, and thus rangers could be somewhat casual about locking up things. State rules required that all offices with petty cash or other valuables be locked up if the building was unoccupied, but the campground buildings were often unlocked unless the ranger was away for a substantial period.

Despite vexing problems, there was great charm to the period, especially in later years. Everything was simpler. Reservations could pretty much be had on the spot for a small fee. Helon Taylor had enough time on his hands to report to the Authority the names of people who received refunds, how much, and the reasons, such as a "virus among group" or death in the family.

Likewise, Austin Wilkins handwrote letters to those who didn't receive refunds, explaining why. Taylor's inventory list of facilities and capital equipment for fiscal 1959–60 was just one page long, reflecting the park's small budget. The estimated cost of what he needed for the season was $3,499 for two bedsprings, three grindstones, two cabinets, one swivel chair, one chain saw, one typewriter, one half-ton pickup truck, five canoes, two aluminum rowboats, one pair of snowshoes, and two stretchers.

▲ ▲ ▲ ▲ ▲

Abol Campground where Buzz was assigned looked essentially the same in 1960 as it does today—a ranger's cabin, storage shed, garage, and woodshed. All the facilities were painted reddish-brown, the park's official woodsy color.

The Abol ranger camp was the newest in the park. There was a screened porch on the front of the cabin with a full-length picnic table. The ranger's desk was just inside, where visitors registered for a site or asked for information about the park. From the porch, there was a clear view to the Abol Slide on Katahdin's flank, thanks to a wide swath that had been cut through the evergreens by the previous ranger, Tom Sprague. At the end of the day, the ranger could stand on his porch to see if there were any hikers descending from the slide.

All the campground ranger cabins had outside posts holding a sign with the name of the ranger. Buzz made his own sign, using a hand router: "Irvin C. Caverly Jr., Ranger." It was the second sign he had made, with guidance from his father, who made signs for the forest service. The first one was Governor Baxter's famous quote:

> Man is born to die. His works are short-lived. Buildings crumble. Monuments decay. Wealth vanishes. But Katahdin in all its glory forever shall remain the mountain of the people of Maine.

Buzz was impressed with the statement, which he thought attempted to answer the question of why the governor had created a park for Maine. Baxter's quote was long, and Buzz didn't have enough board to carve all those letters. He messed it up and then gave up, just taking his ranger sign to the park.

In Buzz's imagination, the ranger's cabin was going to be small and completely primitive. He was surprised by the five-room house—office, kitchen, living room, bedroom, and bath—with the shower and flush toilet Sargent had rigged up. The walls were Sheetrocked; the kitchen was painted yellow, and the other walls light green. The kitchen had an old Serval gas refrigerator, a gas stove, a six-lidded Queen Atlantic woodstove with a warming oven, and there was a small ram-down stove in the living room. "I had read the book about wilderness warden Dan Hubbard, so I was thinking there would be something like a lean-to for me to stay in," he says.

Buzz's first chore was cleaning up the cabin, which had been empty all winter. He could see from the ample droppings that he might as well get accustomed to living with mice. He grabbed two buckets from the sink sideboard and went looking for a brook to get water.

"My mother said to me when she was helping me pack groceries, 'Be sure when you get to wherever you're going, if it's a camp with cupboards, wash the shelves down before you put your food on them,'" Buzz recalls. "She was an immaculate person, and I promised her I'd make sure everything was clean, so I warmed the water on the woodstove and washed each board before I started putting stuff away." His first meal was Campbell's tomato soup and crackers—a favorite of his father's during the mill years.

▲ ▲ ▲ ▲ ▲

It was pitch black when Scott returned to Abol for the first night. Buzz bombarded him with questions all through dinner but then wanted to go to bed because they had a big workday ahead.

There were two cots in the living room. (The double bed in the bedroom was left for guests.) Scott showed Buzz how to douse the cabin's only light—a Coleman lantern—and jump in bed before the mantle went out completely. Scott was a quick deep sleeper, but Buzz kept him awake asking questions.

> "Myrle," I said—and I hear him going "Hmmm, hmmm . . . what?"
> "How big is the park?"
> "One hundred and ninety-three thousand, two hundred fifty-four acres."
> "Myrle, who does the law enforcement?"

Buzz kept on with the questions and, all of a sudden, heard two feet stomp on the floor. Scott turned on his flashlight, lit up his pipe, and told Buzz in his signature drawl:

> Now boy, I just made me a smoke. I'm going to smoke this pipe of tobacco and while I'm doing it, you ask me every single question you can think of. When you're done, I'm going to put this pipe out and you're not going to ask any more questions, and

we're going to get to sleep tonight so we'll be worth somethin' tomorrow.

---

1. *Legacy of a Lifetime: The Story of Baxter State Park,* by John W. Hakola, TBW Books, Woolwich, Maine, 1981, p. 195.
2. "Helon Taylor," *The Maine Paper,* by Lawrence M. Sturtevant, May 1981, pp. 15–16.
3. *Millinocket, Maine,* Appalachian Mountain Club brochure (no date).
4. *Millinocket: Magic City in Maine's Wilderness,* by Dot Laverty, Bond Wheelwright Co., Freeport, Maine, 1973, pp. 39–42.
5. *Legacy of a Lifetime,* p. 137.
6. Letter from Myrle Scott to Austin Wilkins, May 20, 1960.

Primary Document Sources: BSPA Boxes 1, 2, 4, 15, 17, 18 (Location numbers: 2507-0713, 2507-0714, 2507-0717, 2507-0718). The Baxter Park files at Maine State Archives are numbered from Box 1 every time a document deposit is made; thus, it is important to know the exact location numbers in order to find the right file. Maine State Archives is the central repository for original park documents. Baxter State Park headquarters in Millinocket also retains select historical documents. The Maine State Library houses Percival Baxter's personal archival documents, referred to as the Percival Baxter Collection.

Conversations and communications: Ed Beach, Donat Bisque, Buzz Caverly, Jan Caverly, Dalton Kirk, Elmer Knowlton, Rodney Sargent, Doris Scott, Ed Werler.

▲▲▲▲▲▲▲▲

CHAPTER 3

# Summer Ranger

Buzz's excitement was understandable. He was twenty-one years old and had never been away from home and his family for any length of time. His whole life was before him—and in a special place of spectacular beauty.

One of his first explorations of the park was the road system, and at Ledge Falls on the tote road, he came upon one of the last log drives on Nesowadnehunk Stream. Micmac Indians from the Houlton band were on hand to drive the pulpwood. Buzz watched them use their pick poles to fish out of streamside bushes the logs that had jumped the banks.

From the beginning, Buzz was closer to his two "classmates," thirty-eight-year-old Ralph Heath and fifty-three-year-old Wilbur Smith, than to the veteran ranger crew, which was a tight-knit group because they had been with Taylor since the early 1950s. Most of the older rangers were married and had children. Myrle and Doris Taylor Scott were raising four children at Katahdin Stream Campground; Frank and Avis Darling had two children at South Branch Pond; and Irwin and Amber Sargent lived at Nesowadnehunk. Hilda Taylor, a career grade-school teacher, joined Helon on the weekends after teaching in Guilford, their official residence. Rodney Sargent and Owen Grant were single but identified more with the seasoned rangers. Sargent often stayed with the Scott family for companionship.

"We were very close," remembers Ed Werler, who rangered at the park for ten years. The families enjoyed socializing together—picnicking, playing cards, and fishing. The rangers' wives swapped recipes and ways of running a backwoods household without modern conveniences.

Helon Taylor had commented on the overall comradeship in an October 15, 1959, letter to Austin Wilkins. "We work hard and get along well together," said Taylor. "Each man has his place, does his work, knows and respects the other men in the organization, and is always willing to give a helping hand in an emergency."

▲ ▲ ▲ ▲ ▲

Doris Scott remembers Buzz as "green as green could be. He was not used to living in the woods. He was a little bit nervous, and Myrle used to calm him down." Buzz's earnestness was quite apparent. "He wanted to do things right." She helped him with financial reports (fee income from campers). "He didn't want to be a penny short," she says.

Ed Werler wasn't impressed with Buzz. "I didn't think he was going to make it," Werler recalls, but he couldn't put his finger on why he reacted to Buzz the way he did. "He just impressed me as the type who was not going to be a ranger. I didn't take to him." But in time Werler would change his opinion.

Besides Buzz's newness to the Baxter community, what set him apart from the group was being a teetotaler. Most of the others enjoyed their liquor or beer, even supervisor Taylor, and some didn't always wait until they were off duty to imbibe.

Buzz recognized the personal divide between himself and the veteran ranger crew over drinking. But drinking wasn't the only difference that made for difficult relationships among rangers. At any given time, there were rangers whose personalities clashed, and those who found the other rangers' ways of doing things irritating.

Buzz allied himself with Heath and Smith, not just because they started together. "Ralph had a great sense of humor, and Wilbur had a wonderful personality and was also a real storyteller, like Helon," says Buzz. "Wilbur was great at public relations—more so than maintenance [chores]. I loved being around them."

There was a lot riding on Buzz's performance. A young, single ranger hired before him didn't meet Taylor's expectations, and the supervisor lamented to Wilkins that he had "never picked a dud" before. In an October 15, 1959, letter, Taylor reported that he had fired the man and that the other rangers had concurred wtih the action. Wilkins supported Taylor's decision but said he should have followed proper personnel dismissal procedures.

Under the circumstances, there were questions about Buzz. Would he be a disappointment, too? Would he fit in? Even without personality issues, a single ranger was almost a liability in Helon Taylor's eyes.

"He used to say, 'You get two for one if you get a married couple,'" Buzz remembers. "You hired the ranger, and when he was out on patrol, away from the campground, or going to the dump with the rubbish, the wife was expected to register the guests and answer their questions."

The park reservations system, in fact, depended on the wives to run smoothly. Before Helen Gifford in the Millinocket office could book a party, she had to call on the radio to a campground to see if a space was open or whether the ranger or his wife had already filled it. It meant someone had to be in the campground office virtually all the time in order to take the office calls. If a roadside campground ranger was unmarried, he found himself sitting in the ranger's camp for hours on end when he wanted to be outside doing chores and patrolling trails.

▲▲▲▲▲

With his eye on the May 15 opening day, Buzz got up at sunrise the first morning after ranger training ended. He picked up brush and raked leaves, cleaned out campsite fire pits, and put out the picnic tables that had been stored over winter in the shed. The tables and park signs had to be freshened up by hand, and painting was usually needed also inside the ranger's cabin.

Two or three hours were spent before noon on cabin chores. Next, anything needing repair, such as porch screens, was done. If the ranger didn't know how to do the job, he had to find another ranger to teach him. The afternoon was reserved for office time to take care of incoming campers and check on hikers returning from climbing Katahdin.

Buzz was always anxious to finish his chores as quickly as possible so he could study park maps and go on foot patrol. He wanted to know his surroundings thoroughly, especially the "strange lakes and ponds" he had heard so much about.

He learned to be a fast hiker to cover a lot of ground in a day, and his love of "hoofing it" was fortunate; using a park vehicle to ride around was frowned upon at the time because park trucks were in short supply. Rangers had to document their vehicles' miles, and if they were going to use a vehicle for a non-official or partly official trip, they had to get permission from Taylor.

That first week at Abol, Buzz saw his first moose:

In the late 1940s, certainly all through the 1950s, there were no moose in the farming community where I grew up. Helon and I were traveling together one late evening, going over to see Ralph Heath, who was fishing on the West Branch of the Penobscot. We were driving along in Helon's old Chevy wagon. Suddenly there was a cow moose in the road that had just dropped her calf. Helon gave me an education about moose and where I could usually see them in the park. It was great.

Buzz expected a rush of campers. The campground was shipshape, and the weather was good. He was surprised to have only three campers and six day visitors for the first two weeks of the summer season.

Among the park's campers in late May was U.S. Supreme Court Justice William O. Douglas, who arrived at South Branch Pond with "Jake's Rangers," a group of senior citizens and friends led by Maurice "Jake" Day of Damariscotta, Walt Disney's *Bambi* artist. Jake's Rangers (so named by Day because they "ranged" all over Maine in search of the best fishing holes and wilderness) were often accompanied by writer Edmund Ware Smith. Smith wrote up the adventures of the rangers for *Field & Stream* magazine, dubbing Governor Baxter "Mister Maine" and Douglas "Justice Bill."

"They all had a fine time and good fishing," Taylor reported to the Authority. Buzz ran into the Douglas party at the Pogy Pond campsite between South Branch Pond and Russell Pond but had no idea that Douglas was a justice and an eminent wilderness advocate.

▲▲▲▲▲

One of Buzz's first visitors at Abol was Governor Baxter on his spring inspection tour, accompanied by state game warden supervisor David Priest. Baxter's chauffeur, Joe Lee, would drive the governor to Millinocket, where they would meet Priest and Arthur Rogers, another warden supervisor.

Upon arriving in town, Baxter checked in at the Great Northern Hotel. Baxter was always prepared for emergencies with a red-and-black mackinaw and a pair of gum-rubber boots that he kept in his vehicle. After a day looking over campgrounds in the southern part of the park, he would have dinner at the Daicey or Kidney Pond sporting camps. If he spent the night in the park, it would be at Kidney Pond because it had hot showers and flush toilets. The next overnight would often be up north at the Augustine Hotel at Shin Pond.

Buzz greeted Baxter with a "Hello, I'm pleased to meet you," and they sat down on the porch of the ranger's station. Buzz felt humbled to meet Baxter because Baxter was "the man" who had done so much for Maine.

Baxter asked him simple questions, as was the governor's way. Did Buzz like the campground he was assigned? Were the people enjoying their park? Baxter knew a neighbor of the Caverlys in Cornville and his Aunt Emma's brother, and asked how they were doing. It was a short visit, and the governor thanked Buzz for working for the park and "taking care of our guests."

▲ ▲ ▲ ▲ ▲

Buzz rode with Taylor on his campground inspection trips a number of times that first summer. It was a golden opportunity, Buzz figured, to get to know Taylor better, hear some good stories, and get helpful information. "Maybe he was just sizing me up, too," says Buzz.

The first trip was an eye-opener. Taylor was a fast driver, despite the tote road's poor condition. Rocks and boulders jutted out to the edge of the road, and Taylor was barreling ahead when he met a car with three women. "He whipped to the right and staved up his car," just missing the other vehicle, says Buzz. After the dust settled, Taylor looked out the window, tipped his Stetson hat to the ladies, and wished them a good afternoon. Fortunately, Taylor's vehicle wasn't totaled— just damaged. Park policy in those days was to keep equipment going until it was absolutely no good.

The degree to which that was true was driven home to Buzz when he broke an ax handle and learned there wasn't money to pay for another one in the current budget. Nope, Taylor told Buzz, he would have to wait for the next round of funding in July. Or better yet, Taylor advised, Buzz could whittle himself a handle from ash because it would be "good experience" for him. Taylor showed him how to choose a good tree, carve the new handle and a wedge for the head, and soak it in water to swell up tight.

Buzz learned to grind a dull ax to razor sharpness at Taylor's workshop. There was a pedal grinder with a funnel on top for water to seep down over the ax head. As Buzz was sharpening the ax, Taylor warned him against cutting himself. Then Buzz ran his finger across the blade, and blood spurted out of the cut. Taylor smiled and told him, "They all do it."

▲ ▲ ▲ ▲ ▲

The end of Buzz's first month in the park coincided with Percival Baxter's May 20, 1960, letter to Governor John Reed and members of the Executive Council about restrictions on his land gifts.4 Baxter noted that all of the deeds from 1931 to 1959 mandated that the park was to be maintained in its "natural wild state and as a sanctuary for wild beasts and birds." He then introduced a fear which he would repeat often in his communications:

> While I am living I fear no encroachments on the park, but as time passes and new men appear upon the scene, there may be a tendency to overlook these restrictions and thus break the spirit of these gifts.

He mentioned potential bad ideas that could threaten the park in the days ahead, such as "a museum for old lumbering tools" and that "prisoners [might] be put to work there. Any such matters would directly conflict with the terms and spirit of the trust, and nothing should be done that will disturb the peace of mind of our visitors and spoil the free atmosphere of that remarkable region."

The same communication condoned the killing of predators in the park "such as wildcats, bears, and foxes [that] may become a serious menace to other creatures in the park, such as deer and moose, for deer and moose are the chief wildlife attraction in Maine. Such a situation may need correction to maintain this proper balance," he said. "This should be done only by the Authority in cooperation with the wardens of the Fish and Game Department." Baxter, however, had second thoughts about predator killing and later rescinded his approval.

▲ ▲ ▲ ▲ ▲

By the July Fourth weekend of 1960, campers began pouring into the park. Abol Campground was filled, so Buzz allowed people to tent in the parking lot and his dooryard. "If there was a full house and a carload of people drove in, you'd just go find three rocks for a fireplace on your front lawn, try to scare up a picnic table, and get them settled in for the night," he says.

There was actually competition among the campgrounds to book the greatest number of people. Abol's capacity was 64; Roaring Brook, 100; South Branch Pond, 142; and Katahdin Stream, 148. It wasn't uncommon to have 135 to 140 people a night at Abol and more at the three larger drive-in facilities.

Park fees were very affordable, in keeping with Governor Baxter's wishes. In 1960 the overnight fees were raised by the Authority by fifty cents per person to a dollar fifty for bunkhouse accommodations and by twenty-five cents to seventy-five cents for a lean-to. Tenting and trailer space remained at twenty-five cents per night per person. Boat or canoe rental was kept at fifty cents an hour or two dollars for the whole day. Visitor use fees generated over $16,000, or 35 percent of the park's expenditures.

After the season's slow start, there were so many campers that rangers were averaging 78- to 100-hour workweeks. Taylor told the Authority, "It is to their credit that we still have not had a forest fire or a single accident worth mentioning to date this season."

If rangers had voted on the chore they disliked the most, it's likely they would have picked cleaning out the privies. The dark, odorous structures were impossible to keep cleaned, and often people relieved themselves outside the privy, leaving wads of paper on the ground, too.

By 1960 rangers worked six days a week and on the seventh traveled to Millinocket to deposit camping fees, get their trucks serviced, shop for groceries, and do laundry, usually stopping at Taylor's camp at Togue Pond going out or returning. (Rangers at the north end did business in Patten.) Since the town day wasn't really a day off, rangers had to be back at their campgrounds by late afternoon to attend to duties. Personnel rules gave a ranger one day off a month, but rangers accumulated most of their days off so they could be paid for about a week after they left the park in the fall.

Most communication with rangers during Taylor's days was oral, but they also had to turn in a written report weekly to account for how they spent their time. Taylor filled out an account of his day-to-day activities, too, and kept track of other matters, such as inches of rainfall, campfire permits issued, meetings attended, gas and oil used, cost of truck repairs, and so on.

▲ ▲ ▲ ▲ ▲

Hornets and wasps were terrible, even after DDT spraying at campgrounds, during the summer of 1960. Two campers went into comas after being stung but recovered. Taylor himself got a hornet up his pant leg just when Governor Baxter and he were posing for a photograph "for the pretty lady at Roaring Brook. I am glad it was me and not the Governor, but it is hard to smile and look pleasant with a little black hornet brading you in an embarrassing position," Taylor said.

Fortunately for Buzz, the intensity of blackflies, mosquitoes, and midges wasn't a bother. The stings didn't annoy him, and he wasn't allergic. The most common protection other people used to prevent bites was the old woodsmen's fly dope, and a natural remedy was sticking moose-maple leaves behind the ears. Wearing light clothing also helped.

Buzz hated the DDT spraying, thinking it was out of place in a wilderness park, but he wasn't aware of its use until he saw Myrle Scott with a sprayer at Katahdin Stream. Scott sprayed the Katahdin Stream campground before Memorial Day weekend to make the outdoors more comfortable for visitors, as did rangers at other campgrounds.

By the end of the season, Buzz—dubbed the "young squirt" by Ed Werler before he left park service—was interested in expanding Abol Campground to house more visitors. In a memo to Wilkins, Buzz wrote:

> I . . . realized how lax this campground was in tent sites and came to the conclusion that if we could get a bulldozer and grade off the area that Tom Sprague cleared last year, it would make an attractive tenting and trailer area. After talking with Helon, I was pleased to find out that this campground for the last two years has doubled its business and no doubt will continue to do so in the years to come. Which goes to show that we must have more tent and trailer sites.

▲ ▲ ▲ ▲ ▲

Limited vehicle travel made the park's communications system very important. For years, the only way to be in touch was via the telephone network that was started by the landowners in the early 1900s for mountain fire towers and developed by the Maine Forest Service for fire protection. The peak of the network was in the early 1930s, by which time there was about 3,500 miles of ground and metallic circuit lines, according to Austin Wilkins's 1978 book, *Ten Million Acres of Timber*.5 Besides reporting fires, the lines were used for emergency calls, search and rescue, and military activities.

The line going into Baxter Park ran from Millinocket Lake to Togue Pond on poles about ten feet high. The height then dropped to about five or six feet along the park's tote road. It wasn't long before Buzz despised those lines. "They came down with every lightning storm, every car that pulled up to them too far and got hooked on the mirrors, every blowdown, every limb that fell or bushes that grew tall, and every moose that ran into them."

During his first season, a moose died in the lines once a month. Typically, a moose would wander onto the park road, and a car would come along from behind. Instead of giving the animal time to get out of the way, the driver would try to push the moose ahead, and the moose would go from a walk to a trot to a run. If a car happened to come from the other way, the moose would either collide with one of the cars or go off the road and get tangled up in the telephone wire. Moose would wrap themselves up so tightly—sometimes strangling themselves—that the rangers would have to shoot them. The local game warden would dress the animal in the field and take the meat to the hospital or give it to the local poor.

Rangers spent a good deal of their time constantly repairing and maintaining the phone lines, and even then they didn't go as far as Chimney Pond and Russell Pond. While often a nuisance, the lines provided entertainment for the rangers' wives. When not much was going on, listening in to conversations was a regular pastime.

Shortly before Buzz became a ranger, the park purchased two-way, battery-powered radios to use in the field. The Federal Communications Commission required that all rangers be licensed to talk on the radios—a rule that only required that Taylor send in their names to Washington. The radios were good for short-range calling. "But if there was a mountain between you and the person you were calling, no luck," says Buzz.

Each ranger's cabin had a radio box—a dark gray instrument more than a foot long and four inches wide. The radio itself came in a desktop apparatus with a push-button microphone. Three more radios in large boxes were placed in rangers' trucks for use on the road. The trucks had long whip-like antennas. "You would know they were coming down the road because you could hear the antennas hitting the tree branches," Buzz recalls.

Taylor had one of the truck sets in his vehicle to check in with all the campgrounds at the end of the day. He would drive to a knoll beyond his Togue Pond headquarters to gain enough elevation for the radio to work. "He would push the button and clear his throat and say '901, South Branch Pond or Roaring Brook, how is it going today?'" Buzz remembers. "He and each ranger would talk about the campers, weather, or whatever was going on. It took him an hour to complete a calling circuit."

▲ ▲ ▲ ▲ ▲

Once Buzz oriented himself to ranger life, he wanted his own family around him—a tradition for the field staff whether the relatives were seasonal employees or visitors.

At the time, the park had several seasonal staff who were related. In addition to Taylor and Myrle and Doris Scott, the supervisor hired the Scotts' sons to work on the trail crew. Rodney Sargent's father joined the ranger staff at Nesowadnehunk two years after Rodney signed on, and Irwin Sargent stayed for ten years, along with his wife. Frank Darling and Ralph Heath were brothers-in-law. Nepotism, commented Doris Scott, "was rampant." Again, it was just the ways things were done then.

Tim Caverly was eleven years old when Buzz became a ranger and lived with him for much of the summer. Tim stayed at Abol until Polly Caverly thought he needed to have his clothes washed or get a haircut. He remembers, "Buzz was so excited about living in the woods, he would spend half the night talking to me about what opportunities there were and what we would do the next day. There was no electricity and no phones, and you had to be self-reliant, and he liked that. He felt that people were depending on him, and he impressed on me as a kid that I needed to be mindful of that when I was staying with him."

Another relative who spent considerable time with Buzz that summer was his aunt, Elinor Stevens Walker. Elinor had developed lung cancer and was operated on in the summer of 1960 at Eastern Maine Medical Hospital in Bangor. Her doctor told her she would fully recover, but Elinor was convinced she was going to die. Polly Caverly asked Buzz to visit Elinor and give her encouragement.

"She was glad to see me and started in on all her melancholies," Buzz remembers. He interrupted to tell her about Baxter Park and invited her to visit him. "It was almost like a switch turned on. She was a nature lover, and her whole focus turned to the possibility of spending time in the park. She came up the next weekend [after his visit] with a carload of pies and cookies and stayed a week, then she essentially moved in with me for the summer. Her husband would come up on weekends. She'd be up early in the morning, and if I was going anywhere in the truck, she was going with me, or if I were doing a hike, she'd hike with me."

Elinor was so interested in the park that she wrote four chapbooks—*Our Great Mountain Wilderness, In and Beyond Our Great Mountain Wilderness, All About Maine,* and *More About Maine.* Governor Baxter read them and told Buzz they were among the finest descriptive books he had read about the park.

Someone else who showed up at Abol to visit Buzz unannounced was Janice Thompson of Bangor. She was camping with family members and wanted to be introduced to Buzz. Jan had been sweet on Buzz from afar. While getting a hot dog or hamburger at the Big Swig drive-in in Enfield, she had seen Buzz going by on his horse, Flicka, or in his 1951 Plymouth. "I thought he was handsome," she says. Jan had asked a friend who went to high school with Buzz what he was like and whether he drank. She had vowed never to marry anyone who was a drinker.

Jan was disappointed that Buzz was away from the park and was embarrassed when her nephew spilled the beans to Ranger Scott that Jan liked Buzz. But Buzz was enjoying a day off at the Skowhegan Fair, and it would be a few more months before he and Jan would actually meet.

▲ ▲ ▲ ▲ ▲

Buzz was stationed at Abol until the end of August, when he was transferred unexpectedly to Russell Pond. He replaced Ralph Dolley, who was not leaving of his own accord. Dolley got into a ruckus with a camp counselor who was staying at Russell with a group of boys, and the counselor complained about it to Taylor.

In those days, there was no formal administrative process or employees' union to turn to for help when rangers got into trouble. Authority members, as well as Taylor, fired as they saw fit (although Taylor usually consulted with the Authority). "If someone accused you of something, you were out," says Buzz.

Buzz's father had warned him when he went to the park "to be really careful because there are people who will say anything and get a ranger into trouble." Dolley was the third man to be fired by Taylor. Buzz vowed to himself to avoid difficulties that could lead to trouble and turned his attention to the job at hand.

Buzz and Dolley went on a hike together before Dolley said his final good-bye to Russell Pond. Buzz had already hiked in seven miles from Roaring Brook. Now, Dolley led him up the trail another mile to Lookout Mountain and from there several more miles to Six Ponds and the island in Wassataquoik Lake. They had to cross waist-high water at one point, and Buzz kept his clothes on and wound up sopping wet. By the time the rangers arrived back at Russell Pond, Buzz concluded that Dolley had been testing him to see if he was tough enough for the backcountry job.

One of Dolley's idiosyncrasies was his love of snakes. He kept little garter snakes inside the cabin to eat the indoor mice. Buzz was sitting on the front steps after the hike when one of Dolley's favorite snakes came out the cabin door and wiggled across Buzz's boot. Buzz, who had a snake phobia, picked up a rock and killed the snake, making Dolley furious. He asked Buzz what in the world he was thinking. A wave of guilt came over Buzz, who realized he had violated a cardinal park rule against killing wildlife in the sanctuary, but the incident didn't make him ever like to be around snakes.

When Dolley arrived at Taylor's camp to say good-bye, he told the supervisor that Buzz would never make it as a backcountry ranger. Dolley reached in his pocket and pulled out one of his pet snakes, and Taylor quickly escorted Dolley and the snake outside.

▲▲▲▲▲

Buzz had gone from a relatively new camp at Abol to one of the park's original log cabins at Russell Pond, likely built in the 1920s. It had a low roof with uneven roof boards, loose windows, and oakum-chinked logs—anything but weather-tight. The roof was covered in aluminum, as was the one at Chimney Pond. Buzz had already discovered when he was on Katahdin's summit that when the sun hit those aluminum roofs, they were "an ugly, ugly sight." But Helon Taylor was practical when it came time to deciding what materials to use in the backcountry. Aluminum slid well on the snow (and vice versa), and rangers could lug it to the remote cabins more easily than heavy roof shingles.

Buzz felt instantly at home at Russell. It was far from the drive-in campground at Roaring Brook, with all its traffic, noise, and activity. Over the years, Dolley had cultivated a small garden with herbs and flowers that added to the charm of the place. Buzz loved being away from vehicles and taking care of his work all on foot. He also was pleased that the campers he met at Russell were different from those at Abol. "They are what you call real outdoor campers," he mentioned in his season wrap-up report to Austin Wilkins.

Most important, however, he found that he had the autonomy to take off in the early morning and explore before he had to attend to his official daily duties. His favorite trips were Grand Falls, Fort, Tip-Top, Pogy, North Turner, and Mullen Mountains. The untrailed mountains required bushwhacking but sometimes had sections of old logging roads that provided some relief from the spruce-fir thickets. Buzz never liked Davis Pond or even Chimney Pond. He especially felt an "eerie sense" at Davis and didn't like the foggy and rainy days he spent there.

While at Russell, he painted the front of the camp, built new racks for fire equipment, and cleared all trails of blowdown from his station to near Roaring Brook Campground. The fishing was good throughout the season, and at least one sixteen-and-a-half inch trout that weighed just under two pounds was caught by an angler.

One of the never-finished jobs was cutting firewood. Buzz liked burning hardwood but had to expend a lot of effort to get it. He paddled his canoe across the pond, went into the brush to find suitable species, sawed them down by hand, piled them in the canoe and paddled back, then split them and stacked them up.

One of Buzz's campers was William R. Girvan, who would later publish a memoir about his visits to the park. Girvan had been accustomed to spending time with Ralph Dolley at Russell Pond and was surprised to find Dolley replaced by Buzz. He made note of the "trolley on wires" that newcomer Buzz had built across the South Branch of Wassataquoik Stream near the campground.

The device, which Girvan described as "a kind of breeches buoy that the camper can climb into and pull himself across," didn't look all that substantial, so Girvan waded across the stream. Buzz "set me right about it," Girvan wrote, and showed him how to use it.

Girvan noted the presence of Buzz's relatives and the good times they all enjoyed. Buzz often invited campers running low on food to dinner. Girvan was impressed that Buzz and company ate so well in the backwoods, noting one supper of boiled potatoes, pot roast, gravy, homemade bread, baked beans, banana pudding, custard pie, and ice cream. Buzz made fudge on the gas stove, and the ladies made a big kettle of popcorn to finish off everyone's hunger.[6]

▲ ▲ ▲ ▲ ▲

Toward the end of the park season, Buzz had the company of Rodney Green from near Manchester, New Hampshire—the only official camper at Russell Pond during that time. The two hiked about every day for two weeks blazing trails. There had never been a painted trail to Lookout Rock, and Taylor instructed them to do it.

Lookout Mountain was only a 400-foot climb, but it provided stunning views, following past fires and logging operations. To the north, a hiker could see North Traveler, and, turning toward the east, could glimpse across miles of woods and hills the smokestack of the Sherman Lumber Company in Stacyville. On a clear day, Katahdin's North Peak and Knife Edge were visible.

"It was a sunny fall day with full foliage," Buzz recalls. "There are some ledges before you get to the highest outcroppings at Lookout. Rodney and I were standing together looking out at the views, and I saw this nice flat rock surface that was out of the way of direct sight from hikers on the trail. So we autographed it with our names in white paint—'I. C. Caverly and R. Green, October, 1960.'"

Buzz didn't give another thought to the initialed rock, but it would come back to haunt him.

Green went on patrol with Buzz to Grand Falls on the Wassataquoik one morning, and they followed the old Wassataquoik tote road on the north side of the stream to the dilapidated warden's camp. The log cabin was located just inside the Baxter Park boundary and had been built by two wardens to keep an eye on poachers in the Russell Pond-to-Katahdin Lake area. After the illegal hunting was curtailed, the wardens had no more use for the cabin. By the time Buzz and Rodney Green found it, there were just three walls left standing. Inside were a tin stove, a bunk, and makeshift table.

Buzz was impressed with the tall pines growing near the cabin— both in and out of the park. He had a special feeling about the pines and the pristine Wassataquoik Stream, and made a mental note to watch over the area. Green snapped a photograph of Buzz leaning against the cabin, and it surfaced many years later after the pines had reached old-growth status and became a priority for protection by a post-Percival Baxter conservation philanthropist.

▲▲▲▲▲

Another memorable encounter in late fall was with Ruth Butler. Buzz was almost in a run on the trail from Russell to Roaring Brook when he "met" Butler as he was jumping across the rocks at the South Branch of the Wassataquoik. In midair, he looked down into the stream and saw Butler with her face in the water getting a drink. Her full head of wet hair was floating in the stream and fell across her face as she rose up out of the water to look at Buzz. "I'm Ruth Butler," she shouted. "Are you Buzz?"

There was no mistaking Butler, whom Buzz had heard about from Helon Taylor. She had a lip deformity, spoke with a lisp, and seemed what people in those days would have called "mannish." A single woman from New York State, Butler was an example of the numerous "characters" who adopted Baxter Park, and it was only by chance that she discovered it. Disowned by her family at an early age, Butler was homeless for awhile but by sheer determination made a successful life for herself. She found an assembly line job at Currier Air Conditioning in Syracuse while very young, and the work was the foundation of her financial well-being all of her life. She bought a bicycle and traveled to the Canadian Maritimes in 1948. On her way back, she stopped at Baxter Park and was sure she had arrived in paradise.

Butler spent her first vacation at Chimney Pond when Ed Werler was the campground ranger, and then for many years stayed at Roaring Brook. She took lean-to #8, a two-person shelter, every season, staying a month or more, usually part of the summer and part in the fall. She had her own nails and shelving that she put into the shelter upon arrival and took out every time she left.

While in the park, she cleared trails and in general kept watch over things. If she caught anyone doing something that was against the rules, she marched them to the ranger's office and presented her case. She wanted to know how the infraction would be handled. She, like Ranger Ivan Roy, kept an eye on mischievous children, and didn't hesitate to rein them in. While Butler could be domineering, the staff was good to her, and she was particularly close to Werler, Helen Gifford, and Wilbur and Gertrude Smith.

When they met at the stream, Butler had been on her way to meet Buzz at Russell Pond to see what he was all about. He was headed to Roaring Brook, so she turned around and fell in step with him, talking all the way. Butler couldn't hike as fast as Buzz, and when they ran into some other hikers, Buzz left her behind talking to them. He visited with Wilbur Smith awhile and just before he left the campground, Butler came along and asked why he left her. She was not about to be ignored by Buzz, whom she had decided would be a good friend. And she had it her way, developing a long-standing relationship with Buzz and Jan.

▲ ▲ ▲ ▲ ▲

By the end of that first season, Buzz had climbed Katahdin twenty-three times, eighteen of them at night to find hikers who hadn't returned to camp by dark. With a simple flashlight, he sometimes had to look for missing campers on the Knife Edge, the peak's famously dangerous arête between Baxter and Pamola Peaks. Russell Pond and Katahdin took up so much of his time that he didn't get to explore the northern part of the park for several years.

Rangers were without walkie-talkies or any other means to communicate while on the mountain, and generally didn't carry any water or food with them. Sometimes Buzz piggybacked hikers down the mountain alone and other times worked with only one other ranger evacuating an injured person on a stretcher. "Youth and adrenaline were the key factors in being able to do that," he says. No one had died from a hiking accident since the park was created, and rangers lived in denial that it would occur.

Rangers were expected to meet whatever physical demands came their way. Since Buzz had walked to school from Cornville to Skowhegan as a teenager and worked on farms from sunup to sundown, long hiking days were pure pleasure most of the time. "My adrenaline was so high, it wasn't difficult to do all that hiking."

Because he was the Russell Pond ranger, Buzz had to deal with the facility on Wassataquoik Island. The Kaler family, who owned a cabin on Second Lake Matagamon and enjoyed camping on Wassataquoik Island, had donated a tarp-covered wood structure to the park with Taylor's approval. In the spring and fall, Buzz had to haul three heavy tarps three miles to and from his camp. Buzz used an army packboard to carry the 150-pound load. A jill-poke (a pole with a nail in the end) enabled him to raise the tarps to the roof and lower them without hurting himself.

While it was tough labor, Buzz later found that evacuating a person on a litter from a mountain during a rain- or snowstorm was the worst physical job in the park.

▲ ▲ ▲ ▲ ▲

Buzz was pretty quick to notice the laxity of the park's attention to environmental problems. The dump at Russell and the drainwater disposal area was an in-your-face reality.

"I got kind of accustomed to the roadside dump that the sporting camps [and Katahdin Stream and Abol Campgrounds] were using at Foster Field," Buzz recalls. "I was realistic that it was considered the only way to dispose of stuff in those days. But when I got into Russell, this was probably my first consciousness of the need to have some type of carry-in, carry-out rule. I think I was operating on basic common sense. I remember saying to campers, 'If you can bring that soup or bean can in here full, why in the world can't you take it out empty?' They would just look at me and laugh as if it was a totally ridiculous idea to think they would be expected to carry out garbage or litter from the Maine woods."

The dump was on the edge of a very boggy area that was left over from William F. Tracey's sporting camp operations prior to the creation of Baxter Park. "I told Helon I was real disturbed about it," Buzz says. "He just kind of said, 'No, that's part of the operation.'"

Taylor was accepting of a lot of conditions and behaviors that would be questioned or illegal today. For instance, the field crew threw old toxic paint cans into the dumps, took baths with soap in park waters, and pitched laundry wash-water (sometimes with baby poop) into the woods.

Also, when it came to amenities to make things a little easier in the wilderness, Taylor and the Authority seemed to overlook the question of consistency with Governor Baxter's wishes. Rangers who had the inclination or skill to rig up a device—such as a flush toilet—did it without seeking approval beforehand, setting a precedent for other improvements.

In fact, Taylor acquired the first "generator service" in 1960 from Owen Cowen, the forest patrol ranger at the Maine Forest Service camp at Togue Pond. Cowen had received a generator through a federal surplus program and had it installed in his tool shed. It was so powerful that Cowen ran an extra line from his place to Taylor's so the supervisor could truly have running water. Taylor later bought his own Coleman generator, and others were installed elsewhere in the park over time.

Buzz knew his place as a rookie when it came to advocating change, but if he were ever in charge, he knew he would clean up the park. That inherent imperative made Buzz feel different from other rangers.

▲ ▲ ▲ ▲ ▲

Governor Baxter and Buzz met again when Baxter was on his fall inspection trip. Buzz had heard that Baxter was going to be at Roaring Brook Campground, so he hiked from Russell Pond to see the governor, along with ranger Wilbur Smith, his wife, Gertrude, and granddaughter, Karin Wilshire. Buzz and Baxter exchanged pleasantries but not much conversation. Buzz was thrilled to see the governor again. "I told [Baxter] I had just come out of Russell Pond, and that got his attention. He talked about a horse trip he had made from Stacyville to Russell Pond, as well as other horse trips to Basin Pond [lumber camp] depot."

Buzz summed up his first season in the park in a letter to Austin Wilkins: "I had a lot of new experiences and met a lot of new people, and I am proud to say that I never had any trouble with any of my campers. They were a great bunch, and it was very interesting talking to all of them."

By now, the personnel board had turned down Wilkins's request for a three-step increase for Buzz to make his pay comparable to that of Ralph Heath and Wilbur Smith, but Buzz was promised a pay raise for the next season.

▲ ▲ ▲ ▲ ▲

Governor Baxter paid another visit to the park just before it closed, and attended the annual park banquet with the rangers and their wives. Buzz didn't speak directly to the governor, but just enjoyed seeing him.

After the event, Buzz and the other crew worked to batten down the camps and finish fall chores. Buzz offered to help Ralph Heath install shutters on the ranger's camp at Chimney Pond Campground.

The following morning, the pair decided to go on to the summit of Katahdin, another two miles, where they encountered fresh snow. From there, they hiked down the mountain another seven miles to Russell Pond. Buzz wanted to show Heath the old game warden camp and the pines on Wassataquoik Stream at the park boundary—the trip he had done earlier with Rodney Green.

With twenty miles under their belts, they called it a day, sleeping over at the Russell Pond ranger's camp. They lit a fire in the woodstove, turned on the gas lanterns, and warmed up some soup. It was Buzz's practice to pull his cot away from the cabin's support beams because mice liked to run along the stringers and now and then fell down on top of a sleeper below.

Heath had a .22-caliber pistol, and Buzz was awakened in the middle of the night by the sound of Heath calling out his name and firing the gun. "Bang! Bang! Bang!" Buzz saw Heath standing on his bed in his undershorts yelling that he had to get out of there, that mice were crawling all over him.

They gathered up their gear and left for Roaring Brook Campground, another seven miles. Wilbur Smith was spending his second night alone without his wife because he was closing up the camp, and he was known to be uncomfortable alone. As Buzz and Heath walked by the campground garage about 4:00 A.M., Heath fired his gun to warn Smith they were coming in and scared Smith out of his wits.

On October 29, Buzz left the park in good standing. In his November and December reports to the Authority, Taylor praised the performances of Caverly, Heath, and Smith. They "worked in well, all did their share of the work, and they got along well together," he said. "It is a pleasure to work with such a fine crew of men, and it is to their credit that everything went off so well this season. No serious accidents, no fires, and very little confusion."

Taylor's reports were full of camper numbers and dollars taken in.

The total visitation for 1960 was 17,318, plus an estimated 24,911 day visitors. The numbers were huge, compared to 1942 when 582 people signed the register at the two campgrounds, and 1950 when 2,396 visited the four campgrounds. Despite its backwater location, nearly 300 foreigners found their way to the park, presumably because of its notoriety in the new media. The 1960 income was $21,213. Evidence of how important personal contacts were in those days, Helen Gifford reported that she wrote 893 letters and talked with 1,759 people, and Taylor penned 1,044 letters and conversed with 2,179 people.

▲ ▲ ▲ ▲ ▲

Buzz counted the days until he could resume his ranger position. When he left Abol for Russell, he had shifted from temporary status to seasonal employment, making him eligible to go back to Russell Pond. In the summer, warden supervisor David Priest had come to the park and asked Buzz if he was interested in working on enforcement for the fish and game department in the fall. Buzz was gung-ho, and after his park season was over on October 30, he was commissioned a state warden and assigned to Wytopitlock, "the poaching capital of the world," for the month-long hunting season.

Buzz was paired with warden Alden Kennett. Until 1960, wardens used their personal cars on the job and couldn't put more than 16,000 miles on them for work and be reimbursed by fish and game. One night when they were staking out a field to catch night hunters, they saw a suspicious car and chased it a short distance. Then Kennett stopped and turned around because he had nearly used up his 16,000 miles for the year.

When the warden's job was over, Buzz headed back to Enfield to live with his parents and find a winter job. He was anxious to see his girlfriend, Margie Cossaboom. He didn't have a car, so he decided to walk and hoped to hitch a ride. A woman on her way to Milo stopped to pick him up. When she found out that Buzz was a ranger, she told him her husband and she had had sporting camps at Baxter Park before the park kicked them out and burned their cabins. "The state killed my husband," the woman said, and Buzz was flabbergasted to learn that her husband was William F. Tracy, who had operated camps at Russell Pond. "I was never so happy to get out of a car."

Buzz wasn't picky when it came to a temporary winter job. He wrangled work at Irving Tanning Company in the old Atlas plywood mill on the Penobscot River. "I knew a guy there, and he said they had a job there for thirty-five dollars a week for five days a week. I took the job and boarded at home in Enfield that winter." He also found a state trooper who would let him ride around the countryside on patrol, and it helped Buzz forget the distastefulness of working in the tannery.

"The first day I went into the plant, they issued me a black rubber apron, took me down to the cellar, and told me my job was to de-hair the hides. I just couldn't take that—the insects down there, the wet, the filth, and the odor," he recalls. "I worked a couple of hours and went back up to my friend Rolly Hanley and told him I had to find another way to make a living. It was the first time in my life I'd ever taken a job I felt I couldn't stick with."

Buzz was assigned another job in the finishing operation, this time on the third floor. That whole winter he did nothing but pick finished leathers off a grading machine and put them on a "wooden horse." "I'd build those horses up two or three feet high with leather, then move the rack. By the time spring fever closed in in mid-March, I was chomping at the bit to get out of that tannery. I knew I wouldn't ever go back."

▲ ▲ ▲ ▲ ▲

That winter, three thousand miles away, writer Wallace Stegner sat down at his typewriter to make a case for a national wilderness preservation system. His "Wilderness Letter," sent to the Outdoor Recreational Resources Review Commission, awakened a national conscience to the human spiritual need for wilderness. The very idea of wilderness was a valuable resource, he said. Actual wilderness, he said, was a reminder of America's frontier origins that "has helped form our character and that has certainly shaped our history as a people."

> We need to demonstrate our acceptance of the natural world, including ourselves; we need the spiritual refreshment that being natural can produce. And one of the best places for us to get that is in the wilderness where the fun houses, the bulldozers, and the pavement of our civilization are shut out. . . . We simply need that wild country . . . even if we never do more than drive to its edge and look in. For it can be a means of reassuring ourselves of our sanity as creatures, a part of the geography of hope.7

The "Letter" was a strong influence in the shift from traditional "conservation" to a more activist form of preservation that came to be known as environmentalism. It was included in the commission's 1962 report and consequently served as a catalyst to the passage of the Wilderness Act of 1964.

Buzz was unaware (as likely were the other rangers) of Stegner's letter or the national effort toward defining wilderness and expanding the reservoir of federal wilderness lands. Yet in time the remote Maine park would become a one-of-a-kind wilderness area that would attract admirers from around the globe.

---

1. *Legacy of a Lifetime: The Story of Baxter State Park,* by John W. Hakola, TBW Books, Woolwich, Maine, 1981, p. 195.
2. *Changing Maine: 1960-2010,* edited by Richard Barringer, Tilbury House, Publishers, Gardiner, Maine, 2004; Chapter 19, "Maine's Forest Industry: From One Era to Another," by Lloyd Irland, pp. 366–86.
3. The 3.2-mile Helon Taylor Trail, opened in 1963, started at Roaring Brook Campground and followed a westerly direction over Keep Ridge to end at Pamola Peak. Most of the work building the trail was done by Monroe Robinson of Millinocket and his Boy Scout troop, with much help from volunteer Ruth Butler.
4. The council was an anachronistic political holdover from the nineteenth century that had confirmation power over gubernatorial appointments and authority in other political matters until the early 1970s.
5. *Ten Million Acres of Timber,* by Austin Wilkins, TBW Books, Woolwich, Maine, 1978, p. 117.
6. *In Beyond Katahdin,* by William R. Girvan, self-published (no date), p. 199.
7. "Wilderness Letter," Wallace Stegner to David E. Pesonen, December 3, 1960.

Primary Document Sources: BSPA Boxes 1, 2, 4, 15, 17, 18 (2507-0713, 2507-0714, 2507-0717, 2507-0718).

Conversations and communications: Buzz Caverly, Ray Porter, Rodney Sargent, Doris Scott, Doug Scott, Janice Thompson, Ed Werler.

▲▲▲▲▲▲▲▲

CHAPTER 4

# Russell Pond

Buzz was down in the dumps at the beginning of 1961. He had an indoor job he didn't like, and his romance with Margie Cossaboom was over. But an invitation to a local skating party suddenly turned his personal life topsy-turvy. He finally met Jan Thompson, who knew right away that Buzz was her man.

Jan was raised in Lowell, where her father worked as an electrician at the local paper mill. Like Buzz, she went to a one-room school until the eighth grade and then enrolled at Lee Academy, where she graduated in June 1956—three years ahead of Buzz.

Jan's ambition was to run a day care for children. However, a few weeks after going to work at the nursing home in Lincoln, Amy and A. J. Cole of Bangor approached Jan about looking after their daughter, Jackie, who had a bone disease and needed round-the-clock care. The Coles' family trucking business had made them wealthy, and they opened the door to a new world of luxury and travel for Jan.

Nothing, however, would keep Jan from being with Buzz. He was clean-cut, with all-American good looks and a winning smile. He wore white t-shirts and khakis, and preferred white socks even though he knew they looked dorky.

Buzz, on the other hand, was cautious about Jan. He thought she was accustomed to "high society" and doubted she could be seriously interested in him. Jan had to be away during the winter with the Coles in Florida, but she and Buzz kept in touch by phone and mail. "I had never written so many letters in my life—twice a week," says Buzz.

Over the winter, he came to believe a future with Jan was possible. A letter he wrote to her on March 30, 1961, declared his deep love for her. "I think it's going to be the happiest day of my life when you come home," he said. The letter also revealed how strong Buzz's need was to have a family. He had visited a newly married friend in Skowhegan and was "really envious."

*Jan Caverly, 1956*
OLAN MILLS PHOTO, COURTESY OF THE CAVERLY FAMILY

All the time I was at his place I thought about you and how I wished you were with me, as I watched them and saw how happy they were. I can't understand, hon, why it seems so hard for me to get settled down, all I ask for right now is a year-round job, not one that is going to get me rich, just one that will pay me enough to have the one thing I have always wanted, a family, someone to love and share what little I have got. I thought last summer when I was up at the Park I was all set except that I didn't have the one thing that every boy wants, a girlfriend.

▲ ▲ ▲ ▲ ▲

By late April, Buzz was back at the park ready for the spring social and ranger training. He was assigned again to Russell Pond Campground, as he expected.

Buzz had a surprise when he first came in sight of Katahdin. It was his first view of the mountain massif draped in snow—one of the most

*View of Russell Pond*
JAKE DAY PHOTO, BAXTER STATE PARK PHOTO ARCHIVES

beautiful sights he had ever seen. When he had arrived the previous May, there was no snow on the summit, and he had left the park in the fall before new snow had fallen.

"The snowdrift in front of the old forest service camp at Togue Pond beach was so hard and deep that they couldn't get the vehicles through to get up to Helon's camp," Buzz recalls. The rangers used shovels to break down the drifts to the point Taylor's old Willys Jeep could get through. Later, they made a snowplow out of used railroad timbers. They arranged them into a V, bolted on a scraper, and devised a pulley to raise the plow. "Back then we were motivated to be creative because we had scant resources to work with," Buzz notes.

Buzz and Ralph Heath spent the night at Helon Taylor's camp. After supper, Buzz and Ralph Heath were told that they had to go to bed early, and there was no explanation. Snoring away in bunks in the attic room, they were rousted awake about 10:00 P.M., got dressed, and went outside to find out what came next.

Taylor directed them to go to Roaring Brook Campground with Myrle Scott and Frank Darling, now a senior ranger. For the first time, Buzz and Heath rode Taylor's red Polaris snowmobile, which had a notable history. Without asking approval from Governor Baxter or park trustees, Taylor had bought the sled for $854 of his own money so he could more comfortably get around in the park in winter. It was so hard to ride and the metal seats so cold that rangers named it "the old iron dog."

Buzz's maiden ride on "the dog" was body-numbing, with the temperature considerably below zero. The Polaris, with a 7.5-horsepower engine, couldn't go more than ten or twelve miles an hour, but the windchill effect was still enough to make the ride physically daunting. Rangers didn't have the warm, insulated snowsuits and helmets that riders wear today.

When the group arrived at Roaring Brook, Buzz and Heath pulled a toboggan out of the shed and then dug out of the snow a bunch of 200-pound gas cylinders to tie onto the sled. The round cylinders were hard to keep in place for any distance, especially in hilly terrain, and by the time they reached Blacksmith Brook, they hit deep snow.

It had snowed over 115 inches that winter—not a record amount but enough to impress a twenty-one-year-old farm boy. Buzz was accustomed to demanding physical labor in the fields of Cornville but unfamiliar with the winter circumstances in which he now found himself.

Snowshoeing was new, too, and it was especially hard because he was wearing rubber gumboots. In those days, the snowshoes had leather straps that loosened up when wet. In turn, the boots had more room to slip around, making Buzz work hard to get solid footing.

> The way we handled the job was having two of us in front of the toboggan and two of us at the back. When we got into a steep pitch, the ones up front would pull the toboggan up to them and hold it, and the ones on back would get down on their knees and hold it and then the ones on front would step ahead. When they pulled it, the ones in back would push as far as they could reach. You'd fall flat on your face. That's how we would get gas in to Chimney Pond—one tank at a time, one snowshoe step at a time.

Buzz sweated buckets and then some. Every time he pushed the toboggan over a drift, he fell outstretched behind it into the waist-deep snow. He was nervous, hungry, and afraid to stop for long because his cotton clothes were too thin and wet to protect him from freezing. All was silent along the trail except for the low grunts of the rangers and the crunching of their snowshoes in the deep powder.

It was about 2:30 in the morning near Basin Pond, and I was on the back of the toboggan at this point. I gave that shove to push the toboggan up and fell flat on my face. When I brushed the snow off my eyes and looked, I was on the crest of that little pitch before Basin Pond. So when I looked up right in front of me, there was Katahdin—the North Basin, the start of the South Basin, the Saddle area, and a full moon. The clouds had just cleared within those few moments. The moon was reflected on the mountain, the pond, and the snow. I just lay there and said to myself, "My God, I've finally gotten to heaven. This has got to be it!" That was the inspiring first impression that I got of the mountain. My adrenaline really kicked in, because I got over the worst part of that whole trip fine.

▲▲▲▲▲

When Buzz had a chance to reflect on that experience, he felt it as "a calling"—a kind of personal transformation that many recognize as a deep spiritual revelation. He knew he wanted to be in the park the rest of his life and do all in his power to keep it wild the way Percival Baxter wanted it. Unbeknownst to Buzz, the creator of the AT, Benton MacKaye, had had an awakening eerily similar to his.

At eighteen years old, following his freshman year at Harvard University, MacKaye set out on an ambitious hike of northern New England mountains. On New Hampshire's Mt. Tremont in the White Mountains, MacKaye found himself in dire circumstances on a mid-August day in 1897. He and his companions struggled to find the trail to the summit amid thick blowdown and in driving rain. Lightning struck uncomfortably close by, and thunder roared in the heavens as night fell. They waited for dawn in a flimsy shelter they built in the downpour near the peak.

MacKaye awoke before dawn, and the storm had passed. He found his way to the summit, waiting for the sun to rise. In the moment of first light, the inclement weather cleared. Spellbound, MacKaye came the closest to a religious experience as he ever described.

The sight from Mt. Tremont caused "the cold chills" to go up his back, he told a friend. "I saw the sun rise over the mountains making one side of them day and the other night." Mt. Washington and the Franconia range emerged from time to time through the clouds, and he thought it "mystical."[1]

These initial encounters in Buzz's and MacKaye's lives proved fateful opportunities they could never have planned. Although the two never met, MacKaye's experience reached out to touch Buzz through the AT. The last ten miles of the 2,175-mile Georgia-to-Maine path amble through Baxter State Park, terminating on Katahdin's Baxter Peak. Buzz would eventually have oversight of that section for decades and provide untold support for tired thru-hikers trying to finish their journey before winter.

▲ ▲ ▲ ▲ ▲

While Buzz's epiphany on the Chimney Pond Trail was the strongest spiritual experience he ever had, it was not the only lasting one. Russell Pond provided daily inspiration that fueled his passion for the park even after he had left ranger duties in the backcountry.

Almost everyone who visits Russell Pond sings its praises for the penetrating solitude and scenic beauty. It wasn't always that way. Loggers moved into the Russell/Wassataquoik Stream area in the late 1880s, and the first camp on Russell Pond was part of a cluster of depot camps built by Foster J. Tracy and his son-in-law, Hugh Love, in 1883 in preparation for lumbering. They also built new footpaths up Katahdin. Tracy's nephew, William F., reopened the Russell camp in 1927 for sportsmen prior to Percival Baxter's acquisition of the land. Reminders of the Tracy-Love operations and the sporting camp have been visible for many decades in the leftover machinery and household items lying around the woods and the old garbage dump.[2]

To Buzz, Russell Pond was "a vision come true." At their dad's forestry camp in Enfield, young Buzz and Tim had shared a small bunk-room, and there was a picture on the wall of a placid pond, a cabin, a canoe on the shore, and a mountain in the background. Buzz was captivated by the photograph, wondering if he would ever be able to find such a place to live. "I came up over that little hill to Russell, and I saw the trout pond," he recalls. "I felt, 'This is paradise.' I had been envisioning this for two years."

The campground was most easily accessible from Roaring Brook, eight miles away on the Tracy Horse Trail (renamed the Wassataquoik

Stream Trail) or the seven-mile Russell Pond Trail. The hike in from South Branch Pond Campground was nine miles and from the western side of the park along the Center Mountain Trail and Wassataquoik Lake, eleven miles. Once settled in at a lean-to, tent site, or the bunkhouse, a camper was within an easy walk of some of the park's most remote gem lakes and streams, and hiking trails radiated out in all directions.

The deep snowpack that spring required Buzz to have Elmer Wilson fly him in to the Russell camp on May 21, a week after the park's general opening date. "The campground was in pretty good shape overall," he said in a report to supervisors, "although I did lose one lean-to during the winter. I was surprised to find the snow as deep as it was at that date—about five or six feet on all trails. I had another surprise when on that same day I had five doctors from Pennsylvania come down from South Branch Pond. They told me of their trip and how it took them three days to get to Russell crawling on their bellies over the snowdrifts. They were stuck two nights at Pogy Pond."

Buzz had cleaning up to do, making repairs, getting canoes out, and rebuilding the damaged lean-to. He rearranged his cabin to allow for four bunk beds to sleep visiting family and friends, and he perfected his biscuit-making on the cookstove. The ranger's cabin had been added onto over time to the point that there was a comfortable living area, a kitchen, a pantry, and a bedroom. A gas refrigerator had been flown in and dropped on the dock by Wilson in the late 1950s. Gaslights had preceded Buzz's arrival in 1960.

The park allocated the Russell Pond ranger one free flight a month for goods and services. If Buzz needed air service otherwise, he had to pay out of pocket. Wilson charged him fifteen dollars for an extra flight, and, if he wanted a tank of propane, another fourteen. (Rangers paid their own utility costs.) Groceries took the rest of his thirty-nine-dollar-a-week paycheck.

In June, after the trails were finally free of snow, he cleared blowdowns on trails, built a new dock and canoe rack on the pond, and took a wildlife inventory so he could tell campers where moose were hanging out and fish were biting. He started building a replica of a Maine Forest Service fire tower at the pond to be able to demonstrate to campers how a forest fire was located. He abandoned the project, however, when it incensed some other rangers who said it had no place in the wilderness. (Later, another Russell Pond ranger used a chain saw to take down the tower and burned the wood in his camp stove.)

To help Elmer Wilson more easily identify boulders lining the shoreline, Buzz tied white Clorox jugs to some of the rocks. He also cut a swath of trees at the end of the pond toward Deep Pond to give Wilson more clearance when taking off. Buzz extended the "runway" about 250 feet, but it wasn't enough to satisfy Wilson, and Taylor directed Buzz to take down as many trees as the pilot wanted.

Wilson was always nervous about servicing the Russell Pond Campground. He figured that the law of averages would catch up with him, and he would crash. By the end of the year, he threw in the towel and moved away from the area.

▲ ▲ ▲ ▲ ▲

Governor Baxter and his party arrived at Togue Pond on June 16, 1961, for a two-day inspection of roadside park facilities. Buzz didn't see Baxter because he was in the backcountry. Although the blackflies were terrible at the time, Taylor said the governor "seemed to be in fine spirits, good health, enjoyed his trip, and was very pleased with the way things are going here." The campgrounds, the supervisor noted, looked like "young tent cities with 200 people at some of them."

With things back in order at Russell, the fun began for Buzz. Brother Tim, Aunt Elinor, and Elinor's friend Dorothy Whitten were frequent visitors again. Jan came up with family members several times to visit, and she and Buzz dated all that summer when he could manage time off. On one of his forays into town, he stopped at the Millinocket Lake store and bought Jan the first gift he ever gave to her—a white photo album with Katahdin on the front.

Besides family members, campers who returned to the park often became important to him. Some of them were "salt-of-the-earth people," interested in Buzz and able to teach him skills he didn't have, such as how to cut a stovepipe. They developed valuable friendships that would sustain him through thick and thin.

None were more special than Olga and Herbert Nowitsky, who were already friends of Helon Taylor. Buzz was impressed by the New York couple's traditional camper skills and love of the woods—characteristics that he admired. The Nowitskys had fled Germany in 1931 before Adolph Hitler came into power. Veteran campers, they preferred staying at Russell Pond because it was far away from the park's hustle and bustle. The strong attachment Buzz felt to them eventually would lead him to invite Herbert Nowitsky to live on his and Jan's land in East Corinth in 1985 after Olga died.

▲ ▲ ▲ ▲ ▲

One way the rangers blew off steam and created fun was playing practical jokes, and Buzz enjoyed the pranks as much as any of them, especially when he was still unmarried. One of his favorites was setting the outhouse at a tilt on rocks so that when someone was using it, he could sneak behind it and lower it down to embarrass them. "You'd be amazed at the screams from people caught like that."

His most notable joke at Russell Pond was the fake water hole on "Blister Buster Hill," the rise just north of Turner Brook. Summer hikers doing the long hike from Roaring Brook to Russell Pond were usually hot, tired, thirsty, and had blistered feet by the time they reached the knoll.

Buzz drove a galvanized pipe into the ground and screwed onto it an old kitchen pitcher pump that he freshened up with a coat of green paint. He made a wooden trough for it and hung a cup on it, as well as a small sign saying "Tracy's Old Spring." Hikers would stop at the pump and work the handle, but no water would come out. "They would come to me and complain there was no water," says Buzz. "So I'd give them a bucket to get some water from the brook to prime the pump." Once the gullible hikers opened the lid of the box to pour in the water, they saw the sign "No Water. Keep Smiling."

Buzz was as often the target of the jokes as the perpetrator. Buzz, Ralph Heath, and Wilbur Smith worked with a "man-killer chain saw" to clear brush and limbs from trails. One night, they all stayed at Smith's cabin after clearing blowdowns from fifteen miles of trail, and Buzz put the chain saw away in the Roaring Brook shed. They settled down for a supper prepared by Smith and then made music together— with Heath on the guitar, Smith on the harmonica, and Buzz singing.

Before turning in, Heath asked Buzz if he had turned off the toggle switch on the chain saw to keep the battery from draining power, and Buzz shook his head no. He went out to the shed and turned off the button. Heath suggested he'd better go down to Helon Taylor's camp and get another battery.

Taylor's favorite pastime at night was reading. He was a great fan of Western author Louis Lamour and had quite a collection of cowboy novels. Buzz remembers, "Helon was lying there with his Stetson on, reading a western and eating some peanuts, and he asked me what I was doing there so late. I said I needed a battery to replace one in the chain saw. He looked at me and said, 'I've never seen a battery in that chain saw, and I've got the mate to your chain saw. I think you've been had. The boys got you good.'"

Smith's camp was dark when Buzz returned. He tiptoed inside, thinking his pals were asleep, and suddenly he heard them laughing till they cried. "I heard about that for so long—that I had been a real sucker—so I began to tell people about it myself," Buzz laughs.

While gullible and fun-loving in his early years, Buzz was unusually serious when it came to enforcing park rules and state fish and game laws. He energetically handed out summonses for violations. In the backcountry, he had a lot of authority because he was usually the only law around—patrolling fish and game wardens or state forest rangers were few and far between.

▲ ▲ ▲ ▲ ▲

Since Helon Taylor didn't get out frequently to check on his rangers in person, he devised field tests to make sure they were telling him the truth. Now the time was ripe to see how dependable Buzz was. Taylor called Buzz one rainy evening and told him to go check on a party of campers at Davis Pond. Buzz didn't hesitate or ask questions. He remembers the trip well:

Now Davis Pond is five miles from Russell, and it's an uphill walk much of the way. I told Helon I'd go the next morning, and it was still raining hard. I probably had one of the most miserable trips of my life going up to the pond. By the time I got there, the rain had stopped, and the clouds broke, but I'm soaking wet. I looked into that old log shelter that was built by the AMC. It had no windows—just a door—and it was full of spruce boughs people put in there to sleep on and had never pulled out. There was a big old fireplace right at the doorway. If a spark ever flew out of that fireplace onto those dried boughs, nobody could ever get out in time, I thought. The sun got stronger, so I climbed up onto that old building roof to dry out. It had 90-weight tar paper, and I remember lying down on that and how warm it felt, and the heat just penetrated my wet clothes. The steam was coming off me. I was lying there, not a soul around, and I'm thinking to myself, "Boy, this is a great trip." Then I heard footsteps and thought, "Helon's right. There is somebody up here." So I just lay still and heard them coming from down off Katahdin. Whoever it was got closer and closer and pretty soon came around the corner. It was Ralph Heath from Chimney Pond.

Both rangers were surprised to see each other and to find out that Taylor had told both of them the same story. They figured out pretty quickly that Taylor was seeing if they would carry out his orders. They agreed not to let on to Taylor that they saw each other and see what would happen.

Buzz returned to Russell Pond for the week, and when his day off came up, he stopped at Taylor's camp early in the morning.

Helon would get up at 4:00 A.M. and do his paperwork. He was a one-finger typewriter operator, and you'd hear the plunk-plunk-plunk of the typewriter when the windows were open and the birds were singing. He was always congenial. "Come on in, Buzz," were the first words out of his mouth when he saw you drive in the yard, and you'd go in and have a cup of tea. He'd ask how things were going and so forth. "By the way, I sent you to Davis Pond here awhile back," he said. "Did you get up there all right?" I said yes, and then he had asked if I saw anyone else there. I told him that there were no campers there but someone else showed up. He got this smile on his face and said, "Well, thank you. I appreciate you going up."

Taylor never questioned Buzz anymore on the subject but Buzz found out from Heath that the supervisor asked him the same questions. "So Helon was satisfied that Ralph and I had carried out his instructions."

▲ ▲ ▲ ▲ ▲

In the short time that Buzz had known Taylor, the supervisor had become Buzz's ideal image of a ranger. "He was always Tom Grant to me [from *Wilderness Warden*]," says Buzz. "He was of such high character and such a hard worker." Buzz had yet, however, to overly impress Taylor, according to a letter to Austin Wilkins on July 4, 1961. Taylor was comparing rangers. He said that former ranger Tom Sprague saw the need of more tent sites at Abol Campground but requested a bulldozer, trucks, and a power shovel to make them—costs the park couldn't make.

> Last year Irvin Caverly, Jr., was there, saw the need but expected somebody else to do the work and build them. This year Rodney Sargent saw the same need and went to work with what he had to do with and before July first had five new tent sites ready with the access road and a place to park a car at each site ready for use. He had no outside help and there was no extra cost. Last night he had some ninety campers there, all happy and everything under control. That, in my estimation, is what it takes to be a good ranger on this Park.

Two days later, Wilkins replied to Taylor's assessment of the three rangers and came to Buzz's defense. "I do feel compelled to say that Caverly is a very young man and needs guidance as to what to do," said Wilkins. "I believe once he is told he should be able to carry through. Possibly if Caverly was told to go ahead and do this on your orders, he might be doing the same as Rodney Sargent."

▲ ▲ ▲ ▲ ▲

There was an underlying competition between Buzz and Rodney Sargent, who already was "top-notch" with Taylor. Sargent returned from the army in 1961 to take over Abol Campground again. The two rangers worked well together on park projects but weren't personal friends. Yet there were similarities in their Baxter experience.

When Sargent joined the park crew, he was, like Buzz later on, the "baby ranger," and was introduced to Percival Baxter by Taylor that way. He, too, described his first view of Katahdin—at Pockwockamus Hill on the way to Togue Pond—as "breathtaking. Knowing I was going to be working in the mountains that I'd never been to before was exciting," Sargent recalls.

Sargent loved the job because it varied so much. "You never knew day-to-day what you'd be facing," he says. "From 5:00 A.M. until 11:00 at night, you might be helping the Girl Scouts at a campground or carrying people off Katahdin. There was more responsibility than you could imagine—search and rescue, first aid, and law enforcement."

Sargent, like Buzz, tramped all over the park, following old tote roads, bushwhacking through the woods and up mountain peaks, exploring old sluiceways and lumbering camps. Buzz was not the only one who felt "a calling" after he arrived at Baxter Park, according to Sargent. "If a ranger was at Baxter long, he had a calling."

▲ ▲ ▲ ▲ ▲

Letters from park visitors praising Buzz improved his standing with Taylor. For example, on August 30, 1961, Frank J. Hahn of the mathematics department at Yale University wrote Taylor a letter of appreciation for the friendliness and helpfulness of rangers. "In particular Ranger Caverly at Russell Pond was very helpful and seemed quite familiar with the surrounding area," Hahn said. "The camp at Russell Pond was the model of what such a camp should be."

Taylor appreciated Hahn's comments about Buzz. "He is young and needs some experience before he will make a top-notch ranger," replied the supervisor. "Your remarks will help him greatly, and I have some good comments from others this season, too."

Hahn was one of an increasing number of park visitors who were complaining about environmental issues. He called attention to the "desecration" of camping areas around the Fowler Ponds—the refuse, empty beer cans, whiskey bottles, trees stripped of bark, unauthorized fireplaces on the pond shores, and signs peppered with bullet holes.

Elizabeth White of West Hartford, Connecticut, who had spent a month at Katahdin Stream Campground, sent a seven-page diatribe to Wilkins, complaining of overcrowding, traffic congestion, and noise. Her tent site was at the Hunt trailhead, and she was bothered by almost constant foot traffic, she said. The two nearby outhouses "were full almost to the seat."

The general atmosphere of the large open area around the little pond and dam near the ranger station I regarded as none of my business, but I was appalled at the fact that children playing there had imported jumbo plastic ball bats, whiffle balls, and other commercial toys, and many campers had house trailers. The impression was that these were not people who knew how to camp . . . and nothing was done to call attention to the pleasurable natural resources around them. They had brought civilization with them and closed out nature. I was struck by the absence of nature trails, a nature library in this or any of the park's ranger stations, or for that matter, park personnel versed in accurate and complete knowledge of natural phenomena, even including identification of trees and birds.

She also complained about overcrowding destroying the peace and beauty of the park and presenting "a health hazard." White told Wilkins that the rangers should acknowledge that they "have not given full consideration to the wishes of nature-loving campers, any more than you have fulfilled Gov. Baxter's intent."

There was no question that under the eyes of Percival Baxter, the Baxter Park Authority, and Helon Taylor, environmental abuses were overlooked, knowingly allowed to persist, or corrective action was slow in occurring. It was not just a matter of financial and staff limitations. The whole concept of wilderness management and political environmental ethics was just at the beginning stages of development.

Even state agencies undertook programs and actions that were counter to wilderness protection. An example was Austin Wilkins, acting on his own, giving approval to the fish and game department to kill fish in South Branch Pond in the name of "reclamation." Biologists used chemicals to kill the native suckers and minnows and then restocked it with brook trout to provide anglers a better fishing experience. It wouldn't be the only time restocking would happen in park waters without considering Governor Baxter's wildlife sanctuary mandate.

Also, Helon Taylor had allowed fishermen from the sporting camps to build cooking fires for lunch on the shores of a number of the park's remote ponds without permits. Deputy forest commissioner Fred Holt informed Wilkins that the situation put warden Clayton Gifford in a hard spot. Gifford felt he should prosecute the violators but hadn't done so in deference to Taylor. Holt suggested in a letter to all concerned that the park rules on fire permits would be enforced the next season. The Authority agreed, angering sporting-camp owners.

Gifford also called attention to the unlisted and unposted (for a fire permit) campsite at Wassataquoik Lake, which rangers referred fishermen to at times. "Caverly feels he can't refuse [anglers] once they've used it and requested it again this year," related Holt. "It's safe enough—my point is there appears to be too loose control of what goes on . . . and filthy conditions. . . . It seems to me with extremely few exceptions—perhaps only Little Wassataquoik and the Fowler Ponds— all campsites that are not manned should be eliminated. Whatever few do remain should be policed regularly."

Little by little, Buzz began developing a sense of the gap between Percival Baxter's wilderness vision and on-the-ground reality. On that score, DDT spraying was a red flag.

Pesticides were generally considered at the time "miracle" chemicals with no long-term threats to humans. However benign they might be to people using poisons to kill off brush along roadsides, and to kill biting insects at campgrounds, they seemed to Buzz to be in direct opposition to the park's mission. He wouldn't use the sprayer at the campgrounds he managed.

Littering, dumps, and filthy privies were also hard for Buzz to accept for Baxter Park—not only at campground areas but the camps of state foresters, fire tower watchmen, and wardens in the preserve. "Litter was something everybody thought they had to get rid of, and so they just opened the car window and threw it out," Buzz says. Rangers picked up the litter and campers' garbage bags and hauled the stuff to the dumps off the main tote road that were easily accessible by trucks.

There was no dump at Abol Campground. "We had a fifty-five-gallon drum painted green and sprinkled lime in the bottom," Buzz recalls. Rangers emptied the drum daily at the Foster Field dump. Garbage from the Katahdin Stream Campground and the privately run sporting camps at Daicey and Kidney Ponds was also disposed of at Foster Field. Some other sporting camps on the park's borders surreptitiously created dumps inside the park for everything from garbage to trucks, machinery, and bedsprings.

At Chimney Pond, garbage had been accumulating longer than anywhere in the park because people had been camping at that outpost since the early 1900s. The dump, behind the old bunkhouse, was in an area that drained down to a brook, and the odor attracted bears. In 1959 Chimney Pond ranger Nicholas Barth questioned the continued use of the campground he oversaw because of the environmental, as well as sanitary, conditions. Taylor didn't respond to Barth's complaints or recommendations about how to improve the situation. When Buzz saw

*Junior York's Twin Pines sporting camp dump
on Nesowadnehunk Stream, 1960s*
BUZZ CAVERLY PHOTO, BAXTER STATE PARK PHOTO ARCHIVES

the dump location in a wet, mossy area on the edge of a bog, he complained to Taylor that it was a disgrace, but the supervisor suggested that Buzz should accept dumps as necessary to park operations.

Taylor's solution to objectionable dumps (and to worn-out trails) was to move them to a fresh spot. Recreational impacts still were generally minor on the landscape, and the north woods seemed limitless. So Taylor's thinking wasn't unreasonable for the times.

If Buzz really wanted to go to the trouble, he could relocate the Russell Pond dump, Taylor told him. But there was no place to go because of the surrounding marsh. The nearby Turner Deadwater area was too pristine and beautiful, Buzz thought. "I told Helon the only way to improve things was for campers to lug out what they brought in. Unfortunately, people didn't accept the concept of 'carry in/carry out' until later."

▲ ▲ ▲ ▲ ▲

Encounters with bears came in different ways. One afternoon in the fall when Buzz was hiking back to Russell Pond, he stopped on the trail to empty himself of a heavy meal he had eaten in Millinocket. Buzz didn't know when he squatted down that a bear was doing the same thing just feet away behind some brush. When Buzz stood up, the bear ran away, and he looked around to discover the bear's "steaming berries on the ground. It was too humbling to talk about then."

▲ ▲ ▲ ▲ ▲

The 1960s national environmental movement had yet to bloom in Maine. The Maine Chapter of The Nature Conservancy and the Natural Resources Council of Maine (NRCM), launched in 1956 and 1959, respectively, were focused initially on ramping up their organizations, and NRCM was the only environmental advocacy group on the scene for awhile. NRCM cut its political teeth on the controversial Dickey-Lincoln dam and Allagash Wilderness Waterway proposals in the mid-1960s, and didn't turn its attention to Baxter Park issues until the end of the decade.

Consequently, the Fin and Feather Club stood alone on the Baxter activist front when Buzz joined the park crew. Not many weeks went by that the Authority didn't receive complaints, criticism, or special requests from the club. Buzz sympathized initially with the club's hard feelings against the park. The outdoors was what local people lived for, because they spent all their working life in a hot, odorous, oppressive mill.

"I knew about it from my dad in the textile mill," Buzz says. "The only break that a lot of these people got from that atmosphere was fishing, hunting, trapping, and camping. They saw it as their God-given right to use the park the way they always had, and their fathers and mothers before them."

Much was about to change on the environmental front nationally, and events couldn't help but affect Baxter Park over time. Wallace

Stegner's "Wilderness Letter" was gaining traction with the public, awakening the American conscience to the spiritual need for wilderness.

On September 27, 1962, *Silent Spring* hit the bookstores after being serialized in the *New Yorker* magazine. Biologist/author Rachael Carson's investigation of the chemical industry exposed the hazards of DDT to humans and wildlife and gave "legs" to the fledging environmental movement. The Sierra Club published *In Wildness Is the Preservation of the World* with color photographs by Eliot Porter. It, too, increased public interest and support for environmental protection, as had the earlier black-and-white photographic essay by Ansel Adams called *This American Earth*.

Baxter Park rangers, however, were still oblivious to such media and political stirrings. Geographically and culturally, they were far from the mainstream.

▲ ▲ ▲ ▲ ▲

On October 4, 1961, Buzz closed Russell Pond Campground and moved to Roaring Brook to help Wilbur Smith cut cordwood. At the end-of-season banquet at Togue Pond Camps, Buzz had another opportunity to see Percival Baxter, who was accompanied by then-governor John Reed and other state officials. It was a special occasion—Helon Taylor's sixty-fourth birthday. Taylor was pleased with all the to-do over him. "Not everyone can boast that the governor of the state and his [Executive Council and the Baxter Park Authority] flew some 300 miles just to sing them a happy birthday," Taylor wrote in his October park report.

Buzz and Baxter didn't get a chance to talk personally. But rangers Myrle Scott and Frank Darling daringly spoke out to Baxter about banning pets—a smoldering issue. Not only dogs and cats were running around campgrounds, but campers also brought chickens and parrots on occasion.

Domestic pets were a touchy issue, since Helon Taylor and other rangers kept dogs at their camps. Buzz's collie, Bonnie, lived with him at Abol and Russell Pond. Baxter, a well-known dog lover, knew about the practice and condoned it.

Jean Stephenson, executive director of the ATC, had advocated getting all domestic pets out of the park. In a letter to the Authority, she wrote that pets, even on a leash, had no place in a wilderness preserve.

If pets weren't removed, she said songbirds "would be driven away" by the continuing presence of cats.

"Wild" pets were also a park tradition that Percival Baxter condoned. Area wardens brought motherless little animals to Doris Scott and Jeanette York. Helon Taylor and numerous rangers tamed animals with kindness and food, such as the fox, "Frances." One of Taylor's favorites was "Cookie," a doe who would eat out of his hand. Doris Scott's resident doe was "Perky," and bucks named "Pat" and "Mike" hung out at South Branch Pond, where campers offered them chocolate bars and took photos. Ranger Tom Sprague had a fawn living in his Abol cabin, and Buzz inherited a raccoon from Sprague. Ralph Dolley had tamed a doe with soda crackers at Russell Pond, and Buzz took up feeding the deer when he replaced Dolley. Buzz hadn't had problems per se with domestic or wild pets at Russell Pond. He considered it a roadside campground issue.

▲ ▲ ▲ ▲ ▲

Buzz went off the payroll on October 14, and for the second time worked for a month as a game warden. Then a surprise letter came in the mail ordering him to report for a physical exam to be drafted into the army. He drove to Bangor unworried about it, and his nonchalance paid off. He was given a 4-F rating for a reason he never inquired about.

Buzz constantly thought about the park, wondering what was going on. There was little happening because so few people were there. One party showed up for Thanksgiving—a group of twenty-eight outing-club members from MIT—and Taylor sent Owen Grant with them. They prepared a turkey dinner with all the fixings in the bunkhouse at Chimney Pond. No other folks turned up for the rest of the year.

Buzz relocated to Brunswick for the winter to drive an oil truck for Brunswick Coal and Lumber Company (now Downeast Energy). Brunswick was only twenty-six miles from Portland, where Governor Baxter lived. Baxter often said to the park staff that if any of them were in Portland to please stop by and see him. "I was humbled by the invitation," says Buzz. "Here I was a kid from little Cornville, and Governor Baxter had done so much for the state of Maine. I didn't think I'd have the courage to do it. But I thought about it."

Buzz had an unexpected day off when his truck needed repairing. He drove to Portland and thought he would just see where Baxter's office was on Congress Street. The governor had spacious quarters on the top floor of the Trelawny Building. Buzz remembered the office as resembling his dentist's office. The furniture was "really ancient," he says, and the décor included artifacts from Baxter's travels. Receiving visitors was secretary Alice Guerney, who was almost as old as Baxter, then eighty-five. She responded to Buzz's inquiry as to whether the governor was in with, "Good Lord, land sake's, of course he is." The door to Baxter's office was open, and the governor was sitting at his large mahogany desk. The governor, dressed in a three-piece suit, welcomed Buzz warmly.

"He was so pleased to see me, but it took him a minute to find out who I was," recalls Buzz. "He asked how things were going, and he wanted to tell me about his first trip to the park in 1903. I mentioned Russell Pond, and he brought up Chimney Pond, assuming I had been there. I told him about swapping campgrounds with Ralph Heath so that Ralph could do some fishing and I could hike on Katahdin. [Baxter] talked about his trips to the old depot camps at Basin Pond and to Russell Pond with his friend Caleb Scribner."

Baxter was alert and well, Buzz remembers. "He was probably in the best shape I'd seen him." He was not using a cane at the time. Baxter commented on what a fine job park supervisor Helon Taylor was doing and that Buzz should follow his example. "I assured him I would do my best. We had a great visit—about an hour. I got ready to go, and he said, 'Good day.' Then he asked me if I had enough money. I said, 'Yes, I'm all set.'"

As Buzz drove back to Brunswick, he worried that Baxter thought he might have visited him because he needed money. He confided in Taylor, who brushed off the money question. People were always asking the governor for money, Taylor told Buzz, adding that Baxter was clarifying for himself whether he could help Buzz. Taylor's explanation satisfied Buzz, and Buzz tried to visit the governor again in Portland at another time, but Baxter was away from his office.

▲ ▲ ▲ ▲ ▲

While Buzz was delivering oil, Taylor's purchase of the Polaris snowmobile came to the attention of the Authority and Governor Baxter just after the New Year, 1962. Authority chairman Austin Wilkins asked Baxter to reimburse the supervisor. The legislature didn't provide capital funds for such an expense and consequently, Wilkins said he would like to take the money from the park's trust fund. "I have seen this vehicle and believe it is a useful means of winter travel that could very well serve the purpose of rescue, inspection, and law enforcement work," he told the governor. Baxter approved the reimbursement.

There was more to the snowmobile matter than met the eye. Taylor had wanted the sled not just for his use but to make money for the park. He wanted to charge winter visitors to haul their gear on the Polaris—fifty cents per pack, a dollar per person on a regular trip, and eight dollars per trip for special situations. "We have been giving away too much around here, especially in winter," Taylor said. Wilkins agreed.

With the door opened to the first snowmobile by Taylor, others followed. When the machines weren't being used to haul equipment and supplies, rangers had a ball racing them and testing the limits of sled and rider on the snowy slopes of Katahdin.

▲ ▲ ▲ ▲ ▲

As winter came to an end, Austin Wilkins had to fish or cut bait on whether to fund a year-round chief ranger/assistant supervisor position. Myrle Scott was no longer willing to carry out those duties without the official title and a pay raise. Wilkins concluded that the state's general fund couldn't afford the position, possibly for a couple of years. Since Scott needed more income for his growing family, he quit to become director of Lily Bay State Park in Greenville.

Taylor was disheartened to lose his "right-hand man." Scott had grown up with the park, knew it better than anyone else, and would be hard to replace, Taylor said, griping in a letter to Wilkins about the loss of Baxter rangers to the state park system, as well as to schools, Great Northern Paper mills, and other full-time employment. Scott's departure, however, created a leadership hole in the field ranks, making room for someone else to rise to importance. That person would be Buzz Caverly.

▲ ▲ ▲ ▲ ▲

Buzz's second park season had reunited him with Ralph Heath and Wilbur Smith. They worked on projects together and often had to hike miles alone to shovel snow off campground roofs. Buzz recalls break-ing trail by himself in deep snow from Togue Pond to Roaring Brook, a distance of eight miles. It took him until near dark to get to the ranger's station, where he built a fire to get warm and opened a can of beans for supper. By early morning he was shoveling for all he was worth so he could return to Helon Taylor's place.

The battery-powered radios at the ranger camp were dead in the winter, so there was no communication with the outside world if Buzz was injured. When he asked if Taylor was concerned about him, he remembers Taylor saying, "Mister, you're a woodsman. If you can't take care of yourself, maybe you shouldn't be there."

Buzz had to fly in to Russell Pond because the late snow on the ground was too deep to snowshoe carrying supplies. He found "every-thing in good condition." On his to-do list were the usual clearing of trails, repairing bridges, painting, testing fire equipment, cleaning up camping areas, and getting his own home in order.

In his years at Russell, Buzz would explore and re-explore the vicinity of Russell Pond and back south to Roaring Brook, rather than heading north. He didn't particularly like the Pogy Pond Trail to South Branch Campground. In the early 1940s, that area had been cut hard by William T. Tracy, and after that, was hit by fires, leaving it a hot place to hike on humid days.

On Russell Pond and at Wassataquoik Lake, Buzz also practiced gunnelling canoes—standing on the bow and rocking the boat to near capsizing—a new interest that provided exciting experiences for fam-ily, friends, and governors.

Being single and not interested in gourmet dishes, Buzz found he could get by with a lot of dried food, powdered milk, and canned goods. He ate a lot of pancakes, corncakes, macaroni, soups, sardines, and peanut butter. If he had visitors, he made goulash by taking one of everything he had in the cupboards and dumping it in a pot of tomato soup and tomato paste. His culinary salvation was fresh trout from the pond. Now and then, Buzz would hide a cake of ice in with the groceries flown in by Elmer Wilson. He had liked making ice cream from the time he was a kid and took a small churn into Russell Pond with him. By adding vanilla and a baby-food jar of mashed bananas, Buzz had a tasty dessert.

In the summer, Buzz's clan—Tim, Aunt Elinor, and Dorothy Whitten—were back again to live at his cabin. As Tim got older, Buzz let him join the park crew putting out small fires and dealing with wildlife matters. By this time, Tim was dead set on following in Buzz's footsteps.

Jan Thompson visited Buzz twice that summer. The second time, Buzz took her up to Lookout Rock above Russell Pond. Standing there, looking out over the peaceful valley and toward the Northwest Basin, they took in the enduring beauty of the region and, says Buzz, "made a sort of awkward proposal to each other." They acknowledged goals of full-time employment in the park and a lifetime commitment to Baxter's vision.

Tim Caverly viewed Buzz and Jan as a team from the start, and they all got along well as a threesome. One of Tim's strongest memories of that Russell Pond summer was Jan "always hiking behind Buzz," and the smell of Buzz's cherry-blend pipe tobacco in the air. (He smoked just briefly.)

Buzz went to great lengths to interact positively with campers and had an innate interest in people of all kinds, recalls Tim. One camping party asked to leave a trout in Buzz's camp freezer, and the next day another party also left another trout, which was larger. When the first party left, he took the second party's fish, and Buzz hiked after him almost all seven miles to Roaring Brook to give the right trout to the campers.

▲ ▲ ▲ ▲ ▲

Governor Baxter had mulled over the pet problem and allowed a domestic pet prohibition to go into effect for the summer of 1962— with no word to rangers about the feeding and taming of wild animals. If campers were unaware of the pet ban when they arrived, they were allowed to stay one night with their animal. Some people took advantage of the situation. Even at Russell Pond, a lost pet would show up now and then, and when Buzz was transferred to Katahdin Stream Campground in 1964, he was still faced with illegal pets. "We were too many years in getting that rule in full force because someone always said they didn't know about the ban," he says.

Visitors continued to write letters commending Buzz, who received more mention to the Authority than any other ranger. Richard Fleck, Jr., of Greenville, a counselor at Camp Allagash, praised Buzz for the cleanliness of the Russell Pond campsite and his "outstanding" cooperation. Taylor forwarded the note to Wilkins "with great pleasure. I talked to Caverly quite strongly when he came to work last spring and I think somebody else must have given him an earful, too," wrote Taylor. "He has done a much better job this summer than ever before. Clayton Gifford was in there recently and will tell you the same thing. He may make a good ranger yet. I hope he does."

▲▲▲▲▲

An irate camper confronted the Park Authority over what he saw as visitor damage to the wilderness preserve. Richard Leach of Danvers, Massachusetts, was disturbed that a boy had brought a gasoline-powered go-kart into South Branch Pond Campground. The youngster was driving it on the camp road "making considerable noise, stinking the place up with gasoline and oil fumes, and making a lot of dust," Leach said. He viewed go-karts as "entirely out of place and a nuisance" in the park, "the sort of thing that I want to get away from when I go camping."

He also mentioned "Tote-Goats," gasoline-driven vehicles for mountain trails that had reportedly penetrated western wilderness areas. If there were no regulations against such motorized contraptions, what would prevent Baxter Park trails from becoming "super high-ways" for those "outdoorsmen who cannot move around without the aid of the internal combustion engine and gasoline?" Leach asked.

Taylor answered the question in Leach's letter—"what has happened to Baxter State Park?"—on August 16:

> Many things in three years [since Leach's previous visit]. We have just about doubled in attendance and have acquired another 7,764 acres of land. That makes us 201,018 acres in all. However, I see your point. I saw the motor scooter at South Branch Pond. We do not have a rule or regulation to cover such things at present. We will have a meeting this fall and try to correct the situation. Some people find fault that we have so many rules and regulations already but we have to try to keep up with these things. We still hope to keep this a wilderness area.

Confirming the pressure on the park, Richard Pardo of the Maine Forest Service visited Chimney Pond in preparation for writing a park brochure. He observed that the number of campers there was often double what it was supposed to be. "Ranger Heath hesitates to turn anyone away, one reason being the fact that they will camp in unauthorized areas and create even more of a problem than the crowding of the camp areas," he said.

Taylor's 1962 survey of park visitors found that all but two of the 223 people he interviewed that month liked the park. "The other two did not like me, the rangers, wild animals, Baxter State Park, or the State of Maine. I expect their congressman will have us all fired," he quipped. Most park visitors were enchanted with Katahdin, and climbing it was the goal of most hikers. About 2,500 reported they hiked the mountain in the first four months of the season.

▲▲▲▲▲

The park reached a milestone on August 6, 1962, when Governor Baxter purchased from Great Northern Paper 7,764 acres around Togue and Abol Ponds in Township 2 Range 9. It was the last land purchase Baxter made, and it enabled him to reach a little beyond his goal of 200,000 acres to 201,018 acres. The Fin and Feather Club chimed in with a complaint about the "annexation of twelve square miles of T2R9," and registered concerns that it would be closed to hunting and trapping. However, Baxter once again allowed hunting and trapping to continue in deference to local sportsmen.

Governor Baxter returned in the fall for his regular inspection. It was the first time that Ellie Damon, the new ranger at South Branch Pond, met Baxter. Damon recalls that when Baxter arrived at the campground, he went into the cabin to visit and opened the refrigerator door. The ranger thought Baxter was checking to see if he had any liquor or beer. Buzz questions whether Baxter ever intruded into a ranger's business in that manner, but Damon was confident in his memory of the event.

Buzz again went south to work for Brunswick Coal and Lumber and stayed in a boardinghouse. But this time he had family close by. Irvin Caverly, Sr., had been transferred by the forestry department to Bowdoin, and Tim stayed with him.

At Christmas, Governor Baxter always remembered his rangers. Buzz had already received the twenty-five-dollar cash gift on each of the previous two Christmases. Anticipating their marriage, he bought

Jan a hope chest from Knowles and Dressel's furniture store in Skowhegan and put it on layaway. He put five dollars down on the thirty-five-dollar cedar chest and planned to pay the rest as he could save it. Baxter's twenty-five-dollar gift at Christmas 1962 enabled Buzz to pay the balance he owed on the chest.

▲ ▲ ▲ ▲ ▲

When Buzz returned to his ranger job in the spring of 1962, he and Ralph Heath were snowshoeing to Roaring Brook. They had just crossed Chase field culvert, where they had hauled out a dead moose the previous spring. They had just started up the hill when they heard Taylor coming on his Polaris. "He came by and hollered something like, 'See ya at Roaring Brook, boys,' and went by looking back at us. While he had his head turned, he went over what we called a 'Yes, Ma'am' bump in the snow, and Helon sailed off the machine. The throttle was open, so the sled continued to go ahead up the road. Helon rolled over, got caught up on his knees, and reached down to his belt and grabbed that coiled rope attached to the lever and pulled back on it. The deadman throttle worked like a charm and the Polaris drifted to a stop. Helon stood up and dusted himself off, rolled up the rope and hung it back on his belt buckle, got back on the sled, threw the throttle ahead, and took off."

Yes, Buzz surmised, Helon Taylor and the Polaris were made for each other.

---

1. *Benton MacKaye*, by Larry Anderson, Johns Hopkins University Press, Baltimore, 2002, pp. 36–38.

2. *Legacy of a Lifetime: The Story of Baxter State Park*, by John W. Hakola, TBW Books, Woolwich, Maine, 1981, pp. 34–36.

Primary Document Sources: BSPA Boxes 2, 4, 15, 18 (2507-0713, 2507-0714, 2507-0717, 2507-0718); Natural Resources Council of Maine newsletters, 1960-1969.

Conversations and communications: Buzz Caverly, Tim Caverly, Elmer Knowlton, Ray Porter, Rodney Sargent, Doris Scott, Jeanette York.

▲▲▲▲▲▲▲▲

CHAPTER 5

# THE BEST AND WORST OF YEARS

BUZZ AND JAN'S WEDDING DAY was planned for June 16, 1963, and Taylor surprised him by giving him three days off—a generous amount of time given the shortage of manpower in the field.

Buzz and Jan were married in the Baptist Church in Enfield by her brother-in-law, the resident preacher. Buzz couldn't afford a ring, but his Aunt Emma loaned him her garnet engagement ring until he could afford a diamond. Jan had bought a knee-length white satin and lace dress with a jacket from Sears & Roebuck for twenty-nine dollars. Buzz was dressed in a charcoal gray suit his mother had purchased for him.

Park reservations clerk Helen Gifford attended the wedding, as well as Jackie Cole. Governor Baxter couldn't be there because of ill health and sent the couple a check for fifty dollars. The park was so under-manned that neither Helon Taylor nor any of the rangers attended.

After the "I do's," Buzz and Jan took off in their blue 1957 Chevy wagon, decorated with crepe paper streamers and a cardboard sign on the front grill saying, "Just Married." They spent their first night in the Moonglow Motel in Farmington and planned to honeymoon in the White Mountains.

When they arrived in the Whites, they rode up the Mount Washington auto road on a shuttle bus, and while they enjoyed the view, they didn't like the trappings of civilization at the summit. Buzz told Jan he knew "a better place," and they high-tailed it back to Maine.

Along the way, they bought a pack basket for Jan and some gro-ceries, and met bush pilot Ray Porter at Togue Pond. There was a rainstorm brewing, and Porter took Jan and the groceries in his Super Cub to make a dash for Russell Pond, leaving Buzz to wait for the next trip.

Jan had a bumpy twenty-minute flight to her new woods home, and the water landing was scary enough that she would never forget it. The weather became so bad that Porter couldn't return to Togue

Pond, so Jan spent her first night alone as a "volunteer" backcountry ranger/bride. Buzz endured a long, wet night in his car near Windy Pitch on the Roaring Brook Road, waiting for daylight and the wind and drenching rain to end.

He burned up the trail to Russell Pond to get to Jan, and she had a hot breakfast ready and a good story of how she had taken care of the campers during the night.

After they settled in, Buzz wrote Governor Baxter a thank-you note for the wedding gift and put the only stamp he had—six cents—on the envelope. Helon Taylor advised Buzz that he had better steam off the stamp and replace it with a three-cent stamp. The governor was very generous in giving away money, Taylor said, but if he thought Buzz was unnecessarily wasting three cents on the federal government, he would have nothing more to do with him.

▲ ▲ ▲ ▲ ▲

On her second shopping trip to Millinocket, Jan bought the usual supplies and some new clothes. They filled up their pack baskets for the hike back to Russell Pond the long way around—over Katahdin. After a night at Roaring Brook Campground, they slung on the packs—Jan was carrying twenty-five pounds and Buzz, forty pounds—and headed up the Chimney Pond Trail to visit Ralph Heath.

After a big breakfast, Buzz and Jan took the Cathedral Trail to Baxter Peak. At the summit, Buzz noticed two hikers had thrown orange peels down amid the rocks, and he had a few words with the culprits, who promised they would pick up the peels and take them away for proper disposal. The hikers struck out toward South Peak, with Buzz watching them. When they reached the Knife Edge, one of them threw a bag with the orange peels off the cliffs. The bag opened in the wind, and the orange peels dropped back on the mountain.

Buzz was so mad that he ran after the hikers. He was in prime physical condition and caught up with the pair halfway across the mile-long Knife Edge. The hiker who had thrown away the orange peels turned out to be a former high school classmate of Buzz's, but that didn't stop Buzz from giving him a court summons. For Jan, the episode was a lesson in patience with Buzz that she would face a million times in the future.

After the Knife Edge episode, Buzz and Jan climbed down off the

mountain to the Davis Pond lean-to for a snack. Buzz remembers the
rest of the day:

Jan decided to freshen up a bit. She'd brought this new white set
of slacks and a blouse and a new tube of lipstick and hair comb—
she had all that stuff with her. I couldn't believe it. I had never
told her about Lake Cowles and the "land of the ooze" and all that
good stuff. So she comes back and looks like a million bucks—lipstick on, hair's all combed, brand new pair of white sneakers and
white pants. So we started down, and of course, she's getting a little tired by now. She came from the streets of Bangor and never
really had a lot of hiking experience. She was traveling slower
that I thought she should, and if she kept that up, we wouldn't get
to Russell before dark. I figured if I stayed back and let her keep
resting and stopping the way she wanted to, we'd never make it.
So I started moving ahead and found that if I kept ahead of her
just a little bit, she'd stay with me. She didn't complain too bad.
Well, I got a little too far ahead and heard her call out, "Buzz,
wait!" and so I didn't answer her the first couple of times. But I
kept hearing her say, "Buzz, wait. I need to rest." I kept going and
got out of sight. I could still hear her, and then she shouted,
"Buzz, Goddamnit you get back here!" So I went back. She had
tripped and fallen in the land of the ooze and gone in mud right
up to her elbows. Her arms were covered in mud, her face was
covered in mud. She wasn't hurt, but she was some mad. I'd have
given a lot if I'd taken a picture from the time I first spotted her
that day. You talk about a sight for sore eyes! I got her up out of
the mud, brushed off, and the adrenaline she felt from the fall
took her all the way to Russell without asking me to wait again.
She stayed right on my heels. When we got to camp, she went
into the bedroom—I thought to change her clothes. I grabbed the
buckets to get some water to fix supper. I was tired and knew we'd
sleep well after supper. I came back from the pump and no Jan. I
looked in the bedroom and there she is, crossways on the bed,
fully dressed in her muddy clothes and sound asleep—right out
cold. I just moved her over and threw a blanket over her.

Everyone who knew Jan knew how forgiving she was. Fortunately
for Buzz, she didn't ditch him and head right back to Bangor. "It was an

atrocious trip for Jan," he acknowledges now. When Buzz told Helon Taylor of Jan's escapade, Taylor commented, "She's tougher than a boiled owl!"

▲ ▲ ▲ ▲ ▲

Jan soon had another opportunity to forgive Buzz. In a mood to explore the Wassataquoik Lake area, they paddled a canoe across the big lake to the mouth of Little Wassataquoik, hiked to the lean-to, had lunch, and decided to climb South Pogy Mountain. There wasn't a lot of afternoon light left, so they left their pack basket at the lean-to in order to move quicker. They bushwhacked up the mountain, took in the beautiful ridge views, and realized they didn't have time to hike across the back side of the mountain and down into Pogy Notch and back home along the main trail to Russell. Also, their pack basket and canoe had to be retrieved. They decided to make a risky descent.

"South Pogy is straight up vertically, very, very steep so that it would be considered a technical climb if the quality of the rock was not so poor," Buzz says. Both were wearing dungarees and sneakers. He had a t-shirt on and she, a light jacket. They free-handed down the head-wall and never slipped—to their amazement.

It was pitch black by the time they returned to Wassataquoik Lake. They didn't have a flashlight with them—a surprising oversight for a ranger. Jan spent a couple of hours sitting alone in the dark while Buzz hiked almost two miles back to retrieve the pack basket and canoe at Little Wassataquoik.

When Jan heard Buzz coming, they started hollering to each other for direction, and a little comfort. After paddling to the lake outlet at the old dam, they started walking down the 2.6 miles to Russell and got back to camp around eleven at night and hit the sack. "What a day that was!" Buzz remembers. "But it was a very, very dangerous, potentially death-defying trip. All the advice we gave people about carrying lights in case they got stranded on a mountain or in the woods at night—it never occurred to us that this could happen to us. I thought I had every-thing totally under control. I almost think I had this chip on my shoul-der that all these bad things that happened to others wouldn't happen to us."

*View north from South Turner Mountain*
COURTESY BAXTER STATE PARK PHOTO ARCHIVES

▲ ▲ ▲ ▲ ▲

From the day they were married, Buzz and Jan were virtually insepa-rable. If he hiked to Grand Falls on the Wassataquoik or bushwhacked up Turner Mountain, Jan went with him. Whether it was rainy or muddy or snowy, Jan never complained. In fact, after long, hard days following Buzz, she thanked him for the trip. She valued her time at Russell Pond almost as much as Buzz.

About midway along the south shore of Wassataquoik Lake is Greene Falls, one of Buzz's favorite spots. He showed it to Jan and told her that an initiation for a new ranger's wife was to stand under the cold waters of the falls. Buzz was an old hand at withstanding the chill and thought Jan wouldn't last long. He stayed under the falls longer than usual, but she outlasted him. Jan showed Buzz that he had met his match, and he couldn't outdo her easily.

To ready the cabin for Jan, Buzz painted the floor gray. Polly Caverly made the curtains. Elmer Wilson flew in a chaise, as well as a folding rocking chair. For cooking, an old cast-iron, four-burner Atlantic stove had to do.

Wilson also delivered a fifty-five-gallon tank so the Caverlys could have running water. Buzz rigged it up above the eaves of the cabin roof with a gravity-fed water line to the kitchen sink. For washing clothes, Jan had a hand-cranked wringer on a stand with a rinse tub on each side. She would rinse the clothes in a tub and then crank them through the wringer to the second tub before hanging them on the line. She used a heavy flatiron heated on the woodstove to press their clothes. Jan rinsed the washtubs out in Russell Pond and used hand soap to bathe in Turner Deadwater because it wasn't clear yet that the phosphates in soaps were detrimental to water quality.

The Caverlys' evening ritual at Russell was to catch a couple of trout and fry them for supper, and then Buzz would visit campers to see how their day went. The newlyweds would sit on the porch until the whippoorwill started singing. The nocturnal bird's last call just before dawn was their alarm clock in the morning.

Buzz would rake whatever camping sites needed it and clean the outhouses, and Jan would freshen up inside the cabin. Jan learned quickly that Buzz placed a high value on a spick-and-span home.

With the chores over, they would grab their lunches (made the night before in Buzz's organized fashion) and go hiking. They would be away until midafternoon and then return to take care of campground needs, play horseshoes, and repeat the evening routine.

Fourteen-year-old Tim Caverly stayed with Buzz and Jan part of the summer. He was in charge of cleaning outhouses and became quite proficient. Buzz's mother hiked in twice. His dad and older brother Steve trekked in once at separate times.

At Russell Pond, there wasn't much need for cash. Buzz was now earning sixty-three dollars a week. Governor Baxter wanted to increase the salaries of rangers and Helen Gifford by ten dollars a week, but Authority members and state controller Henry Cranshaw were dubious, believing it would conflict with the state personnel board's salary system. The governor, his advisors told him, should give the additional money as a bonus or a Christmas gift. Baxter already had a practice of giving rangers money gifts from time to time, usually from twenty-five to a hundred dollars, depending on the occasion.

▲ ▲ ▲ ▲ ▲

While the Caverlys were having the best summer of their lives, another pond "reclamation" was undertaken by the fish and game department with the approval of Helon Taylor. The project at Abol Pond involved poisoning the pond's unwanted fish—suckers, yellow perch, and chub—and then stocking with hatchery-raised brook trout. But first a barrier dam had to be built to prevent the predator fish from moving back into the pond from Abol Stream.

Buzz disagreed with the project but didn't have any more influence on that subject than he did when he complained to Taylor about open dumps. Taylor was willing to hear differing opinions from his rangers, as long as everyone was clear just who the boss was and understood that the park had minimal funds to "fix" things. Going along to get along was a big part of the way Taylor managed things.

Taylor was enthusiastically supportive of the Abol project. He wanted the fisheries division to clear the project with Austin Wilkins, but legally the agency had authority over waters within the park and didn't need approval of the park. Fish biologist Roger Auclair received approval to use rotenone on the pond, and the Fin and Feather Club built the barrier dam with wooden railroad ties.

Abol Pond's natural environment had been altered for a long time. Stocking of trout had been started in 1937 and continued annually until 1950. It was discontinued for the next decade, when biologists concluded that a "reclamation" was necessary for the trout to survive, and a dam was necessary to keep the unwanted species from migrating back into the pond.

The project was an obvious goodwill gesture to local anglers and outfitters by the Authority. Other trout ponds would also be "reclaimed," and stocking was an ongoing program.

▲ ▲ ▲ ▲ ▲

After a surprise snowstorm in late August, hikers came out in droves to enjoy the clear and sunny weather in September. On just one day, September 1, an estimated (and shocking) 200 people made it up Katahdin. A clear day offered the chance to see the Atlantic Ocean and New Hampshire's White Mountains more than 100 miles in the distance—a view that would disappear in the early 1970s because of air

*Willard Wight and Austin Wilkins visit with Buzz at Russell Pond, 1963*

JAN CAVERLY PHOTO, BAXTER STATE PARK PHOTO ARCHIVES

pollution from smokestacks and and vehicle emissions blown in to Maine from other states, especially from the heavily industrialized Midwest.

Austin Wilkins and his chief supervisor, Willard Wight, made a rare climb to the summit later that month. Wilkins never camped out in the park but visited at least twice a year. This time, however, he was going to overnight at Russell Pond with Buzz and Jan.

After visiting Ralph Heath at Chimney Pond, Wilkins and Wight climbed Katahdin and went off the mountain via the Davis Pond Trail to Russell Pond. Jan had prepared a turkey dinner with all the trimmings, along with blueberry and apple pies. "Austin and Bill walked in the door about 6:30 that night," Buzz recalls. "It was remarkable that Austin, who was in his sixties, had made it. I don't care how young you are—Roaring Brook to Chimney Pond, over the mountain, down by Davis and to Russell—is a tough way to go. He was hurting when he arrived, with cramps in his legs. He asked for water but was unable to eat. It was heartbreaking for Jan, but she understood. Bill made up for what Austin didn't eat. Austin went to bed early, and the next morning seemed to be in good shape."

Deputy forestry commissioner Fred Holt also made a trip into Russell Pond with Willard Wight, and Buzz caught them with the fake water pump at "Blister Buster Hill." Holt didn't see the humor in the setup and ordered Buzz to remove it immediately.

When Holt viewed Greene Falls, he saw it as an accident waiting to happen and wanted Buzz to build a guardrail there for visitors. Buzz summoned the courage to question Holt's thinking. "If you put a rail here, what's going to stop you from putting one on the Knife Edge?" Buzz asked Holt.

Holt responded that hikers knew the Knife Edge was dangerous. "I told him, 'Well, any damn fool that looks at this steep ledge and thinks it's not dangerous is not in touch with where they are,'" Buzz says. He suggested that educating hikers about potential danger was the appropriate action. "I just couldn't see Baxter's wilderness becoming cluttered with safety rails and facilities," Buzz says, and Holt later backed away from the rail idea.

▲ ▲ ▲ ▲ ▲

One of Buzz's campers that summer was a tall, long-haired, bearded fisherman who seemed to know right where to go in Russell Pond to catch trout. Buzz admired the man's skill at fly-casting and his string of fish at day's end. "Buzz's eyes just bugged out because he didn't have as much luck fishing as I did but also not as much time," said the angler. He remembered Buzz was "very affable," and his party hiked up the northwest ridge of Katahdin with Buzz.

Another ten years would pass before Buzz encountered wilderness advocate Charles FitzGerald again, and this time he was clean-shaven and the instigator of a lawsuit against the park—one of several that FitzGerald would file to champion his own vision of what "forever wild" meant in Baxter Park.

All summer, Ralph Heath had been heading up a volunteer crew scouting and cutting a new 3.2-mile trail from Roaring Brook to Pamola Peak to be named for Helon Taylor. Naming the trail for the supervisor was an exception to Baxter's rule against individual "memorials" in the park. Baxter agreed not only to the trail but to naming a pond for Taylor. The Helon Taylor Pond, just after the Togue Pond entrance, gives visitors an exquisite view of Katahdin. Buzz was on hand with Governor Baxter and about twenty others for the September 28,

1963, dedication of the demanding trail, and Baxter praised Taylor for "good management" of the park.

▲ ▲ ▲ ▲ ▲

While still no known deaths on Katahdin, there had been plenty of close calls and injuries. Accidents were frequent during the summer when so many hikers were on the mountain. A near-fatal situation had occurred on Katahdin that was recounted to the Authority by Edward T. Clark, Jr., of the American Youth Foundation in St. Louis, Missouri. He thought that the scary experience of his Camp Merrow Vista staff warranted rangers putting up signs warning of the difficulties of the hike and the unexpected life-threatening weather that people might encounter.

Coming down the Hunt Trail in wind, rain, and cold temperatures, Clark's group happened upon a father and three children in inadequate clothing and quite frightened, and shepherded them down the mountain to safety.

The camp staff talked to an unidentified ranger about posting large signs, such as those in the White Mountains, warning prospective hikers of possible dangers. "His response was a rather nonchalant, 'We don't need them,' and the father should have read the rules," Clark wrote. Another ranger had answered much the same way, Clark added. "I can certainly appreciate how rangers must feel after a full summer of dealing with a public which often is indifferent and hostile to regulations." However, Clark urged the Authority to consider signs and review their safety regulations—a timely appeal, as events would prove.

▲ ▲ ▲ ▲ ▲

The event that turned Buzz's best of years into the worst began to take shape the week of October 28, after the park's official season closure. Two women hikers, Margaret Ivusic and Helen Mower of Massachusetts, arrived to climb Katahdin. They had some experience hiking together elsewhere in New England, but this was their first trip to Baxter Park.

They met Ralph Heath at Roaring Brook and picked up a copy of park regulations. Since the park was only open during the day now, they departed to overnight at a nearby motel. The next day, which continued to be warm and sunny, they backpacked into Chimney Pond and spent the evening talking to Heath.

The next morning, the weather was pleasant, showing no signs of serious change, and the women hiked up the Cathedral Trail to Katahdin's north plateau. Heath and Sargent spent the day working on the Helon Taylor Trail. Buzz was away that day at a rehearsal for his brother Steve's wedding.

Ivusic and Mower ate lunch on the summit, took pictures, and by early afternoon had headed down the mountain. Unbeknownst to the two women, Hurricane Ginny, which had been gathering momentum to the south, had started rushing northward.

At some point, the women began arguing about which route to follow back to Chimney Pond, which looked tantalizingly close from several gullies. Ivusic, the more experienced of the two, insisted on taking a shortcut down from the Knife Edge, while Mower stayed on the marked trail. The acoustics of the bowl-shaped South Basin allowed the women to hear each other's voices for quite awhile. Mower heard Ivusic call out below the serrated ridge but couldn't see her. Ivusic was trapped and couldn't move up or down. Mower then descended the steep Dudley Trail to get help.

It was not until about 8:00 P.M., when Heath returned to his cabin, that he learned of Ivusic's plight. The good weather was still holding, and Ivusic could hear Heath yell up to her from the edge of Chimney Pond. She wasn't injured, so Heath judged that it was best to leave her on the mountain overnight and rescue her in daylight.

By nightfall, Buzz was back in the park at Katahdin Stream Campground, where he, Frank Darling, and Owen Grant were laying a foundation for a new crew camp. They heard the radio conversations between Heath and Taylor about Ivusic, as well as a new weather forecast predicting high winds and heavy snow.

Near midnight, the wind was blowing so hard that Heath got out of bed, packed climbing gear, a poncho, sleeping bag, and food, and started up the Dudley Trail to find Ivusic. But the forty feet of rope he carried wasn't enough to reach Ivusic, so he returned to his camp at 4:00 A.M., letting Mower know that Ivusic was all right and near the main waterfall west of the Chimney.

Heath called Taylor again at 4:45 A.M. to tell him that Ivusic was still on the mountain and it was starting to snow. Taylor directed

Rodney Sargent to head for Chimney Pond to assist Heath. By 5:00 A.M., temperatures had plummeted, and the storm was hitting with hurricane-force winds; a cold rain was falling that would quickly turn to blizzard conditions. Heath knew that Ivusic couldn't last long in that situation, and he headed out again—no one knows for sure which route—to try to reach Ivusic.

Buzz's assignment initially during the search for Heath and Ivusic was to keep the road open from Togue Pond to Roaring Brook by driving back and forth with Taylor's Jeep. That way, support vehicles with chains could get through the snow.

When Sargent arrived at Chimney Pond, he tried to establish voice contact with Heath and Ivusic but was unsuccessful. "The weather was such you couldn't breathe," Sargent remembers. "The force of the wind took your breath away. Above tree line your clothes froze. I knew if Ralph was on the head-wall there was no hope."

A full-fledged search was on for three days with trained and volunteer rescuers from several states, but they couldn't find either Heath or Ivusic. The effort was called off on November 4.[1]

Now the park had its first documented deaths on Katahdin, and Taylor was understandably upset with the losses, especially one of his best rangers. It was worse for Buzz; he was torn apart emotionally. Heath was not only a special friend; Buzz knew it would have been him on the mountain with Ivusic if he hadn't traded days off with Heath. Buzz made a promise to himself that he would never let Heath's ultimate sacrifice be forgotten over time. He became loyal to the lost ranger's memory in word and deed for the rest of his career.

The Heath-Ivusic tragedy was a long-in-coming wakeup call about the inherent dangers of hiking and climbing—an issue that the park had avoided by sheer luck. It pointed to the need for serious search-and-rescue training for Baxter rangers, a detailed search-and-rescue plan, and new winter rules.

Sargent, along with two state fish and game wardens, was sent to New Paltz, New York, to learn rock climbing. Additional technical and search-and-rescue training would be provided in the following years, but the park wouldn't have its own mountain rescue team until 1969. Park rules were changed to require anyone camping or climbing above tree line between October 16 and May 14 to have a park permit, plus proof of competency.

In his monthly report after Heath's death, Helon Taylor commented that "many things were brought to light whereby we could improve our technique. Mostly we lack equipment and training. Also, we need better control of people entering the park during the off-season. This is our first fatal accident on the mountain and we were not prepared for it. The weather was against us from the start."

In Buzz's mind, Heath's death also underscored the need for the right clothing and best equipment for rescues. When Heath went out to look for Ivusic, he was wearing cotton clothes, not wool, and thus was unprotected from the severe cold and wet weather he encountered. "I always thought that Ralph Heath went further than the rest of us would have," says Buzz. "He had courage . . . he certainly was not thinking of himself."

It wasn't unusual for rangers to wear jeans, cotton shirts, and outerwear. Buzz himself was so accustomed to having wet jeans from park work that he didn't think twice about it. Jan saw to it, however, that he got some wool long johns and pants. Buzz vowed to himself after Heath's death that if he were ever in charge of the park, he would make sure that members of the field crew had the gear they needed to see them through the toughest rescues.

With Heath gone, Taylor kept Rodney Sargent for the winter, making him the park's second year-round ranger. Sargent bunked in with Taylor in the supervisor's cabin at Togue Pond. "On a cold night, Helon would offer you a little nip," says Sargent. "A half glass of rum, half glass of Coke. He thought he could loosen you up." Nursing a drink, Taylor would tell woods stories until late at night.

▲ ▲ ▲ ▲ ▲

The hurricane that had led to the deaths of Ralph Heath and Margaret Ivusic had caused a major forest blowdown behind Abol and Katahdin Stream Campgrounds. Approximately 3,000 cords of wood were thrown over by the wind in a 300-acre area, and the situation posed a fire danger, according to Austin Wilkins. He reported to Governor Baxter in early 1964 that there was an "urgent need to salvage," and projected an income of $10,000 from selling the timber. Baxter wanted to see the situation for himself, but Wilkins said there was no time to wait because insect borers would be infesting the wood soon.

Baxter was as stubborn as Wilkins, saying he feared that a salvage operation would set "a disastrous precedent." Nothing should be removed, the governor ordered, unless it was "dangerous to human life. Our park is a wild, rough area and we should leave it just as it is."

But Wilkins wouldn't let the issue alone. He finally pressured Baxter into letting logger Gerald Ladd take out most of the blowdown with horses.

▲ ▲ ▲ ▲ ▲

Buzz left the park payroll on November 2 and missed the hoopla over the first woodland caribou transplant. Twenty-four of the animals from Newfoundland were being relocated to Maine to be reintroduced to the park. Caribou were once native to Maine but had disappeared many years previously.

The idea for reintroduction was started in 1959 by Percival Baxter's old friend Caleb Scribner, Dr. Lore Rogers, and state biologist Francis Dunn, all of Patten. They engineered a trade whereby Maine would swap 320 ruffed grouse with Newfoundland for twenty-five caribou.[2]

A ten-foot-high corral was built at Togue Pond by park rangers to hold the caribou until the release date, and Buzz and Jan went to see the animals and enjoy the crowd of supporters—biologists, game wardens, reporters, photographers, and tourists.

On a raw December 3, eighteen of the animals were tranquilized with darts. Their feet were tied together, and they were loaded one by one onto a stretcher and carried into the holding pen where they were ear-tagged and marked with a number in yellow paint. Then they were loaded onto a pallet that was picked up in a net by the helicopters and flown to Katahdin's northeast plateau, where they were released by another crew during very tough wind conditions. Six other animals couldn't be airlifted because of bad weather and were released at Roaring Brook.

All of the animals disappeared within a short time for reasons that were never determined. Buzz was disappointed that he missed out on providing hands-on assistance. Another reintroduction plan would surface in 1986 and give Buzz a hearty dose of caribou politics.

▲ ▲ ▲ ▲ ▲

While the Fin and Feather Club saw all sporting camp guests as having special privileges in the park, the one who stood out above everyone

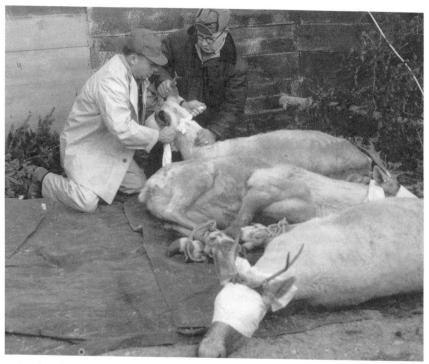

*Caribou being prepared for transport from Newfoundland to Maine, 1963*
BAXTER STATE PARK PHOTO ARCHIVES

was Harold G. Colt, Jr. He and Jake Day were, in effect, park celebrities. When they were there, their presence was telegraphed to park staff, and rangers deferred to them. Buzz enjoyed both men, but his path crossed more often with Colt.

Colt was a wealthy great-grandson of inventor Samuel P. Colt, who founded the famous firearms company that still bears his name.[3] The family had a long history at Kidney Pond, going back to the early 1880s. Harold's uncle, Russell Colt, visited Kidney Pond with his wife, actress Ethel Barrymore, and apparently was responsible for some rare amenities in the middle of the woods—a pool table, an upright Steinway piano, and two bowling alleys.

Harold Colt, Jr., visited the camps at both Kidney and Daicey but was mostly identified with the Kidney Pond cabin known as "The Laura," named for the wife of then-camp owner Roy Bradeen near the outlet. When Buzz checked fishermen at Daicey-area ponds or had other reasons to visit there, he would visit with Colt in the library or the porch and listen to Colt's exotic travel stories.

Colt was a dedicated park volunteer and an eccentric with peculiar mannerisms. A physically small man, Colt drove a fancy Italian car, was an accomplished violinist, a talented photographer, and a world traveler. Kidney Pond attracted a well-to-do clientele like Colt because it featured hot and cold running water in each cabin, flush toilets, showers, and maid service. A generator provided power, allowing Colt to have sound equipment to play his extensive collection of recordings, and a television (with roof antenna). Each season, Colt set up Camp Laura with his own belongings to make it more personal.

There was nothing about the park that he didn't want to know. He studied park history and wanted everyone to know how knowledgeable he was. He enjoyed camp gossip, too, and liked to tattle about the goings-on among staff and guests.

Colt obsessively maintained Baxter Park trails—Doubletop, OJI, Sentinel, and trails around Lost, Lily Pad, and Big Rocky Ponds. "He was constantly using the latest technology," says Buzz, "such as brush saws, long before we ever heard of them—chain saws, axes, any kind of tool you could think of." Colt built a log bridge across a wet area at Big Rocky and erected a sign, "Colt's Crossing," with two crossed wooden pistols.

Once Buzz found Colt near Deer Pond with a weed-whacker cutting the marshy grasses along the trails as close to the ground as a lawnmower would. "He kept those trails groomed like you would find in a New York City park," remembers Buzz. "I went back and talked to Helon about it. Helon said, 'Well, Buzz, he does a beautiful job on those trails,' and left it at that."

Colt's special status at Kidney Pond was reflected in the dining room. He sat at the head of the "pond table" in front of the window with the best view. The other seats were reserved for longtime guests, who would have to go along with the decorum required by Colt. For instance, he wouldn't put up with misbehaving or loud children at the table. Sometimes after dinner, he would set up his projector and show slides of his travels.

Colt loved the park so much that he wanted to be a benefactor in the footsteps of Governor Baxter. He would have that opportunity in the days ahead.

▲ ▲ ▲ ▲ ▲

At the end of 1963 Buzz had to find work again outside the park. His truck-driving experience in Brunswick enabled him to instantly land a job for the winter with O. S. Gonya Oil Company in Millinocket.

The next priority was finding a winter rental. Buzz started knocking on doors on Katahdin Avenue to see if he could find quarters he and Jan could afford. "My mission was to walk the entire length of the street, which is about a mile and a half, and stop at every single house," he says. "I was a bold one."

The house they liked the most was at the corner of Katahdin and Bates Streets, so Buzz knocked on the door. Ralph Shaw appeared, and Buzz related his situation:

> I told him where I worked, that Jan and I had been married a few months, I was getting laid off from the park and had gotten a job with Gonya for the winter. I wondered by any chance if they'd like to rent their house. He had me wait for a few minutes while he talked to his wife. Since we had no children and no pets, they were agreeable. Their house was beautiful . . . as beautiful as my home in Cornville. Ralph Shaw told me we had arrived just in time because his wife's doctor had advised them to spend the winter in Arizona to help Mrs. Shaw's asthmatic condition. I said, "Great, how much do you have to get for rent?" and it was a terrible price he wanted—sixty-three dollars a month, and I'd be responsible for the utilities. We wanted that house bad, but I said, "Well, let me figure things out." Jan and I went back to the car, and drove to Mike's Restaurant on Main Street, where Jan had applied for a waitress job. Sure enough, Mike was going to give her the work, and we took the house.

The Shaws had a black-and-white TV that helped Buzz and Jan relax at night. It seemed like a real luxury, given their tight financial situation. They made enough money to pay the rent and utility bills and put a couple of dollars worth of gas in their car to travel to see Buzz's family at Christmas.

The couple's limited income made holiday gift-giving a challenge. Before marrying Buzz, Jan made thirty dollars a week working for the Coles. With no living costs, she had spending money and then some. One of Jan's brothers referred to her as "moneybags" because she spent more on gifts at Christmas than other family members.

The most Buzz could allocate to Christmas was about fifteen dollars for members of both families. "I'd get so frustrated," he recalls, "but Jan had the patience of Job going into a store and picking out these nickel and dime items. When we were done, there would be no money left. That was a rough transition in our marriage."

Earlier that year, Buzz had purchased an eight-year-old, one-person Polaris snowmobile for a hundred dollars, and on weekends Buzz and Jan would ride in the park. It was the only recreation they could afford.

---

1. *Legacy of a Lifetime: The Story of Baxter State Park*, by Dr. John W. Hakola, TBW Books, Woolwich, Maine, 1981, Appendix 1, Heath/Ivusic accident; Baxter State Park accident file.

2. *In the Deeds We Trust: Baxter State Park*, 1970-94, by Trudy Irene Scee, Baxter State Park Authority, Tower Publishing Co., Standish, Maine, 1999, p. 174.

3. Michael Ressig, Colt Manufacturing.

Primary Document Sources: BSPA Boxes 2, 4, 5, 14, 15, 18 (2507-0713, 2507-0714, 2507-0717, 2507-0718).

Conversations and communications: Bill Bromley, Buzz Caverly, Jan Caverly, Tim Caverly, Chris Drew, Charles FitzGerald, Bob Howes, John Neff, Rodney Sargent, Eric Wight, Elmer Wilson.

▲▲▲▲▲▲▲▲

**CHAPTER 6**

# Katahdin Stream

KATAHDIN STREAM, THE PARK'S MOST POPULAR campground, was viewed by rangers as a grooming post for supervisor. "A posting to Katahdin Stream sent a message to the other staff," according to Abol ranger Rodney Sargent.

In the spring of 1964 there was a vacancy there because Frank Darling, who had replaced Myrle Scott at Katahdin Stream, had left park service. Both Sargent and Buzz wanted the posting. Buzz was ready for new challenges and responsibilities, and he wanted to move roadside because Jan was pregnant.

Buzz was given the transfer, and Sargent was miffed, convinced that Austin Wilkins had favored Buzz because of the connection between Irvin Caverly, Sr., and Wilkins. Buzz rejected the idea of receiving preferential treatment. "Dad was not the type of person to take advantage of that situation, and he was a firm believer that whatever his boys accomplished in life was entirely up to them."

▲ ▲ ▲ ▲ ▲

Buzz and Jan had bought themselves a Bell & Howell film camera and projector. He took the camera with him to Chimney Pond, where he was helping build a new bunkhouse, and filmed the slopes of Katahdin. Buzz kept hoping he would see something that would reveal Heath's or Ivusic's body.

As the snow melted on Katahdin, wardens Elmer Knowlton and Charles Merrill climbed to Pamola Peak to search Katahdin's basin walls with binoculars. Luck was with them. Knowlton spotted a hanging rope attached to Ivusic.

Buzz snowshoed in to Chimney Pond to help the recovery team. When he arrived, warden Glenn Speed told him the technical climbing team needed some rock salt because Ivusic was encased in ice under-

*Recovery of Margaret Ivusic's body on Katahdin, 1963*
BAXTER STATE PARK ARCHIVES

neath about eighteen inches of snow. They had tried chopping the ice around her, but were afraid of hitting her. Now the plan was to use rock salt to melt the ice. Buzz was the youngest, so they asked him to go to Millinocket to get it and bring it back to them.

The next two days were like a marathon for Buzz. He snowshoed back to Avalanche Field on the Roaring Brook Road where his truck was parked. (The road was plowed up to that point because of the blow-down harvest operation.) He went to Millinocket to pick up thirty-five pounds of rock salt, drove back to Avalanche Field, loaded the salt in his backpack, hiked back to Chimney Pond, and headed up Pamola Peak. He worked his way across the Knife Edge and was at Katahdin's South Peak just as the sun came up. Two of the team members met Buzz, took the rock salt, and went back down the ravine to Ivusic's body. Buzz stayed on the Knife Edge, waiting for them to free her, and fortunately for him it was a warm day.

It was about 4:00 P.M. before word came back to Buzz that they had broken Ivusic free, wrapped up her body, and were ready to transport her up to the ridge. It was exhausting work for the strongest men, Buzz recalls.

The Knife Edge is only a mile long, but it's a hell of a long way when you've got a body; there are sheer plunges on both sides of you and you're trying to keep the stretcher fairly level. It was a terrible, terrible walk. Just before dark, we got her over to the plateau near Thoreau Spring. Helon had made arrangements for a Maine Forest Service helicopter to pick her up. We got her strapped to the skids, and the thing took off. Then we hiked back across the cutoff trail to the top of the Saddle. I was the youngest, probably in the best shape of the crew, and had gone through the least stress. The other guys were so tired they were dragging. I was ahead of them 500 feet and got to the edge of the Saddle decline. I thought, Jeez, there's a snowfield all the way down there. If I go step by step, cutting steps with the ice ax, we'll be midnight getting down, but if I just go into a glissade, I could cover that pretty quick.

When Buzz kicked off, he went totally out of control. His ice ax broke loose from his grip as he slid down the entire length of the Saddle Slide to where the blue-blazed trail started into the woods. Fate smiled at him. He had no injuries, not even bruises. "Everything was quiet," he remembers. "I got up, brushed myself off and felt great. I said, 'Boy! That was a good move,' and then looked up to see where the other guys were. I saw Glenn Speed shaking his fist at me and knew he was mad, that I'd better get out of there."

Buzz didn't stop at Chimney Pond to rest. He wanted to see Jan and sleep in his own bed that night. He headed down to Roaring Brook on snowshoes, then jumped on his snowmobile, and, with the throttle wide open, made a beeline to his truck at Avalanche Field to drive the final distance home.

When he later saw Glenn Speed, the warden had calmed down. But Speed let Buzz know in no uncertain terms about the risk he had taken with the glissade, not just for himself but for other members of the rescue party. "He was absolutely right," Buzz says. "It was a foolhardy thing to do, and I got away with it. That had happened to me many times in the woods. I'd done things no person should ever get away with, and the Lord was good to me that way."

Two weeks later, Speed and Sargent joined other searchers to look for Heath's body. They found him about 400 feet above the spot where Ivusic had been found. Buzz wanted to be part of the rescue team, but

Taylor wouldn't let him go because of the two rangers' close friendship. The rescuers later told Buzz that Heath "looked as if he had just sat down and gone to sleep."

Heath was buried in the cemetery at Sherman Mills on May 20, and Buzz was one of the pallbearers. Governor Baxter paid the costs of the ranger's funeral and tombstone. Besides Heath's name and birth and death dates, his epitaph said, "He Gave His Life In An Attempt To Save That Of Another."

In memory of Heath, Westbrook engineer Winston Robbins made a 4 x 4-foot plaster replica of Katahdin that was given by the Maine State Employees Association to the park. Robbins put in over 800 hours on the model. For years, it sat in between the forest service and fish and game quarters in the Cross Office Building. Eventually, it was moved to park headquarters. Fiberglass replicas were later made for the ranger stations at Abol and Roaring Brook Campgrounds.

▲ ▲ ▲ ▲ ▲

During the winter, Buzz and Jan had gone to look at the Katahdin Stream ranger's camp for the first time. Jan wanted to see what household items would be needed to make it feel homey. She was excited about the move because the camp was larger and had more amenities than at Russell Pond.

In the kitchen, there was a newer Atlantic cookstove with a nice warming oven, as well as a gas stove, and a black iron sink with running water. Better yet, in Jan's opinion, the Katahdin Stream camp had a bathroom instead of an outhouse, complete with flush toilet and shower.

Before they could relocate to Katahdin Stream, Buzz and Jan had to retrieve their belongings at Russell Pond. They could have left Russell Pond in a float plane, but they wanted the last trip to be on the trail and they wanted to take their time. Buzz turned for a last view of the camp knowing that he was closing a chapter of his life, and the future looked bright.

▲ ▲ ▲ ▲ ▲

Buzz was so anxious to get started at Katahdin Stream that he and Jan moved into the ranger's station in mid-April, before he went on the

*Buzz Caverly riding one of the park's first doubletracks, 1964*
BAXTER STATE PARK PHOTO ARCHIVES

payroll. Using $298 worth of Green Stamps, they purchased new furniture for the living room and bedroom, and Jan planted tiger lilies and gladioli in front of the porch.

Life was very different at Katahdin Stream. There were different types of campers and more hands-on work, expectations, and needs. At Russell Pond, campground chores and maintenance were limited because there were only four lean-tos, three tent sites, and a bunkhouse. At Katahdin Stream, there were twelve to fourteen lean-tos, an equal number of tent sites, two bunkhouses, and, in addition to campers, from a hundred to a hundred and fifty day visitors, including a trickle of international campers and hikers.

Buzz was constantly reminded of Percival Baxter's dream for the park by a brass plaque affixed to a boulder just before the start of the AT's Hunt Trail. Written on the plaque was the former governor's most repeated statement, one that was memorized and carried forward in the years by Buzz: "Man is born to die. His works are short-lived. Buildings crumble, monuments decay. Wealth vanishes. But Katahdin in all its glory shall forever remain the mountain of the people of Maine."

Buzz's office duties at Katahdin Stream took much more time than at Russell Pond because there were so many more campers and visitors. On top of all the housekeeping chores around the campground, he was often called on to investigate vehicle accidents, attend more meetings, and prosecute more court cases. He was responsible for one assistant ranger and an unlimited number of wilderness patrols.

Airstream trailers and other oversized vehicles were a big headache because they frequently became stuck at the bottom of steep Abol Hill or wound up in the ditch, and then they became Buzz's problem to resolve. The highway commission wanted to tar Abol Hill because it was so hard to maintain with the grader, but this was not something the Authority would seriously consider. Commercial bus companies also ran tours of the park, causing their own particular traffic issues and raising questions for Buzz about visitor overuse.

The human impacts were clear at Ledge Falls on Nesowadnehunk Stream, where the water rippled over sloping granite slabs within inches of the Tote Road. The falls was initially an attraction for fly fishermen. As more families discovered Baxter Park, the site became a heavily used swimming spot.

The Tote Road was located close to the stream's edge because the grade was high on the other side. Highway crews had hot-topped a short section of the road there, ostensibly to protect it from washing out during log-driving days, and Governor Baxter was aware that there was some paving in his wilderness park, at least at Ledge Falls. Over time, the hot-top section was expanded, and Helon Taylor wasn't sure that Governor Baxter would like it because of the visual impact.

On one of the governor's fall inspection trips, Taylor arranged for Baxter's companions—state warden supervisor David Priest or warden Arthur Rogers—to exclaim, "Look at the eagle!" so that Baxter would look out the window and miss seeing the tarred section. Chauffeur Joe Lee would accelerate the car to get across the hot-top. The next spring, on another trip, Baxter surprised his companions. Near the Doubletop warden's camp, Baxter asked if they were nearing Ledge Falls. Taylor confirmed they were, and Baxter told him not to mind the "eagle foolishness" because he had already seen the tarred road.

Besides the Ledge Falls tar, Myrle Scott had the highway crew hot-top two pathways at Katahdin Stream—one going to his ranger's camp and one to the highway commission camp there. Buzz had complained to Scott about the paving as "inconsistent" with wilderness character, and Scott's response, he said, was "small potatoes." In years to come, Buzz would have the tar removed at all sites, with the last of it (in the north end) shoveled up in 1999.

▲ ▲ ▲ ▲ ▲

Helon Taylor kept his eye on Buzz to see how he handled his new responsibilities and informed Austin Wilkins that Buzz was working hard. "I think he is going to be all right there," the supervisor reported. Jan was doing her part, too. She helped with camping reservations, fielded questions, answered the radio, sold firewood, and ran the "store" on the front porch.

The stores evolved in the 1950s as a way for ranger families to earn extra money, and they were popular with campers, who were always running out of supplies. Goods sold included bread, milk, canned goods, candy bars, chips, marshmallows, donuts, and soda. Governor Baxter knew about the enterprises and felt they were different from hot-dog stands or other kinds of commercial businesses. The income helped the Baxter Park families, and in his mind that was justifiable.

Jan stocked the typical store items but didn't bake herself because she already had enough to do in the kitchen feeding rangers. Buzz rigged up an old Coke machine to keep sodas cool. He laid a water line in Katahdin Stream, in front of the camp, and ran it into an overflow tank where he stored the cans. The water chilled the sodas and was channeled back out into the stream. The sodas sold for fifteen cents a can—half of it profit.

The ranger's wives had to keep a record of store sales and submit a report each year. Jan's sales topped $1,200 one season, and it was an important supplement to Buzz's sixty-seven-dollar-a-week salary.

Jan liked to iron in the evening, and at Katahdin Stream, Buzz had provided her with a kerosene iron that had to be pumped up for pressure like a Coleman stove. One night, soon after moving to Katahdin Stream, Jan was ironing and thought she heard someone coming to the cabin. When she looked out the window to see who it was, she found herself staring into the face of a bear. Another bear enjoyed peering at Buzz and Jan through the window over their bed. But getting accustomed to bears at the new quarters was part and parcel of life because some campers left food out in the open.

▲ ▲ ▲ ▲ ▲

During the Memorial Day weekend, park trustee and fish and game commissioner Ronald Speers paid Buzz an unannounced visit. Buzz was eating a hot lunch, after being on Katahdin all night searching for the son of a Maine game warden pilot. It was clear when he opened the screen door that Speers was mad. He started hollering about a pothole in the road leading to the Katahdin Stream tent sites, and demanded that Buzz fix it immediately.

"I just looked at him," Buzz remembers. "The entire park was full of potholes, and the one in the campground had been washed out by rain. I told him I'd take care of it. Out the door he went, and that was my first and last impression of Speers. I didn't like him from that moment on."

Helon Taylor also disliked Speers and later, in a letter to Percival Baxter, threatened to resign if Speers ever became chairman of the Authority.

▲ ▲ ▲ ▲ ▲

While Buzz was rangering at Russell Pond, he was out of sight and out of mind when it came to park politics. But once at Katahdin Stream, he was in the middle of the locals' fight with the sporting camps over fishing opportunities. Bag limits and access had been highly charged issues for years.

After the park acquired T2R9, the Authority proposed to reduce the bag limit on ponds in the Abol/Togue area, new to its ownership, from ten to five fish, in keeping with a greater conservation policy. The plan raised the ire of the Fin and Feather Club, whose members were angry over their perception that their fishing access was already being squeezed by the Daicey and Kidney sporting camp owners. They complained to Buzz frequently, alleging that Junior York at Daicey was trying to spike their vehicles with nails to discourage them from using the sporting camp's parking lot (a charge never proven).

In June, Buzz found out how clever some fishermen were in taking all the trout they wanted. Lying in the duff at Grassy Pond and getting eaten by blackflies, he watched three local men in a boat land one fish after another. When they came to shore, Buzz approached them, asking for their fishing licenses, and one of the men immediately said he had a bladder emergency and ran into the woods. When Buzz checked their catches, the men were within legal limits. Buzz didn't figure out until later how they'd outwitted him. The fisherman who had to relieve himself was wearing a trench coat—the pockets stuffed with illegal fish—and had scattered the evidence in the woods. Buzz found the bones and realized he'd been had.

▲ ▲ ▲ ▲ ▲

Wilderness adventure was a rite of passage for many boys and girls who spent their summers at Maine camps. Baxter Park, the Allagash Wilderness Waterway, and the Rangeley Lakes area were places that Medomak, Kennebec, Chewonki, Kieve, and many other Maine and regional camps sent their older teenagers for "culminating experiences." They learned camp skills, how to identify flora and fauna, and, in general, how to live in the outdoors.

The youngsters were always bursting with energy, even after packing in weighty tins of hamburger, ham, and pineapple to Chimney Pond or Russell Pond campgrounds. Buzz hadn't encountered a lot of summer campers when he was at Russell Pond, but at Katahdin Stream, they were a goodly number of his campground population. They scattered when they hit the trails, leaving their counselors behind, getting lost, and requiring a lot of attention from Buzz. He was so fleet of foot that he left a lasting impression on one Chewonki boy, Don Hudson, who would become a lifelong friend.

Chewonki, whose trips to the park started in the late 1930s in the back of an open truck via Greenville, made a big deal of the outing. Leader Tim Ellis (who became camp director in 1965), would deliver World War II surplus pack boards to the bunks of certain boys during rest hour, just hours before he would announce the campers who would be on the Katahdin venture. The process created more excitement and mystery around the event.

Don Hudson had a leg up in getting the Baxter nod because his father was assistant camp director, but he had to carry his weight on the trip—literally. On Hudson's first trip to the park in 1961, Tim Ellis made him lug a heavy canned ham throughout the thirteen-day outing. "I was the littlest guy on the trip, but Tim thought it was good for me to have that experience with the ham," says Hudson.

To the Chewonki campers, Baxter was a world apart. It took a con-

*Buzz at Pamola Peak, July 1964*
CAVERLY FILES, BAXTER STATE PARK PHOTO ARCHIVES

siderable effort to get there, and the forest seemed to stretch on forever. They knew it wasn't pure wilderness because they hiked through places of former logging operations, littered with rusted pots and old cable lines, and rutted from heavy wagon wheels. They climbed mountains with remnant flumes that sent logs down the slopes into Wassataquoik Stream. But at the summits, there were no tree stumps. "Then you had a real sense you were on top of the world and really in the wild," recalls Hudson, who eventually carried out important alpine plant research on Katahdin.

▲ ▲ ▲ ▲ ▲

With summer's improving weather, the ranger's office was busy from sixteen to twenty-four hours a day. Buzz was often on Katahdin at night looking for overdue hikers.

While Buzz was on the mountain, Jan handled radio communications and kept the office open because relatives, friends, or the press might show up or call. Sometimes, a trip up Katahdin was for nothing because the hikers presumed missing were actually back at camp. Once

Buzz went up the Hunt Trail over Baxter Peak and down the Abol Trail (an eight-mile hike) only to find that the man reported overdue was asleep in his vehicle at Abol Campground.

One of these calls was to help some hikers in bad shape at the Gateway. Buzz found a mother and her daughter, who was recovering from polio. The daughter had made a five-dollar bet that she could climb Katahdin without assistance, but she couldn't make it. Buzz put her on his back, but every time he had to negotiate boulders and rocks, she held on so tightly that she choked him. Eventually they made it down, but Buzz's throat was sore for days.

Jan learned quickly that making a hot meal was her best contribution to an emergency. She and Buzz always kept on hand stores of tuna, hamburger, canned ham, and plenty of brown sugar and pineapple, and various ingredients for cookies, donuts, muffins, and pies.

"She knew that when we'd come off that mountain at 1:00 or 2:00 A.M., that everyone would be hungry and tired," Buzz says. "The first thing they'd want to do is have something hot and good to eat and then hit the hay. She never failed me. I don't care whether I came down off the mountain with just a few people or a big group, Jan would be up and there would be something tasty on the table."

Jan relied on cookbooks kept by Buzz's mother and Aunt Emma, but ranger's wives also shared their favorite recipes. Jeanette York taught Jan how to make her mouthwatering molasses cookies with dates.

Making late-night dinners was much easier for Jan than it would have been had she lived at Abol when Buzz was first there. Buzz had bought the lines and fittings to put in gaslights at Katahdin Stream, paying about eight or nine dollars for five fixtures. Jan could see a lot better to cook and read books. For a time, they had a television for entertainment, but the reception was poor—just black and white "snow." A park rule prohibited a roof antenna.

Buzz enjoyed the public relations part of being a campground ranger. At the end of the day, he would make time to visit every camper—at least those who welcomed a chat. Buzz could tell quickly whether someone wanted to talk or be left alone. If invited to sit down, Buzz would share a cup of coffee or a soda. It could be two hours before he would remember how long he had been out socializing while Jan covered the radio.

Buzz sometimes surprised campers with bean-hole beans and ice-cream treats. Friends provided the beans, and Buzz prepared them. He prided himself on getting forty servings of ice cream out of the wooden churn. When all was ready, he put the bean crock and the churn on the tailgate of his truck and drove slowly through the campground asking campers if they were hungry.

▲ ▲ ▲ ▲ ▲

To make sure that Tim Caverly would still spend part of the summers with them, Jan would drive and hour and a half to Brownville or even all the way to Corinth to pick him up. Tim was still too young to have a driver's license, but Buzz let him drive the park Jeep in exchange for cleaning the outhouses at Katahdin Stream. Tim also helped haul the campground garbage to the Foster Field dump, neaten up the campground, and deal with nuisance bear problems.

Buzz enjoyed children and liked to play jokes on them. A favorite story for kids was about milking the moose. Most of them were skeptical that a moose could be milked, but they always fell for Buzz's invitation to meet him at 6:00 A.M. to milk a moose. He would get up before six o'clock, dissolve powdered milk in a pail of warm water, go out the back door of the ranger cabin, and circle around the campground so that he appeared to be coming out of the woods. With the children in his front yard waiting for a moose to milk, Buzz would inform them that they were too late. The kids were suspicious they had been duped, but Buzz would ask them to stick a finger in the pail and see for themselves whether it was moose milk.

Tim recalls how one little girl, Susan King, agreed with Buzz that it was moose milk. She later lived in the park for several years when her parents, Homer and Joan King, were gatekeepers at Togue Pond. She met Tim in college, and they were married in 1974 after he became a state park ranger.

▲ ▲ ▲ ▲ ▲

One of Buzz's nighttime jobs was patrolling the Tote Road toward Nesowadnehunk Campground until he met ranger Irwin Sargent (Rodney's father) coming south. They were on the lookout for illegal campers or kids from town drinking beer or sitting in their cars necking.

*Buzz having a morning cup of coffee with campers*
*at Katahdin Stream Campground, 1964*
PAUL KNAUT PHOTO, BAXTER STATE PARK PHOTO ARCHIVES

On one particular evening, Buzz carried a .38 revolver with a six-inch barrel. He used it when target practicing with Helon Taylor, who was a national pistol-shooting champion. Just past the AT bridge over Nesowadnehunk Stream, Buzz noticed a car in an abandoned gravel pit and saw the brake lights suddenly light up. The driver had seen Buzz's vehicle pass by and reacted by hitting the brake. Buzz stopped, grabbed a flashlight, and walked back to the gravel pit.

As he entered the area, the driver panicked, put the vehicle in reverse and sped backward. Buzz dove to the ground, and the vehicle missed him by inches. Thinking at first that the driver was trying to kill him, Buzz pulled out his revolver and fired two shots in the air to try to stop them. But the kids kept going until Rodney Sargent stopped them down the road.

When Buzz was working for the warden service in the fall of 1961, he had heard the story of how wardens Irwin Bonnie of Orient and Maynard Marsh of Gorham had sustained broken legs when checking out vehicles in separate incidents. Both men had been run over and left to die.

"When the incident with the kids occurred, my immediate reaction was that these guys were trying to kill me using a car as a deadly weapon," Buzz says. "I hoped the two shots in the air would stop them, but they did not. Later, I learned they were just teenagers 'parking,' who got scared and overreacted."

▲ ▲ ▲ ▲ ▲

Besides night patrol, Buzz had to attend to bear problems at the park's open dumps and campgrounds, and they often occurred during the evening. From 1964 to 1968, he shot a couple of big bears each season at the Foster Field dump and carried them off to the woods, burying them under lime and leaves.

One rainy, foggy night, Buzz dispatched a bruin threatening a campground. There were many old logging roads along the riverbank, so Buzz picked one and backed the truck up to a gradual bluff. The back of the truck was on a downhill, and the slope gave him the momentum to roll the bear off. He knew that the bear would soon become carrion and be eaten by predators. What Buzz didn't realize was that the logging road was just a short distance from Junior York's camp on the West Branch of the Penobscot River. A couple of days later, York stopped by Katahdin Stream and told Buzz that "one of those s.o.b.'s from the Fin and Feather Club" had dumped a bear on his back step. He was furious, and Buzz was silent. Years later, Buzz confessed to York that he was the culprit. They laughed it off, but York never let Buzz forget what he had done.

▲ ▲ ▲ ▲ ▲

Governor Baxter stopped to visit the Caverlys at Katahdin Stream that fall. "He was always cordial and congenial and asked how we were and were we having a good season," says Buzz. "He thanked me for my reports and always asked, 'Are the people enjoying their park?'"

On that particular visit, a snapshot was taken of Buzz, pregnant Jan, and Governor Baxter by local warden supervisor Arthur Rogers—the only photo of the three. Buzz took a photo of Baxter and two couples who were camping. The governor loved the attention. Buzz wanted to take more photos but was too respectful of Baxter, thinking that a camera might be an intrusion that the governor wouldn't appreciate.

*Percival P. Baxter (L), Jan and Buzz Caverly, 1964,*
*Katahdin Stream Campground*
ARTHUR ROGERS PHOTO, BAXTER STATE PARK PHOTO ARCHIVES

In Buzz's end-of-the-season letter to Wilkins on October 31, 1964, he wrote, "On the whole [we had a] very good group of campers. We were very fortunate, as far as accidents go, a few minor cuts, sprained ankles . . . but nothing serious." Buzz also reported that he had kept two men in jail overnight for an illegal fire and camping—common violations during the 1960s.

Making sure that Wilkins and Taylor knew how productive he had been during the season, Buzz listed his major accomplishments at Katahdin Stream, such as building a new camp for the assistant ranger and clearing the Hunt Trail of blowdown. Taylor singled out Buzz for special praise "for taking over at Katahdin Stream, our busiest campground, and doing an excellent job running it."

▲ ▲ ▲ ▲ ▲

Before leaving for the season, Taylor wanted Buzz and park carpenter

Owen Grant to build a crew camp at Togue Pond. Taylor had fought Austin Wilkins on the issue for years, and he was set on having his way so that he and Hilda wouldn't have to keep putting people up in their own quarters.

Hilda Taylor was a schoolteacher and went to the park to see her husband on weekends, which was also when outing clubs and volunteers were around most and always angling for a cot in the supervisor's camp. It was very tiring for Taylor.

He decided to go around Wilkins and ask Governor Baxter directly for permission to build the crew camp. Baxter thought about the situation for awhile and came up with a suggestion. When Taylor ordered wood for picnic tables, he should order a little extra, "and in time you'll have enough stock to build your crew camp," Baxter said.

Taylor liked the plan and sat down to tea with Buzz and Grant to see about getting the new building up quickly. Buzz knew that Taylor was defying Wilkins, but it was okay with him because Baxter had given the green light. Buzz and Grant had the crew quarters finished by the first snowfall.

Buzz was expecting fireworks about the new crew camp when Austin Wilkins paid his annual spring visit to the park in 1967. It was the first thing Wilkins saw when he arrived at Togue Pond. Wilkins flew out of the car and demanded to know how Taylor got the camp. Smiling with satisfaction, Taylor told Wilkins that he built it—and that "Governor B" approved. Wilkins was so angry that he called Governor John Reed's office and set up a meeting of the Authority. Reed had already received an explanatory call from Baxter on the matter, and the subject was closed.

"A couple of days later, I was down at Helon's," Buzz remembers, "and Helon mentioned that 'Austin had a good trip the other day. He found things in good shape. He did get a surprise. But you know, Governor B told me I could build that building if I did it the right way. Austin doesn't seem to understand that. He's very upset with me.'"

Taylor and Buzz had a good laugh about the incident.

▲▲▲▲▲

Construction of the crew camp had ended just in time for the birth of Buzz's first daughter, Cathy, on October 24 at the Millinocket hospital. Buzz was "too chicken" to go into the delivery room. "This thing of going in and helping was unheard-of in those days. We fathers stayed in our place and out of the way of the doctors." Since Buzz had come from a family of boys, he was happy to have a daughter, as was Jan. Governor Baxter sent the Caverlys a baby gift of a hundred dollars.

▲ ▲ ▲ ▲ ▲

The Caverlys again rented the Shaws' house in Millinocket, and Buzz returned to his oil-delivery job at Gonya's during the winter of 1964–65. Jan stayed at home with Cathy, so their winter income was marginal.

Buzz was assigned duty at Chimney Pond in January 1965 to assist winter climbers. This particular winter, he went in with Frank Guertin of Stoughton, Massachusetts, his son, and a couple of other mountaineers who were intent on climbing in the South Basin. Buzz was in the ranger camp when Guertin's son flew in the door to tell him that his dad was having a heart attack on the mountain.

Buzz knew that Guertin had a history of heart problems. He had no radio handy to call for assistance, so he got on his snowmobile to try to get Guertin out.

> I jumped on this little ten-horsepower sled, and I struck out across the pond. I went up that basin and got to a high elevation and ended up on a piece of ledge. I parked the sled and reached down to turn the key off. At the same time I was stepping off the sled, my feet went out from under me, and I went into this sudden free-fall. I was moving fast but caught onto some scrub brush, and it held me. I was really shaken, and then I saw my sled coming at me, rolling right towards my head. So instinctively I jumped into a snowdrift, and the sled bounced around and over the top of me—never touched me—rolled down the hill, and got hung up on another piece of ledge, right up on its side. That engine was still going putt-putt-putt. I heard someone ask if I was okay. It was Frank. He was fine, but it looked like I was in trouble. Frank said he would come help me, so the rescuer became the rescued. I told him I thought he was having a heart attack, but he had just gotten winded and excited.

Guertin put Buzz on belay and lowered him down on a rope to his overturned sled. Buzz grabbed the idling sled and asked Guertin for a little slack in the rope. Buzz dug his feet into the snow and waited for Guertin to come down. The two of them positioned the sled to head straight down the hill.

> I cut her loose, thinking that as long as I could keep those skis straight, I'd be all right. I didn't see any other way to get out of the pickle we were in. Well, I had the most fantastic ride I'll probably ever have in my life. It was like a bullet. It was a matter of seconds from being at the top and reaching the bottom at Chimney Pond. The snowfield was adequate and there were enough openings with no brush, no stubs, no exposed rocks in my way. I may have gone over some rocks, but I was going so fast I didn't realize it. When the sled stopped, I remember hitting the key and shutting off the engine, and everything went dead . . . silent. I was sitting underneath the head walls, trying to reflect on what I'd just been through and how I came out of that experience. I'd never want to do that again, but I'm not sure I would have wanted to miss it, either.

▲ ▲ ▲ ▲ ▲

That spring, while Katahdin was still under snow, Taylor gave state biologist Francis Dunn approval to take a snowsled to the top of Katahdin to retrieve the survival gear (sleeping bags, K-rations, revolvers) that had been left there after the caribou transplant, and to get specimens from the dead caribou that had suffocated during the air-lift. To reach the summit, a trail had to be cut, and Dunn took Rodney Sargent and Elmer Knowlton to help.

One of the trio took a photograph of the snowsleds at the Baxter Peak sign, and the picture wound up on Sargent's camp refrigerator. Buzz saw the image and asked Sargent if he was "out of his mind," knowing what a controversy he could stir up if the public found out about snowmobiles on Katahdin. It wasn't long before the news got out that a state game biologist had cut a trail to the summit without approval.

Austin Wilkins and Ron Speers agreed that if the report was true, the biologist should be reprimanded. Kenneth Hodgdon, chief of the state game division, confirmed that not one but two snowmobile trips had been made up Katahdin, and asserted that Dunn had permission from Taylor.

The *Bangor Daily News* carried an article on the incident and a picture of the sleds by Maine photographer Paul Knaut, purportedly taken at Baxter Peak. The photo prompted a strong response from Don McKay, a papermaker from Old Town. In a letter to the *News,* McKay objected to "these noisy little monsters" invading the "forever wild" park, and he wrote to Governor Baxter about such an "intrusion." "I firmly believe that if this practice is allowed to continue, in a few generations anyone walking in Baxter Park will be out of place."

Governor Baxter contacted Taylor a few days later saying that "these sleds should be prohibited in the park except for one for you as supervisor to use in case of emergencies. I feel strongly about this for they will frighten away the wild animals, and we certainly would not see a caribou again." Baxter continued, "This same reason prompted us to forbid the use of motor boats on our lakes. I can see the damage they would cause. I would be much pleased if the [Authority] would add this to the list of what is forbidden in their regulations . . . this is the time to kill it."

Taylor was irritated by the "petty complaints" about snowmobiles. He claimed that the Knaut photo was taken at Taylor Pond, not on Baxter Peak. Taylor asserted that he and Austin Wilkins could take care of such matters without involving Baxter. "We are the ones who are supposed to be running this park and we wish and strive to run it exactly as you want it run," the supervisor added.

Taylor's position on snowmobiles was perfectly clear. He saw no harm in people using them in Baxter Park, although the state parks commission had outlawed them in parks in its jurisdiction. "Maybe in the future we will have to control it, but up to now it has caused no trouble," he said. "They do not cut our trees, disturb our wildlife, or harm our park in any way. Those who come in summer would never know they had been here unless they were told. I have talked with Austin about this and he and I are agreed that there is no harm in it."

▲ ▲ ▲ ▲ ▲

There were two permanent and eleven seasonal employees in the spring of 1965. Still, with limited funding, the focus remained on campground operations—not wildlife, environmental education, or a forester to manage the township that Governor Baxter had set aside for "scientific forest management" in T6R10, the northwestern corner of the park.

The newest ranger for the season was eighteen-year-old Tom Chase, a friend of South Branch ranger Ellie Damon. Chase's interview with Taylor in the fall of 1964 followed the usual script. "We sat in the coffee shop in Millinocket, and Helon asked me if I liked the outdoors or was afraid of being in the backwoods," says Chase, who had never been to Baxter Park.

Taylor was worried about Chase's age but still hired him to work at Russell Pond. "The first year or two, I didn't have what I could say was a day off," Chase remembers. "We all had to rush around like hell." Like his colleagues, he loved the unplanned nature of the job and the variety of challenges from plumbing to search and rescue.

Although Chase was at a remote campground, he developed a reputation among his peers as a wild man for his youthful and carefree attitude. He loved parties, women, fast driving, and hunting. Chase got away with breaking the rules because of his good humor, likeability, and ability to creatively defend his actions. "His smile could cover up most anything he got involved with," Buzz says.

Buzz and Chase developed a warm friendship, but Buzz drew a line on how far he would participate in certain fun-loving activities with Chase. Alcohol was one. But Chase had a drinking buddy in Wilbur Smith. Smith had a great sense of humor and storytelling ability and was generous with his bottle of vodka, which he kept hidden in the woodpile in the garage. He and Chase would mix the vodka with warm water, enjoy each other's company, and catch up on park news. Chase also enjoyed homebrew at Ellie Damon's. Damon once bottled a batch too quickly and it blew up. He and Chase spent a week cleaning up the mess.

Buzz was impressed with how much Helon Taylor knew about what was going on with his rangers, no matter how far away things happened. The dry-cell batteries for the park radios were kept in a refrigerator at the Maine Forest Service radio lab at Windsor, and the rangers took turns going to get them. On one run, Tom Chase decided to continue on to Portland in the park truck to see the woman he planned to marry.

The next time it was Chase's turn to go fetch batteries, Taylor advised Chase that he'd better not go to Portland on the park's time and dime. The snitch was an I-95 tollbooth operator at the Gardiner exit, who had called the park when Chase went through, alerting Taylor that the ranger was farther south than he should have been.

▲ ▲ ▲ ▲ ▲

Taking care of a baby in the woods might be daunting for some new mothers, but not Jan Caverly. She had babysat from the time she was nine years old, so she knew how to take care of a young child, and she loved being in the park. Jan initially washed diapers by hand, but Buzz soon procured a Maytag gas-powered washer for her—with permission from Taylor.

Jan washed constantly because she wanted Cathy to be as clean as if she lived in town. Jan curled Cathy's hair into ringlets and dressed her in frilly outfits to go outdoors to play. The campers generally made a fuss over Cathy, especially those who returned annually and watched her grow up. It was like a "family affair," Buzz says, referring to the camping families whom he, Jan, and Cathy came to know.

Cathy had a fondness for Helon Taylor and loved the small wooden stools he made. When she visited his camp, she always sat on one. Taylor made her a stool, and Hilda painted it red, decorating it with nursery-rhyme decals.

▲ ▲ ▲ ▲ ▲

Buzz had much more social contact with his fellow rangers and their families when he relocated to a roadside campground than he did in the backcountry. But they never sat around talking wilderness philosophy or how they were inspired about being the stewards of a place as incredible as Baxter Park. "There was too much red-neck stuff going on to talk about wilderness, too much good-old-boy, crazy stuff," he says.

Rangers might quote Governor Baxter now and then, but that's as far as wilderness talk went, Buzz recalls. He never heard Helon Taylor reveal his innermost feelings or thoughts, only "Governor B did this, Governor B did that."

When Buzz rose to his initial leadership position in 1968, he would sing the praises of Percival Baxter and the park but tried to stop short of making people uncomfortable with "feeling talk."

▲ ▲ ▲ ▲ ▲

The summer of 1965 was the beginning of an extraordinary national boom in hiking, backpacking, and general outdoor recreation. An outgrowth of the youth-driven social changes of the era (anti-war, back-to-the-land, drugs, rock and roll music), the surge into the parks and wilderness areas also fueled a transformation in the businesses that produced outdoor clothing, equipment, and gear, such as Maine's own L.L. Bean, Inc., in Freeport.[1]

The park recorded 89,384 visitors in 1965—the historical high—and the number would remain above 70,000 for the next few years. L.L. Bean's growth paralleled that of the park, with a dramatic increase in sales to both catalog and retail store customers. In fact, Bean began a strong identification with the park. In advertising and the naming of products, Katahdin became an integral part of the Bean brand. Buzz and other park rangers eventually became volunteers in field-testing Bean products.

Bean's association with the park had its roots in the friendship between Percival Baxter and L. L. Bean. Any letters exchanged between the two men have been lost or destroyed. But evidence of their personal connection exists in the two photographs that Baxter gave to Bean. One, taken in September 1953, is inscribed: "To Mr. L. L. Bean. We are friends. Percival P. Baxter." The other is dated July 1955, and says: "To L. L. Bean from his long time friend. Percival P. Baxter."[2]

L. L. Bean wrote a handbook on *Hunting, Fishing and Camping in Maine* in 1942, and he showcased Baxter Park in a special chapter. He praised Percival Baxter as "the State's greatest benefactor . . . also to the people of an entire nation has been established a reservation where they may glory in the rugged aspects of nature and where wild life may dwell in peace without fear of gun, trap, or other human encroachment." Bean sent an autographed copy to Governor Baxter.

Katahdin began to appear on the covers of L.L. Bean catalogs, possibly as early as 1929, but definitely in 1966, 1987, and 1996. Products named for Katahdin or Baxter State Park began in 1970 with a Mount Ktaan (Thoreau's spelling of Katahdin) windshirt that was offered briefly. From 1972 on, under Bean grandson Leon Gorman's leadership, the company consistently named products for Katahdin or the park—the Baxter State parka, Katahdin parka, Katahdin fleece, Katahdin tents, Katahdin sleeping bags, Knife Edge boots, and Katahdin fishing nets.[3]

*Baxter State Park Supervisor Helon Taylor (L) and Governor Ken Curtis at the official opening of the new control gate at Togue Pond, 1967*
MAINE FOREST SERVICE PHOTO

Buzz was oblivious to the connection between Percival Baxter and L. L. Bean for a long time. When he was working in Brunswick in the early 1960s, he never even visited the famous retail store.

▲ ▲ ▲ ▲ ▲

Besides recreation, Baxter Park held allure for scientists. Katahdin, with its expansive alpine tableland, was the primary attraction. It had attracted collectors and investigators since the mid-1800s and was reputed to have a lot of rarities, especially alpine plants. No one knows how many specimens the first collectors hauled away, since no one was watching.

When Helon Taylor became supervisor, he encountered a variety of researchers—college students, university professors, and independent operators. Just how much research was typical of the period is foggy, but grant support was very limited. Indications are that Taylor pretty much gave researchers free rein, since there were no rules governing field work, no formal applications required, and no review committee in place.

Geologist Dabney Caldwell, a park regular, remembered that Taylor let him do what he wanted. But Caldwell also knew of someone whose plant fossil proposal in the Trout Brook area had been turned down and the man went ahead with it anyway. The north end of the park was so far away from Taylor's quarters that it would have been impossible to monitor closely.

Buzz became more aware of researchers when he relocated to the Katahdin Stream roadside station, and he was cool to their activities. He saw inquiring scientists as unnecessary interlopers who might harm the natural resources to benefit themselves and their careers.

▲ ▲ ▲ ▲ ▲

The relationship between the park and the Appalachian Mountain Club (AMC) grew more problematic over the summer of 1965, after Governor Baxter became upset over the organization's $5,000 donation for two new bunkhouses at Chimney Pond in memory of Ralph Heath.4 A wooden plaque had been made to commemorate the gift and its source. Buzz and Chimney Pond ranger Laurel Bouchard built the bunkhouses, which replaced dirty hovels that were barely a step up from structures the old river drivers had lived in.

Baxter had been kept in the dark about the donation, and when he learned of it, he called off the dedication ceremony for the buildings. He mailed a check to the AMC that covered the cost of the bunkhouses and some mountain rescue equipment. The AMC felt that the check, in effect, was an invitation out the door.

The situation was wrenching for the AMC because the Boston-based organization had such a rich tradition of involvement with the Katahdin area before and after the park was created. Nine years after its organization in 1876, the club's members first began traveling to Katahdin, sightseeing, hiking, climbing, and working on trails.

A large base camp was built for the club at Katahdin Lake, as well as a smaller facility at Chimney Pond. By the end of the 1890s, however, AMC disappeared from the Katahdin scene, and the two camps burned. The club didn't renew its interest in Katahdin until 1916, starting major expeditions to the mountain and opening up new trails and roads. They signed an agreement with the park in 1941 to maintain 18.5 miles of trail, erected signs, and published the first hikers' guides to Katahdin. Many articles in the AMC's *Appalachia* magazine were about the mountain, thus expanding the public's interest in the area. The club played a major role in planning and locating the Appalachian Trail in the park.

The AMC gave Governor Baxter strong support in his successful effort to block a renewed effort to create a Katahdin National Park. The club's opposition to the national park was particularly ticklish because the Appalachian Trail Conservancy, now chaired by Baxter Park's first environmental critic—Myron Avery—was on the other side of the issue.

And during World War II years, the AMC was faithful to Baxter Park by fulfilling its commitment to maintain trails and rebuild the shelter at Davis Pond.

Some people began to confuse the AMC's role in the park with that of the Baxter Park Authority, and Attorney General Frank Cowan reported that to his fellow trustees and Governor Baxter. They felt the Authority should assert its exclusive administrative responsibility for the park.

Territoriality between the AMC and the park evolved over the next twenty years, as the club's investment in trails increased in man-hours and cash. In the fall of 1960, the club decided that it was time to offer the park an annual contribution for trail work and upkeep of the Davis Pond shelter, and give the job of hiring trail crews to supervisor Helon Taylor.

Tom Deans, a Biddeford native, joined the AMC staff in 1964 as assistant to the director, Fran Belcher. He was well acquainted with Baxter Park, and his family was friends with the Baxter family. While at the University of Maine at Orono, Deans had camped in the park and climbed Katahdin, and he had been a hut man for the AMC in the White Mountains for eight summers. He reflected on Governor Baxter's reaction to the AMC and the Chimney Pond bunkhouses:

> While joining everybody in applauding what Baxter had done in creating the park, we felt a sense of belonging and heritage. We felt we had a right and responsibility to be involved. The last thing we wanted was to offend or get in a pitched battle with the benefactor. I think we all were upset and probably were taken

aback. Why was this such a big deal? AMC had enjoyed a good relationship as partners with the White Mountains National Forest, with huts and trails, and had wanted to do the same thing in Baxter. But we were not appreciated.

When AMC was thrown out of the park, ATC Chairman Avery and Executive Director Jean Stephenson were on the lines cheering, according to Deans. And so was Buzz, who didn't like the AMC and felt that "flatlanders" from any outside group had no business meddling in park affairs.

▲ ▲ ▲ ▲ ▲

With his family growing, Buzz was in a quandary about his income. He and Jan had made do on his ranger's salary and the temporary winter jobs, but now they had a child. Just how fragile their financial state was came home when the park's tote road was washed out by a storm and there were fewer campers at the campground to buy goods from their porch store. With less cash to tide them over the winter, they had to eat the canned food themselves. Buzz was sure he had to have a year-round job for his family to survive.

He went to Helon Taylor and talk over his dilemma. Leaving the park was the last thing he wanted, but he told the supervisor that he needed full-time employment. Taylor told Buzz, "No, there will never be a day when there will be more than two year-round rangers working at Baxter Park." (And at the time they were Taylor and Sargent.) Buzz asked for a letter of recommendation from Taylor to prospective employers. In it, Taylor couldn't recommend Buzz "too highly":

> He is diligent in his work and often goes way beyond the call of duty in an emergency. He is happily married and has no bad habits. He is especially keen in law enforcement, has had more good cases in court than any of the other rangers during the time he has worked. He has a pleasing personality and gets along well with people. I have had many fine letters of commendation about him from our campers. Irvin has also advanced from our most remote campground to Katahdin Stream, which is our busiest one, and I will say that he has handled it very efficiently. Right now, I consider him my most efficient ranger. We would hate to lose him

and he would be a hard man to replace, but if he were to find a better job, since we can only offer him seasonal work, I would not try to hold him back.

Buzz had applied for a permanent job with the Millinocket Police Department, but his heart was in his park job.

Buzz went back to Taylor, saying, "You know, Helon, you're pretty near seventy years old, you've got one ranger working with you, and this is pretty big country. There are a lot of things that need to be done here in the winter. Would you have any problem if I talked to Austin Wilkins about the possibility of year-round work?"

Taylor got a big grin on his face with the idea that Buzz might, just might, be able to get him some more help, so he gave the ranger permission to meet with Wilkins. Buzz met with Wilkins and gave him a list of reasons he should be hired for the winter, and then he waited while Wilkins consulted with Governor Baxter.

Meanwhile, Buzz received a notice from the Millinocket Police that he had been hired. He agonized while waiting to hear from Wilkins, which seemed to take forever. In fact, Buzz finally gave up, thinking that Wilkins had forgotten him or just wasn't going to respond. He drove to Millinocket to accept the police job, and the very minute he put his hand on the doorknob, he heard his radio calling. It was Wilkins, and Governor Baxter not only approved hiring Buzz but wanted him to have a small raise.

Baxter approved taking $2,500 from his trust funds for Buzz to work from November 1, 1965, to April 20, 1966, at the rate of seventy-seven dollars a week. "This man will take some of the burden from your shoulders," Baxter wrote Taylor, "and as you requested this, I could not refuse."

▲ ▲ ▲ ▲ ▲

Buzz and Jan were near neighbors of Taylor for the winter at Togue Pond. With the year-round employment, Buzz and his family were given the gatekeeper's new cabin to live in—free, in exchange for partitioning off and finishing the place. The increase in income allowed Buzz to buy his first insulated boots and wool pants. "I thought I had died and gone to heaven because I knew I could finally be really warm," Buzz remembers.

One of the sacrifices of winter rangers was absence from family at holidays. Every year from 1965 to 1969, Buzz spent either Thanksgiving or Christmas babysitting mountaineers staying at Chimney Pond. It was customary to have a ranger with off-season climbers in case of accidents, and after 1958, the park charged twelve dollars a day for the service.

Katahdin had been a focus of alpinism and rock climbing for thirty years, despite the local atmosphere of disapproval going back to LeRoy Dudley, who thought it was too dangerous except for the most technically skilled. The difficult technical routes provided climbers a taste of what they could expect on Alaska's Denali and the peaks of the Alps and the Himalayas.

A seven-member AMC team (men and women) was credited with the first technical winter ascent of Katahdin in March 1923. They climbed the Chimney, a low-angle snow gully, in the South Basin. Robert Underhill, the most revered of American climbers in the 1920s, was one of the celebrity climbers associated with exploring Katahdin's basins and gullies. Underhill and other alpinists practiced on Katahdin in preparation for climbing in the Alps. After World War II, some diehards climbed Katahdin in winter but most preferred the easy accessibility of the White Mountains.

Katahdin was rediscovered by a new generation of climbers in the 1960s, and Baxter rangers didn't like having to watch over them any more than LeRoy Dudley had.

Buzz pulled the babysitting duty during the holidays in 1965. He snowshoed in to Chimney Pond ahead of his winter parties to open up the ranger's camp and have a warm place when the visitors arrived. A shovel was left hanging on the outside of the building to clear snow away from the door and then make a path to the woodshed.

This particular Thanksgiving, Buzz was stuck with overseeing the MIT Outing Club. He got into the camp after dark, and the mercury was far below zero. He lit the Coleman lamp, started the woodstove, and grabbed a bucket to go get some spring water:

> I figured I'd just run right outside and back. I had stripped down
> to my t-shirt, but I had on pants and long johns. I went without
> my coat, hat, or gloves to collect the water quickly, but when I
> tried to open the cabin door, it was locked. I was immediately in a
> serious situation. If I had broken a front window downstairs to get

in, I would have made the whole camp cold for all the time I had to be there. So I dropped the bucket, waded through the snow around the back of the camp and climbed up the radio antenna that was [screwed] to the roof. My hands were pretty near frozen by the metal, but I got up there and put my foot through a small window of the gable wall and went in, climbed downstairs, got warmed up, and later found a piece of plywood and got the hole boarded up.

When Buzz told Taylor what he had done, the supervisor listened intently. Then he told Buzz to drive to town, buy a pane of glass with his own money, return to Chimney Pond to fix the hole, and then report his progress.

Tending to MIT, Dartmouth, Harvard, and other Ivy Leaguers was about the only job in the park that Buzz disliked. "I resented having to take care of these people from big colleges when I could have been with my own family," he says. Plus, the ranger camp was uncomfortably cold because it was buried in snow, uninsulated, porous to the elements, and the windows were covered by shutters. "It was like being in a cave," he recalls with a shudder.

---

1. *Forest and Crag: A History of Hiking, Trail Blazing, and Adventure in the Northeast Mountains,* by Laura and Guy Waterman, Appalachian Mountain Club, Boston, 1989, pp. 51–60.
2. Percival Baxter photos to L. L. Bean, 1953 and 1955, L.L. Bean, Inc., files, Freeport, Maine.
3. Leon Gorman and L.L. Bean, Inc., catalog files, Freeport.
4. *Legacy of a Lifetime: The Story of Baxter State Park,* by John W. Hakola, TBW Books, Woolwich, Maine, 1981, pp. 190–91.

Primary Document Sources: BSPA Boxes 2, 4, 5, 15, 18 (2507-0713, 2507-0714, 2507-0717, 2507-0718).

Conversations and communications: Walter Anderson, Buzz Caverly, Jan Caverly, Dabney Caldwell, Tom Chase, Ellie Damon, Tom Deans, Leon Gorman, Don Hudson, Paul Knaut, Darrell Morrow, David Priest, Rodney Sargent, Jeanette York, Laura Waterman.

▲▲▲▲▲▲▲▲

CHAPTER 7

# END OF AN ERA

THE GATEKEEPER'S QUARTERS AT TOGUE POND was situated on a slight rise, and the scenery from the living room window was breathtaking. Buzz and Jan had a sweeping, unobstructed view of the southern slopes of Katahdin. They would get up at first light just to watch the sun's play on the mountain. "Look at that mountain!" Jan would exclaim to Buzz time and again.

With Helon Taylor's camp just a stone's throw away, he and Buzz sometimes worked together attending to chores. Mostly Buzz worked alone. His job in January 1966 was to prepare the winter trail from Sandy Stream Pond up through the Widden Ponds deadwater to the South Branch of Wassataquoik Stream and on to Russell Pond.

It was a strenuous job on snowshoes to pack down the trail so the 200-pound snowmobiles could haul the heavy propane gas cylinders to the camps. Trees had to be limbed out, and the brooks had to have snow bridges built over them. Poles and spruce boughs were laid across the brooks and then wet down to freeze. The snow bridge had to be fashioned just so, to prevent the loaded snowmobile from tipping over. Come-alongs weren't in use then to get the sleds back on track. It took sheer manpower to right a machine of several hundred pounds.

Those days out alone were special for Buzz:

I'd work along without a jacket and around 11:30 I'd build a fire and get that frozen tuna sandwich out of my pack. Then I'd stick it on a wire toaster that I carried with me and lay that thing across the coals. While the sandwich was browning, I'd sip on my hot tea and watch the cheese melt on the tuna fish. After I got that sandwich down and the tea put away, I'd start to cool down and go back to work quickly. When I hiked out and saw what I'd accomplished, walking with the ax over my shoulder and my snowshoes on that crunchy snowy, it was always a good day. I was worn out—physically exhausted—but so refreshed in my mind. I'd get into camp where it was warm and eat a hot meal and the next thing I knew, I was sound asleep. I got up the next morning and did the same thing again. Those were not only productive and wonderful times but also very spiritual times.

The winter routine required checking the park's campgrounds and the private sporting camps, and keeping track of day users and campers. Buzz also cut ice from Daicey Pond with Junior York, who stored Buzz's share until he wanted it to make ice cream for summer campers.

During time off, Buzz and Jan snowmobiled all over the park, often venturing in to Chimney Pond. On one of the trips, they rode up into the South Basin. Coming back, Buzz forgot about a boulder they had skirted around, and he drove over the top of it, throwing the two of them off the sled. Neither of them was hurt, but the snowmobile's front skis had been bent double by the accident. Buzz beat on them with his trusty ax until they were straight enough to function.

They took off again to Chimney Pond and then toward Roaring Brook. As they arrived at the bridge at Roaring Brook, Buzz enticed Jan to stay out longer to enjoy the beautiful day. They headed to nearby Sandy Stream Pond, where Buzz took a shortcut onto the pond, and the ice let go, dropping Buzz and Jan into icy water up to their knees. They pushed and struggled to get the snowsled up onto the ice and rode home wet but okay.

Buzz and Helon Taylor had a relaxed attitude about risk-taking. "Helon's basic rule was you go out there, meet the elements and use good judgment, and get yourself out of the messes you get into, and if you can't do it, you're not ranger material," Buzz says. Taylor's own accidents with his snowmobile made him understanding of others' high-jinks.

Governor Baxter kept pondering the presence of snowmobiles in the park. He told Wilkins that "these machines are so noisy and numerous, they should be forbidden to go into the park area. If unrestrained, these noisy machines would frighten the wildlife." But he didn't outright order a ban on sleds, as he would on motorcycles. These were not matters that the Authority wanted to deal with quickly because of their controversial nature.

▲ ▲ ▲ ▲ ▲

In April 1966 Buzz's jobs ranged from taking up old telephone line from Abol Hill to Togue Pond, to cutting firewood and breaking open the snow-covered road to Katahdin Stream. The gasoline-operated washing machine Buzz had installed for Jan at their Katahdin Stream cabin eased her housekeeping chores.

While much of the work was repetitive for Buzz in getting ready for the new season, he was cognizant in the spring of 1966 of how the employee turnover was changing the sense of "park family." Of the ten seasonal employees in 1960 when Buzz started his ranger career, eight of his original colleagues had left. New men were on the scene, and the old social connections were lost. Some of the younger employees were college graduates, not all farm boys, and engaged in new kinds of shenanigans.

"As a group, we weren't 'good old buddies' anymore, so to speak," Buzz recalls. One assistant ranger who worked for Buzz smoked marijuana and raised a ruckus behind the scenes that Buzz didn't know about until after the fact. The assistant brought his drums to practice in the woods, resulting in a lecture from Buzz about wilderness solitude.

Two-year-old Cathy Caverly was walking and talking and happy to see campers return because they enjoyed playing with her. Her first park memories are of swimming in Katahdin Stream and clambering up a small boulder with Baxter's plaque on it. She called the rock "my mountain."

Cathy followed Buzz around the campground, trying to help him with chores, and rode with him on car patrols. His favorite outing with her was gunnelling a canoe on Daicey Pond. He kept a frying pan in the trunk of his vehicle, along with some kindling, so they could cook out at a picnic area if they got hungry. "Dad was everything to me. I loved my mother, but I idolized him," Cathy says. As far as Buzz could tell, Cathy was thrilled to live in the park. Later, when she was older and had a choice, she didn't want to be there, and Buzz felt he had forced the park on her.

After Cathy was born, Buzz and Jan didn't get out of the park to see their parents as frequently as before, and neither did their parents travel to Baxter Park much. Buzz's father, Irvin Caverly, Sr., had more responsibility as head of the forestry department's District 5 headquarters in Corinth, and later, as assistant regional ranger for the eastern division. Irvin Caverly's reassignment to Corinth, a farming community west of Bangor, would later draw Buzz and Steve Caverly to put down roots there.

▲ ▲ ▲ ▲ ▲

Hiker accidents took center stage that summer, when there were more mishaps recorded than ever before, and Buzz was usually in the thick of search and rescue. The most difficult rescue occurred when fifty-year-old Charles Ludwig, of Barrington, Rhode Island, was injured in a fall near where Margaret Ivusic had died in 1963.

When the weather deteriorated on July 12, Ludwig and his sixteen-year-old son, Jim, took a shortcut off the Knife Edge to head back down to Chimney Pond. The elder Ludwig's long fall landed him in a shallow pool of water at the edge of a cliff. His leg was broken, and he couldn't move. Jim Ludwig climbed back up to the trail on the ridge and went for help, reaching Chimney Pond by late afternoon.

Ranger Gary Morse and several volunteers from the campground hiked about halfway up the Cathedral Trail, where they could look across the Great Basin and see Charles Ludwig in his orange poncho in the Chimney, over a thousand feet below Pamola Peak. Because darkness was near, they returned to camp and radioed Helon Taylor about the situation.

By midnight, wardens Glenn Speed and Eric Wight had arrived on the scene. Despite a brewing storm, they headed to the summit to wait for daylight. The next morning, they found Ludwig alive, with broken ribs, a broken leg, and a dislocated shoulder. Needing more ropes for the rescue, Wight stayed with Ludwig while Speed went for help. Worsening weather made evacuation that day impossible. Dancing lightning, furious winds, and water pouring off the mountain threatened both men.

To save himself, Wight left Ludwig. But he found Buzz, Speed, and the rescue team on their way up, just in the nick of time. They returned to Ludwig, helped him out of the water, fed him, and put him in warm clothing.

With a lot of skill and grit, the team got Ludwig 1,400 feet up the side of Katahdin to the Knife Edge in a Stokes litter on ropes, then carried him across the Knife Edge to Baxter Peak and down to the

Tableland where a helicopter was waiting to fly him to the hospital.[1] Meanwhile, Ranger Morse's wife of thirty days had been tested in her own way by having to house, feed, and clothe sixteen rescue workers in their small camp with just the goods at hand.

The rescue took almost four days, and Buzz got another chance to be on Katahdin all night. For Jan, the Ludwig search and rescue seemed to take forever. She waited up for Buzz every night. "I used to worry because I didn't have a radio," she recalls. "Buzz would say, 'See you when I get back,' so I didn't know when I'd see him again." To pass the hours, Jan ironed, knitted, or read William O. Douglas's and Louise Dickinson Rich's books about the north woods. She could never just crawl into bed and go to sleep while Buzz was on the mountain.

Buzz's personal efforts to help Ludwig were praised by George Siter, Jr., a Berkeley Heights, New Jersey, policeman who was camping at Katahdin Stream. Siter was impressed with how well Buzz dealt with freezing rain and wind during the rescue. He also commended Buzz for his "happy personality and efficient manner as he visited the campsites every day. He would always ask us if there were any complaints or problems he could help us solve," wrote Siter in an August 1, 1966, letter to Helon Taylor.

Taylor responded thanking Siter for his "generous letter," and confided that there was "a certain group of people in Millinocket, not the better class, that are out to get Buz [sic], myself and several others fired. Buz is a good man, kind and helpful, willing to work beyond the call of duty." At the same time, Taylor called Buzz "hard-boiled and aggressive as far as poachers and law-breakers are concerned. This is what caused him to be unpopular with this certain element."

▲ ▲ ▲ ▲ ▲

Buzz climbed Katahdin twelve times that summer and was discouraged to find the littering problem getting worse on the mountain. Trash, cigarette butts, glass soda bottles, and cans were left behind for rangers to pack out. There was a hiking register underneath the summit sign in a steel cylinder fixed with a bracket to the sign. "People started saying terrible things in the register and carving on the sign," Buzz notes. Then the register itself was destroyed, with pages ripped out and thrown down over the rocks.

Buzz aided many tired hikers and participated in three stretcher cases that fatigued even the youngest and strongest rangers. He found the Saddle Trail a miserable way to take down a stretcher because of the loose gravel and poorly maintained condition. The Hunt Trail "was no picnic" because of the large boulders at the Gateway and the steepness of the terrain.

Trails in Baxter were blazed with blue paint except for the white-blazed AT. Supervisor Taylor decided that orange was better for visibility and ordered rangers to start switching colors that summer—beginning with the Helon Taylor Trail.

The orange was also used on the just-completed Rum Mountain Trail, a route from Abol Campground that went to Katahdin's South and Baxter Peaks. The Intercollegiate Outing Club Association, a coalition of northeastern college outdoor clubs, had proposed the new trail to Taylor in 1962. Work was planned to start in 1963, but the blowdown storm that fall caused a postponement. Ranger Rodney Sargent had visions of blazing the trail by himself but quickly realized it was more than a one-man job.

Taylor hoped that the new trail would make Abol Campground a more popular site for campers, but the trail didn't last long because of the frequent blowdowns caused by high winds sweeping down from the Knife Edge. After a short time, maintenance of the trail was stopped, and mention of it was dropped from the park's trail list.

Taylor's experiment with orange paint was short-lived. He hadn't taken into account how the orange leaves of autumn might make it difficult to keep the orange blazes in sight, but that quickly became apparent. The paint persisted, however, even into the twenty-first century, on rocks here and there on the now abandoned and overgrown Rum Mountain Trail.

▲ ▲ ▲ ▲ ▲

Down Katahdin's western slopes at 2,500 feet elevation lay the Klondike, the trail-less, almost impenetrable spruce-fir bog that was as wild and remote as the park had to offer. Junior York would bushwhack with his most intrepid Daicey sporting-camp guests into the Klondike, but it was too difficult a venture for most people.

To satisfy his curiosity, Buzz made a trip into the area in the footsteps of Myron Avery, who had explored it in 1928 and described his trip in an article published in a 1929 issue of *In the Maine Woods.*

Twenty years later, F. W. Rungee wrote about his three tramps to the Klondike, lauding it as "one of the few areas in the East unbroken by man-hacked trails" and difficult enough to access to "demand a certain degree of respect from the hiker."[2]

It was surely the wildest place that Buzz had ever seen, but the thick blackflies, tricky footing, and summer heat made it too unpleasant for him to return anytime soon. He thought the Klondike was better off with as few visitors as possible in order to protect its mysteriousness, isolation, and quiet. Later, when he was in charge of the park, he would direct rangers to discourage people from trying to venture into the Klondike and refused requests to lead trips himself.

▲ ▲ ▲ ▲ ▲

When he was assigned to Katahdin Stream Campground, Buzz spent as much time working at night as during the day, patrolling for night hunters. Deer poaching centered on the open fields and meadows. Buzz routinely covered the southern end of the park—McCarty, Nesowadnehunk, Foster and Abol Fields—to see if jacking was going on, usually leaving the north end to other rangers.

It was typical for certain locals to leave work at the mills, go to a bar for a few beers, and then drive up to the park to hunt deer. Sometimes they dropped apples at certain places to increase the chances of finding a deer there later. Buzz didn't catch a lot of violators, and even if they were nailed, the punishment wasn't a deterrent. The fine might be as high as twenty-five dollars—nothing compared to later fines and confiscation of vehicles imposed by the state.

What would make the biggest difference to the poaching problem were gatehouses.

▲ ▲ ▲ ▲ ▲

By the fall of 1966, Governor Baxter had agreed to establishing control gatehouses and building three miles of new park road from Togue Pond to Abol Hill—one of the most important policy decisions of the time. The road, in T2R9, would simplify access into the park from the south and make it possible to control visitation. The route chosen, according to Austin Wilkins, would be "probably one of the best and most scenic roads that could be constructed, showing fine vistas of [Katahdin]."

*Buzz and Jan Caverly at Katahdin Stream Campground*
BAXTER STATE PARK PHOTO ARCHIVES

There was a to-do over the "exorbitantly high" bids for the road, but in the end the state highway commission was authorized to construct the road for an estimated $35,000.

Buzz was excited about the gatehouses—the first pre-fab log buildings in the park—to be erected at Togue Pond, Nesowadnehunk Field, and Matagamon Lake. It would bring order out of chaos. He wouldn't have to go on night patrols to look for illegal campers or fires.

Buzz's year-end report for 1966 documented how he had spent his work time: 1,178 hours in the office, 600 hours of construction, over 200 hours on trail maintenance, 1,143 hours patrolling, and 66 hunters and licenses checked during the hunting season. He had seven court cases, in which all of the accused pleaded guilty and paid fines totaling ninety dollars. Fees of $2,701 were taken in at Katahdin Stream. For Buzz's 3,121 or so working hours, he netted $77.47 a week.

▲ ▲ ▲ ▲ ▲

Helon Taylor heated his Togue Pond camp with a woodstove in the living room and a kitchen stove converted from wood to oil. The stovepipe in the living room went up through the ceiling and ran parallel the whole length of the attic to tie into the kitchen chimney. Taylor stored surplus papers, maps, and other park documents in the attic, and some of the boxes were directly underneath the stovepipe. On January 21, 1967, while the Taylors were in Guilford, the camp and two sheds burned to the ground.

"Jan woke me up in the middle of the night saying the sky was awfully red," says Buzz. "I looked out the window and grabbed my clothes, jumped on my snowsled and raced down to Helon's. By the time I got there, the place was totally engulfed in flames."

Two propane tanks, a 275-gallon oil drum, and hundreds of rounds of ammunition inside the cabin blew up. So did Taylor's new snowsled in a nearby shed that ignited. The cause of the fire was never officially pinpointed.

The financial loss was estimated at $4,800 for the camp and $4,619 for the park equipment, materials, and supplies. That loss of park documents was sobering, leaving an irreparable gap in the historic record of park affairs. "The only thing we could fall back on was to go back to the individuals and ask if they still had this or that report," says Buzz. Having moved so often and discarded a lot of his own park files, Buzz had minimal records to replace those that were burned.

Taylor was notified of the fire by Helen Gifford. He drove to Togue Pond to inspect the ruins. "My camp, No. 1 sled shed, and the woodshed were a complete loss," he observed. "Even my safe was burned out. The only thing I saved out of the ruins was some eighteen to twenty dollars in coin."

The fire also consumed a priceless personal effect of Taylor's—his diary. He had kept a record of his adventures since he was seventeen years old, and the supervisor's whole family grieved the loss.

When Helon Taylor returned to Togue Pond, he had to make do with the new one-room crew camp. He stayed only a couple of days a week during the winter. He lightheartedly drew a chalk line on the floor to delineate "his" and "her" space for the times Hilda visited.

Governor Baxter sent personal checks totaling $2,500 to the Taylors to replace some of their personal possessions lost in the fire and not covered by insurance. Helon Taylor thanked Baxter, acknowledging that "words are just not enough to express our appreciation. We wish there was more that we could do for you."

▲ ▲ ▲ ▲ ▲

Authority member, James Erwin, joined trustees Wilkins and Speers in 1967 and would play a vital role for five years. Erwin, a Republican, had been elected attorney general by the GOP-controlled legislature and replaced Richard Dubord.

A small town probate and real estate lawyer, Erwin had served in the Maine State Senate for one term in 1961–62 and then one term in the house in 1965–66. He ran unsuccessfully against Governor John Reed for the GOP nomination for governor in 1966, when Democratic candidate Kenneth Curtis took the top political job away from Reed. Erwin was a political conservative, as well as an ardent outdoorsman.

At the time, the attorney general's job was still part-time (about two days a week in Augusta), allowing Erwin to continue to run his law practice in York. Indicative of Erwin's formality, he wanted to be called "General" by his Augusta staff.

Erwin was the first attorney general who promised to be an active trustee and not stand back for Austin Wilkins to call the shots. "I liked Austin," recalls Erwin, but he thought the sixty-seven-year-old Wilkins was "a little too old for his time." Wilkins surprised Erwin with his stamina and determination to control the park as much as he could. "He was headstrong." When Wilkins was upset with Erwin, he would call him "the guy from New Jersey." "I did not take that well— that I should be guided by and listen to him because I was not a Mainer," Erwin recalls. "He wouldn't go to the park with me. He wanted to be IT."

Along with his two trustee colleagues, Erwin visited state highway commissioner David Stevens because of the commission's responsibility for park roads. "Dave Stevens was a Napoleon," Erwin remembers. Stevens tried to force people to sit in a certain place lower than his own chair when they went to meet with him at the highway office. "He tried to bully and break people down."

Erwin acknowledges that he didn't have much to do with the park the first year he was on the Authority, but then he began asserting himself. Erwin had met Governor Baxter twice. "He was a tough old nut, kind of a dictator. He made it clear he was in charge. I thought okay, he bought and paid for it. I'm not going to tell him what to do." Erwin felt that his role was "to carry out the dream of one man . . . we had an obligation to carry the dream out . . . to put flesh on the dream."

▲ ▲ ▲ ▲ ▲

Buzz drove hundreds of miles a month on his snowmobile and spent a lot of time checking other sledders. In just six weeks almost 800 sleds were counted entering the park at Togue Pond, and there was no one to keep count of those coming in from Matagamon, Nesowadnehunk, and Abol Ridge. Buzz was frustrated with the lack of oversight of sledders and advocated unsuccessfully for a year-round staff of rangers to deal with all-season recreation.

Snowmobilers were taking advantage of the Roaring Brook Road being plowed for a couple of winters by Great Northern Paper, which was exercising its still-existing cutting rights in the Katahdin township. Logger Gerald Ladd was operating in the Rum Mountain area and had built numerous haul roads to get out the wood.

"People would drive up from southern Maine," Buzz recalls. "It would be nothing to have trailers and cars parked from where Togue Pond gate was and where I lived that winter all the way back down to Caribou Pit [outside the Togue Pond entrance]."

Most of the snowsleds were headed for Chimney Pond to try hair-raising runs up the sides of the basins. The drivers didn't realize how steep the terrain was, and when they turned to descend, they often lost control of the machines and rolled over. "It was not uncommon to find pieces of clothing, broken windshields, and other sled parts," Buzz says. "Logistically, they shouldn't have been up there, but there was no regulation against it." The sledders wouldn't report their accidents or injuries because they didn't want any restrictions on what they were doing.

Helon Taylor was in a mood to promote snowmobile recreation in the park, and he invited a reporter and a photographer from the *Bangor Daily News* to take a trip to Chimney Pond to see what fun it was to ride on the lower slopes of Katahdin. The invitation followed state parks director Lawrence Stuart's announcement that all regular state parks were opening to snowmobiles.

Buzz led an eight-snowmobile contingent that included Rodney

Sargent, Elmer Knowlton, and some Millinocket-area sledders. They headed up Saddle Brook, and Knowlton forged ahead of Buzz, leading the group higher than Buzz thought was safe, given his previous mishaps on the mountain.

"It's so deceiving up there," he says. "You don't have the usual depth perception. I had run my sled to the full extent of its power, and I stopped on a rock ledge, looked over at Elmer, and saw he was in the same situation, only hanging onto some bushes. Another sled was going straight down and I realized we could be in real trouble, but that sled got hung up on some brush. So the situation turned out to be thrilling rather than disastrous."

The *News* carried a half dozen photos of the outing in its February 20, 1967, issue, and the article quoted Helon Taylor calling snowsledding "a great sport." He gave some tips for safe sledding and said, "I only hope that everyone respects [snowmobilers], so we won't have to keep them out." Taylor correctly predicted the time would come when the park would have to put restrictions on snowmobile use.

Buzz looks back on the article as an invitation that brought in greater and greater numbers of sledders. "The minute they got into Chimney Pond and beyond, they'd go back home and tell their buddies about the great snowmobiling," Buzz says. The next weekend there would be twice or three times as many sledders trying out the South Basin. They would get up to elevations beyond their control, and the first thing they knew, they were on a crash course.

▲ ▲ ▲ ▲ ▲

The sporting camps at Daicey and Kidney Ponds were not the only holdings the park had inherited. Four individuals also had camps in the park. Baxter had raised the issue of leases back in 1955, wanting them to be terminated. But until 1967, the different Authorities had delayed taking such action, and Baxter didn't press them to do so. On the table now was a proposal by Kidney Pond sporting-camp owner Charles Lipscomb for the park to buy him out, and the situation prompted Baxter to lean on the trustees again to get rid of private leases because they were possible "infringement[s] upon the *deed of gift.*"

On July 11, 1967, the Authority voted to terminate the leases as of January 1, 1970, but that date was later moved to January 1, 1971. At Austin Wilkins's request, Taylor provided an assessment of the structures. Shorty Budreau's camp on Togue Stream had little value, he said, because the building was "just an old lumber camp office fixed up." The Priscilla Clark camp on Second Lake Matagamon was an old log camp but still in good repair. The Victor Davignon camp was "excessive— board and shingle house, kitchen built on, pump house, power plant, boathouse, hot and cold water, bathroom, and all modern conveniences," Taylor reported. He had never been in the Louis Martin camp on Grand Lake Matagamon, but had heard it was "a regular log mansion."

Taylor wanted to see some of the leases canceled (he didn't say which ones) but not others. "I hope we can make a fair settlement with these people when the time comes," he mused.

▲ ▲ ▲ ▲ ▲

A frustrated Helon Taylor pushed the Authority in early 1967 to make a decision on a new park headquarters to replace his burned cabin at Togue Pond. Taylor favored an office in Millinocket, where he could have a regular telephone, power and water, daily mail, and no road-plowing responsibilities. If the Authority wanted the main office to stay in the park, Taylor said it should be set back from the flow of visitor traffic through the Togue Pond entrance. "I think both Fred [Holt] and Bill [Wright] agree with me," he wrote. "For myself, I like it here at Togue Pond, but my time here is limited."

The Authority approved spending $20,000 of trust fund money for a supervisor's headquarters, and contracted with a building company for the camp. Surprisingly, Governor Baxter balked because he wanted to get the new gatehouses built before deciding what to do for Taylor. The governor had ideas about where he wanted the new headquarters. He didn't identify a specific place, but Buzz believed that it was Round Pond, a little farther into the park than the old office at Togue Pond and with a glorious view of Katahdin.

Baxter also may have dragged his feet on a new camp for Taylor because he had become sensitive to the number of buildings in his wilderness park, despite the regular removal of unnecessary structures. During the discussion about Taylor's situation, Baxter told Austin Wilkins, "I do not want any buildings started without my consent . . . I want to keep everything as it is with no new buildings." The subject evoked his fear that the Deeds of Trust might be violated after he passed on. "While I am here, I can prevent any encroachment but once permission is given it will be hard to call a halt. Please do not allow any mistakes that would make trouble later on. NO NEW BUILDINGS."3

▲ ▲ ▲ ▲ ▲

Taylor's park job had cost him physically. Sixteen years earlier, he had dislocated his shoulder trying to help a Brooklyn, New York, man who had shown up with barrel staves on his feet and thought he would ski in the park. Later, two ribs had been broken when a picnic table fell on him. Working outdoors in bitter cold during the winters aggravated his poor leg circulation, causing one toe to be amputated. Taylor also fell off snowmobiles numerous times, and had had cataracts removed from both eyes.

On top of his other health difficulties, Taylor came down with a bad case of flu that led to pneumonia and a four-day hospital stay. He lost thirty pounds, kept running a fever, and couldn't gain back the weight or his strength. On June 16, 1967, just as the summer season in the park was taking off, he asked for a sick leave.

Taylor hand-picked Rodney Sargent to be acting supervisor. "Rodney is a good boy, and this is his thirteenth year with me on the park so I do not know of a better person to take my place," Taylor said in a letter to Governor Baxter on July 5. He knew that Baxter would be pleased with Sargent. The governor had written Sargent twice in previous years to thank him for his service—rare kudos from Baxter to an individual ranger.4

Taylor soon faced the fact that his health made it impossible for him to return to the park. His years at the park had been "the happiest . . . of my life" and he had "only great respect and admiration" for the men under whom he worked, Taylor wrote Austin Wilkins on July 12. Governor Baxter, Taylor said, "is the grandest man I ever knew."

Baxter resisted the reality of Taylor's situation. He was strongly optimistic that Taylor would recover from his health problems and return to his "usual good form." The ninety-year-old Baxter, who was frail himself, wrote:

> We must not lose you for you are The Park. It is good to know that you have Rodney Sargent to take over temporarily. He seems to me to be a fine young man who will do what is right . . . I

know that you will guide Rodney. He will do his best to follow in your footsteps for the time being. You and I must hold fast, as we are needed. I picture in my mind what is doing at the several campgrounds and I am looking forward to seeing what we have done at the gatehouses and with the new road. Meanwhile we must be patient, as before long we both will be on our feet again. Please keep me informed about everything that goes on. . . . We all have worked to build things up and we must not let ourselves or anybody else get discouraged. When I start my spring inspection, I shall be riding on a cloud and I am sure everybody will be pleased to have us all at work again.

Rodney Sargent had no inkling that Taylor was going to quit, at least anytime soon. "Helon called me to come over one evening, and he was in the process of getting his things together to leave," Sargent recalls. Taylor announced he was going to Guilford and not returning to the park. "'You know where things are' Helon said, and that was it. It was all over in a minute."

Sargent was shocked. He had lived with Taylor during several winters and had even shaved Taylor's face in the mornings because Taylor had arthritis in his hands. He knew Taylor couldn't see too well because he used a magnifying glass to read. Yet Sargent didn't realize the supervisor's health was so poor.

"I didn't spend that much time with him to get to know his problems," Sargent says. "His was a lonely job because his wife was a schoolteacher somewhere else. You would have thought he would have talked to me before he left me in such a spot."

Sargent called the other rangers on the radio and read to them Taylor's letter transferring the acting supervisor's job. Sargent had no grand plan for his supervisory tenure, which he assumed would be short. He had little incentive to do more than take care of the current situation because he had convinced himself that Buzz had the inside track to the permanent supervisor's job.

Buzz wasn't disappointed at being bypassed by Taylor, given Sargent's seniority and the circumstances of the appointment. He felt badly about Taylor's leaving but had been gradually adjusting emotionally to the expectation that his mentor would soon resign. "The writing was on the wall after the fire," he says.

One of Governor Baxter's last letters to Taylor was to explain his opposition to a proposed bill that would give the federal government control of the AT—including the section in Baxter Park.5 Using strong language, Percival Baxter told the chairman of the parks and recreation subcommittee in the U.S. House of Representatives that his consent to federal oversight was out of the question.

"I thought it best to strike hard before these ideas take root and spread," the governor wrote Taylor. "You already may know about this but I want to make sure that our position to keep the Park under complete State control is not trifled with. . . . With you in the lead I am sure that everything will be kept in order."

Wrapping up financial matters with Austin Wilkins, Taylor thanked the commissioner for his kindness and effort in behalf of "our park. Frankly I am worried what may become of it when you and I are both out of it."

Responding to Wilkins's request for recommendations for future planning for the park, Taylor agreed to send along his thoughts. After his retirement was accepted, he added, "I can say anything I want to without risk of getting fired."

▲ ▲ ▲ ▲ ▲

Taylor's resignation was effective on August 19, 1967, the day that the gatehouses officially opened and two months before he would turn seventy years old. His state retirement would be $322 a month. In a letter to Governor Baxter on August 25, Taylor explained that his letter of retirement was one of the hardest he had ever had to write, but his health was at stake. "I feel that my heath was worth more to me than the extra money I would earn if I stayed on longer," he said.

At this point, Baxter didn't try to hide his feelings. "There must be some way to have you remain in command," the governor implored. "Your personality makes the Park and without you, I would lose most of my interest and probably, I would not visit the Park again." Baxter was willing to pay Taylor out of his own pocket or the park's trust fund if money was an issue.

But then in another communication, Baxter was more realistic: "I did not realize the years had passed so rapidly. I do not know what I shall do without you but we must carry on . . . the work you have done to make the Park acceptable is remarkable, and your name will long continue to guide those who follow you. It is strange that I should be crippled at just this time. It is certainly a coincidence as we both move out together. You have laid the foundation, and we have carried on together."

Buzz thought that Taylor was ready to leave the park because he was demoralized by the loss of his camp, and times were changing, making the management of the park more complicated. For instance, the new gatehouses were hard for Taylor to accept, Buzz recalls. "Helon just wasn't used to people having to stop and register, and all of the public complaints and demands that went with that process . . . people being in lines or being told where they could go and what they could do. He didn't like that. He wanted out. He recognized that his time had passed."

Doris Taylor Scott agreed that the fire and the increasing stress of the job finally wore out her father. "Here was a man who had been so strong and energetic, and it was like all the starch had gone out of him," she said.

As for Taylor's replacement, Wilkins told the other Authority members that "it would seen unwise at this time to appoint a successor since we will need to give considerable thought to anyone who will succeed Helon." He figured it would be a long time before they could find anyone who could fill Taylor's shoes. Taylor hoped it would be his son-in-law and former park ranger, Myrle Scott.

▲ ▲ ▲ ▲ ▲

By all accounts, Taylor's resignation was like a bomb hitting the ranger family. Taylor, the patriarch, had been in charge of the park for seventeen years, and the rangers held him in the highest esteem. "Helon was the boss," said former South Branch Pond ranger Ellie Damon. "You knew it, and he didn't have to remind you."

Rodney Sargent was considered by his peers to be experienced and capable, but it was tough to follow in Taylor's shoes. Roaring Brook ranger Leroy Jones recalls that Sargent was "too militant" for his taste. "You did it Rod's way or not at all."

The departure of Taylor meant relocating the park headquarters to 74 Water Street in Millinocket, the residence of Rodney Sargent. But Sargent was usually in the field troubleshooting problems and overseeing operations. He was put on the spot over a blue police light Buzz had bought for his truck for law enforcement—without authorization. Austin Wilkins also thought a blue light on a ranger's truck was going too far, and Buzz had to remove the light and pay for it himself.

▲ ▲ ▲ ▲ ▲

For years, the close connection between the park and the Maine Forest Service hadn't seemed of much concern to anyone. It was now time, however, for a "dividing line," according to Authority member Jim Erwin. Wilkins had been invited to speak at a meeting of The Wilderness Society in the fall, and he appointed his deputy, Fred Holt, to fill in and answer questions about Baxter Park. The event underscored "exactly the blurring of the dividing line between the Baxter State Park Authority and the Maine Forest Service," Erwin recalls. He didn't criticize Holt, but made it clear to Wilkins that he thought it inappropriate to ask Holt to speak for the Authority when he wasn't a member.

In December 1967 the Authority was involved with hearings by the Task Force on Government Reorganization, which was considering merging certain state natural resource agencies. The Authority, under the proposal, would become part of the Maine Parks and Recreation Commission.

Wilkins took a strong position against the idea, noting that Governor Baxter was "quite clear" that he wanted the Authority to be autonomous and that recreation was of secondary importance in the administration of the preserve.

Winston Libby, vice president for public services at the University of Maine at Orono and a key task force leader, agreed with Wilkins. The state, Libby said, "must keep faith with the intent of Governor Baxter in giving this grant to the state. I do not doubt that future generations may urge a breaking of Percival Baxter's intent," Libby continued. "But I do believe it would represent poor faith on the part of any legislative group or upon any task force to circumscribe what he intends will be the administrative organization to oversee the park."

The proposal was subsequently dropped.

▲ ▲ ▲ ▲ ▲

A banquet was held to honor Taylor on December 5, 1967, and the

Taylors were given a painting of Katahdin by Jake Day. Taylor didn't make a speech but later let Wilkins know that he deemed the party "a grand occasion." He felt "highly honored" and couldn't have been more pleased with the painting.

He and Hilda were happy in their new home in Farmington, purchased with Christmas money from Governor Baxter. Taylor received $1,000 each Christmas and put it in a special account that had grown enough to make the $21,000 property purchase. "It is warm, comfortable, and mostly push-button controlled," he wrote. "The nearest to living like white folks we have ever known. Our walls are graced with many things that bring fond memories. Like the paintings of Katahdin, Pamola, and the beautiful clock the park people gave us."

After his retirement, Taylor was asked by Governor Baxter for an evaluation of park employees so that he could know whom to recognize with a Christmas gift. Taylor rated Buzz as "loyal," as were acting supervisor Sargent, Russell Pond ranger Tom Chase, Nesowadnehunk ranger Irwin Sargent, Chimney Pond ranger Bernard Gardiner, Roaring Brook ranger Leroy Jones, and roving ranger Owen Grant. South Branch Pond ranger Ellie Damon and reservations clerk Helen Gifford—and Roaring Brook assistant ranger Richard Frost—were given the highest accolade of "outstanding."

There was no explanation of the standards Taylor used to rate everyone. "I consider [Damon] the very best ranger in our park, and we have all good rangers," he wrote Baxter. Damon surmised that he might have impressed Taylor with his efficient work habits.

After Christmas, Governor Baxter again praised Taylor in a personal note. "You have rendered a great service to the state of Maine and have carried on a dream I have had these many years. To you and Mrs. Taylor, I send my heartfelt thanks for making the park a wonderful place for those who come to our forest. Never shall I forget what you have accomplished."

Not long afterward, Taylor sent a list of management recommendations to the Authority, which had requested them a couple of months earlier. Among Taylor's suggestions were a new park headquarters that would be kept open at least sixteen hours a day, seven days a week; the addition of an assistant supervisor, a year-round forester, and at least one roving ranger to fill in for regular off-duty rangers; more campgrounds throughout the park; and a park museum with a full-time curator.

The summer of Taylor's retirement was the last time Governor Baxter visited the park. While the governor's health and the rigors of travel were given as the official explanations for his absence, Baxter already had said he wouldn't have the spiritual energy to make the trip if he couldn't see his special friend, Helon Taylor.

---

1. "Two Rescues on Mt. Katahdin," *Appalachia*, December, 1966, pp. 409–10.
2. "Exploring Katahdin's Klondike," by F. W. Rungee, *The Living Wilderness*, 1949, p. 12.
3. *Legacy of a Lifetime: The Story of Baxter State Park*, by John Hakola, TBW Books, Woolwich, Maine, 1981, p. 120.
4. Percival P. Baxter to Rodney Sargent, September 20, 1961: "Baxter State Park is fortunate to have a man like yourself." Baxter to Sargent, October 21, 1963: "You are a most conscientious ranger and you take a very active interest in your work. That means everything for the success of our park proposition."
5. The AT corridor is managed by Baxter Park, not the National Park Service.

Primary Document Sources: BSPA Boxes 1, 3, 6, 10, 11, 12, 13, 16, 18 (2507-0713, 2507-0714, 2507-0716, 2507-0718); Baxter State Park Original Authority/Advisory Minutes, Box 16; Percival Baxter Collection (Letters).

Conversations and communications: Buzz Caverly, Cathy Caverly, Jan Caverly, Jim Erwin, Elmer Knowlton, Gary Morse, Rodney Sargent, Doris Scott, Eric Wight.

PART II: THE ROCKY ROAD TO LEADERSHIP

▲▲▲▲▲▲▲▲

CHAPTER 8

# Supervisor Caverly

As Buzz and Jan rang in the New Year of 1968, they were about to become parents for the second time. They left the park in early January to stay with Jan's sister in West Enfield near the hospital. They waited, and nothing happened.

Not one to sit around, Buzz found a part-time job driving a snow-removal truck. But he couldn't stand to be away from the park, so he soon high-tailed it back to Togue Pond.

On January 15 Jan went into delivery at Workman Hospital in Lincoln while Buzz was delivering a generator to the Katahdin Lake sporting camp. The family called the park, and Rodney Sargent contacted Buzz by radio with the news that he had another baby girl. Buzz raced to the hospital. Four days later, Buzz took Jan, baby Tammy, and Cathy to Togue Pond.

That winter would turn out to be Buzz's last season as a regular field ranger, and he put in ten- to twelve-hour workdays carrying out the usual patrols on snowmobile, hauling supplies, and attending to administrative matters.

Living at the gatehouse at Togue Pond, Buzz and Jan saw how much snowmobile use had increased in the park. The first weekend of February, eighty-five sledders went through the Togue Pond gate, plus an unknown number from other directions. Buzz gave out information about park rules and assisted sledders in trouble on the trail. Jan served coffee to those who were cold. Problems of "drinking and littering" came with the activity, causing more headaches for rangers.

Not all winter users came on snowsleds. A University of Maine student drove his car down the unplowed Perimeter Road before sinking in snow to the frame. His intention, as ludicrous as it seemed, was to drive to Abol Campground, climb Katahdin's Abol Trail to the summit, and then return to school in Orono.

Buzz asked him what in the world he was thinking. "Adventure!" the young man replied. Buzz spent most of that day jacking up the car, putting blocking under it, moving it a few feet, and starting all over again as the vehicle sank again to the frame. It was all part of a ranger's day.

▲ ▲ ▲ ▲ ▲

That March, Buzz made his first technical winter ascent of Katahdin, with ice ax, crampons, ropes, and pitons. He was invited to join "Operation High Ski" by George Smith, a personnel officer with the state highway commission, whose climbing resume included ascents in the Rockies and the Swiss Alps. Along also were state forest service engineer Win Robbins; Dr. Bob Ohler, a doctor and former AMC hut man; state marine biologist Dana Wallace; and Dr. Larry Nolan, a Massachusetts physician.

The group took the Cathedral Trail to Baxter Peak and descended the ravine between the Cathedral and Saddle Trails. Buzz, outfitted in a regular work jacket and cotton underwear, was still dangerously dressed by today's outdoor standards. He tied crampons to his rubber boots and they constantly slipped off, slowing down the party. When the trip was over, he decided technical climbing wasn't for him. He didn't like messing with the gear. He much preferred snowmobiling and snowshoeing.

▲ ▲ ▲ ▲ ▲

The Authority's major focus that winter was a replacement for Helon Taylor. Although just twenty-nine years old, Buzz thought that his success in running Katahdin Stream Campground made him ready to step into the top management job.

Buzz was among eleven who applied, and one of three who were finalists: himself, Rodney Sargent, and Harry Kearney, a state district game warden.

Buzz had met Kearney a couple of times at Junior York's and thought him excessively boisterous. Kearney, from Bangor, had gotten to know the Yorks well as a youth camping at Baxter Park, and had worked as a guide at the Daicey camps. He joined the state fish and game department in 1941, served in the air corps from 1942 to 1945, and returned to the warden service after the war. Kearney had a reputation as a difficult personality and was transferred several times by his supervisors. To isolate Kearney until he retired, fish and game commissioner Ron Speers had created a new district in western Maine and moved him to distant Jackman. Speers favored Kearney getting the park supervisor's job as a way to get Kearney out of his agency. But Wilkins and Erwin wanted to give the job to Buzz, at least on a six-month probationary basis. Speers gave in, and Buzz was elevated to the position in May. His pay increased to $156 a week.

Wilkins wrote to former forest commissioner and trustee Al Nutting, who had become director of the School of Forest Resources at the University of Maine at Orono, saying he was "certain that Rodney Sargent was somewhat disappointed, but based on an average of the Oral Board examination and evaluation by the Personnel Board, Irvin Caverly came out first."

Buzz was on cloud nine with his promotion, especially when he received a warm note from Percival Baxter. "Helon Taylor set a high standard for his work, and I want your work to follow along with Helon's as an example," Baxter wrote on May 21. "People look forward to being with us, and we must be careful not to break faith with them. I think of you often," he told Buzz.

In a reflective response, Buzz wrote back to the governor, harking back to his first year as a ranger, his tutelage under Taylor, and his gratitude to Baxter:

> Little did I realize nine years ago this season, when I was fresh out of high school and coming to work as a ranger in this beautiful area, that I would someday become supervisor of Baxter State Park. I feel highly honored and grateful for this opportunity. I also feel very grateful to have had the chance to work under Helon Taylor and feel that the experience, training, and advice that I received from him in these past eight years will always be of great help to me. I cannot express how grateful I am to you for all you have done for the many, many people who come and enjoy Baxter State Park. *I will assure you* that our most faithful reservation clerk Helen Gifford, our fine groups of rangers, and I will do our very best to take care of the needs of the public. But most of all we will work to maintain and preserve this beautiful wilderness that we all love so much.

Helon Taylor exuded pleasure, too, over Buzz's selection. "Nothing could please me more," he wrote. "You have my backing 100 percent, and if there is ever anything I can do to help you, be sure to call on [me]." Taylor confided that he and Hilda were "very happy in our new home and I sure do enjoy working in the garden and wood lot." Taylor ended on a typically humorous note, saying he had to go harvest his crop of rocks to make soup. "Again I say, 'More power to you, Buz.' I am quite proud of my boys. Just remember that you can catch more flies with molasses than you can with vinegar. I am sure no one is going to push you around too much."

▲ ▲ ▲ ▲ ▲

The promotion was the beginning of Buzz's ascendancy, even though his path would wind downhill twice before the last rise. At the time of his youthful appointment, no one would have believed he could survive the twists and turns ahead.

With his first promotion, Buzz was no longer "one of the boys" but the "supervisor of the boys." Privately, he struggled to make the adjustment in relationships with personnel while at the same time facing the most demanding work of his life.

The first time Buzz appeared before the Authority, he was excited and bewildered. Jim Erwin told him to buy a tape recorder so he could keep up with his thoughts about what the park needed. Buzz dutifully bought a recorder and used it for several years.

Buzz accounted for his decisions with typed reports. Many administrators considered paperwork a pain, but Buzz felt that it was a support, and he prided himself on efficiency and order. He had good reason to make written reports a high priority. "After getting into some of the jams I had, I realized I needed to cover myself," he explains.

Buzz had seen that the Authority had given Helon Taylor significant autonomy to run the park, and he "inherited" from Taylor the attitude that he was fully responsible to make everything work smoothly—and should have the level of freedom Taylor had enjoyed.

▲ ▲ ▲ ▲ ▲

The park office moved from Sargent's Water Street house to 307 Katahdin Avenue in May, where it would remain for ten months. Buzz and his family took up residency there, except for the summer months, when they lived in the park at Nesowadnehunk Campground. He had a field office in the crew camp at Togue Pond. Buzz's workdays in the summer were so long that Jan and the children saw little of him. He was usually out of Nesowadnehunk by 5:00 or 6:00 A.M. and not back home until 9:00 or 10:00 P.M. Many nights, he was so tired that he went to bed without supper.

Buzz handled all of his own paperwork and correspondence, with the help of Helon Taylor's old Royal typewriter and *Webster's Dictionary*. When he was back in Millinocket, he had part-time clerical help from Joyce Given, a full-time employee at Great Northern.

After just a couple of weeks on the job, Buzz confided to Helon Taylor that he liked being supervisor and felt that he had full support of the Authority and the Baxter family.

▲▲▲▲▲

Buzz's supervisory appointment generated numerous congratulatory notes and cards, all kept neatly by Jan in a family album. Dr. Ralph DeOrsay of Drexel Hill, Pennsylvania, was one of the many supporters. In a note to Austin Wilkins, DeOrsay praised Buzz for his "boundless energy, hence his nickname, and a becoming modesty in his accomplishments. A most engaging personality and rare insight, judgment, and ability for a comparatively young man."

Buzz had new ideas to improve ranger training in rescue techniques, first aid, and law enforcement and talked them over with DeOrsay. DeOrsay was impressed with Buzz's ideas, as was Austin Wilkins. The young man was "doing an excellent job," Wilkins told Governor Baxter. "I am sure that in time he will begin to fill the shoes of Helon Taylor."

One of Buzz's first actions as supervisor was a small but lasting one. He changed the park seal. "I ran into Jake Day and told him we needed a distinctive patch to distinguish the park from the regular state parks," Buzz recounts. Day produced a design of a moose standing in a pond, with Katahdin in the background. The secretary of state approved the design, and the seal is still used today.

There were many serious management issues that begged for action and had grabbed Buzz's attention in previous years—the dumps, the gravel pits, the outhouses, dilapidated buildings, water pollution, traffic, dams, and overcrowded campgrounds. Now that he was in charge, he began to think about solutions, and his interest in cleaning up the park would grow into a dogged determination, no matter how long it took.

▲ ▲ ▲ ▲ ▲

When the park opened for the 1968 season, local fishermen flocked to the trout ponds. Buzz and Fin and Feather Club stalwart Darrell Morrow were hardly speaking to each other, given the trouble over public access and the coming end to camp leases. About the only time Buzz would speak to Morrow was when he ran into him on the trail. He checked Morrow's fishing license and knew it was irritating to Morrow. "I was probably doing that deliberately, even at times when I knew he wasn't in violation," Buzz recalls.

Now and then, however, there was a short truce. Buzz stopped at Togue Pond one day and saw a dejected-looking Morrow talking to the gatekeeper.

"I felt sorry for him for the first time in my life," Buzz says. "There was something in the look of his face that I knew was wrong, and I hadn't been to blame for. So I said, 'Hi, Darrell. Can I help you?' He said maybe I could and came over to my car. He had a 'terrible problem.' Every year at this time, Darrell got some time off from the mill to go to Nesowadnehunk Lake fishing. He thought he had his camping reservation confirmed but discovered a few minutes before I arrived that he had the wrong dates. It was the first time I had heard Darrell Morrow admit he'd made a mistake, and I was touched by that. I wanted to help him, so I got on the radio and called Helen Gifford at headquarters. We found room for him at the bunkhouse at Nesowadnehunk. He thanked me ten times before he left that day, and we began to have a good relationship."

Based on their improved relations, Morrow asked Buzz for another favor. The park gate at Togue Pond was locked at 10:00 P.M. and not opened until after sunrise. Morrow, speaking for the Fin and Feather Club, asked that the gate be left open so that those who worked at the paper mills could go fishing after their night shifts.

Buzz told Morrow that he couldn't give him a key but would pin (instead of lock) the gate so that fishermen could get in after hours. If that option worked, Buzz was willing to continue it. Buzz and Morrow's cordiality held until the early 1990s, when the park eliminated the West Gate at Nesowadnehunk Field.

▲ ▲ ▲ ▲ ▲

With the new section of Interstate Highway 95 completed to Houlton, tourism became a major economic generator up north. Austin Wilkins expected an influx of visitors to the park, as well as through-travelers headed north to the Allagash Wilderness Waterway. He thought registrations indicated that 100,000 to 125,000 people would visit the park in 1968—an estimate that turned out to be too high by roughly 30 percent. However, Wilkins was reading correctly the soaring interest in outdoor recreation, especially backpacking.

One of the summer visitors was Helon Taylor, who brought his neighbors for a visit to his former stomping ground. A yearling bear promptly paid them an hour-long "friendly visit," posing for photos and enjoying the apple pie and cookies that Hilda Taylor and Mrs. Millett fed him in hopes of luring the animal back again. That evening, the group went to Foster Field to watch feeding bears—but no bears were out.

"We rattled the cans for some twenty minutes trying to call them out and were just about to leave when Mr. Millett happened to glance up and there in a tall spruce tree were two good-sized bears laughing at us," Taylor wrote to Governor Baxter about his park visit. "We talked to them for another twenty minutes or so but they got disgusted with us and came down and went off into the woods. I think they were disappointed that Percy Baxter was not with us."

Taylor also mentioned seeing Buzz, "the nice-looking young man who was the ranger at Katahdin Stream with the nice wife and baby girl. Buz [sic] worked for us eight years under my direction and is the go-go type. If he does not work himself to death or worry himself into ulcers he will make a fine supervisor."

Taylor went on to write about stopping to visit with other old friends and rangers. He assured Baxter, "your park is in good hands." Baxter's reply to Taylor noted that he was "homesick" for the park and didn't enjoy being in Portland "while you and my other friends are traveling over our park."

▲ ▲ ▲ ▲ ▲

As the summer progressed, Buzz was faced with more accidents than at any time in the park's history, including a bizarre fatality at Chimney Pond Campground.

In August, a severe wind- and rainstorm produced unusually severe lightning, and ranger Bernard Gardiner made the rounds of campsites, offering people shelter in his cabin or the woodshed. Scott and Carolyn Newlin of Philadelphia declined his invitation, preferring to remain in their tent.

"The storm intensified to an indescribable fury, both in light and sound," according to Buzz's accident report, "and it struck a tree near the Newlins, traveled through the ground, and hit the Newlins inside their tent. Scott Newlin was killed, and Carolyn Newlin suffered third-degree burns and was in shock.

By just after 6:00 A.M., Carolyn Newlin had made her way to the ranger's station to let Gardiner know what had happened. Buzz could not be reached by radio. By the time he found out the situation, Mrs. Newlin was being carried on a stretcher to Roaring Brook where an ambulance was waiting to take her to the hospital in Millinocket.

The lightning had forked into four or five separate bolts. One stripped the bark off the tree near the Newlins' tent, jumped to a large cook kit, melted a hole in the bottom, and jumped into the tent. Scott Newlin had been outside in the rain prior to the lightning hit, and had crawled into his sleeping bag wet. He went to sleep with his wet arm lying across his metal pack frame, and the frame conducted the lightning to him and then to his wife. It killed Scott Newlin. Of the 116 people in the campground, 22 were visibly burned by the lightning.

With Scott Newlin's death, Buzz learned how mentally stressful it was to console families who lost a loved one in the park, especially if the situation was tragic. As supervisor, he had the job of delivering news about a death to the deceased person's family, most often over the phone. He found that most families wanted to know why a death had occurred, and Buzz found out he had to be ready with detailed information about trail conditions, the weather, and myriad other facts to explain why the deceased person had made certain choices.

▲ ▲ ▲ ▲ ▲

Buzz himself had a scary vehicle crash in his 1968 Ford station wagon on his way to an accident investigation training session he had scheduled for his staff with the Maine State Police. He didn't want to be late for the 9:00 A.M. session and was hurrying along on the narrow park road. South of Doubletop Mountain, his car hit a vehicle driven by a park visitor. The investigating officer was Piscataquis County deputy sheriff Joe Bartlett, whom Buzz knew because Bartlett operated the Togue Pond sporting camp at the time.

Neither Buzz nor the driver of the other car were hurt, but both vehicles were damaged to the tune of $1,400. He accepted the blame for the accident and then went about park business without thinking much about the mishap.

He was relieved to hear from Austin Wilkins that Jan would be put on the payroll temporarily as a gatekeeper during the hunting season to cover for a ranger on sick leave. It was good news to them because of the higher expenses with a growing family.

But while Buzz was going about his normal activities, the Authority was taking a close look at his auto accident. In particular, Attorney General Erwin was alarmed, suspecting that Buzz had been driving too fast. "I think this is serious enough for us to call park supervisor Caverly here to Augusta to account for this," Erwin said in a memo to other Authority members. "In fact, I think he should come prepared to show cause why he should not be removed from office." (In 2003, reflecting on the situation, Erwin didn't remember details of the situation but recalled that he was "disappointed" in Buzz, whom he liked very much. "He did something that could have been serious," Erwin said.)

▲ ▲ ▲ ▲ ▲

The accident brought to light enough rumors about rangers speeding that the Authority asked the chief investigator of the Maine State Police, Alfred Howes, to look into the situation. Inexplicably, Howes interviewed only those who were critical of Buzz, and Erwin didn't want Buzz to be shown a copy of the report until he appeared before the Authority.

Howes interviewed Togue Pond gatekeeper Duncan Peddle, and

Erwin said, "[Peddle] certainly should not have to face any retaliation from Caverly or any other rangers before we talk to Caverly. Furthermore, my personal opinion with respect to Supervisor Caverly will be affected by the manner in which he handles himself and justifies himself prior to any opportunity to talk with and work up some defense with other rangers. This is a very sensitive matter. The meeting with Supervisor Caverly will be difficult for him and for us."

Peddle told Howes that he had been with Buzz and rangers Leroy Jones, David Perkins, and Tom Chase when they operated park vehicles above posted speed limits and at dangerous speeds. He also reported being pressured by Supervisor Caverly, after Ranger Perkins was summoned, to say that he had seen Joe Bartlett drinking beer in the park in violation of park rules. Peddle stated that this was not true, although on one occasion, he had seen a beer bottle in the seat in Bartlett's vehicle. He also reported other incidents of "spinning out with the vehicles and of wise-guy rangers using the vehicles to push the gatehouse around." (The gatehouse was just a small booth sitting on top of the ground so that it could be moved in winter.)

In the past, Bartlett had complained to park officials about certain employees, including Buzz, speeding in and around the park. George Emerson of Camp Phoenix and warden Elmer Knowlton supported the allegations leveled by Bartlett. But Emerson, like Bartlett, didn't like Buzz anyway because of a disagreement over park access for his clients. Oversized vehicles, pets, and motorcycles—all banned in the park— could travel to Camp Phoenix via the Nesowadnehunk Lake gate if they went north directly to the camps. But often they turned south to recreate in the park, and Buzz had taken action to stop the violations.

From Howes's report, it was obvious that the speeding issue was complicated and wrapped up in politics and personality conflicts. Buzz felt the situation had its roots back in 1966, when he and Jan moved to Togue Pond for the winter. Buzz was on patrol near the Rocky Pond area and found Joe Bartlett with a chain saw cutting log-size pines for lumber to be used at his camps. Buzz questioned Bartlett about what he was doing, and Bartlett said he had permission to cut from Great Northern Paper, despite the fact that the company had sold the land to Governor Baxter. Helon Taylor had also given him permission to cut the trees, Bartlett told Buzz. Later, Taylor confirmed that the cutting rights had expired but that he had told Bartlett that he could take some cordwood, not logs. Taylor ordered Bartlett to stop cutting, and Bartlett was mad at Buzz for tattling on him.

Buzz admitted he had made a mistake in speeding. On the day of his accident, he was trying to attend to too many things. There was no chain of command to help him, meaning that he worked seven days a week most of the time.

Helon Taylor read between the lines of Buzz's monthly reports that things were difficult. "I know just what you are up against," Taylor said, commending him for a report that was "in good form, to the point, no excess of words, [and] no mention of those little incidents that stink. More power to you, Buz. I know you are working your head off, but you are young and can take it. Anyway, the worst of it is over for the year."

▲ ▲ ▲ ▲ ▲

Taylor was wrong. The worst was just days away. Buzz met with the Authority on September 3, 1968, in Augusta. Erwin did most of the talking about Buzz's accident and informed him that he was being demoted back to the position of ranger. But his pay would remain the same, and when the position of assistant supervisor was created, Buzz would have it, Erwin promised.

Buzz remembers that Erwin "said I had not developed to the point that I was an effective supervisor of the park but that I had potential . . . and the time would come when I would have learned from the experiences and be able to handle the responsibilities. I remember that I was so emotionally upset that I said to him, 'You can demote me to janitor as long as you allow me to work for the park. I'm going to stay. I love this job.'"

Wilkins escorted Buzz out of the room, and Buzz told him what a shock his demotion was, that he had not been "heads up on this." Buzz returned to the Capital Motel where he and Jan were staying. "I cried my eyes out," he reveals, "and we got that out of our system and moved on with life." Tim Caverly remembers that the demotion "just about devastated [Buzz], but he buckled down" to redeem himself. He was impressed with Buzz's fortitude but not surprised. He knew how dedicated Buzz was to the park and how his attitude was 110 percent positive.

*Katahdin and Kidney Pond Camps from the south shore of Kidney Pond*
COURTESY BAXTER STATE PARK PHOTO ARCHIVES

▲ ▲ ▲ ▲ ▲

The day after meeting with the Authority, Buzz knuckled down to the task at hand—greeting Governor Kenneth Curtis and his party for a visit to the park. State fish and game pilot Andy Stinson flew the governor in to Kidney Pond Camps on September 5, despite the prohibition of planes landing on the water body. (No one objected to the infraction on this occasion.)

That first night he was treated to a steak dinner by camp managers Charles and Ruth Norris. Curtis went fishing after dinner, and then the party drove to Foster Field to enjoy "a show put on by two bears at the dump," Buzz reported. "Many pictures were taken, and all enjoyed watching the bears fight over the food."

This trip was Curtis's second Katahdin climb. He had first hiked up the mountain at ten years of age with his father. Curtis's idea for the return trip was to pay tribute to Percival Baxter.

Buzz joined the group for the hike up the Hunt Trail to Baxter

Peak. On the summit, they ate lunch, took photos, and realized that the weather was getting too foggy to go across the Knife Edge. So the group headed for the Saddle Trail, the easiest way down to Chimney Pond Campground for the night. Curtis's neighbor, Ken Premo, and York County sheriff Richard Dutremble lagged behind the others, and because of the poor visibility didn't see the turn down the Saddle Trail.

Back at Chimney Pond, the group realized that Dutremble and Premo were lost. Curtis wanted to go looking for them, despite the bad conditions, so Buzz guided the governor up the trail to the Tableland, where they encountered fifty-mile-an-hour winds, driving rain, sleet, and thick fog. At one point, Buzz took a fall but didn't hurt himself. He and Curtis returned to Chimney Pond without finding Dutremble and Premo. Luckily, the lost pair found their own way into Russell Pond Campground on the other side of Katahdin about midnight.

The incident prompted Curtis to ask the Executive Council for money from the Contingency Fund to buy a new high-band radio system which included walkie talkies and relay towers to help with future rescue situations on Katahdin. He also paid a visit to Governor Baxter to show him slides of the Katahdin trip. After seeing a couple of the slides, Baxter fell asleep. He woke up at the end of the slide show and told Curtis, "That was wonderful, just like I remember it."

▲ ▲ ▲ ▲ ▲

While Buzz was recovering from his demotion, the Fin and Feather Club decided to champion the cause of snowmobiles in light of rumors that the park planned to ban them. The Authority was concerned over reports that snowmobilers had damaged trees, molested deer, and ignored safety rules; they believed that locals were responsible. Club president Dana Brown denied that "natives" were responsible and laid the blame on out-of-staters.

In his September 20 letter to the Authority, Brown mentioned how popular Buzz was with snowmobilers. Buzz often rode with the sledders and was "a definite pleasure to have along," according to Brown. The park should be seeking "more men of his caliber" to build "a select ranger staff," the club spokesman suggested.

The Authority didn't officially notify park staff until September 27 that Buzz was stepping down from his supervisor's post. The decision was made "with complete accord with members of the Authority," wrote Wilkins, adding, "Buzz Caverly pledges full support to his successor and hopefully this [appointment] will be made on or by November 1. Furthermore, Buzz will be retained as campground ranger with full-time employ, acting as one of the law enforcement rangers during the winter months. I ask that you give the new supervisor your full support and cooperation, and continue relations with Buzz Caverly."

The rangers were upset and wanted to resign in protest. Ranger Bernard Gardiner expressed his disappointment at losing Buzz as supervisor. Buzz's prime concern was "the good of all," Gardiner said. "I could not ask for a better man to work with and under whom to work."

Photographer Paul Knaut contacted Governor Curtis about the demotion, calling Buzz "a man of honesty, integrity, and character, whose first love is Baxter Park and Mt. Katahdin . . . his ambition and life's desire is to care for this park and see that it is run as ex-Governor Baxter has wanted it to be."

In an attempt to head off an intervention from Curtis, Austin Wilkins wrote to Curtis's aide, Howard Cunningham, assuring him that it was "necessary" to demote Buzz. At the same time, Wilkins was optimistic that Buzz might be promoted to assistant supervisor in the future. Furthermore, he told Cunningham, Buzz had accepted his change in position.

Wilkins drafted a letter for Curtis's signature to respond to Knaut's letter, and the governor signed. "I am sure that this whole matter can and will be worked out satisfactorily and in the best interest of all concerned who are interested in the future of Baxter State Park,'" Curtis informed Knaut.

Helon Taylor was still not aware of Buzz's demotion. In a communication to Governor Baxter, he praised Buzz for "doing a fine job running the Park this summer and everybody speaks highly of him. More power to him."

Baxter was always grateful for news because he hadn't been well enough to make his annual visit. "When you were [supervisor] everything went smoothly, and I had no fears as to how affairs were being handled," said Baxter. "You certainly made the Park. I hope that all of us interested can continue along."

▲ ▲ ▲ ▲ ▲

With the park closed for the season and the rangers' fall meeting over, Buzz sent Governor Baxter a copy of a photograph of the field crew and reported that all was well. A foot of snow had fallen, he wrote, and deer, bear, and moose were visible as they looked for food. Junior and Jeanette York were staying at their Daicey Pond sporting camp for the winter and had five deer and two ruffed grouse "that eat meals with them regularly," Buzz wrote. He reported on "a very good camping season," with more than 80,000 visitors, and wished Baxter good health. Buzz didn't mention his demotion.

▲ ▲ ▲ ▲ ▲

In November Buzz was notified by Wilkins that the Authority had offered the supervisor's position to Harry Kearney and that Kearney had accepted. But it would be months before Kearney could take over the job. Buzz would continue in the position until Kearney resigned from the warden service and moved to Millinocket.

Helon Taylor finally got wind of Buzz's situation, but also had heard that Kearney didn't really want the supervisor's job. He wrote Governor Baxter that he hoped Kearney would remain with the fish and game department, where his pay was higher than what the park could afford to pay him. There was always the chance that Kearney wouldn't "fill the bill" at Baxter. "There are a lot of different angles to think about," Taylor said.

Taylor's remarks are interesting, given a letter favorable to Kearney that he had written on February 5, 1952, to then-fish and game commissioner Roland Cobb: "It is the consensus of opinion that Harry Kearney, the warden up around Bethel some place, would be a good man to take Win Foster's place at Millinocket when the time comes for Win to retire. I do not even know the man but I believe he works under Wayne Lindsey . . . Millinocket is one of the hot spots in the state as far as poaching is concerned and we need a good woodsman, a man of good judgment and good character up there."

Jim Erwin viewed Kearney as a mature game warden with potential to be an effective supervisor. The Authority met with Kearney and together agreed that "if he didn't turn out well, he'd walk away."

In discussing the job change with Taylor, Buzz put the best light on things:

> [The supervisor's job] has been quite an experience for me, and I feel I have learned a lot from it, and as a whole I have enjoyed it. I wish Kearney lots of luck and I will do all I can to help him on his new job. I feel that [Kearney] is going to be a good man and I am looking forward to working under him. I also feel that his twenty-seven years of state service will be of great value to him as the supervisor of Baxter State Park.

Buzz also told Taylor that Ron Speers had promised to send him to Maine fish and game warden's school at the University of Maine starting on February 3, 1969. Buzz thought the training would be helpful to his career in the park.

▲ ▲ ▲ ▲ ▲

When Buzz had joined the park crew, he had heard stories from the older rangers about how political certain Authority members were, namely Austin Wilkins and Richard Dubord, who preceded Jim Erwin as attorney general. The whole demotion episode and hiring of Kearney confirmed to Buzz how politics were at the bottom of a lot of goings-on at the Authority level. The moment Erwin had told Buzz that the time would come when he would be ready to head the park again crystallized the situation: Speers wanted Kearney out of his agency, and Buzz's speeding accident had given the Authority an opportunity to appoint a new supervisor.

Despite Governor Baxter's effort to establish a governing board that would not be subject to political shenanigans, the three state officials he chose to be trustees were inherently political. The attorney general was appointed by the majority party in the legislature, and the other two by the governor. As managing the park became more complicated and decisions controversial, the trustees' ambitions and ties to certain constituencies and special interests were clearly reflected in their votes.

Primary Document Sources: BSPA Boxes 6, 7, 16 18 (2507-0714, 2507-0715, 2507-

0718); Percival Baxter Collection (Letters).

Conversations and communications: Buzz Caverly, Jan Caverly, Ken Curtis, Jim Erwin, Harry Kearney, Paul Knaut, Darrell Morrow, George Smith, Rodney Sargent, Dana Wallace.

▲▲▲▲▲▲▲▲

CHAPTER 9

# WE ARE PARTNERS

BUZZ SENT GOVERNOR BAXTER A BIRTHDAY CARD on his ninety-first birthday, and Baxter returned a thank-you note to "Irving" for his kindness. It was in this note that Baxter made the *"we are partners in this project"* declaration that would deeply affect Buzz for the rest of his life:

> These birthdays come and go and we cannot avoid them. In your position at the park you are making good progress and I hear good things about you. I want to keep in touch with you and your [ranger] group in the picture you sent me. I hope they will keep together and make our park stand out, and we will receive good reports of the work you and your associates are doing. I expect to be at home all winter and shall keep in touch with you for you have a most important position. I shall write you and I want you to write me. *We are partners in this project.* Please tell your associates that I depend on you and them to make the park successful.

Buzz shared the May 20, 1968, letter with Helon Taylor, who was glad to know that Baxter was giving Buzz the same heartfelt support he had received himself as supervisor.

▲▲▲▲▲

While after-the-fact, the Fin and Feather Cub was so unhappy about Buzz's demotion that they had local attorney and state senator Wakine Tanous (D-East Millinocket) write all three Authority members for an explanation.

Austin Wilkins responded, explaining that Buzz's demotion was "directly connected with a number of car accidents involving state vehicles and some of our personnel." The Authority acted reluctantly in sending Buzz back to the ranger ranks, but the decision was mutually agreeable, he assured the club.

Fin and Feather spokesman Brown had more to say on Buzz's behalf: "We found him to be courteous and helpful at all times, to resident and non-resident sportsmen alike. He made possible equal access to all available facilities. Regrettably, this was not always true in the past. We think very highly of Mr. Caverly because of his sense of fair play, which has vastly improved the relationship between Baxter Park personnel and the resident sportsmen."

Buzz returned the favor with praise of snowmobilers, many of them club members. In his final report for the year, he said rangers worked hard to keep tabs on sledders but "on the whole, the snowmobilers who come to Baxter are a great bunch of people and have no intentions of violating the rules and regulations, getting themselves into trouble, or doing anything to cause people to worry about them."

However, public pressure was bearing down on the Authority, and in December 1968, the trustees adopted the first regulation (Rule 19) governing snowmobile use. The regulation allowed "snow traveling vehicles" on the park's perimeter road, the Roaring Brook Road and Chimney Pond Trails, the logging roads on Rum Mountain built in 1963 for blowdown salvage operations, and the road from Avalanche Field to Katahdin Lake. Austin Wilkins maintained that the rule had been explained to Governor Baxter. Despite Baxter's declining condition, Wilkins was confident that Baxter understood the meaning of the snowmobile rule.

▲ ▲ ▲ ▲ ▲

Buzz and Jan rented Walter Bouchard's house at 307 Katahdin Avenue in Millinocket for the second winter, and in early January 1969 they moved in. A few days later, they received a call from Harry Kearney, who wanted to meet Buzz at Junior York's house nearby.

"I jumped in my car, drove over, and he met me at the door," recalls Buzz. "He was very social, congenial. I had a nice visit with Junior. We chatted for awhile. I couldn't see any specific reason for my being there, and so I prepared to leave. Harry followed me. We got out to the car and he said, 'Buzz, I want to tell you something. I'm the new supervisor at Baxter State Park. As long as you support me, and you don't buck me, we'll get along fine. But if you do, I'm going to cut your legs right out from under you.' He asked me if I understood. I said, 'Yes, I hear what you're saying.' He became pleasant again after that, and I left."

Buzz knew from that conversation that if he wanted to be anything more than a "yes man," he might end up losing his job. The way that Kearney tried to keep Buzz on a tight rein was to give him assignments day by day, but that didn't prevent them from having problems.

▲ ▲ ▲ ▲ ▲

One of the first incidents that faced Kearney in connection with Buzz was over the Pelletier harvesting road. Great Northern Paper contractor Jim Pelletier had opened up an old horse road for winter harvesting operations past Center Pond in T4R10 that would allow the logger to loop down along Little Nesowadnehunk Stream and out to Nesowadnehunk Field. Wilkins asked Kearney to get a statement from Buzz on why he gave permission to Pelletier to create the loop, off the Tote Road.

Buzz explained that Pelletier had asked for permission to simply use the horse route to Center Pond—not beyond. However, Pelletier had used a bulldozer to make the loop access, and, in the process, had pushed down a lot of trees he had no intention of harvesting. "For the entire 2.7 miles the road is a mess," Kearney said. "The camp area also "is . . . a bit disgusting. There are small dumps along each of the several roads leading away from camp. Cans and garbage flying around not in the least in keeping with Governor Baxter's wishes."

Jim Erwin jumped on the issue with a letter to Great Northern Paper's woodlands manager John Maines, letting him know that the Authority was "considerably upset by this whole matter. In spite of Mr. Caverly's mistaken assumption of authority, this letter is to notify you that the above described road may not be used further."

The Authority reprimanded Buzz in a January 24 letter saying that Pelletier had done "considerable damage . . . the wilderness concept of the Park has been especially disturbed by bulldozer action." Buzz didn't try to defend himself. "I was up to my ears with work as acting supervisor," he explains.

▲ ▲ ▲ ▲ ▲

Harry Kearney began working three days a week for the park in January 1969 while still on the fish and game department payroll. Shortly after Kearney began showing up in the office, Buzz reported for the six-week warden's school at the University of Maine at Orono.

Buzz stood out from the other two dozen participants because he was the only one from Baxter Park—and he was one of the few non-drinkers. "He was a great guy to have along after hours as the designated driver because he would keep us out of trouble," remembers Bill Vail, a classmate from the warden service and a future park trustee.

Buzz roomed with warden Dan Glidden. They were a perfect match because both of them were teetotalers, didn't like to party, and were quiet. Glidden was amazed that Buzz kept in such close phone contact with his family, calling once or sometimes twice a night to talk with Jan and the girls.

Vail and Glidden agreed that Buzz talked all the time about the park. If any of his colleagues uttered a criticism of Percival Baxter, Buzz would get up and leave the room, Glidden recalls, "He couldn't take anyone being disrespectful of Baxter." His classmates "cared nothing about the park," Buzz says. "They just wanted to hear about poachers."

▲ ▲ ▲ ▲ ▲

George Smith and his buddies were unquestionably the most ambitious Katahdin winter climbers of the 1960s. They decided to make the first-ever traverse of Katahdin via the Hunt and Helon Taylor Trails to try out new gear and survival methods in mid-February, 1969. Win Robbins, Bob Ohler, Dana Wallace, and Larry Nolan rejoined Smith for the adventure, and the new member of the party was Walter Anderson, the assistant state geologist for the Maine Geological Service.

The climbers planned to stay on the mountain two nights. Despite the Heath/Ivusic tragedy, Buzz wasn't worried about the traverse because Smith was such an experienced, competent leader. Kearney, on the other hand, was "very nervous about the whole thing," according to Anderson.

The group set up camp in tents at Katahdin Stream Campground and the next day climbed the Hunt Trail and made second camp just below timber line. The next day, they made it to the top and set up a third camp. The group carried extra gear and supplies and buried it under the snow for Smith, who planned to return with another expedition a month later.

A snowstorm that had begun early in the climb gathered steam, creating severe blizzard conditions on Katahdin and disrupting radio communication with Togue Pond gate. The only person they could reach was a radio ham in Georgia. They asked him to let the park know they were okay.

The storm's fury caused the party to descend to Camp 2, below tree line, and they remained there for three days. Plenty of folks were worried about the mountaineers, but Austin Wilkins told Maine newspapers that he had complete confidence that this group could take care of themselves. But Dana Wallace's wife was quoted as saying that she hardly had a fingernail left.

▲ ▲ ▲ ▲ ▲

Kearney started the supervisor's job full-time on March 23 at a salary of $177 a week; that would increase to $186 after his six-month probation period. He immediately pressed the Authority for more staff and equipment. The trustees' hands were tied. Although ill and frail, Governor Baxter was still hanging on, and the trust money he set aside to run the park would not be available until his death and the settling of his estate.

As happy as the rangers were over Kearney's advocacy for more money, they quickly saw what a complicated man the new supervisor was. According to some rangers, he made disparaging remarks about Helon Taylor and began to play one ranger off another; he was suspicious and increasingly jealous of Buzz, whom he saw as a threat to his job; and he knew the law well enough to know when and how to circumvent it. "A lot was going on that [the Authority] didn't realize," Ellie Damon recalls.

Kearney's new dress code for rangers grated on the field staff. "Harry was dressed up all the time," Damon says. "So he wanted us to also wear long-sleeved shirts, neckties, and hats." Damon didn't wear the entire get-up unless he was alerted that Kearney was about to open his front door. State forest ranger Tilly Palmer, who was stationed at McCarty Field, could see all traffic headed north and warned rangers in the north end of Kearney's impending visits.

Kearney was astonished that the rangers weren't spending time checking fishermen and patrolling outlying areas, instead of concentrating on their campgrounds. The rangers, on the other hand, were surprised that he thought they had time for much backcountry oversight, given their limited numbers. The game warden and fire rangers took care of enforcement and fire spotting, they informed Kearney.

Katahdin Stream ranger Dave Perkins was the first one to really get on Kearney's bad side. In early February 1969, Perkins was supposed to show up in the morning to go to Russell Pond with Kearney, Buzz, and Junior York to shovel snow off camp roofs. The trio waited an hour and a half but no Perkins. The ranger had overslept.

When Kearney returned to Togue Pond, Perkins was waiting there. Kearney owned up to the Authority that he refused to speak to Perkins "as I was not in the correct mood." Perkins resigned later, and Tom Chase transferred to Katahdin Stream after four years at Russell Pond. Kearney also refused to rehire ranger Leroy Jones for another season based on "many letters of complaint" about his shortcomings, such as "overbearing manner, improper driving habits, [and] messy campground."

▲ ▲ ▲ ▲ ▲

In April 1969 Kearney settled into a house at 87 Lincoln Street in Millinocket that the park rented for him. Park headquarters was relocated there from Buzz's house.

The same month, an article in *True Magazine* brought bad publicity for Baxter Park nationally and in Maine. The recreational boom that was funneling thousands more hikers and campers into the park had "overrun" it, turning the campgrounds into "slums," writer Michael Frome asserted. He cited a figure of 1,200 as the number of overnight accommodations and 81,000 as the total number of visitors annually. The combination of low overnight rates and housekeeping trailers in camping spaces resulted in the overuse and noise. Cocktail hours, bridge games, battery-run TVs, and blaring radios disturbed the wilderness experience for many, Frome charged.

He alleged that hikers weren't safe in Baxter Park because there were too few rangers to provide guidance and protection. He also highlighted chronic problems such as trail erosion and lack of facilities maintenance.

The *Maine Sunday Telegram* picked up on Frome's allegations, running its own story in the April 6, 1969, paper with the headline "Baxter Park Described As Camping Slum." Austin Wilkins denied Frome's charges, claiming that the gatekeepers were controlling visitor use and making things safer. Harry Kearney countered Frome's figure of overnight capacity, saying there was room for only 587 people.

The cat was out of the bag in terms of extensive public knowledge about the gravity of the park's problems. Buzz was away at warden's school at the time but cringed at the negative publicity for the park.

▲ ▲ ▲ ▲ ▲

When Buzz returned to work, he was ready for a new start. The Authority approved the creation of the position of assistant supervisor, and true to its word, gave the job to Buzz.

Still, Kearney informed Buzz that he wanted the job for Junior York. Buzz stood his ground, telling Kearney that it wasn't Kearney's job to give. Kearney handed Buzz a phone, telling him to take up the matter with the Maine State Employees Association. Buzz made the call. Within a short time, Kearney was informed by Jim Erwin that Buzz was right—the job was Buzz's.

With the new post came responsibilities for all park inventories, vehicle maintenance, ordering supplies, and supervising seven campground rangers and eight gatekeepers. Buzz also oversaw an endless variety of daily projects, ranging from new employee training to law enforcement patrols. For the first time, he also started working extensively with the budget preparation process. "Buzz was a go-getter," states Tom Chase, "and the rest of us were happy being park rangers."

His new job elevated his morale, and Buzz knew he was back in the good graces of the Authority. "I went in with a very positive attitude," Buzz notes. "I was committed to the Authority to do my best and to Harry Kearney to do my best."

Kearney was pleased with the additional education Buzz had received. "I find in discussing various phases of the work with him that he has gotten much good from this school," Kearney reported to the Authority.

*Maine Warden School Class of 1969, (L to R), front row: Clyde Noyce, Glen
Fenney, Buzz Caverly, Tom Bryant, George Chase, Richard Parker; second
row: Norman Moulton, Dan Glidden, Alden Kennett, Mike O'Connell, Bill
Vail, Bob Randall, Maine Fish and Game commissioner Maynard Marsh*

TOM CARBONE PHOTO, MAINE FISH AND GAME DEPARTMENT

▲ ▲ ▲ ▲ ▲

In Buzz's absence, Kearney had hired three new graduates of Unity
College for the summer. Kearney had taught law enforcement and outdoor classes at the Unity, Maine, school, and the trio had been his students. Charles Kenney went to Roaring Brook; Stephen Littlefield to
Chimney Pond; and Rodney Titcomb to Russell Pond.

Another young Unity man, Bob Howes, joined the crew. Vietnam
veteran Loren Goode signed on as assistant ranger at Nesowadnehunk
Field Campground. Kearney had agreed to hire Goode if he shaved his
mustache and earned his high school diploma.

Kenney remembers that the Unity grads were so new to the park
scene that the first time the radio came on, none of them wanted to talk
on the device. The new hires "were all young, were drinkers . . . and full
of vinegar," Goode recalls.

▲ ▲ ▲ ▲ ▲

When the park opened for the 1969 season, Kearney's focus was on showing the public that he was going to strictly enforce park rules. During the Memorial Day weekend, rangers confiscated beer and liquor from visitors watching bears at Foster Field dump and brought charges against them. They prosecuted others for drunk driving, speeding, and violating fish and game laws.

Like Buzz, Kearney was a stickler for cleanliness. Kearney hired high school boys to clear roadside brush and litter and pick up any refuse at the campgrounds. The teenagers picked up a truck full of cans and bottles per mile of park road, and then Kearney ordered his rangers to do the job in the future. Kearney thought the park should charge beer companies an "advertising fee" for every one of their cans thrown away in the park.

Rangers were also busy watching each other. Kearney "would have Buzz sit outside my camp watching me in case I was night hunting," Tom Chase affirms. Or Kearney would call Chase and tell him that he wouldn't be seeing him that day only to arrive a few minutes later. "He was sneaky," says Chase. Ranger Danny Watson was told to be Kearney's "rat" but found ways to avoid that mission against his buddies.

Kearney tried to play ranger against ranger by starting rumors about them, and would test rangers' patience by forcing them to go with him looking for poachers knowing that it was a wild goose chase.

Kearney's first evaluation of Buzz (from January to June, 1969) was full of praise, laced with barbs. "This man is a reliable, honest man," wrote Kearney. "He is dedicated to his work and Baxter Park. He is . . . the first to start and the last to stop. He shows no rancor, or hard feeling for previous difficulties. He does feel it easier to do some tasks than to be a leader and have the work done. I feel that he has a slight inferiority complex. I feel certain [he] will become a fine assistant supervisor. He has difficulty saying 'No' and would rather pass the buck than face a difficult situation. He also finds it difficult to delegate authority."

Austin Wilkins added his own assessment that Buzz was "fully capable and will develop through additional years of experience."

▲ ▲ ▲ ▲ ▲

On June 13, 1969, ninety-two-year-old Percival Baxter succumbed to old age—collapsed veins and possibly small strokes. He had been seriously failing in health for the two previous months and was confined to a hospital bed at his home on West Street in Portland. He was just barely coherent when his great-nephew, Rupert White, saw him a few days before his death. The last words White heard Baxter say were, "Jesus, I'm coming." White was surprised, unaware that Baxter was "religious."

The governor's ashes, along with flowers, were scattered over Katahdin by air. With Baxter gone, the letter he'd written to Buzz saying "we are partners in this project" took on more importance. Buzz framed it to he could read the note every day, and it hung in every office he had from then on.

Baxter's death was momentous for the park—spiritually, operationally, and financially. The creator was gone, leaving a huge vacuum at the pinnacle of the park's leadership. But at the same time, the park benefited tremendously because the trust funds were released to support operations. At the time, the book value was just under $7 million. In just one year, the park went from $83,784 in revenues (most of it from the state's general fund) to $226,625 (from the trust fund).

"Harry came in with the benefit of getting a budget that was sort of unlimited," Buzz recalls. "From his years in the warden service, he knew the ways of getting new uniforms, getting new boats and motors and canoes and generators, and more rangers. My God, he was the only one I ever knew of who could go to an Authority meeting and come out of it adding six new year-round ranger positions to the staff that had had only one or two year-round rangers for many years."

Baxter's will left $7 million to the principal trust to be managed by the Boston Safe Deposit & Trust Company in Massachusetts. Several years later, the Authority implemented a policy that the park would not spend more than "a maximum of" 5 percent of the market value of the fund in any fiscal year. Any unspent trust income was kept in a separate investment income account to further ensure the long-term financial security of the park.

In addition to the Boston account, Percival Baxter left a state-held trust and a land acquisition account, both to be managed by the state treasurer.

▲ ▲ ▲ ▲ ▲

Percival Baxter hadn't been gone long before Kearney was blaming Helon Taylor for the "lenient or even lax way" in which many park problems had been handled—identifying dumps, gravel pits, hovels, deteriorating camps, cutting rights violations, "and other matters you gentlemen know that I can only guess at. I do not mention these matters to run a man down who has done a job long and well and who became old and tired trying to do a big job with so few personnel and so little money," Kearney said.

Then he called attention to the "mistakes" Buzz had made while he was supervisor, the "most glaring" being the Pelletier affair. [T]hey all seem to fit into a pattern similar to the permissive attitude displayed by Helon Taylor. We must remember that Irvin Caverly, Jr., learned to be a park ranger under Helon Taylor, and worked for him for ten years," Kearney continued (somewhat inaccurately). "I am becoming sure that what we consider glaring mistakes only reflect the results of incorrect instruction."

Kearney wanted the Authority to extend Buzz's probation as assistant supervisor another six months in order to "observe his ability to accept our present policies and change his past thinking." Buzz, of course, was suspicious of Kearney's motive. If he was on probation, Kearney could more easily try to fire him.

▲ ▲ ▲ ▲ ▲

Kearney's new rangers—Charlie Kenney, Steve Littlefield, and Rodney Titcomb—rebelled against his dress code when the summer temperatures reached into the nineties. Clearing brush on Pick Pole Hill near Abol, they had taken off their ties, and, when Kearney saw them, he was furious that they had disobeyed him. He blamed Buzz for the rangers' defiant action.

Nesowadnehunk Campground ranger Bernard Gardiner was so upset at many aspects of park affairs that he couldn't remain silent. He contacted the Authority without going through the proper channels and upset them with his allegations. Gardiner railed against the shortage of rangers that made it impossible for the crew to carry out their jobs well. Allowing the hunting of bears in the wildlife sanctuary of the park, unless they were a menace to humans, was not what he thought

Governor Baxter wanted, he griped. Park vehicles were so old and lacking proper maintenance that he suggested they were a danger to rangers.

Gardiner complained pointedly about Harry Kearney's behavior. Kearney overrode Gardiner when he tried to evict campers who possessed liquor and had a Great Dane at their campsite, the ranger said. He criticized Kearney for not identifying himself on the radio and not signaling when he was on or off. Kearney "informs us that it is nobody's business where he is or if his radio is on," Gardiner revealed. The new state employees' union became involved in Gardiner's grievance after Kearney threatened to sack him; it advised that both sides work on reconciling their differences.

Kearney should keep the Authority members informed "of unhappy Rangers working in Baxter Park," Austin Wilkins said, suggesting that the park watch out for "union-conscious" employees. He advised Kearney to follow the official employee grievance procedures and added that he personally had "no sympathy for Bernard Gardiner." Gardiner's days were numbered. He was fired later by Kearney for disobeying orders.

▲ ▲ ▲ ▲ ▲

Baxter Park had a big drug problem during the national "Summer of Love" in 1969. Tom Chase had never heard of drugs in high school. When he found three teenagers sitting on a rock at Basin Pond smoking weed, he was at a loss as to what they were puffing. "They smelled funny," he says. "We arrested them for illegal camping and confiscated the marijuana." One of the boys belonged to the famous von Trapp family in Vermont, and the park called his father, one of the original singers, to come pick up his son.

Buzz theorized that the drugs came into the park initially via the AT thru-hikers, who had traveled through populated places where it was easier to buy pot and hash than in distant Maine. Parks everywhere seemed to be a hotbed for drug use, especially those off the beaten path.

Buzz was constantly looking and sniffing for the presence of drugs, and he was conveniently able to stop any place in the park most days to nose around. As backhanded punishment, Kearney demanded a daily report from Buzz, preferably in person. He required Buzz to drive from his home in Patten all the way through the park to Millinocket for the meeting—refusing to allow him to use the faster way on I-95.

Restricted to traveling no more than fifteen miles per hour on the park's main tote road, Buzz wouldn't get to Kearney in Millinocket until 5:00 or 6:00 P.M., and then he had to drive back over the forty miles south to north at that same low speed, arriving at home at nine or ten at night.

"It was a tough year for Jan and me, and the kids," Buzz remembers. While he agreed with Kearney about the importance of his being in the field as much as possible, the required drive home at night through the park felt retaliatory to Buzz.

▲ ▲ ▲ ▲ ▲

On the morning of July 16, 1969, Buzz was out on foot patrol. The day was hot and humid, and after an eleven-mile hike, he was exhausted when he arrived back home in East Millinocket, where they were living temporarily. He hadn't had time to clean up before he heard a police car with the siren screaming. He guessed there had been an accident on Katahdin. Buzz took his sore feet out of a tub of water, grabbed some dry socks and his muddy boots, and raced to the park.

While Buzz had been hiking Doubletop that morning, a group from Camp Netop in Casco had ascended the Helon Taylor Trail on Katahdin. The party consisted of two counselors, one assistant, and thirteen teenage boys, mostly from the Philadelphia area. About three-quarters of the way up Keep Ridge, one of the boys had to return to the campsite because of knee problems. Counselor William Zimmerman accompanied him down.

The rest of the group continued to Pamola Peak, then across the Knife Edge to Baxter Peak. At that point, the group divided into two, with the other counselor accompanying two slow hikers down the easier Saddle Trail. Assistant Jeff Lang, who was the camp handyman, took the other ten boys down the Cathedral Trail, a path he had never climbed. Descending, the teenagers ignored Lang's efforts to keep them together, and he fell behind them due to fatigue.

When Lang arrived at an area known as the Second Cathedral, he saw two boys on a ledge off the trail and shouted for them to return to the path. However they continued looking for a stream they could hear. Lang went on to Chimney Pond Campground to report that the boys were off the trail, unaware that two more boys—fourteen-year-olds Jay

Barrett and Bert Comfort—also were off the trail. Barrett and Comfort found themselves blocked by a steep, wet, and slippery ledge, and Barrett fell off the ledge to his death. Comfort descended as fast as he could to Chimney Pond to get help.

When Buzz arrived at the accident scene, he helped prepare Barrett's body for removal. "I looked at that child . . . and thought what a terrible, terrible waste of life," Buzz recalls. He was at the back of the stretcher where Barrett's head was during the evacuation and on the way down felt something wet and sticky on his fingers. By this time it was night, and Buzz snapped on his flashlight to see what the fluid was. "It was drainage from the head wound, and I was saturated with blood from my sleeve to the tips of my fingers. It was awful, and I just had to separate myself from my emotions and get the job done of delivering the boy to the coroner. It wasn't until I got back home that I realized how incredibly tired and upset I was."

▲▲▲▲▲

Arrangements had gone forward for Buzz and Jan to purchase the East Millinocket house they were renting. They settled on a date to sign the papers, but it was delayed by the owner until the following day. In the meantime, Kearney called Buzz to say they needed to talk, and he surprised Buzz with new orders to oversee the northern part of the park. That meant a transfer to Patten.

Kearney thought that Buzz had already signed the house purchase papers and would have to quit the park because he couldn't afford to pay for the East Millinocket home and buy or rent one in Patten. Kearney was so sure that his ploy to get rid of Buzz would work that he had already asked his Mason friends who worked at the Great Northern Mill if they could find a job there for Buzz.

Kearney's move was further evidence to Buzz that the supervisor was out to stab him in the back. They were enemies from that day forward.

▲▲▲▲▲

Patten was the town closest (twenty-four miles) to the northern entrance to the park, and it had a special "backyard" relationship to the preserve, as did Millinocket and East Millinocket on the southern end.

A number of park rangers lived and worked in Patten during the off-season. There wasn't as much resentment against the park in Patten as there was in the Millinocket area. Having hunting and trapping available in the park's Scientific Forest Management Area (SFMA) townships softened local feelings.

Buzz and Jan went to Patten and did what they had done in Millinocket—walked down the street and tried to find a rental or someone thinking of selling. They lucked out again on the first knock on the door of widow Theresa Steen, who was putting her house on the market. The price was right—$7,500, with furnishings. With a Farmers Home loan, and a sixty-dollars-a-month payment, the Caverlys could swing it.

Kearney advised the Authority on June 3 that he was requiring Caverly to live in Patten and that Buzz had assured him "this would not pose any great problem with him as he is having a difficult time finding suitable housing within his financial means"—an excuse Kearney concocted.

▲ ▲ ▲ ▲ ▲

At the end of the summer, trustee Jim Erwin proposed the establishment of a ten-member Advisory Committee of "tough-minded park lovers such as ourselves." Not only would a committee be useful for good advice but also to serve as "a kind of buffer to absorb some of the public blows," he said.

Ron Speers thought the idea had "definite merit," but he warned that generally it was "very difficult" to convince an Advisory Committee that its function would be to only offer recommendations. Speers favored setting up the group to serve at the pleasure of the Authority, rather than creating it by legislative act. Then, he said, it wouldn't have "a formal basis for any possible power structure but would actually be a group that the Authority could at its discretion continue or discontinue."

The other trustees took Speers's advice on keeping the Advisory group beholden to the Authority for its existence. They began accepting nominations from the public, including names from the Fin and Feather Club.

▲ ▲ ▲ ▲ ▲

Creation of the Advisory Committee coincided with a major eruption over snowmobiles, sparked by the *Maine Times,* an alternative weekly that was founded in October 1968 by Peter Cox and John Cole.

A freelance writer for the *Times,* Aime Gauvin, caught the Authority planning to secretly open up the heart of the backcountry— Wassataquoik Lake and Russell Pond—to snowmobilers. This was in addition to places off the park's central road that they were already using—the old logging roads on Rum Mountain, the trail to Katahdin Lake, and the path to Chimney Pond Campground.

The September 12, 1969, article provoked a public furor. Defensively, Austin Wilkins explained to Gauvin that expanding snowmobile trails was in response to "the tremendous impact of the [growing sport]." Editor John Cole expressed shock at the Authority's action. Snowmobiles were "one of the most miserable toys man has yet invented," he editorialized. Allowing the sleds to run rampant over the park would be a "blatant insult to the memory of the man who was so recently eulogized as Maine's greatest benefactor," Cole went on. He urged readers to lobby chairman Wilkins against opening new trails to sleds, saying, "Tell him the snowmobiles have the entire state to ruin." The newspaper's plea resulted in a deluge of anti-snowmobile letters from the public.

The debate forced the Authority members to concede they didn't really know how to evaluate snowmobile impacts because the park didn't have a comprehensive management plan. Jim Erwin concluded that snowmobiles should be prohibited in the park, but Wilkins and Speers wouldn't go that far.

On October 15 they voted to continue to allow snowmobiles, but only on the Tote Road, banning them from the three interior trails they had been using. *Maine Times* co-founder Peter Cox attacked Wilkins and Speers for having "no carefully conceived concept of the park's role." The park, he editorialized in the October 24 paper, is no place "to go get drunk or to crowd together in heavy trailers or to zoom around on any type of motorized vehicle. There are plenty of other places for such activities," Cox said, adding that easy access would destroy the park's wilderness character.

*Portland Press Herald* columnist Frank Sleeper accused Wilkins and Speers of breaking faith with Governor Baxter. The park was "meant to be an extreme example of wilderness preservation by a man who had the vision to see something (the rush of megalopolis to Maine) long before most people did," Sleeper wrote on November 5. "An extreme example of preservation calls for extreme measures of preservation—like a total ban of snowmobiles. Halfway steps won't do the job."

John L. Baxter, Sr., the governor's nephew and the family's senior spokesman on park matters, was incensed over snowmobiles being permitted in the preserve. He issued a statement saying he was certain that his uncle would never have approved of the machines, other than "necessary winter use by those responsible for the park," and would have been "deeply disturbed" by the trustees' action.

Jim Erwin aligned himself with the family in deciding that the governor "probably would not have wanted snowmobiles to roam freely in the park." But he emphasized that the issue boiled down to opinion and "valid equities, " adding, "Governor Baxter, himself, stated many times that he was contented that his park be administered by the forestry commissioner, the commissioner of Inland Fisheries and Game, and the attorney general, whoever they might be at any given time. It is inevitable that there will be differences of opinion both within the Park Authority and outside of it."

▲ ▲ ▲ ▲ ▲

There was also more debate among trustees over roads and the role of the state highway commission in the park. The highway crew had been chased out by the rangers for digging new gravel pits too close to the Perimeter Road, and the agency had been tardy in rehabilitating the old pits. Commissioner David Stevens was fed up and ready to get his agency out of the park altogether, and Harry Kearney couldn't have agreed more.

In addition to the conflict between the highway commission and the park over the road crew's modus operandi, the road scrapers and graders were destroying the quiet. A fisherman sitting in the middle of a trout pond two or three miles away could hear the noise of the machines. To boot, the grading tipped up sharp rocks that ruined vehicle tires, and the widening allowed faster travel, causing more accidents and creating more room for larger trailer campers and motor homes.

▲ ▲ ▲ ▲ ▲

Buzz and five-year-old Cathy were in a minor car accident at Patten near the end of the year, but fortunately, neither of them was hurt. The car sank into a soft shoulder of the road and wouldn't budge. They had to hitch a ride to town, despite Buzz's dislike of the practice. Who came along but a car full of long-haired, Janis Joplin-loving young people, recalls Cathy Caverly. Buzz accepted the ride because Cathy couldn't walk the distance to town.

"We got out at the five-and-dime in town and called Mom and walked home," she says. "Dad had this thing about hippies. He was grateful to them for a ride, but he said to me after we got out of the car, 'Don't ever bring one of those home with you.' He liked boys to have crew-cut hair, be straight-laced, and do good and right."

---

Primary Document Sources: BSPA Boxes 7, 8, 13, 16, 18 (2507-0715, 2507-0717, 2507-0718); Percival Baxter Collection (Letters).

Conversations and communications: Walter Anderson, Buzz Caverly, Cathy Caverly, Jan Caverly, Tom Chase, Ellie Damon, Jim Erwin, Dan Glidden, Loren Goode, Bob Howes, Charlie Kenney, George Smith, Bill Vail, Dana Wallace, Rupert White.

▲▲▲▲▲▲▲▲

CHAPTER 10

# KEARNEY VS. BUZZ

BUZZ HAD NEVER LIKED THE IDEA of scientists running around the park scaring wildlife, probing here and there or collecting this or that. He was influenced by Helon Taylor, who "never met a biologist he liked," Buzz says.

In the winter of 1970 state biologists were asking again for approval of another phase of a moose tracking project begun the previous summer. The researchers wanted to go off-road with snowmobiles to locate the animals in their winter habitat and put radio collars on them.

The biologists had already irritated Buzz, Harry Kearney, and the Authority by using motorboats to chase moose feeding in ponds in order to collar them. Park visitors had complained to Buzz and to Kearney, who was sick of hearing about the issue. Ron Speers was frustrated over his agency "knock[ing] heads" with Baxter's rules, and his staff was "up in the air" over whether to write off the park as a study territory. Jim Erwin didn't like the whole affair but agreed with his Authority colleagues to let the survey be completed. The rancor—all out of the public eye—left a bad taste in everyone's mouth.

Buzz kept his head down on the issue, since he was working to get back on his feet from the demotion and trying hard to cope with Kearney.

▲▲▲▲▲

During the winter of 1970, both Buzz and Jan were on the park payroll again. With snowmobile use so heavy, Kearney wanted reliable numbers data. He hired Jan to count the machines entering the Matagamon gate, and rangers covered the other two gates.

Jan took the job because she and the girls could see Buzz during the day. He would drop Jan, Cathy, and Tammy off at Matagamon and go on with his patrol or other duties. Sometimes he could join them for lunch at the gatehouse or on one of the Matagamon Lake islands. The kids were happy to spend all day playing in the snow.

Kearney was pleased with his rangers' winter surveillance, asserting that the park had never been better supervised, and praising snowmobilers for obeying park rules and taking their litter home with them, rather than leaving it in the park. The previous winter, rangers had picked up eighty-two pickup loads of cans and bottles from sledders.

▲ ▲ ▲ ▲ ▲

The park's long-term future was a subject beginning to receive more attention from Kearney and the Authority. They decided it was time to have a Statement of Purpose written into law to reflect the wishes of Governor Baxter and to develop a comprehensive management plan—the latter goal one the Natural Resources Council of Maine (NRCM) had harped on for years.

To start the discussion, Kearney and Erwin evaluated the park's overall condition and suggested ways to correct problems. They provided candid assessments of how the park had been managed—or not managed—under Helon Taylor and the trustees of previous years.

Kearney's ten-page assessment was characteristically blunt, underscoring environmental abuses that occurred under Governor Baxter's nose and undermined his intentions. Most of the degradation was unintentional, in Kearney's view. He pointed to dumps and their emanating water pollution as proof that the Authority had failed its environmental responsibility. "We are in the business of caring for the needs of a small town the size of Harrison or Jackman, so our dumps grow rapidly," he pointed out.

His solution for the pollution of Chimney and Russell Ponds was to close those campgrounds and dumps and build new ones at Basin Ponds and Wassataquoik Stream. For roadside campgrounds and their garbage problems, he proposed the purchase of gas-fired incinerators to handle waste, and he said campers at remote sites should have to pack out their garbage. Kearney wanted a "clean, modern toilet system" that would solve the problems of odor and sanitation.

On the matters of roads and gravel pits, Kearney was adamant that the park should take control from the state highway commission and hire its own road maintenance crew. Widening the roads and straightening curves had encouraged park users to drive faster, which led to more accidents. Kearney advocated a return to narrower roads, stopping the use of calcium chloride to keep down dust, and restoration of the gravel pits.

He lamented the fact that the park was "woefully understaffed" and the employees underpaid. Kearney recommended two assistants (instead of one) for the supervisor, plus other additional staff. Pay raises, improved living quarters in the park, an updated vehicle fleet, more snowmobiles and chain saws, better canoes, and a maintenance shop were also on his wish list.

Kearney's forecast of 192,000 visitors per year by 2000 was quite a bit more than the actual number turned out to be, 74,721. But speculating on that high number caused him to suggest how to deal with a projected shortage of 93,000 camping sites: allow only Mainers to use the park or ignore the environmental problems "and say everything is beautiful . . . and dream on."

In a related document, Kearney proposed new qualifications for Baxter rangers that underscored the importance of personal attributes and public responsibilities. Physical qualifications, Kearney said, should require a ranger to stand at least five feet, eight inches tall, weigh at least a hundred and forty pounds, and be twenty-one years old. No one who had a court record should be considered for the job unless the Personnel Board waived the record, he recommended.

Kearney stressed the need for rangers with a high sense of honor, a reputation for honesty and integrity, self-control, courtesy, and belief in the importance of the job. He offered a list of nineteen "general orders" that a ranger should follow, such as being on duty at all times unless on leave, refraining from drinking while on the job, and not using park vehicles for personal reasons.

▲ ▲ ▲ ▲ ▲

Authority chairman Jim Erwin shared many of the same concerns as Kearney on practical matters. In the realm of policy, Erwin thought the Authority needed to decide whether the "forever wild" concept meant that "scientific forestry" should or shouldn't be practiced in the park. "In other words, should we allow deadfalls to remain deadfalls except where they fall on buildings or block trails, or should we practice some kind of timber harvest in the park?" In his opinion, timber harvesting and management were "not within the concept of 'forever wild.'" He said:

> In the long term, we are faced with the problem, really, of maintaining something. All of our efforts should be directed at that aim. The governor has given us something which may well be unique in the entire world. It is incumbent upon us to keep it that way. Therefore, every decision that is made now by us or later by our successors must start with the fact that this is a unique wilderness area to be preserved at all costs against all of the pressures of politics, mechanical advantages, and technology, so that a hundred years from now, or even five hundred years from now, Baxter State Park will still be recognizable for what it was when Governor Baxter died.

Erwin's willingness to oppose timber harvesting in the two townships set aside for scientific forest management was singular in that he was the only Authority member to ever take that position publicly. Buzz would come to agree with Erwin about the Scientific Forest Management Area (SFMA), and Buzz would be the one who ultimately initiated action with the Authority on recommendations initially made by Kearney and Erwin, from ending water pollution from open dumps to taking charge of the road system.

Because of the sizable backlog of campground rebuilding and maintenance projects and the awful outhouse situation, Erwin boldly suggested that the park close for a year, especially if enough trust fund income was available to pay for the needed work. He wanted crews hired to refurbish and clean up various campsites and build "some kind of acceptable, decent, well-concealed sanitary facilities. I do not believe that the concept of 'forever wild' has to mean that we must have the rank privies and other toilet facilities presently existing in the park," he said.

Buzz thought at the time that Erwin's recommendation to shut down the park to do all the work at once was politically courageous. "I felt it would be wonderful to have a year to do nothing but improvement and maintenance work, but no one took seriously the idea of closing the park for a year," Buzz remembers. "I think there would have been a public outcry."

▲ ▲ ▲ ▲ ▲

By this time Erwin realized that Kearney didn't like Buzz. Kearney viewed Buzz as "a handshaker and apple polisher," criticized him for "never having an original idea," and told stories that Buzz wanted his job "so damn bad he'd cry."

Despite what Kearney's opinion of Buzz was, Erwin felt that Buzz was "too good a person to throw away, he was a good ranger, and some-day he would make a good head man—but he needed more experi-ence." Again, he advised Buzz to accept the disappointment of being removed from the superintendent's post and "stick with the park." Buzz would be head of the park one day if he was patient, Erwin reas-sured him.

One of the new rangers under Buzz's supervision, Danny Watson, also felt that Kearney's dislike of Buzz was unfounded; Watson dis-trusted Kearney based on his own experience with the supervisor. On the other hand, he loved working for Buzz, whom he fully trusted. "Buzz was a big kid at heart and liked to have fun," recalls Watson. "He made the work enjoyable. He was honest, there was no guile in him. But he was pretty good at giving you the dickens . . . without getting out of line with his approach."

▲ ▲ ▲ ▲ ▲

The business operations of the park up until now had been handled by Bill Cross, an accountant at the Maine Forest Service. But with the influx of significantly more income from Governor Baxter's trust funds, the park needed a full-time business manager. Insider Cross, an old-fashioned fiscal conservative, slipped into the new job.

Like good soldiers, Cross and Buzz got along on the surface. However, when Buzz later returned as supervisor, they struggled for power, and sparks flew. In Buzz's opinion, Cross considered his position a step higher than the supervisor's and second in importance behind the Authority.

Like Kearney and Erwin, Cross had strong opinions on the park's status and what should be done to improve things. Cross was a force to be reckoned with because of his access to all the three trustees in the capital. His office remained at forestry's headquarters in the State Office Building in Augusta, and there was hardly a day that he didn't have contact with Austin Wilkins or the fish and game commissioner. Cross poured Wilkins's coffee every morning, which gave him easy opportunity to lobby the commissioner on park spending matters. If Cross wanted to talk to the attorney general, he just had to walk a few minutes away to that office in the State House.

In his new job, Cross began extending his fingers from financial matters into operations, which Buzz claimed as his domain. Cross was a nit-picker, and a constant irritant was the use and expense of park vehicles. For most of the 1960s, rangers drove park-owned trucks to Millinocket to buy supplies, do errands, and go to park headquarters. In the late 1960s, the year-round rangers began moving out of the park because their children were starting school. They were allowed to use their vehicles to drive back and forth to the park in accordance with a law providing that state employees holding certain positions could do so. Still, Cross didn't believe it was an expense the park should bear.

There would be enough trust income for the park to grow, but Cross cautioned the Authority constantly to go slowly in spending. He advised the Authority to continue paying for operations with state general fund revenues and not switch to trust fund income until July 1, 1971, the start of the new fiscal year. He estimated the income from all the trust accounts to be approximately $310,000 a year, plus another $30,000 from visitor fees. The price tag on park operations was about $150,000, leaving $160,000 in the reserve fund for capital improvements and land acquisitions.

One expenditure that Cross was enthusiastic about was putting the wives of rangers on the payroll for about twenty hours a week, since they were, in effect, working for the park already. Alma Chase, Ida Damon, and Janet York were given the title of assistant campground rangers and paid about thirty-two dollars a week.

In 1971, when operating entirely from trust funds, Cross recommended that the park should open an office in Augusta for the business manager and hire an assistant to handle all fiscal matters, purchasing, and related matters. "[Then] the problems of the park could be taken from the Forestry Department where they now lie and all work of carrying out the policies of the Authority would lie in this new office, entirely divorced from either the Forestry or Fish and Game Departments," he wrote the trustees.

▲ ▲ ▲ ▲ ▲

Appointing the first members to the Advisory Committee moved forward in 1970, with the Authority ready to charge the panel with developing a draft Statement of Purpose and then assisting with a master plan for the park.

From a list of twenty-three names, the Authority and Harry Kearney chose ten members: Dr. Bob Ohler, chief of staff at Togus Veterans' Administration Hospital in Augusta; Augusta dentist Dr. Alonzo Garcelon; *Bangor Daily News* outdoor writer Bud Leavitt; Bangor attorney Norman Minsky; *Maine Times* editor John Cole and Baxter nephew John Baxter, Sr., both of Brunswick; state representative Walter Birt (R-Millinocket); photographer Paul Knaut of Dover-Foxcroft; and former governor Horace Hildreth.

Baxter family patriarch John Baxter, Sr., was wary of Cole. "He is often critical when no criticism is justified, but I think he would be a useful, although perhaps difficult, member of the Committee," Baxter said. Ironically, the committee meetings occurred on Cole's publication day for *Maine Times*, and the group wouldn't change the day for the editor's convenience. Thus, Cole didn't last long on the committee. Jim Erwin recalls that Cole would "rather shoot bullets at me" than be on the committee. In fact, in a *Maine Times* interview, Erwin, mentioning the public complaints about banning motorcycles and motorbikes, said that "if I were a smart politician, I would resign from the Baxter Park [Authority] as quickly as I could."

Austin Wilkins explained to the committee that the job of writing a Statement of Purpose was to have a policy and plan that would leave "no question of [Governor Baxter's] intent when administration duties fall upon our successors." Bob Ohler was elected chairman of the Advisory Committee and appointed a subcommittee (John Baxter, Walter Birt, and Norman Minsky) to work on the policy statement. In his acceptance letter, John Baxter wrote Wilkins that he had a "pretty good understanding of [Uncle Percy's] wishes about the park . . . that it would be preserved as a wilderness area." Perhaps at times the governor took "extreme" positions, but John Baxter thought he did so out of "fear that one relaxation would lead to another until eventually the Park would become a recreation area similar to many other parks."

A long-term park user and state entomologist, A. E. "Doc" Brower of Augusta, was elated at the establishment of the Advisory group but offered a warning worth remembering. Many national and state parks had been created with "high aims and resounding phrases" like Baxter's but had declined due to overuse and development, he observed.

"The bureaucratic administrators of these have opened both mind and ears to the clamor and aims of a part of the public whose motives are scarcely above the land developer at whom the finger is now being pointed," he noted. "Now many spots in parks are so completely despoiled that the real reason for these being in a park is gone."

Brower agreed with the Authority's intent to establish policy priorities and urged that Governor Baxter's plan that the park be a "wild area . . . be carried through." There are other areas in Maine "equally or far better suited" for other users, from fishermen to snowmobilers and others who want to "let off steam," he wrote.

Brower cautioned the trustees about too much "maintenance," a term he believe was synonymous with developing and enlarging facilities to make them "more attractive, more city-like, easier for more human beings who have less and less concern for the natural environment." Supporters of more and more development can never be satisfied, he asserted, and the greater the degradation of the wild, the "greater the clamor to open up additional areas for the same fate."

▲ ▲ ▲ ▲ ▲

Although the park was not going to shift completely to trust funds until fiscal 1971, there was a large infusion of money for the upcoming season. Equipment had started arriving in Millinocket, and Kearney said that "some of the rangers look like children on Christmas morning." Buzz was happy to receive better outdoor clothing, protective gear, and a new snowmobile.

"With thanks to an Authority who desires to see the park well cared for, I am sure no ranger will, by necessity, have to wish for anything in the way of material or equipment," Kearney wrote the Authority. The park was going to be able to hire eight permanent and twenty-four seasonal employees—a giant step from 1960 when there was only one year-round and eight seasonal crew.

Several large one-time expenses were on the books for the year—$52,500 to purchase Kidney Pond Camps; $25,000 for boundary work; $32,000 to start work on a new park headquarters; $30,737 for a new radio system to improve communications among staff involved in search and rescue situations; and $5,000 to University of Maine/Orono professor John Hakola for work on the first history of the park.

Perhaps mindful of Governor Baxter's warning against new buildings, neither Kearney nor the Authority set their sights on more park housing and support facilities. Some development was unavoidable, but the main emphasis then and into the future was reducing the number of structures and better maintenance of the remaining buildings.

▲ ▲ ▲ ▲ ▲

Harry Kearney had been supervisor for one year by March 1970, and he penned an evaluation of his "progress":

"There have been times when tempers have been worn thin, and mistakes have been made, but generally the year has been marked with good feeling, strong support, and a grand feeling of accomplishment," he wrote the Authority. Kearney credited his rangers for the good job despite the long hours, low pay, "and not even the dignity of a steady job." Yet his men were dedicated to "something they believe in but would have a hard time explaining even to themselves. . . . On the other hand, you three men who have one full-time busy, primary profession which normally would take all your time . . . accept the thankless, demanding extra work of being the Baxter State Park Authority with pride," Kearney said. "When I say thankless, I am not mentioning the inward pleasure that you must receive knowing that you work for all people are perpetuating Governor Percival Baxter's great dream."

▲ ▲ ▲ ▲ ▲

At its spring meeting, the Authority voted to ban self-contained campers. Rangers had discovered that the owners were driving the vehicles into gravel pits and emptying the toilet contents on the ground. Baggage trailers and pop-up tent trailers were allowed as long as they didn't have toilet or kitchen units.

Besides prohibiting the self-contained units, the trustees banned motorcycles and other similar machines, such as motorbikes and all-terrain vehicles. Governor Baxter had asked for the prohibition in a letter to Austin Wilkins on April 18, 1966. "I understand that there are several motor scooters and motor cycles in Millinocket that may be taken to the park," Baxter wrote. "These machines are so noisy and numerous, they should be forbidden to go into the park area."

Buzz was especially glad to see motorcycles and their cousins banned. While he was rangering at Katahdin Stream, the machines had raised havoc in the evening. Riders liked to speed up and down the campground road, making a lot of noise, stirring up dust, and irritating campers. A couple of times a week, he would have to ask riders to park their bikes to stop the havoc.

The ban received little public criticism, and that came primarily from the Fin and Feather Club. The group condemned the decision, questioning whether "legally registered and licensed vehicles" could be blocked from using the state-maintained park roads. The trustees stood their ground, and for Buzz, the decision removed an irritant.

The trustees were roundly criticized, as well as applauded for their actions. William Nickerson of Livermore Falls wrote that he was "extremely unhappy" being excluded from the park because he had a travel trailer. "Among other things this [ban] strikes me as some kind of weird discrimination," he said. On the other hand, Dorothea Marston of Augusta praised the trustees for translating Governor Baxter's wilderness vision "into practical working regulations."

The rules changes included other revisions important to good visitor management and would remain on the books. They included regulation of speed, parking, washing and bathing, check-in and check-out times, reservation payments, and litter disposal. People couldn't bring paint into the park or mess with trail signs—a response to graffiti being sprayed on rocks. Liquor was banned. Camp groups were required to have a counselor or leader at least twenty years old for every five campers, whether for a day hike or overnight. The pet prohibition was modified to allow pets to travel in vehicles *through* the park, but not to stay. The ban on aircraft and outboard motors was loosened to allow them for "official search and rescue operations, law enforcement, or the administrative requirements of the park"—in other words, as park officials saw fit. As the result of pressure from the Fin and Feather Club, the trustees made day-use facilities at campgrounds available on a first-come, first-served basis.

▲ ▲ ▲ ▲ ▲

Advertising Baxter Park to the rest of the world was frowned upon by all park officials because Governor Baxter had been against publicity. In disapproving the cutting of a Christmas tree from the park for the White House in 1959, the governor had said, "In my opinion it is best not to advertise the Park because it sufficiently advertises itself by those who visit it. If we bring in more people there will be confusion for we have not the facilities to take care of them."

Yet Governor Baxter had approved and paid $1,000 for a "guide booklet" on the park in 1963 for the Maine Department of Economic Development (DED) to distribute to tourists. It was a popular item and Austin Wilkins approved a reprint of 35,000 copies in November 1965 without expressed approval of Governor Baxter. "I saw no reason why his initial approval wouldn't justify the reprinting," Wilkins wrote to state controller Henry Cranshaw, explaining that the cost of the reprint would be shared by DED and the Maine Forest Service.

Now DED wanted a movie about the park. Paul Fournier, an agency consultant, asked for permission to film an individual skiing down Katahdin. However Wilkins, Speers, and Erwin agreed that such a film would commercialize the park and rejected the idea. Other similar proposals in the future all were to meet with the same "no" by the trustees, and Buzz agreed that word-of-mouth "advertising" was enough.

▲ ▲ ▲ ▲ ▲

In mid-June 1970, Ron Speers resigned, pressured to do so by Governor Curtis. Speers was running for the GOP First District seat in Congress. The newly enacted federal Hatch Act made it illegal for a government employee to run for public office if he administered federal funds. Speers didn't want to leave his state job before he knew the outcome of his political race, but Curtis was adamant. The governor even promised that if Speers lost the election he could have the fish and game post back.

Speers didn't win and didn't want the job back, and Curtis was just as glad. While duck hunting together on Merrymeeting Bay, Speers had shot what Curtis believed to be an endangered species.

Speers's deputy, George Bucknam, replaced him as fish and wildlife chief. Buzz was elated to hear of Speers's departure. "I was never a drinking man, but that night I would have gone to a party," he recalls.

A schoolteacher by training, Bucknam set a personal example of ethical hunting and fishing. Buzz respected Bucknam as a country gentleman who was "totally supportive, professional, and kind."

▲ ▲ ▲ ▲ ▲

The park's first rules and regulations made no mention of climbing. Visitors could do as they pleased. By 1959 the Authority had adopted Rule 17 that addressed climbing in "hazardous conditions." The regulation banned climbers "without adequate equipment and proper wearing apparel," with the "final decision" resting with the appropriate ranger. The rule applied to individuals, not those associated with outing clubs.

In the wake of the increase in climbing and deaths on Katahdin, Harry Kearney wanted much stricter rules, especially winter rules. By 1970 Rule 18 was in place and applied to climbers *and* alpine skiers. It was harsh and sweeping. Visitors were required to follow a detailed list of "proper wear and equipment" prepared by the park and it gave the supervisor or his designee the authority to allow or disallow peoples' planned activities "during hazardous conditions." Off-season or technical climbers had to jump through an additional hoop—they had to submit a use permit request a month in advance for off-season or technical climbing and provide a backup rescue team in the event of an accident.

The climbing community was upset about the new regulations, especially the backup team requirement. That particular rule was modeled after one established for Alaska's Mount McKinley, and climbers felt it was far too onerous for Katahdin. A rock climber from New Jersey let park leaders know in no uncertain terms how outrageous he felt the rule was and how incompetent he felt the rangers were in overseeing climbers.

"First, our equipment was inspected by a ranger, who obviously did not know a piton from a carabiner," David Leppard wrote. "What he expected to determine from his 'inspection' of our equipment still remains quite unclear." As for the requirement of having a backup team in case of an emergency, Leppard pointed out that the rule was no longer in effect for McKinley and that nothing like it was required for the notorious Eiger in Switzerland.

Just trying to get into Baxter Park through its system of "passes and permits was incredible," Leppard complained. "It should be easier to get into Fort Knox." The "fuzzy-faced Ranger-Gods ruling with an iron hand" at Chimney Pond provoked campers over reservation and shelter issues to the point that there was "near revolt at the dictatorship," he continued. "It completely destroyed the spirit of [such a] lovely place."

Much was changing outside the park that would pressure relaxation of climbing regulations. The recreational surge that started in the mid-1960s, improvement in outdoor wear and equipment, and the growth of retail outfitting stores, such as L.L. Bean, Inc., were attracting more people to the sport and ultimately to Katahdin.

Maine's climbing community in 1970 had almost no influence with park officials. Climbers' numbers were very small, with pockets of aficionados in the Bangor, Camden, and Augusta areas. Michael Opuda, who was in charge of an outdoor program through the University of Maine at Orono, brought together a group—Jerry Cinnamon, Ken Clark, Tom Davis, and John Leonard—to climb the Barber-Cilley route and the Armadillo Buttress in winter and look for new ascents. "We probably had aspirations beyond our skills," says Cinnamon. Climbers worked to get around rules by making friends of the Chimney Pond rangers, or just ignored as many of the regulations as possible.

No matter how enthusiastic the Mainers were at the sport, they saw themselves in the shadow of the more "professional" boys from New Hampshire who lived and played on Mount Washington. It was the New Hampshire group who began to free some of the hardest, never-climbed ice on Katahdin and fired up wider interest in the mountain.

▲ ▲ ▲ ▲ ▲

After lengthy negotiations with Junior and Jeanette York, the Authority purchased the Daicey Pond sporting camp, including twenty-four buildings, for $45,000. Kearney then assigned Junior York to be the ranger at the new Trout Brook Farm, the park's last campground facility to be allowed per Percival Baxter's directive.

The park also purchased the Davignon camp on Second Lake Matagamon for $5,000 and with it came an ATV—the park's first. Not long after those two purchases, the more substantial Martin camp, on Grand Lake Matagamon, was sold to the park for $10,000. The Davignon camp, across Second Lake near the outlet of Webster Lake, was accessible only by boat and plane. It was turned over to the fish and game department for use as a patrol camp. The Martin camp, on a red pine ledge on the south side of Grand Lake, was reachable by vehicle and was held for park employee housing.

With one ATV in hand, Kearney purchased another to have some company on the trail. He and Junior York had a ball. Buzz watched them run up and down the trails along Wassataquoik Lake. One day he had been at Russell Pond and was hiking back out toward Center Mountain on an old logging road when he heard "laughing and hollering and whooping." Kearney came around the corner on a yellow four-wheeler—a Scrambler—and bragged that it was his new vehicle.

Buzz didn't like ATVs and later got rid of the two machines Kearney had purchased. He also would block attempts by rangers in the future to use ATVs for any purpose on the grounds that they were out of keeping with a wilderness park.

Another hot summer of Kearney's long-sleeve dress code for rangers caused Buzz to openly oppose his supervisor. Buzz gathered rangers' signatures for a petition to the Authority asking that they be allowed to wear short-sleeved shirts and no neckties, and it was approved. When Kearney heard that Buzz was behind the move, he accused him of insubordination and acting "in a manner completely out of context with his position." However, this time Kearney didn't concoct a way to punish Buzz.

▲ ▲ ▲ ▲ ▲

Buzz had been interested in being a Mason, but his long work hours had caused him to give up attending meetings. Red Perry, who ran the Gulf gas station in Millinocket and was an active Mason, approached Buzz in the summer of 1970 about taking up the Masons again. He had an application in his car, gave Buzz a three-dollar lodge meal ticket, and took him to come meet his fraternity brothers.

Buzz was elated. Although membership meant more nights away from home, to Jan's chagrin, he couldn't turn his back on the Masons again. Within a couple of months, he had moved through the different steps to "master mason" and the power of inclusion by the "brotherhood" affected him deeply.

▲ ▲ ▲ ▲ ▲

On October 29, Kearney wrote a second evaluation of Buzz covering the period from June 1969 to November 1970, giving him "good" to "very good" ratings in nine categories, such as skill, cooperativeness, and dependability. Despite their mutual animosity, Kearney again complimented Buzz for his "dedication to his job" and said Buzz's "morals are above reproach."

However, Kearney wrote that Buzz sometimes forgot that "he is in a supervisory category and tries to be one of the boys." He reiterated his previous observation that Buzz didn't want to "accept responsibility and enjoyed having someone else to do it," but Buzz had made progress in "saying no" to employees under him. "A marked improvement in his attitude and ability has been noted in recent weeks," Kearney stated. "His personal neatness and care of park equipment is exemplary."

In the summer of 1969 Kearney had recommended Buzz for a merit increase. But an October 1 evaluation of that year had given him a rating that would downgrade his salary. Austin Wilkins viewed the two ratings of 1969 and 1970 as so inconsistent that the state personnel board wouldn't approve the latest salary proposal. He asked Kearney to review the situation, saying, "We should not penalize Buzz unduly because we have not made out a proper rating sheet." Buzz did receive the merit increase, giving him $155 a week.

▲ ▲ ▲ ▲ ▲

To fulfill his need to know what was going on, Kearney directed Buzz to be vigilant in watching rangers and park guests. For instance, Buzz recollects having to spy on a ranger who was a friend of Kearney's. Another time, in the fall of 1970, Buzz says Kearney ordered him and Tom Chase to go out on a rainy night to Webster Lake to observe some guests of Bangor Hydro president Robert Haskell at the dam camp. Kearney was concerned the party might be night hunting. Buzz and Chase drove down the Black Brook Road to within a mile of the lake, and hiked to a big pine tree on the shore, where they stood all night. The lights went off in the cabin by 11:00 P.M., and to stay awake, Chase repeatedly recited the poem, "The Cremation of Sam McGee."

The only time the men came out of the camp the next morning was to use the outhouse. "We were just standing there waiting for them to do something illegal," Buzz says. But nothing happened. By 3:00 P.M., Buzz and Chase were exhausted. They walked over to the camp and knocked on the door. There, hanging on poles, were several dead deer. The hunters had already killed the animals before the rangers arrived, and they were legally tagged.

Buzz learned that the rain and fog had kept a plane from picking up the hunters. The meat was spoiling, and he was surprised and upset that they would sit in the cabin playing cards and not salvage the meat. The hunters told him they didn't eat deer, that they were just "sports hunters."

▲ ▲ ▲ ▲ ▲

In Kearney's year-end report, the supervisor brought up personnel and other problems, such as petty theft and illegal marijuana smoking. Kearney then related a couple of stories that, if true, should have sparked an investigation by the Authority.

Kearney claimed that white female counselors had been raped by black youths in their charge at Avalanche Field. The group was from a Massachusetts camp specializing in rehabilitating black teenagers from South Boston. Their supervisors were six white women in their early twenties, according to Kearney. Fourteen of the boys, in their late teens, "raped or attempted to rape the six white girls," he stated. "A call was received at about 11:00 P.M. on this matter. The rest of the night was spent trying to regain some order. The girls would not sign complaints or admit that a rape had been consummated for fear of retaliation from this group of knife-wielding thugs."

Kearney took credit for calming things down by telling the group that dangerous bears were staring at them from the woods and would eat them alive if they didn't get into their bus. Ranger Danny Watson, however, claimed to be the investigating officer and his work activity notebook for July 1 documented that it was he, not Kearney, who answered the disturbance call. Watson reported the situation involved black and Puerto Rican boys threatening each other with knives—and no girls or women were involved.

Kearney's report also stated that nude hikers were climbing Katahdin. A ranger, he said, had met a young couple on the Knife Edge, and both were nude except for a bra the woman was wearing. Kearney quipped, "It is my belief that she had not been liberated." Kearney referred to a discussion with the supervisor of the White Mountain National Forest, who had told him that naked hippies were wandering the trails there.

"This seemed far-fetched to me, but shortly thereafter I received a complaint from a girls' camp group swimming at Ledge Falls," Kearney said. "A Volkswagen bus from Arizona had pulled into the parking area, and some ten men and women swarmed out of the vehicle, stripped to the buff, and made a big show of sunbathing on the rocks in front of these ten-year-old children. One of our older gatekeepers, a man of retirement age, approached a car entering the park and was cheerfully greeted by a young lady, completely naked, sitting behind the wheel. (He immediately applied to work next year.)"

Kearney wrapped up the statistics for 1970: between 95,000 and 100,000 vehicles and 68,535 persons. The figures didn't jibe because the gatekeepers didn't count everyone in the vehicles, he explained. Many people were turned away for lack of overnight accommodations, according to Kearney. Many of them stayed at private sporting camps outside the park, helping those enterprises enjoy a banner season. One of the operators was so happy with the summer overflow that he put on a steak and corn feed for the park staff.

"With the many complaints received at the opening of the season, my nerves were taut and bare," Kearney continued in his report. "I am sure that my temper was equally taut. If I have said or done anything that has hurt feelings or caused embarrassment to any of you gentlemen, I apologize, and again repeat what I have said in previous reports: I am honored to be able to work under and with men as dedicated to the continuance of Governor Baxter's beliefs and wishes as you men obviously are."

Replying to Kearney's report, Jim Erwin called it "an excellent piece of work" and didn't mention the alleged rapes or nudes. "Even though your Irish fingers wouldn't handle the German typewriter as well as you might have wished, the job is thorough, interesting, and a damn good report"

The archival absence of any response to Kearney's accusations remains a mystery.

Primary Document Sources: BSPA Boxes 9, 10, 11, 12, 13, 14, 16, 18 (2507-0715, 2705-0716, 2507-0717, 2507-0718).

Conversations and communications: Buzz Caverly, Tom Chase, Jerry Cinnamon, Ken Curtis, Dave Getchell, Sr., Harry Kearney, Michael Opuda, Jim Tierney, Ben Townsend, Danny Watson.

▲▲▲▲▲▲▲▲

CHAPTER 11

# Supervisor Buzz Redux

The "hippie" culture expressed itself among the park staff in the long hair, sideburns, and beards that some of the younger employees started sporting. Buzz, with his self-described "state trooper/Marine Corps image," thought the unkempt look was inappropriate—a position that Harry Kearney shared.

In January 1971, Buzz asked to the Park Authority to ask for a rule requiring employees to be clean-shaven and have short hair. The trustees gave him permission to ban beards. Hair could be worn down to the collar but not over it, and sideburns couldn't be longer than the center of the ear.

▲▲▲▲▲

For months, the Authority had mulled over changing the name of the park to Baxter Wilderness Park. The idea had first been raised by some legislators, according to Austin Wilkins, back in the early 1960s. In a February 14, 1963, letter to Governor Baxter, Wilkins said the proposed name change "would give strength to the statements you have made that the park shall forever be kept wild and in its natural state with no encroachments." There is no evidence that Baxter responded one way or another.

Ron Speers had taken up the matter again in 1970 with the support of John Baxter, but no concrete action was taken by lawmakers. Jim Erwin pressed the issue a third time, and the Authority went forward with a bill. Conservationists, confused about the bill's intent, didn't actively support it, and the matter was tabled.

From a practical standpoint, Buzz favored the name change. Park records don't contain the answer as to why the issue was dropped. There may have been a legal impediment to the proposal. Governor Baxter's Deeds of Trust to the state contained the phrase mandating that each parcel "forever shall be known as Baxter State Park," and changing the name would have been a violation. The Natural Resources Council's Baxter Park Committee pursued the name change later but didn't get anywhere with lawmakers.

▲▲▲▲▲

Buzz, like other rangers, enjoyed his winter days off to polish his snowmobile skills. He was a first-rate sledder, a master of body English. He loved driving his sled up to the highest point of steep gravel-pit walls and racing down. But his real daredevil nature showed on the risky slopes of the Great Basin at Chimney Pond. He would compete with anyone to see how high up they could drive their snowmobiles before rolling down the mountain out of control and at great risk to life.

When the rangers were in the mood for lower-altitude hi-jinks, they raced on the road from Togue Pond to Roaring Brook. Tom Chase had perfected the trick of driving up on the right of another man's sled, then reaching over and turning off the key to the engine. Another favorite was to see how far on the edge of the road or trail one snowmobile could force another without tipping over.

Chase taught Buzz a new mountaineering skill—glissading down the Saddle Trail. It also was hair-raising fun and a quick way to get down the mountain in the shortest possible time. Buzz would always try anything once.

▲▲▲▲▲

By the spring, the rangers' discontent with Kearney—his behavior and treatment of the staff—had reached a peak. Jim Erwin wanted to get to the bottom of it, especially since Kearney was such a close friend.

Erwin drove to the park and interviewed Buzz, ranger Tom Chase, and gatekeeper Ernest Burhoe. When he arrived at the Caverly house on Gardner Street in Patten, Jan slammed the door in Erwin's face. She didn't mean to be rude, but he had surprised her with her hair in rollers.

When Jan sheepishly opened the door again and apologized, Erwin announced he was there to investigate the park staff concerns about Harry Kearney. "I'm not going to fire Harry Kearney, but I may you," he told Buzz. "But I'm going to give you the opportunity first to tell me your story."

Erwin and Buzz sat on the couch talking for two hours. "I spilled my guts," Buzz remembers, recounting to Erwin "shenanigans"that Kearney had pulled that made life tough for him and the field rangers, such as requiring them to work in neckties in the heat of summer.

When Buzz was at warden school, he remembers hearing complaints about Kearney from men who had worked under him. "We'd sit around the room at night and talk about our work," he says. "Like an idiot, I went back and told Kearney what had been said because I thought the stories were entertaining. But he put some of the guys on probation. He was working the left against the right, and never let peace prevail. The guy was an aggravator."

Ellie Damon also told Erwin about things Kearney did without asking for permission from the Authority. For instance, Kearney had the rangers build a camp at Webster Lake to be used by patrolling rangers overnight, and as a place to hang out with each other during days off.

After the interviews, Erwin concluded that "Harry fouled his own nest. [The rangers] didn't like him or trust him. It was so bad, I was appalled. He alienated the rangers, gatekeepers [and their wives]. He played [people] against each other and tried to divide and conquer. Ninety percent of those I talked to said Harry Kearney called it 'my park.' Harry the emperor. It went to Harry's head. No one would tell him what to do. He didn't want advice. He was not concerned with policy. The park was bleeding to death inside."

Erwin returned home knowing that Kearney had to go. Wilkins and Speers agreed. Erwin was surprised that Wilkins didn't fight against firing the supervisor. "I told Austin I could back up [the reasons]. It was the hardest thing in my life to tell Harry he had to go," Erwin states. "I said, 'Harry, you haven't got a friend in the park. Not one.' He didn't want a hearing."

On May 18, 1971, Kearney resigned, effective nine days later. News reports quoted Erwin saying that Kearney was leaving for personal reasons, without explanation.

▲ ▲ ▲ ▲ ▲

Buzz was in his 1968 Ford station wagon near the Telos gate when he received a call on the park radio that Austin Wilkins wanted to talk with him immediately. He found a pay phone at Shin Pond. Wilkins

*Buzz, Jan, Tammy, and Cathy Caverly, 1971*
Olan Mills photo, Baxter State Park Photo Archives

told Buzz that Kearney was resigning and asked him to become acting supervisor again.

Buzz wanted the job badly but hesitated. The family had just settled in at the house in Patten. Cathy was in her first year of school, and Buzz wasn't sure that he could uproot Jan and the girls again.

Wilkins guaranteed Buzz that the park would build the Caverlys a house, pay the utilities, and make it possible for them to hold onto their Patten property. And Wilkins emphasized there was an important change from the previous time that Buzz was supervisor: a bigger budget, thanks to the trust fund income.

Buzz accepted the temporary position and called the rangers together for a meeting May 19 at the Hamlet Motel in East Millinocket to inform them of the change in supervisors. The rangers were happy to get rid of Kearney and have Buzz back in charge. Buzz promised to improve communications among everyone and work toward a better organization.

Austin Wilkins sent out notices about Kearney's departure to several "friends of the park," such as Robert Haskell, Bangor Hydro president. He confided that although Kearney was given "the opportunity to resign for personal reasons, actually the case was leadership incompatibility." Buzz, Wilkins said, would run the park "so much more smoothly" while a wide-ranging search would be made to find a new administrator. Wilkins was not behind Buzz as park chief for the long haul.

The Fin and Feather Cub praised Buzz's promotion, as it had in 1968, optimistic that his experience and "courteous and cooperative attitude" would result in a better relationship between users and park staff.

▲ ▲ ▲ ▲ ▲

Buzz, now thirty-three years old, felt determined to measure up to his new responsibilities, even if he wasn't assured the job full time. He yearned to be permanent supervisor but wasn't sure he'd stand a chance against college men whom he was sure would apply for the post.

Wilkins soon stepped down as Authority chairman after a remarkable fifteen years in the position, and was replaced by Jim Erwin. Buzz was concerned how the change might affect him because of Erwin's friendship with Kearney. Kearney had buffaloed Erwin as far as Buzz was concerned. He knew Erwin could make his life difficult if he wanted to but was relieved at Erwin's affirmation of staunch support.

Erwin told Buzz again that he had never considered Buzz's earlier demotion as a punishment for misdeeds. Buzz just wasn't experienced and skilled enough when he had first served as supervisor in 1968-69, Erwin said. Now, two years later, Erwin thought that Buzz was more mature and ready to "take off like a big bird."

In response to being free of Kearney, park rangers' morale greatly improved. Buzz applauded them for going "far above and beyond the call of duty" in getting the campgrounds and roads into good shape for the beginning of the 1971 summer season.

▲ ▲ ▲ ▲ ▲

Buzz and Jan decided not to keep the Patten house and sold it for a nice profit. They packed up their belongings and moved to Millinocket. The Caverlys temporarily rented a house at 413 Katahdin Avenue, and Buzz set aside a room in the house for the supervisor's office. Again, he had the help of part-time secretary Joyce Given. The park headquarters moved from the Maine Forest Service building on Central Avenue to 260 Aroostook Avenue in the Gonya Oil Company building.

Cathy Caverly knew her father was important because they had a new home and each girl had her own bedroom for the first time. The phone rang off the hook much of the time to the point that the girls answered, "Grand Central Station," and were surprised once when it was Governor Curtis on the line. At that point, Buzz dispensed some "customer service" education to the girls.

The house was near a mobile home park with a playground, and the Caverly girls found many friends there, as well as at school.

"We had the first semblance of a regular family life there, and the girls had a regular child's social life," recalls Buzz. "But my working hours still prevented normal activities. I was still leaving home early in the morning and not getting back until late and working in the office until late at night—often because of the regular drug busts in the park. I wasn't always able to get to church on Sundays with the family. I missed the kids' birthday parties, playground activities. It was a major sacrifice. I was young and naïve enough to think the park came above everything else. Jan understood that when we got married, and she did well, very well, at tolerating my absences."

▲ ▲ ▲ ▲ ▲

Regardless of how busy he was, Buzz still made time to climb Katahdin because he felt it was important for hikers to see the park boss on top of the summit.

Meanwhile, business manager Bill Cross was working on a new job description for a permanent supervisor—one that would eliminate Buzz from consideration. Cross's description required the park supervisor to have a four-year college degree and "an extensive knowledge of professional forestry and wildlife principles and practices . . . of equipment and principles used in managing forest and recreational areas." Also, Cross recommended that the supervisor have "considerable experience" in professional management.

Cross's proposal was not adopted then because Buzz had the inside track for the permanent supervisor's position. But it wasn't the last time that Buzz would hear about job requirements he couldn't meet.

*Buzz Caverly at Basin Ponds viewpoint*
BAXTER STATE PARK PHOTO ARCHIVES

▲ ▲ ▲ ▲ ▲

Showing his leadership capabilities, Buzz moved forward quickly on a number of fronts that would enhance the park's wilderness character. First, he tackled the controversial issue of closing Chimney Pond Campground in favor of a new one at Basin Ponds.

Chimney Pond was a poster scene for problems created by the backpacking craze. Besides the water pollution from dumps, there was crushed vegetation and peeled trees, soil erosion at tent sites and along the pond's shoreline, and filthy outhouses. Harry Kearney had started the ball rolling to abandon the site in favor of Basin Ponds, and the Authority accepted his relocation plan in 1970. Kearney left the park before the project was too far along, although some lean-tos had been built.

Opposed to the relocation, Buzz went forward to try to reverse the Authority's decision—with the support of Chimney Pond ranger Danny Watson and forest service fire control officer Clayton Gifford (the husband of park secretary Helen Gifford).

Watson and Gifford were confident that the Basin Ponds area was a fire hazard because of tinder-dry duff covering the ground, and the shoreline was littered with driftwood and dri-ki. Winds were higher and gustier than anywhere in the Katahdin area, according to Watson, "and scrub growth is filled with blowdowns on the verge of being explosive." To make the place "reasonably safe" would require a costly cleanup involving bulldozers, Watson and Gifford estimated.

Buzz agreed that Chimney Pond had terrible visitor abuse problems but emphasized that it was "perfectly safe" from fires. Starting with the 1971 season, he had already made some improvements at the campground: the number of campers had been reduced from one hundred a night to thirty-five, and shoreline lean-tos had been torn down so there was only tenting near the pond.

Buzz recommended to the Authority that two new bunkhouses be reopened at Chimney Pond and the number of total campers be limited to sixty per night. He also proposed to change the eroded Chimney Pond Trail from Roaring Brook back to the more stable rocky stream bed (the current way). The Authority wanted time to mull over the Basin Ponds issue but approved the trail relocation.

▲ ▲ ▲ ▲ ▲

Buzz then took action to save the Daicey Pond cabins. After purchase, the buildings, many of them on the shore, had been closed while a decision was pending on how to use them. The options ranged from burning them down to maintaining them as commercial sporting camps. Neither choice was acceptable at the time.

Buzz told the Authority that if the aging structures were not opened up to air, they would quickly fall apart. He recommended that the most dilapidated camps be torn down and the others opened for rental by midsummer. The trustees agreed.

Although praised for his action in preserving much of the sporting camp, Buzz had second thoughts in hindsight years later. He speculated that if he had not intervened as soon as he did, the camps might have sat unused and rotted to the point where the Authority would have ordered them burned. Then there would have been the option to put in lean-tos and tent sites or let the area revert to its natural wild state.

On other fronts, Buzz proceeded with removing obsolete and dilapidated buildings. One of the first to go that belonged to the state fish and game department was the warden's camp on Black Brook Road. The building seemed a disgrace to Buzz. The front porch was virtually sitting on the road, and occupants had thrown their garbage and cans down the steep drop out the back door. Buzz arranged a trade of the Black Brook camp for the Davignon cabin on Matagamon Lake.

▲ ▲ ▲ ▲ ▲

The 1970 ban on self-contained trailers and campers with toilets had eliminated sizable vehicles on park roads but didn't prohibit large, multi-canoe trailers, oversized boat trailers, and buses. In Buzz's estimation, those kinds of vehicles were particularly dangerous, and he prohibited them in 1971, letting the Authority know after the fact.

His order banned any vehicle twenty feet long and seven feet high or wider than an average-size car or truck. The only exception would be an organized group traveling to an area they had reserved previously, if the oversized vehicle was their only means of travel. In those cases, a ranger would escort them, and the vehicle couldn't leave the parking lot in that area until the end of their stay.

Buzz acknowledged to the trustees that he might have overstepped his position, but he was willing to take that risk because without action "we are going to have accidents with serious personal injuries." Letters of both protest and praise followed Buzz's move. The rule stuck.

▲ ▲ ▲ ▲ ▲

Proof that Buzz's return as boss was successful was a statement issued by the park staff and the Advisory Committee on July 29, lobbying the Authority to make his position permanent. Buzz was someone they trusted, respected, and were willing to work with, his supporters said. He trusted the rangers to do their jobs without checking on them all the time, and none had "abused that carefully placed trust," they declared. Jobs the staff didn't particularly like in the past were different under Buzz because he worked with them or asked them pleasantly to carry out a chore, explaining the reasons for doing it. "Whether or not Buzz or anyone else realizes it, he'd make an excellent psychologist," they enthused.

The staff and Advisory mentioned how Buzz had worked his way up through the ranks, was unquestionably dedicated, knew how to run a campground, was skilled in handling the public, and knew how to deal with court matters. "He knows the book work of a campground, each job, how to take care of equipment, all the trails and territory of the park, and probably most important he knows his personnel and they know him," the staff added.

For all those reasons, they said, they wanted to "suggest, request, or plead, if necessary, that Buzz be appointed permanent supervisor of Baxter State Park." Among those signing the petition were reservations chief Helen Gifford and fish and wildlife warden Elmer Knowlton, Jr.

▲ ▲ ▲ ▲ ▲

Lee Schepps joined the attorney general's office in August 1971 as an assistant attorney general in the environmental division. Formerly with a large law firm in Dallas, he took on representation of all natural resource agencies, including the Baxter Park Authority, where he became involved in a wide range of matters, from regulations and personnel to enforcement and interpretation of Baxter's trusts.

When Schepps met Buzz, he was surprised at how "cop-like" he seemed for a place like Baxter Park. But as he worked with Buzz, he began to gain respect for him, recognizing that Buzz was a first-class woodsman, a hard worker, always prepared to discuss issues at hand, and extremely knowledgeable about the park.

The two developed a personal relationship partly through ski trips with former trustee Jon Lund and another assistant attorney general, Marty Wilk. Buzz intuited that having an ally so close to the Authority was important as he and the park matured. He was right.

▲ ▲ ▲ ▲ ▲

As it grew, the NRCM took the initiative in August to establish a stronger relationship with park officials—a move that unnerved trustee Austin Wilkins. Buzz was as wary of environmentalists as the trustees were because they could insert unwanted interference in park affairs and produce negative publicity.

Writing to Chairman Erwin, NRCM Vice President John McKee said that during the ten years the organization had been around, it was not always sure what the Authority's guiding philosophy was and what the management goals were. Also, he noted there were instances where decisions were made that seemed at odds with protection of the park's wilderness character, and the public didn't have "adequate opportunity" to be involved in park matters.

In 1969 the council's board of directors had adopted a resolution calling for a comprehensive study and master plan for the park to be developed by an independent consultant, and in 1971 had opposed the use of motorized vehicles and overland vehicles. Most recently, McKee noted, the board went on record opposing development of a campground at Basin Ponds "unless it can be shown that these will not alter the wilderness character of the pond area and will not affect the environment adversely."

The council's Baxter Park Committee had explored the implications of management and recreation in the park, and McKee said the panel would like to meet with the Authority to talk over the issues.

Austin Wilkins revealed to Chairman Erwin what he thought privately about NRCM and other activist groups. "To my way of thinking, this is just another aggravation similar to that of the Fin and Feather Club, Sierra Club, and other 'do good' organizations," he wrote in an August 16 letter. "I know you will have to prepare a tactful reply but it seems to me as an Authority together with the Advisory Committee, we are doing the very things they are outlining in their letter." Wilkins viewed ad hoc environmental committees as worrisome because "these outside groups . . . think they know more about handling Baxter Park than we do. . . ."

▲ ▲ ▲ ▲ ▲

When the fish and wildlife department showed up again in the park to "reclaim" another pond, Buzz didn't try to intervene and borrow trouble. The project this time was to "reclaim" the South Branch ponds by dynamiting the outlet and poisoning the unwanted fish species. Biologist Roger Auclair blew up a rocky gorge on the outlet of Lower South Branch Pond to create a vertical drop—in effect, a barrier, so that

*Looking south to Katahdin from North Traveler Mountain and
over Upper South Branch Pond*

COURTESY BAXTER STATE PARK PHOTO ARCHIVES

trash fish couldn't continue to populate those waters. Again, he used toxic rotenone to kill off the "assortment of rough fish," and introduced sunapees, also known as blueback trout.

---

Primary Document Sources: BSPA Boxes 9, 16 (2507-0714, 2507-0718); BSPA Original Authority minutes, Box 15; Percival Baxter Collection (Letters).

Conversations and communications: Roger Auclair, Buzz Caverly, Tom Chase, Ellie Damon, Jim Erwin, Harry Kearney, John McKee, Lee Schepps, Danny Watson.

▲▲▲▲▲▲▲▲

**CHAPTER 12**

# TRIALS AND SKIRMISHES

JANUARY 12, 1972, WAS A MILESTONE for Buzz. His six-month probation as acting supervisor was over, and the Authority made the position
permanent. He was elated that he had the confidence again of the
trustees.

Buzz had convinced the Authority that his twelve years of experience, including four years as the park's boss, qualified him to be the
permanent supervisor. He was fully knowledgeable about the park, the
staff, and operations, and he had initiated successful on-the-ground
management actions. The Authority agreed that all that counted more
than the college degree that Bill Cross thought the supervisor should
have.

Jim Erwin congratulated Buzz on the appointment and an increase
in pay to $11,000 a year, a substantial amount above an average
ranger's salary. "This move is obviously made on the judgment, by the
Authority, that you have done, and are doing, an excellent job," Erwin
told him. "It leaves open, for a future decision, the matter which we
mentioned to you earlier, about someday having a Park director. Keep
up the good work."

Buzz responded with a thank-you letter, appreciative of "the confidence that the Authority has placed in me . . . I will do my best to work
for Baxter Park's interest in that position. I am aware at times there are
going to be problems when I will have to continue to come to the
Authority for answers, but I will try not to be too much of a nuisance."

▲ ▲ ▲ ▲ ▲

In the middle of the night shortly after his appointment, Buzz received
a phone call that made him break out in a sweat. "It was 1:00 or
2:00 A.M., and the voice said, 'Are you the I. Caverly who has his name
painted on the rock?' I said 'Yes,' and he hung up."

The call worried Buzz so much over the next hour that he jumped out of bed, grabbed a wire brush and headed for Russell Pond. His stomach churned in anxiety all seventeen miles from Millinocket to the park, the seven miles to Russell Pond, and the final mile to the top of Lookout.

"In October 1960, my first fall in the park, I was single and gung-ho," he recalls. "Rodney Green from near Manchester, New Hampshire, was camping at Russell—the only one there. He stayed two weeks, and over that period we talked a lot and hiked about every day. He helped me with trail work and freshening up the blazes on trees. There had never been a painted trail to Lookout Rock—and Helon said do it, so we did. It was a sunny day, with full fall foliage. There are ledges before you get to the highest point. We were standing looking out on the lower rocks, and I saw a nice flat surface that was out of direct view of hikers. Rodney and I autographed it with our names, I. C. Caverly and R. Green, October 1960. We then climbed to the top and life went on."

Several years later, Buzz had been on Lookout and remembered the graffiti. He had checked it out, noting that the paint was barely visible at the ledge itself and not from the trail at all. But now, as he stood on the ledge in the early morning light, Buzz could see that his and Rodney Green's names had been re-lettered in new bright blue paint. He spent hours scrubbing it off.

When finished, Buzz hiked down to the ranger cabin where Bob Howes was stationed. Howes was surprised to see him, and when Buzz told him why he was there, Howes admitted that he had done the re-lettering, thinking it would please Buzz. "I could have died," Buzz remembers, "but Jan thought I got what I deserved."

▲ ▲ ▲ ▲ ▲

Jim Erwin's first evaluation of Buzz had covered only three months, from November 1971 to January 1972, and Buzz had received "outstanding" ratings in the categories of effectiveness and cooperativeness and "very good" in six of seven other categories. Erwin assessed Buzz as "average" in planning.

But the next evaluation covering the following year to January 1973 reflected Erwin's increased confidence in Buzz and Buzz's stronger performance. He received "outstanding" marks in additional categories, and Erwin wrote that Buzz was "doing a remarkable job."

While solidifying Buzz's position as supervisor, the Authority was also moving ahead with Bill Cross's recommendation to create the new job of park director and preserve the supervisor's position as number two in command.

Buzz knew that the director's position was being considered and didn't necessarily count himself out of the running for that job. Even if he wasn't a trained planner, he thought his career record might get him over that hurdle.

Austin Wilkins, however, was not thinking about Buzz as director material. In a note to Erwin, Wilkins sent a copy of Bangor Hydro's Haskell letter mentioning Telos dam keeper Clair Desmond's praise of Buzz as "a great guy. . . . Seems like, in forty-five years, this is just about the only time old Clair has had a complimentary word for any-one in the state 'establishment.' So you just about must have a good man," Haskell wrote.

Well, Wilkins told Erwin, he was pleased with the support for Buzz "but I am very strong in the opinion that we will need to look for a higher-caliber type as an administrator." After the park's top job was classified as director by the state personnel board and the salary set, "we then can move into the area of trying to do something for Buzz," Wilkins added.

▲ ▲ ▲ ▲ ▲

For Buzz, 1972 was an intense time. Park expansion was on the fast track, as the numbers showed. Just two years previously, before the trust funds were released, the park had only eight year-round staff and twenty-four seasonal employees, and for 1971–72 the number had grown to fourteen permanent employees and twenty seasonal workers, plus the new positions of assistant supervisor and business manager. Park salaries also showed the growth: In 1969–70 pay totaled $25,886, and for 1972–73 it had grown to $143,807. The park also purchased in-town property for its first permanent headquarters.

While Buzz was overseeing the increase in staff and operations, a number of controversies swirled around him that involved the Authority: chemical spraying, timber-cutting rights, drug use, and environmental damage by so many visitors.

▲ ▲ ▲ ▲ ▲

Reporter and avid cross-country skier Bob Cummings made his usual winter trip to Chimney Pond, and this time he was angered by the proliferation of snowmobiles—the ones park rangers rode. He learned that rangers had driven 2,000 to 3,000 miles patrolling the park. That was excessive, in Cummings's opinion, and he felt that the snowmobiles' roaring sound, smell, and smoke were a blight on the park.

His party had climbed Katahdin and could see three park rangers racing snowmobiles on Chimney Pond and doing loop-the-loops. At South Branch Pond, he reported, the ranger revved up his snowmobile five times one afternoon and evening for the fifty-yard round trip between his cabin and the pond.

It was clear that Cummings thought the rangers were playing, rather than hauling supplies or water. Buzz defended the rangers' high level of snowmobile use in general as necessary for good management. But Cummings's impression was that the rangers were "local kids into motors, not wilderness." Later evidence of that to Cummings was a ranger who overlooked more than a dozen snowmobile recreationists showing up at Chimney Pond in violation of the rules. The party wasn't cited then, and Cummings thought there were other similar times that the rangers allowed snowmobilers, especially the ones they knew, to get away with driving wherever they wanted to go.

▲ ▲ ▲ ▲ ▲

Ranger training was always a focus of the early spring schedule, and Buzz augmented the education of the operations crew. Rangers went to warden school, mountain rescue training school, forest fire control school, pistol training school, drug enforcement school, and to snowsled maintenance and Red Cross first-aid workshops. Since Ralph Heath's death, Buzz's philosophy was "the more training we can get, the more we want . . . it makes for better men who will do a better job when the time comes to act in a hurry," as he said in a speech to the Maine Forestry Department.

▲ ▲ ▲ ▲ ▲

Because of the controversy over DDT in the 1960s, chemicals had been banned by the Authority, and roadside brush was flourishing. By 1972 there were about 85,000 people traveling the narrow and winding park roads annually in 27,000 vehicles. Vehicle accidents had increased to between fourteen and twenty each season. Austin Wilkins and highway commission chief David Stevens wanted to reinstate limited spraying, with a different herbicide, out of traffic safety concerns.

The plan was to have the brush cut by hand, chipped, and blown into the woods as mulch. Then 2,4,5-t (mixed with kerosene or diesel oil) would be applied to the stubs and stumps from a backpack tank. Thus, there would be no roadside browning or killing of grasses and ferns.

The spray's active ingredient, 2,4,5-t, had been widely used in Vietnam to defoliate trees. The federal Environmental Protection Agency had banned the sale of the chemical in 1970 because of its link to birth defects in experiments with rats and mice. But in 1971 it was allowed on the market again for use in recreational areas.

The Maine Arborists Association and the Maine Chapter of the Society of American Foresters supported the spraying project. Opposed were the Natural Resources Council of Maine, Maine Audubon Society, and the State Biologists Association. First District Congressman Peter Kyros, a park user, jumped into the fray too, asserting that spraying would be "unconscionable." He opposed the "submission of this natural environment . . . to automobiles and chemicals."[1]

Despite Buzz's opposition, Jim Erwin defended the plan. The Authority had backed away from dealing with roadside brush for years "so as not to disturb the late Honorable Percival P. Baxter while he was alive," he recalls. Wanting to avoid a public battle with environmentalists, the Authority met with the three leading anti-spray groups and Don Mairs, supervisor of the State Board of Pesticides Control. Mairs was brought to the meeting to explain the effects of 2,4,5-t. Mairs said that the chemical, when used according to label directions, was not hazardous to public heath and was essentially nontoxic to wildlife. When applied to stumps, it killed only the root crown and sprouts but was more toxic to broad-leaf vegetation than grasses, he explained.

After weighing all the pros and cons, the Authority surprised everyone. They voted against spraying. It wasn't pressure from environmental groups or scientific evidence that forced the trustees to back off. They concluded that the issue itself had become harmful to the park. "The park needs more friends—not more enemies," the

Authority declared in a press release. "We want an end to the controversy and have a strong alliance to serve and protect Baxter Park."

▲ ▲ ▲ ▲ ▲

Up to this time, neither the park nor any state agencies had employed a woman as a ranger or warden. Fieldwork was the unchallenged domain of men. But in the spring of 1972, Barbara Downey met with Buzz to inquire about being hired as a ranger. "It was the most insulting response I've ever gotten," she remembered years later. He didn't think a woman could handle the job, especially the physical work, she asserted. "He was disgusted at the idea. How did I think a woman could move those [200-pound] gas tanks to get them into Chimney Pond and Russell Ponds? I said just like any ranger—tow them behind a snowsled. But he wasn't willing to consider it."

Buzz doesn't remember the situation. In retrospect, he admits he might not have been "enlightened" enough at the time to hire a woman. Up until then, the highest ranking woman in the park was reservations chief Helen Gifford. Alma Chase and Ida Damon were still in the positions of assistant campground rangers because they were the wives of rangers.

Baxter Park wasn't unusual in being slow to hire women in field positions. The fish and game department waited until 1978 to hire its first woman game warden and the Maine Forest Service, until 1985 to employ its first woman ranger. The Allagash Wilderness Waterway's rangers were all men until 1984.

▲ ▲ ▲ ▲ ▲

After interviewing twenty-five candidates, the Authority chose thirty-year-old Philip McGlauflin from Presque Isle as Buzz's assistant. McGlauflin had started working with the state parks agency at Aroostook State Park at sixteen and had moved up from grass-mower to manager.

The park now had district rangers supervising campground rangers, and Buzz assigned McGlauflin to work with each district ranger until he had covered every trail, visited every campground and campsite, and could understand the issues facing rangers and the administrative staff.

McGlauflin arrived in time to help with an unusually busy June. People were overwhelming the reservation staff with calls and letters, and dozens of people (primarily locals) stood in long lines to get their favorite camping sites. Visitors violated the speed limit to the point that rangers set up a radar unit between Abol Hill and Nesowadnehunk. In two days before the radar trap, twenty court summonses and sixty-six warnings had been issued to speeders. Afterward, the speeding frenzy stopped.

Buzz reported to the Authority that there were a lot of complaints that the park's rules and regulations were "stupid" and that the park should have trained ecologists on staff. But the alleged shortcomings didn't stop 91,157 people from visiting in 1972 and leaving just one *written* complaint at headquarters.

▲ ▲ ▲ ▲ ▲

Bob Cummings continued his critical newspaper articles about Baxter's environmental problems. Topping his list of abuses were the perennial issues of overcrowding, litter, rutted trails, foot-damage to the fragile alpine area on Katahdin, snowmobile trails punched through the heart of the park, reduction in backpacking campsites in favor of more auto camping sites—and, of course, herbicides to eliminate roadside brush.

Referring to his February 1972 winter trip, Cummings complained about snowmobiles packing down the snow to the point that it made him feel like he was walking on a paved highway. During that visit, he encountered two rangers and two forest wardens on snowmobiles just out sightseeing between Roaring Brook and Russell Pond. Cummings felt this was in violation of the rule against snowmobiling on the Roaring Brook access road that the rangers had used to get to there.

Cummings also was offended that one ranger who accompanied his party didn't know where emergency rescue equipment was kept and was unfamiliar with pitons. Furthermore, he claimed the rangers didn't know the weather for the next day.

The articles may have angered the Authority, but the trustees didn't respond in writing.

▲ ▲ ▲ ▲ ▲

Writer Aime Gauvin was becoming a full-fledged activist on park issues and, in an April 10, 1972, column in *Maine Times*, appealed to Jim Erwin and Ron Speers to show their conservation colors in their respective fights for the Republican gubernatorial nomination. He urged them to prove they are "apostles of conservation" as they claimed in debates for the nomination.

Gauvin wanted the candidates to go further with stricter rules and regulations to stop all long-standing abuses, such as allowing the Perimeter Road to be an all-night highway.

The rule changes already adopted by the trustees provoked the Fin and Feather Club to again present them with a list of old and new grievances that largely focused on improving use for Mainers, especially locals.

The club asked the Authority to eliminate the use fee for Mainers and to keep all entrances open twenty-four hours a day, attended by gatekeepers. They wanted all private, commercial operations ended in the park to prevent "discrimination" against non-clients.

Taking into consideration the big picture, the club supported phasing out use at Chimney and Russell Ponds to allow them to recover ecologically, and establishing new campgrounds. They wanted the last purchase of Governor Baxter (T2R9) designated for hunting and trapping instead of wildlife sanctuary, and asked for a pre-season course for rangers on Baxter's Deeds of Trust and enforcement procedures so that rangers would not try to impose their own interpretations of rules.

Other requests were that official complaint forms be available at all campgrounds to be mailed directly to the attorney general's office; that the park hold public meetings once a year to discuss issues; that the park be classified into three categories—wilderness, auto camping, and special regulations (specifically the 28,000-acre area set aside for scientific forest management).

The Authority took the requests under advisement. Eventually they eliminated the day-use fee for Mainers, ended the private operation of sporting camps in the park, increased pay and benefits for rangers, and established an annual meeting with the public in Millinocket.

▲ ▲ ▲ ▲ ▲

The beginning of one of the park's historical defining moments came in a routine letter dated June 16 from Austin Wilkins to Ralph Currier of

Great Northern Paper on the subject of cutting rights.

The company had sold 7,764 acres in T2R9 to Governor Baxter in 1962 but had retained the right to log there until December 1, 1973. In addition, cutting rights to 8,000 acres were still active in T3R9, which Baxter had purchased in 1954. The land encompassed nine ponds and the slopes of Abol and Rum Mountains, off Katahdin's southern slopes.

Currier's letter indicated that Great Northern would harvest timber in both townships before its rights expired, and its access would be via the Roaring Brook Road. There was no question that the planned cutting would have a visual impact on park visitors.

Wilkins asked if Great Northern would consider selling the cutting rights. "I am sure that further cutting is going to create a false public image in which you as well as the Authority will be criticized for cutting in Baxter Park and violating the 'forever wild' and other conditions in the deeds of trust," he told Currier.

Currier was willing to contract with the James W. Sewall Company to carry out an inventory of the stumpage volume and value and get back to Wilkins on a price by the end of the summer. The matter was then put on the Authority's back burner.

The market value of the park's endowment funds by June 30, 1972, was $11,397,101. The Baxter trust, at $8,346,013, was the account to be tapped in the event of a buyout. The value of the other accounts was: the state-held trust, $2,182,044; the invested income account (interest and dividends from the Baxter trust), $869,044; and the park's checking account, $118,580.

▲ ▲ ▲ ▲ ▲

On July 1 Buzz and Jan moved out of their Katahdin Avenue rental house to one on Bates Street for just a month, anxious to finally move into their new park house. After packing up to leave Bates Street, they were told at the last minute that the park house still wasn't ready, which forced them into a short stay in the park. A month later, they moved into the new home at 55 Tamarack Street, where they would be during the week for more than thirty years.

Not living in the park meant that Buzz and Jan had to be more attentive to getting the girls out into the park. Picnics at Rum Brook were popular with them. Since Tammy was just a baby when she lived in the park, she doesn't have as many memories of family times there as Cathy. But Easter at Rum Brook was one that stuck in her mind because of the tasty ham and fried eggs that Buzz cooked for them at the water's edge. He kept a cast-iron frying pan in the back of his vehicle for just such occasions.

The Russell Pond adventures with the girls were also memorable. Buzz and Jan would fly with them to Wassataquoik Lake, hike the nearly three miles to Russell, and then finally out to Roaring Brook—a total of ten miles. "I whined the whole way, and Dad told me to toughen up," Cathy Caverly recalls.

▲ ▲ ▲ ▲ ▲

Marijuana use was at an all-time high, and Buzz was aggressive in finding and prosecuting culprits. By the end of August, more than a hundred campers had been taken to court and most pleaded guilty, paying several hundred dollars in fines. Among the young people caught smoking at Katahdin Falls was the son of a town official. Ranger Howard York picked up another seven youths in Baxter Park, and Buzz reported to the Authority:

> The group was in a circle and they had taken an orange, put a roach in the center of it, and were passing it around the group. They also had a bag of grass and cigarette rolls in their possession. In the years I have spent in Baxter Park, I have not seen as many cases taken to court in such a short period by our Park Rangers. The boys are working day and night in hopes they will be able to put a stop to it, but it seems to be an endless battle. If we don't start getting some of the family people back camping and less of the hippie groups, our problems are going to increase. I guess the hippies drove the families out. I sometimes wonder what hippies are allergic to, and whatever it is, we should import some into the Park. Pamola doesn't think much of these people and he has had it rain a good part of the summer, but it still doesn't do any good!

Jim Erwin thought the law enforcement situation had gotten out of hand and ordered Buzz to stop arresting so many people and just give them court summonses. Hauling so many people to Dover-Foxcroft for arraignment was an undue burden on rangers, he said. Erwin suggested not arresting anyone unless the person was violent or otherwise upset to the point of damaging the park.

Erwin even advised that any summonses given should be aimed at a certain day, such as a Friday when the judge was at the nearby district court in Millinocket, and that one ranger be given the responsibility for all the cases—unless trials were ordered. Erwin was clear that he didn't want "the boys to let up on marijuana and other drugs," but thought that more efficiency in the enforcement process was needed.

▲ ▲ ▲ ▲ ▲

The park's organization chart was an important document. It was a hierarchical ranking of employees based on position. Buzz believed it was the supervisor's job to revise the chart as needed, but, true to form, Bill Cross wanted a hand in it, too. In 1972 Cross tried to change the position of supervisor to director and have the director be assigned to Buzz's free living quarters on Tamarack Street in Millinocket.

Buzz disagreed with Cross on changing the job titles but was most upset about the possibility that he would be forced out of the Tamarack house. If he had to relocate—possibly to the park for financial reasons—"I would have to divorce my family, as I have a school age child and could not afford to transport her to Millinocket daily and pay tuition," Buzz wrote Cross. He pointed out that Jan had lived in the woods six years and that she had worked free for the park for four of those years. After such service, Buzz said that Jan had earned "a home where there are modern facilities and schools available."

As for Cross wanting to cut the field crew, Buzz said the number of workers was already thin and short on equipment.

"I resent this because I feel we have an effective, workable system in the park," Buzz wrote, "and it is the responsibility of all Baxter Park personnel to work to upgrade our department and work toward the preservation of Baxter Park, and it is especially your and my responsibility to supply this personnel and equipment necessary to do the job."

Buzz sent a copy of his response to Cross to Jim Erwin, writing, "It bothers me when [Cross] takes it on himself to try and change our system of operation. Regardless of what I talk to him about, if I don't agree to change to his way of thinking or if it isn't his idea, it is no good."

At this point, Cross was well on his way to becoming Buzz's in-house enemy, a situation that would persist until Cross retired not only from the business manager's job in 1978. but also from the Advisory Committee he would serve on from 1978 to 1994. The issue of changing titles for the head of the park simmered for a decade.

▲ ▲ ▲ ▲ ▲

Buzz's salary became an issue again, and Erwin rose to his defense. The Authority wanted to raise Buzz's pay by two levels. But personnel department commissioner Nicholas Caraganis said no, due to a regulation technicality involving the motor vehicle division.

Erwin explained that the lower pay Buzz was receiving was arranged only to accommodate Harry Kearney, and it discriminated against Buzz. No law Erwin knew of prevented reestablishing the pay range back to what it was originally for supervisor. He asked Caraganis to review the matter personally. "I feel that a great injustice is being done to Mr. Caverly, who is being punished by the fact that his predecessor had a set of financial circumstances different from his and that he now is trapped by an accommodation made for the convenience of someone else." Erwin's effort convinced Caraganis to restore Buzz to his rightful salary level.

Buzz didn't like to haggle about money, but his family expenses were increasing. He could still remember when he was supervisor the first time, and was so short on cash that he didn't have enough money in his pocket to buy a sandwich while on the road.

▲ ▲ ▲ ▲ ▲

The increasing crowds of park users in August had become so chaotic that seasonal staff started to leave before the 1972 Labor Day holiday to escape the work pressures. Buzz was faced with a field-staff shortage when ten seasonal employees gave their departure notices, contending they had to return to college, had enlisted in the military service, or were taking a year-round job before Labor Day.

"We are more short-handed than ever, and the bad part about it all is that we don't have the applicants to choose from," Buzz reported. "The type of young people available today who are qualified for Rangers in Baxter Park do not like the sound of a sixteen- or eighteen-hour day, six days a week. This is one of the reasons I asked for fifteen additional positions in the budget for the near future, to cover for men on days off and to try and get our employees who are tied down to a campground or an office and other routine jobs onto an eight-to-ten-hour workday. I would hope that a schedule of this type might encourage our people to work for a career with the Park and avoid an excessive turnover of personnel."

▲ ▲ ▲ ▲ ▲

One of the late seasonal hires was Jan Caverly, who became a reservations assistant and the second highest-ranking woman employee. Another new employee was twenty-five-year-old Chris Drew of Island Falls. He was familiar with the park from camping there with his grandfather in the 1950s and 1960s. Drew had spent two years at Central Connecticut State College and had worked in the woods for Maine Public Service Company, an electric utility, for several years before deciding to try out a park job.

Buzz sent assistant Phil McGlauflin to interview Drew, and McGlauflin reported back that the young Drew was top-notch and "we ought to grab him." They offered him sixty-nine dollars a week as a gatekeeper at Togue Pond. Drew was married and the father of two young children, but he accepted the low-paying post and went on the payroll on September 11.

To Drew's surprise, that first assignment lasted only one week, and then he was sent to Chimney Pond to cover for a vacationing ranger. After a short stint in the backcountry, he was transferred to Daicey Pond to cover for another ranger, Art York, and then was sent back to Togue Pond for a week. After that, he substituted for rangers at Chimney Pond, Daicey Pond, and at Trout Brook Farm Campgrounds.

It was a crazy month-and-a-half, but Drew got to see and know the park unlike any other employee in so short a time. While at Trout Brook Farm, he was handed a job application form for a year-round post, despite the fact that he had been told he didn't qualify for one because he had less than a year's experience.

Drew got the job of commissioned ranger stationed at Chimney Pond with just four months of seasonal experience. He would continue to move up the ranks and quickly became Buzz's right-hand field man for more than thirty years.

▲ ▲ ▲ ▲ ▲

Like his colleagues, Drew relished the outdoors and the diversity of park work—lots of maintenance projects, trail clearing, putting in gas and water lines, and coping with the challenges of blackflies, mosquitoes, and troublesome bears. "And there were always campers on your doorstep, generally at mealtime," he recalls. He discovered quickly why people got the Chimney Pond post: "Because you were new and didn't know any better or you screwed up and were punished. I went in because I was new and came out because someone screwed up."

Drew fit in well from the start because he was a good storyteller with an infectious sense of humor. He had caught his sense of humor from his father who was "half gypsy and half nomad." Drew was intrigued with the park's storytelling tradition.

Chimney Pond caretaker LeRoy Dudley was the park's earliest storyteller. Some of his tales had been published in *Appalachia* magazine. Fred Ward at Trout Brook Farm and Wilbur Smith at Roaring Brook were also talented yarn-spinners. Drew felt that storytelling was a positive way to deal with the public—and his peers.

Fred Ward's tales were largely embellished lies but entertaining ones. Drew says, "Fred didn't just go catch trout. He caught ten- to fifteen-pound trout. He never shot anything under 300 pounds. There were so many coyotes on deer trails up his way that they beat a quarter-mile-wide trail through the woods. His snowmobile was the best because it had a million miles on it and he still hadn't changed the spark plugs. Campers from Boston didn't have a clue how much he was pulling their legs."

Drew also appreciated the stories of Bob Gould, the assistant ranger at Roaring Brook, who carried a big knife and claimed that the mice at his camp were the toughest. "Bob claimed he threw his knife once and slit one of those mice right clean in half and the hind end passed the front end going out the door," Drew laughs.

▲ ▲ ▲ ▲ ▲

More unneeded buildings in the park were burned down on Buzz's initiative and with the knowledge of Jim Erwin. "There were forestry camps at Matagamon landing, and the Chub Foster garage," Buzz says. "I was very careful . . . sure to consult with the chairman of the

*Burning of the Budreau, Morrow camp*
BUZZ CAVERLY PHOTO, BAXTER STATE PARK PHOTO ARCHIVES

Authority. It was not just Buzz Caverly going out with a match and touching off a place."

The park had finally gotten rid of the private camps of Budreau, Morrow, McQuarrie, Steen, and Clark, as well as the two wardens' camps on Black Brook Road and Foss-Knowlton Pond. The remaining wardens' camps had become a problem for the park. Wardens didn't use them any longer for overnight accommodations when they were on patrol far from home. There were more roads in the backcountry now and no mileage limit on wardens in carrying out their duties. So the cabins at Katahdin Stream, South Branch Pond, Doubletop, Roaring Brook, and Davignon's at Matagamon became recreational spots for gatherings of wardens, families, friends, and Augusta office personnel. At the Davignon camp, accessible only by boat or plane, the logbook showed that 90 percent of use was by off-duty wardens hunting and fishing.

During the summer at the Doubletop warden's camp, Chris Drew discovered hordes of cars and tents covering a large open area to accommodate a big party. Buzz felt strongly that the camps shouldn't be used for social gatherings. Too, the events circumvented park policy against personal use of cabins.

▲ ▲ ▲ ▲ ▲

One of Buzz's most important hires was Gerald Merry of Stacyville, who joined the staff as park carpenter. Not only was Merry a fine finish carpenter, he was a gifted amateur naturalist and photographer. Merry also was patient and quiet, and he and Buzz hit it off immediately.

Buzz developed complete trust in Merry, allowing him wide range in his park duties. Merry was always taking photographs and making notes about the park's resources. Before long, he had assembled the park's first slide show as a way to educate the public about the ecological and scenic beauty of Baxter Park. Merry was on his way to becoming the park's first naturalist in practice, although not in official title until 1979.

The more knowledgeable Merry became about the park's resources, the more he agreed with Buzz that scientific research shouldn't be allowed.

▲ ▲ ▲ ▲ ▲

The scientific research issue heated up in 1972 as more permit requests were made. Despite his personal feelings, Buzz's professional position made him inclined to issue a permit if the proposed project seemed reasonable, in the park's interest, and not a threat to wildlife.

Evaluating a black bear study request from Ray (Bucky) Owen, Jr., an assistant professor at the School of Forest Resources at the University of Maine at Orono (UMO), Buzz decided it didn't pass muster with the park's guidelines. (The request was for Owen's graduate students.) In saying no, Buzz pointed out that a similar study of moose by the fish and game department had been terminated because "the whole operation was found to be in violation of the concept of 'forever wild.'" There would be no research, he said, that disturbed wild animals in their natural habitat. Confrontations between bears and people in the park weren't a problem "except in those rare instances when people become foolish at a dump site," Buzz wrote Owen.

Buzz had known Owen since 1968, when he was a student of Owen's at warden school and had enjoyed his classes. The research denial created the first tension between Buzz and Owen, and there would be more to come later when Owen took a leave from the university in 1994 to become head of the Department of Inland Fisheries and Wildlife and a member of the park Authority.

Owen's research request prompted Buzz to ask the Authority to clarify the permit process. The upshot was a simple rule that proposals had to be submitted in writing to the Authority, and collection of specimens would be considered in light of the wilderness concept. Like the employee hiring process, decisions on research went back and forth between the Authority and the supervisor. Unless it was an unusual situation, Buzz made the call.

Ralph Lutts, curator of collections at the Museum of Science in Boston, was the first applicant after the revision of the permit process. He wanted permission to hike into the Klondike to gather certain specimens and carry out photographic work. Authority chairman Jim Erwin told Lutts no, unless his project qualified as the exception to the rule. The exception allowed research for "bona fide scientific expeditions made by proper institutions for public purposes and for knowledge to be entered into the general public domain," wrote Erwin.

If Lutts's project fit the bill, Erwin suggested that Buzz could give him a permit to camp in the Klondike rather than hike into the rugged area daily from a distant campsite. Lutts didn't pursue the study, and Buzz would have been hard pressed to allow the Klondike to have been used, since he considered it *the* park's wilderness gem and didn't want anyone exploring there.

While Owen and Lutts went away quietly, one researcher created a stir by going ahead with projects that involved excessive removal of rocks and plants. An out-of-state scientist took a truckload of shale from the riverbank west of the Trout Brook bridge. The paleobotanist claimed to have permission from Buzz, although Buzz did not remember giving his approval. What the researcher discovered in the material were some of the most complete fossils of Devonian land plants—the first vascular plants to live on earth. He was able to describe a new genus, *Pertica*, from the material and thus achieve professional fame. *Pertica* was later made the official state fossil by the legislature.

Buzz's most exasperating research situation to date started in 1972 but didn't play out to its conclusion until 1973. Christopher Campbell, a graduate student at UMO, proposed that the park help fund his documentation of the flora of Baxter Park. The Authority denied the request for money and free accommodations at several campgrounds.

Campbell notified the Authority by letter that he would go ahead anyway with his project, promising that his plant collection "will in no way threaten the existence of any rare plants." Buzz was worried that park research rules were not tough enough to dissuade collectors or make enforcement meaningful.

▲ ▲ ▲ ▲ ▲

There were increasing complications in getting supplies airlifted to the backcountry. The bush-pilot heyday was ending. Increasing FAA regulations and insurance costs were forcing small operators out of business. Too, the need for them was decreasing because a rapidly developing logging-road network created vehicle access where there had been none. And almost all of the river log-driving was over by the early 1970s.

As the bush planes left the scene, Baxter Park relied more on helicopters to haul supplies—especially in winter—to the backcountry. The park had used the old "banana-style" helicopters during Helon Taylor's tenure to move construction materials and firewood to Chimney Pond. They had been used for the first time in a search and rescue operation to evacuate the bodies of Ralph Heath and Margaret Ivusic. The Maine Forest Service chopper had been used now and then—once dropping a prefab outhouse at Togue Pond. The park also had hired pilot Al Averill, who had a M.A.S.H.-type helicopter, to move supplies for several years, but by 1972 he didn't want to take on such risky work because of high liability insurance costs.

Environmentalists didn't challenge the wilderness ethics of using helicopters or other aircraft to haul supplies, and Buzz endorsed their use. He felt that helicopters were not damaging to the natural resources, except for short periods with noxious air emissions, and snowmobiles would have had a greater impact in terms of pollution and noise; also, it would have taken snowmobiles more time than a helicopter to carry out any given job.

▲ ▲ ▲ ▲ ▲

Like Harry Kearney and Jim Erwin in 1970, Advisory Committee Chairman Bob Ohler and the NRCM came forth with separate proposed objectives for the park in the absence of a master plan.

Ohler recommended "no further manmade changes other than those of a rudimentary nature such as rough hiking trails and primitive campsites of limited capacity." He favored no further expansion or improvement of the road system, eventual strict limitation on the use of motor vehicles, and the possibility of closing certain roads. Ohler even raised the possibility of allowing only foot traffic in the park.

He agreed with Buzz that the Klondike was one area that should not even have a trail in order to preserve this island of true wilderness. He proposed expanding mountain trails in the northern half of the park to spread out hikers' impacts on Katahdin.

On the question of who should be park director, Ohler suggested a land use planner/administrator with experience in wilderness preservation, public relations skills, and a commitment to Governor Baxter's ideals for the park.

NRCM, concerned about overuse, feared that the park would be ruined without a comprehensive management plan. When Governor Baxter had created the park, the population of the country was approximately 100 million, and outdoor recreation was generally a pastime of the reasonably affluent, the council observed. Park use wasn't high enough to even keep records before 1950.

From 1950 to 1972, the nation's population had more than doubled, to 210 million, and recreation had undergone a radical transformation. Camping and hiking skyrocketed, as did sales of car campers and snowmobiles. Peoples' mobility and middle-class affluence increased, and superhighways were built across the nation. All of these factors combined to make the problem of overcrowding in Baxter Park a reality in 1972, NRCM asserted.

The council's first two recommendations addressed the wilderness nature of the park. To reduce public confusion over whether the preserve was just another state park, a name change should be pursued to clarify that it was Baxter Wilderness Preserve or Baxter Wilderness Park, as initially proposed by Authority member Jim Erwin. State promotional and informational literature should be reviewed to make sure it emphasized that the park's first priority was wilderness protection, not catering to public recreational desires.

The Authority couldn't make "sound management decisions" without a master plan, NRCM contended, pointing out that all major parks in the U.S. already had such plans or were working on them, and noting that AMC and other environmental groups had been calling for a plan for years. Rather than continuing to debate the need for a plan, NRCM asked the Authority to immediately retain a consulting and planning group, appoint a broad-interest steering committee that included members of the Baxter family, and budget up to $150,000 for a plan.

On other matters, NRCM proposed that the Authority acquire options on land around the Togue Ponds to prevent commercial exploitation near the park's southern entrance. A new state park should be created at Millinocket Lake to cater to car camping and act as a buffer zone for the park. Furthermore, the park should close all open dumps after the 1973 season and improve the handling of human waste and litter. The possibility of banning vehicle traffic was raised, but NRCM believed such a step would necessitate construction of a perimeter road outside and around the park for motorized access. Until the road issue was dealt with, the council said there would be no "real" answer to trail abuse, especially the most popular trails up Katahdin.

Mountain safety in the park was still inadequate, the council said. A review board of the best mountain safety experts in the Northeast should be convened to evaluate the training and knowledge of park personnel, the available equipment, plans for prevention of accidents and for rescues, and park policies toward public education in mountain safety.

Austin Wilkins wrote a note to Ohler congratulating him for "a very excellent broad approach" to some of the park's problems. The Authority was willing to listen to outside ideas, he said, but wanted to do things its own way in its own time. NRCM never received a response from a park official.

With unrelenting demand for management planning, the Advisory Committee formed a subcommittee to look at various ideas and come up with some interim objectives. The group proposed reducing vehicle traffic, putting less emphasis on camping, and encouraging more hiking and backpacking. NRCM supported the recommendations as a good start.

▲ ▲ ▲ ▲ ▲

Tom Deans, associate director of the AMC, and Robert Proudman of the ATC attended an Authority meeting in the park in August—an attempt at smoothing over long-standing tensions. Deans outlined the historic relations between the AMC and the park, noting that the club had held over a hundred major explorations into the Katahdin area since 1876 and had established many of the original trails in the park. Until 1961, the club had maintained at least a half dozen trails but that year had sent funds for trail work so the park could hire a crew to do the job.

With so many more hikers on the trails, there were many questions about how to deal with erosion and the protection of trailside resources and how to educate users on "not injuring" the outdoors, Deans said. He noted that the AMC had no relationship with the ATC except for the similarity in names.

The Authority was cordial, but there was no indication that the meeting caused trustees to change their opinions about the groups and their interest in having a foothold in the park.

▲ ▲ ▲ ▲ ▲

The cutting rights issue was back in front of the Authority in the fall of 1972 with a vengeance, and it commandeered front-page headlines at every turn and twist. After weighing all the pros and cons, the trustees and Great Northern agreed that a timber swap was the best solution. Great Northern could exercise its cutting rights in the two northwestern townships that Governor Baxter had set aside for "scientific forest management"—T6R9 and T6R10. In theory, it would be out of the public's sight and spare both the park and the company from public criticism.

The Advisory Committee unanimously supported the land swap because the specter of harvesting in the Katahdin area was so offensive. Chairman Ohler stated that a trade would be "the best possible solution to a bad situation." Buzz agreed with the swap, believing that an exchange of locales would preserve the beauty of the park's most popular Katahdin area. Also, it would open up logging roads in the north end that would be used for years to come when the park was ready to develop it for scientific forest management. The Authority saw great financial benefit to the park in letting Great Northern develop the road system.

"Those of us who had been around awhile were accustomed to cutting in the park," Buzz notes. "There had been two winters of operations on Rum Mountain by Gerald Ladd and major salvage harvests around Abol and Katahdin Stream from the 1963 blowdown. Lyle Chamberlain was cutting around Avalanche Field and between Katahdin Lake and Roaring Brook. If you looked far enough back, to 1884, there was heavy cutting in the Russell Pond area. And all that land recovered, and we were sure that the southern or northern part would also recover, whichever Great Northern cut."

The public reacted angrily to the deal. Two surprising opponents were Great Northern logging contractors—most prominently, Lyle Chamberlain of Lincoln—and former park supervisor Harry Kearney. They contended that the company had already cut most of the merchantable timber in the southern end and were putting the squeeze on the park to secure more valuable timber in the north.

Indeed, the 1972 timber appraisals by the James Sewall Company revealed that the timber in the southern townships was valued at $861,813 while the northern townships had stumpage worth $2,329,000. The Authority maintained that the logging roads that Great Northern would construct at its own expense would have a considerable value to the park later on in accessing timber not included in the swap agreement. Another rationale for the deal—this time from Erwin—was that it would keep logging away from snowmobilers. Wilkins contended that it would also help protect the park from the spruce budworm epidemic beginning to invade the northern townships. (He had to later say he was wrong on that score, because the budworm onslaught wasn't as immediate as he had claimed.)

NRCM and wilderness activists were outraged. Charles FitzGerald joined other opponents in a protest march in Portland, and there were several threats of court action against the park. William Osborn, who was writing a Ralph Nader book on Maine's timber industry, informed the Authority that he would take them to court if they didn't make public the contents of a Sewall Company timber appraisal of T6R9 and T6R10 that Wilkins was withholding from reporters. Wilkins conceded, but would only let the document be viewed at his office.

Governor Curtis, who was unhappy about the timber swap, stepped in to ask the Authority to go slowly because of the cloud over the cutting plans. Overall, however, he agreed with the Authority and the Advisory Committee that it was the best way out of a no-win situation.[2]

In mid-November, amid the turmoil, the Authority voted unanimously to give Great Northern until April 1, 1975, to exercise its cutting rights. Erwin termed it a "good faith effort." The Baxter family stood by the Authority's decision. Wilkins boycotted the signing of the agreement because he had felt "abused" by the attacks against him by opponents.

Still to be determined was the actual cutting plan.

Bob Cummings wrote articles about the timber swap almost every other day in November for the *Portland Press Herald* or *Maine Sunday Telegram*. Austin Wilkins penned a memo to Jim Erwin and Maynard Marsh about an interview with Bob Cummings on the proposed timber swap. "The main thrust of our discussion centered around his thought that the Northern would never have cut the wood in the remaining time and therefore the state would have inherited a gift of wood to the value of $700,000 plus," reported Wilkins. "The line of questioning was lengthy, and we disagreed on several points. I have no idea how he will treat my answers."

After reading the articles, Erwin wrote to Wilkins, "You know now, Austin!"

▲ ▲ ▲ ▲ ▲

Austin Wilkins retired in turmoil as the spraying and timber rights issues became explosive. In a letter to Wilkins, Buzz commended him for his forty years of service to the state. He thanked Wilkins for his advice and assistance over the years:

> I remember well the day that I first met you at the three-day school we had at the Great Northern Hotel in Millinocket during the spring of 1960. I also remember the trip that you and Bill White made up over Katahdin and into Russell Pond during one of the summers I was stationed there as Campground Ranger, and your trips over Katahdin with Governor Curtis and his party. You have always displayed a deep interest in Baxter Park and its operation. I always looked forward to the inspection trips you made to the Park with Governor Baxter, David Priest, and Arthur Rogers. I am grateful that I had the opportunity to meet Governor Baxter on each of these trips during the later years of his life.

Wilkins wrote Dr. John Hakola to see how he was coming on the park history project, but he had an ulterior motive. Wilkins wanted to review Hakola's manuscript before publication, knowing that final approval had to be made by the Authority.

"I would add at this time that I would take a very serious view of any references made by former park supervisor Harry Kearney which may appear in your papers," Wilkins wrote. "This individual has in recent newspapers attempted to discredit the Authority and me personally and I want no part of his quotes in the Baxter Park History. This is not a case of revenge but one of what I consider a proper course of action."

▲ ▲ ▲ ▲ ▲

On the heels of Austin Wilkins's departure, Jim Erwin left office. His last official act in December 1972 was to sign a policy statement that's still in place allowing park staff to sport mustaches and beards in winter but not in the summer.

Erwin's last evaluation of Buzz rated him even higher than eleven months earlier. Buzz was simply "outstanding," according to Erwin. "[He] is doing a remarkable job. He is growing well in his responsibilities. His maturity is improving rapidly. We are completely satisfied with his work and especially pleased with his attitude."

A retirement party for Erwin was held at the Senator Inn in Augusta, and Buzz drove him home to Randolph.

> So I'm driving and he'd give me directions, and Erwin said, "I want to tell you something. You know this incident a few years ago when you were asked to step down?" I said, "Yes." He said something to the effect that "you were young and you had some growing up to do and you had some unfortunate situations. But that wasn't the entire reason that you were asked to step down. The reason you were asked to step down and retained at your same rate of pay—and the reason we created the assistant supervisor's job to give you a promotion—was that Ron Speers was very much interested in getting Harry Kearney out of Division J in Jackman."

Buzz was grateful for the reaffirmation that there was more to his demotion than his past mistakes and lack of experience.

▲ ▲ ▲ ▲ ▲

Republican Jon Lund was elected attorney general, replacing Erwin. Lund went into the job opposed to the park's cutting rights deal. Lee Schepps had recommended to the Authority while Erwin was still a member that he file a suit against Great Northern to stop the cutting in T6R10, and Erwin refused. But Lund gave the go-ahead.

Before the state could file, Charles FitzGerald, David Flanagan, Stuart White, and Richard Smith went to court against the park and Great Northern Nekoosa (parent of Great Northern Paper) on December 27, 1972.

▲ ▲ ▲ ▲ ▲

Buzz was too busy to notice the progress of the environmental movement outside the park—indicative of the long-felt sense of isolation there. However, things were moving in concert toward a greater public consciousness of the natural world and environmental degradation—change that would support what Baxter Park was all about.

In Maine, the Portland Natural History Society morphed into the Maine Audubon Society; the Maine Coast Heritage Trust was founded to protect offshore islands; the Maine Land Use Regulation Commission was created by the legislature to control development impacts in the vast unorganized territory; and the Maine Site Location Law was enacted to regulate major development projects in cities and towns. On the national front, Congress passed the landmark Clean Water Act, the National Environmental Policy Act, and the Endangered Species Act.

Together, the state and private environmental organizations and strong wildlife and anti-pollution laws established a foundation from which to seek solutions to society's increasingly damaging effects.

---

1. *Maine Times,* March 24, 1972, p. 9.
2. *Maine Times,* April 14, 1972, p. 7; November 3, 1972, p. 27; December 8, 1972, pp. 10–11; December 15, 1972, p. 6.

Primary Document Sources: BSPA Boxes 9, 11, 16 (2507-0715, 2507-0716, 2507-0718); BSPA Box 1 (2112-0717); BSPA Original Minutes Box 14.

Conversations and communications: Cathy Caverly, Buzz Caverly, Jan Caverly, Bob Cummings, Ken Curtis, Tom Deans, Barbara Downey, Jim Erwin, Charles FitzGerald, Jon Lund, Phil McGlauflin, Darrell Morrow, Bucky Owen, Bob Proudman.

▲▲▲▲▲▲▲▲

CHAPTER 13

# The Surviving Link with Percy

When Jon Lund and Fred Holt, Jr., joined fish and game commissioner Maynard Marsh on the Authority in January 1973, it was a singular moment. For the first time, no one on the Authority had known Percival Baxter personally. Buzz was now and forevermore the only residing park leader who could assert that special connection. Moreover, Buzz had been told directly by Baxter that he had his confidence.

Tom Chase was the only other park employee at the time who had even met Baxter. The young ranger had shaken hands with Baxter twice after he joined the field crew in 1965, but the two never talked.

Over time, old and new critics of Buzz would object to his using his relationship with Baxter to signify that he knew what was best for the park. However, Buzz was not to be dissuaded from "channeling" the governor. Unquestionably, the relationship carried weight when it came time to make a tough decision. But Buzz didn't simply use the connection for political purposes; he carried a deep emotional belief that he had been chosen by Baxter to defend his vision.

As for Jon Lund, Buzz already knew him as a regular park visitor, and the two had a cordial relationship. As a result of many fishing and camping trips in the 1960s, Lund knew the park's actual terrain better than either of his two Authority colleagues. Lund's recollection of Buzz from those trips is "a very dedicated, sincere, and honest person who was very much devoted to what he saw as his vision of the park."

Buzz was pleased that Lund was not going to be a "drive-through or fly-in" trustee, and hoped to make an alliance with him to further Percival Baxter's goals for the park. Fred Holt was well-known to Buzz, too, but they were not close. Buzz was wary of Holt from past run-ins and disagreements. As deputy forestry commissioner, Holt had a history of overstepping his position into park matters.

Lund was an unusually principled man, conscientious, unpretentious, and Maine's first full-time attorney general. From the beginning, he made it known that he was a strong environmentalist and cared deeply about Baxter Park and its future. While a member of the Maine House of Representatives, Lund wrote Governor Baxter a letter of reassurance in connection with the defeated bill that would have changed the makeup of the Authority to include representatives from Millinocket and Greenville. Lund told Baxter that he didn't want the governor to worry "about things like this. People will keep their eye on [the park]," he promised.

Lund's first environmentally related action was dramatic: he released the controversial public lots report suppressed by GOP rival Jim Erwin.

The public lots were thousand-acre lots set aside by each town for the support of the local schools. Between 1850 and 1870, the state sold the timber and grass rights, and over time the lots were forgotten. During the Curtis years, the issue resurfaced. Some 400,000 acres of forestland were at stake. The governor ordered a study, part of it falling into Jim Erwin's lap.

Erwin appointed Lee Schepps to research the matter. Schepps concluded that the sale of the timber and grass rights was a one-time deal for what was standing at the time and did not apply to future growth. Reporter Bob Cummings was closely following the issue and pressured Erwin for a copy of the report. Erwin refused, releasing only a summary.

There were only two copies of the report—Erwin's and Schepps's. Erwin asked his subordinate to give his up, but Schepps refused. Instead, Schepps gladly turned it over to Jon Lund, who made it public. The forest industry sued the state over ownership of the timber and grass rights, and the state countersued and won. The Department of Conservation then began to swap lands with industry to consolidate the new state "reserved lands" in choice locations.

Buzz got to know Lund better on a cross-country ski trip into Billfish and the Fowler Ponds in the north end of the park, as well as into the townships Great Northern planned to cut. Buzz hadn't done a lot of skiing, and it was noticeable to Lund. "He would walk on the skis like he had his snowshoes on," Lund recalls.

Buzz advised the Authority that cross-country skiing was increasing, and there was no apparent conflict between skiers and snowmobilers. In fact, he was beginning to notice a drop-off in use by sledders. The

*Baxter State Park staff: (L to R) front row: Supervisor Buzz Caverly, ranger Lonnie Pingree; ranger Tom Chase; ranger George Blackburn; assistant supervisor Phil McGlauflin; ranger Bob Howes; second row: ranger Charlie Kenney; ranger Mike Porter, ranger Art York, ranger Barry McArthur; carpenter Gerald Merry; ranger Loren Goode, 1974*

BAXTER STATE PARK PHOTO ARCHIVES

new models of snowmobiles were designed to go faster and faster. To take advantage of the speed capability, snowmobile clubs were grooming trails on other public or private land. Consequently, the ungroomed, slower Baxter Park trails were less enticing.

▲ ▲ ▲ ▲ ▲

The park's most significant issue of 1973—the swap of Great Northern Paper's timber-cutting rights—swirled around Buzz but didn't involve him in his supervisory role. He was busy on other fronts. He made two important management decisions: ending the sale of food and drink at the ranger posts and organizing the park's first (and only) mountain rescue team.

The porch stores had evolved during Helon Taylor's tenure, and many visitors relied on them for items they forgot to pack or ran out of, from bread to soda. Buzz and Jan had fond memories of their store experiences, especially because of their social nature. When campers showed up on the doorstep to make a purchase, the Caverlys often invited them in for a cup of coffee and conversation. But as a manager, Buzz had to deal with the downside. "The litter issue had become a big problem—pop cans, bottles, cigarette butts. It was time to get rid of them." Buzz also thought that some rangers were paying more attention to squeezing money out of the stores than in keeping their campground up to par. Visitors could still purchase park-related books at the ranger's camp, and they could buy groceries and other items from the nearest stores at Nesowadnehunk and Matagamon Lakes.

The growth of winter recreation prompted Buzz to form a resident mountain rescue team. He brought in climbers George Smith and Harold Taylor to train a half dozen rangers to handle search and rescue. At its organizational meeting, ranger Tom Chase was elected to lead the team that included Mike Porter, Lonnie Pingree, Charlie Kenney, Al York, and Chris Drew. The team had already participated in mountain rescue training courses with AMC for several years, so they were a capable group.

Buzz and Jan climbed Katahdin with friends in the winter of 1973—a nine-hour trip and her last time on the peak at snow time. "Pamola was cooperative and kept the sun shining while we were there," Buzz reported.

▲ ▲ ▲ ▲ ▲

Electing fish and wildlife commissioner Maynard Marsh chairman of the Authority was the first item of business on the trustees' agenda for 1972, and then it was on to details of the timber swap. They appointed Gary Morse, a former Chimney Pond ranger who now worked for the Maine Forest Service, to serve as liaison with Great Northern, and assisting him was state game biologist Francis Dunn, who had been involved in the caribou transplant project.

At the time, Morse thought that the compromise plan was one that could mitigate a "heavy hand." Trees to be cut were supposed to be marked to prevent high-grading, and Morse successfully pressured Great Northern to change their road-building policies enough to ensure that the new roads would gently curve and be more scenically pleasing thirty or forty years after the harvest—instead of running in a straight line.

Bad weather forced a delay in Great Northern's cutting operations—only 180 cords of wood had been harvested. It was a fortuitous postponement for the park. Forester Morse reported that Great Northern had done some "very heavy marking" on 240 acres and if the area were cut as planned, "it would be excessive under good forestry practices." In other words, it would be a typical commercial operation.

A rigorous "scientific forestry" standard was supposed to govern cutting in the two northern townships known as the Scientific Forest Management Area (SFMA).The term was used in discussions about Great Northern's harvesting plans, but in fact there was no real definition. Heretofore, no effort had been made by the park to develop the area as Governor Baxter envisioned.

Jon Lund was skeptical of the whole timber swap situation, especially after a disturbing memo from assistant Lee Schepps and viewing the area to be cut in person. Schepps advised Lund that the contract between the park and Great Northern had been changed between the original draft and the signed document. No longer did the Authority have the same controls over harvesting, road-building, and other aspects of the operation that had made it palatable to the trustees. And the agreement didn't meet the scientific forestry standard of the day, Schepps noted.

The Authority—at Lund's behest—informed Great Northern that they couldn't proceed until both parties agreed on practices that could meet the "scientific forestry" principles. However, Lund was compelled to go even further to protect the park. He decided that his office should oppose the whole deal and file suit against the Authority to stop the cutting.

Lund then dropped out of participation on the Authority with regard to the harvesting controversy. Buzz was impressed by Lund's decision: "A lot of people condemned Jon Lund for stepping up as the attorney general and saying, 'Look, this is wrong, it shouldn't be done, and if you, Maynard Marsh, and you, Fred Holt, proceed with this ridiculous idea, you'd better hire a lawyer because I am not going to represent you. I'm going to sue you.' That was what turned it around. I always respected that decision."

In late January, Superior Court Judge Albert Knudsen granted

Attorney General Lund a temporary restraining order halting the harvest, followed by a preliminary injunction and refusal to limit NRCM's issues in the case. A hearing for a permanent injunction was scheduled, and the state and NRCM's suits were joined for the trial. With Lund as a plaintiff, the state had to hire an outside lawyer to represent the park, and Jon Doyle agreed to be counsel.

The judge and the attorneys needed to have a "status meeting" to discuss the issues that would be brought up in the trial, and since Judge Knudsen was holding court in Ellsworth at that time, the lawyers traveled there on a Sunday. The closed bar at a local motel was picked as the meeting place.

NRCM's Clifford Goodall disclosed to the Great Northern attorney and the judge that he planned to put scientific forestry under a microscope to see how the paper company's harvesting plan measured up. He said he would demand that before any cutting occur, a timber inventory be done of T6R10 and T6R9, and that the park develop a master plan that would conform to Governor Baxter's wishes.

The potential for Great Northern and the park to be embarrassed and for cutting to be delayed for years was obvious. The attorneys conferred and decided that an out-of-court settlement seemed like the best way out. Marsh and Holt agreed, settling for far less than the value of the timber contract the Authority had entered into with GNP. Still, some interests felt that any amount was too much and looked like a "payoff."

Park business manager Bill Cross was furious. He thought the payment would bankrupt the park, and the park staff shared that opinion. Why not just let Great Northern take the wood because the park would recover, as had happened before? The deal was a defining moment for FitzGerald. "I realized I couldn't trust the Authority because they were political appointees and were willing to participate in a payoff," he remembers. "I thought it was a sham. It was a shock to me that this was how things worked, but it was so transparent."

Governor Curtis rationalized that the monetary settlement was the best solution, and the check was handed over to Great Northern on March 12. The funds were taken from the park's invested income account, leaving it with just over $100,000. The logging road was closed in T6R10, and the small amount of wood that had been harvested was sold by the park to GNP. With that, all commercial harvesting rights in the park were extinguished for good.

▲ ▲ ▲ ▲ ▲

While the cutting rights issue was still hot, Jon Lund volunteered to make an appearance before the Millinocket Chamber of Commerce near the end of April 1973. Members of the Fin and Feather Club were present and challenged him on a variety of issues, from snowmobiling to a new warehouse for the park. In retrospect, Lund thinks it was a foolish appearance because he had "irritated all kinds of people in Millinocket" with his suit against Great Northern:

> I cannot remember any situation where I had gone to speak to people where I had seen greater overt hostility and lack of warmth . . . from the minute I got there. No one thanked me for coming. I felt very uncomfortable and came to realize that people in Millinocket saw Baxter Park as their backyard and were unwilling to recognize that there were other interests. Their interests were in maximizing day-use facilities, and easy access to where they wanted to go. Bud Leavitt wrote a very unflattering description of my presence at that meeting, although he wasn't in attendance.

In his April 30 "Outdoors" column, Leavitt, a member of the Advisory Committee, described Lund's appearance as "cold and stiff." Lund's statement that construction of the planned $350,000 headquarters, vehicle maintenance facility, and warehouse would be postponed due to the cost of buying Great Northern's cutting rights "are rattling bitterly around the Magic City business community," Leavitt went on. The facility would have solved "a thousand and one problems related to managing" the park and had met the standards of the previous Authority and the Advisory Council, he said. "The word circulating around Millinocket is that Lund's nose got bent out of shape in the Baxter vs. Great Northern hassle and he has chosen to call off construction as a back-of-the-hand swipe at GNP and Millinocket."

Lund says that newly elected Governor James Longley's new building moratorium in the face of state budget problems forced the delay of park headquarters, not some retaliatory act connected to the Great Northern payment.

▲ ▲ ▲ ▲ ▲

While Buzz was not always involved in the park's defining issues and events, those matters had lingering effects into the future that he would have to face. One example is the Advisory Committee: Buzz had no role in the politics around its formation but would eventually find it a major ally in his management objectives.

The Advisory's role in park affairs up to now had been limited. Since its formation at the start of 1971, some members' attendance at Authority meetings had been spotty. No one from the Advisory attended the first eight meetings of the Authority in 1973, apparently due to the fact that the group hadn't been notified that the trustees were meeting.

Advisory member Walter Birt had complained to Austin Wilkins in mid-1971 that the committee wasn't being invited to Authority meetings, which discouraged the membership. On March 26, 1973, John Baxter raised the issue again, asking Maynard Marsh why the Advisory Committee hadn't heard from the Authority for so long. Was the Authority going to let the committee "wither away?" he asked. "You know from experience what an exceptionally dedicated and useful committee it has been . . . I strongly believe that the discontinuance of the committee . . . would be a bad mistake, one which would hurt the future of the park."

Jon Lund, however, thought the Advisory Committee was unnecessary and was miffed at their wholehearted support of the timber exchange with Great Northern and then the cutting rights buyout. Buzz wasn't privy to the Authority's discussion about the Advisory, sensing that the trustees wanted to keep the issue close to the chest.

Bud Leavitt defended the Advisory as people with "capable and trusted talents" who had provided "dedication and keen enthusiasm." The council provided a way for the public to communicate with the Authority, Leavitt said, and Millinocket people remembered "when there was virtually no way" to talk directly with the trustees.

Lund came around to supporting a smaller, reconstituted committee. On April 27, on a motion by Lund, the Authority appointed seven people to the Advisory (four of them holdovers) to serve for a year and to meet at least once a year. Again, their attendance at Authority meetings was sporadic.

A special seat was reserved on the committee for the superintendent of Maine's Acadia National Park. No record exists of who instigated the appointment, but it likely was the Authority. The idea was that the Acadia leader would be an asset because the two parks dealt with similar issues, from increasing visitor pressures to trail abuse.

▲ ▲ ▲ ▲ ▲

On the heels of the public uproar over the timber swap and the 1972 roadside spraying, the Authority planned another 2,4,5-t brush-spraying project. This time, the trustees kept the spraying quiet, and Buzz didn't blow the whistle on them. In fact, he wanted the brush and stumps killed off for safety reasons.

The public didn't find out about the project until June, about a month after the spraying was all done, and earlier spraying opponents held their fire. Jim Erwin defended the secrecy, owning up to his resentment of "the fact that the newspapers and the politicians jumped all over me and Austin when [spraying was proposed] in openness and honesty," but they didn't react to the clandestine project.

Phil McGlauflin was in charge of the operation that began at Nesowadnehunk Field and reached the foot of Abol Hill. His crew used twenty gallons of 2,4,5-t and achieved about an 80 percent kill. Some passers-by questioned the crew, but McGlauflin reported "as yet no drastic criticism."

▲ ▲ ▲ ▲ ▲

During the summer of 1973, five-year-old Tammy Caverly almost stepped on a bear at Katahdin Stream, and the outcome was unfortunate for the bear.

Ranger George Blackburn had been complaining to Buzz about the bear, telling how it was hanging around the Katahdin Stream Campground and had walked into one camper's site and taken food from the frying pan. He wanted to kill it but Buzz told him not to be too quick to pull the trigger. Sometimes bears just wandered off if left alone, Buzz advised, and they should be patient.

A few days later, Buzz was traveling through the park to pick up cash receipts at the campgrounds and had his family with him. At Katahdin Stream, he went into the office to see Blackburn, and Tammy went to the outhouse. Suddenly, he heard her screaming, "Bear, bear,

bear!" Buzz rushed out to find Tammy in tears, and Jan was upset. "I told George, 'Shoot that bear,'" says Buzz, "and we got in the car and left."

Blackburn shot it, and Buzz found out later that the bear hadn't done anything. The animal was simply lying down by the outhouse, and Tammy didn't see him until they were almost face to face. Blackburn spread the story that the park supervisor wouldn't let him shoot bears until they scared his daughters.

▲ ▲ ▲ ▲ ▲

Because he was supervisor, Buzz was on call night and day when he wasn't officially on duty. If he received a phone call in the middle of the night, it was usually due to an accident on Katahdin or a missing hiker. His home phone number in Millinocket was readily available through Information, and before the number was changed in 1973, he and Jan were sometimes awakened by people wanting to make camping reservations or ask about the weather. After the number was unlisted, they could go to sleep knowing that when the phone woke them out of their dreams, it wasn't likely to be someone asking, "Sir, could you tell me if it will be sunny on Katahdin tomorrow?"

▲ ▲ ▲ ▲ ▲

Hikers experienced the usual fatigue episodes and minor accidents while climbing Katahdin, and often disregarded good planning. One district ranger had to tramp up the same trail on the mountain four nights in a row to help bring people down after dark who didn't have flashlights and/or were simply scared.

Writer Aime Gauvin was on the Chimney Pond Trail at Basin Ponds when he had a heart attack and had to be evacuated by rangers. Buzz and the rangers were gathered at a district meeting at the Martin camp in the north end of the park when the call came in that Gauvin needed to be rescued.

"Eight rangers tore out of the driveway in different vehicles and made an emergency run," Buzz remembers. "They had their sirens and blue lights on and sped out of the park to Patten, down to Millinocket, and back up into the park at Togue Pond. They grabbed a litter at Roaring Brook and hiked to Basin Ponds. When they got up there, he was still alive. They treated him, warmed him up, put him on a stretcher, and lugged him down to a vehicle for the hospital."

Gauvin recovered enough within a month to attend an Authority meeting, where he publicly criticized various rangers who had helped save his life. "One of the rangers said to me in jest, the next time we have a meeting and a call comes in to rescue [Gauvin], let's not interrupt it," Buzz recalls.

▲ ▲ ▲ ▲ ▲

In the 1960s AT thru-hikers who made it to Baxter Park were few and far between. Only thirty-seven made it the whole way to Katahdin during the decade, and that low number didn't pose problems. The ATers trudged into the park without accommodations and stayed at Katahdin Stream before their final push to Baxter Peak. Some of them took their dogs, despite the no-pet ban of 1962.

In the 1970s the thru-hiker traffic increased—especially groups—to the point that there wasn't enough room to squeeze them in unannounced at Katahdin Stream. At Buzz's urging, the Authority diverted the long-distance hikers to Daicey Pond Campground. Two lean-tos were placed in the field away from the cabins and designated for thru-hikers at no cost. More capacity was added as use of the AT exploded, but some thru-hikers still camped illegally in the park.

In 1973 eighty-nine thru-hikers completed the route, and a social divide had developed between the thru-hikers and Daicey cabin patrons. The thru-hikers were a disheveled sort. They arrived dirty, skinny-dipped in Daicey Pond, and monopolized the dock. Then they hung their wet sleeping bags and clothes on the rafters of the quaint library (to the consternation of other users) and peeked into cabin windows.

▲ ▲ ▲ ▲ ▲

Drug use in the park just wouldn't go away. Hundreds of users at pot parties were nabbed by rangers during the summer—some of the park officers actually dressed in long-haired wigs and torn jeans to mingle among the hippies. With Buzz's approval, rangers and sheriffs' deputies spied on campers at night, springing from behind trees and bushes and yelling to the surprised culprits to "drop that roach."

Park ranger Hal Wilkins (no relation to Austin Wilkins) embarrassed Buzz and the Authority by telling the *Maine Times* that some rangers "got off" on law enforcement because it was more exciting than pulling speeders on park roads.[1] Buzz was mad that the prevalence of drugs was driving out individuals and families who visited the park for a wilderness experience, not to encounter the "illegal [and] immoral" use of drugs.

The Authority differed with Buzz's gung-ho attention to the drug issue—concerned with how much of the rangers' time and effort should be spent catching and prosecuting violations. Jon Lund felt that only warnings should be issued and that persons caught with drugs should be asked to leave the park. Lund's position would prevail, downplaying Buzz's preferred emphasis on the problem. Although drug use was already illegal under Maine law, Buzz saw to it that the prohibition was added to the park rules effective in 1974.

Besides marijuana, day use was an unrelenting headache for Buzz. He didn't understand why most visitors wanted to put up with the congestion at Katahdin when the north end of the park had such wonderful attractions, such as the Freezeout Trail and the Traveler Mountain range.

In the two weeks before the park closed on October 15, there were almost 10,000 visitors. The high use generated plenty of complaints that went to Buzz: too few visitor facilities, too many non-Mainers, no telephones, and hiking restrictions in bad weather. Most of the dissatisfaction came from people who wanted "to run at-large and were not allowed to throw their weight around," Buzz reported.

▲ ▲ ▲ ▲ ▲

Buzz was happily self-assured in the acting supervisor's job, although he knew the time was drawing near when a new chief would be on the scene, and he would be someone's sergeant again.

The Authority explained to Buzz that the director was going to focus on development of a long-term park management plan and oversee policy matters. The supervisor's position was being retained, and he would continue to run everyday operations. The new man wouldn't step on Buzz's toes, the trustees promised.

Since Buzz had no planning credentials and believed his job responsibilities would not change, he didn't apply for the director's job. Not yet. The national search for a director in 1974 resulted in seventy applicants. Out of those, the Authority interviewed four: national wildlife refuge manager Arthur "Lee" Tibbs from Branchville, New Jersey; former Baxter Park ranger Ed Werler of Saco; state parks planner Tom Cieslinski of Augusta; and Fred Bartlett, facilities manager for the state Bureau of Public Lands of Augusta.

Tibbs, thirty-four, was tapped for the director's post. Ironically, he wasn't a trained planner but rather a scientist; his planning capability was experience-based. Tibbs had a forestry degree from West Virginia University at Morgantown and a master of science degree in wildlife management from Pennsylvania State. He had worked for the U.S. Fish and Wildlife Service, in management jobs at a number of national wildlife refuges on the East and West Coasts, including Moosehorn National Wildlife Refuge (NWR) in Washington County, Maine. His federal jobs had given him hands-on training in planning, such as revising refuge management projects and strategies.

Tibbs was aware that he would be at a disadvantage in relation to Buzz because he hadn't known Percival Baxter and was unfamiliar with the park. Moreover, Tibbs was sensitive to the fact that Buzz had been head of the park twice and that Buzz might find it difficult going from first to second in command.

Tibbs didn't start his new job for several months, so that he and his family would have time to relocate. Meanwhile, Buzz continued to run the park, with little time to contemplate the personal implications of Tibbs's hiring. As events had already proved, Buzz was a survivor, and he continued to score management successes, such as augmenting safety and search-and-rescue procedures and regulations.

▲ ▲ ▲ ▲ ▲

Before Tibbs's appointment, however, 1974 had already started off ominously for Buzz. A climbing disaster struck on February 1 that was a defining accident for Buzz and Baxter Park. The situation involved six present and past employees of the AMC. The most inexperienced climber died, and the others sustained varying degrees of frostbite.

Buzz's attitude about search and rescue since Ralph Heath's death was to provide all the assistance necessary but not put his rangers in undue danger. He had to depend on winter users to take care of themselves in most situations, and it was from that perspective that he dealt with what became known in park annals as "the Keddy accident."

Bob Proudman, Paul DiBello, Tom Keddy, Page Dinsmore, Doug George, and Mike Cohen had left Chimney Pond to ascend two different gullies on the side of Pamola, with three climbers on each team. Three of the six were current AMC staff —Proudman (AMC's trails supervisor), DiBello (a mechanic at the Pinkham Notch headquarters), and Keddy (a member of the Pinkham crew).

Proudman and DiBello were already familiar with Katahdin, having made first ascents on the mountain in the winter of 1973 and as recently as January 1974. They had planned to take other experienced climbers on the February expedition. But when some of the men they invited couldn't make it, they asked Keddy and Dinsmore.

The weather was relatively warm but unsettled with some rain. The morning the team left camp, the sky was a foreboding red. They figured they had twelve to eighteen hours before severe changes occurred, and were confident they could do the climb and return safely. Not anticipating a night out, they carried no gear for a bivouac. DiBello left behind his big down parka in favor of a lighter polyester jacket.

Proudman led the first team, which included Cohen and George. They lost sight of the second team about midday and stopped for lunch in early afternoon. The second team, with DiBello in the lead, encountered unexpected difficulties and didn't stop to eat. By late afternoon they were fatigued, and Keddy was aware he was in over his head.

The two teams finally made verbal contact at nightfall. DiBello asked Proudman to wait for his climbers since they had only one headlight. So Proudman remained where he was on a narrow ledge, and George and Cohen were below him—all secured with pitons and ropes.

A few hours later, as the two teams were about to converge, a storm of fierce winds and heavy snow engulfed the climbers, but everyone managed to reach Proudman on the stony, precarious perch. The men who hadn't eaten were either very tired or near exhaustion. They all tried to eat some food and put on extra clothing in wind gusts of up to a hundred miles an hour that sent windchill temperatures plunging to killer levels. The party spent the night doing isometric exercises, singing, and yelling "Endure!" to keep their spirits up. Dinsmore's face became white from frostbite, and he told his friends he was freezing to death. Keddy hardly moved or spoke.

At daylight, the winds were still roaring, and the climbers' clothes had frozen solid. They couldn't manipulate buttons, snaps, or ropes.

DiBello could no longer stand and had to be held up. Keddy fell over the cliff side twice and was pulled back up. Dinsmore climbed up the cliff and into the fog to try to save himself.

Proudman and Cohen, unable to free all their frozen, tangled ropes, decided that Proudman would take their one free rope and go for help, while Cohen stayed behind to work on untangling the remaining gear. Proudman caught up with Dinsmore, and they descended together. They reached the Chimney Pond trail just below Basin Ponds in mid afternoon of February 2.

As they headed toward Roaring Brook, they found ranger Art York's snowmobile about a half mile from the Chimney Pond campground. Proudman sent Dinsmore on down toward Roaring Brook while he turned back up the trail to find York. Meanwhile, DiBello, Cohen, and George decided that they, too, had to evacuate themselves, even though Keddy wasn't able to go.

York had tried to sound the alarm that the climbers were missing the night of February 1, but, unable to raise anyone at the Millinocket office, he didn't reach Buzz with the news until the next morning. Buzz wasn't overly worried because the group was well-equipped, knowledgeable, and had mentioned to him that they might spend a night on the mountain, possibly going over the summit down to the Davis Pond lean-to in the northwest basin.

"I didn't think we were looking at a tragedy, not at that point," he recalls. But prudence led him to Loren Goode's Millinocket apartment to see if Goode knew more about the climbers' plans. Goode had talked to the party at Chimney Pond before going off duty and agreed with Buzz that they shouldn't be concerned yet. Buzz decided to give the men until about midday to show up before he organized a search-and-rescue mission.

Before 1:00 P.M., York called Buzz for help. By this time, Doug George had just reached Chimney Pond and was in serious condition, and Buzz knew he had a grave situation happening. Buzz couldn't find all of the park's mountain rescue team and turned to the warden service for assistance. He also called George Smith's central Maine climbing group and the AMC in New Hampshire. In the early afternoon, Buzz received a call from Dinsmore, who had reached Roaring Brook, saying he was in rough shape and needed help, too.

For the first time in the park's history, the National Guard's 112th Unit in Bangor was called. Buzz directed the Guard to pick up

Dinsmore in a helicopter, deliver him to the Millinocket hospital, and return to Chimney Pond to pick up other survivors. Buzz was on hand at the hospital to help lug the climbers from the helicopter to the emergency room.

DiBello miraculously made it down the steep Dudley Trail to Chimney Pond about 6:30 P.M. Descending in the dark, he had lost the trail at one point and fell off a sixty-foot cliff into snow and trees, scratching his eyes with tree limbs. Snow-blind, he somehow went the right way, bumped into a building at Chimney Pond, and fumbled his way to the ranger station. He was in critical condition and was pretty sure that Keddy was dead.

Warden Eric Wight and former park ranger Danny Watson, now a warden with fish and game, were part of the twenty-five-man search-and-rescue crew. The Guard tried to get three of them into Chimney Pond the afternoon of February 1, but the winds were too strong. The pilot, fighting fifty-knot winds, put them out at Avalanche Field, more than five miles from Chimney Pond.

Wight and his buddies had to jump out of the chopper a good distance from the ground. "It was just at the edge of dark," he said. "The wind shrieked and moaned in the hardwoods. We had to hang onto each other and walk backwards just to make headway." It took them until 7:00 P.M. to reach Chimney Pond.

Wight was stunned by DiBello's appearance. "His eyes were frozen shut," Wight said. "We took his boots off, and his feet were frozen solid. His feet and toes were like sausages, with ice between them." The rescuers took DiBello on a litter to a snowsled ambulance at Roaring Brook, where he was taken out of the park to the hospital.

AMC director Tom Deans arrived on the scene that night. "I was very upset," he said. "They were our people. I had worked closely with them . . . been on many rescues with them. Buzz and the staff at the park were incredibly helpful and concerned."

On the morning of February 2, rescuers climbed Katahdin to locate Keddy, but the weather was still too brutal to remove his body without risking the lives of others. The team secured the body to the ledge, and Buzz pulled everyone out of Chimney Pond to rest and wait for better conditions.

On February 5 the body recovery was completed without problems. Buzz oversaw the operation from Chimney Pond, and by early evening all the crews were safely down to Togue Pond and a hot meal. Buzz tallied up the rescue cost. The total came to a record $984, including four helicopter trips, fifty gallons of gas for snowmobiles, and motel and food expenses.

George Hamilton, who wrote an article about the accident for *Appalachia* magazine, called the rescue effort by Buzz "worthy of commendation" because of the swift response.[2] He concluded that the tragedy was preventable. The climbers made mistakes, Hamilton said, when the group went ahead without enough weather information; didn't leave base camp early enough; took along a climber of Keddy's limited experience; and didn't carry emergency gear.

Rangers and climbers offered numerous recommendations to the Authority on how to prevent future accidents: a sign-out sheet so rangers would know where climbers were and when they expected to return; a requirement that climbers carry radios to communicate any problems; and assignment of a technical climber to Chimney Pond for quicker reaction to accidents.

Buzz also made two proposals. First, climbers should be required to camp overnight at Chimney Pond. "If these people had been required to camp at Chimney Pond," he said, "we might not have prevented them from getting caught on the mountain, but we would have known about fifteen hours earlier that they were in trouble and could have had rescue teams . . . organized and ready to go at the first moment the bad weather broke." Buzz's proposed rule would eliminate the possibility of confusion as to whether the party was intentionally camped on the mountain or in trouble.

The second recommendation was for the park to have a direct line to the Air National Guard official in charge of dispatching a helicopter. From the time Buzz called for help, there was a forty-five-minute delay before red tape was cleared and approval given for the chopper. Time is critical in search-and-rescue missions, Buzz emphasized, and forty-five minutes can make the difference between light and darkness, a change in the wind, or life and death.

The Authority accepted Buzz's recommendations.

▲ ▲ ▲ ▲ ▲

After the Keddy tragedy, there was another death in the park that required an extensive search during the July 4 holiday—the largest since Ralph Heath's death. Eighty-six-year-old Augustus Aldrich was determined to climb Katahdin, despite foggy and rainy conditions. He ascended the mountain alone and then disappeared.

Underscoring the importance of the park's search and rescue mission, Authority chairman Maynard Marsh showed up to support Buzz in any way he could, such as providing fish and wildlife personnel help. "He wasn't looking to do any Monday-morning quarterbacking," Buzz recollects. "His message was 'whatever you need from me, I'll give.'"

When there was no sign of Aldrich by the second day, Buzz called in more volunteers, as well as air support and a search dog. Buzz and game warden Leonard Ritchie rode in an Air National Guard helicopter, rising in stair-step fashion up the head-wall of Katahdin to see if Aldrich was stranded on a ledge. It was a hair-raising experience, Buzz recalls, and was for naught because there was no sign of the lost man.

Buzz was on duty virtually twenty-four hours a day for a week while the search went on, coordinating field crews and support services and working late at night on routine business matters he didn't have time for during the day.

Aldrich's nephew, Hollister Kent, arrived to help but died of a heart attack en route to the search. Search parties looked for Aldrich for a week without success, and his body was never found.

The Aldrich death forced a greater realization by the park staff that there were going to be all kinds of fatalities as more and more people visited the park. Up to this point, it's fair to say that the park had been just plain lucky that less than two dozen people had died in the park (not counting victims of airplane crashes). Only four had died on Katahdin before Aldrich. Some park employees favored closing Katahdin to hiking as a safety measure. But that seemed too extreme to most, especially since so many more people died in other ways, such as highway accidents.

▲ ▲ ▲ ▲ ▲

Buzz was not one to talk about his personal party politics. But when former trustee Jim Erwin became a Republican candidate for governor for the second time in 1974, he let Erwin know he was cheering for him. "Janice and I are behind you all the way and wish you the best of luck," Buzz wrote. "We are confident that you are not only going to be Maine's next governor, but you are going to be one of the best governors this state has ever had."

Erwin still visited the park frequently for fishing, as did former trustee Jon Lund. Lund generally went unguided into the backcountry, while Erwin preferred the company of Buzz or a ranger. Once Buzz took Erwin into Widden Pond, a long enough hike to have time to talk to Erwin about park affairs. When they arrived at the pond, the dam was out, and the water was little more than a mud puddle. "Jim looked at me and said, 'You're a hell of a good supervisor, but I wouldn't hire you as a guide!'"

Erwin's longtime rival, Democratic Governor Ken Curtis loved the park as Erwin did and in the summer visited with his friend, Vermont Governor Thomas Salmon. It was always a big deal for the park to host a governor, and Buzz's job was lead guide.

The governors had fishing on their minds, and Buzz took Curtis and Salmon to Wassataquoik Lake and Six Ponds. He felt comfortable, mischievous, and in control enough to subject them to his infamous canoe gunnelling. He didn't tip the governors over but came so close that Authority chairman Maynard Marsh lectured him later. "Maynard was bent out of shape," says Buzz. "He shut the office door and said, 'What the hell did you think you were doing? If you upset the canoe with two governors in it. . . !' I asked him if he didn't have more confidence than that in me. I surely had confidence in my ability to gunnel."

▲ ▲ ▲ ▲ ▲

One of the park's chronic problems was the road network—the most important physical "structure," and one that took a lot of Buzz's time and attention. In his early ranger years, he had helped scrape, plow, and level it; fill and refill potholes; shovel sand and gravel; and listen to visitors' endless complaints about it. As supervisor, he still pitched in at times to work on the road, but mostly oversaw the maintenance by state highway employees.

The struggle between Buzz and the road graders was a small war, with each side determined to have its way. Buzz's primary interest was keeping the roads, especially the Tote Road, narrow and in keeping with Percival Baxter's vision of wilderness character. The graders had their own ways of doing things, and, if their way was to clear too much roadside brush in the name of safety, so be it.

The 1950s had been punctuated with clashes between Percival Baxter and the highway commission over excessive maintenance and the creation of unsightly gravel pits. Disputes increased as the park grew and there was more need for maintenance. Grader operators lived in the park in the summers, and, in time, came to be considered part of the park family.

Gene Crosby, hired in 1974, was the longest-term grader, and he and Buzz came to know each other pretty well and had to find middle ground. The two got off to a rocky start, though. Buzz found Crosby sitting in his pickup in the north end of the park on July 4 drinking beer. Crosby had thrown his bottle out the window, and Buzz told him in no uncertain terms that he wouldn't stand for such conduct. The only reason Buzz decided not to give Crosby a summons was that they had to work together.

Crosby's feisty reputation had preceded him. Bald, short, and unkempt, he was also gruff, with an opinionated way of doing things. Among sportsmen, he was something of a hero because he had stood up to a black bear near Burnt Mountain. The animal had crawled up in the back of Crosby's new pickup, and Crosby had picked up a board and slapped the bear on the rear end. The bruin ran off, and the incident became a favorite tale among rangers and woodsmen.

Crosby irritated Buzz because he used a larger grader that widened the roads even more than his predecessors had. If a tree, a tree stump, or brush was growing in closer to the road than Crosby felt it should be, he eliminated it as a hazard to vehicles. He and Buzz had sharp words plenty of times over grading.

But Crosby was a man after Buzz's own heart in that he would hand-pick rocks out of windrows graded into the middle of the road, thus sparing travelers a punctured tire or dents from flying projectiles. Buzz also thought a lot of Crosby and his wife, Diane, because they had a close marriage. The Crosbys rode together in the grader, Diane putting out the "road repair" warning signs. While waiting for her husband, Diane Crosby would pick berries in the woods or read a book in the cab. She put on bean feeds for park crew and visiting highway officials.

Buzz tried to talk highway officials into buying a smaller grader to lessen the maintenance impacts in the park. But they weren't interested, believing that less-powerful equipment would not have enough power to get up Abol Hill or Windey Pitch and would be unable to cut out potholes effectively.

Road politics was hardly a subject of interest to visitors. But to

Buzz, it was a never-ending source of irritation and obsession. Besides the potential for the big grader to create a "highway" in the preserve, the need for in-park gravel pits grated on him. He had been successful in 1970 in getting the highway officials to allow the park supervisor to approve the location of a pit, the building of a road to the pit, and the restoration of the area.

Buzz made the case against using calcium chloride to keep down dust. He and Harry Kearney had agreed that the chemical should be banned in the park because it polluted streams and endangered wildlife. But neither Buzz nor Kearney prevailed while the highway agency maintained the roads. Even after the park took control of the roads, calcium chloride was used to keep dust down around certain high-traffic areas, such as gatehouses.

▲ ▲ ▲ ▲ ▲

The name of the primary park road, the Tote Road, was changed to the Perimeter Road in 1974. There is no record of how it came about. Buzz thought it was a decision made by the highway commission. Perhaps the commission thought that "perimeter" more clearly described the road to the public because it ran along the southwestern and western boundary and then easterly in the north end and out of the park. The name would stand for twenty years until Buzz ordered the old Tote Road name reinstated. He thought the Tote Road better described what the road was realistically and hopefully would encourage drivers to go slower.

▲ ▲ ▲ ▲ ▲

Daniel Doan, author of *Fifty Hikes in the White Mountains,* and Claude "Huck" Sharps, a veterinarian, paid a return visit to the park for the first time since 1931—the year that Governor Baxter made his first purchase of the Katahdin township. Both seventeen years old on their maiden hike, the two boys had climbed the mountain via the Hunt Trail—after walking in ten miles from the end of the auto road beyond Ripogenus Dam.

On that sunny day in 1974, they sat at a Katahdin Stream picnic table eating breakfast and reminiscing about the changes that were obvious since 1931—so many more campers and the noise of pulp

*Boy Scout dinner, Stoughton, Massachusetts: (L to R) Debbie Guertin,*
*Frank Guertin, Emily Guertin, Baxter State Park carpenter Gerald Merry,*
*Jan Caverly, Baxter State Park supervisor Buzz Caverly, 1974*

F. E. MAIOLI PHOTO, BAXTER STATE PARK PHOTO ARCHIVES

trucks roaring over the West Branch's Abol Bridge.

Their 1931 arrival had required two days' journey in a Model T
Ford to cover the 320 miles from Orford, New Hampshire, hauling
tent, ponchos, tarp, cook kit, knapsacks, canned beans, corned beef, and
other groceries, spare tires, tubes, tools, and motor oil. They had followed the gravel road from Greenville that led to a slope of muddy cor-
duroy logs that narrowed into a woods path.

The boys saw plenty of partridge, rabbits, a bald eagle, and a deer
along the way. They stopped at a cluster of log cabins and shacks used
by guides and their trout fishermen and stayed for the night, shivering
in thin blankets but happy for the respite from blackflies. The next
morning, they took off for Katahdin, stashed their packs at the start of
the Hunt Trail and made a "flying afternoon climb and descent,
equipped with [only] chocolate bars." They didn't see anyone else that
day.

The 1974 venture was quite different. On this trip, they had to
pass through a gate and pay a two-dollar fee, and then obey twenty-

five park rules, one forbidding hikers to start up the Abol Trail after 11:00 A.M. The Perimeter Road enabled them to drive all the way to their campsite at Abol Campground. They had to register to climb the mountain and identify which trail they were using and the time they departed (and arrived back).

On the hike, they wore packs loaded with gear, food, and water to survive an unexpected bivouac above tree line. For old time's sake, Sharps carried his Sears, Roebuck canvas knapsack that had cost four dollars in golf-caddying money in 1928. At the top, the weather was perfect, and they lunched on beef jerky, hardtack, dates, and water. One bearded young hiker offered his butterscotch—the only item he carried. "With mixed feelings, I realized that forty-three years hadn't changed youth from being foolish and confident enough to attack Katahdin with pocket candy," Sharps said.

Along the trail, they passed a line of uniformed camp girls, people with long and short hair, people in shorts and t-shirts, dungarees, sneakers, some carrying nothing, some with heavy frame packs and bags. On Baxter Peak, they counted twenty-five people taking photographs, eating lunch, attending to foot blisters, and lounging on the rocks. "It was a parade," Sharps observed.

▲▲▲▲▲

In the wake of the cutting rights settlement with Great Northern Paper, the Authority initiated steps to harvest timber in the SFMA. An estimated 10,000 cords of wood were available for cutting annually in the 29,584-acre area. Authority records indicate the trustees were more interested in the forest as a potential source of new income for the park than in experimenting with scientific forestry—shortsightedness that would come back to haunt future trustees.

One of Buzz's responsibilities was to make sure the park boundary was secure and to keep tabs on harvesting incursions, poaching, illegal entry, and garbage dumping. In the fall of 1974, Chris Drew ran the western border and discovered that the boundary line of the sanctuary actually cut across the Camp Phoenix land and took in some of the buildings. He also found a dump the camp had created on park land and learned that George Emerson's clients were hunting in the part of the field owned by the park. "They were sticking apples under the apple trees that had already shed," remembers Drew, explaining that the practice was designed to attract deer to shoot.

Buzz and the Authority already knew about the boundary problems because they were long-standing. Buzz and Emerson had clashed
for years over Emerson's illegal use of park land for dumps. But
Emerson was influential with Austin Wilkins and thus had delayed resolution of his problems.

The Camp Phoenix incursion wasn't the only one from bordering
commercial operations. There were trespassing violations caused by
Emerson's Matagamon Wilderness campground at the north end of the
park and from his camps at Nesowadnehunk Lake and Thissell Pond.
And Joe Bartlett's clients at Togue Pond used park land as a toilet
because the outhouse facilities at the sporting camp were so awful.

Bootleg trails were forever cropping up from private lands into the
park. Emerson had a trail cut from Camp Phoenix across park property
to Little Nesowadnehunk Lake and painted blazes on the trees. He put
the trail on a map he sent out to clients. At Matagamon Lake, Don
Dudley put a trail from his place to Middle Fowler Pond, Billfish, and
Frost Ponds for use by his campground guests. Bowlin Camps on the
East Branch of the Penobscot River maintained a cabin within fifty feet
of the park boundary and cut a trail to Traveler Pond for fishing clients.
Bush pilots brought in fishermen, who, by bypassing the gates, were
able to avoid registering and paying for campsites.

The difficulties with neighbors respecting the park boundaries
went back to the days before the park was created. Sporting camps had
mutually agreed upon land lease arrangements with private landowners and "rights" for their clientele to recreate on outlying grounds.
When townships were acquired by Baxter for the park, the change was
a hard pill to swallow for sporting camps suddenly inside the park or on
the border. The park established rules that forced the businesses to
operate somewhat differently and in keeping with protecting wildlife
and other natural resources.

The sporting camp owners' sense of "territoriality" and protection
of their livelihood was triggered, and conflicts with the park began—
many of them involving Buzz when he was a ranger, supervisor, and
director. "Wherever there were sporting camps, there were issues until
those ownerships were phased out," Buzz says.

▲ ▲ ▲ ▲ ▲

On November 21, a near catastrophe landed in Buzz's lap. A monster wind- and snowstorm battered the park, leveling 3,000 acres of trees from Rum Mountain southwest to Daicey and Kidney Ponds and the park's border.

The gatekeepers at Telos were marooned for two days before Bangor Hydro sent in a skidder to fetch them and the dam keeper. The three-foot snow depth forced the skidder to go so slow that it ran out of fuel, and the evacuees had to trudge five hours to reach safety. Two rangers were trapped at Nesowadnehunk Field and Abol, and hunters' vehicles were buried at Avalanche Field and their owners marooned at Katahdin Lake Camps. It took three days of cutting blowdown and plowing roads to get everyone out.

Ranger Bob Howes was cleaning up his camp, getting ready to move to Togue Pond for the winter, when he heard the radio report about a wet snowstorm on its way. En route to Togue Pond from Katahdin Stream Campground, Warren Nelson called Howes to tell him trees were coming down all over the place. "It looked like a tornado was striking," says Nelson.

When Howes got up the next morning and went out to get his personal truck out of the garage to drive to Togue Pond, he couldn't help but notice that the winds were picking up. Howes thought he'd better take his chain saw with him in case there was a tree on the tote road. The first blowdown was actually so close to camp that he hardly got beyond sight of the cabin when he had to start cutting in winds up to 100 miles an hour.

Because the winds weren't as high in Millinocket, no one at park headquarters knew how severe conditions were until Howes reached Buzz by radio. He told Buzz he was stranded and to come get him. By now the garage at the campground was shaking, the doors blew off, and two lean-tos had blown over onto their roofs. Howes nailed the doors back on the garage and went to bed exhausted.

The next day, there was heavy, wet snow covering everything. Roads and trails were obliterated by the fallen trees. It took six crewmen to cut through the blowdown from the southern entrance to reach Howes. The blowdown was piled so high that Howes said it looked like a teepee over the road when he was able to drive his truck out through it. Buzz's reaction to the impact was "unbelievable." Surprisingly, there was little damage to buildings at Abol and Katahdin Stream Campgrounds.

It took time for everyone to grasp the extent of the blowdown. Irvin Caverly, Sr., then district ranger for the Department of Conservation, flew over the area on December 12. "If this could be observed and publicized as many storms are in populated areas, it would be declared a natural disaster," Caverly Sr. reported.

Some 100,000 cords of wood were on the ground. From below Ledge Falls through Abol, the trees were all uprooted and laid in the same direction. In places, the blowdown was ten feet high. To find out what the damage was at Daicey and Kidney Ponds, Chris Drew thought he could walk through the blowdown to the camps. But he had to crawl—literally—to get over the downed trees. He met a deer crawling toward him. The surprised deer went one way and Drew went the other.

Buzz was in a panic about the AT. He assumed the blowdowns were bad enough to force a closing of the trail, and imagined a controversy on his hands when thru-hikers started arriving in the summer. But a survey of the situation by a MATC trail group in January found that, for the most part, the AT had been spared extensive damage.

The question of whether to salvage timber from the blowdown was one the Authority was forced to share with the public. NRCM urged the trustees to leave the downed wood alone, emphasizing the need to have a management plan to deal with such catastrophic events. Jon Lund was leaving the Authority, and, as he departed, he wrote a letter urging that the "cleanup" of the blowdown area not be undertaken but be left to natural forces.

Joe Brennan replaced Lund as attorney general and trustee, and he joined Maynard Marsh and Fred Holt in approving a salvage operation in T3R10, encompassing the campgrounds at Daicey and Kidney Ponds, Abol, and Katahdin Stream, with the hope of finishing it by June 1975, in time for the summer season. Private consulting forester Vladek "Kim" Kolman was hired to oversee the salvage effort.

1. *Maine Times,* August 24, 1973, pp. 1–5.

2. "The Katahdin Tragedy, January 31–February 1, 1974," by George Hamilton, *Appalachia,* December 1974, pp. 123–37.

Primary Document Sources: BSPA Boxes 11, 13 (2507-0716, 2507-0718); PSPA Box 1 (2112-0717), BSPA Original Minutes, Boxes 12, 13.

Conversations and communications: George Blackburn, Buzz Caverly, Tammy Caverly, Bob Cummings, Ken Curtis, Tom Deans, Chris Drew, Charles FitzGerald, Clifford Goodall, Bob Howes, Jon Lund, Gary Morse, John Neff, Warren Nelson, Bob Proudman, Lee Schepps, Lee Tibbs, Danny Watson.

▲▲▲▲▲▲▲▲

CHAPTER 14

# Headaches, Grievances, the Indian Sit-In

Lee Tibbs took up his new duties as park director in March 1975, and Buzz shared an office with him at the Aroostook Avenue headquarters. Tibbs appeared to be laid-back but was determined to be the boss and not be intimidated by his second-in-command.

One of Tibbs's first directives was the standardizing of reports to make it easier to find information—a move that immediately irritated Buzz. Routine matters that were important to Buzz, such as rangers' patrols and snowsled repairs, wouldn't be included anymore in order to reduce the volume of reports.

Buzz had been a stickler for recording as much of park life and activities as possible, not only to ensure "protection" to himself and others, but for historical reasons. He was always mindful of the fire that had destroyed Helon Taylor's reports and letters. The matter of reports would continue to surface over the years and eventually represent a power issue between Buzz and a park trustee.

Being in the same office raised the heat between Buzz and Tibbs. Neither one was bashful about raising hell if one got in the other's way. Sometimes they disagreed so much they ended up shouting at each other. Buzz's duties in the field allowed him to escape the office, get some breathing room, and complain to sympathizing rangers.

After their fights, Tibbs often wrote memos asserting his position over Buzz. But Tibbs had to be careful because the operations staff worked for Buzz and was loyal to him, plus Buzz knew how to make things happen and how to slow or stop things, if he wanted to. Chris Drew recalled how challenging it was for rangers to work for Tibbs, too. Some didn't like Tibbs because he was an outsider "and we weren't going to cut him any slack," recalls ranger George Blackburn. Others complained that Tibbs managed "by the book" and wasn't a good listener.

As Tibbs settled into his job, Buzz was privately apprehensive that the supervisor's job might be scrapped, despite assurances to the contrary from the Authority. Eliminating the position would save $30,000 a year, plus benefit costs. "My fear was that I would lose the privilege of working in the only place I wanted to be," he says.

In 1975 Jan received a promotion from seasonal clerk to year-round assistant to Helen Gifford. Since the Caverlys lived behind park headquarters, Jan could still provide close supervision of the girls when they weren't in school. Buzz had little time to oversee his daughters' raising. He was always on the go—in the park or traveling farther than ever from Millinocket for speaking engagements or meetings.

▲ ▲ ▲ ▲ ▲

The blowdown salvage was the park's primary issue throughout 1975, and it gave Buzz more experience in dealing with controversy, Authority politics, public demands, and being in the media spotlight. For Buzz, what to do with the blowdown was an easy call. If the wood wasn't removed, he was sure a major fire would erupt, so he wanted it gone.

The trustees joined Buzz to unite behind the salvage. Buzz's sense of representing what Percival Baxter wanted was strengthened by Baxter's 1964 approval of blowdown cleanup along roadsides with horses. A decade earlier, Baxter had been wary of establishing "a precedent" in salvaging because it might "disadvantage" the park in the future. Later, after discussions with Authority members, Baxter backed off, allowing "acts of nature or carelessness of man" to be dealt with by the trustees.

There had been another shift in the Authority makeup again, when Democrats made gains in the legislature and were in position to elect the attorney general. They picked Joe Brennan, who had served a total of ten years in the Maine State House of Representatives and the Maine State Senate, to replace Jon Lund. Traditionally, the job was a potential stepping stone to governor, and there was no doubt that Brennan wanted to be chief executive. Some of his office underlings thought he had a short memory for anything that didn't have to do with becoming governor.

Brennan obligingly attended most Authority meetings, but he was a city boy, raised in Portland, and he didn't pretend to care about the park beyond his official duties.

Brennan went along with Maynard Marsh and Fred Holt in moving forward on the salvage. Expecting the issue to become high-profile, they agreed to hire a consulting forester, advertise for bids, and develop a management plan.

Buzz's role in the salvage issue early in 1975 was to provide the Authority with an assessment of the blowdown's impact on park operations. He advised that Katahdin Stream and Abol Campground use would have to be curtailed for at least part of the season, that no new reservations would be accepted for the two areas, and when they opened it would be on a day-to-day basis. Also, Foster Field would have to be off-limits to campers because it might be needed as a base camp for salvage workers.

Plans were made to obtain help from federal CETA (Comprehensive Employment and Training Act) workers to help remove slash from the roadsides, and the AMC and other trail groups offered to aid in the clearing of blowdown on hiking paths. As preparations were made, the Authority was continuing to keep an eye on the massive spruce budworm infestation that was getting more of a foothold in the park's spruce and fir stands, especially in the SFMA.

The first job of rangers and bush crews during the winter was to make a snowmobile trail through the blowdown on the main road. The job was daunting: working with chain saws in snow up to their waists. Chris Drew spent weeks cutting through the pile of downed trees in the southern end of the park to Foster Field, while other rangers worked their way down from the north. The blowdown was so high in places that as Drew cut through it, the opening looked like a tunnel.

As expected, the Perimeter Road and southern end campgrounds were closed in the blowdown area at the first of the summer season due to hazardous conditions. There were so many calls to park headquarters from the public that the staff had to put the telephone lines on hold just to take a break.

Before Jon Lund had left office at the end of 1974, he had hired Sarah Redfield to be an assistant attorney general, and she was assigned by Joe Brennan to be counsel to the Authority. Redfield was the first woman attorney for the park and the first one to sit in on park meetings on a regular basis.

Redfield became aware quickly that Brennan was pretty much uninterested in the park. He hadn't read the Deeds of Trust and didn't understand the intent of Percival Baxter, she remembers. On the other hand, Redfield was fascinated with park issues, particularly the blow-down—a matter that mandated that she read all of the trust documents, communications, and laws.

Just before Labor Day, consultant Kim Kolman presented his proposal to the Authority for cleaning up the blowdown, estimating the gross income from the project at $250,000 and the net income at about $200,000. The Authority wanted to go ahead with the salvage but agreed to hold a hearing at Kidney Pond Camps to give the public a chance to be heard on the issue.

About seventy-five people showed up at the session, many of them opposed to removing the fallen timber. But Authority members seemed to have made up their minds prior to the gathering, and immediately after the public meeting ended, they voted to proceed with the salvage. The decision angered environmentalists.

On November 20, five citizens—among them Charles FitzGerald and Aime Gauvin—went to Kennebec Superior Court asking for an injunction to stop the salvage. FitzGerald had persuaded Charles Dayton, a Minnesota lawyer involved in the Boundary Waters Canoe Area, to take the case.

One of the first legal issues was whether the plaintiffs had standing to sue. In a break for the activists' side, the attorney general's office decided not to challenge their right to do so, and Sarah Redfield was successful in convincing Superior Court Justice Lewis Naiman to allow the case to go forward.

FitzGerald viewed the standing issue as critically important for the future. It set a precedent for any citizen to bring a suit and made the Authority vulnerable to the public in a direct way. FitzGerald saw Redfield as an ally and called her "instrumental in a lot of my education about Percival Baxter." On the other hand, FitzGerald knew Buzz was not in his corner and had no contact with him over the blow-down suit.

The salvage controversy was the beginning of FitzGerald's long, litigious involvement as public defender of the park. Like Buzz, he had a sense of "calling" to protect Percival Baxter's "forever wild" dream for the park. "I recognized something in Percival Baxter that I felt close to," FitzGerald remembers. "I felt like him. I identified with him. He became my mentor."

FitzGerald also was close to Baxter's niece, Ethel Dyer. While he was visiting her once in Fairfield, she gave FitzGerald a silver llama that

*Baxter State Park assistant supervisor Buzz Caverly (L, kneeling), and park director Lee Tibbs (kneeling); back row (L to R): business manager Pete Madeira and Baxter Park Authority members Maynard Marsh, Joe Brennan, and Fred Holt, 1975*

BAXTER STATE PARK ARCHIVES

had sat on Baxter's desk in Portland. In a letter to FitzGerald, Dyer said that Baxter always recognized that animals carried burdens for humankind, and she was glad he was willing to carry the burdens of Baxter Park.

The court could not rule on the injunction request until the salvage actually began, and in the meantime, plaintiff Ronald Davis, a University of Maine at Orono biology professor, sent out a letter seeking contributions to the new Baxter Park Defense Fund. Davis's pitch was based on the trustees' failure to develop a wilderness management plan. Without a master plan, wrote Davis, wilderness advocates were forced to use the courts to protect the park.

Critical responses started pouring in to the Authority, as well as to

Governor Longley. Lee Tibbs was assigned the task of answering them, and he let his temper fly, suggesting that since Baxter's "forever wild" park didn't meet the 1964 federal definition of wilderness, the park wasn't really a true wilderness. He also advised the letter writers that park issues were very complicated and maybe they weren't qualified to give advice to the trustees. Buzz says the situation was "a disaster, and I told him so."

▲ ▲ ▲ ▲ ▲

During the salvage debate, NRCM pressed the Authority for the umpteenth time to forge ahead with drafting a park master plan. Council President Chris Herter, also on the Advisory Committee, even offered to have NRCM help pay for the work.

Tibbs agreed that the plan was a priority and confessed his lack of familiarity with park operations. He thought he needed more time to educate himself about the park before beginning the master plan. Tibbs indicated it would take two years to bring a plan to final approval, an estimate that was overly optimistic, as things turned out.

Buzz spent a lot of time in 1975 familiarizing Tibbs not only with administrative matters and field operations but also with the landscape. They drove the roads, hiked the trails, and flew by plane so that Tibbs could literally see his realm. Buzz saw in their travels that Tibbs was not a director who wanted to know all the nooks and crannies of the park as Buzz did. Tibbs was most at home behind his desk.

The two also attended a workshop together on collective bargaining, and visited Acadia National Park and Moosehorn National Wildlife Refuge to learn about management procedures and visitor center operations that might be helpful to Baxter Park.

Despite their disagreements on operational matters, Buzz and Tibbs enjoyed their travels together. "Socially, Lee was quite patient," Buzz says, and Buzz's philosophy during Tibbs's tenure was "one day at a time, one trip at a time."

Leaving policy matters to Tibbs, Buzz's workdays were filled with inspection of park facilities, patrolling with his rangers, supervising the bush crew working on blowdowns, search and rescue, staff meetings, public relations, interviewing job candidates, personnel problems, rules and regulation proposals, and an endless array of desk work.

Buzz's concern over park dumps was shared by state environmental officials. Laws governing dumps were more demanding than ever, and the state told the park that something had to be done to clean up refuse areas. Tibbs advised the Authority that there were several options. Dempsey Dumpsters, costing $2,000 each, were the best solution, but the vehicle needed to collect the garbage was too large under park rules governing use of the roads. A private contractor could be used to take the garbage away at a cost of about $325 a trip. Using the town dump would cost between $1,800 and $3,000 a year, depending on the volume.

The Authority couldn't decide what to do. In the meantime, rangers were shooting dump-feeding bears that eluded trapping, despite the "sanctuary" designation of the land containing the dumps.

▲ ▲ ▲ ▲ ▲

Helon Taylor's attitude about ranger antics had been "boys will be boys," and pranks were still popular among rangers. They would give each other a false report that someone had jacked a deer nearby just to get a colleague to go out in his vehicle to see what he could find. Other common ones were throwing water in each other's sleeping bags and placing a pail of water above a cabin door so that it soaked the guy entering. At Katahdin Stream, water-bucket fights were so intense among rangers that campers took their lawn chairs to the picnic area to watch the antics. Rangers tossing each other into streams or rivers was almost routine.

Firecrackers were a favorite, too. Sleeping rangers—even those fresh off a tiring rescue on Katahdin—were wakened by firecrackers set off near their heads. Charlie Kenney was known as a "jumper" because if aroused out of a dead sleep, he would pop up with clenched fists ready to hit anyone nearby.

Even as supervisor, Buzz was subject to pranks. After Buzz and some rangers treated Bob Howes at Abol to a water-bucket dump, Howes sprayed a can of Mace on Buzz's vehicle defroster and turned the fan button on high so that when Buzz turned on the ignition, the truck fan would blow out the chemical. Howes was sitting quietly on his porch when Buzz and the other pranksters took off in his vehicle. In a couple of minutes, he heard Buzz's voice on the radio saying, "You got us!" For the next couple of days, their eyes were so bloodshot that Howes almost felt sorry for them. At other times, ranger Warren

Nelson says Buzz wouldn't take jokes very well. "There would always be payback," he says.

As the number of employees increased, there was greater opportunity for romance among staff. Liaisons, even extramarital ones, were tolerated to a certain point and then quietly resolved by giving the ranger the choice of resigning or being fired. To a lesser degree, some rangers tried to romance park visitors, and out-of-the-way camps became rendezvous for love trysts. Buzz knew about the goings-on, since numerous complaints were made by staff and park users. But good rangers were not easy to come by, and those who were hard workers escaped serious consequences for a long time.

▲ ▲ ▲ ▲ ▲

Lonnie Pingree had developed the reputation of being the park's honest-to-goodness "character." Pingree had always wanted to be a Texas Ranger and as a youth belonged to a quick-draw club, enjoying competitions for the "fastest gun in the West." He had a hair trigger on his Colt pistol and swaggered around "walking tall" and wearing sunglasses. Unfortunately, he had a knack for accidents.

Pingree shot himself in the foot because he forgot to put the safety on the hair trigger. Although he was trained as an emergency medical technician, he passed out when he saw his own blood. Not long after he wounded himself with a bullet, he cut his foot with an ax, which prompted his brother to write a poem:

Lonnie Pingree took an ax
And gave his left foot forty whacks.
When he saw what he had done
He shot his right foot with his gun.

When Buzz took Pingree for his first snowmobile ride, Pingree broke his leg. Chris Drew was on hand at Daicey Pond when Pingree flipped himself over in a canoe, and then he injured his back trying to lift the boat out of the pond while it was half-filled with water.

Pingree and Buzz got along so well that Pingree became, for awhile, a dependable assistant. The two enjoyed playing on their snowmobiles, and Pingree was wowed by Buzz's snowsled expertise. Once, Buzz stood up and leaned over the front of his snowmobile to prevent it from tipping over. Pingree tried the antic, but neither he nor the other rangers could master it.

▲ ▲ ▲ ▲ ▲

Most visitors to the park wanted to see and photograph moose, and rangers made it easier by keeping salt licks around the campgrounds. Tibbs thought that licks were inappropriate for a wilderness area and wrote a memo to rangers to remove them.

Ranger Joe Cushman was one who was slow to obey the directive. He had a salt lick just ten feet from the parking lot at Nesowadnehunk, and a neighborhood moose liked to lie down beside the block and enjoy it. When either Buzz or Tibbs was about to visit a campground that had a salt lick, rangers would be alerted by their buddies that the bosses were on the way, and they'd hide the block until the coast was clear.

Rangers had continued feeding other wild animals, following the practice of their predecessors, and they also kept on killing pesky mice and squirrels. So did some visitors. Ranger George Blackburn accidentally stepped into a mousetrap that had been set by a camper at Katahdin Stream. The camper had a line of six traps in various places, even one in his car.

As protector of park resources, Buzz had given a lot of thought to what that designation meant. Sure, he had shot some of the animals he was hired to defend, namely dump bears. That action seemed defensible at the time, and it was how things were done. Now, however, he saw that anyone who took life in the park was out of line and in violation of Percival Baxter's "sanctuary" mandates. His evolved position would put him on a collision course with coyote haters and pine marten researchers in the future.

▲ ▲ ▲ ▲ ▲

On September 2, 1975, Buzz went into high gear over a nineteen-member AT thru-hiking party that wanted to finish their journey by summiting Katahdin—the last five miles of the 2,175-mile journey. Because it was a cloudy, rainy day, the park had closed the trails, and the conditions were considered hazardous.

The hikers, most of them students from the University of Connecticut and the first organized group to reach the end of the long journey, were quite chagrined and wanted special permission to climb anyway. Buzz advised Katahdin Stream ranger George Blackburn that no exceptions would be made.

Twenty-five-year-old Warren Doyle was an energetic, determined group leader who wouldn't take no for an answer. In 1973, he had speed-hiked the AT in a record sixty-six and one-third days. This was his first group thru-hike, and he thought Buzz was being unnecessarily obstinate.

At 8:30 A.M. Doyle appeared at Buzz's office "extremely upset." Buzz sympathized with the hikers' desire to complete their climb but wouldn't let them jeopardize their safety on hazardous trails. Doyle went over Buzz's head and talked with Tibbs, who also denied the party its climbing request. Then Doyle started on Buzz again but to no avail. Doyle left the office determined to climb, and Buzz called all commissioned rangers available to gather at Katahdin Stream Campground in a show of force.

Buzz explained again to the hikers why they couldn't climb the mountain. Doyle's party talked among themselves for two hours. "They milled around, made motions indicating they were advancing up the trail, but at the last minute they turned back," Buzz says. Then they dispersed.

It was "a bitter pill to swallow," according to Doyle. "After 109 days of unrestricted foot travel through the Eastern mountains, we were stopped by the well-known oppressive atmosphere surrounding Baxter State Park." While stopped physically from summiting Katahdin, Doyle felt that the group had "completed our journey in spirit." Doyle wrote in the Katahdin Stream register: "It is a shame that a beautiful, free mountain such as Katahdin is in a state park such as Baxter."

It wasn't the last that Buzz would hear from Warren Doyle.

▲ ▲ ▲ ▲ ▲

Buzz's relationship with park employees and his maturity as a manager came into sharp focus in early 1976. It was a hard, yet pivotal, wake-up call—personally and professionally.

The park staff, including those who worked directly under him, filed a collective grievance against him. Their problems dealing with Buzz had been building for more than a decade, and they were fed up. The aim of their complaint wasn't to force Buzz out but to make him wake up to some of his unthinking behavior and the way he affected people negatively.

When confronted with a number of specific accusations, Buzz's response on every one was to apologize to the employee or employees involved and promise to change.

Chris Drew told Tibbs that the staff wasn't after Buzz's job, "and in no way are we pulling a Harry Kearney." They wanted Buzz to stay. But they needed him to understand that old, hard feelings needed to be put to rest, and Buzz had to improve his interactions with people.

Buzz's problems weren't necessarily "greater than some of those we [in the ranks] have," Drew said, and even Tibbs admitted that he, too, had been "guilty of some of these things" due to the pressures of his own job. Both felt that bringing things out in the open and facing them would result in fewer problems in the future. Buzz offered his appreciation for the staff making an effort to improve their relationship. "I take it as an eye-opener and not as basis for dismissal," he said.

Tibbs didn't reprimand Buzz. Everyone went about his or her business as usual, with the staff satisfied with Buzz's responses and assuming he would shape up. "It was time to move on," Buzz says.

Importantly, the employees' petition didn't call into question Buzz's park management initiatives thus far. Disagreements the staff had with the direction he was taking the park were kept out of the grievance meeting. Like him or not, employees knew Buzz had the experience to run the park. The Indian demonstration proved that again.

▲ ▲ ▲ ▲ ▲

Buzz took a short vacation after the grievance face-off, only to return and be confronted with the park's most notable event of 1976: the ten-day Indian sit-in at Abol Campground.

On April 15 Buzz received a call from warden supervisor Leonard Ritchie that "some militant Indians were on their way to Baxter Park." Yet by the time he got the word, twenty-plus Passamaquoddy from Washington County had already sneaked into the preserve via Togue Pond and occupied Abol. (The park was closed to the public between April 1 and May 15 for mud season and ice-out, but the roadside blow-down cleanup was still going on, so the Perimeter Road was open.)

Chimney Pond ranger Warren Nelson was covering Abol at the

time, and the Indians handed him a slip of paper saying they were the Abenaki people and the park was their native land—a reference to their larger land claims suit being fought at the time in court. They declared their intention to clear trees, plant crops, build an encampment, and use Katahdin for ceremonial purposes.[1]

Tibbs had prior plans to go on vacation and didn't want to postpone his trip. He had talked to the Authority and felt that the sit-in would be worked out peacefully after a negotiation period. So Tibbs left town, glad to hand the problem over to Buzz. Tibbs, Buzz recalls, was "very timid about controversy and such pressures . . . and he wanted to get out of Dodge, leaving me to become Matt Dillon for several days."

Buzz escorted tribal governor Allen Sockabasin and tribal attorney Tom Tureen to the park to meet with the sit-in group, and he joined them for coffee to hear their requests. He gave them permission to move their vehicles from the parking lot to the lean-to area so they could get their supplies more easily, but he wouldn't allow them to receive any more food because their activities violated park rules. He warned the group about damaging the campground and asked them not to climb Katahdin because of safety concerns.

On one matter after another, Buzz was advised by park counsel David Flanagan as the sit-in continued. "A lot was happening," says Buzz. "The Indians were using slingshots and shooting lead balls, and one of them hit a tree just above a ranger's head. They were snaring rabbits and cutting green trees everywhere to make their sweat lodges and lean-tos." Several Indians wore knives or tomahawks and carried bows and arrows. Buzz says several of the group "gave the impression they would become militant with the slightest provocation and perhaps were dangerous."

It was all frustrating and upsetting to Buzz because, in his mind, the Indians were "desecrating . . . the principles of the park. It was insulting, he felt, that they said they were going to till up part of Katahdin to plant corn like their ancestors because their ancestors had respected and feared the mountain.

The news media demanded to be allowed into the park to see for themselves what was going on, but the Authority forbade it. Buzz stayed on duty almost twenty-four hours a day, seven days a week. "I'd go home, take a shower, change clothes, and leave for the park again," he remembers. "It was like that for the blowdowns, the Indians, and any other big event."

What most people didn't know was that Buzz had received a call threatening him, Jan, and their daughters. "We took the girls down to their grandparents' in Corinth for two or three nights," he said. Cathy was twelve and Tammy, eight.

Some Indians were sneaking into the park, and there were rumors of carloads more about to arrive to support their compatriots. Buzz called in all law-enforcement rangers to prepare to stop anyone else from joining the sit-in, and he told all women living in park quarters to move to town.

When it was clear that there was not going to be a confrontation, Buzz went with rangers to search the woods near the Togue Pond entrance and found a number of Passamaquoddy, among them Governor Sockabasin. Buzz told him he was "completely disappointed in him and had lost what respect I had for him. He made it very clear that he could care less what I thought."

The park staff remained nervous that violence might erupt at any time, and Buzz ordered his rangers not to harass the Indians under any circumstances. However, Chris Drew found two Indians with bows and arrows and confiscated them; later one of the same Indians took the law officer's badge from Drew's warden coat.

Indian Affairs commissioner George Mitchell arrived on the scene to help work out a settlement between the park and the Indians' leaders. Tom Tureen bargained for land and visitor rights to the park for the Indians, and asked that charges be dropped against those tribal members arrested in connection with the sit-in.[2]

But on April 22, when Tureen realized the Authority wasn't going to concede and was ready to physically move the Indians out of the park, he told the group to pack up and head home. As the Indians reached the park exit at Togue Pond, they stopped to have a long ceremony, and Buzz became "very impatient. The straw was ready to break the camel's back," he recalls.

Buzz was greatly relieved that the incident ended without injury to anyone, but the following day, he was alerted that more Indians were on their way to the park, as was an NBC television crew. State troopers, deputy sheriffs, game wardens, and park rangers gathered in force and prepared for a standoff. It was a false alarm, and all the law enforcement people went home, but in Buzz's official report, he predicted there would be more incidents in the future.

▲ ▲ ▲ ▲ ▲

At the end of the sit-in, Buzz and Jan's spirits were lifted—and their lives changed—by Irvin Caverly, Sr. The district forestry headquarters was on Route 15 in Corinth, and the elder Caverly bought a nearby twenty-acre farm on McCard Road in East Corinth in anticipation of retirement. He offered just over three acres to Buzz and Jan. They took it, thinking they would build a woods camp for weekend getaways. However, it was so refreshing for them to get away from Millinocket that they decided to build a permanent home there.

The McCard Road property was former farmland with a fringe of woods. Besides his father next door, Buzz's brother Steve and his family had built a house a half mile down the road. Buzz soon purchased a ten-acre woodland next to Steve where he could go to be alone and enjoy some peace and quiet.

The Caverlys wouldn't have chosen East Corinth if they hadn't been given land there, but Buzz would have insisted on living in a rural area like Cornville, not in the far north wildlands. Socializing was important to Buzz, and he relished the neighborliness he found in East Corinth, such as morning coffee gatherings at the local corner store. People were more interested in what was going on in their community than in badgering him about park matters—a great relief to him. Buzz didn't put a phone in the house for three years, in order to preserve the peace and quiet.

▲ ▲ ▲ ▲ ▲

Snowmobiles and the blowdown salvage were the other hot-button issues of 1976. Buzz looked askance at the continuing public debate over snowmobiles. Being such an avid user, he thought the idea of prohibiting the sleds was extreme—and wrong. He saw snowmobiles in general as no different from motor vehicles in the park—and, in fact, causing less damage to natural resources than autos.

Assistant attorney general Sarah Redfield thought an inquiry was in order. With the backing of attorney general and gubernatorial hopeful Joe Brennan, she launched a review to determine if snowmobile use violated Percival Baxter's Deeds of Trust, and conferred with Buzz on various issues. After spending months delving into every facet of the matter, she concluded that Rule 19 allowing snowmobiles was inconsistent with Baxter's mandates. Her advisory opinion recommended that snowmobiles be limited to use by park staff for administrative purposes and in emergency situations.

The Authority agreed to consider a ban and scheduled a public meeting. The discussion in July 1976 was passionate, with snowmobilers and environmentalists railing at each other. The fight was so intense that the Authority decided a cooling-off period was in order before they voted on what to do.

The Authority looked to Tibbs to make a recommendation. Tibbs didn't want to take sides, so Buzz presented the employee position of support for snowmobiles. With Brennan strongly in favor of a prohibition, trustees Maynard Marsh and John Walker followed. Their September 7 vote prohibited snowmobiles, except for administrative purposes, and they left it to Buzz to interpret how much the field crew could use their sleds.

Buzz established snowmobile operating procedures designed to account for use, such as emergencies, hauling supplies, patrolling, and accompanying winter parties. Rangers had to file a report on miles driven and maintenance work. After awhile, however, the accountability process weakened as oversight diminished.

▲ ▲ ▲ ▲ ▲

While the snowmobile debate was going on, the blowdown salvage had begun (about 160 cords removed from roadsides) before the superior court ruled on the injunction petition. The Authority had awarded the salvage contract to Stanley Sproul, a prominent Augusta contractor and city mayor.

Finally, in mid-1976, Justice Lewis Naiman handed down a ruling that, in effect, gave the opponents a victory. He didn't prohibit the salvage but did ban the use of heavy equipment, including skidders. The alternative was horses, and no contractor was going to use that mode to get the wood to market.

Buzz thought that horses would be fine to use, except by the time they could get the wood out, it might be full of worm holes and less marketable. "To me, it was all unnecessary interference and would hurt the park in the long term."

Both sides of the salvage issue appealed Naiman's decision, and Sproul was let out of his contract by the Authority. The Maine

Supreme Court upheld the lower court ruling, allowing the salvage but with no heavy equipment. The matter died then and there for good.

The salvage problem left the park with a $90,000 deficit. The financial loss prompted the Authority to move immediately on hiring a permanent forester to begin developing a management plan for the SFMA. George Ruopp started work in 1978 shortly after Kim Kolman's forestry services contract with the park ended. Tibbs bounced back and forth between working on the park's management plan and keeping up with the blowdown salvage and SFMA.

After retirement, as Buzz weighed the Authority's decision to develop the SFMA, he concluded that it was the wrong idea; he thought every square inch of the park should be managed as sanctuary. If he had had access to Governor Baxter and the wisdom of his later years, Buzz didn't doubt that he would have used all his powers of persuasion to convince the governor to change his mind on allowing harvesting. It would have left the park wilder, less roaded, and more compelling for recreationists, he believed.

▲ ▲ ▲ ▲ ▲

Fred Holt's replacement on the Authority in the summer of 1976 was John Walker, the new head of the Maine Bureau of Forestry. Walker, like some of his predecessors, wasn't keen on having to serve on the Authority. The long months of boundary work in the park in 1970 more than satisfied his interest in spending time in Baxter Park. But the experience had endowed him with hands-on knowledge of the park.

One of Walker's first actions was to join Brennan and Marsh in approving budworm spraying that summer. The forestry bureau recommended spraying 54,000 acres in the park—28,000 acres in the SFMA and the rest in two southern park townships. The Authority felt it had no choice but to sanction some spraying. Advisory member and NRCM president Chris Herter was the strongest in-house opponent, arguing that no spraying should take place until the much-delayed park master plan was done.

Herter had other concerns. He observed that Brennan was often absent from Authority meetings, that Walker didn't seem to be engaged in park issues, and that Marsh ran the show. From the way the decisions went, Herter thought the trustees discussed issues before the public session and knew ahead of time how each other would vote.

On the staff side, Herter thought it obvious that Tibbs and Buzz didn't get along beyond a public cordiality. "Buzz was a Mainer and had grown up here," Herter says. "His expertise was field operations. Lee was comfortable with the Authority and the Advisory but not comfortable with Buzz and the gang." At Authority meetings, Herter read Buzz's body language as an expression of his discomfort with decisions that didn't go his way. "He had a certain way of doing things and looking at things. If the Authority's rulings didn't line up with his historical or philosophical perspective, he didn't agree with them."

▲ ▲ ▲ ▲ ▲

Like his mentor, Helon Taylor, Buzz made note of animal sightings in his monthly reports. He had been lucky enough to spot an elusive Canada lynx when he was a ranger at Russell Pond in 1960, and in 1976 saw another one—this time at Abol Stream.

Lynx didn't have a breeding population in the park, as far as anyone knew, but coyotes were returning to make a home there. Chris Drew reported seeing coyotes in the Nesowadnehunk area for the first time. Pine marten were increasing, and beaver had thrived after trapping them in the park had been banned and poaching had stopped.

Still, the safety of animals was not guaranteed in Baxter Park. Some rangers and game wardens killed coyotes or beaver willy-nilly. They looked at the animals as nuisances or worse. A few men hated coyotes so much that they would go out of their way to drive the predators onto frozen lakes or ponds, run them to exhaustion, and then finish them off with repeated hits with their snowsleds.

Beavers aggravated rangers by rebuilding their dams in road culverts time after time. After a few instances of having to tear out a dam and maybe relocate a beaver, some rangers lost their patience and shot the animals to solve the problem.

Buzz was on the side of the coyote, the beaver, and all the wildlife in the park, large or small, and the rangers knew it. Consequently, Buzz didn't know about the wanton killing of coyotes and beaver until after the fact. Although no disciplinary actions were taken against the guilty rangers, Buzz let them know in no uncertain terms that he wanted it stopped, and problem beavers had to be trapped and relocated. In his younger days, he says he would have fired a ranger who shot an animal or bird in the park's sanctuary.

▲ ▲ ▲ ▲ ▲

Strict drug enforcement had prompted the question of whether rangers were more law enforcement or conservation oriented. It was answered in an August 26, 1976, memo from Tibbs to all commissioned rangers:

> While law enforcement is a necessary part of park management and thus a part of your duties, it is not your primary function to be policemen. The law enforcement policy of Baxter Park is one of low-profile, preventive enforcement with an absolute minimum of authoritarian enforcement. This type of policy in the long run will be the best for Baxter Park, for park users and for the park staff. Certain recent events have indicated that some commissioned rangers may be leaning too far toward authoritarian enforcement and using some procedures that may not be the best that could be employed. If so, this is not in the best interest of Baxter Park, and we must correct these practices.

Buzz's job was to evaluate, in consultation with rangers, the law-enforcement procedures used in the park and make recommendations in keeping with the policy. He disagreed with law enforcement being relegated to a lower profile, but in time recognized that conservation of park resources benefited from the change.

▲ ▲ ▲ ▲ ▲

In early fall, the new park headquarters on Balsam Drive was completed, and Buzz and Lee Tibbs finally had separate offices. About two hundred people turned out to celebrate the completion of the building. A large crowd and "a lot of proud people" were on hand, Buzz remembers. "We had waited a long time for the building and were happy and relieved to start working in it." The building, however, had its defects and faulty workmanship, and it plagued the occupants for years.

During the year, Buzz was constantly on the road to Augusta to work on changes in pay scales proposed by Governor Longley's 1976 Hay Study. The study looked at job reclassifications, pay, administrative procedures, and a host of issues that related to an expanding state government. It caused considerable reaction and opposition among state employees, including Baxter employees, over the raises proposed and the perceived inequities among similar jobs in different agencies.

One of the proposals that took center stage was a forty-hour work-week. It had serious implications for Baxter rangers, who had always spent as much time on a job as it took, regardless of the hours. Now, more than forty hours would mean overtime pay and higher costs to the park. A reduction of services to the public was guaranteed by the Longley effort, and many rangers didn't like it, even though it assured them more time off.

Buzz was frustrated with the Hay proposal's lack of transparency on pay scales. The only way a disgruntled park employee could get a straight answer on why his or her pay was set at a certain level was to file a grievance, and he felt it was a "poor way" to treat his staff.

▲ ▲ ▲ ▲ ▲

On November 2 Millinocket native Anne Erickson opened the doors to a new local newspaper—the *Katahdin Times.* She was a stringer for the *Bangor Daily News* and a photographer. From the start, she was very interested in what was going on in Baxter Park. She had been going to the park since she was five years old, and the park was part of her family's recreational history. Erickson had testified against the proposed prohibition on the public use of snowmobiles when the Authority debated the issue in 1976 and subsequently approved the ban.

The paper's first edition had a four-column photo of Katahdin's snow-covered cap, plus a page-one story about rangers using snowmobiles in the park and another article on the new park headquarters building.

Erickson's investigative streak was apparent in the November 16 issue that used large bold print to charge: "Baxter Park Airlifting Wood to Chimney Pond: violating 'forever wild' concept." In the front-page article, she pointed out that the park was using a professional helicopter service to airlift hardwood to the ranger station, despite a rule that prohibited aircraft within park boundaries. Buzz thought Erickson was trying to pick a fight with the park because of the ban on snowmobiles.

Buzz didn't pay much attention to the *Times* or to any other newspaper's coverage because he didn't read it. However, the *Katahdin Times* proved to be an untiring watchdog within a stone's throw of the park itself, and it provided a ready forum for local people to express their opinions on park management. Erickson was openly conservative and critical of environmentalists such as Aime Gauvin. Over the years, her paper took on an anti-park tone, even though Erickson personally thought Buzz was doing a good job.

▲ ▲ ▲ ▲ ▲

As a plan for the SFMA was given the go-ahead, a fire plan was also completed. Buzz was one of the fifteen members who drafted the proposal, which called for vigorous fire control, rather than fire management. It rejected in general the idea supported by environmentalists that fire was a natural part of nature's scheme of things and should be allowed—at least in places.

Regardless of its weaknesses, the plan was more than the park had had before. Just how unprepared the park was for a major conflagration would soon become apparent.

---

1. The mythical bird spirit Pamola was the God of Thunder and protector of Katahdin, and climbing the mountain was taboo among the Abenaki Indians. John Neff devotes the first chapter in his 2006 book, *Katahdin,* to the relationship between the Native Americans and the mountain gods.
2. *Maine Times,* April 4, 1976, p. 26.

Primary Document Sources: BSPA Box 1 (2112-0717); BSPA Original Minutes, Boxes 11, 12.

Conversations and communications: George Blackburn, Buzz Caverly, Ron Davis, Warren Doyle, Chris Drew, Clint Dyer, Anne Erickson, Charles FitzGerald, Chris Herter, Phil McGlauflin, Warren Nelson, Lonnie Pingree, Sarah Redfield, Lee Tibbs.

▲▲▲▲▲▲▲▲

CHAPTER 15

# CONFLAGRATION

ON JULY 17, 1977, BUZZ FACED A CONFLAGRATION that threatened the very heart of Baxter Park—Katahdin and the southern end of the park—like no other natural event. From the beginning, he was like a general in wartime commanding his troops, according to volunteer Lester Kenway.

It was another situation, like the Indian sit-in, that showed Buzz had the right stuff to lead the park—even if he, in the eyes of two respected wilderness advocates, was repressing "freedom of the hills" in Baxter Park.

Buzz was at South Branch Pond as the sun went down when he was alerted that lightning had started a fire at Lost Pond in the southeast area of the park near the border with Great Northern Paper. Another strike and a second fire were reported shortly thereafter.

Ranger Bob Howes hooked up with regional Maine Forest Service ranger Roger Milligan (later fire boss) to take a close look-see at the quickly spreading blaze. Blowdowns and boulders made it extremely difficult for them to hike in the woods. When they found the blaze near midnight, it was cherry red, and they knew they had a major fire—and a twenty-mile-an-hour wind whipping it in a southeasterly direction.

Buzz had dashed down the Perimeter Road to the fires with emergency equipment, and, once he knew the fire sites, began dispatching men and tools. He also immediately directed evacuation of camps, especially those at Daicey and Kidney Ponds because they were on dead-end roads. In the ensuing chaos, he saw a spot fire behind Abol Pond and used a spade to dig into the ground and throw dirt on the blaze.

The fire jumped over to Great Northern land by sunrise of the second day. Two Beaver airplanes were dropping water on the fire, and two bulldozers were trying to establish a line along the Foss Knowlton Trail.

Lester Kenway was working on trails for the Youth Conservation Corps (YCC)—his first summer in Baxter Park—and was at Russell

Pond when the fire broke out. He helped get campers out of the park via South Branch Pond. Driving them down I-95 to pick up their vehicles at the southern end of the park, Kenway was awed by the sight of a smoke plume rising one and a half to two miles high over the Katahdin area.

Kenway returned to the park to work in the makeshift kitchen to feed the firefighters. Having worked in a resort hotel in Bar Harbor for a couple of summers, Kenway was an expert meat slicer, even though he had a broken wrist in a cast. He sliced hundreds of pieces of ham and cheese for sandwiches. The fire crew showed up in the kitchen covered in black charcoal, grabbed some sandwiches, and dived into a barrel of crushed ice and sodas. The ice was black when they left, Kenway remembers.

Buzz hated fires, but Kenway was impressed by the "military" way that he marshaled resources to respond to the crisis. "If there is a talent for being a commander, he had it," Kenway says.

Charles FitzGerald managed to slip by park security to take photographs. "We went roaring in," he says. "There was a frantic period where park people were chasing me. I drove by Buzz and will never forget that stare of his—he has a wonderful round face and big eyes. It was like the stare of an owl. He suddenly realized who I was. I wanted to show in my photos the Great Northern lands south of the park boundary [that had been harvested]. I discovered a moonscape from clear-cutting—slash and roads as far as eyes could see."

During the fire suppression effort, the *Bangor Daily News* ran an article about FitzGerald's threat to sue the park for trying to put out the blaze. It provoked one unidentified person to call FitzGerald and threaten to burn down his house, and some state foresters complained to him that he was trying to take their jobs away.

Lee Tibbs stayed away from the fire scene for the most part, driving to the park every now and then to talk to the forest service fire boss. For Buzz, one day ran into another. "The whole episode was like one long day," he remembers. When he was able to get a little sleep, he would wake up in a panic that he had been away from the fire front too long.

Buzz's father, an instructor on forest fire control management, also worked on extinguishing the blaze. He would go to Buzz's house exhausted after hours and hours on the fire line and try to catch a few hours' sleep. Buzz was busy evacuating people and hardly taking a rest, so they didn't see much of each other.

Bill Vail, Buzz's former warden school classmate and now the warden supervisor in Greenville, joined the firefighting force. He helped sink canoes in Daicey Pond so they wouldn't burn and removed furnishings from the cabins. Fortunately the fire didn't get to Daicey.

As with the Indian sit-in, the Caverly girls were affected by the fire, with Tammy being sent to Buzz's parents' and Cathy to a cousin's house. At one point, though, Buzz let thirteen-year-old Cathy work with Jan at Togue Pond in the field kitchen and ride with him in a forestry helicopter to view the fire.

Chris Drew hardly slept for two weeks. At one point while fighting the fire, he was surrounded by flames and had to be evacuated. The worst accident during the fire was a skidder running over Warren Nelson, the Chimney Pond ranger. Nelson had been on a lengthy hiking trip on Katahdin with Art York the previous day and hadn't had much sleep when he had to pitch in to work the fire. He stayed up all night getting equipment in to the fire and then was on the end of a fire hose for hours. Fatigue caused him to sit down, and the ground was so soft, he fell asleep. He didn't hear a skidder coming close, and it backed right over him. What saved Nelson was that one of the tires rolled up on a rock and the skidder pushed him down into the bog. Despite a shoulder injury and broken ribs, he was able to get up and run along beside the skidder and shout to the driver that he had been run over. Then he fainted.

One guy jumped off a tank truck onto a broken tree with the stump sticking up. It was razor sharp and he impaled his foot. The fire was coming at him and he couldn't move. The crew sprayed water on the ground around him, and someone got a chain saw, cut the stump, and took the man to a hospital—his foot still impaled on the wood.

At the peak of the suppression effort, sixteen bulldozers, six tank trucks, 200 men, thirty pumps, seven skidders, six Beavers, three helicopters, and one CL-215 air tanker were working straight out to control the fire.

The fire burned a total of 3,000 acres—1,900 acres in the park and the remainder on Great Northern land. The immediate impact on the public was the closing of campgrounds and fire-damaged areas to day users. The total cost of the fire was about $745,000 or $209 an acre. Warren Nelson was the most severely injured firefighter, and another forty-four people sustained minor injuries.[1]

While the 1977 fire was the largest in park history, it wasn't the worst one to suppress for Buzz. His most difficult blaze had burned Lord Mountain, north of Wassataquoik Lake, in 1966. It stuck in Buzz's mind not only because it was a tough fire to contain but because the in-park state forest warden refused him a ride back to his vehicle, leaving him to trudge back on sore feet for several miles and late at night.

▲ ▲ ▲ ▲ ▲

The good news about the 1977 fire was that it didn't destroy park buildings, and recreational areas were still in good shape. A lot of the blow-down problems had been taken care of because all the woody debris on the forest floor had burned up, lessening fire danger in the years ahead. However there were serious environmental impacts. Bulldozers had created fire lines and access routes that scarred the land for decades. Streams were altered by the machinery and waters diverted.

The Maine Forest Service and the Department of Conservation held public sessions with a six-person board reviewing the impacts. The review board concluded that the presence of heavy, dry fuels on the forest floor—plus strong, shifting winds, boggy and bouldery terrain, and lack of existing access roads—contributed to the intensity and difficulty of controlling the fire. Buzz and others who had supported the blowdown salvage felt vindicated. The panel also pointed out that the park's procedures for dealing with fire were minimal and urged the park to draw up a substantial plan within the year. The need to upgrade firefighting equipment and aircraft—and the training of firefighters— was also underscored. As for environmental impacts, the review board recommended that efforts should be made to minimize adverse effects on the land, and a policy should be adopted establishing who was responsible for repairing damage in the aftermath of fires.

▲ ▲ ▲ ▲ ▲

After the fire and twenty-two years in the park, Helen Gifford retired, and Jan became acting reservations chief. Gifford's departure was a milestone. She was the park's first woman on the staff and the first clerical worker. She had begun as a summer employee in 1957 and handled ever-increasing reservations and correspondence under Helon Taylor, Harry Kearney, Buzz, and Lee Tibbs, and she left the park as a legend in her own right. She had worked the longest of any woman employee.

Jan wanted Gifford's job permanently, but Buzz told her she was too shy to get the post. Jan dug in her heels and decided she would beat out her three competitors—all women. On the hiring committee were Tibbs, Tom Chase, Alice Crabtree, and newly hired business manager Pete Madeira. They asked Jan why she should have the job. "I told them I had worked for Helen and had lots of experience," she said. Madeira thought Jan was the best qualified, hands down. Buzz was taking some vacation days in East Corinth when Jan and the girls arrived with Cathy hanging out the window shouting that Jan had gotten the job.

Politically, Jan's rise in the headquarters hierarchy was noteworthy. There was no overt adverse reaction from the staff, despite the potential to read nepotism into the situation. Nepotism had flourished in the park system during Buzz and Jan's early years there, and they saw nothing out of the ordinary with her promotion. She had competed aboveboard for the job, and Buzz was not involved in her appointment.

With Jan as head of reservations, they became the only married couple to ever ascend to top management. The positions of the Caverlys gave them elevated standing to influence decisions and create or block directions the park would or could take.

▲ ▲ ▲ ▲ ▲

The Indians were back at the park's doorstep, at least figuratively, and it was the beginning of a determined, long-term effort to acquire "cultural rights" within the preserve. Penobscot tribal representatives, with support from the Passamaquoddy, appeared before the Park Authority asking to use the park for certain traditional ceremonies.

The Indians believed that their ancestors had had a village on the east side of the flat land on Katahdin's western plateau. They would resettle there when their pending land claims case was won, they asserted. In the meantime, the Indians wanted to visit the park for up to 100 days over the summer and fall for feasting, praying, and purification in sweat lodges. They were possibly willing to accept an isolated area in lieu of an established campground for ceremonies, but insisted that it must include a direct view of Katahdin. The Authority put off the tribes by asking them to submit their requests in writing.

The issue was on the back burner until the fall of 1978, when the

Penobscots approached the Authority again for special permission to use the park for spiritual purposes. The tribe contended that Indians had an "inherent right . . . to . . . walk freely on mother earth and on the spiritual mountain, K'tahdin."

▲ ▲ ▲ ▲ ▲

On June 2, 1977, Buzz set his personal best record for hiking from Roaring Brook to Russell Pond. Hoofing it at the end of a rainy day, he covered the seven miles in two hours and five minutes—but not better than Tom Chase's amazing hour-and-a-half time a decade earlier.

The following month, Buzz was back at Russell to spend several days looking over the area—going to some places he hadn't been to since he'd left there as a ranger in 1963. "Quite a difference in thirteen years," he observed, referring to removal of the old bunkhouse and hovel and the new ranger's camp.

Buzz was doing more patrolling in the backcountry. Because the forty-hour workweek limited rangers' time on the trail, there was more litter along the trails because no one had come along to pick it up. Another effect of the workweek rule was to remove gatekeepers and put the Telos and Nesowadnehunk entrance booths on the honor system.

▲ ▲ ▲ ▲ ▲

One of Buzz's satisfactions was the unusual security the park afforded visitors from attack, theft, and other misbehavior. Once the control gates were in place, the public knew that access to the park was under much greater scrutiny. Hikers and campers, especially women, had little or no fear of being physically harmed by strangers. They could leave their wallets and possessions in their cars or tent and find them still in place later. Fellow campers looked out for each other. Every now and then, a domestic incident occurred at a campground, but such upset was a rarity.

Park signs, however, were a popular item to steal, but it was usually locals who tore them off posts when they were in a hell-raising mood. A group stole sixteen signs one day in 1977, and because the gatehouse had their license number, Chris Drew tracked them down and got the signs back. When he raided their Island Falls house, he not only found the park signs, but state, town, and Camp Phoenix signs.

Usually, the park didn't recover stolen signs. They would end up in someone's backwoods camp.

▲ ▲ ▲ ▲ ▲

Warren Nelson was on light duty after his fire-related injuries and was assigned to Roaring Brook. One fall day in 1977 he was looking over the guest register and thought he saw Governor Longley pass by. A couple of hours later, he received a call from Chimney Pond that Longley had hiked all the way up to the campground to see how Nelson was getting along. The governor turned around and hoofed back down to Roaring Brook to pay his respects to Nelson. "He was very personable," says Nelson. "He came twice a year to see me. I don't know why. We'd sit and talk about how things were going."

Longley, the Independent who marched to his own drum, didn't seek out Buzz on any of his trips, and the two never met. Gatekeepers told Buzz that Longley showed up with his children, driving his own vehicle, and wanted to keep "a low profile." Longley was the only governor to visit the park between 1960 and 2005 with whom Buzz had no contact.

▲ ▲ ▲ ▲ ▲

On October 7, 1978, there was another significant park resignation. Bill Cross announced he was leaving after over thirty-one years of service. Cross had been associated with the park since 1959, when he had transferred from the Public Utilities Commission to the Forestry Department. In those days, due to limited funding of the park, forestry handled all the park's financial, personnel, and related matters. Cross noted: "I have seen the park go from a small operation in 1959 to a major one in 1977." Some of the comparisons he gave were: "The budget, from $50,093 to $584,857; expenditures from $45,867 to $567,803; permanent employees from two to twenty and seasonal from thirteen to thirty; vehicles from one to twenty-two; campgrounds from seven to nine."

Typical of Cross, he left behind an eye-opening report for Tibbs and the Authority on the way financial records were being kept, and cast blame on Buzz in an October 13 memo:

Another year has gone by without the proper data for a reconciliation between the field and the official inventory records in Augusta. This has been going on for several years and, as indicated previously, I believe it was 1969 when the records were last reconciled. Every year there has been one excuse after another as to the reason why the data could not be furnished the Augusta office, and it is about time that someone was made accountable for this situation—the Supervisor [Buzz] has been responsible during this period for which nothing has been done! I have explained the proper procedures to be taken practically every year both in writing and verbally, but it has done no good. I know you are aware that this item of reconciliation has been of major concern to the auditors in recent years and to date I have given them one reason or another, but this past year we were written up in the audit report. It is imperative to have a complete inventory taken of every location except Kidney Pond, which is another problem.

Cross wanted a full accounting, with any overage or shortage reported and the reason for it. "In the past, many items have been condemned and taken over as personal property, which is strictly against all rules," he said. The only way equipment could be written off the books legally was by auction sale, transfer to another department, or condemnation if the item was in too poor shape to bring a good price. It was the junk "that brings good prices these days," Cross added.

While some of Cross's cronies may have thought that his concerns deserved more attention than they received, neither Tibbs nor the Authority took any action..

▲ ▲ ▲ ▲ ▲

Long before the park was created, its mountain summits lured hikers and climbers. There were 150 miles of mountain and lowland trails—paths that invited visitors to explore. But the trail network had never been well maintained. On Katahdin, trails were gullied several feet deep, and remote trails were overgrown or even obscured by flooding.

From a budget standpoint, trails were only one need among many, and Tibbs and Buzz were always worrying about how much work was affordable. In 1978 the park trail crew numbered only four, and there was limited assistance from rangers and other park employees.

Volunteers from the AMC and the MATC worked primarily on Katahdin trails, but their contributions were irregular.

On foot, Lester Kenway undertook a first-ever survey of the trails in 1978 and concluded that they were in a critical state overall. Because the park couldn't hire a larger trail crew or invest staff time in trails planning, Tibbs applied to the AMC's Murphy Fund Committee for $70,000 to pay for major trail improvement, upgrades to trail signage, and development of a trail volunteer program.

Kenway's survey was shocking as to the actual condition of the trail system parkwide. Only sixty-one trails were officially maintained, and there wasn't standardized blazing or directional signage parkwide. As well, trail signs were a hodge-podge of different colors and letter sizes, from attractive routed signs on Traveler Mountain and the AT to hand-made signs crafted with magic markers and unpainted boards. There were still many signs on the Katahdin trails labeled *A.M.C.*, despite the fact that the club hadn't been responsible for maintaining the Katahdin trails for more than a decade.

The survey listed as the most pressing problems overgrown trails, serious erosion, lack of cairns, and/or lack of a well-defined footpath above tree line. The condition of trail "treadway" was terribly neglected, with extensive mud holes, eroded gullies, and trampled alpine areas. Kenway estimated that just the backlog of needed work was more than thirty years—a job that could see him into retirement without adding any new trails or having to deal with significant trail damage from Mother Nature.

By the time the Murphy Fund approved the request, Kenway (a chemistry graduate from Bates College) had been hired as the new and first trail crew leader. In addition to his YCC work in the park, Kenway had helped relocate long sections of the AT in western Maine, and thus was well-experienced.

▲ ▲ ▲ ▲ ▲

Just before the 1977 fire, well-known mountaineers and writers Guy and Laura Waterman had spent the day with Buzz to interview him for articles and a book on wilderness ethics. They wanted to hear from him how the park's wilderness character was being protected, although they already had a sense of the situation from past visits they had made to technical-climb Katahdin.

In the October and November issues of *New England Outdoors*, the Watermans published their findings. Their first article, "Anthem for Katahdin," talked about the park in glowing terms. The follow-up, "Requiem for Katahdin," was highly critical—in fact the strongest journalistic criticism of the park in print thus far. Although they didn't single out any person by name, it was clear to anyone who knew Buzz that he was the primary one when the Watermans talked about "park managers."

The Watermans were "freedom of the hills" advocates, and they charged that the park was overregulated; in fact, Katahdin was the most overregulated mountain in the U.S. They quoted Paul Petzholdt, founder of the National Outdoor Leadership School (NOLS), who had visited the park in 1970 and said it was "like a prison camp to me," but added, "These regulations are not the result of blind police-state thinking. Quite the contrary, the managers of Baxter State Park are conscientious and dedicated men who love the Mountain and the wilderness."

Safety consciousness was an obsession, the Watermans asserted. "Nowhere else in the Northeast, maybe the whole country, do land managers try so zealously to protect the hiker from himself, to the point of imposing restrictions that stifle enjoyment of the Wilds." They referred to their beloved White Mountains and many western hiking areas that were as rugged and exposed as Katahdin but none "so hemmed in with rules at every turn." An element of risk, unpredictability, and adventure were part of the wilderness experience, they argued, and in trying to exorcise possible hazards, the managers were "destroying this very spirit of wildness."

The examples they gave were the entrance sign that bid visitors "welcome," immediately followed by the admonition "observe all rules." A list of seven prohibitions were posted and a sign at the gatehouse itself stated that sometimes mountain trails were closed. The only other place in the Northeast that was ever closed was Mt. Washington when serious avalanche risk occurred, they stated. In midsummer, why would a trail be closed, they asked. And they were stunned to learn that "cloud cover" was the answer. In 1976 Katahdin's summit trails were closed more often than open, and this turned away visitors from afar and those who were finishing their thru-hike over the last five miles.

The bad weather policy was only the beginning of bad regulations, the Watermans asserted. They pointed to the restriction on departure times for hiking Katahdin—7:00 A.M., which meant crowding on the trail. "Gone are the quiet moments of walking alone up the trail in the solitude of the early morning." They termed the rule "ridiculous."

"Rules such as Baxter Park's seek to impose a Procrustean standard on all hikers regardless of experience, stamina, equipment, judgment, and determination," they wrote. "Park managers want to be 'fair' to all—but what is proper for the less-qualified hiker is absurd and intolerable for the Hillarys and Unsoelds of this world, not to mention a lot of the rest of us duffers who fall somewhere between those extremes."

The Watermans lamented the stringent winter rules as too burdensome for climbers. Other criticisms were greatly over-blazed trails—"official graffiti, we would call it"; relocation of the old crestline route on the Knife Edge to make it safer; and the police-like behavior of rangers. They said there was little or nothing in Governor Baxter's stipulations that related to safety, just about preserving the natural state of things. The contributing factors, they said, were a reaction to the increasing number of visitors; overreaction to accidents, including deaths, on the mountain; political pressures on the trustees; and the remoteness of Katahdin.

A case in point involved Warren Doyle, who'd had the confrontation with Buzz in 1975 over climbing Katahdin. In early January 1978, Doyle and his friend Steve Messier climbed Katahdin without registering, and Messier was injured coming down from the summit on the Abol Trail. The two men were cited by rangers for illegal climbing and fined twenty dollars each in Millinocket District Court. Rebellious Doyle refused to pay and went to jail for twenty-four hours—a symbolic resistance to regulations and to make a point that it was possible to be jailed for climbing mountains in America. While in jail, Doyle wrote a poem, "Katahdin," in which he lamented the ways that mortals had "imprisoned" the mountain with rules, and prayed for the day of liberation for the massif.

The Watermans concluded that the park was "out of touch with contemporary trends in wilderness management elsewhere in the Northeast." They suggested more education and advisory warnings, as opposed to flat prohibitions, thus "restoring a sense of the freedom of the hills."

There was no response to the articles from Buzz or any park official, which was puzzling to the Watermans. When they wrote something critical of the White Mountains National Forest management, they received a response from supervisors there. "There was a good give and take, and we sometimes influenced their thinking," recalls Laura Waterman.

Buzz didn't read the articles, but when he had personal conversations with the Watermans, he appreciated hearing their wilderness perspective and the "diplomatic" way they presented it. "No matter how much we agreed or disagreed, Guy and Laura were always congenial, never adversarial," Buzz says. However he felt they "were not well-informed about the challenges of mixing wilderness and public recreation."

Guy Waterman never returned to Baxter Park, and Laura Waterman did only once. But they still had plenty to say against the park's strong regulation of visitors in the books they published in the 1990s on mountaineering, woods history, wilderness ethics, and backpacking ethics. They also recommended that AMC not carry out rescue-training workshops in the park in winter because Katahdin's terrain was too scary for students. When their book *Wilderness Ethics* was reprinted in 2005, it continued with the same critical refrain against park management.

▲ ▲ ▲ ▲ ▲

The park was still providing a house on Forest Avenue for the park director, and Joe Brennan felt the Authority should get out of the housing business. Maynard Marsh, John Walker, and Win Robbins agreed. They felt Buzz's house on Tamarack Street could be justified better than others because he was there to watch the headquarters, maintenance building, and other facilities. The trustees voted to sell Tibbs's house.

At Tibbs's urging, the trustees also decided to move the park's business office in Augusta to Millinocket. The relocation would allow the park director and business manager to be in daily face-to-face contact, and the move would save $1,800 a year in rent.

▲ ▲ ▲ ▲ ▲

Buzz's performance ratings for 1977 and 1978 by Lee Tibbs were positive, since Tibbs felt that Buzz was improving on all fronts. His judgment and decision-making were better, Tibbs said in the 1978 evaluation, which was mostly a repeat of the one for the previous year. When in the field, Buzz's directives were "especially good" when he was directly supervising on-site. Buzz had made "a noticeable effort" to improve operations by "more judicious delegation to subordinates" and better follow-up. But Tibbs thought Buzz could improve employee management even further with "a little more aggressive follow-up."

Buzz had made "a good effort" to reduce costs, but Tibbs thought that if he were "more thorough," he could improve efficiencies, and thus, savings. Buzz was "very effective" in organizing and planning projects he was personally involved in. However he still had "a tendency to occasionally" allow subordinates to plan and organize their own work to such an independent degree "that the best interests of the department are not always served." He recommended that Buzz provide closer oversight.

Buzz had instituted more frequent meetings with employees to discuss their performance. Tibbs felt Buzz had a tendency to focus only on the good points of an individual in his written evaluation without identifying the areas the employee needed to improve.

Tibbs commended Buzz for taking steps toward self-improvement and said he could "profitably spend more time" keeping informed about new management and supervision techniques. As for communications skills, Tibbs felt that Buzz was already doing quite well, but, of course, could do more. Great Northern Paper was sponsoring a Dale Carnegie course for some of its employees, and Tibbs arranged for Buzz to participate. Buzz was a fan of U.S. Senator Hubert Humphrey because of the effective way the Minnesota Democrat could speak in public, so Buzz jumped at the chance to improve his public speaking.

Buzz was much more relaxed about his relationship with Tibbs four years into Tibbs's tenure. Practically speaking, he operated pretty much as he had prior to Tibbs's arrival, and Buzz figured he could outlast Tibbs and be in line for the director's job. "My attitude was have patience . . . this too shall pass," Buzz says.

▲▲▲▲▲

One of the highlights of Buzz's 1977–78 winter was chasing bears with state biologist Roy Hugie. Lee Tibbs had approved a bear survey project by the fish and game department, and Buzz agreed with it because the data collected was necessary to getting rid of open dumps.

Buzz and Hugie located one of their subjects in a den just off the Roaring Brook Road at Rum Mountain, but the animal escaped through a getaway hole before they could tranquilize him. Buzz and Hugie chased the bear on snowshoes for two miles cross-country but were unable to catch up. They tried tracking another bear across the side of Rum Mountain to the base of the Knife Edge but never got that one, either. Still, it was great fun for Buzz to be out in the woods instead of behind a desk, and whenever he had a chance to return to hands-on work in the field, he took it.

▲ ▲ ▲ ▲ ▲

The Authority took another step in bringing some order to scientific research requests. Prompting the move was an alarming request from a Bates College professor to collect twenty-four species of mammals in the park. The trustees agreed that a formal permit process was needed. They approved a new standing committee to consider collection permit applications and make recommendations on whether to approve or reject them.

Three Advisory Committee members were named to the panel, but in reality, Buzz continued to call the shots on research requests. He remained resistant to research efforts, scuttling a proposal to include certain rare park plants in a Maine Critical Areas Program catalog that would be available to researchers and the public. Buzz was suspicious that the Critical Areas Program represented a way for an outside entity to gain some management control over park resources.

The case in point involved a prime rare fern area in back of Billfish Pond. The park's unofficial naturalist, Gerald Merry, thought researchers were already trampling vegetation there and warned Buzz of the greater damage that could result from drawing more visitors and the taking of samples. Previously Buzz had refused to allow a proposed hydrologic study in the Billfish Pond drainage because the University of Maine researcher wanted to drill a small-diameter hole to analyze groundwater. In Buzz's judgment, the information to be gained comparing the impact of people in the north end drainages to those in the south didn't justify damaging park resources.

Buzz had a few exceptions to his research position, and allowed geologist Dabney Caldwell to take geologic samples from the park. He knew Caldwell was quite conservative in his collections, and Buzz felt that he could trust Caldwell's judgment.

▲ ▲ ▲ ▲ ▲

No matter what management position he was in, Buzz used his routine monthly reports to emphasize the wonderful aspects of working for the park. It was a chance to set an upbeat tone, no matter what problems or troubles the park and its employees were facing. To him, Baxter was a one-of-a-kind place and everyone there was privileged to work there.

"One of the great advantages an employee of Baxter State Park has is the opportunity to start a new season each year with tremendous expectation of a full year of accomplishments," he wrote in his May-June report. "It is true we never know what is ahead that will interfere with our plans and accomplishments. However, regardless of what takes place, whether it is a blowdown, a fire, fatalities, Indians, drugs, or the bears, we know that in one sense or another we are going to succeed in contributing to the pleasure and answering to the recreational demands of our visiting guests."

In the early summer, Buzz was busy with staff interviews and hiring boards, job standards, revising operating procedures, and an affirmative action plan. District rangers and other staff were responsible for the orientation of work/study students and YCC groups.

One of Governor Baxter's three trust funds for the park was earmarked for land purchases through the Maine Forest Authority. The trustees had bought a 200-acre lot in Mt. Chase plantation and 200 acres in Harpswell in the early 1970s. Importantly, the Authority had decided that $50,000 was to be set aside each year for land acquisition even though no money had been available yet for that purpose.

▲ ▲ ▲ ▲ ▲

After Bill Cross's departure, the park had kept the business manager's position vacant for six months to save money, but in 1978 had hired Peter J. Madeira, Jr., to fill the post. Tibbs recruited Madeira, who was the office manager for AMC in Boston. He didn't know Madeira personally but knew his father, Jay, who was on the Advisory Committee, and Tibbs wanted someone who was a hiker and interested in being in the park, not just sitting behind a desk.

Madeira had big shoes to fill, and he was only thirty years old—a political science and public administration graduate from the University of Maine at Orono. He had worked for AMC for three years.

Madeira had already met Buzz briefly when he first went to the park in 1963 on a backpacking trip with his parents and brothers. He was impressed that Buzz had risen in the ranks with a limited education, and that rangers looked up to him. "Buzz had figured out how to make things work, and he used his relationship with Percival Baxter and his understanding of the Deeds of Trust to steer him in the right way," recalls Madeira.

After Madeira had been on the park staff for awhile, the rangers told him they were sure that Tibbs had hired him to be a "mole." Eventually, they changed their perception.

Madeira's initial observations of the Tibbs administration were that the emphasis was on income generation more than responsiveness to visitors, and rangers were still rude to complaining users, telling them they could leave if they didn't like the rules and regulations. Madeira thought that commissioned rangers spent too much time on law enforcement and riding around in their trucks. The park rule about closing the mountain to hiking and climbing on bad weather days drove him crazy.

A rite of passage for new park staff was a snowmobile ride with Buzz as soon as the weather allowed. Madeira had never been on a snowsled, and Buzz put him on a new, fast machine. Buzz liked to see how far he could push novices, so he told Madeira to follow him.

Buzz zigzagged along the park trails, and when Madeira came to the bridge at Abol Stream, he froze from fear of toppling over the side. Buzz talked him into trying it, and Madeira was successful, but he crashed later trying to follow Buzz's S-turns. Madeira was a good sport and climbed back on his machine and followed Buzz for a hair-raising ride to Chimney Pond.

Bill Cross had been asked to be a consultant to Madeira if Madeira needed help with the business office, but Madeira ignored his predecessor. Cross then criticized Madeira's job performance, as he had Buzz's.

▲▲▲▲▲

The much-awaited draft master plan was finally ready for public comment, and expectations were high, especially in the environmental community. The one who was most skeptical was Buzz, who thought Tibbs didn't have what it took to lead a successful process. Buzz declined to have much to do with the plan, not believing in the need for it to start with and not wanting to be tarred by it if—or rather, when—it showed itself to be a failure. Buzz's position all along was that Governor Baxter's mandates constituted the only plan necessary.

The plan was supposed to represent Baxter Park's attempt to come of age with wilderness thinking. It didn't come close. It was nearly fifty pages of dry, bureaucratic script. In general, the document was a conceptual framework for managing the park. In identifying the two main goals, the plan stated the obvious: protecting the natural wild state in keeping with Baxter's Deeds of Trust, and providing recreational use in accordance with the park's wild character.

There was a new element in the plan: a geographical division of the park into five management zones: existing roads; recreation areas; the wildlife sanctuary, compromising most of the park; the SFMA; and wildlife areas, such as ponds, where the park shared jurisdiction with the fish and wildlife department. The policies and criteria for managing the zones were so broad that they provided little meaningful direction—at least in the initial plan.

Five public meetings were held across Maine for citizens and representatives of special interest groups to comment on the draft. The feedback was awful, with most people calling the effort a waste of time. The plan was assailed for being so vague that a truck could drive through it, and it was deemed useless because of adherence to old, ecologically questionable practices. Former Authority member Jon Lund was one of the strongest critics, saying the plan had no vision for the future and noting that it didn't even try to define wilderness or carrying capacity.[2]

While Buzz stayed out of most of the discussion, he was instrumental in getting an obsolete building removal policy included in the plan—one that grounded his mission to get rid of all structures that were not essential to field operations.

Despite the public rejection of the plan, there was a lot of self-congratulation among those who drafted it: they were relieved a document was in hand, and they could go on to other work. The plan was supposed to be updated every five years, but that schedule wasn't met.

For Buzz, the value of the master plan was that it established for the first time a Standard Operating Procedures (SOP) manual. Tibbs gave Buzz the job of writing the document—a how-to guide that interpreted the master plan and provided the details necessary to carry out jobs and operational activities. Being in charge of the SOP was "almost as good as being director," Buzz discovered.

▲ ▲ ▲ ▲ ▲

Tibbs floundered with what to do next. With the plan a failed effort, Tibbs's critics became more vocal, in and out of the park. Environmentalists in particular viewed Tibbs as just another bureaucrat with little concept of wilderness management and no passion for the job, especially after the planning process. They wanted a new director.

One of the lasting stories about Tibbs from Jim Tierney was that he never climbed Katahdin but pretended he did. Even Authority members told the tale as evidence that Tibbs was a fish out of water at Baxter Park.

When Tibbs began horning in on field operations to keep himself busy, tensions intensified with Buzz, who didn't like the intrusion, and the rangers, who were closer to Buzz than the "college dude."

"We went through some very rough seas," Buzz says, "but overall Lee was a diplomat, and we managed our disagreements." Buzz didn't know that Tibbs viewed his park job as a short-term one until Helena Tibbs told Jan that her husband had never stayed in a job more than seven years. By that calculation, Buzz could hope that Tibbs would resign by 1981.

▲ ▲ ▲ ▲ ▲

As a result of the 1977 fire, blueberry bushes were growing in profusion in the sandy, open burned areas in the southern end of the park. Buzz and Jan had always enjoyed picking wild berries and edible plants. Rangers were quick to find natural foods to supplement their camp larder and take to park staff social gatherings.

Besides blueberries and fiddleheads, there were raspberries, cranberries, serviceberries, and mushrooms to harvest in the summers. Blueberries grew all over the park, from the roadsides to the slopes of Katahdin and the other mountains. The North Basin of Katahdin and the south side of Traveler Mountain had the best cranberries. Serviceberries thrived at the South Branch parking lot. There was a large fiddlehead area in a hardwood flat south of Wadleigh Mountain to Trout Brook Farm on both sides of Webster Stream. For a time, the park allowed local people to harvest the fiddleheads, but when some began to sell them commercially, public foraging was stopped.

Buzz loved a peppermint tea plant he found at Little Wassataquoik Stream. Gerald Merry had special places to pick wild greens for salads. But the most determined forager was Chris Drew, who was passionate about everything edible, whether wild or in his impressive vegetable garden in the park.

▲ ▲ ▲ ▲ ▲

Road access in the north end of the park was much greater in 1979 than it is today. By fording Trout Brook, people could drive all the way up the Freezeout Trail to the Little East campsite at the convergence of Webster Stream and Second Matagamon Lake. They also used the Black Brook Road to drive to Webster Lake, and then they could connect to a logging road all the way out to Telos.

Getting in and out at multiple spots was of particular interest to hunters and poachers who used the so-called Legal Mile. That stretch was between Trout Brook Crossing and Wadleigh Brook in the southeast corner of Township 6 Range 9, where the northern hunting zone (in the SFMA) bordered the sanctuary and the Perimeter Road. In fact, the zone included woods on both sides of the road, and it was a magnet for deer and partridge hunters. It was hunters who originated the name "Legal Mile."

Buzz's first reason to dislike the Legal Mile came in 1968 when he was supervisor for the first time. The South Branch Campground dump was on the Legal Mile, and hunters flocked to it because of the easy opportunity to kill bear—with tourists looking on. Buzz felt it was a public relations disaster and got the dump relocated to the sanctuary zone.

Deer and partridge hunters both liked to go after game on the Legal Mile because of the easy access, and Buzz was haunted by the illegal hunting going on. He didn't have enough rangers to keep close watch on the road and was sure that if hunters saw an animal in the sanctuary area on the way to or from the Legal Mile, they probably shot it. "The temptation was always there for a fish and game violation," Buzz remembers.

Toward the end of any November hunting season, people desperate for deer would shoot a moose instead if they came upon one—ignoring the fact that there was no moose season in the park at any time. Some hunters engaged in thrill shooting—leaving the dead animal for the rangers to deal with.

Rangers laid traps for known poachers. They stationed themselves north and south of the Legal Mile at Trout Brook and Nesowadnehunk, just as Buzz had done earlier in his career. Gatekeepers let the rangers know when so-and-so ventured into the park so the men could be watched and/or stopped for a vehicle search.

▲ ▲ ▲ ▲ ▲

At the end of such a hectic and sometimes volatile decade, it was hard to know whether the 1970s would go out like a lion or a lamb. A new confrontation on snowmobiles was imminent, and anything could happen. One thing was for sure: Buzz and the rangers wanted snowmobile use to continue, and Buzz used his influence toward that end.

Joe Brennan left office in 1978 for a successful gubernatorial run and was replaced by Republican Richard Cohen, who had been deputy attorney general and head of the criminal division. Maynard Marsh and John Walker also left office, and two "acting" heads of the fish and wildlife and forestry agencies became temporary trustees for several months. Snowmobile advocates thought that new blood on the Authority might bode well for their cause of getting the ban removed, and they counted on Buzz being in their court.

▲ ▲ ▲ ▲ ▲

One of the novice seasonal employees for the summer of 1979 was Ben Townsend, who was assigned to Chimney Pond to be assistant campground ranger. From the start, Townsend was not a Buzz "loyalist." In fact, he quickly went over Buzz's head on an issue—a radical action for a ranger, new or old.

Townsend had been at Chimney Pond only a short time when Buzz flew over in a helicopter to identify potential landing zones for search-and-rescue choppers. Lester Kenway happened to pass along the Davis Pond trail that same day and saw a prominent boulder freshly painted by Buzz with orange spray paint.

Townsend heard about the paint and was curious enough to hike over the mountain to see for himself. He was upset enough to go directly to the forest service to report the matter. "I don't think Buzz was happy," Townsend says.

That was the beginning of Townsend's skepticism about Buzz's capabilities as a wilderness manager. During Townsend's six years at Chimney Pond and even more years on the Advisory Committee, he came to believe that Buzz had too many personal limitations, such as a sense of insecurity and defensiveness. Those traits "could pop up at the oddest times when dealing with him on park issues," Townsend remembers.

He believes that Buzz manipulated information that affected the Authority's decision making and thus was an effective lobbyist in getting what he wanted from the trustees. As a case in point, Townsend points to Buzz's successful efforts in removing so many park buildings on the grounds that they were unnecessary or obsolete.

▲ ▲ ▲ ▲ ▲

Buzz had waited a considerable time to hire a full-time park naturalist, and funds were finally available in 1979 to fill the new position. Buzz was instrumental in moving his protégé Gerald Merry up to the spot. Merry had no college training, but Buzz felt that he was knowledgeable and talented enough to handle the job.

Indefatigable, Merry's first priority was to inventory park flora and fauna. Merry spent a tremendous amount of time developing the park's educational and interpretive materials and a slide show presentation for interested groups throughout Maine. In fact, it seemed there was hardly any administrative task that Merry couldn't do.

Merry and Buzz hit it off so well that he became, in effect, Buzz's unofficial assistant. Buzz's promotion of Merry was not well understood among the staff, and some didn't like it, but Buzz defended Merry's wide-ranging work as highly valuable to the park. Three years later there was still enough internal unrest about Merry that Buzz explained in his annual report how "lucky" the park was to have him and suggested that anyone who had questions should come to him personally.

▲ ▲ ▲ ▲ ▲

On June 4, 1979, Glenn Manuel of Littleton was named commissioner of the Department of Inland Fisheries and Wildlife (formerly Fish and Wildlife), replacing Maynard Marsh. Manuel was an Aroostook County potato farmer, businessman, and inventor, but he was no stranger to fish and wildlife issues. Like Buzz, he had grown up on a farm and spent his youth outdoors fishing and hunting. Manuel had served in the state senate, was chairman of the Fish and Wildlife Committee, and was also on the department's advisory council for most of the 1970s.

There was no fish and game commissioner who bested Manuel on personality. He had a lot of country humor and spoke his mind, regardless of the occasion. He loved photo ops and being in the political limelight. Because of their common backgrounds, Buzz and Manuel felt a natural bond. Buzz figured correctly that Manuel could be a valuable ally.

▲ ▲ ▲ ▲ ▲

In preparation for a new debate on snowmobiles, former Maine Snowmobile Association president Beverly Rand had polled former trustees and park staff about their positions on snowmobile use. Buoyed by their responses, he went to the Authority as expected to ask for removal of the prohibition.

Rand, a retired potato and dairy farmer from Island Falls, emphasized at the September 1979 meeting that snowmobiles were now quieter, more dependable, easier to ride and handle, and a more sophisticated machine than the earlier models. He argued that it was discriminatory to allow vehicles in the summer but not snowmobiles in the winter.

The Authority was given a letter that Rand had solicited from past park leaders, including former trustee Jim Erwin, who noted that he had been the lone dissenting vote on snowmobiles earlier. Erwin saw things differently now.

"I have to say now in all honesty that all through my tenure, the snowmobilers caused the Park no problems, they did no damage, they chased no game, and they carefully obeyed all the park rules," he wrote. "Each spring when the perimeter road was again opened to vehicles, they toured the entire area in pickup trucks to be sure no litter had been overlooked. In short, they were good citizens. In my judgment, they earned the privilege of using the road."

Governor Baxter, Erwin continued, had created the road to enable citizens to get into the park. Erwin, like Buzz, thought it was unfair to say that cars, pickups, and other vehicles could use the road but not snowmobiles. "This seems especially so since we know that when they were allowed to use it, they behaved thoughtfully."

Former supervisor Harry Kearney also weighed in with his pro-snowmobile position. He emphasized that Governor Baxter was "well aware of and pleased with the winter use of the park" by snowmobilers, cross-country skiers, and hikers. "He was, however, adamant that the snow machine use be restricted to the road systems that were maintained and used for summer travel."

NRCM and other environmental groups opposed a return to snowmobile use as a violation of the "forever wild" mandate, and prepared for a court fight. Buzz had notified Richard Cohen that he had polled the park staff and found that a "large majority" of them thought the machines should be allowed on the Perimeter Road for much the same reason as Erwin argued.

The administrative use of snowmobiles wasn't an issue yet, and if rangers had been polled on that particular subject, they likely would have felt even more strongly. Getting supplies to the backcountry campgrounds and search-and-rescue operations would be much more difficult without snowmobiles, as the field crew had come to see.

The Authority tabled the snowmobile question for two months and then voted unanimously to reconsider the ban and petition the Maine Superior Court for guidance on their power to regulate snowmobile use and that of other motorized vehicles.

Governor Brennan appointed Ken Stratton to head the Maine Forest Service just in time to head off environmentalists' concerns that the Authority was moving ahead on the snowmobile issue without a key trustee.

▲ ▲ ▲ ▲ ▲

The snowmobile issue aside, the 1979 season was one of the park's best years—no fatalities, no fires, few drug problems, no Indian problems, relatively good weather, and good fishing. Lost fishermen or hikers were found or walked out safely on their own.

Buzz concentrated on developing and implementing an SOP manual for search-and-rescue activities—the park's first. The in-house mountain rescue team had been disbanded by now because there were fewer rangers eligible due to personnel department restrictions, and money was tight. Also, the rangers were getting older, making it physically harder to meet the demands of rescue operations. Buzz lined up outside volunteer organizations to carry the burden of search-and-rescue missions, but he made sure that park rangers continued to receive first aid and other specialized training to assist rescuers.

---

1. *Maine Times*, August 12, 1977, pp. 1–3; September 23, 1977, p. 20.
2. *Maine Times*, August 26, 1977, pp. 18–19; September 2, 1977, p. 6.

Primary Document Sources: BSPA Box 1 (2112-0717); Box 2 (2507-0801) BSPA Original Minutes Boxes 9, 10, 12; Maine Land Use Regulation Commission's Togue Pond Camps file.

Conversations and communications: Dabney Caldwell, Buzz Caverly, Charlie Cogbill, Chris Drew, Charles FitzGerald, Bill Gormely, Chris Herter, Bob Howes, Don Hudson, Lester Kenway, Pete Madeira, Warren Nelson, Lonnie Pingree, Sarah Redfield, Ben Townsend, Lee Tibbs, Bill Vail, Laura Waterman.

PART III: TRANSITIONS AND POWER

▲▲▲▲▲▲▲▲

CHAPTER 16

# OPPORTUNITY KNOCKS

WHEN KEN STRATTON WAS APPOINTED to head the Maine Forest Service and took his seat on the Authority at its January 10, 1980, meeting, he was the first member from the Millinocket area since the era of the Authority's predecessor—the Baxter Park Commission—in the 1930s. But anyone who thought that Stratton would fall in line with whatever the locals from Millinocket, East Millinocket, and Patten wanted were surprised. Stratton had a mind of his own about park affairs, partly because he had spent so much time roaming around the preserve as a boy.

The major contention at that meeting was over Dr. John Hakola's park history book, started five years previously. There was dissension among the Advisory Committee's history review subcommittee over whether it should be printed. Some of subcommittee members thought the book was dull and repetitive; others were dissatisfied with it because it ignored controversies that questioned management of the park.

As head of the review panel, former Authority chairman Austin Wilkins wielded considerable power on the matter. He was on the "publish it" side, but insisted that the book downplay snowmobile use, spruce budworm spraying, and other hot-button political issues.

Buzz's concern about the book was not over its readability or whether controversies were included, but rather how heavy AMC's hand was in the writing of it. Pete Madeira was friends with Hakola, was a long-standing member of AMC, and was editor of the AMC's *Maine Mountain Guide*. Madeira, as well as Tibbs and Bill Cross, had worked with the subcommittee in both general editing and non-editing capacities. In fact, Madeira had suggested the title, and Hakola had accepted it: *Legacy of a Lifetime: The Story of Baxter State Park*.

Tibbs and Madeira were well aware of Buzz's animosity toward AMC—and not just from the past. Some AMC members would occasionally try to get special privileges or access, using their membership as justification. The request would start in the field with a ranger or campground personnel and escalate to Buzz or other staff at park head-quarters; the AMC members' approach was not appreciated.

Because the legislature wasn't interested in funding the book, the Authority decided to use Baxter trust money, to be replaced by sales revenue or other sources. The trustees voted to print 5,000 copies and sell each hardcover book for sixteen dollars.

When *Legacy* was finally published in May 1981, there was no one for whom the book turned out to be more important than Buzz. He had begun familiarizing himself with Governor Baxter's writings in the early 1970s and had a basic understanding of the protections and regu-lations. However, *Legacy* provided Buzz for the first time with good knowledge and interest in what the trust provisions were and what Baxter's vision was. It galvanized his interest in seriously studying the directives to the point that he obtain his own copies of the Deeds of Trust and Baxter's communications. His personal copy of *Legacy* was quickly marked in red, highlighting passages that he wanted to remem-ber and would refer to repeatedly for the rest of his career.

▲ ▲ ▲ ▲ ▲

Despite Buzz and Tibbs's clashes, his annual evaluations didn't suffer. Authority chairman Maynard Marsh had served as Buzz's rater in 1976–77 and had given Buzz eighty-six points out of a possible hun-dred in seven categories, from managing employees to communications skills. Tibbs's evaluations covering 1977 through 1980 were even better and likely important in the Authority's future decision on whether Buzz was ready to succeed Tibbs.

Tibbs gave Buzz eighty-seven points in 1977–78 and by December 1980, ninety-six points, just four shy of a perfect score. He elaborated on the areas that Buzz could improve. Tibbs's remarks in three differ-ent evaluations provided deeper insights into Buzz's management habits and inclinations than had been referred to in past reviews. There was always room for a little more improvement, but Tibbs left no doubt that he thought Buzz's general performance was "of the highest cal-iber." Not only did he give Buzz the best rating ever, but especially noted his "above average" judgment and decision making, his "fair and objective" method of coaching and evaluating subordinates, and his "consistent efforts" to improve resource and staff efficiencies.

Buzz received a merit increase the following year for improvement in the areas suggested by Tibbs. But he continued to struggle with delegating too much authority to subordinates.

▲ ▲ ▲ ▲ ▲

True to Tibbs's seven-year job itch, he gave notice in August 1981 that he was going to leave later in the year and go into private business. Tibbs confided to Buzz that he had resigned. Buzz was thrilled.

Glenn Manuel and Tibbs had never hit it off and, in fact, were confrontational. Many times Manuel visited headquarters, and he and Tibbs ended up hollering at each other. Tibbs was tired of the politics, the changing membership of the Authority, and the increasing administrative responsibilities. Much of the time the director was caught in the middle between demands of the trustees and the staff.

Buzz asked Tibbs to recommend him, but Tibbs declined. Tibbs thought it was important for Buzz to compete on his own. "Buzz was quite mad at me," Tibbs recalls. Buzz confided in former Authority member and now NRCM president Jon Lund that he was seeking the director's position. Lund had reservations about Buzz but encouraged him. NRCM board members were alarmed at the possibility of Buzz being the permanent director because of his lack of higher education and some of his past behavior.

▲ ▲ ▲ ▲ ▲

While the Authority filed a snowmobile petition with the courts, the SFMA was an ongoing subject. Because of his responsibility for park operations, Buzz couldn't help being involved in SFMA field oversight, discussions, and plans. Forester George Ruopp had written a management plan designed to promote the objectives of scientific forestry and had set goals. Buzz was very much aware that he knew nothing about forestry science and didn't offer any objections to the proposal.

The ten-year plan proposed the clear-cutting and selective harvesting of almost 14,000 acres of the 28,527-acre SFMA and the building of forty-four miles of road to access the stands—all in the first five years. Environmentalists thought it was outrageous.

At a public hearing in July 1980, the plan drew strong opposition from Jon Lund and past Land Use Regulation Commission member

Whit McEvoy. Both charged that Ruopp's proposal differed only slightly from a commercial operation, with its skidder damages to the land and use of pesticides and herbicides to prevent unwanted species growth. Jon Lund noted that almost a decade earlier, he had seen a previous Authority willing to allow non-scientific forestry in the specially designated townships. Now it could happen again if Ruopp's plan was accepted.

Charles FitzGerald didn't testify at the hearing but wrote Tibbs, stating that the Authority would be agreeing to nothing more than an industrial-style harvest if it accepted Ruopp's recommendations. Referring back to Great Northern's proposed 1972 timber swap from the Katahdin area to the SFMA and the commercial blowdown salvage of 1974, FitzGerald said both were "disguised as 'the cleanup and restoration of the forest to its natural wild state.'" The language of both plans claimed to fulfill the purposes of the park covenants when in reality both were "ordinary commercial logging plans."

He urged a plan "both cautious and imaginative, separate from any influence of the forest industry. . . . [T]here is no need for the instant development of the entire SFMA area, or for any large-scale experiments based on so-called 'modern' forestry techniques." If the Authority wasn't careful, he suggested they would be looking at another court suit.

▲ ▲ ▲ ▲ ▲

Returning to his early stomping ground was guaranteed spiritual renewal for Buzz, in good times and bad. In early spring, 1980, Buzz and Jan returned to Russell Pond for a couple of days. It was the last time Buzz would be at his former post so early in the spring. He did a little evening fishing, some hiking, and watched moose, savoring the familiar, tranquil surroundings.

The rest of Buzz's spring was routine and relatively quiet—office work, meetings, patrols, speaking engagements, investigating accidents, search and rescue. But something always came along to cause a stir. This time it was an $18 bill from the park business office to Charles and Ruth Norris at Kidney Pond Camps for an American flag issued from park supply. Buzz was mad and in "despair" about the situation, given the park's close relationship with the Norrises and the fact that Kidney Pond was owned by the park. It stung his sense of patriotism.

In a memo to Tibbs and Madeira, Buzz said that a flag flying at Kidney Pond was an asset and seen by "patriots" from all over the country—naming army general William Westmoreland and NBC newsman Tom Brokaw. "It is pretty small potatoes" for the park to ask for payment for a flag in stock, Buzz wrote business manager Pete Madeira. "The flag should be provided . . . anyway." He declared his commitment to seeing the Norrises didn't have to pay.

"A wise old Maine guide told me many years ago that 'when you live in the woods, you work together if you wish to succeed,'" Buzz concluded. "I believe strongly in this theory and these words of wisdom." The bill was canceled.

▲ ▲ ▲ ▲ ▲

Moose in Baxter Park lived a life of Riley, having no one to fear. Efforts had been made in the legislature to approve an open season on moose, and the bill introduced in 1975 by Representative John Martin (D-Eagle Lake) failed by only one vote in the Maine Senate. With the moose population on the increase as the result of commercial forest clear-cutting, which produced good browse for them, and a forty-year ban on hunting the animals, an open season was virtually guaranteed the next time around.

In 1979 an experimental season on moose was approved for the northern half of the state, to begin in the fall of 1980. Baxter Park was exempt from the start. Just before the first season on moose began, Buzz wrote a memo "to all Baxter State Park Moose" that might wander out of the preserve to open hunting grounds, and he had copies tacked on bulletin boards at park headquarters and gatehouses:

> BEWARE! Next week, Sept 22–27th, humans with thunder sticks will be stalking your tracks in an all-out effort to skin your hide [outside the park]. These same people who have marveled over your magnificence and have snapped many pictures of you to show friends and relatives your beauty are now ready to hang you up. Stay deep within the boundaries of Baxter State Park; trust no one; and we will try to protect you from would-be violators of the law. However, we need your cooperation. In the interest of your preservation, we urge you to keep a low profile for this six-day period. Please spread the word among your kind.

Welcome them to join you deep within the heart of Baxter Park; otherwise, one of those six days could be the shortest of your life.

Buzz had talked with Maynard Marsh about having a protective buffer—one township wide—around the park to give Baxter moose greater protection. It would take care of the problem of hunters luring moose across the park line onto private hunting land. But Marsh thought it was too thorny an issue for his department and the park to take on, and there was no natural boundary for enforcement purposes.

▲ ▲ ▲ ▲ ▲

As the park closed in the fall, rangers breathed a sigh of relief. Visitors had been unusually cranky, complaining about poor road conditions, no park map handouts, and the prohibition of pets, motorcycles, and over-sized vehicles.

Buzz and Helon Taylor were still exchanging letters and reminiscing about their park days together. Buzz reported seeing old park friends, such as Ed Werler and Myrle Scott, who was leaving his supervisor's job at the Allagash Wilderness Waterway. Buzz passed on news about ongoing issues he thought his mentor would be interested in:

> As you are well aware, Baxter Park has become very controversial since Governor Baxter's death, and nothing is simple anymore. Everybody appears to have a different interpretation of the Deeds of Trust. Many people he never even knew proclaim to be long-time friends, or even relatives, and yes, even John Baxter and Ethel Dyer speak loud in honor of the family name. Other Baxter family representatives keep a low profile and appear only during a sideline highlight once in a while. It is unfortunate, in my opinion, that John and Ethel did not show more interest during the Governor's lifetime. I wonder why they waited until he was gone before speaking up. The snowmobile issue, the Scientific Forest Management Area, the road system and the operation of the facilities are all debatable subjects now, each in their own sense. Yes indeed, we have become very complicated within our operational system. However, I and other Park personnel continue to see our jobs as a challenge and enjoy much satisfaction in accomplishments we are able to achieve toward our daily operation.

▲ ▲ ▲ ▲ ▲

Dick Cohen left the attorney general's office and the Authority at the end of the year. Cohen was the sixth attorney general who had served on the Authority since Buzz had been in park employment. Cohen and Jim Erwin stood out for taking "a sincere interest in Baxter Park operations," Buzz wrote the departing Cohen. "I hold you in the highest esteem and appreciate your interest, effectiveness, understanding, and the help you provided each of us as we carried out our operational responsibilities."

Before Cohen departed, he shared with Buzz his hope that wealthy Harold Colt would come to the financial rescue of the park. Colt was known to want to make a major contribution, and, like Percival Baxter, leave an enduring legacy.

Cohen felt the way to go was a substantial endowment fund. So as not to "corrupt" Baxter's influence, such a fund would not be used to expand programs, but rather would simply generate interest money to cover the park's ongoing costs. When Cohen learned that the Baxter family would oppose the idea, he dropped the matter. Colt, however, had an idea of his own that he would try later.

▲ ▲ ▲ ▲ ▲

Despite his retirement, former park business manager Bill Cross continued to press his concerns over spending. Costs were up for numerous reasons—inflation, collective bargaining, the SFMA startup investment, and heating system breakdowns at park headquarters. In a letter to his friend and fellow Advisory Committee member Win Robbins, Cross let the Authority "have it" verbally for not, in his estimation, paying enough attention to their fiduciary responsibilities.

During Governor Baxter's lifetime, "the governor personally approved almost every expenditure" from his trust funds, but after his death, the fiscal control was "very lax or nearly nonexistent at many times," Cross wrote. "It should be remembered that during his lifetime most of the Authority members were career people and rarely spent a lot of time and effort looking after the park, but in recent years the makeup of the Authority has changed from career to politically oriented people with varied interests other than Baxter Park," Cross continued.

When he was in the Augusta business office "there was never a day that I was not in contact with the chairman talking about the park, and operational fiscal control was lost when the business office was moved to Millinocket," Cross contended. If "something" wasn't done to rein in expenditures, the park wouldn't be able to go on operating and spending at the same rate as the recent past, he warned.

In another letter to Robbins, Cross reiterated his unhappiness with the Authority and the Advisory over budget problems, and he laid out a laundry list of other wonderings, opinions, and long-held suspicions.

He raised the question of why the attorney general had so much influence over other Authority members. "Yes, this is a very touchy subject but one of great concern to many others too, but leave it to me to put it in writing," Cross said.

He questioned whether the Authority should be kept "fully informed of operational problems such as [staff] grievances, dismissals, investigations, etc. Whereas, in my opinion, the Authority is responsible for the public image of the park, I feel strongly that they should be fully informed of all problems within the park." He wondered if it was true that "Governor B never intended for the A.G. to become chairman of the Authority but to only act on legal matters for the park."

Often revisiting the $725,000 compensation in 1973 to Great Northern, Cross voiced his suspicions over the necessity of paying that much. "Information and data available at the time indicated that the volume shown was questionable and impossible to remove within the time frame of the deed," he asserted, "but these facts were never considered—it is very sad that the case did not go to court as there is no doubt in my mind that about $500,000 was paid for stumpage which could not be removed, or more important, should the agreement have been allowed to stand, the park would today have a road system available to use for the removal of wood in the area." Cross called his ruminations "quite a lot of food for thought" and added there was more he could say. "Although some of the items might be taken in the wrong vein by some, I truly feel that they are all items of concern to many persons, so I am again willing to be the fall guy and bring them up if it will help to result in better Park operations in the future."

▲ ▲ ▲ ▲ ▲

As Superior Court Justice Dan Wathen prepared to hear the park's snowmobile case in 1981, Jim Tierney was elected by the Democratic majority in the legislature to be the new attorney general. At thirty-three years old, Tierney was the youngest attorney general in the country and on the move politically. "I was young, driven, fast-talking, glib, very partisan," he remembers.

Tierney yearned to run for governor. But first he had to repair the combative reputation he had gained during his years as majority leader in the Maine House (when he was just twenty-nine years old), reorganize his new office, and attract a top quality team of lawyers. With so much already on his plate, Tierney was simply horrified to learn that he was automatically a member of the Baxter Park Authority. His reaction was to order his chief counsel, Rufus Brown, to get him off the Authority or it would drive him crazy. "I was the attorney general to make the world better," he says. "This Baxter thing seemed like it could take me down."

Brown's "bad" news was that Tierney had to remain on the Authority and attend the meetings; he couldn't delegate his duties. He also had to put up with calls from Buzz about the most minor issues and drop-in visits from Baxter Advisory Committee members. In his first few days on the job, Tierney was visited by Win Robbins, who wanted to talk about a blowdown at Windey Pitch. "I said to Win, 'What am I supposed to do with that? Get a chain saw and cut it up?' Win said he was just calling on everyone on the Authority to let them know about the situation."

Once Tierney really understood that he was committed by law to the Authority, he took his role seriously. He hauled home Baxter's Deeds of Trust, correspondence, and other documents to read, decided to give it his best effort, and quickly discovered that he relished being part of the Baxter Park clan and taking his own large family there for vacations.

Tierney's assessment of his Authority responsibility was primarily to enforce the trust. "I read all the cases," he says. He could see that Governor Baxter took different positions at different times and "was not a god." Tierney's opinion on the Authority setup was that it was brilliant in terms of checks and balances. On the other hand, the staff organization was dysfunctional, in his view.

"All the rangers were the same age as Buzz and all had been hell-raisers, had great old times," he recalls. "They were wonderful public servants living in the woods with a high school education and no law-

enforcement training and no wilderness training. The lines of authority were mixed. Everyone had hugely strong feelings about the park, so
they gravitated toward Ken [Stratton] and myself to solve problems.
There were people in the environmental organizations who didn't like
Buzz because they thought he was 'a yahoo, a cop, because he'd always
wanted to be a state trooper.'"

Tierney was from a working-class family like Buzz's. His parents,
like Buzz's mother, didn't graduate from high school. So environmentalists were treading on thin ice with Tierney over Buzz's lack of formal credentials. He liked Buzz, seeing him as "very transparent. I saw
capacity in Buzz."

Tierney was struck by the "Taj Mahal" (as the park headquarters
was called) and inquired how in the world a previous Authority could
have located such an expensive building beside something as crass as
McDonald's and miles away from the park. He wondered if association
with Baxter Park made people "a little cuckoo."

▲ ▲ ▲ ▲ ▲

The chairmanship of the Authority passed to now-senior trustee Glenn
Manuel. In one of Tibbs's last trips to Augusta, he and Pete Madeira
met with Manuel to brief him on park operations and finances. Madeira
had developed charts on revenue trends and other information that
would give "the new boss" a picture of what was going on. He and
Tibbs expected a lengthy meeting, but Manuel wasn't interested in a
long-winded explanation of finances and operational details. After just
a brief summary, Manuel said, "Well boys, that's all good, but I'll manage the park the way I want." The commissioner's reaction convinced
Madeira that he wouldn't be working for Manuel very long.

▲ ▲ ▲ ▲ ▲

Buzz was always thinking about how to tighten up the park's boundaries and end old access "leaks." He was in the right place at the right
time and had the right relationships to bring to fruition in 1981 a plan
he had been ruminating about for a long time. The subject was Bangor
Hydro's Telos Dam property at Webster Stream. Buzz wanted to bring
the lot into park ownership to stop public traffic and preclude the
potential for future construction of a major dam. (The old deteriorating

dam was not a functioning structure.)

The Black Brook Road access to the dam was used not just by Bangor Hydro employees and guests, but by the public. People drove jeeps as well as horses to the dam, and hauled in lots of beer. The remoteness of the area allowed hunters to get away with baiting bears with cow carcasses, and night-hunting deer from the road was also a problem. The road had a number of wet spots, and the traffic caused deep ruts and erosion. The small bridges along the route fell apart, and essentially, the road became unsafe to drive.

"I was in a good mood one day, and I decided to ask a big favor of Bob [Haskell, president of the utility]," says Buzz. Haskell, a supporter of Buzz's, understood correctly that Buzz wanted the utility property turned over to the park. Haskell told him, tongue in cheek, that if the Authority would make him permanent director, Haskell would cooperate. There couldn't be any deals like that, Buzz replied. But a few days later, Buzz was notified by Tierney's office that Bangor Hydro had turned over the dam lot deed to the park. Haskell gave up the company's ownership of twenty-five acres, including flowage rights on Webster Stream and the easement on the Black Brook Road from the park's Perimeter Road. The park immediately stopped public access.

▲ ▲ ▲ ▲ ▲

As seasons came and went, the spruce budworm infestation improved and worsened. No budworm spraying had been needed in the SFMA in the 1970s, so the infestation was strengthening again. Forester George Ruopp recommended protecting 7,000 acres with a spray containing *Bacillus thuringiensis* (Bt), a microbial insecticide. Buzz was nervous about spraying because it would take $105,000 from the park's already strapped bank account. Startup costs of the SFMA had pushed the park's 1981 budget up 7 percent (just under $52,000) to $798,108.

With Tibbs making the staff cut down on the number of pencils they used, Buzz thought the park couldn't afford insect spraying—that operations were "deteriorating." He wanted everyday needs to take priority over salvage or any SFMA startup activities. The Authority, however, was pushed by Glenn Manuel to go along with Ruopp's advice to spray.

In response to public criticism of Ruopp's draft SFMA management plan, it had been revised to include sections on fisheries, wildlife, and recreation. Ruopp felt the park was now ready to send the unit revisions out for another round of public critique—one of the last hurdles before cutting could actually start. The Authority and Tibbs wanted the plan to be implemented as quickly as possible to generate new revenues.

▲ ▲ ▲ ▲ ▲

The park's income needs set off a debate over increasing user fees. Fees hadn't been raised for a decade. It was the easiest way the Authority knew to offset the effects of inflation, which had eroded about 30 percent of the trust fund's value since Percival Baxter had died.

A subcommittee of the Advisory panel looked at old and new fees, including whether to institute a fee for Maine residents—heretofore a no-no because of Governor Baxter's wishes. Before the panel could complete its report, state senator Charles Pray (D-Millinocket) announced that the Penobscot County delegation would fight a move to charge Mainers, especially after wasting so much money on such an expensive park headquarters.

Subsequently, the subcommittee backed down from the idea of a resident fee and recommended a dollar increase for each type of existing fee—a hike that would generate about $75,000, or 40 percent more for operation needs. Ideas such as voluntary contributions, adopt-a-trail donations, and other ways to meet annual operating expenses were rejected.

Buzz supported an across-the-board fee hike for various types of roadside facilities but didn't want fees raised for backcountry sites, which were not high-maintenance. He also opposed a hike in the day-use fee in order to keep attracting people with "moderate means," as Governor Baxter wanted.

Bill Cross jumped into the debate, advising Authority chairman Glenn Manuel that the park had the "cart before the horse." The park needed to know "the true cost of Park operations" before fees were increased, he argued.

Cross contended that little had been done for a decade to review or hold down costs and that if the rate of expenditure continued to rise at the same pace, "no affordable fee increases will cover these costs . . . and even the proposed [$75,000] fee increase will not cover the anticipated increased costs." He stood firm on the need for a resident fee dedicated to road maintenance. The highway funding level of $32,000 hadn't been raised since 1969, and the park was almost desperate for more road money.

▲ ▲ ▲ ▲ ▲

With every expense examined closely, there was in-house lobbying against retaining the naturalist position held by Gerald Merry, who had also become Buzz's unofficial administrative assistant and was commissioned as a law enforcement officer. Phil McGlauflin, Bill Cross, and Win Robbins thought that Merry was wasting money traveling around the state to give slide presentations and educational talks about the park to "little old ladies."

In a May 21 letter to Robbins and Cross, Buzz was adamant that the position be retained, and defended Merry's many skills, his talents, and his statewide traveling engagements—engagements he gave prior approval for. "Gerald has worked hard, and I feel he can be credited with many good projects and some excellent public relations for the Park," Buzz wrote. Older Mainers who couldn't climb mountains or hike the backcountry deserved to have the park come to them through presentations by Merry, Buzz said, declaring that Governor Baxter didn't "necessarily restrict" the park to young people in good physical shape. He explained that Merry worked closely with the district rangers on education for interpretive programs at campgrounds and had plans to work with campground personnel to "expand their knowledge of the natural beauties of the park so they can better explain them to the public."

Merry had made it clear to Buzz that if the naturalist position was eliminated, he was not interested in returning to carpentry work. Buzz asked the Authority and the Advisory Committee to take a close look at the situation before making a hasty decision. Buzz prevailed and Merry's job was retained.

▲ ▲ ▲ ▲ ▲

The short funding had led to Buzz and Lester Kenway butting heads over trail funds for the summer. Lester Kenway felt so strongly that the trail crew program needed certain supplies that he went around Buzz and Phil McGlauflin to seek needed items and had Tibbs approve purchase of the supplies. Buzz called Kenway's action of going to Lee Tibbs "a dangerous precedent." In an April 30, 1981, memo to Tibbs, Buzz said he was concerned that Kenway would feel he had "a blank checkbook" and that if he needed anything, he would just "go to Lee. I am concerned that there will be repercussions from field personnel, basically Chris and Bob [Howes], who had to cut items and live with it."

Kenway responded, explaining that McGlauflin had given him permission to write to Tibbs, and denying that he felt he had a blank checkbook. He pointed out that he received only $140 out of a requested $750. "I am shocked that you think I maintain such an attitude," Kenway said. Buzz stuck to his position that Kenway needed to follow the chain of command structure.

As for the "blank checkbook" statement, Buzz told Kenway that he had "a tendency to insist on getting what you want regardless of the sacrifice." It was true that the trail program was minimal, Buzz acknowledged, but until funds and manpower were available, there was "little that can be done about it."

▲ ▲ ▲ ▲ ▲

After three years of managing Cobscook Bay State Park, Buzz's brother, Tim Caverly, wanted to move back to the north woods. In the spring, he applied for the position of supervisor of the Allagash Wilderness Waterway. During his job interview, he was asked how much he would let Buzz influence his decisions at the waterway. Tim assured the supervisor that he would be his own man.

Tim was hired, he moved with his wife, Sue, to Umsaskis Lake in May 1981, and in a few days, Buzz, Jan, and the girls showed up for a visit. Buzz was very proud of his younger brother. They took time out from the family gathering to paddle up the lake to look around and talk about Tim's new challenges. "Managing for wilderness was fairly new to me," recalls Tim Caverly. "I didn't know how to even talk about it."

It was unusual, if not unique, in the whole country for brothers to head one state's two premier wilderness areas. Tim and Buzz would find themselves challenged like never before in the complex and difficult arenas of management and politics.

▲ ▲ ▲ ▲ ▲

On June 12, there was a landmark ruling from the court. Superior Court Justice Daniel Wathen ruled that the Authority had the power to allow snowsleds within the preserve, thereby dashing the hopes of environmentalists for a snowmobile-free Baxter.

Maine newspapers gushed with stories and opinions on the decision, and the state's two leading dailies in southern and northern Maine took opposing views, reflecting the divided public opinion. The *Portland Press Herald* editorialized that the ruling was "disheartening." If the Authority was committed to honoring Percival Baxter's intent, it will choose to ban snowmobiles, the paper said.[1] On the other hand, the *Bangor Daily News* editorialized that there was "nothing destructive or inherently evil about snowmobiles traveling through the park."[2] Again, the *Herald* said that if the Authority allowed snowmobiles, it would "break faith brazenly" with Baxter, no matter what the condition. "And faith is at the heart of his magnificent gift."

But the "to be or not to be" about snowmobiles was not settled yet, because the litigants were intent on appealing the ruling to the Maine Supreme Court.

▲ ▲ ▲ ▲ ▲

During that summer, Buzz was in the unenviable position of denying wheelchair athlete George Murray of Millinocket permission to land on Katahdin in a helicopter. Thirty-four-year-old Murray was the first person—but not the last—to test park rules for the disabled.

Murray had traveled more than 4,000 miles cross-country in his wheelchair and asked Buzz to allow him to complete his journey on the mountain. (Murray had lost use of his legs at age fourteen in a hunting accident in the shadow of Katahdin.) Buzz denied the request based on the park's rule against aircraft landing in the park except in emergency situations. Ignoring the prohibition for Murray would set a precedent, Buzz said. The Authority agreed.

A *Kennebec Journal* letter writer, who didn't sign a name, pointed out that the rule had already been broken for well-connected visitors. The late Supreme Court Justice William O. Douglas flew in to the north end of South Branch Pond, and Governor Ken Curtis had landed twice on Kidney Pond. At times Buzz offered politicians and other people flights in to Wassataquoik Lake.

But Buzz didn't budge on Murray, who protested the ruling by emptying a bottle of Pacific Ocean water into Katahdin Stream outside the park boundary.

▲ ▲ ▲ ▲ ▲

On October 31 Governor Joe Brennan headlined an event at Stearns High School in Millinocket marking the fiftieth anniversary of the park. He recounted the long effort of Percival Baxter to create the park and said, "Percival Baxter could see what many others could not, that a park including Mt. Katahdin was a worthwhile investment that would be cherished by future generations."

The Authority and some legislative leaders attended, as well as Buzz, the park's most senior employee, and Tom Chase, the most senior ranger (sixteen years). Harold Colt showed up, and Glenn Manuel mentioned that Colt was "probably the only person here who has visited the park in each of the fifty years and climbed to Baxter Peak every year." Ruth Butler, a devoted park user for thirty-two consecutive years, wouldn't have missed the occasion for anything, and there were a handful of other park faithfuls.

"Baxter Park," Brennan continued, "is a public gift without equal in the annals of Maine history. That one man, using his own funds, assembled this, the fourth largest state park in the nation, over a period of forty-four years, is an accomplishment as grand, as awe-inspiring, as magnificent as Katahdin itself. As is so often the case with visionaries, time has proven him right . . . and Governor Baxter's vision must have been extraordinarily clear, his commitment extraordinarily strong to overcome the obstacles to establishing the park."

▲ ▲ ▲ ▲ ▲

The park's budworm-ravaged woods caused considerable roadside blowdowns in the central park in 1981, through the McCarty Field, Center Mountain, and Nesowadnehunk areas. About 10,000 feet of pine and spruce lay on the ground, available for salvage at $125 per thousand feet—an enticing windfall for the park.

Buzz kept strict watch over the roadside operation and over every log. The rangers could use a cable winch that reached about 65 feet into the woods to snag a downed tree and pull it roadside. If they had to cheat the distance rule, Buzz made them leave the log.

There was an especially big pine that Charlie Kenney thought was worth $150, but it was 75 to 80 feet into the woods. Buzz pointed out that if he allowed Kenney to get the tree, "the line will creep and creep." Although Buzz agreed the tree was worth a lot of money, he told Kenney it was worth a lot more right where it was. Another huge pine went down at Grassy Pond and the rangers wanted to salvage it. It was within the cable length but in such a high-profile location that Buzz wouldn't let them get it.

While the roadside salvage got underway as planned, scheduled cutting in the SFMA was delayed. The paper companies cut back on the volume of wood they planned to buy, and logging contractor Quentin Smart couldn't find crews and equipment to do the job in winter, causing a major setback of at least six months for the SFMA.

▲ ▲ ▲ ▲ ▲

In the wake of Tibbs's and Madeira's resignations, Bob Cummings wrote a scathing article in the *Maine Sunday Telegram* alleging that the pair quit because they were in disagreement with park operations policies.[3] Since operations was Buzz's bailiwick, they must have been referring to him.

The article, however, didn't explain specifically what Tibbs was unhappy about. He was quoted worrying about budget matters and whether his master plan for the park would be ignored after he left the director's post. Mostly, Cummings focused on remarks by Madeira, who was critical about the way park rangers spent their time. He claimed they were too busy enforcing minor regulations and thus not helping visitors understand why Baxter was different from ordinary parks—a backhanded slap at Buzz. They should be educating visitors on goals of Baxter and how they could help, rather than spending time with rules and regulations and having rangers chasing people over nitty-gritty little violations, Madeira said. Buzz had once sent a memo to his rangers, praising the work they were doing and urging that they "keep those arrests coming in," Madeira said. (Cummings didn't contact Buzz for comment.)

Tibbs and Madeira had been anxious for the Authority to retain the director's job and to hire a professional with a background in park planning, according to Cummings. That concern also was a slap at Buzz without saying it directly.

Buzz thought that Madeira had taken pot shots at him because he couldn't stand the idea of working under him instead of Tibbs. "We had our mutual irritations with each other," Buzz remembers, "as did Tibbs and I." Buzz also felt at arms length with Madeira's father Jay on the Advisory Committee, because of his AMC affiliation. Both Madeiras were active in the club, and Buzz continued to believe that, given half a chance, AMC (or ATC) would assert a territorial claim on the park for its own needs.

Madeira left thinking the park needed to be more creative in how to give people access to the northern end of the park. A shuttle system might be the way to go, he thought, but Madeira didn't believe Buzz was interested.

▲ ▲ ▲ ▲ ▲

Tibbs finally left the park officially in late 1981. Buzz was clear that he was not interested in being acting director while the Authority took its time to find a replacement for Tibbs.

"To say the least, I am somewhat disappointed with the [acting director] proposal," Buzz wrote the Authority. "After twenty-two years of service to this Department, and during those years being subject to several political shakeups, I am not now about to be interested in a new title such as 'acting [supervisor],' which has a possibility of requiring that I serve six to nine months, probably without any consideration during this period of a pay raise. . . . As park supervisor, I am willing to take on additional responsibilities to assist the Authority in any way possible, however, what I need most now is job security and the confidence and support of the Authority."

Buzz's reaction was short-lived. He ate his words and accepted the "acting" position—all in hopes of being tapped for the permanent job.

▲ ▲ ▲ ▲ ▲

The snowmobile appeal period had passed with no filings by opponents of Justice Wathen's ruling. Consequently, it was up to the Authority to vote. Prior to a final resolution of the controversy, the trustees had held a series of public hearings across the state in August. Buzz was still an enthusiastic supporter of the machines being allowed in the park, as was Chris Drew. Both testified, as did dozens of other Mainers on both sides of the issue.

Ethel Dyer, grandniece of Governor Baxter, made an impression on the audience when she stood up to say she didn't know what the Baxter family was going to do if the Authority let snowmobiles back in the park. "What is the family going to do with that mountain and all that land we're going to have to take back?" she asked. Dyer was suggesting that if snowmobiles were approved, the family might possibly sue to get the park land back on a breach of trust charge. No one took her seriously, but it got some people thinking "what if?"

Glenn Manuel and Ken Stratton had a lot of friends who wanted snowmobiles back in, while Tierney was lobbied by staff and friends who were opposed. Park counsel Rufus Brown lobbied strenuously against snowmobiles but couldn't change Tierney's mind. At the Authority's November 19, 1980, meeting, the trustees voted 2-1 to welcome snowmobiles back into the park.

Stratton was the holdout. He felt that Governor Baxter had made it clear in a 1965 letter that he opposed snowmobiles and that it was the Authority's responsibility to "subordinate our wishes" to those of the park donor. Manuel and Tierney, however, contended that Baxter's wishes on snowmobiles were not clear and felt that snowmobilers could use the park without harm.

Snowmobilers had asked to use the entire eighty-mile road system, but the Authority limited the machines to the Perimeter Road and Webster and Matagamon Lakes. They were banned from the shorter roads going to Roaring Brook and South Branch Pond Campgrounds, and to Daicey and Kidney Pond Camps.

Tierney was the swing vote. He had read Sarah Redfield's advisory opinion. He knew that Brennan didn't like snowmobiles and thought Redfield's paper was contrived to shut out snowmobiles from the park to help Brennan politically with environmentalists.

Tierney's friends were against snowmobiles, but he wasn't listening to them. Most important, in the opinion of some Tierney observers, was his view on how snowmobiles intersected with his gubernatorial aspirations. He framed himself as the friend of blue-collar families and believed their support would be influenced by his vote. So he voted to allow snowmobiles, claiming that a plea from a Bucksport paper mill worker to allow snowmobiles pushed him to side with Glenn Manuel.

When he returned to the office after the meeting, Rufus Brown was crushed. "The moon and stars had fallen," said Tierney, remembering Brown's reaction. "I said, 'I know you don't like it. Go ask the investigators, five or six cops, what they think,' and he came back and reported 'They said Tierney did the right thing.' I said, 'Rufus, the governor wanted the park for everybody.'" Tierney made the record clear that if there were violations, he would revisit the snowmobile issue. "Maine is a very small state. If there are complaints, they would get to me."

The *Portland Press Herald* condemned the trustees, accusing them of betraying "the memory of the man who gave the park to Maine as a wilderness recreation area. . . . It was a "lamentable decision," the paper said. The "Baxter legacy has been carelessly and needlessly violated."

The *Kennebec Journal* opined that "the Baxter State Park Authority has made a serious mistake." Manuel and Tierney wouldn't "heed the arguments of the Authority's third member, forest service director Kenneth Stratton, and likewise ignored Baxter's own words about the park—and about the use of snowmobiles there." Tierney and Manuel were unworthy of Baxter's trust in their judgments and integrity."[4] On the opposite side of the fence was the *Bangor Daily News*, which complimented the two men for rising "above the single-minded rhetoric and exercise[ing] common sense."[5]

The *Ellsworth American* came down hard on Manuel and Tierney. The two trustees "may go on 'constructing' until the end of time but the plain fact is that they have consciously, deliberately, willfully disregarded the lifelong wish of the donor of the park and defeated his plan and explicit desire to keep out every snowmobile but that of the supervisor. If Tierney and Manuel construe Baxter's wishes for a decade, the only thing about the Park that will still be 'wild' will be their construction of the English language, their interpretation of the law, and their reading of the document by which the Governor conveyed his land to the state of Maine," the paper said.[6]

Charles FitzGerald's answer to the Authority's vote was to challenge it in court. He was instrumental in founding the Northwoods Alliance to serve as the organizational vehicle for the fight and to help raise money to pay the legal bills. The *Kennebec Journal* wished FitzGerald luck in righting "a serious wrong. . . . If he succeeds, Maine will be the big winner."

Just before Christmas, the Authority met to adopt a rule governing the use of snowmobiles in the park, requiring that they obey the twenty-mile-per-hour speed limit.

▲ ▲ ▲ ▲ ▲

Chairman Manuel wanted to officially welcome snowmobilers back into Baxter, so he called Buzz to arrange for the two of them to be at the gate to celebrate with the sledders as they motored through the Togue Pond gate. The news media was on hand too, and Buzz arranged things to make Manuel look his best.

Buzz had a very stable double-track snowsled that he thought might be best for Manuel to use because Manuel didn't know how to ride the machines well. Buzz thought he would ride the new single-track, a faster, more nimble sled. But when Manuel saw the bigger, heavy-duty machine, he wanted to ride that one in order to look good in front of the media.

Manuel and Buzz joined the snowmobilers and leaders of the Maine Snowmobile Association for an outdoor barbecue, including hot dogs and toasted turkey sandwiches, at Katahdin Stream Campground. "This is as close to heaven as you can get," Manuel said, referring to the mountain scenery. The clouds parted to give the celebrants a good view of Katahdin, and Manuel received generous praise from the snowmobilers for working to lift the ban.

---

1. *Portland Press Herald*, June 16, 1981, p. 4.
2. *Bangor Daily News*, June 19, 1981, p. 14.
3. *Maine Sunday Telegram*, November 15, 1981, p. 25A.
4. *Kennebec Journal*, November 20, 1981, p. 12.
5. *Portland Press Herald*, November 21, 1981, p. 10.
6. *Ellsworth American*, November 26, 1981, Section 2, p. 1.

Primary Document Sources: BSPA Box 1 (2507-0801); BSP Annual Report, 1981; Caverly Files; Austin Files.

Conversations and correspondence: Rufus Brown, Buzz Caverly, Tim Caverly, Chris Drew, Charles FitzGerald, Charlie Kenney, Lester Kenway, Pete Madeira, Sarah Redfield, Ken Stratton, Lee Tibbs, Jim Tierney.

▲▲▲▲▲▲▲▲

CHAPTER 17

# Director Caverly

INSTEAD OF MOVING QUICKLY to replace Lee Tibbs, the Authority dragged its feet. It was an important "take a break" time to discuss park leadership needs in the 1980s. Was it time to eliminate the supervisor's position and save $30,000 a year plus benefits? Would the park be better served by someone from the ranks moving into that job or an outsider? Were a college degree and professional training critical requirements?

Discussions went on for a couple of months among the Authority, the Advisory, and a park hiring committee. Unable to reach a consensus, the trustees went ahead at their January 12, 1982, meeting and gave Buzz the official title of acting director. Buzz didn't want another temporary appointment. But he didn't really have a choice, mindful that if the supervisor's post was eliminated before a full-time director was chosen, he could wind up without a job.

Park staff rushed to Buzz's defense. Some employees wrote to the Authority with enthusiastic support, citing his experience and his ability to learn from mistakes. Books and college degrees didn't necessarily make good leaders, wrote Chimney Pond ranger John Gordon and Jean Hoekwater, who had briefly worked at the park briefly and would eventually become the park naturalist. "Getting one's hands dirty and learning from the bottom up can give one the broader view—the long view that mere book learning cannot develop." In a memo to the trustees in April 1982, seventeen rangers and other employees (almost all the year-round staff) gave Buzz a vote of confidence, emphasizing his "twenty-two years of unquestioned loyalty to Baxter State Park." A major change in administration "could have a strong negative influence on employee morale and productivity," they warned. "We trust that men of your capabilities will carefully weigh all factors before making any . . . changes."

Buzz responded to the staff with an appreciative memo. "Thank you for bearing with me," he said. "Thank you for assisting me, and thank you for your team effort." He quoted the "partners in this project" letter from Baxter, telling them he always found it "encouraging."

▲ ▲ ▲ ▲ ▲

One of Buzz's first decisions as acting director was to close the park because of critically cold weather, a move that the more rugged winter users saw as a "nanny" response.

There were five feet of snow on the ground at Chimney Pond, the destination of most people in the park at the time. On January 18, 1982, the wind at the campground was so strong—fifty to ninety miles an hour—it blew out a window of the ranger's camp. "Even with a good fire going in the stove, a bucket of water sitting on the floor froze solid," Buzz reported. The thermometer registered forty below zero, and the windchill temperature was colder than 120 degrees below zero.

Chris Drew had a party of eight with him at Chimney Pond, and all were safely inside with enough food for three or four days. Intrepid mountaineer Clarence LeBell was in the park somewhere with eight friends. But no one knew their whereabouts—a situation created by the reduction in field staff and inability to check on all parties at night.

The LeBell party had been exposed to the bitter cold for two days, and Buzz decided they needed immediate attention. His authority to make such a call, even if the winter users didn't want his intervention, irritated the climbing and skiing die-hards.

Buzz called a Millinocket pilot, but he was forced to turn back by high winds. Buzz then called for help from the Air National Guard, met the helicopter at the local airport and flew to Nesowadnehunk Field to see if there was any smoke or tracks from the LeBell group. After checking other areas and finding nothing, they returned to the airport for refueling and there were notified that the LeBell party had been located by ranger Barry McArthur at Russell Pond.

Three of the party had severe frostbite and were evacuated. Buzz was on the second chopper and ordered everyone else out and to leave their gear behind for the time being.

After dealing with that situation, Buzz oversaw the evacuation of another climber with frostbite at Katahdin Stream Campground. A total of twenty-three people were evacuated from Chimney Pond, Russell Pond, and Katahdin Stream.

It was the second time that LeBell, a highly experienced winter camper, had to be rescued from Maine's winter fury. Buzz began to keep a file on leaders who had demonstrated bad judgment during use of the park. He also gathered data on the number of people lost and the amount spent on them to make a case for greater restrictions. For instance, from July 1, 1959, to June 30, 1960 (the fiscal year), 323 persons were lost, and it cost the park only $3,560 to find them. By 1980–81 the figure was 308 visitors lost, and the cost had soared to $54,353.

Buzz felt that the forty-hour workweek was at the heart of the "lost visitors" problem because the park just didn't have the necessary manpower anymore to track people. In the early 1970s there were five base camps available for winter use and eight to ten rangers available to accompany parties staying overnight. Rangers were working a non-standard workweek and stayed with folks as long as necessary.

Increasing winter use led to an expansion of facilities available to the public—from five to nineteen. With the workweek limit in effect and overtime a financial concern, several ranger jobs were cut. Field crew retained had to take two days off per week, making it unusual to ever have more than two rangers in the entire park. Those on duty couldn't possibly keep up with the whereabouts of all hikers, campers, and skiers.

Buzz's solution to protect visitors from their own bad judgment was a class day system based on weather forecasts, similar to the one he had already implemented for the summer season. Class Red designated a situation where temperatures were fifty degrees below zero and meant that all recreational entrance to the park would be restricted. Anyone in the park would be confined to camp. Class Yellow defined a day where the weather would be deteriorating and allowed visitors to proceed with their plans with caution. Class Green was for a normal day with no threatening weather.

As a result of lobbying by climber Dave Getchell and climber/rangers Ben Townsend and John Gordon, Buzz relented on some of the harsh winter rules. The revisions no longer required climbers to have physical fitness certification or arrange for a backup search-and-rescue team. No more need for permission in writing to climb. No more inspection of equipment and supplies. The leader was allowed to be responsible for the experience of group participants. Climbing parties no longer had to have four members who stayed together but instead were allowed to be apart, just "within reasonable sight and sound" of each other.

▲ ▲ ▲ ▲ ▲

By early spring 1982 Buzz was ready with his plan to expand campsites—a directive from Glenn Manuel to increase park income and accommodate more people. Buzz had thought long and hard about how to please Manuel but not at the expense of the park's wilderness character. Dealing with Authority orders he didn't think were necessarily in keeping with Percival Baxter's vision was a good test of Buzz's creativity.

Buzz went looking for campsite options in the less-used roadside campgrounds and remote tenting areas, rather than opening up more sites in the crowded Katahdin area. He picked out walk-in spots at Trout Brook Farm and South Branch Pond Campgrounds in the north end, and proposed enlarging the group area at Nesowadnehunk Field. Half of the new sites were outlying in the Fowler-Long Pond, Webster Lake, Matagamon Lake, and old Katahdin Paper dam areas. The plan provided an increase of twenty-six campsites, which would allow overnight accommodations to rise by 105 people to 1,305.

Advisory and Baxter family member Ethel Dyer observed that the park should be careful it wasn't moving toward "building a Yosemite." Glenn Manuel defended the expansion as a way to better balance visitor use, although it would be an uphill effort to convince more visitors to use the north end.

▲ ▲ ▲ ▲ ▲

Lester Kenway was convinced that volunteers were the only way to obtain enough labor to begin to tackle the gargantuan trail work needed. He was successful at getting the needed approval from Buzz and the Authority to participate in the Student Conservation Association (SCA) program, and in the summer of 1982, the first interns came. The following year, 83 percent of the trail work was being done by volunteers. The SCA became the core of the trails program for the rest of Kenway's twenty-three years in the park, and beyond.

Coordinating the adjunct staff for 4,000 hours of work in 1983 "pushed me to my physical and mental limits," Kenway reported.

Besides the SCA, the Sierra Club, the American Hiking Society, the Maine snowmobile clubs, and individuals provided the most hours. Having so many volunteers in the park worried the employees' union. The fear was that free hands would replace employees in time, but that concern proved to be unfounded.

Conditions for the trail crew were often challenging, from rain, cold, and biting bugs to chain saws that wouldn't work. Crew members were always being faced with fixing things they had never fixed before and in rough backcountry.

Kenway tried to keep the crew's spirits up with hot food. When they were camped at a roadside, there was no limit on what meals they could prepare. In the backcountry, food was brought in by air.

With a dozen people having a base camp at a certain place for a week, they could be assured that mice would find them. Kenway came up with a resourceful way to get rid of them. He filled a gallon or two-gallon jar with a few inches of water, smeared peanut butter down the side of the jar and built a ramp up to the top of the jar. The mice would travel up the ramp and fall into the water and drown trying to reach the peanut butter.

▲ ▲ ▲ ▲ ▲

Underscoring the overuse issue was a request from Republican gubernatorial candidate Charlie Cragin that blossomed into a full-fledged commotion. He wanted to take about 100 to 150 people on a day hike up Katahdin, although park rules limited groups to twelve. Cragin wanted to make a film and take the press along. Buzz worried that it was too many people, and that they would have to go in two groups on two different trails. Win Robbins admitted he had violated the rule for years, taking as many as thirty-six people to the park. But he thought the Cragin hike would create a precedent for commercializing Katahdin and opposed it, a position shared by Jim Tierney, Ken Stratton, and Glenn Manuel. Bob Ohler mentioned that the park had turned down people who had wanted to hold revival meetings in the park.

Cragin said he had been climbing Katahdin for several years and was always struck "by the beauty and grandeur of the mountain and surrounding plain. In fact, the scenic vista and wilderness climb have always been an inspiration to me." He wanted to take other office seekers and office holders, he said, because he thought it was difficult for people making public policy decisions affecting the environment to understand Maine's natural heritage unless they saw firsthand the "beauty and splendor" symbolized by Katahdin. He didn't contemplate making the climb a media event but wanted to create "an enjoyable and congenial day" for people to come together to develop "a keener aware-ness of the beauty and expansiveness of Maine's magnificent natural resources."

After conferring with Buzz, Cragin reduced his entourage to sixty, and compromised on many other logistical details to reduce the impact of the hike. The trustees thought Cragin had responded responsibly to concerns and approved the hike—without filming but with press par-ticipants. All the publicity didn't help Cragin win the GOP nomination. Democratic Governor Joe Brennan handily won a second term.

▲ ▲ ▲ ▲ ▲

While Buzz was stewing in limbo over the director's job, the long-persistent issue of donations to the park came to a head. The Baxter family was opposed to outside contributions as "public charity."

Win Robbins had asked John Baxter to support publishing a park brochure soliciting public contributions to help the park's financial con-dition. Baxter was horrified, responding that "Uncle Percy's ghost would haunt us all" if such a step were taken. Buzz agreed.

The issue wouldn't go away, and it was discussed at Authority meetings now and then. The family remained entrenched. When the brochure matter arose in 1982, John Baxter reiterated, "To have others join in endowing [the park] would entirely change the nature of the park's endowment and the unique character of his generosity." Jim Tierney thought it was silly of the family to view donations as "charity," and thought it was time to allow park lovers to con-tribute.

It always struck Tierney as interesting that Percival Baxter, "who was humble and didn't want memorials in the park had an awful lot of things named for him. . . . The guy was clearly focused on his immor-tality," Tierney believes, adding that the famous photo of the governor standing sideways in front of Katahdin "was clearly posed."

It would take more time for the Baxter family to come around to appreciating donations as gifts from the hearts of park lovers, not as competition for Percival Baxter's legacy.

▲ ▲ ▲ ▲ ▲

As Percival Baxter had passed from the scene, so was John Baxter preparing to do so. He was now over eighty years old and wanted the younger generation to take over representation of the family. He did his best to educate his nephew, Eric Baxter, about the issues confronting the park, but the best "course" Eric had in Baxter Park was the unfinished drafts of John Hakola's book. The author had sent them unfinished chapters to peruse while the Baxters were flying here and there together.

John Baxter had been on the Advisory Committee since 1970; Ethel Dyer, since 1976; and Hartley Baxter (their sibling), since 1979. Hartley, Eric's father, left in 1981, making room for his son. Eric's cousin, Connie, had been interested in the park in the early 1970s and had been part of a winter climbing group which was marooned on Katahdin in early 1971. She was taking photographs for a book, *Greatest Mountain: Katahdin's Wilderness*, which was published in 1972. She left Maine soon afterward, eventually to return to take an interest in one of the park's most difficult issues in the 1990s.

▲ ▲ ▲ ▲ ▲

By the time Eric Baxter was officially appointed as family representative, he was put on the committee assigned to interview prospective candidates for park director. "I went right into the fire pit," he recalls. "By the time that job was done, I felt like I knew the park."

Eric Baxter was not acquainted with Buzz prior to joining the committee, despite the numerous times he had camped in the park with other Baxter family members. He recalls being "seduced" by the impressive resumes of the candidates for director. The state personnel department had selected the finalists and sent eight candidates to the committee: Gordon Mott, with the U.S. Forest Service and member of NRCM's board of directors; George Ruopp of the Maine Forest Service; Fred Bartlett of the Bureau of Parks; and consultant Kim Kolman, the former Baxter Park forester. Only one candidate was from out of state with park and forestry specialties.

"They had unbelievable backgrounds in forestry and life experience," Baxter recalls. He was most impressed by Gordon Mott, a U.S. Forest Service forester who was well-respected by the environmental

342

*Chief ranger Chris Drew building a footbridge*
*across Trout Brook, 1982*
BAXTER STATE PARK PHOTO ARCHIVES

community. "He carried himself well," says Baxter, whose vote was going to Mott before Buzz came before the committee at the end of the selection process.

"It was like night and day when Buzz came in to talk with us," remembers Eric Baxter. It was clear to him that Buzz was a natural leader. "What Buzz lacked in curriculum vitae, he had in spades in heart and soul and conviction. There was no doubt in my mind that he was the one, the right man. I surprised myself, and I still have that feeling today that it was an enlightening moment. I didn't even question myself about my feeling for Buzz, and it was interesting to see the others reach that same conclusion, that he was the right man."

Although Buzz didn't know the Baxter tribe well, they trusted his commitment to Percival Baxter and the park and respected his record, which had already proved his administrative and managerial capabilities. They also liked him—not a small consideration. Buzz was a man of extraordinary energy and huge goodwill, which everyone could see. He had a booming voice, a big smile, and a warm handshake that made him an attractive ambassador for the park. And, he was a familiar and trusted figure to thousands of loyal campers and hikers.

Choosing a director from within the ranks, especially one with such a long history with the park, was uppermost on the minds of the Authority and the Advisory Committee given the disappointing experience with outsider Lee Tibbs. Buzz was the only candidate who was ready to go from day one, the only one who didn't need training wheels.

The Advisory Committee surprised no one by backing Buzz, despite criticism from the AMC and the Sierra Club about the hiring process. These groups felt that the director's job had not been advertised widely enough outside Maine. The search should have been conducted on a national scale, the clubs asserted.

Also, as expected, NRCM was a major opponent of Buzz's. Board members worried that Buzz, in reality, was a conservative red-neck, lacked intellectual depth, and might not have the strength to stand up to local special interests and the greater snowmobile community. NRCM believed that it was time for the smartest, most capable visionary the Authority could find to take the helm because this was a turning point in the park's history.

Buzz and Maine Sierra Club chairman Ken Spaulding argued face-to-face about whether Buzz's twenty-two years of park service and on-the-ground education should make up for a classical education. Buzz used Helon Taylor's reasoning about college degrees. "Helon used the line with me early on that the director of the park didn't necessarily have to be a forester, didn't have to be a molecular biologist, didn't have to be a recreation manager, but did have to be a person who could fill those positions with qualified personnel," Buzz remembers.

Former NRCM president Rob Gardiner, who had moved on to head the Bureau of Parks and Lands, spoke up in Buzz's behalf. The park director didn't need to be someone with a lot of creative ideas but an understanding of the big picture, an ability to work with the Authority, a "good sense of his own compass," and a lot of integrity, Gardiner contended. Buzz had those qualities, and moreover, he said, "Buzz was Baxter's soldier."

Reporter Bob Cummings alerted the public that there would be a new director soon. He mentioned criticisms of park management for its focus on enforcing minor public safety-related regulations and its failure to devote adequate time in creating and preserving the wilderness character. He didn't single out Buzz in print but privately thought that Buzz would be a bad pick to succeed Lee Tibbs. In Cummings's opinion, Buzz and his rangers were too addicted to motorized equipment and not committed enough to protecting important wilderness values like silence.

▲ ▲ ▲ ▲ ▲

What would make a good park director? The Authority asked the question, and Buzz's response reflected his credentials: someone who had a deep feeling for the park and respect for Percival Baxter, who was down-to-earth and could work directly with people and stimulate their faith in the park.

At the end of the Authority's August 3 meeting, the trustees went into executive session. When they emerged at noontime, they announced that forty-three-year-old Buzz Caverly, who had spent half of his life in the park already, was the new park director. Glenn Manuel said, "No man living in the state of Maine today has anywhere near the knowledge of the park that man has." He praised Buzz for running "a top-notch operation" during his supervisory term.

Buzz asked point-blank if the vote had been unanimous, and was assured that it was. Full, not divided, support from the Authority was important to him. He thanked everyone, saying he felt the same exhilaration that day as when he had first climbed the mountain as a ranger in 1960. John Baxter declared that Buzz was an excellent choice.

Jim Tierney had been offended at environmentalists' attempts to derail Buzz. Their efforts were "personal, mean-spirited," and came from "very wealthy Maine residents," he feels. The specific issue was Buzz's lack of education beyond high school. "I said, 'Buzz, you've got to learn to speak, listen, talk to professors, read and think about new things,'" Tierney recalls. He emphasized to Buzz that he was "going to be the personification of the *park*—not the Authority members" and thus the most crucial link between the park and the public in a time of expanded environmental awareness.

Buzz didn't want to have to move back to Millinocket full time. Tierney told him, "Buzz, you're the boss. I don't care where you live. You take care of the park. I'm not going to doubt your commitment to the park. You just go do it."

On his drive home, Buzz had time to let his victory sink in. He had had two trial runs as head of the park, had honed his skills, and now he had the opportunity he had been praying for—permanent director. Jim Tierney's words reverberated in Buzz's mind about needing to reach out to more people. Too, he knew that the more supportive he was of the Authority, the more supportive they were likely to be of him.

Buzz also couldn't help but think of his mentor, Helon Taylor. Taylor's words of advice to Buzz about his future in the park rang as clear as when the old supervisor had said them twenty-two years earlier: "As you go through your career, as you accept the opportunities for promotion, keep a clear vision of Governor Baxter's objectives, surround yourself with competent people who you and the park can depend on, and maintain a course for park values."

Although he knew the park so well, Buzz was facing a harder job and a much different era than in his previous years at the helm. Governmental regulations covering all aspects of the park from the office to the field were ever-changing and ever-demanding. New technology was knocking at the door and had the potential to revolutionize the way the park carried out its administrative and business affairs. Could Buzz change with the times? That was a question that only time could answer.

▲ ▲ ▲ ▲ ▲

The morning of August 4, when Buzz went to park headquarters, there was no official party marking his elevation to permanent director. After all, it was the third time he had stepped up to the top job. But Buzz was showered with congratulations from well-wishers, some of whom had stood behind him through thick and thin. One of his staunchest supporters, Jim Erwin, wished Buzz many years of continuing success. "Some of our earlier conversations from the Harry Kearney days come to mind, and I am pleased to remind you that I'm a good prophet,"

Erwin wrote Buzz. "I told you that you had all the stuff to do the whole job, if you had the patience and the character to stay with it. You have amply demonstrated both."

Buzz's former Lee Academy principal Fred Dingley told him, "[T]he honor and the responsibility are now yours, earned the hard way." To Bud Leavitt, Buzz's "obvious superior talents" led the Authority to make him director. In Leavitt's mind, there was no reason to look beyond Buzz. "For twenty-two years, he has been a leader. The man knows his job. He is a genuine professional in all aspects, including the all-important matter of managing people." The Authority, he said, made the right decision "naming a Maine product to manage a Maine product."

It was exciting to Buzz to envision the days ahead, and, as well, he felt relieved that "the expectations were over." This—this director's position—was it, what he had been working for all his adult life. He intended to stay the course, just like Percival Baxter.

Buzz's office was downstairs at park headquarters, while Tibbs's had been upstairs. Buzz decided to remain in his first-floor office so he could more easily interact with staff and the public.

Buzz's office décor in 1982 remained about the same throughout his tenure. The freshly painted walls were covered several years later with a wildlife-design wallpaper, the same as the wallpaper in his East Corinth living room. On one wall hung a framed USGS map of Katahdin he had had since 1963, and on another wall, the old #3 map from the Appalachian Trail guide.

Buzz had kept the 1960 #3 map in his desk at Russell Pond. After fishing a hiking party out of Wassataquoik Stream and feeding them a hot meal, Buzz had been asked by the leader of the group, a man named Doubleday, if he could do something for Buzz. The man worked in a framing shop, and Buzz took out the #3 map and said he would like it protected. It became a frequently used historical reference for Buzz in the years ahead.

His other map was a framed copy of Governor Baxter's original vision of a park covering 57,232 acres and containing all of Katahdin and Katahdin Lake. Buzz would study that 1921 map for years, wondering why Baxter couldn't convince the owner of the Katahdin Lake township to sell, and if there would ever be a way to purchase it. That original map would play a critical role much later in the successful acquisition campaign.

*Helon and Hilda Taylor, 1983*
RINIA FARMER PHOTO, COURTESY OF APPALACHIAN TRAIL CONSERVANCY

The famous photo of Governor Baxter with Buzz and Jan (pregnant with Cathy) from 1964 hung on one of the wood-paneled walls in the office, along with a couple of Jake Day paintings of the park acquired later on. Buzz did his endless paperwork at a state-issued gray metal desk, and the metal bookcases on the sides held his copies of Baxter's letters, the Deeds of Trust, and other essential park documents.

Buzz was "prideful" about his office, keeping it neat and spick-and-span at all times. He might not be able to control "messes" on his different secretaries' desks, but he set an example in case they wanted to follow it.

He had already established a daily routine, regularly interrupted by unexpected visits and events. But on a "normal" day, he was in the office by 7:30, spent the first hour or so with staff and visitors who dropped in, and then dealt with correspondence and phone calls. After lunch he spent time on the park budget or drove to the park to talk to rangers and look at various projects. There were reservation issues to deal with throughout the day. A search-and-rescue call would take precedence over everything else.

It wouldn't be long before employees heard Buzz singing one of his favorite country songs as he entered the headquarters door in the morning—so happy he had achieved his goal of director.

▲ ▲ ▲ ▲ ▲

In his final rise to the director's post, Buzz took with him the confidence of a dozen trustees that comprised seven different Authorities over two decades of park history. Proof of the confidence in him was the annual evaluation. Buzz's rater was the Authority chair, except when he was second in command, and then it had been Harry Kearney and Lee Tibbs. All of his evaluations had been positive, and they were better and better after he was named director.

Buzz made sure that every chairperson reviewed his job standards—an opportunity for the Authority head to suggest changes. Buzz also had another impetus for going over his duties: he wanted there to be no doubt or surprise about what his responsibilities were.

From the time the Baxter State Park Authority had been created, the law had vested its three members with the responsibility of establishing policy and running the park. There was no mention of a supervisor or director who would have to handle the day-to-day affairs of the park and how his responsibilities would differ from those of the Authority.

But having a supervisor/director on-site to oversee daily park operations was practical and necessary for the Authority, and Percival Baxter had been well aware of the operations man's role—from Hal Dyer to Helon Taylor to Buzz. There is no evidence that any Authority delegated that power in writing. It just happened because of the way things were "back then"—a park geographically distant from Authority members in Augusta, limited communication with the park boss, and the fact that the trustee job was one that many members shirked.

A review of park history would show that major policy issues, such as snowmobiles, were brought to the Authority for a decision or a formal vote. But matters that were not politically sensitive or were minor policy issues were handled by the director/supervisor. Thus by the time Buzz became director, there were more than thirty years of this kind of dual policymaking between the Authority and the park chief.

Buzz knew there was a line beyond which he shouldn't go when getting into policymaking himself, although no one knew exactly where that line might be. However, Buzz didn't plan to compete with the Authority. The established order meant a lot to him.

Buzz agreed with Percival Baxter that the Authority was the best oversight structure for the long-term good of the park. The only problem he saw with it was that the Maine Forest Service director no longer was a cabinet-level position like the other two Authority members, and Buzz thought that resulted in an inequality of stature among the three that could cause problems.

There was a huge difference between the time when Helon Taylor was park supervisor and the modern political era that faced Buzz. Indicative of how much had changed nationally was the will of the public and Congress on environmental protection. Since the end of Taylor's tenure in 1967, laws had been passed establishing protections for a wide range of natural resources, such as clean air and water, trails, marine animals, endangered species, and coastal barriers. Earth Day, begun in April 1970, was a popular celebration from Maine to California.

▲ ▲ ▲ ▲ ▲

As much as Buzz was publicly identified as a wilderness advocate because of his job, he was not one personally—beyond advocating for Baxter Park's wilderness. He was not a member of NRCM, the Sierra Club, The Wilderness Society, or other environmental organization— with one exception for a short time (the Maine Appalachian Mountain Club).

Reflecting back on his days as ranger and supervisor, Buzz feels that some kind of wilderness philosophy was forming before he knew how to define the concept. It was an instance where an academic background could have helped him, he surmises. What he could articulate from a philosophical perspective in 1982 was that he "liked to see things pretty much left alone and see what would happen over time."

He had spent a lot of time in the backcountry alone, having his senses filled with the sights, sounds, smells, and wonder of the forests, bogs, streams, and mountain wildflowers. "Something happened to me internally when I immersed myself in nature," he says. "It was almost a religious experience."

Bottom line, he was a nuts-and-bolts ranger who loved being outdoors. He was driven to keep going after the park's top job because of his relationship with Percival Baxter, and he was confident he could do better than anyone else on the scene in upholding the "forever wild" mandate.

As director, Buzz had to think deeply about wilderness preservation because it was at the foundation of every decision he made—and he would have to explain this to the Authority, employees, and to the public. The environmental movement was much more of a force in 1982 than during Buzz's two other times in the park's top job.

For Buzz, the director's appointment was his personal summit. In his mind, the name change seemed to elevate the job to a higher executive level. "I wanted to prove to myself that this one-room schoolhouse graduate from Cornville could meet the challenges, face the PhDers and say, 'I can do this job,'" he recalls.

Following Tierney's advice, Buzz met with the leading Maine and New England environmental groups—NRCM, Maine Audubon Society, the MATC—and discussed roadside mowing, chemical spraying, trail maintenance, day use, and reservation problems. He also traveled to the White Mountains National Forest in New Hampshire and the Green Mountain National Forest in Vermont, where officials were eager to find out how Baxter Park was dealing with a crush of day-use visitors.

▲▲▲▲▲

Bob Cummings was impressed that Buzz reached out to leaders of environmental organizations who opposed or doubted him. "He said the right things—that he would carry on the wishes of Governor Baxter," Cummings reflects. "In retrospect, I also think that it would have been very hard for an outsider to have pushed Baxter's dream the way Buzz could do as an insider." Buzz was unaware at the time that his efforts to make friends with environmentalists irritated some of the rangers, who looked at his behavior as capitulation to the enemy.

But he was politically savvy enough to know that he should keep the park out of the public limelight to please the Authority. His in-house strategy was: "Don't let the world hear what's going on in Baxter Park through bitching and complaining . . . document it. Put it in writing. If someone questions policy, put it in writing." He wanted "clear policy and clear communications." He reflected that if such procedures had been in place when he ran into Joe Bartlett in the woods cutting trees in 1966, he wouldn't have gotten into so much trouble over speeding.

With more responsibilities than previous directors, Buzz needed close associates he could trust and depend on. At headquarters, he looked to Gerald Merry to run operations and to the new business manager, Robert Williams, for financial matters. "I gave Bob one instruction: keep us in the black. Don't ever come to me expecting me to take to the Authority a proposal that is going to overspend. I didn't have to worry."[1]

With the supervisor's position eliminated, Buzz wanted to create a new position that would be distinctive. He remembered former supervisor Hal Dyer's idea that the park should have a chief ranger (and, in fact, Dyer had that title on park stationery). Buzz latched on to that position as the right one to replace the supervisor's job. It also was a way to improve the career ladder in the park. The park staff backed Buzz, as did the Authority.

Ranger Loren Goode, a thirteen-year park veteran, was upfront with Buzz that he wanted the job, but Goode wasn't comfortable with being in the public eye. Chris Drew, who was outgoing and a natural at public relations, also applied for the new job. Buzz wanted a chief ranger who was in it for the long haul with him, and he wanted a pledge of personal loyalty. He instinctively thought Drew had what it took. Buzz had hired Drew a decade earlier as a seasonal employee and knew he was a doer and a very religious person. Buzz didn't think Drew would deceive him.

Prior to deciding which man would get the new post, Buzz sat in his truck with Drew. "I told him that if I was going to be successful, I needed people who could get things done and not undermine me. I wanted to know if I could count on him to do that. He said yes, and then told me something that convinced me Chris was my choice." When Drew had moved to Trout Brook Farm, he shot a deer in the field, having been lied to by other rangers who said it was okay because there was a special provision in the flowage rights that allowed it. The rangers teased and harangued him for his wrongdoing, and they blackmailed him for years over it. Drew told Buzz the story at his chief ranger interview, and Buzz let it go. "I said that's behind us," Buzz remembers. "I've done things I shouldn't have, too."

Drew was to be Buzz's counterpoint and the pivotal figure in his relationship with the staff. "Buzz had to be separate because he was the boss," says Drew. "I'm sure he felt isolated from those guys who couldn't see the big picture. It must have been difficult."

▲ ▲ ▲ ▲ ▲

The congratulations were still coming in when Buzz received the news that Tim and Sue's cabin on Umsaskis had been burned down by an arsonist. The fire occurred on September 12 while the Caverlys were away for a state parks picnic (and baby shower for Sue) at Reid State Park. It was a traumatic time, and Tim and Sue had to move to a cabin at Chamberlain Bridge. Shortly afterward, Sue gave birth to daughter Jacquelyn.

Buzz provided Tim space at Baxter Park headquarters to set up the Allagash office temporarily. State Parks and Recreation director Herb Hartman didn't want Allagash mail being sent in care of Baxter Park because it might be perceived as too close an association, so Tim changed the Allagash address to a post office box number, and that was all right. The Allagash office was moved after about a month to quarters at South Twin Lake outside Millinocket (and later to town and then to Churchill Dam.)

There began a cooperative relationship between Allagash Wilderness Waterway and Baxter Park staff. It wasn't long before Buzz approved having the Allagash radio frequency in the Baxter system so that rangers from both parks could talk to each other. Buzz and Tim encouraged their staff members to exchange information. Tim held his spring and fall training sessions at Baxter headquarters. Once the Baxter rangers went to Allagash headquarters for their bear management training. The two staffs also borrowed equipment from each other.

During the time Tim was living at Chamberlain Bridge, he and Buzz saw a lot of each other, since the northern end of Baxter Park was only about five miles from Tim's cabin.

▲ ▲ ▲ ▲ ▲

Buzz figured if he could stay focused on what Governor Baxter wanted for his park, he would be okay. He began to study Baxter's trust provisions to figure out how he could best interpret and implement the park's policies and regulations. "Baxter wanted us not to break faith with the people and wanted the park used to the fullest extent, without harming the resources, and those kinds of words started to have an impact on me," Buzz says.

As for the Authority, it was "a psychological game" dealing with them, especially the chairmen. Glenn Manuel was a strong supporter of Buzz's, and he stopped by the park headquarters often on his way down to his office in Augusta or back home to Mapleton to develop a relationship with Buzz and give him advice. To help Buzz avoid budget mistakes, Manuel had his department business manager double-check the work of business manager Bob Williams and Buzz. But it wasn't long before Manuel told Buzz not to send the papers to Augusta anymore because he and Williams were doing fine.

Manuel liked to ride with Buzz into the park on patrol and would spontaneously bring up ideas for changes in the park. "One day we rode by some blowdowns," Buzz recalls. "Glenn looked at those downed trees and thought it would be great to bring in a sawmill and saw them up right on the spot." Buzz knew that Governor Baxter had specifically said he didn't want a sawmill in the park, but he also knew that Manuel didn't want to hear Buzz say, "We can't do that." Consequently, Buzz told Manuel that it was an interesting idea and he would get back to him after researching the Deeds of Trust. When he informed Manuel that Baxter didn't want a sawmill, the chairman agreed that it was fine to use a tractor, winch, and truck to remove the blowdown.

Another time, the two were driving through the same area, south of Rum Mountain, and Manuel proposed building a road from the summit, over the ridge connecting to Katahdin, and up to the Tableland. "He said, 'We're all getting old, Buzz. A road would be nice for senior citizens to drive to the top.'" Buzz squelched that idea, too, with Baxter's own words against new roads in the park.

The interactions with Manuel helped Buzz hone his personal skills in political maneuvering. Buzz had seen Lee Tibbs provoke fury in Manuel by directly opposing the chairman, so Buzz's strategy was a soft, agreeable approach. "Glenn was so congenial with me, always," Buzz remembers. "So I can't be too hard on Glenn Manuel. My working relationship with him overall was good." The esteem that Manuel had for Buzz would be reflected in his yearly evaluations of Buzz from 1982 to 1986. He gave Buzz ninety-six out of a hundred possible points every year.

▲ ▲ ▲ ▲ ▲

Just because he was director didn't deter Buzz from continuing his self-improvement efforts. Since he had taken the Maine Criminal Justice Academy's law enforcement course in 1968, he had returned every year to take refresher training courses in a variety of subjects, such as first aid, firearms, firefighting, defensive driving, and bear handling. After his promotion, he trained in search and rescue, personnel management, and more law enforcement. He joined the board of directors of Unity College in 1983. The small environmental school in Unity, Maine, had been important to the park in that numerous students had worked as interns or seasonal employees. Buzz headed up a fundraising campaign, which provided experience that would serve him beyond his wildest imagination after his career ended at Baxter Park.

▲ ▲ ▲ ▲ ▲

The personnel department required job standards for Baxter Park's director. Although unusual, Buzz wrote an eight-page draft of standards for his own job, using those for Lee Tibbs as a guide. Glenn Manuel questioned why Buzz needed standards, telling him that he would "do what I tell you. He was so used to telling Lee something and Lee protesting it, that he thought I was starting down that track," says Buzz.

Buzz asked Manuel to just look over the job description and consider it. A couple of days later, Manuel gave his approval and never said anything about the subject again. At the end of the mandatory six-months' probation period for director, the commissioner of personnel approved permanent status for Buzz at the request of Manuel. Buzz was "doing an excellent job in coordinating the activities and managing the operation of Baxter State Park," Manuel wrote on the probation report. "An exceptional employee!"

1. The park's trust funds were handled by professional managers at Boston Safe Deposit & Trust. Throughout Buzz's tenure, the invested funds performed well, even in rocky stock market periods. The Authorities followed the sage advice of the trust advisors to spend only a small percentage of the interest income in order to grow the principal. The value of the assets grew from $7 million in 1969 to $74.2 million by early 2008. The trust is now managed by Bank of New York Mellon.

Primary Document Sources: BSPA Box 1 (2507-0801) BSPA Original Minutes 9; BSP Annual Report, 1982.

Conversations and correspondence: Eric Baxter, Buzz Caverly, Bob Cummings, Tom Chase, Chris Drew, Dave Getchell, Sr., Loren Goode, Lester Kenway, Gary Morse, Rob Gardiner, Ken Spaulding, Jim Tierney, Ben Townsend.

▲▲▲▲▲▲▲▲

CHAPTER 18

# Management's Bumpy Road

WITH NEARLY FIFTY EMPLOYEES and a budget that had grown to just under $900,000, Buzz was facing complicated leadership challenges. Updating administrative operations took up much of his time in 1983 and 1984, and he was fortunate that there were no public controversies to distract him and only one major Katahdin accident. There were signs of stormy weather ahead, but it wouldn't arrive until later in the 1980s.

Jim Tierney, reflecting in 1984 on his four years on the Authority, said he was impressed with the "tremendous stability of park affairs" during the period Buzz was getting his feet under him in the new job. Glenn Manuel agreed with Tierney, expressing how "extremely happy" he was with the job Buzz was doing. He mentioned how tight park finances had "pretty much straightened out," staff morale had improved, and public gripes had declined. Yes, things were going "first class," he said, joking in his inimitable way, adding that the three "bulls in the Authority china shop" were working very well together.

By necessity, director Buzz spent less time in the park, although by nature he wanted to be aware of every leaf that dropped and wished he could be in two places at once. The impossibility of it was obvious, but that didn't keep Buzz from trying. Former director Lee Tibbs had criticized Buzz for too little oversight of field crew; now the staff felt that Buzz was going the other way and trying to micromanage.

As much as the Authority members enjoyed their park duties, they didn't always show up for their regular meetings—a situation that grated on Buzz. The trustees' regular jobs were so demanding, they marginalized their part-time park duties when possible, leaving it to Buzz to make sure all was well.

▲▲▲▲▲

Communications between the director and employees was an important issue—made more complicated by ever-changing laws, state personnel rules, employee contracts, and park organizational politics. After his retirement Buzz would say that personnel problems dogged a director more than management or public issues, and required a significant amount of his time in trying to sort them out. "Everyone [on the park staff] had an opinion," he recalls. Initially employees were enthusiastic and their morale was high, but after a while they "became territorial and opinionated and were more than willing to share their opinions."

Employees' support of Buzz as director eroded as chain-of-command communications suffered. He depended on his supervisors to relay details of park affairs and activities to subordinates. Buzz thought he was clear with what information should be passed along. He later found out that the attitude of some supervisors was "the less [the underlings] know, the better," leaving employees out of the loop. It was human nature for rangers to speculate, worry, and pass on gossip about problems, and it was easy for everyone to blame Buzz.

Hirings and promotions, in particular, became sensitive issues as the park staff expanded. From the time he became a manager (first as supervisor), Buzz's job description gave him responsibility for hiring and training employees. In 1968, he had fourteen employees to oversee. In 1971, when he had his second turn as supervisor, he had forty-five employees—the increase due to the financial boost to the park from Percival Baxter's trust fund. When he became director, the number increased to more than fifty but then fell back to the high forties.

Buzz started a staff newsletter as a way to improve communications and try to renew the sense of "park family." It gave Buzz a forum to take up management issues and share current and former employee news, such as promotions, awards, travels, births, and deaths. The newsletter, the spring and fall training sessions, and other events with staff were additional opportunities to also pass on the inspiring story of Percival Baxter's work to create the park. Buzz wanted park employees to also have that feeling of connection to the founder. It was all about enhancing park stewardship in the ranks and forging a distinct park culture.

Buzz's goal wasn't easy. Communications wasn't the only problem some field crew had with him. There were small, irritating matters.

They didn't like his hard line on beer and alcohol in the park. It wasn't uncommon after a search-and-rescue mission for rangers and other crew to return to one of the campgrounds and have a cold beer. Buzz didn't like it and told them to stop. So they made sure he wasn't around before they drank their beer. Buzz also didn't like dirty outhouses, and kept pressing them to do more cleaning. And he was insistent on staff being well-groomed, like the park donor had been—short hair and no beard or mustache. "I believed so strongly in the mission and the reflection of the mission in how we kept the facilities and behaved as park employees," says Buzz. He remembers that Percival Baxter had been "so well-groomed . . . a professorial appearance."

▲ ▲ ▲ ▲ ▲

The big difference between Buzz's first two times as park boss was the size of the park budget, with it considerably larger in the early 1970s because of the influx of trust funds. The major difference when he became director was Tibbs's master plan. Although the plan had been heavily criticized as weak and disappointing, Buzz actually thought it was useful once it was in hand.

The plan, he said, "brought a consciousness" to management decisions and priorities that had been missing. For example, if Buzz had wanted a trail in a different location when he was supervisor, he would have just moved it to where he thought best. The master plan provided guidelines that required a process to be followed in making such decisions.

The plan's overview of the five management zones also defined how much the campgrounds, roads, and other human impacts had compromised the very wilderness character that Buzz and the Authority were responsible for protecting. As director, Buzz wanted to reduce those impacts.

▲ ▲ ▲ ▲ ▲

A vexing problem facing Buzz in the early 1980s was spending in the SFMA. The SFMA's large development costs and minimal harvesting income threatened the park's financial stability. From 1979 to 1982, SFMA spending reached $261,808. At the same time, the cumulative loss of purchasing power over the last ten years was just

*Jan and Buzz in his park headquarters office*
JEAN HOEKWATER PHOTO, BAAXTER STATE PARK PHOTO ARCHIVES

under 54 percent, partly due to inflation.

Besides the financial issues, the SFMA was a mess on the ground. SFMA contractors had created unsightly stump dumps and waste wood piles along the primary access road, and had poorly installed road culverts. Buzz led the trustees on a trip to the SFMA in 1981 to see what was happening, and Ken Stratton confirmed that they saw operations that "were not sensitive to the public face of the woods in Baxter Park. Anyone going into the area would say, 'This is a mess.'"

Just how big a mess would be determined much later. Suffice it to say that the trustees had a limited picture of where the whole enterprise was going. The concept of scientific forestry was vague to them, and much more so to the loggers who were accustomed to rough harvesting and cutting pretty much as they pleased.

The original plan called for hitting the high fir areas affected by spruce budworm in order to salvage as much value as possible before the trees died. But with markets glutted with fir from industrial salvage operations, the harvesters primarily hammered the SFMA's big spruce.

Glenn Manuel had taken on the role of point man for the SFMA, and Buzz was happy for him to deal with the problems and repercussions. Buzz followed orders and tried to stay out of the line of fire. The trustees continuously discussed the problems but primarily wanted to keep the cutting going to recoup some of the expenses. Projected revenues of $50,000 to $60,000 a year were tantalizing.

Ken Stratton's answer to the SFMA troubles was to have the Maine Forest Service take over the harvesting and he volunteered forester Fred Rooney to take George Ruopp's place. Ruopp had resigned his park forestry position after losing his bid to become director.

Buzz was concerned about having the Maine Forest Service take over SFMA operations, since it was an outside agency. In a move to protect the park's oversight powers, Buzz insisted on revising the contract with the agency to make himself (as director) responsible for overall coordination of all uses of the area.

Rooney increased road-building and buried the worst stump piles. The trustees praised his leadership. Rooney was in charge for only a few months when Ken Stratton replaced him with another forest service forester, Kim Kolman. Stratton had great faith in Kolman's abilities. Kolman had been trained in Prague at one of the oldest forestry schools in the world and cared much about the park. Stratton believed that Kolman could create the sustainable forest that Governor Baxter had wanted.

Buzz recommended using the Black Brook Trail as the first demonstration area, but Tierney wanted to hold off on showing the SFMA to the public. He was worried, repeatedly explaining that the purpose of the SFMA was "not to make money for the Authority . . . [but] to practice the very best possible forestry practices."

▲ ▲ ▲ ▲ ▲

Jim Tierney was an effective lobbyist with legislators, and Buzz decided to use Tierney's talent to see about increasing the park's autonomy from state government. Buzz's interest was in enhancing operational efficiencies and savings. The first issue he and Tierney tackled was commodity buying of equipment and supplies, and they were successful.

Buzz's experience with a Chevy Citation car was an example of why the park needed to be in charge of its own purchases. The Bureau of Purchases had sent all state managers a Citation, a small, low-frame vehicle, but it was inappropriate for the rough, potholed roads of the park. To get the Authority on his side, Buzz had taken them on a ride in the Citation. They were thrown around so much by the bumps and potholes that at the end of the trip they were convinced that Buzz needed a more appropriate, heavy-duty vehicle. The governor's office let him have what he wanted, an AMC American Eagle, a larger sedan with four-wheel-drive capacity.

The purchases bill approved by lawmakers allowed Baxter Park to buy independent of the bureau when it benefited the park, but to use the state when it was to the park's advantage.

Buzz also began to press upon legislators the need to double the Department of Transportation appropriation for the upkeep of park roads. Although roads were considered by many people to be a dry, uninteresting matter, they were of utmost importance to Buzz—and perhaps to park visitors after encountering eroded, potholed roads.

Unusually heavy rains during the spring and summer of 1983 had made road maintenance a nightmare, and repairs were critical. The park, however, had already overrun the $32,000 road budget by $15,000. DOT was threatening to stop maintenance if the park didn't pay up. The park reimbursed DOT, and Buzz used the overrun situation as proof to legislators of how much the park was in need of a road budget increase.

▲ ▲ ▲ ▲ ▲

In the spring of 1983, Buzz learned that the neighboring Nesowadnehunk Wilderness Campground was for sale. Because there was a dam at the lake outlet there and he didn't want the park getting into ownership of dams, he didn't approach the Authority about purchasing the campground.

After the Daisey family sold Camp Phoenix to George and Beryl Emerson in 1955, the Emersons had leased additional land next to the dam from Great Northern in 1959. They were the ones who established the campground and built a store. The property was later sold a couple of times and finally ended up in the hands of Jim and Beth Mahoney, who would own it until the mid-1990s.

The Perimeter Road ran off park property and by the Nesowadnehunk campground and store and crossed the dam, so the Mahoneys thought the facility was a good investment. For instance, the store did its biggest business in July and August when park visitation was at its highest. Besides ice and t-shirts, customers could buy beer there.

In addition to the forty-eight campsites on the lake, there was a cabin and a workshop—buildings that had been moved there from an old logging camp. The Land Use Regulation Commission had given permission to put in showers, and the Mahoneys brought in two more cabins from the old Harrington Lake camps in 1985.

Park business manager Bob Williams saw all sporting camps on the park's boundary as threats because of the danger of uncontrolled access to the park. But Buzz saw more potential problems in owning properties with dams and thus passed up the opportunity to bring a strategic property into park ownership.

▲ ▲ ▲ ▲ ▲

Buzz's personal connection with campers who returned to the park year after year, decade after decade, didn't end because he was director. Keeping in touch—whether they stopped off to see him at headquarters or he surprised them at their campsites—was important to him. He considered many of them part of the greater park family.

In the summer of 1983, he held a small celebration recognizing the thirty-fifth anniversary of Ruth Butler's camping in Baxter Park. She had become a legend because of her lengthy stays, volunteer work, and eccentricities. Buzz enjoyed hearing how things had gone for her back in Syracuse. Butler impressed him with her frugality through the years and how she managed to acquire just about anything she wanted.

When he had first met her in 1960, she was driving a Mercedes-Benz—a long way up from a bicycle. She traded her vehicle for a new model every few years. Butler had bought a small house, too, as well as a number of Jake Day paintings of the park. She must have met Day in the park because she visited him in Damariscotta to see his paintings and purchased them for no more than a few hundred dollars each.

Butler had been the target of abuse from men during her life and carried a small gun to protect herself. She claimed that Helon Taylor had given her permission to carry it in the park. One day Buzz found her doing some target practice at Rum Brook and had to put the kibosh on that.

▲ ▲ ▲ ▲ ▲

When Buzz was a ranger and on Katahdin in winter, he had often heard a hollow echoing under the snow. He had seen avalanche slides down the basins and knew that climbers and snowmobilers on the mountain had the potential to cause a snow release. But Buzz had never seen the situation as a real and present danger to people. That is, until February 8, 1984.

Buzz was with Chris Drew and Tom Chase at Trout Brook Farm Campground when they received the call that a five-man party had been swept down Katahdin's Great Basin by an avalanche.

Bob Esser and Ken Levanway had been to Chimney Pond four years before and had done extensive outdoor technical climbing on Katahdin. Rick Cumm, Steve Hilt, and Peter Cochetti had winter climbing experience. Their first day, they warmed up on some easy slopes to test out the stability of the snow.

The next day, Esser, Levanway, and Cumm set out early to climb the Cilley-Barber route. But they returned in a couple of hours, reporting that conditions were too dangerous and they would join Cochetti and Hilt on their climb up to Baxter Peak via the Cathedral Trail. The group was about fifteen minutes out of camp, approaching the First Cathedral, when the avalanche occurred.

The climbers were wearing goggles and face masks and, with the high winds, couldn't see the avalanche coming. Cochetti was knocked on his back, completely covered, and swept down the basin. He wound up under about eighteen inches of snow and managed to claw his way out. Fortunately, he had no broken bones.

Once out, he saw Rick Cumm, who yelled that there was someone underneath him. Cochetti started digging but realized he wasn't going to be able to get to the other climber without a shovel, so he had to go for help. He ran as fast as he could to the ranger's cabin, got Charlie Kenney and shovels, and the two made a beeline to the accident scene.

Time was critical. Kenney and Cochetti worked to free Esser's and Cumm's heads so they could breathe. Then they dug out Levanway and Hilt and administered CPR but were too late. Esser and Cumm had broken bones and severe injuries but were responsive. Buzz took charge of the rescue-and-recovery operation from headquarters, as other park staff, search-and rescue teams, and volunteers arrived to help.

Esser and Cumm were taken to Chimney Pond, given medical attention, and airlifted out to the hospital. Rangers moved Hilt and Levanway to the Chimney Pond ranger station, where they were loaded onto tote sleds behind snowmobiles and taken to the Perimeter

Road for pickup by the Millinocket funeral director.

Later, it was determined that the weight of the climbers triggered the avalanche. The two-foot snowpack was sitting on a thin layer of granulated snow, and it didn't take much to release it down the mountain. The cost of the rescue was estimated at $4,935.

More important than the cost, the double fatality drove home the avalanche danger on Katahdin. Buzz thought of how often he had been on the mountain alone in gum-rubber boots and loose crampons and had heard that hollow sound under his feet. "I didn't know how much danger I was in," he says.

Buzz promised himself he would make sure his rangers received avalanche training to help keep themselves and winter climbers out of harm's way. But it would take until the winter of 1986 for that specific training to be put into place.

▲ ▲ ▲ ▲ ▲

A long-standing problem was illegal camping on Webster Lake, and it hailed back to the days when folks could do almost anything they pleased in the Maine woods.

Popular with fishermen, the lake is half in the park and half out. Flying services in the region had long landed within Baxter's portion of the lake to drop off fishermen, and the anglers then commandeered park camping sites without registering with headquarters or paying fees. They were sloppy about littering, and the high traffic was pressuring the trout population.

Buzz wanted it stopped. He and his top staff met with flying service owners in the winter of 1984 to discuss the situation, and the pilots promised to collect camping fees from clients and forward them to the park. If their clients refused to pay the fees, they agreed not to land them within park waters. The agreement was honored by some and not others, and the problems continued for years, despite the park setting aside a landing site at Matagamon.

Buzz had to pick his priorities for resolution, and illegal camping and commercial guiding were two that sat on the back burner. He knew from experience that unexpected opportunities arose now and then that led to relatively easy solutions to vexing issues. Waiting was a way that he protected himself and the park from unnecessary attack.

▲ ▲ ▲ ▲ ▲

A reintroduction of caribou was gaining momentum among some veterans of the previous effort, and Authority chairman Maynard Marsh decided it was time for a look at what food sources the animals would have on Katahdin. He contacted Don Hudson, who had earned his PhD in ecology and evolutionary biology at the University of Indiana and was now working in the park on old-growth and alpine plant projects under a state contract.

Buzz was enthusiastic about a second reintroduction possibility and welcomed outside funding support for the research from the AMC's Evelyn Murphy Fund. Hudson and Vermont plant ecologist Charles Cogbill agreed to take on the study project and climbed Katahdin in the summer a half-dozen times to have a look-see.

Buzz was very protective of Katahdin's Tableland because of the fragile alpine environment. He wanted to personally oversee anything going on there, and he could be counted on to nit-pick anyone's research proposal. A matter that Hudson and Cogbill had to clear with Buzz was how to permanently mark transects on the Tableland to be able to evaluate the impact of grazing caribou. (A transect is a cross-section of a habitat being sampled in order develop a profile of the study area.)

Buzz hiked up to Chimney Pond to meet with the researchers. The idea of using steel pins or nails was not acceptable to Buzz because they would mar the rocks, and neither did he want cairns built to mark the sites. What the three negotiated was marking the underside of dinner plate-sized rocks at the ends of the transects with spots of lemon-colored paint. That way, the paint spots wouldn't be visible to hikers. Cogbill was impressed with the length to which Buzz would go to be engaged with issues big and small.

▲ ▲ ▲ ▲ ▲

The weekend of October 17, 1984, was one Buzz wouldn't forget. He was away from Millinocket on a week's vacation when DOT's Division 3, based in Bangor, showed up just outside the park with equipment to pave the three miles of gravel road from the park line to the state road. He was fighting mad when he found out about it.

From a legal standpoint, DOT had authority to do what it wanted because the road (known simply as "the park road") was owned by the state. DOT's Division 3 superintendent, Walter Munn, had warned Buzz a couple of years earlier that the department was considering paving the road. He asked if Buzz wanted DOT to tar by the gatehouse at Togue Pond to keep the dust down, or tar Abol Hill or Windey Pitch—the two steepest road sections in the park that became "washboardy" during extreme dry or wet times. They routinely needed to be graded during the busiest months and were a sore point between park staff and DOT.

Buzz remembers telling Munn, "Let's get one thing straight right now. Don't you come within smelling distance of the park's land. I don't want hot-top to come anywhere near Togue Pond because I see it as a creeping blight." The park didn't own the land on the ponds at that time. Walter replied, "Okay, I guess you're not too excited about this idea of tarring."

When Buzz returned to park headquarters after vacation, no one mentioned that DOT had gone ahead with paving the gravel road to Togue Pond. A couple of days later, he drove out to the park, made the right-hand turn, and faced a new hot-topped road all the way to the beach area. He blew his top to his car passenger, Del Higgins, a retired post office employee who sometimes rode around in the park with Buzz.

Buzz later recalled that Munn's successor, Bill Gormely, told him that the paving happened at that particular time because a crew became available for a few days. Thus, the only gravel road left in Division 3's area of responsibility was tarred.

There was no objection from environmental groups. It was a done deal. Buzz acknowledged that the ride was surely smoother. He recalls that when he first worked for the park, there were a lot of gravel and dirt roads all the way from Millinocket Lake. "There was really an opportunity for about eight miles before you got to Togue Pond to get mentally set into a backcountry frame of mind. That opportunity was diminished, maybe eliminated, by the hot-topping."

▲ ▲ ▲ ▲ ▲

Buzz exchanged his park uniform for a dress suit and Jan donned one of her best dresses to attend a Christmas party at the Blaine House in Augusta in December 1984. It was the couples' first visit to the governor's mansion. They had never been asked before, and Buzz credited Glenn Manuel with making sure they were put on the invitation list.

In a letter to Governor Joseph Brennan, Buzz wrote, "It was an experience we will always remember." They went every year while Brennan was governor but were never invited again.

---

Primary Document Sources: BSPA Original Minutes Box 9; BSPA Correspondence Boxes 1, 2; BSPA Annual Report, 1983, 1984; Maine Land Use Regulation Commission Togue Pond files.

Conversations and communications: Buzz Caverly, Chris Drew, Charlie Cogbill, Charles FitzGerald, Bill Gormely, Don Hudson, Richard Leduc, Jim Mahoney, Lonnie Pingree, Ken Stratton, Lee Tibbs, Jim Tierney.

▲▲▲▲▲▲▲▲

CHAPTER 19

# The SFMA and Pockwockamus

The SFMA had a visitor in the summer of 1985. Former logger, union activist, and wilderness advocate Bill Butler from Aurora wanted to see for himself what was going on. He figured the township was being high-graded and otherwise treated like a commercial operation—he was an old cynic about such things. So he wasn't surprised at finding exactly what he expected, and he was mad.

Butler didn't go see Buzz; instead he went to Charles FitzGerald and landowner/logger Mel Ames to take a look, and they agreed there was nothing "scientific" about the cutting operation. Butler then went to the *Maine Times* to report what he had seen in the SFMA and took a reporter to the site to generate immediate publicity about the situation.

The *Maine Times* exposé charged that contractors had cherry-picked the woods of the best trees—ones that would bring the highest dollar from timber buyers. The loggers had dragged whole trees to roadside, leaving deep ruts and tearing apart seedlings; gashed sizable standing trees; cut "den" trees needed by wildlife; and left mounds of slash by the wayside.

For the Authority and Buzz, it was a bad day when the cover story was published on October 11, 1985. It was the first bona fide controversy since Buzz had been appointed director, and it made him wish he could turn back time and speak to Governor Baxter about allowing harvesting anywhere in the park. He regretted that Baxter had set aside land for uses other than wildlife sanctuary. With his years of experience in the park, he knew then what a nuisance and obstruction the SFMA was to the rest of the park and had no idea if it would ever change.

Glenn Manuel, Ken Stratton, and Kim Kolman reacted sharply to the charges of abusive harvesting practices, defending the operations and telling the public there was no reason for alarm or concern. Kolman went so far as to indicate that the questioning was emanating from people who didn't know a lot about forestry.

Buzz stayed out of the spotlight. Since the Authority had taken such a direct interest in the SFMA operation and management, the criticism fell at their doorstep and that of the Maine Forest Service rather than Buzz's. He was lucky that his reputation and public image were not tarnished by the controversy.

Private forestry consultant Gordon Mott, who had been a candidate for director in 1982, had been on the SFMA Advisory Committee when it developed the management plan, and he was the first professional forester to criticize the operation following a visit to the site for *Maine Times* and NRCM. Mott confirmed that high-grading and short-term economic gain appeared to be the guiding motivation for the operations.

Mott and NRCM's Jerry Bley, who also had been on the site visit, called for an immediate review by outsiders, and *Maine Times* demanded a stop to the harvesting. NRCM leaders and Mott faced the Authority at the November 21, 1985, meeting, with the news media waiting for the sparks to fly.

After NRCM's Brownie Carson took the Authority to task, Jim Tierney screamed at him for publicizing their concerns and scolding the trustees publicly. The trustees said the council should have sat down with the Authority in private to voice their concerns. (Years later, Tierney acknowledged that he had made a mistake in assuming the forest service was doing the right thing in the SFMA. He was so busy with politics that he didn't give full attention to his trustee responsibilities, he recalled. Consequently, he set about to correct the wrongs in the SFMA, and part of his strategy was to give Carson a hard time.)

"Glenn and Ken were ready to give [SFMA opponents] nothing," Tierney says. "If I hadn't screamed at Brownie, I wouldn't have had the votes I needed to appoint a special investigative committee. I had to prove I was on the side of a very defensive Authority who let me down." When it was clear that Tierney had won over Manuel about a committee, Stratton joined them to make it unanimous.

The SFMA debate spilled over into 1986. Bill Butler and FitzGerald, on behalf of Friends of the Maine Woods, went to court to challenge the SFMA harvesting. While waiting for a ruling, the SFMA committee and the Authority agreed on a 3,000-cord harvest to be ended by February 1, 1986. Then cutting would stop for mud season, and the review committee would consider further steps to be taken.

At a January 9, 1986, meeting, the investigative committee concluded that Gordon Mott was essentially correct, and recommended that the harvesting operation be suspended until all silvicultural prescriptions were completed. "The evidence was pretty clear that [the harvest operation] had been mishandled," said NRCM's Jerry Bley. The committee called on the Authority to hire a resource manager and establish a permanent SFMA Advisory Committee.

FitzGerald wasn't happy with the report, accusing the special committee of "whitewashing" its recommendations by removing criticism of the Maine Forest Service—a face-saving gesture for Ken Stratton. The Authority refused FitzGerald's demand to reinstate the language in question in the final recommendations.

When the committee's report reached the Authority, Tierney and Stratton voted to stop the cutting, terminate the contract with the Maine Forest Service, and establish the proposed SFMA standing committee. Glenn Manuel abstained from voting.

Within days, an irate Manuel called the committee members to his office and informed them that the Authority just wasn't going to implement the recommendations the trustees had approved in public. When Tierney got wind of the confidential session and Manuel's position, he forced Manuel to back down. The Authority couldn't lie to the public about what was happening in the SFMA, Tierney insisted. The issue was already terribly embarrassing for the Authority, and Tierney didn't want it to be a further political liability. Manuel remained angry about the whole situation, branding as "crap" the charges of mismanaging harvesting operations.

The Authority adopted the investigative committee's recommendations, in effect taking full responsibility for the harvesting debacle. The contract between the Maine Forest Service and the Authority for harvest operations was canceled June 30, and it was obvious that things were in too much upheaval for logging operations to resume in 1986.

The Authority and the new SFMA Advisory Committee agreed it was urgent that a resource manager be hired. The roadside slash problem needed immediate attention, a new management plan was critical, and then the park could get on with making the SFMA into the "exemplary" productive forest that Percival Baxter had wanted.

A plus for Buzz from the SFMA debate was his new friendship with park counsel Paul Stern. During the controversy, Buzz had to trust in the advice given to him by Stern, who had assumed legal

*Buzz Caverly and Helon Taylor's last visit, 1981*
GERALD MERRY PHOTO, BAXTER STATE PARK ARCHIVES

duties for the park right at the time the SFMA issue exploded. Buzz and Stern developed a good working relationship that led to mutual respect and a closeness unlike any other Buzz had known with previous park attorneys.

▲▲▲▲▲

Buzz's twenty-fifth anniversary year in the park had started out badly for him. Helon Taylor's health problems finally got the best of him, and the old supervisor died on January 2, 1985, eighteen years after leaving Baxter Park. Buzz and several park staff attended the funeral in Farmington. It was Buzz's last trip with Gerald Merry, who soon learned he had fatal cancer. Within a few weeks, Myrle Scott died, too. Those three deaths represented the passing of iconic figures associated with the park and with Buzz.

The last time Buzz had spent time with Taylor was at Taylor's Farmington home in 1981. Buzz took Merry with him for a visit and found Taylor laid up with a bad foot. Taylor had been shoveling snow from his roof and had fallen off. He didn't go to the doctor, instead putting an herbal "bag balm" on the injured spot. A year later, his foot was still hurting, and he found out that he had broken the foot, which was now twisted to the side. The doctor wanted to re-break it and set it, but Taylor said no, he had lived with it okay so far.

Buzz asked Taylor if he still had the snowmobile that survived the 1967 fire, and Taylor affirmed that it was in his shed. He limped outside to a bright red ATV, climbed on board, juiced it up so much the machine stood on its back tires, and roared over about twenty feet to the shed. "You comin'?" Taylor said, looking back at Buzz. Recalling the incident, Buzz says, "My mouth was open, but it was so typical of Helon, what with all his motorcycle and snowmobile experiences in the old days."

As Buzz started to leave, Taylor told him how proud he was of his ranger "boys." "I'm most proud of you, Buzz," Taylor said. Buzz drove away with tears in his eyes.

▲ ▲ ▲ ▲ ▲

Buzz had long harbored a strong desire for the park to acquire the land and sporting camps at Togue Pond because it was the primary gateway into the Baxter preserve. Without owning the properties, the park would continue to be vulnerable to inappropriate development on its doorstep.

Once Buzz was director, he began to inch toward acquisition of the camps and toward a long list of leadership initiatives that would enhance the park's wilderness character.

The Togue Pond Camps came up for sale in 1984, and ironically the person the park had to deal with was former park supply manager Lonnie Pingree. When Pingree had left in 1977, he'd moved back to Dallas, Texas, to go into business with his brother. But when he heard the camps were for sale, he jumped at the chance to return to Maine, buying the property for $63,000 in April 1980. He leased the fourteen acres of land under the camps from Great Northern for just a few hundred dollars a year.

Under the previous owners, the sporting camp facilities had declined. The dozen rental cabins, a recreation hall, a store, five bunkhouses, thirty-one tent sites, and various outbuildings were mostly in poor condition. The camping sites on the shore of Lower Togue Pond were suffering from soil erosion and overuse. There were numerous old individual cesspools and wooden septic tanks serving the buildings.

A lot of upgrading (including installation of a new septic system) was needed, and Pingree tired of the situation. He put the camps up for sale in 1984, and the park came calling. Months of negotiations led to a purchase contract for $130,000—a price Rufus Brown—still park counsel at the time—opposed as too high.

Buzz also was uncomfortable with the price, especially given the rundown condition of the camps. But he was convinced that of all four sporting camps on the park's border, the one at Togue Pond was the most crucial to acquire. The deal was signed on July 1, 1985.

Buzz would have preferred tearing down the camps but thought it would be politically difficult. So he presented an ambitious restoration plan to the Authority, with some cabins to be ready for renting in January 1986. However, as the work proceeded, Buzz made a 360-degree turn. He decided that only two buildings were in good enough shape to repair, and that all the others had to be razed.

Jim Tierney thinks that Buzz wanted to tear down the camps to get rid of local troublemakers who had a history of building fires on the beach and raising hell. If the camps were removed, Buzz's rationale was that the social disruptions and potential fire threat to the park would disappear. The Authority went along with Buzz, and surprisingly, there was no public reaction.

Chris Drew discovered that the camp clients had used adjacent Baxter Park land to relieve themselves over the years because of the terrible condition of the outhouses. He found over a hundred piles of human feces near the Upper Togue Pond beach shore.

While the demolition of the Togue Pond Camps was going on, Buzz also wanted to get rid of the Maine Forest Service building on the Lower Togue Pond side of the main park road. State forestry service pilots flew in when people were using the beach, would turn the aircraft around, and blast sand onto the people and their blankets. Buzz thought it was time to stop the practice.

Knowing more about the backdoor ways to get things done, Buzz invited Jim Tierney, state representative Pat McGowan (D-Canaan), and representative Paul Jacques (D-Waterville) to the forestry camp to see what was going on. McGowan quietly attached an authorization to turn the camp over to the park in a state budget bill—without forest service director Ken Stratton's knowledge. Buzz had the building moved to Pine Cove where it was used by volunteers and to store supplies.

The Camp Phoenix Sporting Camps on Nesowadnehunk Lake were up for sale at the same time as Togue Pond Camps. Buzz, however, didn't see the need to buy that property, despite the very long and complex boundary disputes and other problems. Neither did the Authority pursue discussion on the matter.

▲ ▲ ▲ ▲ ▲

On the heels of the Togue Pond Camps cleanup, another mess was uncovered that, this time, put Buzz in an uncomfortable spot. He had to confront the Boy Scouts of America for letting their facilities at Abol Pond deteriorate to substandard conditions.

The Scouts—guests of the park with special privileges ever since leases were canceled in 1971—had been allowed to maintain the area free of park oversight. Chris Drew just happened to discover how much in disrepair the facilities were when he was looking around the park for a place the Penobscot Indian Nation might use to revive its spiritual practices.

Shelters, toilets, and fireplaces at Abol needed immediate attention, and Buzz informed the Scouts that the site would be closed until the facilities were brought up to park standards. After the area was put back into use, a ranger would inspect it regularly to make sure things were being properly cared for.

In addition to the Abol site, the Scouts' Maine High Adventure Program had special use of a camping area on Second Lake Matagamon. Penobscot Indian leaders picked up on those Scout privileges, returning to Buzz to argue that they should be afforded equal consideration to meet their spiritual needs. They had begun to reestablish their ancestors' connection with the mountain in 1981 with the "Katahdin 100" race, which followed the Indians' ancient seasonal migration route along the Penobscot's West Branch to Katahdin Stream Campground. Held on Labor Day, the 100-mile race attracted an increasing number of participants, and the tribe felt it needed a private site that could be used for various spiritual purposes during the year. But it was a request that wasn't easily settled between the tribe and Buzz and the Authority.

However, Buzz was able to settle the issues with the Boy Scouts. It was an example of an opportunity presenting itself because of an out-side pressure, not pressure from the park director. The Scouts' special privileges were extinguished, and they had to compete for reservations elsewhere in the park like everyone else.

▲ ▲ ▲ ▲ ▲

Baxter Park was a most desirable place for Maine college students to spend as winter or summer interns and earn credits. Primarily they came from recreation and environmental studies and work/study and cooperative education programs at the University of Maine branches at Presque Isle and Machias. They assisted campground rangers and sometimes worked at park headquarters.

The lucky ones got to spend some time with Buzz, who enjoyed mentoring young people. He took them on patrol and educated them about the park, hiked with them to his favorite spots, and invited them to have a meal with him at his house. The association with Buzz made a deep impression on some, such as Mike Boucher from the university's Presque Isle campus. Twenty years later, Boucher would have a chance to show Buzz how much that experience had meant to him.

Buzz traveled to the interns' colleges to speak to their classes and try to excite students about careers as rangers. Over the years, some of the interns became year-round Baxter rangers, and others served in state and national parks around the country.

Members of the news media were also welcomed by Buzz and given his personal attention. They usually provided an excuse for him to get from behind his desk and go on a hike, sometimes for a couple of days.

On August 20, Buzz and Chris Drew took *Yankee* magazine writer Mel Allen for one of the park's classic day treks covering twenty-five miles—Roaring Brook to Chimney Pond to Davis Pond to Russell Pond. By the time Allen finished the last eight-mile stretch from Russell Pond to Roaring Brook, he had impressed Buzz and Drew with his stamina.

Allen's article, "The Governor and the Ranger," was one of the more memorable accounts of Buzz's career in the park and his rela-tionship with Percival Baxter. It was illustrated by the full-page photo of Buzz, a pregnant Jan, and Governor Baxter taken in 1964 at Katahdin Stream—the only one taken of Baxter and Buzz together.

▲ ▲ ▲ ▲ ▲

Worries about visitor overuse plagued Buzz—it was the most intense problem in the Katahdin area. An Advisory subcommittee recommended that a staffed kiosk be placed at the intersection of the Perimeter and Roaring Brook Roads to manage the crush of traffic, especially on weekends and holidays.

Buzz wholeheartedly supported that idea, and it was approved by the Authority. But the related proposal of a shuttle system, to be called into service only at the busiest times, was a harder proposition—expensive and complicated to run. Buzz didn't think it was the right solution, yet he was willing to give it a shot if there was consensus it could work. There wasn't enough support for it within the Advisory, and the shuttle idea was squashed.

The *Bangor Daily News* blasted the park for not having already solved the overuse problems that had started with the hiking and backpacking boom in the late 1960s. Climbing Katahdin in the summer of 1985 was about as much of a wilderness experience as a trip to Coney Island, the paper editorialized. "It's a tribute to the park staff and most of the hikers that the mountain and its approaches have not become a wasteland of trampled flora and granola wrappers."

A shuttle system might cut down on vehicle traffic but wouldn't help the people jam on top of the mountain, the *News* said. The only way to solve that problem would be to strictly limit the number of day users, as well as campers, using the approaches to the peak. In the long run, limiting people would give everyone a better experience of Katahdin, according to the paper. "After all, it should be an experience, rather than a spectacle."

▲ ▲ ▲ ▲ ▲

Amid the upheaval of 1985, Buzz and Jan flew to New Jersey to move their friend Herb Nowitsky to their property at East Corinth. Nowitsky's wife had died, and he was lonely. In 1969, on a ride with the Nowitskys to Mt. Chase, as they all looked across at Katahdin in the distance, Buzz had told them that when they were ready to retire, they could move in with him and Jan.

Nowitsky was eighty when he decided to take Buzz up on the offer. Buzz and Jan found Nowitsky in his three-story home in Alpine,

New Jersey, waiting for her to pack all his things into boxes. She spent three days sorting out what he could take and loading up a U-Haul truck.

The idea had been to move him into their own house, but at the time Nowitsky arrived, Buzz's parents were in a difficult situation with Polly Caverly suffering the effects of Alzheimer's. Things felt too chaotic for Buzz and Jan to share their residence, so they helped Nowitsky buy a trailer to put at the end of their driveway on McCard Road. Buzz did all the necessary carpentry work, plumbing, and electrical work, and Nowitsky lived there for the next twenty years, with the Caverlys watching over him and never being sorry they had extended the invitation.

▲ ▲ ▲ ▲ ▲

Snowmobiles and the SFMA had sobered Buzz about the ever-present reality of politics in park affairs. In 1986 he felt ready to step out front for the first time and take the heat to defeat a development proposal on the park's doorstep—Pockwockamus Pond.

Wayne Hockmeyer, the father of the whitewater rafting industry in Maine, wanted a company base on the forty-six-acre pond in order to have close access to the state's most difficult whitewater, the Cribworks on the Penobscot's West Branch. As the property was only two miles south of the Togue Pond gate, Buzz believed the project would pose a clear threat to the already overcrowded park. Hordes of rafters would undoubtedly want to visit Maine's most revered park and climb Katahdin, he surmised, and he asked the Authority to take a firm stand against the project.

The importance of the moment can't be understated in light of Buzz's subsequent actions to battle proposals and activities he believed would undermine the park's wilderness character and impose greater strains on staff and natural resources.

Whitewater rafting began as a new recreational sport in 1976. Outfitters had started out on the Kennebec River, but as the industry grew, rafting expanded to other rivers. To minimize transportation of clients, a new base was needed close to the West Branch.

Buzz took Glenn Manuel on a flight over the pond to Katahdin and regaled the chairman with why the park should oppose the project. Manuel told Buzz to go ahead and speak out against it, even though the trustees were concerned about angering neighboring landowners. Ken Stratton, in particular, didn't want Great Northern Paper to think the park was trying to create a no-development buffer around the park. The Authority was concerned only about the potential negative "shadow effect" of the Pockwockamus development, Stratton recalls.

Buzz notified the Land Use Regulation Commission that the park was opposed—naively believing that LURC would act in the park's behalf first. His efforts against the Pockwockamus proposal upset some management people at Great Northern Paper to the point that a company official, Paul McCann, went to Buzz to ask him to back down. When Buzz refused, McCann washed his hands of Buzz and would hardly speak to him again.

Meanwhile, Hockmeyer went to the Authority to assure trustees and Buzz that his development wouldn't harm the park as they imagined. Hockmeyer promised that the facility would be built carefully so that it would blend into the surrounding landscape and be invisible from the mountain. All sixty-one camping sites, the mess hall/shower house, and related facilities at Pockwockamus would be used by his clients, not the general public, he said.

Buzz still didn't believe that the development would be benign. He had climbed Katahdin twice to look down at the pond and envision what might be seen of human activity after the development was built. Buzz expected, at the least, to see activity on the pond and campfires.

Buzz delivered an impassioned speech against Hockmeyer's proposal at LURC's public hearing—with the trustees' knowledge. True to form, Buzz injected Percival Baxter into the debate. "If one citizen of Maine felt so committed to building such a heritage, don't we as resource managers and citizens have an obligation to put forth every effort we can to protect that area?" he asked.

Park defender Charles FitzGerald and NRCM, as intervenors in the case, asked LURC to impose a special protective zone, to be called a Natural Character Management Subdistrict, on lands within two miles of the park's main entrance, including Pockwockamus Pond. FitzGerald also called on LURC to place an interim moratorium on development around the park and to appoint a study committee to consider ways to protect the border over the long term.

LURC, however, approved the development and it wasn't long before Hockmeyer was back before the commission wanting to do exactly what Buzz feared—expand the development and open it up for use to the public. By 2005 LURC still had not used the politically charged Natural Character zone to protect wild lands anywhere in its vast jurisdiction.

Although Buzz couldn't stop the Pockwockamus project, his offensive gave him confidence in his powers of persuasion with the Authority. The environmental community was buoyed by Buzz's show of strength and determination to fight for the park. From then on until Buzz retired, there would hardly be a letup in conflicts affecting the park, and this would shape his leadership and legacy.

The question of how to insulate the park against negative impacts from neighboring lands was raised for the first time by the Pockwockamus development. While Great Northern Paper owned most of the land around the park and there were few roads in the region, the park had been well-buffered. However, when the river log-drives ended in the early 1970s, Great Northern and other landowners began building thousands of miles of roads to truck their wood to market. The roads opened up the Maine woods like never before. Although the land continued to be managed for timber, the haul roads meant that small tracts, especially on water bodies like Pockwockamus, could be sold for development.

▲ ▲ ▲ ▲ ▲

Buzz sailed into the excitement of the second caribou transplant project. He was an ardent supporter, partly because he knew Governor Baxter had supported the 1963 reintroduction effort. Another reason Buzz was so enthusiastic was that his boss, Authority chair Glenn Manuel, was thrilled with the idea. Manuel literally beamed with happiness when he envisioned "reindeer" running around on the top of Katahdin. Manuel's IF&W staff were forced participants in the project.

The new caribou transplant project was first raised as a possibility by Dr. Daniel McNichol of Bangor, who was inspired by the 1963 effort and began seeking support at Maine sportsmen's shows. In 1986 McNichol was invited to talk with Manuel about the venture, and the more Manuel thought about it, the more he saw the reintroduction as his last hurrah as an Authority leader.

Manuel assembled a quasi-governmental group to charge ahead. Dr. Ladd Heldenbrand, the chairman of the 1963 project, joined the team, as did state conservation commissioner Dick Anderson and state

*Buzz snowshoeing at Daicey Pond, 1986*
ED DWYER PHOTO, BAXTER STATE PARK ARCHIVES

representatives Pat McGowan and Paul Jacques.

It was quickly apparent that there weren't enough state funds for the project, so it became a totally private enterprise. In September 1986, former governor Horace Hildreth contributed $50,000, and the caribou enterprise began. The caribou to be relocated were to come from the Avalon herd in Newfoundland—animals that were relatively nonmigratory. The plan was to establish a nursery herd on Betsy Wyeth's Allen Island off Port Clyde and then transplant the animals to the park.

IF&W biologists didn't have a coordinating role in the caribou roundup for Maine but reviewed plans for the animals' transport. They were concerned about the possibility that the Newfoundland herd might be affected by the lethal brainworm parasite carried by white-tailed deer, or infected by a nematode parasite brought with Scandinavian reindeer in past years. IF&W was also concerned (as was everyone) that the caribou might acquire the lethal brainworm parasite from Maine white-tailed deer.

Mark McCollough, a recent PhD graduate of the University of Maine at Orono, was hired as project leader in mid-October 1986. He was under great pressure from Glenn Manuel to make the project happen in short order before the end of the year.. Democrats Manuel and Dick Anderson were going to be out of office at the beginning of 1987 because Republican John McKernan had won the 1986 gubernatorial election.

Manuel wanted the caribou in Maine by late October, but it was an impossible target date due to the international arrangements that had to be made between Maine and Canada. Their strategy was to create a "nursery herd" from which animals would be eventually released into the wild.

Baxter Park was discussed as the eventual release site, but a location was needed for the nursery herd. An aging deer-research facility at the University of Maine at Orono was selected as the home for the caribou. The proposed capture of animals for October was postponed to early December to allow for repairing the Orono facility and to finalize the difficult logistics for capturing and transporting the caribou. Allen Island was eliminated from the program to save time.

Buzz's job was to make everything the park was responsible for go as smoothly as possible. He looked forward to being involved because he had felt a little deprived at missing out on the first reintroduction effort. He began attending caribou transplant meetings and joined the Caribou Transport Corporation—writing the first check for a hundred-dollar donation.

At the beginning of December, Buzz traveled with other core project leaders to Newfoundland to round up animals for relocation. Bad weather made the plane ride bumpy and scary to him. He felt sick witnessing the shooting of caribou with tranquilizing darts. He felt worse when nine animals died from stress-related causes during the capture and pen-holding.

However, Buzz stuck with it, helping to get the twenty-seven caribou back to Maine by truck by the time Manuel left office, and

Manuel gushed that it was a great way "to cap off" his career. (Manuel then joined the CTC team.)[1] Two more caribou had died en route to Maine, and three more shortly after arrival. Twenty-two caribou (two stags and twenty females) survived to start a nursery herd.

Amid public criticism of the high mortalities, Buzz joined the crew refitting old deer pens at the university in Orono for a caribou corral and started to raise funds for the project. In his 1986 annual park report, Buzz called the reintroduction "worthwhile and [a] challenging venture." He thanked Manuel for giving him the "privilege" of being involved.

After Manuel's departure from office, IF&W continued to play a role in the transplant—to assure that plans for the transplant and post-release monitoring of the caribou were developed, and to see that protocols were in place to try to prevent the introduction of brainworm. The department, however, did not take a pro or con position on the reintroduction.

The caribou produced sixteen calves in the spring of 1987; seventeen were born the following spring, and by the fall of 1988, the captive herd numbered forty-five. The Orono corral unfortunately included habitat that had been used by a high population of brainworm-infected deer. None of the caribou died from the parasite while in the pens. McCollough recalls explaining to the CTC boar and the Authority that there was a risk that the caribou would pick up the parasite while inhabiting the corral. But so far, so good. The project moved forward, with the news media following all the ups and downs of the enterprise.

▲ ▲ ▲ ▲ ▲

The Maine Supreme Court pleased Buzz and Maine snowmobilers on May 6, 1986, with a five-to-one vote that led to the return of the machines to the park. The high court's majority spoke firmly that the Authority had the power to allow snowmobiles to use the park or to ban them, thus upholding the 1981 ruling of the superior court. Justice Louis Scolnik was the only dissenting justice.

In his twelve-page opinion, Scolnik viewed the snowsled issue not as an access question but one of recreational use. Allowing snowmobiles would frustrate Governor Baxter's "clearly expressed purpose of creating the park as a refuge against the encroachments of mechanized society," he said. "Any recreational activity permitted in the park must be harmonious with, and not encroach on, the trust's primary objective of preserving the wilderness experience."

On the other hand, Chief Justice Dan Wathen, writing for the majority, said that the Authority's decision was "a rational accommodation between the dual goals of the Baxter State Park Trust." Rule 19 allowing snowmobiles, "while enhancing wintertime access to the park, at the same time protects the public's opportunity to enjoy the wilderness experience," he wrote.

The 1981 finding of the superior court found that access and wilderness protection were legally compatible. Neither that decision nor that of the Maine Supreme Court settled the snowmobile debate, and after five decades, it ranked as the park's number one battle.

As the fight over snowsleds evolved, Buzz changed sides. His snowmobile opposition revolved around his belief in the higher value of solitude, protection of the resources, and soft use by visitors. He still strongly favored administrative use of snowsleds by park personnel. Accustomed to the convenience and efficiency of the machines, he wouldn't think of forcing rangers to return to the old days of hauling supplies and carrying out search-and-rescue missions without them.

▲ ▲ ▲ ▲ ▲

Besides Katahdin, Baxter Park's greatest attraction was moose. Several thousand visitors walked the half-mile to Sandy Stream Pond from Roaring Brook Campground each year to take photos of moose feeding on aquatic vegetation. The huge mammals seemed so tame.

Moose had been prevalent in the park since Buzz's arrival, and no one enjoyed watching them more than he and Jan. During the winter of 1986, the tables were turned when a cow moose put her eye on Jan.

The Caverlys had bought some pizzas, wrapped them in newspapers to keep them warm, and gone to Abol Campground to give them to Dave Getchell, Sr., and some friends who were there to climb Katahdin. Buzz and Jan drove their snowmobiles to Stump Pond, parked them so the climbers wouldn't hear the machines' noise, and skied the last distance to Abol. Getchell was astonished to see the smiling Caverlys standing on the stoop with steaming pizzas. It was the kind of thoughtfulness that Buzz and Jan were known for.

On the way back out of the park on their snow machines, Buzz led the way and didn't immediately see the cow that bounded out of nowhere toward Jan. When moose are low on food, they can be aggressive toward people moving past them, and Jan must have looked tasty. The cow moose was so close to Jan that she heard the animal's teeth snapping and felt a nip on her snowmobile suit.

▲ ▲ ▲ ▲ ▲

Motorcycle use was front and center again in 1986. This time, the community of cyclists—led by United Bikers of Maine—was far greater in numbers. Also, the machines had undergone change over the years, especially in reducing noise levels. But Buzz and the Authority's stand against lifting the ban on motorcycles was immovable, given Percival Baxter's 1966 directive to keep them out of the park.

During the months of discussions, Buzz was confident of the outcome—a pleasant change from other battles. He and the Authority listened patiently to the bikers' arguments, but Jim Tierney told proponents that without overwhelming evidence to the contrary, the trustees would continue to prohibit motorcycles. He speculated that the next Authority might even restrict automobiles.

"A lot of things have changed since 1966 and 1949, and the overwhelming problems of summer usage in the park threaten to rob [it] of much of its special character," Tierney said. "During our discussions of buying the Togue Pond area, we talked about forcing people to leave their cars outside the gate and running busses in." Buzz also went on record stating that he had "serious reservations about any further expansion" of vehicles, considering the problems of traffic and day use.

Although they lost another round, motorcycle advocates didn't stop going to Buzz to continue to press their position.

▲ ▲ ▲ ▲ ▲

In 1986 Buzz targeted the park's unsightly roadside gravel pits for restoration—an important effort to improve the park's scenic resources. The first effort was the pit at Trout Brook Farm, where $10,000 was spent resloping the pit walls so they could retain soil and be replanted with red pine. Other sites closed and restored were those at Slaughter Pond, Foster Field, and Windey Pitch.

Disregarding Buzz's directives, rangers or the highway crew sometimes reopened a pit for their convenience. For instance, Buzz found out after the fact that a crew had reopened the Grassy Pond pit because the commercial gravel source was so far away. He reluctantly allowed its use, and the pit was still an unrestored eyesore when he retired.

▲ ▲ ▲ ▲ ▲

In the wake of the SFMA nightmare, Buzz and the Authority had to address the hiring of a resource manager. The primary mission of the person hired would be to transform the hard-hit woods into the exemplary model of scientific forestry.

The Advisory Committee, worried about the impact of the additional job on park finances, fought hiring someone immediately. But Buzz and Jim Tierney thought the credibility of the Authority had already been stretched too thin on the issue and rejected an eleventh-hour effort by the Advisory to delay advertising the job. The ad went into publications across the country, and a federal forester in Oregon saw it in a college publication.

Jensen Bissell, thirty-three, was ready for a change. After college, he had worked on private lands, then at the state tree nursery, and had done a little logging for himself. In Oregon, he worked for the Bureau of Land Management on some of the most productive timberlands in the world. After ten years with the BLM, it was time to decide whether to continue with the BLM and possibly move to Washington for management training.

Bissell and his wife, Sheilah, were Easterners. He had grown up in Saratoga Springs, New York, and his wife in Rochester. They had expected to be in Oregon for just five years, and she was ready to move back to the East Coast to be closer to family. Just any place wouldn't do. They didn't like cities, preferring small, rural settings.

Bissell liked the sound of the ad that promised a job not simply growing trees but being involved in broadly based resource management. He called the park office and talked to Chris Drew, asking some general questions. Bissell figured he would be flying east on his dime and wanted to know the job hadn't already been promised to an in-house favorite son.

He was assured the job was available. He called the park again, talked with Buzz and asked questions. He was assured again about the equity of the process, so Bissell decided to apply for the job, and he was invited for an interview. He had broken his leg playing soccer and was in a cast and on crutches when he arrived in Maine.

Bissell knew nothing about Baxter Park. He flew to Bar Harbor to stay with his sister a couple of days before the interview and planned to read up on park matters at the University of Maine at Orono library. There he came across the *Maine Times* articles about the cutting controversy. "I spent the evenings reading those and understanding the culture of the park and controversial issues of the SFMA, and getting to know the players," he recalls.

When Jan Caverly saw him for the first time, she pinpointed him as "the one" and told Buzz. Bissell was impressive enough to wow everyone. "He came across as very sincere, very intelligent, well-studied on the SFMA, and well aware of the controversy," remembers Buzz. "He was confident he could turn it around."

There were thirty-nine candidates for the position, and the screening process took it down to six. Buzz was not on the interviewing committee but was the appointing authority, and after receiving the committee's recommendation in favor of Jensen Bissell, Buzz called to offer Bissell the job, with one caveat: Bissell would have to shave his beard.

SFMA Advisory member Jerry Bley was surprised the Authority was willing to hire someone from Oregon and the federal government. "But Jensen just sort of rose through the process," he recalls. "I don't think we consciously decided we needed a new and different outside objective perspective. But as we interviewed, he was a breath of fresh air, and it seemed it would be good for the park—not just the SFMA. He was young, progressive. Yet I think we tried to find ways to dismiss him. He wouldn't go away."

The committee didn't try to sugar-coat the difficulties of the job or the place he would be living. They were upfront about the realities of conservative, backwater Millinocket where "all the loggers speak French." However Bissell was undeterred. "This is the challenge I want," he told them.

"Even when we hired him, we were less than 100 percent certain that this guy would be able to pull it off, given the history of the situation," remembers Bley. "We were taking a chance in the end, and we all felt like he was worth taking a chance on."

Bissell came to Maine with the intention of staying put in Baxter Park for the remainder of his work life. However he would have to prove himself to Buzz, who worried that the SFMA couldn't be turned around and would continue to be a financial liability and an area of controversy that would continue to reflect badly on the rest of the park.

In effect, however, Bissell was to become Buzz's protégé and the person whom Buzz, now forty-five, eventually felt was most qualified on the staff to succeed him when he retired.

Bissell took small steps in the SFMA, didn't spend a lot of money at once, and little by little began to make headway in the townships. And in so doing, he began to heal the wounds between the SFMA and the rest of the park and proved that the SFMA could live up to Percival Baxter's hopes. The biggest job was convincing Buzz and the rest of the staff that the SFMA could be an asset to the park and not a liability.

Bissell was fortunate to take on the task in the late 1980s, rather than in the first part of the decade, because the ability to generate revenue was completely different. The markets had improved and harvesting techniques were improving. Logging equipment was changing, getting more high-tech and nimble, and thus having less adverse impact on the land.

---

1. *In The Deeds We Trust: Baxter State Park* 1970–1994, by Trudy Irene Scee, Tower Publishing, Standish, Maine, 1999, p. 186. Scee devotes an entire chapter to the caribou project, pp. 173–208.

Primary Document Sources: BSPA Original Minutes Boxes 9, 10; BSPA Box 1 (2112-0717); Boxes 2, 3 (2507-0801). BSP Annual Report, 1985, 1986, 1987.

Conversations and communications: Mel Allen, Jensen Bissell, Mike Boucher, Buzz Caverly, Jan Caverly, Chris Drew, Charles FitzGerald, Pat McGowan, Gordon Mott, Lonnie Pingree, Rick Scribner, Ken Stratton, Jim Tierney.

▲▲▲▲▲▲▲▲

CHAPTER 20

# Kidney Pond

As with all gubernatorial elections, the winner mattered to Buzz because of who would be on the Authority. Republican John McKernan's defeat of Democratic nominee Jim Tierney led to the departure of Brennan appointees Glenn Manuel and Ken Stratton. Although Buzz was a registered Republican, he voted for Tierney because of their long-standing friendship. But McKernan's replacements gave Buzz his Dream Team.

First, since the Democrats retained control of the legislature, Tierney resumed the reins of the Attorney General's Office and returned to the Authority. McKernan appointed career warden Bill Vail to head the Department of Inland Fisheries and Wildlife and Georgia-Pacific helicopter pilot John Cashwell to lead the Maine Forest Service. As senior trustee, Tierney became chairman of the Authority.

One of the first congratulatory calls Vail received was from Buzz. Vail hadn't even remembered that he would be on the Authority but was happy to be there because of his long association with Buzz. The two had seen a lot of each other after warden school in 1968 because Vail had been assigned to the East Millinocket district for two years. He covered the East Branch townships on the east side of Baxter Park, participating in dozens of search-and-rescues there. Even when he relocated to the Greenville district from 1974 to 1978, he still helped with finding lost hikers in the park. So he knew the park—and Buzz—well.

On the other hand, Buzz didn't know Cashwell at all, and likewise Cashwell knew little about the park. He had climbed Katahdin once with friends, but that was it: he was unaware of the park's history or the Authority's responsibilities.

Buzz, Vail, and Cashwell had a common bond as farm boys. Vail and Cashwell had also experienced war. Vail had been a helicopter tail gunner in the Vietnam War, and Cashwell had piloted a chopper in Vietnam. Neither had elective office ambitions, unlike Tierney. But all three were Type A personalities, and for Buzz that was good news. "He could bring a problem or issue to the table, and it got dealt with," remembers Cashwell. "We could get things done and do it unanimously."

The stars must have been in the right alignment for the trustees to click because after they organized themselves, they relished their Authority job. Vail and Cashwell appreciated Tierney's considerable political knowledge and instincts, and he helped them think about issues outside the lines. "Jim was the consummate issues digester," Cashwell says, "and it helped us understand the landscape we were in."

When they were together, their mutual interest and enjoyment was apparent for all to see. They looked forward to Authority meetings in the park as mini-vacations. Vail eagerly hiked to remote ponds to fish, while Tierney and Cashwell enjoyed socializing with park staff and friends at camp.

No matter how uneven their park knowledge was at the beginning, the Tierney/Vail/Cashwell team would become one of the park's most memorable Authorities, and arguably the most effective. The trio discovered to their surprise and pleasure that they could put party and constituent politics aside and work like a well-greased machine. The first issue they tackled was Kidney Pond Camps, one of the most publicized controversies in park history.

▲ ▲ ▲ ▲ ▲

Before he became director, Buzz had tried unsuccessfully to convince Lee Tibbs to take immediate action to fix problems with the septic system at Kidney Pond Camps. Win Robbins had reported the deteriorating situation to Tibbs, and finally, as he was leaving the park, Tibbs reported "serious" problems to the trustees. He urged the Authority to review the Kidney Pond operation immediately and remedy the problems by the summer of 1982.

The Authority had different fish to fry at the time and ignored Tibbs's recommendation. In 1983, Robbins again tried to get the trustees' attention, telling them that one of the septic tanks was actually leaking badly enough that effluent was polluting the pond. The runoff was hardly the only problem at the camps. The whole campground (thirty-eight buildings) was a mess, with old electric lines running haphazardly, old dumps still visible, an overcrowded shoreline of deteriorating cabins, poor maintenance, and wild raspberries growing through cabin floorboards.

Buzz explained the trustees' postponement of action in the early 1980s as connected to Austin Wilkins's continuing influence with trustees and leading Republican politicians. Wilkins was close with the brother of Kidney Pond Camps owner Charles Norris and protective of the Norrises' retaining the lease.

But when Charles and Ruth Norris's lease came up for renewal in 1987, Buzz wanted action on the pollution problem and favored the park taking over the whole operation. He knew for sure he could improve the situation drastically, and it was on the Kidney Pond front that Buzz proved he had matured into a politically astute manager.

In June 1987 Buzz took the Authority on a tour of the Kidney Pond facilities to look at the septic issues and the dilapidated facilities. Buzz explained that the toilet and gray-water wastes from the cabins were held in cedar barrels buried in the ground, with straight pipes into the pond. The effluent was leaking straight into the trout-rich pond without settling out in the holding barrels.

Buzz took the trustees to a storage shed and pointed out the dynamite and boxes of poison sitting on the shelves. "Everything that had been invented in the nineteenth century to kill or blow something up was in there," recalls Cashwell. "Buzz's tour was a defining moment for the three of us. We looked at each other and said, 'This place does need to be cleaned up.'"

Kidney Pond wasn't just any place in Baxter Park. It was sort of a private club with a well-heeled, influential clientele. There were generations of families who summered at Kidney Pond, virtually tying up reservations a year in advance to the exclusion of the "public."

The camps had private baths with flush toilets, hot showers, electric lights, catered meals, ice-making machines, laundry services, and a central dining room. No one had more conveniences and electrical contraptions than top guest Harold Colt, the only one with a television (the antenna nailed to a tree) and a sophisticated sound system. It cost fifty dollars a night per person to stay at Kidney Pond, compared to six dollars a night per person at one of the park's campgrounds.

The full-service operation was comforting to the older clientele of the camps. Without the indoor utilities and special treatment, they wouldn't be able to vacation there, they claimed. The other facilities— lean-tos and no-frills cabins at Daicey—were too Spartan for them.

The decision to clean up the camps meant they would have to be closed for the 1988 season because the needed work couldn't be done in winter. The Authority easily agreed. But the third step—what to do with the camps after the cleanup—was obviously going to be a tough and emotional one. To look at all the options, the Authority appointed a special nine-member committee to study the situation and make recommendations.

A question about the camps' historic nature still lingered. Win Robbins was among the advocates for placing Kidney and Daicey camps on the National Register of Historic Places. In 1987 he had asked the Maine Historic Preservation Commission to review the two sporting camps' eligibility for the register, and Kidney Pond Camps was deemed intact enough—but not Daicey.

However, due to the constraints such designation would place on the park, the Authority opted against proposing Kidney Pond Camps for the register. Enter George Kerivan, a Harvard, Massachusetts, history teacher and Baxter Park user. He contacted Buzz, among others, in late 1988 to urge that the camps be preserved as they were and that historical artifacts be kept in the library building for visitors to see. A meeting between Kerivan, Buzz, and Jean Hoekwater led nowhere, but Kerivan would continue his effort.

▲ ▲ ▲ ▲ ▲

Over the course of several months, Buzz and his senior staff developed a proposal on alternatives for how the park would operate Kidney Pond Camps. The special review committee then began discussions and public meetings that, at times, were the most entertaining in the park's history.

The alternatives were: upgrading the camps and returning them to private management; canceling the lease and turning the facilities into a park-managed, Daicey Pond-like operation; or removing the buildings altogether and replacing them with lean-tos and tent sites.

Buzz urged the committee to "put your emotions aside, put the [camps'] tradition aside and special interests aside, and ask one question—what is in the best long-term interest of the park?"

Buzz's personal preference was to raze the buildings and make the area into a more wilderness-like setting, with lean-tos and tent sites. But that was too bold a step for the Authority, he reckoned. Thus, he and his top aides took the position that it would be best to terminate the Norrises' lease, downsize the number of buildings from thirty-eight to nineteen, and convert the cabins to simple, Daicey-like accommodations. The two most involved Baxter family members, Eric Baxter and Rupert White, agreed—a big relief to Buzz.

Buzz made an eloquent and convincing case for a Daicey Pond-style operation. To start with, he pointed out that it would cost $150,000 to $200,000 of trust fund money to upgrade the camps. Even if the park had no money concerns, he said, the priority shouldn't be to have flush toilets and dining facilities at the expense of greater park needs, such as a full-time naturalist, an educational interpretive program, more seasonal employees, and better, newer equipment.

Buzz asserted that Percival Baxter's vision was a park that was preserved as simple, where people could enjoy nature; it would be available to people of moderate means; and it shouldn't be "locked up" for one special group or another. Anything more than a Daicey Pond-type operation would be "a threat of commercialization; expensive, deprive other aspects of park operations; separate park users; and potentially violate the Deeds of Trust."

If the Authority members approved a no-frills operation, they wouldn't be sorry, he promised, thereby virtually staking his career on the outcome. NRCM supported Buzz's choice, as did the Fin and Feather Club. The AMC didn't take a position but sent a letter of interest in taking over management of the camps to the Authority. Club planners thought it was one of the best locations the AMC could ever find. Bo and Jeff Norris (no relation to Charles and Ruth Norris) made a proposal to run Kidney Pond Camps similar to the way they operated their cross-country ski facility in Rockwood.

The park's new business manager, Beth Gray Austin, objected most to the AMC's proposal because it was a special-interest group with desires for a full-service camp (with individual showers and toilets replaced by central facilities). If AMC invested $100,000 in capital improvements, what would be the difference between that and paying for a bunkhouse at Chimney Pond, she asked, referring to the latter dispute with Governor Baxter in 1965. Austin favored Buzz's Daicey Pond-style operation at Kidney Pond.

Rob Gardiner, chairman of the review committee and former Advisory chairman and NRCM executive director, disagreed with Buzz's choice. Gardiner felt that Governor Baxter, who had stayed at the camps himself sometimes when he visited the park, would have been "entirely content" to have the private operation continue. Gardiner recognized that there were pressing maintenance matters and described himself as "squarely in the middle" of several alternatives.

The issue was so hotly debated that Gardiner delayed the committee vote for awhile to give the Kidney Pond clientele time to express themselves to the Authority. And Harold Colt had a card up his sleeve.

At a special meeting in October 1987, Colt announced that he had found "someone" who would spend $250,000 to upgrade the camps to park standards, even if it meant raising prices for guests and increasing the lease revenue equal to the income from Daicey Pond camps. A ten-year lease from the park with a ten-year renewal option was needed to make it a doable project, Colt said.

The unidentified party was assumed by everyone to be Colt himself. Buzz opposed the initiative because he thought it was sneaky. "I don't see how anyone can possibly conceive of $250,000 as not a donation," Buzz said at the meeting. "It's a claim to a portion of Baxter State Park. We're all nice guys, but face it, no one gives anything for nothing. Baxter Park will be asked to pay the price," he predicted. "It's going to come back to haunt us if we go down that path." He was convinced that "special interests should not monopolize one tiny acre" of the park.

When the committee finally voted, it was split evenly. Three members voted to maintain Kidney Pond as it was, three favored a Daicey Pond-style operation, and three wanted a "modified plan" that would retain some of the amenities preferred by the older clientele. Rupert White jumped sides to help promote the modified plan. Under that scenario, running water would be maintained in one-third of the cabins; meals would continue to be served three times a day; bed linens would be provided; and laundering would be done, but outside the park. Electricity would be replaced with gaslights. The two-thirds of the cabins without running water would use the outhouses and wash-basins, as at Daicey Pond.

John Cashwell remembers the Authority "lying on our stomachs in the grass at Kidney Pond and messing around with stuff on the ground and just talking about things. Three grown men there saying what in the hell are we going to do?"

Bill Vail thought that he and Cashwell were "pretty pragmatic" about what should happen—change the operation to the Daicey Pond type. But Jim Tierney was sensitive to the politics of the issue, as always. He lobbied his fellow trustees and Buzz for a solution that would please the largest number of people. "Cashwell and I joked that Jim knew we had those two out of three votes so that we could get him over a difficult hump," Vail notes. Tierney joined them in a unanimous decision for a Daicey Pond-style operation.

The trustees felt badly for Harold Colt. Cashwell sympathized, "We're fixing to terminate something he valued probably more than any single individual on the face of the earth: the tradition of his family and the tradition of his spending summers on the pond." But Colt was always thinking ahead and would have another plan to present to the Authority later.

In light of unexpected costs for the SFMA and new road-building at Nesowadnehunk Lake, Buzz budgeted the conversion of Kidney Pond at a low level. It would progress on a "pay as we go" basis, even if it meant taking a few years longer than projected.

Kidney Pond showed how far Buzz had come in the art of leadership and proving himself to his superiors. From then on, the chemistry felt among the trustees included Buzz. It was as if nothing could stop the four of them. Bring on the problems, and they would have the boldness and stamina to solve them.

All three trustees were unusually mindful that they were transients on the scene, and that it was in the park's best interest to support the one steadying force—Buzz. "Buzz's true strength was his incredible belief in the park," reflects Cashwell, "and he made us believers."

▲ ▲ ▲ ▲ ▲

Meanwhile, in the SFMA, Jensen Bissell had started work on February 2, 1987. With Sheilah's family in the Ellsworth area, they decided to locate in Milo, the right size and type of town he'd grown up in, and within easy reach of Ellsworth, Augusta, and Harpswell, the latter the site of a small woodlot owned by the park.

The remoteness of the park and SFMA didn't bother Bissell. He loved the park at first sight, and it offered him the opportunity of a lifetime—to practice "showplace" forestry in a place that would not change ownership or directions. What also "clicked" for him—made him want to take the job—was the way Governor Baxter had set up the park to be self-sufficient and independent of other state agencies.

As things unfolded, what no one had predicted was that the two SFMA townships would become an entity almost unto itself. Bissell would have a chance to leave a legacy of his own making of an ecological kind—separate from that of Governor Baxter, Helon Taylor, and Buzz Caverly.

Bissell's assessment of the SFMA cutting controversy was that well-intentioned, capable, and good people were involved, but unfortunately the process of solving the problems derailed amid acrimony. The park staff was well-versed with park management and recreation management, he concluded, but not in forest management. The Authority's solution was to give management to the Maine Forest Service, an outside agency. Other circumstances that played into the situation were bad markets, a developing spruce budworm infestation, a sense of urgency, and a lack of consensus on how the forest would be managed. "All of these things collided in a train wreck for the park," Bissell recalls.

Soon after Bissell was hired, he and Buzz were driving in the park when Buzz commented that it probably would have been better for the park not to have started development of the SFMA and thus fragment the management mission. Bissell took that statement as a reflection of the inherent difficulty of managing with a double mandate—one requiring that some of the park be managed for timber harvesting and for hunting and trapping, and the other directive requiring the majority of the land to be protected in its natural wild state.

Regardless of how Buzz felt about the SFMA, Bissell felt the director was "totally committed" to the Deeds of Trust and to the SFMA mandate. "He was willing to give me as much autonomy as I needed to try to make that happen," Bissell recalls. As well, the SFMA Advisory Committee wanted him to succeed. They were "battle-weary" from the big 1985 controversy, he remembers, "but unshaken in their belief of what the SFMA could be."

The old SFMA plan that Bissell inherited called for developing the area quickly, and he knew it wasn't a realistic or wise goal. He prevailed in getting everyone to slow down and make sure things were done right.

Road access to the SFMA brought Bissell and Buzz to an early disagreement over bridging Webster Stream. Buzz was against it. Webster was one of the very few canoe streams in the state where one could canoe the entire length (eight miles) without obstructions. "In my opinion, we must maintain the integrity of this stream and its relationship to the recreationist to the fullest extent possible, while meeting the mandates of the SFMA," Buzz wrote Bissell in a memo.

Buzz also wouldn't approve using the Perimeter Road from Black Brook to Matagamon for hauling wood in winter. The Perimeter Road was a seasonal tote road and was to remain as such, according to Governor Baxter's wishes and the Deeds of Trust, he explained. "To convert to a hauling road would require extensive ditching, bridge repairs, and widening," Buzz said. "Also the road is a portion of the only access snowsledders and other winter recreationists have to the north portion of the park during that season. We should not make that access physically impossible by plowing the road."

Buzz was aware of the hardship of the road decisions on Bissell's efforts to gain easier access to markets north and east of the SFMA and to make the SFMA a more attractive work site to local contractors. At the same time, he told Bissell that he would just have to find his way around those kinds of management obstacles. Bissell did just that.

▲ ▲ ▲ ▲ ▲

After five years as director, Buzz finally had a full-time secretary, Roxie McLean of Millinocket. Their offices were so close they could talk to each other from their desks. Now and then Buzz made her so mad she cried, but overall she found him a pleasure to work for.

McLean's sense of humor went a long way to help Buzz relax and be able to be teased—especially over the color red. One of Buzz's quirks was a dislike for red, and McLean liked to wear the color. Every time she wore a dress with red in it, he would make a dig about it. He wouldn't let her use a red pen because, in his mind, red ink meant there was financial trouble. She got fed up quickly and found ways to create laughter around red. When he decided to wallpaper his office, she picked out a design with gaudy red flowers and enjoyed the startled look on his face and the way he stuttered, "You're kidding." She was.

Buzz had become sensitive to politically correct speech. When McLean and the other women in the office talked about "the girls" doing this or that, Buzz corrected them with "women"—the result of his "retraining" over the years. To get her attention from his office across the hall, he would toss pencils into her room. She stopped that by getting a soft fuzzy snowball for him to pitch.

McLean felt that Buzz was fair in listening to the staff about their feelings on administrative and operational matters, but the older employees particularly complained about having to do things Buzz's way. While he claimed to have an "open door" policy, some rangers thought it was a ruse because he had a closed mind. He sometimes refused to see them, they said, just because he didn't want to, not because he was too busy.

▲ ▲ ▲ ▲ ▲

The military found Baxter Park an alluring place to carry out training exercises, and every time they tried, Buzz was like a bull in the doorway. No, he would say politely—to the army, the Marines, and the Canadian government at different times—Baxter's wilderness park was an inappropriate venue for such activities. Every time there was a change in command at Loring Air Force Base in Limestone, the new chief would approve "top gun" jet training over the park until Buzz got on the phone and set him straight.

In mid-1987, the navy proposed to test unarmed Tomahawk cruise missiles over a corner of the park. Before Buzz could react, Jim Tierney and U.S. Senator George Mitchell jumped on the situation, successfully pressuring the navy to plan a route around the park.

Military aircraft weren't the only problem. Low-flying single-prop planes buzzed the park, too, especially around Katahdin, and Buzz complained to the state Aeronautics Division that the dangerous terrain and downdrafts made flying by fixed-wing aircraft in the Chimney Pond area dangerous. More and more, the planes were carrying moose-seeking tourists who wanted photographs as close as they could get.

▲ ▲ ▲ ▲ ▲

The connection between Baxter Park and L.L. Bean, Inc., had increased. Bean extended to Baxter employees the 33.3 percent discount that Maine wardens and foresters had been given years previously. Buzz and other park staff also became field testers for Bean clothing and equipment.

As part of L.L. Bean, Inc.'s seventy-fifth anniversary, the company introduced the new Katahdin logo: the "Spirit of 75" with the sun rising over Katahdin. The label symbolized the "beliefs" and "traditions" that L.L. Bean had represented for so many years, the company said, and used it on gift certificates and credit cards.

It was typical for tourists to stop by the Freeport store to buy a pair of Bean boots or a flannel shirt before heading up to the park for their vacations and perhaps to stop back again on the way home. Likewise, L.L. Bean leadership teams and employee groups began to make organized trips to the park in the mid-1980s.

By the late 1980s, Percival Baxter, L. L. Bean, Baxter State Park, and L.L. Bean, Inc., all had a mystique about them, promoted by the media. Both men and their legacies represented something mythical and nostalgic about the great Maine outdoors. People wanted to make pilgrimages to the park and the retail store to be part of it all.

---

Primary Document Sources: BSPA Original Minutes 8; BSPA Minutes Box 1 (2112-0717); Boxes 2, 3 (2507-0801); BSP Annual Report, 1987.

Conversations and communications: Eric Baxter, Jensen Bissell, John Cashwell, Buzz Caverly, Rob Gardiner, Leon Gorman, Roxie McLean, Paul Stern, Jim Tierney, Bill Vail, Rupert White.

▲▲▲▲▲▲▲▲

CHAPTER 21

# Getting the House in Order

Buzz emerged from the Kidney Pond controversy as "the voice of Baxter Park." He had proven with the Kidney Pond and Pockwockamus controversies that he was an assertive director willing to speak out, to take political risks.

From Kidney Pond on, Buzz was a darling of the news media in and out of Maine. Benefiting from his public speaking courses, he felt comfortable before a microphone or on a podium. Buzz had the blessing of the Authority as the man out front. His job description called for him to be the park spokesman and in charge of news announcements. He honed the skill of staying on message—the Percival Baxter message.

The public and media demands of the park director had changed light-years from the days of Helon Taylor, Harry Kearney, and even Lee Tibbs. In the 1950s and 1960s, when the supervisor's job was much more circumscribed, Taylor did his job largely outside the public eye. If he wanted to affect a decision, he discussed things with Austin Wilkins or Percival Baxter—not the news media. Likewise, the media was only intermittently interested in the park, mostly during controversies or natural events like the 1977 fire.

Interest in the park from all quarters had increased in the 1970s, as the park grew and the recreational boom and the environmental protection movement took hold. Kearney and Tibbs, as well as the Authority, had more visitors, diverse organizations, and different media to answer to than ever before. *Portland Press Herald* reporter Bob Cummings, freelance writer Aime Gauvin, and the *Maine Times* saw a lot to question, and offered criticism about park management. They provided ongoing coverage of park affairs, with other newspapers, magazines, and television stations jumping into park issues occasionally.

The more Buzz was in the headlines or on nightly TV, the more he was publicly identified with Percival Baxter. He quoted the governor or the Deeds of Trust to support his position on a particular matter or to underscore the importance of protecting the park from new and old threats. In time, he moved from being just the "voice" of the park to also being the "conscience" of the park.

As John Cashwell got to know Buzz, he saw "three Buzzes. There was the public Buzz trying to keep order, the spiritual Buzz who could hold sway on issues, and the human Buzz who could cut to the chase on stuff and talk in plain English. Buzz could wander up and down that ladder of the three Buzzes on an issue, depending on who the audience was and depending on his confidence in what to use to do the right thing—or the thing he wanted."

▲▲▲▲▲

With Jensen Bissell in place, Buzz's top administrative priority in 1988 was to hire a new naturalist and thus fill out his senior staff. The selection process, however, was not smooth.

The position had been vacant for three years because of budget constraints, and two park employees jumped at the chance to move up the limited career ladder. Jean Hoekwater, a human ecology/natural sciences graduate of College of the Atlantic, had a diverse resume. She had worked at the park as a gatekeeper in the early 1980s, earned a whitewater guide's license, worked on seabird conservation in Quebec Province, taught school, and ran educational programs at AMC's Pinkham Notch headquarters.

Her rival was South Branch Pond ranger Keith Smith, who, like Gerald Merry, was a talented, self-taught naturalist and had been working in the park since 1980.

Buzz sat in on the hiring committee interviews, and the panel unanimously recommended Hoekwater as the first choice for naturalist. Instead of accepting the recommendation, Buzz took Hoekwater and Smith to meet the Authority, and afterward he continued to delay choosing one over the other, causing unrest among park employees who were divided over who should get the job.

Buzz thought a "cooling off" period was necessary because the competition for the job was intense, and Gerald Merry's death was still weighing on him. Both candidates used correspondence from Merry to support their candidacies, and bringing Merry into the discussions revived Buzz's grief, making it hard for him to go forward.

Hoekwater was eventually Buzz's pick, and Smith filed a grievance against the park with the technical services bargaining union that would take three years to resolve. The union contended that the Authority—not Buzz—was the "appointing authority" for the naturalist position. However, arbitrator John Burgess found no evidence that the trustees appointed anyone but the park director, "who in turn [was] responsible for all other appointments among the park personnel."[1]

The meeting of Hoekwater and Smith with the Authority was "a mere familiarization step," Burgess concluded. "They (the Authority) did not select and did not claim the right to select the person for the park naturalist position." He added that the purpose of the hiring committee was to make recommendations to the director, who was the appointing authority. Thus, Burgess found nothing improper about the selection of Hoekwater as the naturalist.

Burgess's ruling on the "appointing authority" for new employees was the first time that the issue had surfaced. Like the law that established the trustees as the policymaking entity for the park, so did the statute designate it as the appointing authority. In the days of Authority chairman Austin Wilkins, he and Helon Taylor discussed who would be hired for the new season. But Taylor also acted autonomously on hirings, as well as firings. With the comings and goings of Authority members over time, the hiring of full-time and seasonal employees was given over to the park supervisor/director. Again, there was no legal delegation of the responsibility. But neither the Authority, the employees' union, nor the employees themselves raised a question about who hired or fired them.

Hoekwater, Bissell, and chief ranger Chris Drew jelled quickly in the late 1980s. They would be a formidable group behind Buzz and essential to his management goals. They were not only supporters of Buzz but confidantes. In carrying out their jobs—with a loose leash from Buzz—they would become among the best in their professions. They would initiate and carry out enlightened projects and activities that would reflect well on Buzz and expand the park's excellent reputation. All three would remain with Buzz for the rest of his career.

However, the Hoekwater/Smith issue caused undercurrents among park employees for years. Employee rankings in the chain of command and the difference in postings—at headquarters or in the field—made for unrest and upset. Some rangers felt the field crew was considered "a little less than" those who worked at headquarters. When Buzz took minor actions, such as ending the after-season lobster parties where beer was consumed, it was easy for them to feel that Buzz didn't trust them to behave responsibly.

▲ ▲ ▲ ▲ ▲

While the naturalist issue was going on, Jensen Bissell was getting squared away, trying to understand the Maine and eastern wood markets and what needed to happen in the SFMA first.

The ugly slash piles were easy, compared to his other challenges. He covered them to dry so they could be burned later—a move seen by others as amazingly innovative. Bissell's more difficult move was to get the park out of the state's low-bid contracting requirements so that he could choose the operator he wanted—one he thought would do the best job in unusual circumstances.

Bissell and the reconstituted SFMA Advisory Committee were a good match. With pugnacious Charles FitzGerald and strong-minded professionals on the committee, "we had finger-shaking, vein-popping arguments," Bissell remembers. However, their mutual vision was to get the next phase of SFMA development right, and to do that, they were willing to be team players and go slowly.

Buzz was confident enough in Bissell to give him autonomy to do what he felt was necessary. Bissell was the professional forester, the scientist—educated and trained in areas Buzz knew nothing about—and Buzz was glad to be out of the muck of the SFMA. In the summer of 1989 Bissell would resume cutting operations after a three-year hiatus.

▲ ▲ ▲ ▲ ▲

As the spotlight on the SFMA controversy faded, the caribou reintroduction project again took center stage. Buzz's initial excitement had faded. In February 1989 he resigned from the board of the transplant corporation. He was frustrated by the administrative and logistical problems of the project and disheartened by the decline of the caribou.

The Authority was still hanging in with the project and allowed fourteen young caribou to be taken to a park holding pen and then set free (in secret) on May 3, 1989, before the summer camping season started. Two of the caribou died en route to the park, and ten more succumbed by late autumn—from predation by bear or coyote or brain-

*Caribou in holding pens during the second reintroduction attempt, 1986*
BAXTER STATE PARK PHOTO ARCHIVES

worm disease. And there were other deaths of calves born in captivity in Orono.

The deaths stirred more controversy about the project, with media criticism turning harsh. *Maine Times* had been the only Maine newspaper to oppose the reintroduction from the get-go. The caribou deaths prompted other papers to urge ending the project. Animal rights groups also jumped into the fray, contending that the release program amounted to animal cruelty.[2]

Mark McCollough and other project leaders wanted to take what was left of the nursery herd and release the animals into the wild outside the park in 1990 and return to Newfoundland for more caribou and transport them directly to Baxter Park. Their preferred site was Rum Mountain, but they faced opposition from Buzz.

Buzz didn't want to open up the mountain's old logging road because it would invite hikers and sightseers. He believed the place with the least long-term impact to the park was the Klondike, but that site was totally out of the question because the Klondike was the most pristine wilderness in the park. The caribou would have to be airlifted to that location and their movements tracked by plane. Buzz could only imagine how many things could go wrong.

In fact, Buzz had had it with the caribou transplant idea by the end of 1989. It just didn't make sense to him anymore. Buzz discussed the situation with Bill Vail and Jim Tierney, urging them to join him in parting ways with the project.

At the Authority's January 1990 meeting, Mark McCollough reported that a post-mortem examination of five caribou showed that they had died from the dreaded brainworm, which the animals had picked up because of the infected deer previously at the university corral.

Jim Tierney was taken aback by the information. He thought the Authority had been assured that the caribou didn't have brainworm. McCullough insisted that no one knew at the time of the reintroduction that some of the animals were sick. He explained that the assurance biologists gave the Authority about the health of the caribou had to do with the European nemotode parasite, which the herd had been tested for. Furthermore, the caribou had been treated with ivermectin, a drug that biologists believed would not only rid the caribou of any exotic Euyropean parasites but also prevent them from acquiring the brainworm nematode from white-tailed deer..

Bill Vail surprised himself—as well as McCollough—by suddenly withdrawing his support from the project. Tierney and John Cashwell were fed up enough, too, to make the vote unanimous. Cashwell responded, "Thank God. We're not doing this again."

Buzz expected a public reaction, but there was none—except that the project leaders were bitterly disappointed. Because of the problems with the deer brainworm, project leaders and biologists decided to release the remaining twenty animals from the Orono facility. They received permission to release the caribou on private land on the eastern boundary of Baxter State Park in April 1990. As with the 1988 release, the caribou were radio-tagged and monitored daily. All of the caribou died by October, about half from bear predation and half from neurologic disease caused by the deer brainworm parasite acquired in the University of Maine facility.

McCollough's hopes of continuing the project outside the park were dashed when the private financial and moral support dissipated. Newfoundland agreed to provide additional cariboou, but in the end, many of the private backers discontinued their funding. It was easy to see that the reintroduction suffered from insufficient planning and unrealistic promotion of the positives of reintroduction to enhance fundraising. It was another example of where the political aspects of the situation—starting with rushing to carry it off before Glenn Manuel left the Authority—undermined the effort.

McCollough concluded that reintroduction was "at best a very costly venture with a high probability of failure and that the limited funds available should be spent on protecting and preserving extant endangered [species] populations."3

▲ ▲ ▲ ▲ ▲

When Jim Tierney became chair of the Authority, he assumed the job of rating Buzz's performance. The last year of the evaluation point system, 1988, gave Buzz an even higher score than previously—ninety-seven out of a hundred possible points. Tierney's only personal comments were to praise Buzz for his dedication to the park and his commitment "to all of the people who use it . . . he is a great asset to our state." In subsequent evaluations by Tierney, Vail, and Cashwell, all would commend Buzz for remarkable qualities and capabilities, not once pointing to an area that Buzz could improve upon.

▲ ▲ ▲ ▲ ▲

Behind the scenes at the end of the 1980s, Buzz was awaiting progress on an important front. He was privy to Harold Colt's plan to purchase Camp Phoenix and give it to the park when he died. Getting control of the development would give the park an opportunity to convert it to a Daicey Pond-type facility, as Buzz had done with Kidney Pond, or remove the buildings and let nature restore the area to the wild.

First, however, Colt had to wrest it away from the new owners, T-M Corporation, a shrewd group that had been involved in controversial developments in northern Maine. The sale of the property on January 8, 1988, had happened before Colt could act, and ongoing purchase and sale talk was a game of cat and mouse.

Before the Authority knew anything about Colt's plan, it had become alarmed at T-M's announcement that it could convert most, if not all, of the nineteen camp structures at Phoenix into condos. A presale was advertised in *Yankee* magazine, hawking the Phoenix compound as representing "The Essence of Maine."

The Authority called an emergency meeting to discuss the new threat on its border. Litigation over boundary issues with Camp Phoenix was still pending, and the Authority questioned whether it should try to stop the sale until the boundary dispute was resolved.

T-M's Bill Holland and Gary Merrill had some questions of their own for the Authority, since the park's Perimeter Road was their only vehicle access. At a meeting on January 20, 1989, they asked for permission to use heavy equipment on the Perimeter Road to transport materials to rebuild Phoenix's old septic system. Park rules forbade vehicles taller than nine feet or wider than seven feet, and thus the Authority would have to make a special exception.

Buzz and park counsel Paul Stern already were aware of T-M's road needs, and they didn't see eye to eye on what the park should do. Buzz didn't want to make an exception on road travel for T-M; he thought it would set a terrible precedent. Stern thought it would be in the park's best interest to allow use of the road. If park officials cooperated with T-M, Stern felt they could prevent a commercial store, require a covenant in the condo deeds requiring compliance with all park rules and regulations, settle the boundary dispute in an acceptable manner, and probably obtain a deeded right to enforce the covenants that would ban dogs and ATVs.

Buzz reluctantly went along with Stern, as did the Authority, telling T-M they could use the Perimeter Road as long as their vehicles were in compliance with park rules and regulations. Buzz would say later on that it was a good decision because the owners of the condos turned out to be strong allies of the park.

The fact that T-M was moving ahead on the development plans didn't deter Harold Colt from proposing to immediately take the property off their hands—for a nice profit. T-M was interested. Colt's vision was to purchase Camp Phoenix and operate it with the amenities desired by the elderly and no longer available at Kidney Pond.

After Buzz informed the Authority of Colt's proposal in February 1989, they waited for months while Colt and the developers forged a deal. According to park officials, the two parties reached agreement on a price, but T-M upped the ante when Colt appeared for the closing and signing of papers. Trustee John Cashwell talked to Colt, who told him that T-M had tried to extract $250,000 more from him than he had agreed to pay. "Harold said go to hell, and that was it," he remembers

In any event, Colt lost out once again. But he was still undaunted. When he learned that Penobscot Pond Lodge Camps were for sale, he tried to buy those too—again to run them like the pre-conversion Kidney Pond Camps. But the price was raised on him once more at the last minute, and Colt washed his hands of the project. From then on, Colt stayed at the West Branch Camps on the Penobscot in the summers, and he lived another seven years. The Land Use Regulation Commission allowed T-M to convert the Phoenix facilities into twenty-two condo units, install a new septic system, and bring in new generators. The potential impacts to Baxter Park were not addressed.

▲ ▲ ▲ ▲ ▲

Colt had been a visible potential philanthropist poised to add to Percival Baxter's park legacy. There was also another park devotee who, like "trailmaster" Colt, was a dedicated volunteer and wanted to leave something of significance behind at his death. Frank Trautmann of Islesboro only knew Buzz in passing for many years, but he saw what Buzz's leadership and spirit had wrought, and he felt the park's wilderness character was evolving in the right way.

Trautmann, a skilled carpenter, had first visited the park in 1978. Learning about the new Wassataquoik Stream bridge project, he offered to help, and this was the beginning of almost two decades of service on Lester Kenway's crews.

Trautmann, known for his patience and helpful ways, worked all over the park, from roadside to the backcountry, often packing his own tools with him. He never complained—not about the cold, the rain, the bugs, or minor injuries. Approaching sixty years old in 1981, Trautmann could still carry heavy loads of sixty to a hundred pounds up some of the taller mountains, doing better than many twenty-something crew members.

Trautmann had a 1977 Chevy Suburban, and he parked it at Togue Pond and cooked and slept in it for quite a few years during volunteer work. The big vehicle came in handy in the late 1980s when new lean-tos were needed for Togue Pond and Little East sites, and the park didn't have the money for them. Trautmann cut trees on his farm, turned them into lumber with his portable sawmill, and loaded the wood in the Suburban for a ride on the ferry from Islesboro to the mainland and up to the park. At Togue Pond he assembled the lean-tos and then moved them to their respective sites.

Trautmann also teamed up with Kenway on the AT, as Kenway was the overseer for the trail's Katahdin district. Trautmann assumed maintenance of the AT from Katahdin Stream to the southern park boundary in the early 1980s, clearing blowdowns and brush and painting blazes.

Harold Colt and Trautmann never met, but Trautmann felt like he almost knew him because of Colt's "large presence" at Kidney Pond. Trautmann was tapped by ranger Bob Howes to remove all the electric power lines from the campground and modify cabins when the downsizing began in 1988.

In 1985 Trautmann and his wife, Margery, had written their will. If they were fortunate enough to accumulate any amount of money, they had decided it should go to Baxter State Park. Trautmann anticipated that it would be a simple contribution, having no idea what his intentions would lead to in time to come.

▲ ▲ ▲ ▲ ▲

The Wilderness Society (TWS), the fifty-four-year-old organization that Percival Baxter once belonged to, rolled out the proposed Maine Woods Reserve to the public in March 1989, and opened a Maine office to promote it. The 2.7-million-acre future federal park would surround Baxter Park but didn't envision a "taking." Regardless, neither Buzz nor the Authority welcomed the idea and publicly distanced the park from the proposal.

The idea of a federal preserve in addition to Baxter Park was anathema to most northern Maine residents. The Allagash Wilderness Waterway, a federally designated Wild and Scenic River, was enough experience with Washington for local residents, and they equated federal ownership with a loss of traditional rights to hunt, fish, and trap.

The Maine Woods Reserve plan, which became the project of a new group called RESTORE: The North Woods in 1992, was just one of several mega-conservation plans to come forth from different nonprofit organizations as huge changes appeared on the horizon for the forest industry.

Throughout the national pulp and paper industry, land divestiture had started, along with relocation of mills to the South and to other countries with cheaper labor and better tree-growing conditions. Rural land speculators were scouring the north woods for real estate opportunities, along with conservationists, something that had already occurred on the Maine coast.

An increasing number of people believed that it was a critical time to enlarge the public domain before the vast timberland tracts were completely fragmented and in the private hands of wealthy individuals or investment groups. Forest economist and consultant Perry Hagenstein, a former president of the American Forestry Association, estimated that ten million acres of the northern forest would be up for sale by the year 2000—most of it in Maine—a prospect that few Mainers could imagine as realistic.

There would be "a sea change in forest ownership in northern New England," he warned, adding that the value of the lands "was increasing as real estate for recreation, tourism, and subdivision."[4]

▲ ▲ ▲ ▲ ▲

Continuing to move on his determination to control access to the park, Buzz had pushed forward on relocating the three miles of the Perimeter Road that were outside the park on Great Northern Paper land. The rebuilt section was officially opened on July 18, 1989.

At the same time, the old Telos Road and Nesowadnehunk Field gates on the park's western border with Great Northern were closed. Since this it made it more difficult for locals to reach Nesowadnehunk Wilderness Campground, the park opened West Gate on Nesowadnehunk Lake. The decrease in access points from five to three rankled area sportsmen and increased their feelings against Buzz.

The Fin and Feather Club pointedly complained that the gate wasn't open long enough to satisfy mill employees with long shifts, who liked to go fishing before or after work. Buzz and Chris Drew disagreed on how to placate the club. Buzz thought an honor system during the gatekeepers' off-duty hours, such as was in effect at Togue Pond Gate, was the best solution. It would allow the locals to self-register. Drew figured it wouldn't work because people wouldn't register, would illegally transport their pets into the park, and would use oversized vehicles. But they did it Buzz's way for awhile.

▲ ▲ ▲ ▲ ▲

Approaching his fiftieth birthday, Buzz was in good health, fit, and able to get into the park frequently, sometimes just to enjoy being alone at some of his old haunts and other times to pay unexpected visits to campgrounds.

On one such occasion in the summer of 1989, he hiked to Russell Pond and found a sign on the crew camp, "Jack's Shack." Buzz was furious. He informed assistant campground ranger Jack Sheltmire that the sign was territorial and memorial-like and had no place in the park. The sign came down.

Sheltmire, a University of Maine at Presque Isle professor, was educated in wilderness recreation management, and he liked to regale his ranger friends with the ways Buzz and Chris Drew didn't know how to manage a real wilderness by the textbook.

▲ ▲ ▲ ▲ ▲

Veteran mountaineer Clarence LeBell returned to the park in the summer to investigate the possibility of a new trail that he wanted to name for Buzz, raising the "memorial" issue again. LeBell focused on the possibility of a connector trail from The Owl to Katahdin's Tableland via the mountain's west flank and Saddle Spring. It would offer hikers an exciting new route and a closer view of Witherle ravine and the Klondike.

Buzz told LeBell that he would be "very hesitant" to add more trail miles since the park had more to maintain than it could already, and Buzz was "extremely concerned" about the impact to alpine vegetation. Having a trail named for himself would be "flattering," Buzz said, but he reminded LeBell that Governor Baxter didn't want trails or natural features named for individuals—except in situations that Baxter himself approved or that were already in place when he bought the park lands.

The Caverly Trail idea died on the vine then, but memorializing Buzz was an idea that would be impossible to put down later on.

▲ ▲ ▲ ▲ ▲

Although in his early ranger years Buzz may not have thought women could shoulder the job, he was in the "equality" camp by the time he was director. In the early 1970s, when Governor Baxter's trust funds were released, the wives of campground rangers were put on the payroll as assistants—a job they'd been doing already as wives. During Lee

Tibbs's tenure, single women began filling the ranks of assistant rangers and trail crew, proving they could do the same "heavy lifting" as the men.

Esther Hendrickson, who had been on the trail crew, broke the ranger "glass ceiling" in 1985 when Buzz hired her as the first woman ranger. Her assignment was noteworthy because it was Chimney Pond, the park's toughest backcountry post. But Hendrickson had already proven herself as assistant ranger at Chimney Pond during the 1984 season.

Buzz wasn't present at Hendrickson's hiring interview but she had to pass muster with him. He had heard she was fully capable of assuming the job. Small in stature, Hendrickson had pulled off a hiker rescue below the Knife Edge with no problem, showing any doubters that she had the strength to meet the physical demands of the job. Ranger Ben Townsend was impressed with Hendrickson's work, affirming her "incredible" work ethic and her quickness in learning how to be comfortable on Katahdin's steep slopes.

Another "first" was reached in 1989 when Christine Trefethlen joined Hendrickson at Chimney Pond as assistant campground ranger. Campers enjoyed having two women managing the campground. During Hendrickson's ten years at Chimney Pond, she experienced only one instance of unwanted male harassment.

Buzz and Hendrickson had interesting similarities. She, like him, was a stickler for obeying rules and was stern with campers who violated them. "I was very strict," she recalls. "After all, the park was a wilderness area." She also wasn't afraid to refuse the boss a favor when it seemed a personal encroachment.

Park perks were dispensed by Buzz to members of the Authority and Advisory Committee, bureaucrats, and certain "friends" of the park. He gave reservations on-the-spot for Chimney Pond, usually for the crew camp, but sometimes for the ranger's cabin. The ranger and/or assistant were sometimes asked to carry the gear or equipment or fix meals for the visiting important people.

"It all rubbed me the wrong way," remembers Hendrickson. She went along with what Buzz wanted to a point, but she drew a line at his offering her own bed to guests. No way, she said, and she prevailed. Hendrickson noted that Buzz wouldn't force campers out of their paid sites to make room for dignitaries.

▲ ▲ ▲ ▲ ▲

Throughout the history of the park, important documents had come and gone. Boxes of Percival Baxter's records had been lost. Helon Taylor's papers had been destroyed when his camp burned. Park headquarters had moved so many times that an untold volume of documents had been misplaced or hauled to the dump. No one had a clue as to what records had survived in nooks and crannies of back rooms and cabinets at the office or in the attics of rangers' camps.

The state had started to protect government records back in 1880, but storing an increasing volume of archival documents was a space and administrative problem. In 1930 the law was amended authorizing the secretary of state to destroy records more than five years old. Twelve years later, certain officials were given authority to approve destruction of records in their possession as they saw fit. Practically speaking, none of these laws affected Baxter Park because no one there was paying attention. Keeping or discarding records was haphazard.

Many interesting park documents from the 1960s and 1970s, especially correspondence between Authority members and with supervisor Helon Taylor, were sent to the Maine State Archives, the official repository for government papers. No record was kept by the park of what was destroyed. However, the limited volume of material preserved tells the tale to anyone researching park history.

In the park's 1982 report, Buzz mentioned planning as a priority to "purge . . . archives files" to delete "unnecessary" documents. The task didn't get done for years. A lot of files were stored in boxes in the old bunk-room at headquarters, and Buzz asked business manager Beth Gray Austin to take charge of the "purge." According to him, she threw out most of the files, not checking with Buzz about the historical importance of one box full of papers or another.

In 1988 the Maine State Archives developed a document retention program with recommended time periods for keeping papers. For instance, park correspondence was required to be kept only two years, and the naturalist's papers, five years. There was no rule about e-mails. Employees from the different agencies were trained in the nuts and bolts of record retention and record elimination. Buzz designated his secretary and a clerk to be in charge.

Periodically, the park record overseers would give Buzz a list of documents to be destroyed, and he had to sign the order. Now and then, the historical nature of some documents would be brought to his attention, and he would direct them to be kept at park headquarters (e.g., the Daicey Pond files), sent to Maine State Archives, or be destroyed. Many times he would just "glance" at the list of papers ready for disposal.

It seems reasonable that the park would eliminate the file drawers of old forms, sales-tax records, vacation slips, training notices, and the like. But important documents went into the trash, too: correspondence between Buzz and the Authority; between Buzz and environmental groups; Advisory Committee correspondence; Great Northern Paper correspondence with the park; ranger meeting discussions; and documents related to many controversies such as snowmobiles, the 1974 blowdown, Pockwockamus Pond, the caribou reintroduction, motorcycles, scientific research, Native American requests, and handicapped access. Some of the 1970s materials destroyed were files donated by Advisory Committee members, information about the old park dumps, church services at Katahdin Stream, and the Civilian Conservation Corps in the park in the 1930s. All would have been valuable to historians, journalists, and authors.

Later, after Buzz had retired, efforts would be made to establish protocols to help park managers decide what to retain and what to dispose of without interfering with the historical record. Yet the appropriateness of those subjective, in-house decisions was not reviewed by an independent party.

While Buzz let important documents go to the local waste disposal facility, he was foresighted in compiling annual reports to the Authority to leave a permanent record of operations. Buzz started making a yearly report to the Authority in 1981. These sizable documents are interesting to read not only for the details of field work, visitor statistics, and budgets but for how they reflected Buzz's growth and changes in the job.

Buzz always wrote an overview of the year's events and his activities, followed by division and other staff operational details. He included various letters of interest that addressed issues, and by 1985 was adding "concluding remarks" about what was likely to come up in the following year. His communications became more personal and expansive in the 1990s, seemingly reflecting his greater self-confidence and growth as a manager.

The reports also were a forum (like the park newsletter) for expressing appreciation to other park leaders, staff, volunteers, Baxter

Park trust officials, and long-term park friends, and for tracking the deaths of people strongly connected to the park, starting with John Baxter in 1984. Besides being nostalgic, Buzz was sentimental. He felt strongly about honoring others for their deeds. When marking the deaths of special friends, Buzz often related stories that reflected on the history of the park and the hardships endured by early employees— hoping to instill in current park employees an interest and appreciation for past contributions and sacrifices.

In the inaugural annual report in 1981, Buzz reinforced the park's mission to employees. "[Percival Baxter] entrusted us [with the park] as responsible people and was confident we would never let him or his gift down," wrote Buzz. "WE WON'T!" As a reminder to staff, Buzz said he had ordered new stationery with these words prominently printed across the bottom: "TO PRESERVE AND PROTECT." In the 1990s, Buzz included more references to Percival Baxter's gift and his expectations of park employees to keep faith with the Deeds of Trust and help visitors enjoy the park "in the right, unspoiled way."

Buzz's reports, more like booklets, grew to nearly two hundred pages in following years. In 1992 he mentioned that the 172-page report might seem to be "excessive paperwork." He reflected back on the "extraordinary loss of information" when fire had consumed Helon Taylor's cabin and contents in 1967, and he had seen Dr. John Hakola's "struggle" to document certain years of park history in *Legacy of a Lifetime*. "It is essential, in my view," Buzz asserted, "that we document as much as we can about the details of our operations because it is this well-distributed and accountable documentation that will help future historians in maintaining an ongoing history of Baxter State Park."

▲ ▲ ▲ ▲ ▲

At home, Buzz and Jan were experiencing an "empty nest," with both daughters having graduated from high school and left for work and college. Buzz's mother, Polly, died in an elderly care center in Bangor, leaving Irvin Caverly alone. He wouldn't move in with Buzz and Jan, and within two years had to move to a nursing home in Skowhegan.

Buzz turned fifty in 1989 but didn't think twice about it. He wasn't big on celebrating birthdays, especially hallmark ones. He was feeling strong and healthy and was just as enthusiastic about his job as when he'd started as a ranger in 1960. He still sang country music tunes when he went to work in the morning, and his mischievous streak was alive and well, as he showed his buddies when they went into the park.

1. State of Maine and Maine State Employees Association, Case Number AAA#113900014189, arbitration findings and decision by John Burgess, May 6, 1991.
2. *In The Deeds We Trust: Baxter State Park* 1970-1994, by Trudy Irene Scee, Tower Publishing, Standish, Maine, 1999, pp. 194–202.
3. "Lessons in Reintroduction Policy from an Attempt to Restore Caribou to Maine," by Dr. Mark McCollough, unpublished paper, 2008.
4. *The Future of the Northern Forest,* edited by Christopher McGrory Klyza and Stephen C. Trombulak, University Press of New England, Hanover, New Hampshire, 1994, p. 95.

Primary Document Sources: BSPA Original Minutes 6: BSPA Box 2 (2507-0801); BSPA Box 1 (2112-0717); BSP Annual Report, 1989.

Conversations and communications: Ron Ahlquist, Jensen Bissell, John Cashwell, Buzz Caverly, Chris Drew, John Graham, Jean Hoekwater, Jim Henderson, Esther Hendrickson, Bill Holland, Linda Ives, Gary Merrill, Nina Osier, Jack Sheltmire, Keith Smith, Paul Stern, Jym St. Pierre, Jim Tierney, Ben Townsend, Frank Trautmann, Bill Vail.

PART IV: BATTLEGROUNDS

▲▲▲▲▲▲▲▲

CHAPTER 22

# West Gate and Pine Marten Research

THE 1990S WERE VOLCANIC FOR BUZZ and for the north woods. It would be the decade when he came into his full maturity as a manager and a champion of Percival Baxter's wilderness objectives. Buzz led the charge on multiple new fronts—further restricting vehicle access, preventing the killing of wildlife through research, ending the storage of private boats on trout ponds, improving the trail system, and achieving management autonomy from the state. He went out on an especially slender political limb with a bold vision for how the park could become "Wilder from Within."

As Perry Hagenstein had correctly forecast, it would be a decade of tectonic upheaval in the large timberland ownerships around the park. The enduring old ownerships were broken up and sold to multiple corporate entities with aggressive, short-term profit goals, stirring the emotions of people throughout Maine. The sale of Diamond International Paper's 800,000 acres of lands in Maine in 1987 had presaged the shocking changes to come, and while nightmarish for many, there would be expansion opportunities for Baxter Park that Buzz wanted to seize.

The reality of a new world order in the papermaking business struck Millinocket in 1990 when one of the industry giants, Georgia-Pacific (G-P) Corporation carried out a hostile takeover of Great Northern Nekoosa, including its Great Northern Paper division. In less than two years, G-P spun off Nekoosa's Great Northern mills and lands to another conglomerate, Bowater Corporation.

The two ownership sales opened the door to the conservation of lands around the park through nonprofit organizations that would help buffer the park from development and other potentially damaging enterprises. The park was able to acquire two small but strategic parcels on the southern end of the park that secured the Togue Pond entrance and the Abol/West Branch border.

The Togue Pond purchase sailed through with little public reaction, but the second one in 1997 sparked a donnybrook over traditional uses, one that would bring into question whether any future park acquisitions could be made without allowing hunting and trapping. Buzz threw all of his weight into battling for sanctuary designation for the West Branch parcel and lost. He would consider the West Branch fight his greatest defeat.

However, the experience provided valuable lessons for Buzz in a future park land acquisition battle in 2006. Although he was no longer director by then, he was arguably the single most important advocate for the purchase of the bejeweled Katahdin Lake tract. Again fighting the hunting and trapping lobby, Buzz worked untiringly in support of the land being included in the park's sanctuary. That time, he was on the winning side.

▲ ▲ ▲ ▲ ▲

The relationship between Buzz and the Authority came into much sharper focus in the 1990s due to increasing polarization of the two leadership camps.

Buzz's stellar Authority team of Tierney–Vail–Cashwell remained in place until the beginning of 1991, when Tierney ended his remarkable ten-year membership and was replaced by Michael Carpenter, a former legislator and Houlton attorney. Cashwell and Vail left state service within a couple of years and their positions were filled by Sue Bell at the Maine Forest Service and Bucky Owen at IF&W.

The strength and support of senior staff loyalists Chris Drew, Jean Hoekwater, and Jensen Bissell was a huge plus as they headed into the choppy waters of the new decade. The senior rangers, several of whom had spent more than twenty years on the job, also provided important stability (and institutional memory) in the field crew. Tom Chase had twenty-five years of service, just five years less than Buzz. Charlie Kenney, Loren Goode, and Bob Howes had twenty-one years each, and Barry McArthur, nineteen years. The older rangers had pretty much grown up together in the park, and like Percival Baxter and Buzz, felt territorial about the place.

On the two occasions when Buzz had been elevated to supervisor, the park staff had heartily supported him, and those on board in 1982 had rallied around him when he was appointed director. But since then, a lot had changed. True to human nature, change was not always welcomed, and it added to disgruntlement in the ranks typical of any agency or organization. As park boss, Buzz was a close and convenient target to blame.

The park, including everything from personnel to policy, was even more complex at the start of the 1990s than when Buzz became director in 1982—the result of expanded staff and operations, increased bureaucracy, visitor demands, and more special interest and user groups. In earlier days, for example, the little band of rangers had a relatively simple job and lots of room to do things as they pleased. But when Percival Baxter's trust funds began flowing into the park in the early 1970s, personnel and personnel supervision increased. Eventually everyone was watched by someone else. Accountability and paperwork were required at every turn, from toilet cleanings to visitor contacts.

As the chief enforcer, Buzz was responsible for making sure that things ran as smoothly as circumstances allowed, that changes were implemented from top to bottom, and that personnel kept their eye on the prize—staying true to the vision of Percival Baxter.

Baxter's bedrock guiding principles for the park were critical for employees "to buy into," in Buzz's mind, and at spring and fall meetings with the full staff, Buzz consistently stressed the history of the park and called attention to the connection current staff had with those of bygone years. At weekly and monthly meetings with senior staff, he emphasized how operations should be carried out to meet Percival Baxter's vision and directed them to educate employees whom they supervised, and on down through the ranks.

Some supervisors met Buzz's expectations of bringing along subordinates, but others didn't. At times, the result was counseling or reprimands. Buzz couldn't fire all those who didn't buy into the Baxter mission, marched to their own drumbeat, or complained about him to park users. There was too much work to do, which forced compromises and a "moving on" approach.

The philosophical differences employees had about the park were evident when their opinions were solicited on controversial subjects such as the West Branch lands. Some sided with Buzz in believing that all new lands should be designated sanctuary, while others wanted hunting and trapping and vehicle access to continue on newly acquired properties.

Regardless of the internal difficulties at the park, Buzz's annual evaluations were sterling and reflected well on his relationship with park employees. "Buzz continues to perform in a highly professional manner," Authority chair Jim Tierney said in his 1990 report. "His dedication to Baxter Park and his commitment to all of the people who use it is remarkable. He is a great asset to our state." Tierney noted that Buzz was "able to deal with his employees on a face-to-face basis so remarkably that complaints and grievances are minimal." As for in-house promotions, Tierney said Buzz identified employees with management potential and "brings them along in his own careful way . . . insuring the long-term future for the park that he loves."

▲ ▲ ▲ ▲ ▲

The national economic recession of the 1980s had reduced the investment earnings from the park trust. In 1990 Buzz projected a shortfall of about $58,000. Rather than lay off employees, he wanted to eliminate the new West Gate, although he knew this would stir up local interests, including the Fin and Feather Club. Buzz's proposal was the start of a lengthy push and pull that got ugly and, in a bizarre twist, ended up damaging Governor Baxter's bust in the State House.

West Gate, located on the park side of the dam at Nesowadnehunk Lake, had been established to replace two access points south and north at Newsowadnehunk Field. Yet only 5 percent of park visitors, most of them locals, used that entrance, and only $7,000 was collected in fees for 1988 and 1989 combined. Buzz felt that staffing the gatehouse (a small cabin relocated from Kidney Pond) was a waste of limited resources. If the entrance were closed, he promised, it would decrease wear and tear on park roads and give the park greater control of its access points. He didn't have to work hard to convince the Authority.

In April 1990 the trustees agreed to close the gate, effective July 1, 1991, and the decision touched off anti-park sentiment across Piscataquis and northern Penobscot Counties. In particular, there was angry reaction from three sporting camps on the park's borders—Pray's Cottages, Frost Pond Camps, and Nesowadnehunk Lake Campground. Senator Charles Pray (D-Millinocket), whose family owned Pray's Cottages on the West Branch, retaliated by filing a bill to slash by $60,000 a year the state highway budget for park road maintenance.

Maine newspapers gave the fight coverage at every turn. Buzz invited news media attention to explain the issues and generate public support for removing the gate. He portrayed business interests, including Pray's, as selfishly trying to compromise the best interests of the park. Environmental groups and some private citizens, such as former Authority member Jon Lund, joined the debate supporting Buzz.

In a rare move, Buzz went to the legislature to lobby against Pray's bill to cut park funding, informing lawmakers that the park wouldn't be blackmailed. Even if the funding was reduced, the park would close West Gate, he declared. Pray prevailed—to a degree. The legislature declined to eliminate the full $60,000 road budget, but allocated $20,000 per gate per year. The effect was to reduce the road budget to $40,000 annually. The *Kennebec Journal* called Pray's move "nakedly political . . . a power play . . . legislative blackmail of an independent agency."[1]

Pray continued to lead efforts to get Authority members to change their minds on closing the gate. Michael Carpenter was a good friend of Pray's, and when Carpenter joined the Authority in January 1991, he tried unsuccessfully to get West Gate reconsidered. Buzz pushed hard for the Authority to stand by its vote.

Fighting about the gate closure lasted over another year. There was hardly a day that went by when a local resident didn't call Buzz or visit him at the office to challenge the rationale for eliminating the gate. Buzz used every opportunity, whether at a Mason's meeting, church, or social event, to explain the park's position.

The issue was finally put to rest by unanimous agreement of Vail, Cashwell, and Carpenter in late 1992.

▲ ▲ ▲ ▲ ▲

A matter very close to Buzz's heart was resolved in late April 1990. Stephan Bunker, representing the Law Enforcement Memorial Committee of the Department of Safety, informed Buzz that his proposal to add Ralph Heath's name to the memorial in memory of officers who had died in the line of duty had been accepted.

It was a coup for Buzz. One of the creators of the memorial had felt that because Heath was a ranger, he wasn't eligible. But Buzz argued the point that rangers were duly sworn to be law-enforcement officers with police powers, and he thought Heath was as eligible as anyone. The department researched the matter and agreed with Buzz.

After Heath's death, Buzz had made an annual trip to Sherman on Memorial Day and placed flags on Heath's grave, along with a plaque explaining the honor for one who had given the supreme sacrifice. He took several law-enforcement rangers with him and placed the U.S. and Maine flags at the grave. At the end of seven days, Buzz and Jan picked up with flags and plaque for safekeeping to use the following year.

▲ ▲ ▲ ▲ ▲

Since the 1970s, parks throughout the country had been working away on their mounting waste and garbage problems. At the latter part of that decade, Baxter Park began to shift responsibility to visitors by initiating a carry-in/carry-out policy at backcountry campgrounds. In the summer of 1990, carry-in/carry-out was instituted parkwide, and it would result in a 55 percent reduction in trash just that season.

There were other chronic issues that demanded attention, too— illegally blazed and painted trails, unsafe bridges, and underground fuel tanks. Rangers painted out the trail blazes to Frost Pond and Twin Ponds, and crews removed the underground fuel tanks at Togue Pond, Nesowadnehunk Field, and Trout Brook Farm, and installed above-ground tanks at Abol gravel pit and Trout Brook. The Wassataquoik Stream bridge was removed for safety reasons, and the Foster Field dump was finally closed. It was the last big dump in the park and its closing was a day of celebration for Buzz, who had first complained about the dumps to Helon Taylor back in 1960.

Waste disposal areas, however, were still necessary for some materials—a justifiable concession in Buzz's mind. A small burn area was created off Roaring Brook Road for old wood. There was also a storage tank for human waste from Chimney Pond Campground.

Chimney Pond had an experimental composting outhouse to try to better deal with the volume of waste. But in winter, the rangers couldn't turn over the waste so it would decompose. The only solution was to haul it out. A catch basin was put in the toilet hold, and the feces froze in the cold temperatures. The rangers wrapped the holding tubs in canvas or garbage bags and drove them down to the Roaring Brook area on snowmobiles. In March and April, when the removal occurred, temperatures were warm enough that the material melted somewhat. Once when Loren Goode was hauling a tub, the cover came off, and a shower of slop hit him from behind. "He came into the office and said no one should be assigned to a job like that," says Buzz. The answer was better containers that were sealed and wrapped tightly.

▲ ▲ ▲ ▲ ▲

As thru-hiking the AT became more popular, Buzz's worries about late hikers' safety increased. Besides the higher numbers, there were hikers with disabilities who were setting new benchmarks for long-distance hiking. The media was also more involved in covering adventures gone wrong, especially if there were fatalities.

Consequently, Buzz was very anxious about Bill Irwin, the first blind hiker who had attempted an end-to-end journey. Buzz didn't want to interfere with Irwin and his guide dog, Orient, completing the historic trip. More importantly, Buzz wanted it to be a safe finish and not a search and rescue that would spark a media frenzy. Irwin already had taken hundreds of falls and broken a rib, and the Hunt Trail, especially if icy, could be dangerous.

Buzz came up with a flip-flop plan for Irwin that would establish the way the park handled all post-season thru-hikers from then on. He arranged a phone conversation with Irwin to propose that he pick Irwin up at Stratton and deliver him to the Hunt trailhead to summit Katahdin. Buzz told Irwin he would return him to Stratton to finish the AT to Katahdin Stream.

After pondering the proposed turnabout, Irwin agreed, and Buzz and Jan picked him up and took him to Daicey Pond to stay in the ranger's cabin the night before the hike. Irwin and Orient climbed Katahdin on October 24, but no one but a few park people knew it. On Buzz's orders, Irwin's name wasn't mentioned on the park radio, and no other hikers were allowed into the park that day. Buzz gave Irwin a celebratory dinner party in Millinocket that night, and then drove him back to Stratton the next morning.

Buzz's thoughtfulness didn't end there. He let Irwin borrow a park radio to keep in touch as he hiked the remaining miles to the park, and arranged for him to stay at a private camp one night because temperatures were so cold. Buzz and Jan even showed up with pizzas and junk food that night to keep Irwin going—food he relished under the circumstances.

Irwin and Orient finished the AT thru-hike on November 21, 1990. Buzz and Jan and a group from Irwin's family and church were on hand

*Bill Irwin and guide dog Orient complete their 1990 thru-hike
of the Appalachian Trail*

JEAN HOEKWATER PHOTO, BAXTER STATE PARK ARCHIVES

to rejoice with him at a party at the inn at Millinocket Lake, and Buzz presented Irwin with a gift from the governor. Buzz's response to Irwin's multiple expressions of thanks was his characteristic rejoinder, "Small job."

▲ ▲ ▲ ▲ ▲

The vexing question of scientific research in the park was an issue whose time had come, and it came to the fore over the elusive pine marten. Tom Chase was patrolling the Webster Lake areas with local district warden Randy Probert on January 6, 1991, when they stopped at the former gatehouse on the Telos Road hoping to chat with the winter residents—pine marten researchers from the University of Maine at Orono. They didn't find anyone around but did spot the bodies of two pine marten frozen to the windowsill of the gatehouse porch.

That evening, Chase told district ranger Barry McArthur about the pine marten, and the two went back to the camp, finding Bill Guiliano, a UMO graduate student, inside. He told the rangers that the marten had died after being radio collared for tracking purposes. McArthur advised Guiliano that the marten carcasses should be pulled off the windowsill and placed out of sight of park visitors.

Discovery of the frozen marten was the beginning of several years of frustration and turmoil over the proper role of research and its impact on park resources. It was so divisive that it led to university wildlife scientists abandoning the park for years as a research area.

For chief ranger Drew, the pine marten controversy was the most personally painful experience of his career. He was the staff person most directly involved in the ongoing difficulties that became personal between him and the UMO researchers. Buzz supported Drew fully as the issue developed, and when it reached the Authority, Buzz took center stage. Pine marten research became a referendum on whether the trustees would sanction killing of animals in the park's wildlife sanctuary.

To back up to the start, in the summer of 1989, Dr. Dan Harrison, professor of wildlife ecology at the University of Maine at Orono, had begun the marten research project on logged-over land owned by Great Northern on the west side of the park. He wanted to use Baxter Park as an uncut control-study site. Specifically, he had chosen an untrapped area without timber harvesting in the northwest corner, west of Trout Brook and north of Nesowadnehunk Field. Harrison proposed to live trap about thirty-five marten and ear-tag and radio-collar them for tracking.

The goal was to better understand the population dynamics of marten. Most marten in Maine were found on private lands. A habitat specialist, the marten depended on old conifer-dominated forest, and with the high level of harvesting going on in northern Maine, the question was how could the marten survive. Already, the animal had become extinct on Prince Edward Island, was threatened in Newfoundland, and in decline in Nova Scotia and New Brunswick. The Orono university researchers wanted to know the impact of logging, road-building, and timber harvesting, and had come up with proposed ways for landowners to maintain profitable harvests and, at the same time, maintain viable marten populations.

Trapping the marten to collar or re-collar the animals carried a risk of mortality that concerned Buzz, Drew, and naturalist Jean Hoekwater, as well as the researchers. From October 1990 through March 1991 one animal died from capture-related stress. Four others died of unknown causes, five from predation, and two were legally killed outside the park. Hoekwater informed Buzz of the deaths. The researchers changed their trapping protocol in response to the one capture-related stress death, and the research continued.

When the project moved to the park, the researchers stayed at the state warden's camp below Doubletop Mountain and then, in September 1991, at the Telos gatehouse. Rangers had assisted the students by cleaning up the Telos building, which had been vacant for awhile, and providing them with firewood, tools, and a radio. Buzz allowed them to take showers at headquarters in Millinocket and gave them access through old entries closed to the public.

Ranger McArthur and DOT road foreman Gene Crosby had complained about Bill Guiliano to Chris Drew back in October 1990, for lax behavior. According to the reports, Guiliano had habitually parked his vehicle in the travel section of the Perimeter Road while checking live traps. The DOT personnel resurfacing the Morse Mountain portion of the road with gravel had to stop their work because of Guiliano's vehicle, forcing a delay. Drew spoke to Guiliano and his assistant, Midori Saeki, about the importance of adhering to all park rules; that conversation occurred just two days before Tom Chase reported finding the frozen marten carcasses.

On January 10, 1991, Drew was going toward Telos to ski in from Thissell Pond to meet with the researchers to discuss the proper storage of pine marten bodies. He met Midori Saeki and talked to her alone, learning that the marten carcasses had been left on the porch three days and were in the cabin two days or so. Then Drew went to Nesowadnehunk Field to check on a University of Maine at Orono group, including wildlife professor Bucky Owen. "They were cheerfully tracking animals and braving the cold very well," Drew reported. The facilities were in good shape. Then he headed north again to ski to the Telos facility. Drew was incensed when he found the camp filthy.

Drew made a report on the situation to Buzz and Jean Hoekwater. He was torn about the project—thinking on one hand that it was having a negative impact but believing the information being gathered was significant. But if the researchers couldn't take better care of park facilities and tools, Drew felt that the housing and other benefits should be curtailed.

In the spring, Drew found that the grounds outside the Telos facility "were left in shambles" when the researchers vacated. Park staff had to clean up the property. Ten days later, a ranger complained about a lot of plastic flagging (forty-one flags in the first mile of road) along the Perimeter Road in the marten project area. Drew found *hundreds* of roadside flags. Then he learned that the marten researchers had taken two padlocks and the pin from the Telos gate when they went through—a breach of trust, in Drew's mind.

He met with project personnel to see if the issues could be resolved, but things didn't improve. In fact, more problems cropped up, and Drew had had enough. He recommended that if more problems surfaced the park should terminate the project. In addition, he proposed limiting the use of park facilities for research groups to no more than two weeks, banning plastic markers and flagging, restricting the use of Telos Gate by resident marten personnel, and requiring that all future researchers be interviewed and screened by park management before being allowed to use the park.

Dan Harrison met with Jean Hoekwater on July 2, 1991, and apologized for the unlocked Telos Gate and "substandard maintenance of facilities within the park." He reported that he had instructed one of the researchers to clean up the property and cabin at Doubletop and remove unnecessary flagging. Harrison personally inspected the Doubletop and Telos cabins and the telemetry stations on the Perimeter Road and the access road to McCarthy Field.

His disappointment in the Telos situation caused him to suspend access for Guiliano and his fellow researcher. He told them to walk or bike to their project vehicle for access to study sites in T4R11 and T5R11, and ordered a reduction in flagging. The cabin and facilities at Doubletop, Harrison said, would be maintained within park standards at all times, and he asked for the park to inspect the cabin by July 15 and let him know if further improvements were needed. He promised that the Telos cabin and grounds would be revisited and improved, vehicles cleaned biweekly, park speed limits observed strictly, and all park policies regarding alcohol would be met.

Buzz wrote to Harrison thanking him for trying to correct "a negative situation." He referred to a visit by Guiliano a few days previously when the student was "aggressive, confrontational, and accusatory." He showed disrespect for Chris Drew and the park, Buzz wrote. "I . . . will not expose any of my key management people, park employees, or the general public to this type of abuse. There was a total lack of respect, and such an outburst of this type in the future will jeopardize the pine marten project." Buzz said that Guiliano failed to understand that "research in Baxter State Park does not fail because of Baxter State Park . . . [but] because the priority of the project attempts to supersede the mandates of our gift."

It was not the last of the pine marten controversy. The issue continued in the background and erupted again in 1995, causing Buzz and new trustee Bucky Owen to butt heads and agitating their relationship. What reactivated problems was a new proposal by Harrison's group to expand their research to study prey availability for the marten.

Harrison's plan projected that 50 percent of the shrews caught would be killed and 1 percent of other small rodents that would be trapped. To Buzz, one dead shrew was one shrew too many. His mission—to not allow harm to the park's resources—extended to every living critter, no matter how small. And he reminded others that Percival Baxter was a passionate antivivisectionist, as well as an outspoken critic of plain old animal abuse. Bucky Owen felt that research was good for the park. In the case of the pine marten project, he viewed the mortality risk to prey as very low and the value of the project to science potentially high. There was no discussion of the earlier pine marten's death from capture-related stress. Concern about whether the little radio collars slowed down the marten trying to get away from predators was not addressed.

Given the disagreement between Buzz and Owen, the Authority sent the issue back to the director's research committee. The committee, most of them researchers, voted six to one in favor of allowing the new phase of the marten study and recommended that the Authority approve it. The only one against it was Jean Hoekwater, who joined Buzz in public opposition to the prey study.

At the Authority's July 11, 1995, meeting, Hoekwater speculated that if the proposal involved killing "just a few moose" instead of tiny shrews, there would be an outcry. She believed a value judgment was being made based on a difference in size and popularity of the species. Park counsel Paul Stern joined in the anti-prey effort, noting there was nothing in Baxter's writings that indicated he was interested in using the sanctuary for scientific research.

But Owen, bolstered by the support of a new trustee, Maine Forest Service Director Chuck Gadzik, prevailed when it was time for a vote.

Attorney General Andrew Ketterer opposed approving the study.

Buzz was livid, and he confidentially asked for help. Shortly afterward, Jym St. Pierre, Maine director of RESTORE: The North Woods, challenged Owen's participation in the vote because of Owen's professional ties to the research applications—IF&W and the University of Maine's wildlife ecology department at Orono.

Three days later, Owen notified Buzz that he had an appearance of a conflict of interest and thus would have to nullify his vote. Consequently, the vote on the prey study was tied—Gadzik in favor and Ketterer in opposition. The project could not proceed and was halted officially on July 14, 1995.

▲ ▲ ▲ ▲ ▲

At the Authority's fall meeting in October, Buzz stated that the Authority's vote showed that "some in the wildlife division at the University of Maine at Orono were not satisfied with my judgment and appealed my [denial] to the Authority." Frank Clukey of East Millinocket, vice chairman of the park's Advisory Committee, was more candid about the intrusion of political influence. He told Bucky Owen in public that university researchers "took advantage" of Owen and Gadzik. "They had some place to go [to contest] Buzz's decision," Clukey said. "That was wrong."

Chairman Owen responded that he had "rather stay away from that," and the matter was dropped. However the gap between Buzz and the research community had widened, and Buzz was concerned about Chuck Gadzik's agenda as an Authority member. Gadzik acknowledged that he wanted to look at park issues with "fresh eyes," and just how that would play out was a worrisome unknown to Buzz.

What was clear was that it was time to finally tackle the questions around research in the park in hopes of avoiding future conflict and animosity.

How to revise the research guidelines kept the Authority and the Advisory and research committees going round and round for months. Members were divided. Some were on the side of allowing research (especially non-invasive projects), pointing to the much greater impacts from recreationists and road-building). Others thought that any research was inappropriate because it made Baxter a "guinea pig," in Buzz's words.

Buzz's position on research had been consistent. He opposed it personally but had begrudgingly approved numerous projects that followed the park guidelines. Between 1972 and 1988, ten research projects had been carried out and reports completed. Between 1986 and 1993, eight proposals were denied—all by Buzz with the support of the research committee.

In a December 7, 1995, memo to the Authority, Buzz described how he had reviewed Percival Baxter's discussions on the sanctuary, cruelty to animals, protection of wildlife, and "the need for nature to interact with itself" without interference from people. "I am convinced," he wrote, "that activities by humans to terminate a life for the sake of research within the [sanctuary] is as serious an offense as removing a life from the [sanctuary]. Anyway you cut it, the species is dead, and that, by any stretch of the imagination, is inconsistent with Governor Baxter's intent for his game sanctuary."

Former ranger Ben Townsend was a member of the Advisory Committee during the marten research debate. He accused Buzz of showing "belligerence and hostility toward scientific research." Townsend directed his remarks to park naturalist Jean Hoekwater instead of Buzz, the Advisory chair, or the Authority. He wrote her that Buzz's position "strongly suggests that comments that do not agree with his preexisting conclusions will be not be entertained"—in other words, Buzz didn't have an open mind.

"While I understand that Buzz holds strong views in this area," Townsend responded, "I believe he has an adequate forum for expressing those views to the Authority without imposing his own conclusions on the Advisory Committee . . . quite frankly, I do not see the value of a review process under which only those comments and suggestions that conform to Buzz's views are included in the final recommendations to the Authority."

Advisory chairman Roy Farnsworth, an ally of Buzz's, wrote to Townsend that he was "very disturbed" by Townsend's criticism of Buzz, and thought that sending the letter to Hoekwater was "out of place. I believe if you are at odds with a person you should address that person directly, certainly you can with Buzz."

By January 1996, after three drafts of research revisions, consensus was reached. The new guidelines established three levels of approvals based on impact to the park's natural resources, and these were still in place in 2008. Category I applies to short-term projects and requires approval of the park director; Category II needs a six-month lead time for the research review committee and the director to study the proposal; Category III requires a nine-month lead time to ensure the full involvement of the Authority, the director, and the research review committee.

Buzz prevailed on the most important research issue—the taking of life. The guidelines prohibit killing wildlife in the sanctuary area. They also ban research that would remove or destroy geological specimens or features, and prohibits construction of permanent structures, alteration of the terrain, and permanent markings. Bucky Owen and Chuck Gadzik had lobbied for a provision allowing consideration of research of importance beyond the value to the park. The committee did not accept that provision. The new guidelines have slowed down research but haven't stopped it.

During and after the research debate, scientists who were staunch allies of Buzz and the park found the rationale for denying them opportunities for studies disingenuous. They pointed to the development in the park—cabins, campgrounds, roads—and intense human use as disturbances much greater than those from research. They also pointed to the killing of bees, hornets, wasps, bats, and mice by rangers or campers as "inconsistent" with the park's no-kill policy.

Furthermore, researchers claimed that Buzz was willing to violate his own policy when it suited him. Geologist Dabney Caldwell received Buzz's approval for a study project over the objection of the park's research committee, adding to the notion among some that Buzz played favorites.

The value of the research debate was obvious in the record of research committee meetings after 1995. Discussion showed a thoughtful, probing give and take among members in sorting out difficult issues. For instance, the pine marten project had changed its duration and format in midstream to include the killing of the shrews, and that alerted the committee that they needed more detailed questions in the permit applications to better assess projects and to let researchers know more specifically what the park considered impacts.

▲ ▲ ▲ ▲ ▲

While the pine marten issue was going on, there were many other significant events in the life of Buzz and the park. Evidence of how much

Buzz was held in esteem by wilderness advocates came in 1991. The Wilderness Society (TWS), which Percival Baxter had turned to for support in the late 1930s, honored Buzz for twenty-two years of "uncompromising commitment" to the values that led to the creation of the park.

When he was notified there would be an event at the Asticou Inn in Northeast Harbor to present him the award, Buzz knew he would have to make a speech. He was trying to find something to say that was catchy, and remembered a phrase that had "popped" out of him during an interview with photographer/writer Bill Silliker just days earlier. Silliker had asked Buzz for his definition of wilderness, and Buzz's response was simple—"nature at peace." The more he thought about those words, the more he felt they captured the essence of the park. The phrase became his mantra.

TWS presented Buzz with the coveted Olaus and Margaret Murie Award. He was the fourth recipient of the award, first given in 1988. Olaus Murie was a renowned federal wildlife biologist and a former executive director of TWS, and Mardy Murie was an acclaimed author and conservationist who had been on the society's governing council since 1976.

"A lot has changed in our world in the more than three decades since the day Buzz reported for duty as a ranger at Russell Pond," said TWS's spokesman Jym St. Pierre in announcing the award. "But in the heart of Maine, one thing that has changed very little is BSP. That's good; there's not much you can do to improve that special place. The two people who deserve the most credit for protecting this natural gem are former governor Percival Baxter and Buzz Caverly. They shared a belief in protecting our natural heritage, and their persistence and integrity have kept that vision for Baxter alive and well."

He mentioned how Governor Baxter had written Buzz, "I hear good things about you," several years after Buzz had been on the job. "The fact is, everyone who cares about Baxter State Park hears good things about Buzz Caverly," St. Pierre said.

The award praised Buzz for fighting "degradation of the wilderness values of the park and [has] faithfully carried out the ideas expressed by Governor Baxter when he donated the land to the people of Maine— that this park be preserved forever wild. The vital contributions of Buzz and others like him to the proper management of our public lands often go unnoticed. The Wilderness Society has presented its 1991 Murie

Award to publicly acknowledge Buzz Caverly for his tireless efforts toward preserving one of the most spectacular places in the eastern United States."

At the reception, Buzz expressed deep appreciation for "this vote of confidence" and his own admiration of the Muries, who "truly blazed the trails in identifying and educating people in the values of wise stewardship of natural resources by their examples, their writings, their love and respect for nature." He expressed lasting gratitude to Governor Baxter and Helon Taylor for giving him the opportunity to spend much of his life in the park. He would "work and support Governor Baxter's dream and reality in whatever capacity" he could, Buzz promised, adding that whatever he or anyone did in that respect would be comparatively minor compared to what the creator had accomplished.

"The experiences I gained from starting to work at BSP under the supervision of a true woodsman, a man of integrity, high character, and the bottom line straightforwardness of Helon Taylor were of extraordinary value," Buzz said. "Among many things, he instilled in me the value of an ax when traveling in the Maine woods and that it, like every other tool, should be respected and used with discretion as a comforter for travelers of the forest. 'It must be sharp and in good shape, for a dull ax is dangerous and unproductive.' When traveling, I frequently carry this message to co-workers; some are more receptive to the concept than others," he quipped.

Buzz related stories that underscored the values of the park, thanked his staff for their "loyalty, dedication, and commitment," and he recognized many friends for their support.

Jim Tierney was among those supporters weighing in with a letter of congratulations:

> I am very proud of your lifelong commitment to the Park. Since those early days when you spent hours with Governor Baxter on his regular visits to his monumental gift, you have carefully nurtured an ever-growing love and dedication to Baxter State Park. I have watched you reach out to all of those who care about and use the park and listen to their needs and concerns. You understand better than anyone the competing pressures inherent in Governor Baxter's wish that the park be both accessible to those who would use it and that it remain 'forever wild.' You have con-

ducted yourself with great dignity while working to carry out
Governor Baxter's legacy. Working tirelessly with your wonderful
wife, Jan, to whom you proposed high on a cliff overlooking
Russell Pond, you have stood firm in the face of immense public
pressure to keep the dream alive.

Mardy Murie wrote Buzz from her home in Moose, Wyoming. "I
have a special feeling about Baxter State Park," she said. "It happened
that in 1936 I was back home in Alaska on a Yukon River stream and a
fellow passenger was Gov. Baxter . . . that has always been a very pleasant memory." Murie called Baxter "a very charming gentleman."
(Interestingly, there is no evidence in the Percival Baxter archives that
confirms he was ever in Alaska.)

The Murie Award brought Buzz to the attention of wilderness leaders beyond TWS. As a "player" now on the national level, he received
invitations to speak to large gatherings of wilderness managers. His
theme was always what Percival Baxter did for the state of Maine and
the work it took the governor to create a wilderness park in the middle
of an industrial forest landscape.

The Murie Award was followed in 1994 by an award to the park by
the U.S. Humane Society in recognition of "Sir Percival Baxter for his
precious gift of land, and in recognition of the citizens of Maine for
their commitment to the preservation of Baxter State Park." The society particularly wanted Buzz to receive the plaque. Unlike the Murie
Award, the October 14 occasion received no publicity in Maine. Buzz
was grateful because it gave him a chance to speak his mind on animal
cruelty without worrying that he would get in trouble with Millinocket
locals or the Authority.

He brought up the subject of coyotes and appealed to the society to
try to stop trapping of the animals in Maine. "I was lucky to not get in
the doghouse," he said years later. "The coyotes and I won that night."

▲ ▲ ▲ ▲ ▲

In just its second year of taking over Great Northern Paper, Georgia-
Pacific wanted out and began negotiating with Bowater Company. Even
before ownership was transferred, Bowater began talks with environmental groups about a huge land conservation deal around Baxter Park.

Bowater wanted to gain the support of environmentalists for the relicensing of the six dams on the West Branch of the Penobscot River. Relicensing by the Federal Energy Regulatory Commission (FERC) was critical to the expansion of the company's coated paper production capacity—the reason for Bowater's acquisition of Great Northern.

Bowater's offer was to give a time-limited conservation easement on the 800,000-acre watershed of the West Branch. The company also offered to give the state an option to purchase at fair market value or exchange equivalent land for 13,000 acres in Rainbow Township surrounding Rainbow Lake; a donation of 5.5 miles of permanent river and lakeshore development rights to fill in gaps in previous deals; and creation of an advisory council to consider management practices on lands adjacent to Baxter Park. A company memo put the "hard" cost of the proposal at millions of dollars.

Although the life of the easement was tied to "timely and viable" renewal of dam licenses, it seemed an enormous protection opportunity. In the early to mid-1990s, there was much uncertainty over the future of the West Branch watershed lands surrounding Baxter, difficulties in raising money for large-scale land acquisitions, and the prospect of waterfront land sales on high-value lakes such as Rainbow and Chesuncook. The idea of raising the money needed to purchase outright even a non-development easement on 800,000 acres around the park didn't appear likely or imminent.

The easement plan would have prevented development of most of the West Branch watershed, particularly to the south and west of the park, and it would have mooted the prospect of Baxter becoming a kind of protected island, as it would create breathing room for a permanent solution and probably facilitate further protections.

The environmental coalition met with Bowater for more than two years but couldn't come to an agreement. The major obstacle was over the easement being tied to dam license renewal. There was a lull in negotiations. It became evident that the 1993 license renewal would be delayed quite a while and the new license would impose conditions that would increase the cost of Great Northern's hydro power.

Consequently, Bowater redirected its initiative to focus on the area of company ownership that was of greatest interest to environmental groups—the Debsconeag remote recreation area that included the Rainbow Lake area and 41,000 adjacent acres containing several undeveloped lakes. The new proposal retained the transfer of "fill-in" development rights along the 5.5 miles of river and lakeshore, and added a proposal for bald eagle habitat expansion. It also retained a multi-year option for the state to purchase the Rainbow property and proposed a purchase option for the Debsconeag land—a way to connect Baxter Park, and the state-owned Nahmakanta Lake Unit, and a highly scenic stretch of the AT.

Environmentalists saw the opportunity to broaden their list of goals that would strengthen conservation gains, and a fattened conservation proposal made it all the way to the Bowater board of directors. The company's media office was preparing an announcement with Governor John McKernan and Bowater's chairman when the proposal fell apart within the coalition.

In the end, Bowater made deals with commercial whitewater rafters and the Fin and Feather Club in exchange for their support, and the dams were relicensed. Some years later, a conservation easement on 200,000 acres of Great Northern land on the west side of Baxter Park was acquired by the state, and The Nature Conservancy also purchased the Debsconeag/Rainbow Lakes area—giving the park at least some of the breathing room from development threats it would have obtained under the failed 800,000-acre initiative.

---

1. *Kennebec Journal*, June 25, 1991.

Primary Document Sources: BSPA Box 2 (2507-0801); BSPA Original Minutes 4, 5; BSP Annual Report, 1990,1991; *Maine Times*, December 7, 1990, pg. 16; June 14, 1991, p. 15; *Bangor Daily News*, August 7, 1991, pp. 1, 2; *Maine Sunday Telegram*, August 11, pp. 1A, 12B.

Conversations and communications: Buzz Caverly, Michael Carpenter, Tom Chase, Chris Drew, Roy Farnsworth, Loren Goode, Dan Harrison, Chuck Gadzik, Bob Howes, Chris Herter, Bill Irwin, Charlie Kenney, Andrew Ketterer, John Loyd, Gordon Manuel, Bucky Owen, Charles Pray, Jym St. Pierre, Jim Tierney.

▲▲▲▲▲▲▲▲

# CHAPTER 23

# Protecting Togue Pond and Coyotes

THE END OF BILL IRWIN'S AT THRU-HIKE in 1991 was the beginning of Buzz's most special friendship with a park visitor since Herbert and Olga Nowitsky in the 1960s. The cooperation between Buzz and Irwin to make sure that Irwin completed his Katahdin climb before winter gave Buzz a sense that "it was almost fate" that they had come together—that he had been put in the right place to help. Irwin inspired Buzz with his determination for success and his religious faith.

Irwin returned to Maine in 1992 to see Buzz and Jan at East Corinth, Millinocket, and the park, and they talked almost every week on the phone. On one of Irwin's visits in the winter of 1992, he gave Buzz a photograph of Orient's paw print, and Buzz hung it at the entrance to his East Corinth house. Irwin also surprised Buzz with an autographed photo of himself and Clayton Moore, TV's Lone Ranger. Watching cowboy movies from his youth was still one of Buzz's favorite off-duty pastimes.

Later, Buzz and Jan visited Irwin in North Carolina. Buzz was a fan of country singer Loretta Lynn, and Irwin's uncle in Tennessee happened to be a friend of Lynn's husband. The connection resulted in Buzz and Jan visiting the uncle and Lynn's farm. They didn't see the singer but did pay a visit to the Grand Old Opry for an evening's entertainment.

While on the trip Buzz was mistaken by a convenience store customer for Buford Pusar of the movie *Walking Tall*.

When Irwin published his account of the AT hike, *Blind Courage*, in the spring of 1995, Buzz and Jan helped drive Irwin to speaking engagements in Maine. "Buzz went out of his way to do things others couldn't do and never abused that authority," Irwin says.

When Irwin married in 1996, Buzz and Jan were the only outsiders invited. That summer, Bill and Debra Irwin stayed with the Caverlys while they purchased land in Sebec. Up to his old tricks, Buzz gave the

Irwins a "Hee-Haw" outhouse—all crooked, just like the one on the TV show. Buzz knew the Irwins didn't have plumbing and would need it to stay at the camp on their new land while they built a house.

▲ ▲ ▲ ▲ ▲

Ever since the park had purchased the sporting camp facilities on Togue Pond in 1985, Buzz had been quietly maneuvering behind the scenes for acquisition of the land. His efforts were not appreciated by some higher-ups at Great Northern Paper, and woodlands manager Jim Giffune visited Buzz at park headquarters. The land could become part of Baxter Park one day, Giffune told him, but not until some opponents within the company retired.

Buzz backed off, biding his time. The sale of Great Northern to Georgia-Pacific stirred his hope that a deal could finally be made, and an agreement was reached in relatively short order. In early December 1991 he was ecstatic about announcing the purchase, which included 1,047 acres of woodlands and Upper and Lower Togue Ponds. Although the property was priceless to the park because it bordered the main entrance, G-P was willing to sell it for below market value—$200,000.[1]

The acquisition was the first addition to the park since Governor Baxter's last purchase in 1962. No longer would park officials have to worry about development at the park gateway or along the ponds' shoreline.

While Buzz had worked hard for the purchase, John Cashwell was the linchpin because of his past connections with G-P. Cashwell had been a helicopter pilot for the company at its Woodland mill. When he became director of the Maine Forest Service, his contacts with the paper industry expanded, especially at the higher levels. When it came time to talk turkey about the Togue Pond land, Cashwell knew just who to contact at G-P.

Park discussions with G-P coincided with the company's confidential negotiations with Bowater to purchase the Millinocket mills and almost one million acres of timberland. Cashwell approached John Rasor, G-P's group vice president for forest resources, about holding out the Togue Pond lands from the Bowater sale so that the ongoing negotiations with the park could continue. Cashwell also persuaded Rasor and two other officials to visit the park and see the situation themselves.

*Buzz speaking at a news conference on the purchase of the Togue Pond*
*lands, 1991; back row: Georgia Pacific vice president John Rasor;*
*Eric Baxter; Governor John McKernan*
BAXTER STATE PARK PHOTO ARCHIVES

Buzz, Cashwell, and Chris Drew were tour guides for the Rasor party, and the G-P executives were duly impressed with the extraordinary natural resources of the park. They agreed that the Togue Pond property should rightly become part of the park.

Following the visit, a G-P representative sat down with Buzz and Cashwell to hammer out an agreement. The purchase included two private in-holdings—Clark Island and Camp Natarswi (the Girl Scout facility)—and four private camp lot leases. At the same time, G-P conveyed a 2.5-acre parcel to the Millinocket School Department that had been under lease to the school for an educational and municipal recreation program.

By the time the deeds were signed on December 16, 1992, Cashwell was not on the Authority any longer, and Bill Vail signed the papers. "I took a great deal of pride in that I was one of the few who signed a deed for Baxter Park besides Percival Baxter," Vail recalls. The park was now 202,064 acres.

Robert Shiners of Newport, Rhode Island, offered to sell the acre his camp was on to the park. The log cabin on the south shore of Lower Togue Pond had a commanding view of Katahdin. He wanted $80,000 for it, but Buzz was able to get it for $30,000 in 1994. The cabin was converted to an administrative camp for the park. The other individual camp leases were purchased in subsequent years, but the in-holding lots remained in private ownership.

An in-house dispute arose over the use of the Shiners camp after some associated with the park used the facility for vacationing with family and friends. Buzz went to the Authority for backup on a policy he issued on November 8, 1995, which spelled out allowable uses. It limited Advisory members, staff, volunteers, and others to accommodation for no more than three days at a time "while they gain more insight into and assist the park." The director was given "discretion" over the uses.

▲▲▲▲▲

As much as Governor Baxter loved animals, he had wavered on protection for predators in the sanctuary. The issue had come up first in 1952 when Baxter agreed with the Authority and Helon Taylor that predators should be eliminated. Upon reflection, Baxter changed his mind, worrying about setting a precedent. Then in 1954, a question arose about whether predators were increasing in the park to the point of threatening the deer and moose populations. If that were the case, Baxter initially agreed that the problem should be dealt with by the Authority and IF&W. Again, he backed off from approving any action against predators.

Whether coyotes were the threat in the 1950s was not specifically mentioned in Baxter's correspondence. But by the early 1990s, the animals' population had recovered from eradication efforts throughout the country to have a resurgence in Maine.

Buzz had first heard about coyotes returning to Maine when he was in warden school in 1969, and in 1970 he thought he saw one at Second Lake Matagamon. Chris Drew was sure he had seen coyotes on the fringes of the park border.

It was legal in Maine to bait and shoot coyotes, and in 1992 Drew had reported to Buzz that sixteen coyotes had been killed on Matagamon Lake—some of them run down from behind with snowmobiles.

About that time it came out that in the 1991–92 winter in T6R9, IF&W district warden Randy Probert had authorized a licensed coyote trapper to go into the SFMA to trap the animals because of alleged high deer predation there. The trapper reportedly snared fifty to a hundred coyotes in the park.

Buzz had known nothing about the trapping, and he was sickened by it. IF&W's predator control officer Henry Hilton had assumed Buzz knew about the trapping. When Hilton learned differently, he figured there had been an unfortunate breakdown in communications. He also had suspicions that Buzz had been intentionally left out of the information loop.

As expected, Buzz put his foot down hard, sending a firm anti-trapping message to the hunting community. As long as he had anything to do with it, coyotes wouldn't be killed in Baxter Park without proof they were a threat. Buzz recalled that some people had wanted to eliminate bobcats because of their predation on deer. "But our park is about predation as well as other interactions of nature, so I am inclined to leave it alone and let it work," he stated.

Buzz called for a meeting with state agency people—rangers, wardens, biologists, predator control agents, and a university coyote specialist. At the session Buzz denied IF&W permission to snare coyotes in the park in the winter of 1993 and thought that more investigation of the issue was needed, especially since some park staff, warden staff, and others wanted some degree of predator control. He assigned Bucky Owen, chair of the university's wildlife department and an Advisory Committee member, to form a subcommittee and take a broad look at predator control overall in the park.

After listening to pros and cons, Owen reported back to Buzz that the panel believed predator control would be "untenable" to the public. Bill Vail let Buzz take the lead on the coyote issue because Vail's IF&W constituency favored eliminating coyotes. Buzz believes that Vail's willingness to step back on the issue kept it from developing into a major controversy.

Buzz and Chris Drew were on opposite sides of the coyote issue— a rare circumstance for the two colleagues. Drew had promised Buzz loyalty, and he never wanted to embarrass Buzz publicly by being in an opposing camp. Consequently, he felt stung when Buzz ordered him to remove the stuffed animals from his office wall. Drew's office was the largest one at park headquarters on the second floor. He had several deer and moose mounts on the walls and had traced on paper thirty to forty fish he had caught with the dates of the landings. Someone on the park staff complained to Buzz, and Buzz directed Drew to remove them.

Drew didn't argue with Buzz. He just stopped showing up at the office as much. In a couple of weeks, Buzz noticed Drew's absences and commented on his being away so much. Drew told him, "I'm a country boy. I've had an office with no windows for eleven years, and I despise the paperwork. I got a lot of pleasure just looking at those mounts and the fish and thinking about the outdoors. You took that away."

That being said, Drew and Buzz put the matter behind them. Working closely together for more than twenty years, they had found a way of dealing respectfully with disagreements so as not to threaten their relationship. Buzz had the same strength of loyalty to Drew that Drew gave to him.

▲ ▲ ▲ ▲ ▲

There were old stomping grounds in the park that Buzz returned to time and again to renew his spirit and let off steam. Some were near the roadside, such as the little sand beach near Slide Dam and underneath Doubletop. Others were miles into the backcountry, like Greene Falls and Wassataquoik Stream. No place was more special to him than Russell Pond, and he continuously returned to his former summer home.

Buzz's beloved ranger's camp at Russell Pond had been converted to a bunkhouse as the campground facilities had been reconfigured and upgraded over the previous twenty years. But it was time to remove that last old building, and Buzz joined a work crew in early April 1992 to destroy it. Since the structure contained asbestos, state experts were called in to remove, contain, and transport out the hazardous material.

"Boy, I didn't want to see the building destroyed," Buzz recalls, "but I also didn't want anybody doing it but me. Bernard Crabtree started for the camp with some birch bark to put on the floor to start a fire. Just as he got to the door, I called out to him to say, 'I'm going to do this one.' I lit the match, and I hope nobody saw me because I cried as I did it." It was a humbling moment for him. The camp had been his home for four years and his and Jan's honeymoon cabin.

The fire effectively ended the Tracy-Love era that began in 1883, when the two men started lumbering on Wassataquoik Stream. They had built camps twice to house their loggers, and both times the structures burned down. William T. Tracy then built a sporting camp facility on Russell Pond, and it was taken into the park when Percival Baxter purchased the land in 1941.

Most of the structures that Tracy had constructed were removed in time. One of the three buildings that were kept—the dining/kitchen facility—became the park ranger's camp that Buzz lived in. In 1972 a new ranger's cabin was raised, and the old camp became a bunkhouse. All of that history flowed through Buzz as he watched the structure burn and heard in his mind Percival Baxter's words about how buildings crumble and the only thing that lasts forever in the park are the natural resources.

In the fall of 1992, Buzz and Jan flew in to Wassataquoik Lake with game warden pilot Alan Ryder to spend three days at Russell Pond filling in as campground rangers. "It was like returning home after a long trip away," Buzz says, remembering the feel of carrying weighty backpacks and hearing the cry of loons from the lake.

After making sure that the campground facilities were clean and orderly and that campers were happy, Buzz and Jan hiked to a high place on the North Peaks trail, visited all of the nearby ponds and Wassataquoik Stream, fished a little, and reminisced a lot.

▲ ▲ ▲ ▲ ▲

Buzz's perpetual program of removing old and deteriorating buildings grated on George Kerivan. A history teacher from Harvard, Massachusetts, Kerivan had first visited the park as a kid from Camp Kennebec. In fact, Buzz had met him then at Daicey Pond, where the group was camping.

Kerivan loved sporting camps. He wasn't visiting the park during the time when the Togue Pond Camps were purchased by the park and subsequently torn down. He was on the sidelines of the Kidney Pond conversion debate, supporting the change to rustic camps. In the aftermath of the Authority's decision to convert the camps, Kerivan wrote Buzz and others urging that the camps be preserved as they were, and urged that artifacts of the sporting-camp years be displayed museum-like in the library.

Kerivan didn't get anywhere with the proposal at the time, but he approached Buzz again in 1991 about putting Kidney Pond and Daicey Pond Camps on the National Historic Register. The two talked more than once about the matter in a friendly way, but Buzz was uncomfortable about the idea from the start. He opposed any government historical designation for sites in the park and discouraged Kerivan, but Kerivan didn't give up. He gathered 286 names on a petition that asked the legislature to request that the Authority put the camps on the register. The petition noted that in 1987, when Kidney Pond Camps was turned over to the park, the Maine Historic Preservation Commission was considering a request to have the camps recognized as national historic preservation sites. The Authority had refused at that time to allow the request to be made. Win Robbins had also asked the Maine Historic Preservation Commission to evaluate Kidney Pond Camps for potential register listing, and the commission had agreed the camps were eligible. But formal action was not taken.

This time, when Kerivan asked the commission to evaluate both Kidney and Daicey Camps, the commission felt that Kidney Pond was still eligible, despite the removal of half of the thirty-eight original buildings—but not Daicey because there had been so many renovations. However, without the Authority's approval, no camps could be listed.

Buzz wrote architectural historian Kirk Mahoney on April 12, 1992, making it "clear the park was to preserve natural resources not cultural resources. Alien and limited as that may seem to someone in your position, that limited focus is the reason for whatever success we may lay claim to today as park managers . . . [Percival Baxter] created a monument to nature and not to human work and accomplishments. The park is a place for humans to be humble, to recognize the vastness of time and glorify in wonders beyond the mastery of human beings."

A listing would set a bad precedent for another agency or organization to make policy regarding matters that were the responsibility of the Authority, Buzz emphasized. "Governor B clearly did not want that responsibility eroded over the years," he said. Park counsel Paul Stern offered a legal reading of the park's mission that supported Buzz's position. "Our mandate is to preserve and protect the natural resources of Baxter State Park and not to memorialize buildings or people," said Stern. "Although we respect the development and operation of the sporting camp era and people involved, our park is forever, not its buildings and people."

The Authority voted June 2, 1992, against any historic listings for the two camps. But Kerivan wasn't about to give up on his preservation effort.

▲ ▲ ▲ ▲ ▲

Aircraft was banned from landing in Baxter Park except for operational purposes. However, the airspace above the park was controlled by the government.

During the years Buzz was a ranger, the drone of float planes had been an integral part of the soundscape in the backcountry. Some of them were tourist flights and others were bush planes dropping supplies off at Chimney or Russell Ponds. In the 1980s, there had been several incidents with low-level military aircraft in and around the park that Buzz contended negatively affected wildlife and the experience of visitors.

Low-level military flights over the park were again proposed by the U.S. Air Force in late spring of 1992, and Buzz and the Authority didn't have to think twice before raising objections. The Air Force wanted to create the Great State of Maine Military Operation Area (MOA), which would include the mountain areas of the state and the Allagash Wilderness Waterway. The plan proposed to allow single-seat F-16s to fly as low as 100 feet above the ground during nearly 3,000 annual training flights.

There was sharp public reaction against the proposal. Loring Air Force Base officials held a public meeting in Presque Isle, and Buzz joined the crowd in voicing unanimous opposition to the plan. Buzz said the flights would be "very disruptive" to Baxter Park and offensive to the memory of Percival Baxter.

Former park director Harry Kearney was as blunt as ever. "You know nor care nothing about northern Maine," he told the Air Force officials. "Maine has everything to lose and nothing to gain in this intrusion of our lifestyle." The Air Force dropped the plan, promising that the Air Force and National Guard would maintain minimal altitudes of 2,000 feet above ground over the park and other Maine wilderness areas and designated wildlife refuges.

Low-level flights, however, continued to be a concern, provoking Buzz to request again that they be stopped.

▲ ▲ ▲ ▲ ▲

There wasn't much of significance that escaped Buzz's attention in the park. But in 1981, unbeknownst to him, Barry Dana, a Penobscot Indian, had run solo a hundred miles from the tribe's reservation at Indian Island, near Old Town, to the park. It was a trial run for Dana to see how difficult the endeavor was and to assess whether he could gain the interest of other tribal members to reconnect spiritually with Katahdin, the Penobscots' sacred mountain.

On Labor Day 1992 Buzz was driving down Abol Hill when he heard someone yell, "Buzz, is that you?" It was tribal leader Butch Phillips running up the hill as part of the hundred-mile run, which by now had become an annual Labor Day event. The encounter woke Buzz up to the tribe's growing interest in the mountain. If the run increased to the point that Penobscot leaders dreamed of, they already knew they would want a special place of their own in the park to convene and hold their ceremonies. Soon, Buzz would be traveling with them throughout the park to look at potential sites and negotiating sensitive Native American issues.

▲ ▲ ▲ ▲ ▲

At the end of each year, Buzz could look back and count dozens of speeches he had made as Baxter Park's emissary to schools, colleges, environmental, civic, and social organizations, government conferences, trail groups, nursing homes, and churches. Public speaking had become easy for Buzz because he concentrated on his favorite subject, Percival Baxter and the park, and he could speak extemporaneously for hours if necessary.

Buzz typically related some of the most entertaining stories about Governor Baxter—the childhood "fish account," an encounter with raccoons, the dog Garry Owen. He talked about the challenges Governor Baxter had met in trying to create the park, his own first meeting with Baxter in 1960, the fragility of the park resources and the central mission of park stewards to preserve and protect, and various political controversies. He also emphasized Baxter's request to not break faith with the visitors.

Another regular way Buzz had to remind the public of the park's mission was at his public communications meetings. He had instituted them shortly after becoming director as a way to make himself known throughout the state and to be available to individuals and interested groups to answer questions about the park and his decisions. For years, meetings were held in the spring and fall in Millinocket and Augusta, and sometimes in Portland. In the 1990s, there was a drop-off in attendance, and Buzz held the sessions only in Millinocket until public interest in that one also petered out. So many people, among them environmental advocates, felt that Buzz was managing the park so well that they could just trust him to do the right thing.

▲ ▲ ▲ ▲ ▲

After thirty-three years with the park, the question of when Buzz might retire was a subject of so much speculation among employees that he answered it in the August 19, 1993, staff newsletter. "Bottom line is, I don't got [no] plans," he wrote.

Fifty-four-year-old Buzz noted that former supervisor Helon Taylor had worked until he was seventy, and Governor Baxter had completed his last land purchase when he was nearly eighty-five. A goal of fifty years' service to the park for himself "wouldn't be bad," Buzz wrote, which, if achieved would mean he would retire in 2010 at seventy years old.

Retirement was getting to be a bigger issue for Buzz as he grew older, given the charge that Percival Baxter had given him in 1968: "We are partners in this project." Buzz routinely read the letter to his staff at spring training to fire up the newcomers and the entire crew. At the same time, it reminded people what was driving Buzz. Some of the older employees were weary of hearing about Buzz's connection with Baxter. Times were different, Baxter was long gone, and some of them felt that "channeling Baxter" was a way that Buzz exaggerated his own importance.

However no one questioned the fact that the park was Buzz's whole life and that he would be lost without it. He had not developed outside interests as some of his veteran rangers had. For example, Tom Chase had a hunting guide service, Charlie Kenney had a hog and beef farm, and Loren Goode was a woodcarver. The closest Buzz had gotten to a hobby was the ten-acre woodlot near his house, where he cut trails and cleared a site for a cabin.

Trustee Sue Bell, who had replaced John Cashwell on the Authority

*Jan Caverly hauling firewood to Chimney Pond, 1993*
JEAN HOEKWATER PHOTO, BAXTER STATE PARK PHOTO ARCHIVES

in 1992, had casual conversations with Buzz about retirement, but he never indicated to her that he was interested in pursuing the subject. Bell thought he was doing a great job and assumed he would stay as long as his health allowed. Buzz was still improving professionally, she reflected, and "he was getting about, had fire in the belly, was energetic and engaged."

▲ ▲ ▲ ▲ ▲

Shortly after Cashwell departed, Bill Vail left unexpectedly. Governor John McKernan's proposed budget cuts for Vail's agency were so deep that Vail refused to go along with them, believing that they would do irreparable harm to his department.

Vail resigned in March 1993, leaving Buzz with a great sense of loss. He and his Dream Team had faced up to tough problems and left an indelible mark on the park with their decisions to convert Kidney Pond Camps, close West Gate, purchase and clean up the Togue Pond Camps, bring the last section of road outside the park boundary to within the Baxter borders, and resolve a host of other important administrative and operational matters. It had been a heady time, and Buzz steeled himself for the days ahead.

The state budget problems, forcing "furloughs" of employees in order to save money, hit Baxter Park, too. There were temporary lay-offs of all but "essential" employees, causing Buzz and other senior staff to cover for campground employees and gatekeepers in the park to avoid severe disruption of summer operations.

▲ ▲ ▲ ▲ ▲

Other than the employee turmoil over layoffs, Buzz and the reconsti-tuted Authority had a relatively quiet 1992–93. Several issues could have easily caught fire without careful handling.

A key decision on Buzz's part was to not seek sanctuary status for the new Togue Pond parcel, but to let traditional uses, such as hunting and trapping, continue. There were so many in-holdings in the parcel, unlike the other tracts that Percival Baxter had acquired, that he fig-ured he would leave well enough alone and save his fight for another day.

The biggest use issue that emerged at two public hearings was whether snowmobiles could continue to be used on Togue Pond. Locals used the machines to access ice-fishing sites. Opponents, especially in-holders, asked for a ban on snowmobiles. The upshot was a ban on snowsleds, except to supply lessees' camps in winter.

As for other uses, Buzz was able to get some important restrictions approved by the Authority. Motorboats were limited to ten-horsepower engines, aircraft were prohibited from landing on the ponds, pets were banned, and beach access was closed between 10:00 P.M. and 6:00 A.M.

The Fin and Feather Club felt sold out by the plan and charged it had been hatched in secret. They blamed Buzz, as usual.

Motorcycles returned to the forefront for the first time since 1981. The bikers were given a sympathetic ear but Buzz and the Authority repeated their predecessors in explaining that Governor Baxter specifi-cally directed that the machines be prohibited.

Buzz also guided an important access change at the south entrance to the park with virtually no adverse reaction from the public. The gate booth was moved a short distance from where it had sat for years to the "y" junction of the Perimeter and Roaring Brook Roads. The new loca-tion enabled gatehouse attendants to directly observe vehicles headed in both directions and to control Katahdin-bound traffic. No more sneaking into Roaring Brook, where parking was limited, to access the trails up the mountain.

▲ ▲ ▲ ▲ ▲

One of the "traditions" in the park was watercraft storage on trout ponds. A number of local fishermen liked to keep their canoes close to the shoreline—sometimes on racks nailed into live trees—during the off-season. It was one of the lingering special privileges that was not well-known by the general public.

Chris Drew had grown increasingly dissatisfied with the situation because of the large number of canoes being stored (especially at Rocky Pond), the trash left at the sites, messy fire rings, and illegally cut trails. He pressed Buzz to end the storage practice, even though both knew it could be a volatile matter among anglers.

Buzz was more than ready to clean up the situation. It was one of those problems that had been on his back burner for a long time. The park ponds were valuable for multiple reasons to more and more users. If it became widespread knowledge that locals were keeping boats in the park, others could assert that right, too. Buzz wanted to handle the change with sensitivity and aim for consensus with boat owners to avoid a major controversy.

The boat storage tradition on park lands dated back to when Irvin Hunt had built the sporting camp at Kidney Pond. Millinocket- and Patten-area fishermen flocked to the area because of the high concentration of trout ponds in close proximity to Kidney and Daicey Ponds in the south end of the park and the Fowler Ponds in the north end. Private landowners allowed the practice without charge, and it became a privilege of convenience, especially for Fin and Feather Club members.

Buzz used the Advisory Committee to evaluate the situation and make recommendations. He included local fishermen in the discussions. Most accepted the inevitability of it all. For some, their more active fishing days were already over.

▲ ▲ ▲ ▲ ▲

Buzz's wealth of experience as a user himself resulted in small management actions that could only have been carried out by someone with an intimate knowledge of the park.

In 1993, he had enough "extra" money to order the purchase of new, quieter canoes for park ponds. The old Grumman aluminum boats made a loud echo when a paddle hit the side, and Buzz wanted plastic Old Town Discovery craft for a more peaceful trip.

The money for several canoes came from the park's new donation fund. After years of wrangling over whether the park could receive donations from the public, Buzz and the Authority agreed that small donations were appropriate. At the beginning, the yearly amounts donated were in the $10 to $25 range, and Buzz tapped $1,000 for the canoes. The National Guard airlifted the canoes to remote locations, such as Russell Pond, during their routine training exercises.

Buzz also directed that anything newly named in the park would be designated for natural features, not individuals. New roads in the SFMA were given names, such as Hazelnut Brook and Blunder Bog. Old sporting-camp owners at Daicey and Kidney Ponds had been naming cabins after loyal patrons, and after the park acquired those facilities the names were changed there, too. (Historic names, such as Davis and Cowles Ponds, were not changed.)

With as much as Buzz had on his plate on any given day, the degree to which he would put himself in the visitor's shoes and try to ensure the highest quality of wilderness experience was remarkable. The minor decisions didn't make headlines, but they made a difference and provided Buzz with great satisfaction

▲ ▲ ▲ ▲ ▲

After approving the development of a rafting base at Pockwockamus Pond and then allowing it to change from private to public clientele, another expansion proposal was in the works. The new plan called for more campsites, a larger lodge, a new garage and more parking, and a 40 percent increase in overnight customers to 300.

Buzz was itching to get involved again. He had facts to present to LURC that he felt were evidence of the existing development's negative impact on the park. In the summer of 1992, unruly clientele from the rafting center showed up at the Togue Pond sand beach and park campgrounds, and rangers kicked them out. Buzz believed a larger development would mean more trouble for the park.

Although he had been allowed to speak up at the original Pockwockamus Pond permit hearing, this time the Authority said no. As chair, Sue Bell delivered the order forcefully over the phone to Buzz to stay out of this outside issue and mind the park.

NRCM, The Wilderness Society, and activist Charles FitzGerald fought the expansion. Even the Fin and Feather Cub was against it. The LURC staff recommended denial of the proposed expansion on the grounds that it would violate LURC's own comprehensive plan designed to protect ponds and lakes from overdevelopment—and agreed with Buzz that the enlargement would put visitor pressure on the park.

However, the plan garnered the support of the majority of LURC commissioners because three rafting companies had now clustered their operations at Pockwockamus and were operating from the site as Penobscot Outdoor Center. Two of the companies had relocated from the heavily used Big Eddy area on the West Branch.

The question of a buffer for the park came up again during the expansion debate. Bell opposed getting involved in buffer issues, questioning how wide a buffer would have to be to work successfully. Her priority was not to stir up problems with border owners but to be good neighbors and sensitive to their needs.

LURC commissioner Elizabeth Swain, who voted in favor of the expansion, advocated that her agency draw up a comprehensive plan for the perimeter around the park, but it was never done.

▲ ▲ ▲ ▲ ▲

Sue Bell's assessments of Buzz for 1993 and 1994 mirrored those of all the other chairs of the Authority who held Buzz in the highest regard. Bell was one who commented generously about Buzz's attributes— "his commitment to his duties goes far beyond the requirements of the job," "effective in managing employees and utilizing resources," "thoroughly understands the duties and skills necessary to operate and maintain the park," "sensitive to the importance of local relationships in daily operations," "effective working relationship with members of the Authority and works to develop effective strategies to deal with issues confronting the park." Bell mentioned nothing of concern and had no recommendations for improvement of Buzz's administration.

1. *Maine Times,* December 25, 1992, p. 8.

Primary Document Sources: BSPA Original Minutes 2; BSPA Box 1 (2112-0717); BSP Annual Report, 1992, 1993; BSP Staff Meeting Minutes, 1992, 1993.

Conversations and communications: Sue Bell, Buzz Caverly, John Cashwell, Chris Drew, Chuck Gadzik, Henry Hilton, Jean Hoekwater, Andrew Ketterer, Bill Irwin, John Loyd, Darrell Morrell, Bucky Owen, Wiggie Robinson, Jym St. Pierre, George Smith, Paul Stern, Bill Vail.

▲▲▲▲▲▲▲▲

CHAPTER 24

# Buzz and the Authority

By 1994 Buzz had worked for seventeen different Authority groups as a manager—either as director, supervisor, or assistant supervisor. Suffice it to say, the part-time policymaking board was inherently a musical chairs arrangement. The longest any three trustees had served together was six years. It was unusual if they met more than six times a year, just twice in the park. Often they hadn't had time to prepare for the meetings due to the demands of their day jobs. Consequently, the importance of the park director's continuity and leadership couldn't be overstated.

In certain respects, the Authority's job was similar to that of a corporate board of directors—to make decisions on matters their executive director brought them. Buzz always prepared the meeting agenda and sent it to the chairman for review. The Authority preferred short meetings so they could hurry off to other commitments. Most of all, they didn't like surprises, although the agenda item "other" could produce unexpected issues raised by citizens or organizational representatives.

The situation of so many unengaged or lukewarm trustees was made for a tough-minded, long-experienced director like Buzz filling the leadership void. Each Authority, to one degree or another, had deferred to Buzz's command and control for their own convenience.

Of course, everyone knew that Buzz worked for the Authority and was supposed to defer to them. But reality was reality. He knew far more about park needs and operations than they did on any given day, and some trustees were happy with being rubber stamps, relieved that Buzz could lessen the time they had to devote to park business. On the other hand, if anything he did went awry, he was accountable to them.

Percival Baxter could not have foreseen a Baxter Park director with as much power as Buzz accumulated in the absence of committed Authority members. During the 1950s and 1960s, when the park began to evolve administratively, respective Authority chairmen Al Nutting and Austin Wilkins dominated oversight over other trustees. The long-time field man during Baxter's life, Helon Taylor, bore little resemblance to Buzz from a management point of view.

Ironically, things reverted to Percival Baxter's vision of a fuller, assertive Authority as the period in which Buzz had held so much sway collided with shifts on seminal fronts—the increase in the park's public status, the stronger influence of special interest groups, the deepening divide over wilderness politics, and the arrival of younger trustees with different ways of viewing issues and a desire to be involved.

The bellwether of change was Bucky Owen, who was appointed fish and wildlife commissioner in 1994 by Independent governor Angus King. Owen had a long history with the park and with Buzz from wildlife research projects, the caribou transplant project, and memberships on the park's two standing committees—the Authority's Advisory Committee and the SFMA Advisory Committee. Owen intended to be an active Authority member, and he was willing to tangle with Buzz.

The Owen Authority was uncomfortable for Buzz, and the Authorities that followed ranged from unpleasant to downright scary—light-years away from the halcyon days of Tierney, Vail, and Cashwell. Some of the park's most divisive battles were yet to come, and Buzz believed to an increasing degree that he and the Authority had opposing philosophies about how to shepherd the park forward.

By the end of the decade, it was apparent that Buzz's star had reached its apogee. Some trustees yearned for him to quietly retire and put closure on a distinguished career.

▲ ▲ ▲ ▲ ▲

The situation that Buzz faced in 1994 was unexpected, given his and his predecessors' history with previous Authorities. The relationships between the supervisor/director and the trustees had been formal and distant, with the notable exception of Austin Wilkins.

Shifts in Authority membership didn't bother supervisor Helon Taylor during his seventeen years in the park. He dealt almost exclusively with Austin Wilkins, and if Taylor disagreed with the chairman, he would get satisfaction from Governor Baxter himself. The other Authority members from 1960 to 1967—Roland Cobb, Frank Hancock, Ron Speers, and Richard Dubord—were more names on park letterhead than active policymakers.

Buzz had little personal contact with the Authority when he was a ranger. That changed when he was appointed supervisor in 1968. Like Taylor, he dealt with Austin Wilkins, who remained chairman until June 1971. Using Taylor as his example, Buzz tried to avoid bothering Wilkins with park affairs any more than he had to. He was too busy in the field trying to keep his head above water.

During Buzz's second, longer supervisory period, from June 1971 to April 1975, his main Authority relationship was with Jim Erwin, who succeeded Wilkins as chairman. There were five new trustees during that four-year period—George Bucknam, Maynard Marsh, Jon Lund, Fred Holt, and Joe Brennan. Buzz had good rapport with all of them, although he most enjoyed Erwin and Lund because they were enthusiastic park visitors.

The Wilkins–Erwin–Speers Authority was memorable for the proposed timber giveaway to Great Northern—the deal that their fellow Republican Lund helped nix. But that situation was beyond the realm that involved Buzz.

The mid-1970s were significant development years for Buzz as a manager, and his experience gave him the confidence to assert himself—for example, in his successful effort to retain the campground at Chimney Pond instead of relocating it to Basin Ponds. The more trustees he worked with, the more he saw a fundamental disconnect that some members had with Percival Baxter and Baxter Park.

During the next five-and-a-half-year period, when Lee Tibbs served as director and Buzz was second in command as supervisor, there were five other new Authority members—John Walker, Richard Cohen, Glenn Manuel, Ken Stratton, and Jim Tierney. Buzz interacted with the Authority at meetings but otherwise concentrated on field operations.

The snowmobile and caribou reintroduction issues during the Manuel–Tierney–Stratton years were examples of proposals made to the Authority from the outside and the park director's position was inconsequential. On snowmobiles, Manuel wanted to please the snowmobile clubs, and gubernatorial candidate Tierney wanted voter support. On the caribou transplant, Manuel convinced Tierney and Stratton that it would bring positive publicity to the park and the state and set a precedent for transplanting the animals to other northern states—if all went well. In the face of such adamant Authority positions, Buzz would have had no standing to resist backing the Authority. Fortunately, for him, he favored both snowmobiles and the reintroduction.

Manuel, Stratton, and Tierney were the Authority that hired Buzz to succeed Tibbs. As the ones who promoted Buzz in the face of environmentalists' opposition, the trustees were invested in his being successful. All of them developed a good working relationship with him. They had faith that Buzz would live up to his potential and that the park was in good hands.

▲ ▲ ▲ ▲ ▲

The stars must have been in a fortuitous alignment because the Tierney–Vail–Cashwell Authority and Buzz jelled like none other before or after. They were fortunate to have an unusual amount of time together—five years—to mesh their personalities and styles. They enjoyed themselves and their park duties, and saw problems as opportunities to move the park forward. They spent memorable time in the park at the twice-a-year meetings there, rather than fleeing back to their bureaucratic duties in Augusta the minute the gatherings were over. They became a team. Buzz, in effect, became a de facto member of the Authority in the eyes of some close observers.

Tierney, Vail, Cashwell, and Buzz's joint achievements have remained unparalleled in park history, and it was Buzz who initiated all of the bold, successful proposals. Their actions underscored their operating principle that the park's interest was paramount, not that of a special constituency. Tierney redeemed himself and didn't allow politics to influence his voting as it had in the 1980 snowmobile decision.

The camaraderie with trustees made it hard for Buzz to see them depart one by one from the Authority. When Tierney left the Authority in 1991, he was replaced by Michael Carpenter, a former legislator. While both had started out unenthusiastic about their park responsibilities, Carpenter, unlike Tierney, never developed an interest. Carpenter joined the Authority on the tail end of the West Gate issue. Mindful of his northern Maine constituents' position, he favored opening up that can of worms again, and his first visit to the park was as a guest of the Fin and Feather Club. But Carpenter saw quickly that everyone had moved on from that squabble, and Cashwell and Vail prevailed on keeping the gate shut.

*(L to R), Buzz Caverly, Authority chair Sue Bell, park counsel Paul Stern,*
*and Authority members Bucky Owen and Mike Carpenter, 1994*
JEAN HOEKWATER PHOTO, BAXTER STATE PARK PHOTO ARCHIVES

Sue Bell and Bucky Owen followed Cashwell and Vail in 1992 and 1994, respectively. After West Gate, Carpenter was next in line to become chairman but handed off the job to Sue Bell, who had been on the Authority for just four months. Carpenter was happy to let "the professionals" run the park, and never strayed from what was recommended by Buzz. From that standpoint, he was the epitome of a trustee who never got in Buzz's hair.

Buzz and Bell had known each other when the Caverlys lived in Patten. Bell had moved to town from Houlton when she was sixteen years old and had spent a lot of time with high school friends camping and hiking in the park. She arrived on the Authority with experience as a park user and with a long-standing interest in the Authority job.

Yet Buzz was concerned that Bell might have an "attitude" about the park because of her ties with Patten. Bell was sensitive to the park's treatment of locals and to the way changes in park policies were explained to the public. She felt that the park had mistreated Louis Martin of Patten in terminating his camp lease on Matagamon Lake in

1970. He had been given the option of a lifetime lease but decided to take the park's buyout offer, and the community grapevine saw almost any lease purchase as a raw deal for the seller.

Because Bell was chair of the Authority, Buzz had to pay attention to her perspective. The chair had more power over the park director than the other two members because of the yearly evaluation. The chair also provided guidance for the other Authority members in determining policy and business priorities.

Buzz ran into Bell's power over him about six months after she had joined the Authority, when the park was faced with the proposed expansion of the Pockwockamus Pond rafting facility. Buzz wanted the Authority to oppose the plan, again for the potential negative impacts to the park. But Bell disagreed. Buzz remembers her yelling at him on the phone to stay out of the Pockwockamus affair. He conceded.

Otherwise, he and Bell had a cordial relationship, and there was a serendipitous pause in political controversies. In 1993 and 1994, she wrote two of the best evaluations of Buzz's management that he ever received, praising him for his "effective" relationship with the Authority and his management of employees "fairly and consistently," and calling attention to his "capable management team."

When IF&W commissioner Bucky Owen joined the Authority, Buzz had high hopes for a close, Vail-like relationship with him. But it was not to be because of philosophical and personality conflicts. Like Buzz, Owen was passionate, assertive, spoke his mind, and liked to be in control. Once Owen got to know Buzz more, he saw him as "far more a preservationist" than Owen had realized. He respected Buzz but felt that Buzz "didn't understand current public park management" and was stuck too much in the past. The tensions between them spilled out in the open at Authority meetings.

Owen's number one priority as a trustee was buffer protection of the park through new acquisitions or conservation easements—lands open to multiple uses rather than designated as sanctuary like most of the park. He also felt strongly about the park being less restrictive to scientific research and allocating more funds to trail maintenance. All three issues pushed Buzz's buttons.

Andrew Ketterer, who replaced Carpenter and served with Bell and Owen in 1995, was much like his attorney general predecessor in "not being tuned up on the history of the park" and relying on Paul Stern for navigation. He recalls arriving at the Authority meetings with just minutes to spare, making decisions "without knowing a lot," and then "closing the [agenda] book" and going home. "There were so many things on my plate I didn't have the luxury of time for the park," he says.

Unlike some other trustees, Ketterer didn't find it difficult to be the attorney general and a park trustee simultaneously. It was clear to him that when he was acting on park business, he was 100 percent a trustee. All other interests were set aside, including his own personal preferences. Needless to say, Buzz felt he could rely on Ketterer to uphold Baxter's vision.

The Owen–Bell–Ketterer grouping was the last Authority where Buzz felt he had only one trustee who was on a different page from himself. From then on, it would be two trustees of the three who would be problematic for him—hardly a comforting place to be. He would have been floored at the time to know that the day would come when all three Authority members would line up against him.

▲ ▲ ▲ ▲ ▲

Throughout Buzz's ups and downs with different Authorities, he always had the Advisory Committee to turn to for advice and support. The panel had become an institution (and an institutional memory) in its own right by the time Buzz became director.

Buzz was far more adept at reading situations than his high school education would have indicated, and he astutely saw that the Advisory could help him achieve his management goals if he handled them carefully. A supportive Advisory could give his proposal extra weight if it was politically sensitive for the Authority. Also, if Buzz didn't want to stand out front first on an issue, he could have the Advisory do it for him and thus escape potential flak from the Authority.

The Authorities, with one exception, had accepted the Advisory as a necessary player—although such a group was never contemplated by Percival Baxter. Back in 1972, after Jon Lund "fired" the Advisory for a few months and it reorganized, it steadily solidified its position as a fixture on the scene. Membership became a way to reward enthusiastic park users and special interests. For a time, NRCM, the Fin and Feather Club, and local interests had seats on the committee. Special slots were reserved for representatives of the Baxter family and Acadia National Park. Eventually an ad hoc level was established for newcomers or those who didn't have time for full membership or for newcomers to ease into an Advisory seat. Later, an emeritus role was added to allow the oldest Advisory members, such as Win Robbins and Bob Ohler, a continuing connection with park leadership.

When Jim Tierney joined the Authority in 1979, he shared Jon Lund's perspective that the committee was unnecessary. Tierney looked at the panel as "a group of old men. They were very nice and very nice to me, but I wasn't going to take their advice on much of anything," Tierney recalls, though he did have exceptions to that opinion. He relied on Win Robbins on matters such as bridges because Robbins was an engineer.

As Tierney developed an understanding of the park's many issues, he changed his mind about the Advisory, believing it was important to have a sounding board—but a younger, more professional one. Consequently, Tierney began asking people in their thirties and forties with legal and financial expertise to serve. In the 1980s, the Advisory and the Authorities functioned the smoothest they ever had, according to some former members, and the committee's work on various issues was valued by the trustees.

As Buzz's interest was to have the Advisory in his corner, he made sure he had loyalists on the panel to reflect his positions. Some former committee members said he courted them with favors, such as camping reservations, private tours of the park, or special vehicle stickers to bypass lines at the Togue Pond entrance. But the rewards were always connected to a task the member carried out for the park and one Buzz knew the person would enjoy doing. If the Advisory became disagreeable with Buzz, he might slow down or stop sending work for them to do—a show of his disappointment in them. When all was said and done, it was rare for the Advisory to oppose Buzz.

The Advisory's regular meetings were typically scheduled just prior to those of the Authority, and Buzz was usually there to discuss the issues to come before the trustees—just to make sure all the ducks were in a row to obtain decisions he wanted. If he could not join the Advisory, he sent a senior staff member to keep close tabs on things.

In the 1990s, the relationship between the Advisory and the Authorities became less comfortable due to the Advisory's evolved sense of self-importance as a "mini-legislative" group.

A major internal Advisory issue in the 1990s became the size of the group and the length of service. Authority member Andrew Ketterer viewed the Advisory as being too large and its members having served too long. He wanted a smaller panel with set term limits. Buzz agreed with Ketterer that it was time to revamp the Advisory. The size was reduced to twelve, and members were limited to three two-year terms. The emeritus category was eliminated, and membership on the ad hoc panel was no longer a guaranteed path to the Advisory.

One result of the change was that Authority members began putting forth names for membership for the first time since Jim Tierney. Institutional politics entered the appointments process. The departure of veteran members diluted the Advisory's institutional memory, as well as Buzz's influence with the panel. But no matter who the member was, Buzz took care in developing as close a relationship with him or her as they would allow.

The Advisory shakeup didn't touch the permanent memberships for representatives of the Baxter family and the superintendent of Acadia National Park. The Baxters were 100 percent behind Buzz. He was a dedicated friend whom they trusted. As well, the Acadia superintendents were strong supporters of Buzz.

Robert Reynolds, who had previously headed up Bryce Canyon National Park, viewed Buzz "in many ways as a purist," who at times was "too stiff-necked, too stiff-backed." Reynolds heard "grumbling" from the staff about Buzz's "old style." However, in the long run, he surmised that Buzz's way of doing things was what kept Baxter Park largely unchanged and true to Percival Baxter's vision.

Reynolds was struck by Buzz's recognition that his experience, although deep, was limited to "one place, one environment." Buzz knew "his shortcomings," Reynolds said, and knew the value of "picking others' brains." Jack Hauptmann admired Buzz's firm managerial style and willingness to take risks.

Reynolds, Hauptmann, and Paul Haertel were amazed at Buzz's level of autonomy from the Authority, compared to their situations with National Park Service leadership. "Buzz did things I never could have done at Acadia," Haertel recalls. "We operated in different arenas. Mine was a public arena governed by the rule of law, and Buzz's was governed by what Percival Baxter wanted—and God bless him for it."

At times, Haertel thought Buzz's decisions, such as prohibiting people from climbing Katahdin in adverse weather, would surely be challenged legally. Buzz's assertive management and job survival were testimony to his effectiveness, Haertel thinks. "It was very unusual to see a person grow up in a park, move through the ranks, become supervisor and then director and stay on for years. It's is almost unheard of in national parks because of outside pressures from special interest groups."

▲ ▲ ▲ ▲ ▲

While the Advisory Committee played a key role in helping Buzz achieve his goals, his senior staff was indispensable too. The successes of Jensen Bissell, Jean Hoekwater, and Chris Drew reflected so well on Buzz that their professional achievements frequently received notice in Buzz's year-round evaluations by the Authority chairperson. The trio individually received recognition in their respective fields and in the news media.

Testimony to the importance of Buzz and Chris Drew's long relationship was their mutual respect and praise for each other's character and work at the end of the journey. Drew was a dedicated problem-solver. There was hardly a day over the twenty-five years they worked together as director and chief ranger that they didn't talk or meet face to face. One of Drew's favorite stories about Buzz was how Buzz would hike up to Halfway Rock on the Chimney Pond Trail to meet him when he was the ranger at the remote campground in 1972–73. It became a metaphoric reference to tell others how fair Buzz was in resolving issues. "Buzz would always meet you halfway," says Drew.

Drew, who had been with Buzz fifteen years longer than Bissell and Hoekwater, knew the park like the back of his hand and had a sixth sense of what was going on almost everywhere. He was crafty, clever, and could smell a person's character for what it really was rather than what it appeared to be. He made it tough for hunters to get away with poaching or cutting illegal trails on park land, or for lazy field crew to last through a season. He stopped neighbors from dumping on park land and spearheaded new trail-building. Drew was thorough in his operations reports. He honed his gift for storytelling and was able to handle many difficult problems with tall-tale humor. He was as well-respected in his job as anyone who ever worked for the park.

When Jean Hoekwater was appointed naturalist, the park didn't know the extent of its resource base. There was "an alarming lack" of baseline data on the condition, variety, and amount of plant and animal life, she told a reporter. Consequently, the park's understanding of its "carrying capacity" was primitive, she said, based on "feelings and experience" rather than quantitative information.

For ten years Hoekwater had no assistant as she worked to develop an information and education division and a comprehensive resource database. Along the way, she established the visitor information center at the Togue Pond entrance in 1994; set up protections for moose and upgraded viewing sites for park visitors; developed plant monitoring stations for species to track climate change; and better defined the park's relationship with the AT, ATC, and MATC. She instituted the alpine steward program to interpret the alpine environment and species, shared Leave No Trace principles with hikers on Katahdin, and brought college students into her office to expose them to park conservation principles in a way that spread Percival Baxter's example of conservation out into the world at large.

Forester Jensen Bissell was, in effect, Buzz's deputy director. He forged ahead with Baxter's vision for the SFMA, instituting innovative forest management practices that would allow the once-controversial woods to become "green" certified. Bissell stabilized and increased annual revenues from timber sales and developed specialty markets. The result was an important new stream of income to the park. He also oversaw forest management of the park's outlying parcels in Mt. Chase Plantation and the Austin Cary Lot in Harpswell.

A multi-talented manager, Bissell relieved Buzz of numerous responsibilities the outside world was forcing on him. Bissell handled the duties of business manager when that job was vacant from 1991 to 1997. He educated himself about the park's trust portfolio and became a knowledgeable, articulate source of information. He also assumed responsibilities for working with DOT on the maintenance of the park roads and bridges.

Bissell had a steady hand, and he impressed those who interacted with him with his composure and thoughtfulness. While Buzz was a man of passion, Bissell was calm and deliberate, and the longer he was at the park, the more people talked about him as Buzz's likely successor. However, neither Bissell nor the other senior staff were competitive with Buzz—a situation that made their working relationships comfortable.

Buzz met with Drew, Bissell, and Hoekwater once a week to go over projects and activities. At times all four would go on a road trip into the park together to look at a project on site and discuss how best to handle it. But when not on the job, Buzz and his staff didn't socialize. All of them lived in different directions and had different family responsibilities and interests.

Park counsel Paul Stern was not on Buzz's staff per se, but he played a singular role for Buzz on legal matters involving policy. Buzz and Stern had developed a close relationship—the most trusting that Buzz had ever shared with a park lawyer. With Buzz so close to park affairs, Stern helped him to see things from a larger perspective and to separate personalities from the goals Buzz wanted to achieve. Stern believed that Buzz was so familiar with Percival Baxter's words that when there were options from which to choose, Buzz would choose the best one.

▲ ▲ ▲ ▲ ▲

In the mid-1990s, only a half dozen of the older park generation was still on board. The park had representatives of the Silent Generation, the War Generation, the Baby Boomers, Generation Jones, Gen X, and Gen Y. The differences in education, work ethics, and basic handyman skills were wide, causing Buzz and the oldest rangers to wonder how the park would fare after they were gone.

Buzz was struck by how "extra good" the younger, highly educated job applicants did in interviews. The younger ones hired for seasonal jobs, though well-versed in how to use computers and other tech devices, didn't necessarily know how to use an ax properly, operate a chain saw, or maintain a vehicle. It meant more maintenance and safety training by supervisors than ever before.

Also, Buzz generally viewed the younger field crew as more interested in their labor contract than in what they could contribute to the park. He recollected one accident where a hiker had broken a leg, and a campground ranger helping with the evacuation suddenly said he had to leave or be paid overtime. "I thought to myself, what kind of person would worry about overtime in this kind of a situation?" he says.

As much as Buzz would shake his head comparing the young whippersnappers to his generation of rangers, the Xs and Ys and iGens represented the future caretakers of the park and Percival Baxter's vision, and training them well was essential.

▲ ▲ ▲ ▲ ▲

By the mid-1990s there was more undercurrent about Buzz's hiring practices, which some employees continued to feel was based on favoritism rather than required personnel rules. Employee discontent stayed in-house except for the infrequent times it turned into a grievance with one of the employee unions representing park staff. The longtime union reps' perspective on Buzz was harsh: he was vindictive, arrogant, and hired the least qualified, they claimed. Buzz wasn't surprised at the union's opinion of him, since they were usually on opposite sides of the table on issues.

Buzz ranked personnel issues as *the* most difficult—more so than visitor use and Authority politics—because they involved resolving disputes, counseling, and sometimes having to take disciplinary action with employees whom he considered friends. In 1993 personnel matters were so challenging that Buzz referred to them in the annual report. While complying with confidentiality requirements, he mentioned investigations of two complex situations that involved disciplinary action. Those cases created "a year of turmoil throughout the ranks," he revealed.

None of Buzz's employee critics went to the Authority or to the news media with complaints. Park trustees, with large staffs of their own to manage, didn't solicit complaints about Buzz from the staff. Their focus was park policy, and they had to be confident that the director was managing his people well, knowing that all state agencies had internal conflicts and ongoing personnel issues as a matter of course.

▲ ▲ ▲ ▲ ▲

From a visitor's standpoint, getting a reservation in the park at a favorite spot had become increasingly difficult. Competition for lean-tos at Chimney Pond and the handful of cabins at Daicey and Kidney Ponds, especially for the spring and fall fishing seasons, was fierce.

Locals had an advantage in getting the spaces they desired because they could show up at park headquarters when the door opened and pay their money, beating the crowd that sent in reservations by mail. Most reservations were made by mail, and Mainers had an edge in that their letters were opened first. Reservations could not be made by Mainers or outsiders over the phone yet.

When Buzz was first a ranger at Abol Campground, sites were generally available around the park at any time of the year. Reservations didn't become tight until about the time of Helen Gifford's retirement in 1979, and she left complaining about how time-consuming the process had become for clerks.

In the late 1980s, as the competition for popular sites increased, out-of-towners began showing up on the doorstep at headquarters the night before opening day, so they could be among the first in line. All reservations for Chimney, Daicey, Kidney, Russell, and even South Branch Pond could be snapped up on that first day, leaving would-be visitors to hope for cancellations so they, too, could camp at a choice site.

Buzz remembers arriving at the office early one morning in 1989 to find a man from Vermont who had spent the night outside headquarters to be first in line. A few more stalwarts showed up in the next year or two, and the New Year's camp-out, sometimes in bitterly cold temperatures and snow, began to attract news media attention—which, in turn, prompted others to join the night-long wait and huddle in down sleeping bags or set up a tent outside the park office. Buzz and Jan got into the fun of it by greeting people and serving them coffee and doughnuts. Soon, Buzz was calling the event a "tradition," happy to socialize with return patrons and feeling that all the personal contact benefited the park.

The crush of people ultimately caused Buzz to restrict reservations in 1990 to just one at a time and then returning to the end of the line, hoping it would bring a little more fairness and order to the process. Still, the lines became longer and longer, creating congestion and sanitation issues. In 1994, when 350 people showed up the first day, Buzz moved the group from headquarters to a large motel across the street. There, determined registrants could wait in the sunroom and dining room and be warm and comfortable until they were called to go to park headquarters to make their reservations.

The system, although better for clerks handling the rush, still didn't solve the problem of fairness. Those who were able to get to the park on opening day still had a leg up, and clerks worked for twelve to fourteen hours to satisfy requests. It would be another decade before the system was revamped to solve the equality issue.

▲ ▲ ▲ ▲ ▲

In 1994 the park was offered free of charge two other dam properties by Bangor Hydro. The Nesowadnehunk Lake and Matagamon Lake dams controlled the flow on the East Branch of the Penobscot River. The Matagamon dam property had about 200 acres to go along with it.

"Without even contacting the Authority, I said, 'No, we're not interested in doing that because of what it entails,'" Buzz recalls. "I didn't want to get into the physical responsibility for dams. It was too controversial, too much of a challenge to maintain, too much overhead, and too much contrary to what we were supposed to be representing."

Buzz's position was that the park could achieve more in protecting the land that was already in the preserve than spending limited funds in acquiring more territory that would irritate "another whole group of people." He referred to users of the private campground on the East Branch of the Penobscot near the Matagamon entrance to the park and the retirees' campground and Camp Phoenix on Nesowadnehunk Lake. The Authority didn't override Buzz this time, but the issue would come up again ten years later.

▲ ▲ ▲ ▲ ▲

In another small but important decision, Buzz ordered a name change for the park's major gravel thoroughfare in hopes of improving road management. Since 1974, it had been called the Perimeter Road because it ran along the western park boundary. Buzz reversed the name back to the original Tote Road to emphasize the park's primitive nature. Buzz thought the change would send a message to visitors that the road was a "wild forest woods" road, not a speedway.

▲ ▲ ▲ ▲ ▲

Buzz was finally rid of Bill Cross in 1994 when the former business manager resigned from the Advisory Committee. Finance Committee chairman Jim Garland sent Buzz a note saying that he shared some of the frustrations Cross had highlighted "and hope[d] to remember some of the things you've pointed out (for example, independent, outside audit of the books). The park has a variety of new problems, mostly spelled p-o-l-i-t-i-c-s."

While not always agreeing with Cross's perspectives, Garland told Cross that he "had more good ideas than most other committee people, showed your concern for the park, and in general, were more alive at our meetings than a half dozen other committee members put together."

Cross told Garland that Buzz had asked him to resign from the Advisory Committee because Buzz wanted someone "more in line with their thinking, as well as from a political standing." Win Robbins, who had left the Advisory in 1991, also was persona non grata, Cross indicated. "Guess we have been around too long and know too much as to the goings-on at the park."

Cross felt there were "very few on the Advisory and none on the Authority that really understand or care about the internal workings of the park, especially as it pertains to finances and operations. I am sure that most have the best interests of the park in mind but really don't want to get into the hard facts of operations and the associated problems, especially when they are not politically expedient."

As an emeritus member of the Advisory, Cross planned to be "able to speak freely and write dirty." But he didn't follow up that intent.

---

Primary Document Sources: BSPA original Authority and Advisory Committee minutes, Box 1 (2112-0717); Boxes 1, 2, 3 (2507-0801). BSP Annual Report, 1981-1994.

*Maine Times,* three-part series: November 14, 1986, pp. 2–5A; November 21, 1986, pp. 18–22A; December 5, 1986, pp. 20–22A; four-part series: April 2, 1998, pp. 4–7; April 1, 1998, pp. 20–21; April 9, 1998, pp. 18–20; April 23, 1998, pp. 7–9, 15.

Conversations and communications: Sue Bell, Mike Carpenter, John Cashwell, Buzz Caverly, Brendan Curran, Chris Drew, Tom Doak, Chuck Gadzik, Paul Haertel, Jack Hauptmann, Andrew Ketterer, John Loyd, Keith Miller, Robert Reynolds, Jym St. Pierre, Paul Stern, Jane Thomas, Jim Tierney, Bill Vail, Ron Wye.

▲▲▲▲▲▲▲▲

CHAPTER 25

# WILDER FROM WITHIN

BUZZ HAD MANY SLEEPLESS NIGHTS over the ongoing large timberland sales in the north woods, especially as timberland investment groups and "kingdom buyers" replaced the patriarchal paper company owners. He mulled over potential impacts and contemplated "what-if" development scenarios. He was mindful of Bill Vail's caution to stay out of issues outside the park and concentrate on what he wanted to do inside the park. In the face of an unpredictable future, the only way the park could sustain its wilderness character—even enhance it—was to become wilder inside, Buzz concluded.

Buzz thought it was within the parameters of his responsibilities to share his ideas for the park over the next fifty to a hundred years—and he had always felt free to speak his mind, no matter who was on the Authority. So he went forward on his own to propose a "Wilder from Within" approach—a bold vision that immediately incensed some of his longtime critics and excited his supporters. (His senior staff was not involved in the proposal.)

Buzz felt that the cumulative human impacts and heavy hiker and auto traffic in concentrated areas around Katahdin were pushing the park toward the brink of overuse, something that had concerned him off and on for years What the pressures pointed to, in his mind, was the failure of passive rationing of Baxter's wilderness through existing rules and regulations. The numbers supported his fears.

In 1994 trail registers listed 39,636 people ascending Katahdin (and there were more who didn't sign in). There were unconfirmed reports of approximately 700 people climbing the mountain on the July 4, 1995, weekend. The great crowds created visual clutter, noise, and eroded trails. They damaged alpine flowers and mosses on the Tableland to the point that a low-profile stone walkway had to be built to guide people along a single path to Baxter Peak. Serious erosion was occurring on the Saddle Trail—a scree slope and the easiest trail to the summit.

In 1994, 31,337 vehicles drove through the Togue Pond gate. Traffic jams abounded during peak summer months. Motorists ran into each other and ran over wildlife as they traveled the narrow roads, pulling over for a view or racing to and from a trailhead. When the designated parking areas were filled, visitors parked their cars illegally at roadside turnouts, damaging vegetation. Moose watchers at some roadside ponds had destroyed bog mosses and plants, forcing the park to build wooden walkways to Cranberry, Rocky, and Round Ponds. Park rangers worried that sightseers were disturbing moose at Sandy Stream and Russell Ponds.

Buzz's Wilder from Within concept offered three solutions and expanded Percival Baxter's original vision. One proposal recommended stopping the Roaring Brook Road at Windey Pitch, about four miles short of the campground and the most-used trails to Katahdin. Only a limited number of hikers would be allowed to drive to Windey Pitch, park their cars and trek to Roaring Brook Campground or continue 3.3 more miles to Chimney Pond Campground. In time, the entire Roaring Brook Road would be off-limits to motorized traffic, forcing campers to hike nine miles from the Togue Pond gate to Roaring Brook. Those who couldn't or didn't want to walk the distance would have motorized access to other places in the park closer to a road and often under used by visitors.

The second proposal suggested eliminating a twelve-mile stretch of the Tote Road along the western side of the park linking the southern and northern entrances. The effect would be to create an extensive unroaded area in Nesowadnehunk Valley between the turnoff to Camp Phoenix near Nesowadnehunk Wilderness Campground and Trout Brook Crossing in the north. Taking out the road segment would force people to change the way they used the park. Backpackers would be the major beneficiaries, since they would have a much larger area in which to roam without disturbance, and wildlife would enjoy greater safety from vehicles.

The third recommendation focused on making Kidney Pond Campground a walk-in facility by removing the vehicle bridge over Nesowadnehunk Stream. Campers would park on the east side of the stream and walk over a footbridge to their site, about a mile. There would be carts to help them transport their bags. Such a change would make Kidney Pond a much more remote experience, enhancing the quiet for visitors and wildlife alike.

Before going to the Authority with his ideas, Buzz floated them in articles in *Maine Times* and *AMC Outdoors* magazine and then began speaking about them in friendly settings with other wilderness park managers and environmental and trail groups.[1]

The environmental community at large didn't rush to publicly embrace Buzz's proposal, sensing that it could be counterproductive in the anti-wilderness atmosphere at the time. But Jym St. Pierre, Maine director of RESTORE, was one who agreed with Buzz that Baxter Park had become "a threatened island," pointing to the changes around it.

Clear-cutting had devastated large tracts of forest on the west side of the park, and commercial development had expanded near the south, east, and west borders. On the east side, old-growth forest had been harvested, and new roads had been built along the south and east borders. At the same time, the demand for public recreational use continued to outstrip the capacity of the park to provide the great outdoor experience that people "desperately need," St. Pierre said.

The acquisition of the Togue Pond area was "very good news . . . [but] the alarming news is that more and more, we are realizing that Baxter Park is no longer big enough, and this small addition alone will not protect the park from development, harmful forest practices, and other problems," St. Pierre added.

There was no immediate reaction from the Authority members. The plan guaranteed them bad publicity with local interests, so when they found out about it, they hoped it would just go away. Two of the trustees were about to depart anyway. Independent Angus King had replaced GOP governor John McKernan, which led to new appointments to the Authority in 1995. Carpenter was replaced by Andrew Ketterer, and Chuck Gadzik replaced Bell. As the only holdover on the Authority and the one with most park knowledge, Bucky Owen became chairman.

Buzz's timing to go public with Wilder from Within was not calculated—or he wouldn't have gone forward then. Northern Mainers were especially sensitive about proposals they felt would "lock up" the Maine woods from them because of the fight raging over the proposed Maine Woods Reserve, the uncertainty generated by the big timberland sales, and deepening doubts about the future of the state's paper industry. In such anxious times, the word *wilderness* had become a dirty word, thanks to the efforts of the forest industry and sportsmen's organizations, which opposed RESTORE's vision for the region.

Buzz's detractors swarmed over Wilder from Within. It was new evidence to critics that Buzz was an extreme wilderness advocate. In his "Native Conservative" column in the *Kennebec Journal*, George Smith, executive director of the Sportsman's Alliance of Maine, called Wilder from Within a "thought-provoking radical concept." If Buzz's proposal were put in place, Baxter Park would become an "elitist hiker's paradise," Smith contended, and he doubted if "ripping out roads and bridges" was what Governor Baxter would have wanted.

Smith (no relation to climber George Smith) claimed that most visitors he met in the park were not interested in hiking. They liked to see the mountains and moose and get on to the next scenic attraction. "We should let them," Smith wrote. "There's nothing at all wrong with that." If limits were to be placed on people, he suggested they target the hikers—"those who intrude on the innermost sanctuaries of the park—and non-residents, to keep the park available and open to all Mainers who wish to visit." Smith wasn't completely negative toward Buzz. He praised the director for doing "a superb job of keeping society's playthings, such as cell phones, pets, and large RVs out of the preserve."

Buzz's arch-critic George Kerivan unleashed a vitriolic attack against Buzz personally. Writing an op-ed article in the *Bangor Daily News*, Kerivan called Buzz "a self-serving autocrat," and accused him of "grandstanding."[2] Buzz, he said, "cannot resist the temptation of leaving the stamp of his own ego on all that he surveys, all the time posturing as a concerned environmentalist." Kerivan charged that Buzz's "actions go unhindered as he enjoys the trappings of power that have been granted him over the years by the Authority."

In Kerivan's view, Buzz was "fond of casting himself as the anointed, hand-picked successor to Governor Baxter. Taking the rhetorical moral high ground, he uses fear of an eroding wilderness to justify his czar-like pronouncements. Judging from the public acclaim he has received, he has a lot of people fooled."

Kerivan harkened back to his own effort to have Kidney Pond Camps considered for the National Register of Historic Places. It was "now clear why Buzz resisted," he said. "By using politically correct sound bites like a 'wilder Baxter' and 'limited access' and raising the specter of 'overuse,' he is playing to the big wilderness lobby to further his own agenda." Buzz was "on a mission to write himself into the history books as sole protector of Baxter's will," Kerivan added. "He should step aside and allow others with a wider vision to advocate for wilderness in the true spirit of Governor Baxter."

Interestingly, there was no public response, indicating that neither Smith nor Kerivan was convincing to anyone but an audience already anti-wilderness or anti-Buzz.

Environmentalists of different degrees expressed interest in the Wilder from Within concept, and some were instantly supportive.

Sue Bell viewed Buzz's proposal as a "statement of conscience." She also believed the proposal signaled a change, in that Buzz stepped forward with a position he arrived at by himself, rather than working with the Authority and his staff. "I thought it was atypical that he did not have faith in the Authority or try to convince the Authority, and went his own way," she recalls.

After so much publicity, Authority members still didn't initiate talk with Buzz about his ideas or go on record publicly. Bucky Owen remembers the proposal as "hitting [the trustees] blindsided." He thought the road closure ideas "were so far out there that I don't think we took them seriously." However Owen did favor removing the Kidney Pond bridge.

Andrew Ketterer accepted Wilder from Within as representative of what Buzz was supposed to do for the Authority—come up with concepts and future plans. He was interested in Buzz's vision, whether or not he agreed with it.

The Authority didn't get a pass on the subject for long. DOT deemed the Kidney Pond bridge unsafe, and Buzz took the opportunity to put all the options before the trustees, including one from Wilder from Within. Again, counsel Stern sided with Buzz on removing the bridge altogether in favor of a smaller footbridge. Buzz acknowledged that it was a big step and would need a lot of planning and discussion with locals, who would be upset with the loss of motorized access.

DOT engineers wanted to build a new bridge at a cost of approximately $200,000—a price that floored the Authority and Buzz and was dead on arrival. But the Authority wasn't ready to seriously entertain Buzz's preferred option either. His fallback position was repairing the bridge so that the removal option could perhaps come up again, not too far down the road. He found a local contractor who agreed on repairs that would keep the bridge safe for about fifteen years at an affordable cost of $6,200. The Authority accepted that plan.

The bridge was only part of the Wilder from Within proposal that the Authority considered during Buzz's tenure. Bucky Owen, looking back on the plan years later, said the Authority or Buzz should have asked a subcommittee of the Advisory Committee to study the ideas and make recommendations. "Closing roads was a huge issue," he says. "If we had had a Friends of Baxter Park at the time and used the Advisory Committee, I think there would have been more of a chance for discussion by the Authority."

Chuck Gadzik joined the Authority several months after Buzz went public with Wilder from Within. In reflection, he thought Buzz had "needed to convince the Authority that [Wilder from Within] would be a thoughtful, collaborative, inclusive discussion about tough issues. While I was there, it came on the heels of difficult issues where Buzz had been clear he did not like the decisions of our Authority. This was not the atmosphere to take on a major new initiative. In the end, there would have had to be a lot of trust, and Buzz was clear he did not trust the majority of the members," Gadzik says.

Whether Buzz could have gotten further with the vision if the park had a formally trained planner was a question that advocates discussed among themselves later. A planner could have been an effective ally on Buzz's senior staff. But neither Buzz nor the Authority considered adding such a position.

▲ ▲ ▲ ▲ ▲

Another situation arose in 1995 that gave critics ammunition against Buzz as a wilderness activist. He gave Mike Wilson, a grassroots organizer for the regional Northern Forest Alliance, permission to talk with hikers in the park and ask them to sign a petition. The petition called for the protection of forest land from Maine to New York State from development, and the public purchase of ten outstanding areas that merited special protection, including a large area around Baxter Park. Buzz approved the activity with the condition that hikers not be required to fill out a long form.

Forest industry representatives complained to the Authority about Buzz's role in the petition drive, raising suspicions that his underlying "mission" in going along with the campaign was to support the proposed Maine Woods Reserve.

Bucky Owen directed Paul Stern to look into the free-speech aspects of the issue. Stern, noting that Percival Baxter was "a great believer in freedom of speech," said the park would run into First Amendment problems if it tried to ban solicitations. The upshot was the designation of Pine Cove at Togue Pond for individuals or groups to exercise their free-speech rights.

▲ ▲ ▲ ▲ ▲

The renovations that Buzz had begun at Daicey Pond in 1971 and at Kidney Pond in 1988 were finally completed in 1995. Buildings had been removed, relocated, jacked up, leveled, and painted. Sills and roofs had been replaced and porches rebuilt. The old campground dumps had been cleaned up, vehicles removed from brooks, and hazardous chemicals and pollutants removed from the shorelines and buildings.

Buzz sighed relief at reaching such a milestone, but dealing with the park's "built environment" was a never-ending need and constant expense. More dilapidated buildings were scheduled for removal, and there were still some old privies that needed replacement. Buzz had expected concrete vaults to be a solution to the need for better toilets. But they leaked and were hard to clean and had to be replaced with sealed stainless steel vaults.

Tens of thousands of gallons of waste were collected from the toilets, and where it was sent was secret. But in early summer of 1994, a near emergency was created when serious disposal problems came to light. A *Katahdin Times* reporter was in the park on her way down the Katahdin Stream Road and saw toilet paper in the ditch. She took a photo and confronted Buzz about it. The two of them got in his vehicle and went to see what was going on.

There were seven authorized sites in the park for waste pumped by rangers from the vault toilets. High-water conditions had caused the waste dumped in an old gravel pit near the Katahdin Stream Campground to run into a wet area and then into the ditch. Other disposal areas had similar problems. "I had egg on my face," Buzz acknowledges, and he dreaded reporting the problem to the Authority.

In an effort to save money, Buzz had directed that waste be kept in the park rather than hauled out by a private contractor at several hundred dollars a load. With about 60,000 gallons of waste annually from the roadside toilets, outside disposal would have cost the park thousands of dollars. In 1995 Buzz had to reverse the disposal arrangement. He ordered the in-house dumping stopped and the waste was sent to a commercial facility in Lincoln. Then he asked the Advisory Committee to look for a long-term solution.

The committee came up with two sites in the park where the material could be spread safely on the ground, and they met the space requirement: a minimum of 45,000 square feet. The most suitable soils were in or near the SFMA.

The area in the park that Buzz and the Authority chose was on the Black Brook Road on the south side of the SFMA. To accommodate a disposal area there, the Webster Lake trail had to be relocated. At the same time, the gated Black Brook Road, used only by park employees, SFMA harvesting crews, or other approved personnel, was resurfaced with gravel to allow for light vehicle traffic.

Buzz was firm that improving the road should not lead to misuse by people for personal reasons such as hunting and fishing, or as a shortcut to Telos. But it wasn't long before Buzz learned that some rangers and Advisory Committee members were ignoring his restricted-use policy by using the road for hunting access in the SFMA.

---

1. *Maine Times,* June 3, 1995, pp. 10–11; *AMC Outdoors,* January-February, 1995, pp. 15–18.
2. *Bangor Daily News,* October 13, 1995, p. A13.

Primary Document Sources: BSPA Box 1 (2112-0717); BSPA Original Minutes Box 1; BSP Annual Report, 1995.

Conversations and communications: Buzz Caverly, Bucky Owen, Andrew Ketterer, Sue Bell, Chuck Gadzik, Jym St. Pierre, George Smith, John Loyd, Paul Stern.

▲▲▲▲▲▲▲▲

CHAPTER 26

# Trail Blues

From the start, Baxter Park trail czar Lester Kenway knew he had an impossible job restoring the trails on Katahdin. In the mid-1980s, he had estimated that it would take at least thirty years to repair the then-existing damage. He simply had to do the best he could with his single crew working just one month a year.

By 1996 Baxter Park had 188 miles of trails ranging over more than half of the 46 mountains, and none were as important as the half dozen routes up Katahdin. The mountain was not just a goal for hikers in general but an overpowering visual icon for AT thru-hikers. It was the most spectacular peak seen from a distance on the entire 2,175-mile footpath. And legendary, too, because of its resident god, Pamola, and the fact that trails were off-limits for a good part of the year because of weather and park rules.

Probably no one knew more about Katahdin's weather than Lester Kenway. It was "a hostile climate day after day" that made trail work exhausting, he said. "We saw clouds and cold, and sun and heat over and over. There were very few comfortable days, so it was important to feel that each day counted because the end [of the restoration] was never to be seen."

Trail work was the hardest of any park job, paid the least, and offered cramped housing. It was not easy to attract crew who would stay all season. It was common for trail workers to shift to easier, better-paying seasonal jobs if they opened up unexpectedly.

Besides the work site difficulties, the trail budget was a chronic problem. No more than 5 percent of the annual park budget was ever allocated to trails during Kenway's years as trail supervisor. Buzz did approve measures to keep trail crew working longer, but the ongoing scarcity of financial support was disappointing and irritating to Kenway. By the mid-1990s, he knew that Buzz would never make significant funds available for trail work. Trails were secondary to campgrounds in Buzz's mind, Kenway believed. Chris Drew, Kenway's supervisor, agreed that trails always got the short stick, and he was thrust into the role of "peacemaker" between Buzz and Kenway.

An issue that brought Kenway and Buzz into persistent conflict was trail design. The only way to restore and maintain Katahdin trails was to harden them with rock, and the degree to which Kenway felt hardening was needed went against Buzz's grain. To boot, a lot of rock was needed to build steps and water bars and riprap areas, and the source of the material was the mountain itself.

Katahdin challenged Kenway to pioneer new techniques for moving rock from one spot to another in the ecologically fragile environment. The Griphoist cable system he developed nimbly lifted large, heavy rocks and boulders through the air and accomplished that end. Buzz felt that the cumulative impact of the rock relocation was almost to the point that it was changing the face of Katahdin. The rock work, he thought, was an over development that eroded the park's wilderness character, something he had vowed to prevent.

▲ ▲ ▲ ▲ ▲

When Buzz joined the park in 1960, the trail network extended 150 miles. There was no trail crew to clear footpaths from blowdown and brush and maintain them. Campground rangers—if they had some extra time—took their loppers and chain saws to nearby trails to keep them open. But there were no uniform standards. On the whole, the trails were overgrown and excessively blazed.

Trails' low priority was not unusual for that decade across the country. The high-profile causes—the greater environmental movement, the anti-Vietnam War movement, and the women's movement—were taking most of activists' energy. Trails were somebody else's responsibility. It took the hiking boom in the late-1960s and early 1970s to put the spotlight on the crisis of trails and spark the organization of hiking clubs and hiking magazines.

Little by little, and with the help of many volunteers, Baxter Park's trails were improved and expanded as visitation increased. Most of the degradation occurred after 1960, and the first erosion control project ever done in the park was not until 1974 on the Chimney Pond and Hunt Trails.

Kenway started work on Katahdin's Saddle Trail in 1980, but

Gerald Merry didn't like his idea of lining the trail with stones to define the edges, so Buzz put the work on hold. In 1982 heavy rain and runoff caused massive erosion on the Saddle, and rangers Ben Townsend and John Gordon managed to get Buzz up on the trail for a look-see in hopes that he would take action. The outcome was that Buzz directed Kenway's crew to install rock water bars, some stone steps, and riprap to stabilize the trail. Kenway worked on the Saddle until 1986, after which he turned his attention to the Hunt/AT Trail from the Gateway to Baxter Peak.

Working under Buzz—first as trail crew leader for a decade and then supervisor of trails for seven years—had grown increasingly frustrating for Kenway. Both men were stubborn, and neither liked to be told what to do or be corrected by anyone else. Kenway was a tireless worker, highly organized, and with a well-planned timetable for accomplishing his trail goals. The park was a chaotic planning enterprise because of the nature of the unexpected events with visitors, facilities, and Mother Nature. Buzz often asked Kenway to set aside his trail priorities and attend to pressing parkwide operational needs.

Some work could have been done faster if Kenway had been provided the equipment he requested. It took ten years for Chris Drew to get approval from Buzz for a rock drill for Kenway. Drew said Kenway would give him twenty pages of requisitions for a season's trail work but that he dared to pass only a few of them at a time to Buzz because of limited funds.

The trails up Katahdin from Chimney Pond had been laid out by caretaker LeRoy Dudley, and they went almost straight up. By the late 1980s, the new thinking about trail-building advised a more gradual grade that involved building "benches." That technique was challenging for soils. Buzz preferred to have trails with as much "natural character" as possible and reined in Kenway's trail "slabbing" technique. Buzz also didn't like the drilling of holes for anchors and didn't like the way Kenway laid riprap like shingles. It all detracted from the scenic values of the mountain, in Buzz's view.

Kenway first used his Griphoist winch on Katahdin's treeless upper reaches during the summer of 1989. It was an adaptation of the "Yankee Hoist" that the park had acquired in 1979 for the trail crew and used to drag rocks and logs on mountains below treeline. Such hoists, popular in Europe, had been used in construction and ski-lift building.

Buzz recalls seeing Kenway, who was skilled in metalwork, working on his Griphoist prototype in the park's maintenance building and wondering what in the world it was. Kenway's system necessitated fixing steel tripods into the rock to keep the winch cable above ground, since there were no trees to use. He started working with it first on the Saddle Trail in 1992, then on the top of Cathedral for four seasons, and then redoing parts of the Saddle Trail that weren't holding up well.

The most successful restoration work was to build stone steps to secure Katahdin's loose soils. The plateau soils were weathered granite gravel with the consistency of dried peas. When the trails were lined with rocks (there were never any rock walls) erosion would accelerate due to the concentrated foot traffic, and water bars were difficult to maintain due to the loose soils.

The early 1990s budget problems brought on by the national recession forced additional cuts in Kenway's trails program. He protested, pointing out how hard he had worked for years with an unfunded program. Investment in trails had slipped to less than 2 percent of the park budget. Kenway reported to Chris Drew, "I don't think we can be very proud of that trend when user surveys indicate that 80 percent of park visitors come to use the trails."

▲ ▲ ▲ ▲ ▲

Competing for time and money with Kenway's Katahdin projects were new trails—short spurs and long stretches. Buzz decided in the fall of 1991 that the AT had to be relocated to finally deal with long-standing problems between thru-hikers and campers at Daicey Pond Campground. The new route, along Blueberry Ledges between Abol Bridge and Katahdin Stream, would bypass the historical seven-mile river walk along the West Branch and Nesowadnehunk waters, as well as Daicey. Also, the thru-hiker accommodations in the field at Daicey would be shifted to a wooded site called The Birches across the Tote Road from Katahdin Stream Campground.

Besides taking money from the trails budget, the relocation caused immediate tensions between Buzz and the ATC, the MATC, and the National Park Service that oversees management of the AT, and there was a blowup of considerable proportions between Buzz and the trail interests at a November 1991 meeting of the parties. Trail groups didn't want to move the trail from Daicey because it provided northbound hikers their first up-close and panoramic view of Katahdin, and the relocation dropped three miles of the AT. However Buzz prevailed, banking on his belief that all the parties would agree in the future that it had been a good move.

Another skirmish was over the International Appalachian Trail (IAT), the idea of former state conservation commissioner Dick Anderson. Without consulting Buzz, Anderson publicly announced plans for an IAT—a project to, in effect, extend the AT to the end of the Appalachian mountain chain. Initially, Anderson's trail would have taken a route from Katahdin through the north end of the park and then would either follow old woods ways or cut fresh to Quebec's Gaspé Peninsula.

Anderson's plan upset Buzz. Camping sites at Davis Pond and Russell Pond—which would be along the IAT route—were already over-pressured, and he had been considering closing the little-used North Peaks Trail down to Russell Pond Campground.

Furthermore, Buzz opposed the idea because it was another example of an outside organization wanting to take advantage of the park's resources. He met with Anderson to discuss the potential problems of the IAT going through the park and the impact it would have on Russell, and Anderson backed off. Ultimately, the IAT board of directors agreed to keep the IAT south of the park and route it to the east long the East Branch of the Penobscot River. In 2000 the IAT was extended to Newfoundland's Bell Isle—a total distance of 1,400 miles from Baxter Park.

Just to make sure the North Peaks Trail wasn't surreptitiously used by IATers, Buzz closed it.

▲ ▲ ▲ ▲ ▲

Bucky Owen saw the park's trail system as the backbone of the visitor's experience. As he reviewed budget allocations, he was shocked to discover how little money was being allocated to trail maintenance. He faulted Buzz for spending so much to remove buildings and maintain roads at the expense of trail work.

Owen, an avid hiker, took more interest in trails during his tenure than any other Authority member preceding him. He tried to intercede in Buzz's decisions for the 1996 trail work plan. At a meeting between Kenway, Buzz, and Drew on December 5, 1995, Kenway reviewed the plans he had submitted for the 1996 season. Buzz was particularly interested in the progress on Katahdin's alpine trails, and Kenway told him things were going well but it would take decades more to complete the restoration at the current pace.

Buzz asked Kenway and Drew to make a proposal to address the issue, and their recommendation was to increase the number of SCA interns to staff two full crews, add a six-month trail crew leader position and other staff, increase the budget for tools and equipment, provide the trails group an additional vehicle, and improve housing at Kidney Pond and Roaring Brook. The plan would have both crews working on the Tableland for four weeks each, taking turns so as not to overly fatigue the workers. And it would mean having crews work out of the Chimney Pond crew camp continuously for two months.

Buzz took the proposal to the Authority in January 1996, and they endorsed it. But Buzz asked for a delay in implementation until 1997 to soften the cost impact. Bucky Owen objected to postponement, given the trail conditions.

The challenging situation was reflected in the report that Kenway and Drew had given to Buzz. It stated that the trail crew had worked 7,800 hours in the previous twelve years redefining and rebuilding the alpine portion of the Saddle, Hunt, and Cathedral Trails on Katahdin. Kenway projected an additional 19,500 hours to complete restoration of eroded alpine paths.

With the current crew of ten people working four weeks a summer, Kenway estimated it would take twenty-seven years to complete the restoration of just the three most popular trails, but under the new proposal, it would take only seven years. Of course, volunteers would be needed to supplement the trail crew, he added.

Kenway proposed splitting the work on alpine trail restoration and routine trail maintenance. The cost of the seven-year program would be approximately $66,536 the first year (mostly for labor) and the next six years would cost $62,036 a year.

Buzz agreed that trails were important, but he was concerned about cost sacrifices that would have to be made in other programs. He wanted a lot of logistical planning before Kenway's stepped-up trail work began. The Authority decided to compromise and do what Buzz wanted—start the work within a year but go slower toward completion than Kenway proposed.

On July 24, 1997, Jean Hoekwater organized a hike over Katahdin for Buzz to see what Kenway's crews had accomplished and to discuss the next phase of projects. Buzz hadn't climbed the mountain since 1994. The group ascended Katahdin on the Abol Trail to Baxter Peak and then down to the Saddle Trail and back home via the Hunt Trail—a twelve-mile, twelve-hour venture.

Buzz thought the plateau they viewed was in "good shape" from Kenway's "substantial efforts." He commended Kenway and his cadre for the "extreme hard work" in hardening trails and controlling hikers by the use of stone-bordered walkways that "made it clear where people should be walking to protect the alpine zones." The incredibly difficult stabilization efforts from Baxter Peak down to the upper end of the Cathedral Trail was working well, Buzz observed, agreeing with Kenway that the work was necessary.

Buzz also saw the changes to the mountain's natural features as looking too manmade. Soon, he said, the incremental changes would alter the face of the mountain. Buzz looked upon the stones, rocks, and boulders on Katahdin as deserving just as much "protection" to remain naturally in their environment as the alpine plants or Katahdin arctic butterflies.

Buzz didn't stop Kenway's rock work cold turkey, but cautioned him to "avoid alterations of that magnitude [the Chimney Trail] at other locations" on Katahdin. They agreed that Kenway would focus other work below the upper reaches of the Cathedral and Saddle Trails. Yet when all was said and done, Kenway said that much of that project ended up being canceled. The Authority didn't realize what had happened because the trustees didn't follow up.

It took about 3,000 hours of labor to restore 500 feet of alpine trail. During a fourteen-year period, the resources provided to Kenway enabled his crews to reconstruct only 13 percent of the Katahdin trails. He felt that some of the work done between 1983 and 1999 "was of high quality" and required "very little maintenance," including portions of the upper Hunt Trail and the uppermost Cathedral. Other areas, particularly the Thoreau Spring Trail and the middle portion of the Saddle Trail, deserved more work or annual maintenance, he felt. The trails on Hamlin Ridge, Pamola, and Northwest Basin were never worked on, he noted.

Besides trails, Buzz and Kenway clashed over other matters. Buzz thought that Kenway went overboard in building and replacing bridges—for instance the larger ones at Basin Pond and across Grassy

Pond outlet. Buzz felt that it wasn't appropriate to replace backcountry bridges at all if it was just for the convenience of park visitors—it was too expensive and created an unnecessary liability. He supported bridge construction to access facilities or protect fragile zones but was firm that they should be built of natural materials that lasted only ten to fifteen years, when there could be reconsideration of whether to replace them or not.

Kenway, along with a couple of rangers, had wanted to put in a concrete base and steel timbers for the Basin Pond bridge, but Buzz intervened to stop it, telling them it was overkill and that they shouldn't be using anything but natural materials. The eight-foot-wide wooden bridge that was built was oversized for summer hiking but Buzz concluded it was needed for snowmobiles hauling propane tanks and supplies to Chimney Pond in winter.

The Grassy Pond bridge was a high, attractive structure that the AT crossed at the outlet. Buzz found out about it when he first saw it in one of Bill Silliker's annual calendars, strapped on his snowshoes, and went to view it for himself. He blamed the overbuilt bridge on Kenway and had it dismantled.

How did large bridges get built without Buzz's knowing about it? The designs should have been given to him for approval, he said, but the protocol wasn't followed. It was "human nature" for park employees to ignore following the rules all the time and taking initiatives on their own. Besides the bridges, Buzz pointed to a cement-walled root cellar built at Trout Brook Farm that he didn't know about for years.

Buzz and Kenway also disagreed about accommodations for the trail crew working on Katahdin. Kenway wanted to house them in crew quarters at Chimney Pond and at visitor sites elsewhere in the park. Buzz felt that the impact of housing the trail crew at Chimney Pond for two months was environmentally unacceptable, and that reserving public facilities for trail workers eliminated the opportunity for varied other uses. Kenway actually built an A-frame structure on a wooden tent platform at Chimney Pond, and Buzz ordered him to remove it.

Regardless of the job struggles, Kenway's annual evaluations by supervisor Chris Drew were consistently impressive—"top-notch worker . . . exceptional planning and organizational skills . . . excellent reports . . . extremely conscientious . . . strives for harmony among crew he supervises." Drew said Kenway's trail construction and maintenance skills were of the highest professional level and called him "a valuable asset to Baxter State Park."

Kenway resigned in February 2000 after twenty-two years over-seeing the trails. It was not just years of friction with Buzz that caused forty-six-year-old Kenway to leave, but knee and back problems from working so long and hard in the field. Kenway wanted a less physically demanding job, and he became program director of the Maine Conservation Corp and established his own consulting company, Trailservices. He was a big loss to the park.

Kenway's legacy was substantial. His alpine restoration and trail reconstruction on Katahdin left an enduring mark, and he greatly improved the trail connections throughout the park by adding new links. Kenway always looked for opportunities to create loops and elim-inate the old dead-end fishermen's and loggers' routes. He relocated trails in swampy areas to higher ground and upgraded them. It was Chris Drew who pushed to get Kenway's back burner trail link built in the north end of the park—construction and extension of the Center Ridge Trail over Traveler Mountain and north to connect with the existing North Traveler Trail, a ten-mile loop that includes a mini-Knife Edge. Some of the trail connections allow backpackers to go from one end of the park to the other without having to travel on park roads.

With limited resources, Kenway instituted a highly successful stu-dent and volunteer cadre to give him the labor that was essential to carry out the difficult work. Hiking clubs, especially the MATC, gave Kenway significant support and praised him as an effective organizer, planner, and positive boss. In 2005 he was honored with the annual Alpine Steward award by the Guy Waterman Fund, created to protect the alpine areas of northeast mountains. He was nominated for the award by his successor, Paul Sannacandro.

Kenway's reputation extended far beyond Baxter Park because of his Griphoist device. It gained him the attention of state and national parks elsewhere, and he became the go-to consultant for major moun-tain trail construction.

▲ ▲ ▲ ▲ ▲

Besides trails, another area of chronic discontent for Buzz was Katahdin Lake Wilderness Camps. For decades the park had extended special privileges to the remote camps. The various owners and their clients had been allowed to access the private facility from a trailhead in the park at Avalanche Field. The old 3.5-mile logging road was the only open way to reach the remote camp except by float plane. Bushwhacking on an old logging track from the east was possible, but almost no one did it.

Before the park was created, then-landowner Great Northern Paper allowed the camps to have a garage on the Roaring Brook Road near the trailhead, but that had been torn down long ago. What still stood in 1996 was a small hovel at the Avalanche trailhead to store hay for horses used to haul supplies to the camps.

Al Cooper, who took over operation of the camps with his wife Sue in 1975, irritated Buzz with his housekeeping deficiencies. Cooper kept oil and gasoline near the hovel to fuel the snowmobile he used in winter to supply the camps, and park staff had growing concerns about the spilling of oil and gas on the ground and Cooper's disposal of empty cans in the woods. For a long time, however, the Coopers and the park had managed to patch up their cooperative arrangement when problems threatened to end it.

In the winter of 1996, Craig Gordon of Brunswick focused attention on the situation. He had asked Cooper to pack down the trail so he could easily cross-country ski to the camps. Cooper said no and made Gordon mad enough that he asked Buzz to cut off Cooper's access from the park.

"I believe Governor Baxter would be especially resentful of the commercial nature of Katahdin Lake Camps' encroachment on his park," Gordon wrote on March 13. Requiring campers and hikers to travel on foot and allowing Katahdin Lake owners to use snowsleds "smacks of elitism," Gordon maintained. In a follow-up letter, he raised the pollution issue, telling Buzz that Cooper's snowsled was dropping oil-caked pieces of ice on the ground, raising the possibility for groundwater contamination. Gordon also asserted that the trail packed down by the snowsled provided predators an easy way to attack park wildlife and frighten deer.

The issue festered for awhile before Buzz took the issue to the Authority in the fall, and they gave it back to him to resolve. Buzz directed Cooper to clean up the hovel area and advised Cooper that a containment tank would be installed above ground to house Cooper's toxic substances. As uncomfortable as it was for Buzz, the privileges to Katahdin Wilderness Camps under Cooper would continue for another decade, when the situation changed dramatically.

▲▲▲▲▲

Buzz had never been absent from an Authority meeting in his fourteen years as director. But the trustees approved his absence at their October 10, 1996, session in Millinocket because Governor Angus King and his family were visiting the park. It was the first meeting between Buzz and King and the first opportunity Buzz had had to show a governor around since Ken Curtis's last trip in 1974.

After King was elected in 1994, the governor's chief of staff, Chuck Hewett, had met with Buzz, Authority chairman Bucky Owen, Paul Stern, and John Loyd to talk about park issues and plan a meeting between the park leaders and King. Buzz was anxious to talk to King in hopes he would vet possible appointees to IF&W and the Maine Forest Service about their responsibilities as Baxter trustees. It was the first time park representatives had ever initiated such a determined effort to have the governor recognize the importance of those appointments to the park. The meeting, however, never happened. King says he didn't talk to his appointees because he knew the Authority was an independent agency, and he thought he should not interfere.

But King was high on Percival Baxter and Baxter Park, even though he had never visited the park. He had included the park in a film shown at his inaugural address. In it, King called Baxter Park "one of the greatest acts of generosity in the history of the United States." He ordered Percival Baxter's portrait to be hung in the cabinet room at the head of the conference table, and enjoyed telling visiting school children about Baxter and Katahdin. King was thrilled for Buzz to take him and his young kids on a park tour.

Buzz drove the Kings to some of his favorite spots, and they talked about regional economic problems. King pointed out that the Millinocket area needed a replacement for the wood economy, and the park was part of the solution. He was interested in how the park could accommodate more visitors—a line of conversation that irritated Buzz.

Buzz educated King on the point that Percival Baxter didn't want any more campgrounds and the fact that day use was already out of control. King tried another proposal—giving free access to the park for Mainers—also not knowing that they already had it. By the time King left, Buzz doubted if the governor was a real friend of the park.

King was in office for eight years and didn't return to the park.

▲ ▲ ▲ ▲ ▲

October 18 found Buzz and Jan in Philadelphia to attend the annual meeting of Katahdin Medical and Philosophical Society (KMPS). The organization, founded by surgeons from a Philly hospital, had started going to Baxter in 1957, and the trip became a tradition that resulted in forming KMPS.

Buzz had met the doctors in his first season at Russell Pond in the fall of 1960. His first days in the backcountry were very busy, but during a downpour, he was taking care of paperwork in his cabin when the doctors arrived for their four-night stay in the old bunkhouse. On that trip were Drs. Roger Fox, Ralph DeOrsay, Ernie Jordan, Hunter Neal, and Dick Mintz.

Just before leaving the office to settle in for the night, Dr. Fox pulled what Buzz referred to as the "Columbo technique," turning and saying to Buzz, "Oh, by the way, can we take our lantern now?" and pointing to a shiny new Coleman single-mantle lantern in the corner of the room. Buzz didn't know whether Fox was kidding, and Fox went on to tell him that they had brought the lantern up on their previous trip so they would have light during their stay, instead of the old kerosene lamps. Ralph Dolly had just "stored" it for them, Fox said.

Buzz had just filled the lantern with white gas, installed a new mantle, pumped and primed it. Impressed that they were doctors and "men of their word," Buzz gave them the lantern, and they dutifully returned it to him empty prior to their smiling departure. A couple of weeks later, Buzz mentioned the lantern incident to Helon Taylor, asking if the park could afford to buy its own lantern for the camp. Taylor informed Buzz that he had bought such a lantern the previous winter and carried it to Russell Pond on a snowshoe trip. "I'm afraid they pulled a fast one on you," he told Buzz.

The doctors enjoyed Buzz so much they made him an honorary member of KMPS and invited him to Philadelphia every year to join them at their annual banquet. Although he didn't make it until 1996, some of his old campers (Roger Fox and Hunter Neal) were still around and overjoyed to see him.

The gathering was a black tie and tuxedo event for the doctors, and Buzz was in uniform (never having worn a tux up to now). It was a special event that helped Buzz realize how deep peoples' love for the park was and how far-reaching Governor Baxter's impact was.

▲ ▲ ▲ ▲ ▲

Bill Irwin returned to the park to climb Katahdin with a new guide dog, Brownie, and suddenly he was in the middle of controversy. Hikers on the Hunt Trail saw that Brownie's feet were bloody and complained to rangers, asking why the park would allow such mistreatment. Buzz heard it from Eric Hendrickson, who had a group of students from Presque Isle on the summit. Hendrickson saw Irwin and Brownie at Baxter Peak, and complained that "the dog's feet were badly cut. . . . The more we traveled the more depressing the vision of what the dog must be going through became." He said Irwin's pushing the dog onward was "wrong. Plain and simple. Dogs have no place on the mountain and if they were allowed, they should be treated as working people, and people would never be treated in this fashion," he wrote.

Irwin and his party stopped by Buzz's house in East Corinth the day after the climb, and Buzz remembers that Irwin's knees were skinned up from scrambling over the granite, and Brownie's pads were in bad shape but not bleeding. Irwin told Buzz that the blood was from Brownie's toenails, not from the dog's pads. Orient's toenails also had bled on the trail, Irwin explained. Buzz accepted Irwin's belief that he was a responsible dog handler and took seriously his commitment to his dog's welfare.

The matter went before the Authority at their fall meeting, and Buzz advocated for Irwin. Consequently, the trustees declined to interfere with a blind person's judgment about using animals, which would have necessitated their defining animal abuse. The state's Animal Welfare Unit looked into the hikers' complaints and concluded that nothing inappropriate had happened.

---

Primary Document Sources: BSPA Original Minutes 2; BSPA Minutes Box 1 (2112-0717); BSP Annual Reports, 1981-1994; Lester Kenway Files.

Conversations and communications: Buzz Caverly, Chris Drew, J. T. Horn, Lester Kenway, John Loyd, Angus King, Bucky Owen, Nik Rogers.

▲▲▲▲▲▲▲▲

CHAPTER 27

# The West Branch: A Bitter Pill

In early 1997 Buzz was looking forward to the celebration of another important land acquisition which he had been working toward for a long time: the so-called West Branch lands on the West Branch of the Penobscot River.

Buzz had been talking to officials at Bowater Company and previous landowners for years about trading a ten-acre parcel of Great Northern Paper land on Abol Hill for an equal tract of park land on the other side of the West Branch bordering GNP ownership. The reason was that a quarter-mile of the Tote Road on Abol Hill ran onto Great Northern land. His goal was to secure that little sliver of ground for the park. "It makes so much practical and common sense," he wrote in the 1991 annual report. "I will continue my endeavors to persuade people who might assist me in accomplishing this."

When Chuck Gadzik became a trustee, Buzz and Bucky Owen pressed him to use his influence in the industry to facilitate a trade with the park. Gadzik had a bigger vision—one that would extend the park's southwestern corner boundary down to the West Branch and take in 2,669 acres of T2R9.

Gadzik and Bowater's woodlands manager, Marcia McKeague, discussed a deal, and negotiations began. Bowater was ready to let the property go for a reasonable price based on the timber value. The recreational/development values of the property had not really surfaced in areas such as Abol. Thus, negotiations were minimal, and the result was a $490,000 agreement ($184 an acre), with the funds coming from the park's land-acquisition account.

Park leaders and staff representatives, environmentalists, and reporters gathered with Governor Angus King in his cabinet conference room on April 7, 1997, to sign the deed transfer. Buzz told reporters that when he walked by Baxter's bust in the rotunda, "He winked at me. It's a great day."

*Buzz Caverly, Lost Pond Trail, 1997*
JEAN HOEKWATER PHOTO, BAXTER STATE PARK PHOTO ARCHIVES

King observed that the West Branch land was "not just any [river] frontage. It's a spectacular and very special piece of property—a logical extension of Governor Baxter's vision." The triangular-shaped property included five miles of frontage on the West Branch, one of Maine's most valued rivers for whitewater rafting, paddling, and fishing, and four miles of the AT. Much of the land had been burned over in the 1977 fire that spread into the park, and it had produced a new cover of hardwoods.

How the land would be managed by the park was not mentioned in the sales agreement. However, Bucky Owen, who was a negotiator of the West Branch deal for the park, maintained that during discussions there was a "verbal request" by company representatives that there be consideration of continuing hunting and trapping on the parcel. "There were no strings attached," said Owen. "There was some concern [on Great Northern's part] about not wanting to alienate people up there."

Owen thought it was a "foregone conclusion" that traditional uses would continue, whereas Buzz assumed the land would be designated part of the wildlife sanctuary with no hunting, trapping, or motorized access.

The ink on the deed was barely dry when the Fin and Feather Club began pushing the "traditional uses" issue—hunting, trapping, vehicle access, snowmobiling, and canoe storage. They were adamant that such uses must be preserved or the park would have a bruising fight on its hands. Buzz informed the group that a special park committee would study the issues and make a recommendation.

The West Branch Lands Committee spent several months taking inventory of the property and holding workshops in four areas of the state to seek public opinion on potential uses. The more discussion there was, the more heated the debate became, with charges and threats from SAM's executive director George Smith.

Smith had begun working for the Sportsmen's Alliance of Maine in 1993, and his interest in park issues increased the longer he owned his Camp Phoenix property. Not only was the park in his backyard, but Bucky Owen was one of his neighbors. Smith had supported Owen's position in the pine marten research fight.

SAM hadn't ever been involved in park issues, but this time the Fin and Feather Club "borrowed" Smith's influential organization to help them battle Buzz and the Authority. The coalition was potent and represented a new strategy for local sportsmen to augment their influence with the Authority, especially the trustee from the state fish and wildlife department.

SAM elevated the controversy by portraying the preservation of traditional uses on the West Branch parcel as critical to the future of sportsmen all over Maine. Traditional uses had been retained on the previous Togue Pond acquisition, Smith noted, and he asserted that the decision set a precedent for future park additions. The effect of not following the Togue Pond designation would be to "ban" sportsmen on the West Branch—a theme Smith would use again when management of the bitterly fought Katahdin Lake lands came up in 2006.

The West Branch management issues dominated Buzz's emotional and administrative energy. It was the biggest fight since the Kidney Pond conversion in the late 1980s and an important test of Buzz's influence with a different Authority.

With the sportsmen pushing the Authority one way, environmental and trail groups pushed in the other direction, toward sanctuary status. Yet the sanctuary supporters' efforts fell far short of the publicity and passion the sportsmen put into their campaign.

Upping the ante, SAM presented an ultimatum to the Authority at the public meetings on the West Branch uses. If the trustees banned vehicle access, and hunting and trapping, SAM would oppose the purchase of any more public conservation purchases by the state's highly touted Land for Maine's Future Program, Smith threatened. Fin and Feather Club spokesman Ray Campbell affirmed they were behind SAM on that score, too. Environmentalists were outraged and urged the park not to fall victim to intimidation.

The last public meeting, on October 16 in Millinocket, was one of the ugliest public demonstrations ever involving park leaders. Adding to the tensions was an announcement by the West Branch Lands Committee at the outset of the three-and-a-half-hour meeting that it favored sanctuary status for the lands, with an exception to allow the administrative use of snowsleds and to permit camp owners to supply their facilities. Also made public was a survey of park staff reporting that twenty of the twenty-nine park staff members sided with a ban on hunting, and seventeen of eighteen favored no motor vehicles on the lands. The full Advisory was not ready to make its recommendation until Lee Perry came on board in November in the footsteps of Bucky Owen.

About a hundred people crowded the park headquarters conference room for the session chaired by Chuck Gadzik. Trustee Andrew Ketterer also was present. Gadzik had taken time to research the history of Percival Baxter's land purchases and spent time talking with Baxterphile Herb Adams, a Portland legislator. The conversations with Adams convinced Gadzik that Percival Baxter "was not a strident idealist—that his conservation values were simple and evolving and not deeply researched. I found these views at odds with some of the characterizations put forward by others who felt they could speak for Percival Baxter," Gadzik recalls, "and I became more skeptical."

Once the Millinocket session was underway, accusations flew from local traditional-use advocates against park leaders, staff, and environmentalists. The oddest one was from local resident Keith Beaupain, who suggested that the Authority or staff was taking money from out-of-state visitor fees and burying it for their own use. That charge provoked Ketterer to jump to his feet to take on Beaupain. After yelling at each other, Ketterer told Beaupain, "control yourself."

Ketterer then said calmly, "If people here think the way to convince the Authority is to malign [us], they have made a mistake." And, directly addressing Beaupain at the podium, Ketterer said, "In my mind, you have made a serious error in judgment. Name-calling does not have a place in this meeting." Beaupain apologized and then used his testimony time to protest park management decisions as far back as the closing of the West Gate in 1990.

Other locals voiced hostility toward outsiders. Jimmy Busque, vice president of the Fin and Feather Club, told the trustees that the park shouldn't accept statements from RESTORE: The North Woods because "it's an environmental terrorist organization from Massachusetts bent on destroying our American heritage of hunting and trapping. They should have no say on how we manage our state park."

Ray Campbell challenged the idea that Percival Baxter would not want motorized access and hunting and trapping. "That park was founded for the people of Maine," he declared. "It wasn't given to the AMC or someone from New Jersey. The people of Maine should come first, not the AMC." Stu Kallgren of the Maine Leaseholders Association alleged that the park wanted to squeeze out West Branch leaseholders Tony York and Pete McPheeters and give the park "to southern Mainers and out-of-staters."

Cathy Johnson of NRCM urged the trustees to "fold the [West Branch lands usage] into the grand scheme" of the park by giving it sanctuary designation. She countered the idea that the park was for Millinocket area residents. The park "was given to us all," she pointed out.

Buzz was the last to speak, and he began his appeal by declaring that Governor Baxter's "thrust in creating the park was to fulfill the primary objective of 'forever wild' and that he firmly believed in nature at peace."

As a matter of balancing different interests, he reminded the Authority that they had most recently favored traditional uses over sanctuary designation on the Togue Pond lands purchased in 1993. In fairness and respect for Governor Baxter, Buzz said the West Branch lands should be managed as a sanctuary. "The pressures for special interest use of these lands are great," he said, "but I recommend a conservative plan for its use. I sincerely believe that this recommendation is in keeping with Governor Baxter's intended use of additional lands purchased with land acquisition account money. He once said, 'It is for those who love nature and are willing to walk.' Otherwise I submit that if past uses of the acquired land become current and future practice, what was accomplished by spending one half million dollars of trust fund monies?"

Bucky Owen thought that Buzz had spoken basically as a citizen and thus his statement was "totally inappropriate." He also believed that Buzz was privy to Great Northern's request to allow traditional uses and had chosen to ignore it.

In early December, the Advisory Committee unanimously joined the sanctuary designation advocates, as did the Baxter family. Park counsel Paul Stern went on the offensive with a ten-page memo addressing issues raised during the months of "vociferous arguments," and coming down on the side of sanctuary.

Stern observed that Percival Baxter allowed hunting and fishing in limited portions of the park only when it was unavoidable. "The [wildlife] sanctuary restrictions were generally the rule," he wrote, "with hunting being allowed only where it was necessary to purchase specific additional land; hunting lines were confused and hunting prohibitions would adversely affect the livelihood of local guides, or when it was specifically part of the SFMA or was necessary to purchase the parcel itself." Stern pointed out that none of those situations applied to the West Branch tract, and reminded the trustees that Bowater "did not make as a condition of sale the continuation of hunting or any other particular activities."

As anticipation grew over what the Authority would do, Lee Perry joined the fray. All eyes were on him as the deciding vote. Upon arrival in Maine, Perry had spent a day in the park with Buzz and Jensen Bissell to get their perspectives and see the West Branch lands for himself. He also was lobbied by SAM, the Fin and Feather Club, and other proponents of traditional uses.

Of all Authority trustees, the fish and wildlife commissioner was the one with the most active constituency. It was clear the commissioner's first and foremost job as a park trustee was to put his day job aside and work only in the interest of Baxter Park. Lee Perry, however, believed his priority was to represent the interests of Maine sportsmen. Much later, a member of the Advisory Committee recalled a conversation with Perry in which Perry told him that he was going to wear his IF&W "hat" on the Authority, not the park's. Perry said he didn't remember making such a statement. However at a subsequent Authority meeting Buzz reacted to the "hat" story by giving out park hats to the trustees and telling them that he hoped they would only represent the park—not agency constituents—when dealing with park issues.

The Authority gathered on January 15, 1998, in Augusta for a decision before an uneasy audience. In an eleventh-hour move, Buzz tried to have the matter postponed to give the Authority some breathing room for further rumination on the issues at stake. But the trustees were in no mood to wait.

Chuck Gadzik stated his reasons for supporting traditional uses of the West Branch lands. He based his position on past evidence that Percival Baxter was a practical man who had shown tolerance and sympathy for local residents' impassioned feelings about traditional uses. Andrew Ketterer responded, "In part, what you're saying is that Baxter would not want to antagonize this number of people." Ketterer said he couldn't dismiss the position of "those who know more than I do"— referring to the park staff and Advisory Committee, and also acknowledged that he was influenced by the Baxter family's position and Paul Stern's legal interpretation.

Lee Perry was the man of the hour, but he didn't say much except to cast his vote with Gadzik in favor of keeping the West Branch tract out of the sanctuary zone. He explained his vote as in keeping with the precedent that Percival Baxter set when deviating from his "personal feelings" at times to benefit local people.

The Authority separated the votes on hunting and trapping and motorized access. On the question of hunting and trapping, Gadzik was a yes vote and Ketterer a no. Perry's tie-breaking vote was yes, too. The motorized access decision was more complicated.

All three trustees voted to allow motorized access to continue with a big caveat—as long as the existing Abol Road and Abol Stream bridge were safe. The trustees further agreed not to spend park money to repair the deteriorating road and bridge—a decision that pleased Buzz. How long the road and bridge would be usable was unclear, although locals speculated it could be years. The road had been built originally by Great Northern Paper during the 1977 fire. But it hadn't been maintained, and even if the parcel wasn't sold, the company had no intention of spending money on improvements in the future—a position that assured the eventual demise of vehicle access.. The Abol Bridge was already shaky because it hadn't been repaired either. Another bridge over Katahdin Stream, about a quarter mile beyond Abol Bridge, had washed out, and park officials had recently blocked access because it was unsafe.

After the vote and the meeting ended, Lee Perry approached Buzz and extended his hand, saying, "I think you're doing a wonderful job, and I want you to keep up the good work." Buzz lashed out at Perry, accusing him of making "a terrible decision. This is a terrible day for Baxter Park," Buzz told the new trustee. "You've made a big mistake, and you have to know it." Buzz went on to say "some other things I probably never should have." Perry, he remembers, "just got a little smile on his face, which was a very diplomatic way of dealing with me. He didn't get harsh. He basically made it clear that he did what he felt he should do."

Buzz told one reporter that the vote was political and a slap in the face to the park staff who had dedicated their lives to managing the preserve. John Loyd, vice chairman of the Advisory Committee, called the vote evidence that the Authority had broken with the past tradition of deferring to park staff on difficult issues. "Not only did two of the three members ignore the people who know best [but] in my mind, they ignored the overriding control each Authority needs to work with— that of self-control."

Sporting groups were elated with the hunting and trapping vote and disappointed at the vehicle access decision. However, George Smith called the trustees' actions "nearly a complete victory for sportsmen."

In the following days, Buzz and Perry's relationship worsened. Buzz blew up with the commissioner during a telephone conversation, and he was called to Augusta for an oral reprimand by the Authority. Around the same time, Buzz received an unsettling e-mail by mistake between Gadzik and Bucky Owen.

Owen praised Gadzik for doing "the right thing." Buzz's statement in the *Bangor Daily News* about the vote being a mistake "was totally out of line," Owen wrote. "[Buzz] is appearing more and more as 'the' person who knows what is right and who should be making the final decision." Gadzik responded that "it was heartburn enough for me, but the complications for Lee were much worse. I worry about Buzz, too, not sure what to do about it."

Gadzik felt that the West Branch issue had revealed how impatient Buzz had become with the Authority and an unwillingness to deal with the complexities inherent in major disagreements. Despite Gadzik's and Owen's extensive relationship with the park, Buzz viewed them as short-term political appointees with limited knowledge and interest in the park, according to Gadzik, "and it did cause some stress. On good days, I was sympathetic to Buzz's passion," he reflects. "On bad days, I was very cautious to find broader counsel."

Jym St. Pierre of RESTORE let Buzz know he shared Buzz's disappointment over the West Branch outcome. "While the Authority has not always decided issues to my liking, in the past I felt that at least they made their decisions based on carefully considered logic," he wrote. "In this case, it is clear that a majority of the Authority abandoned logic and bent to the demands of a noisy mob."

St. Pierre feared for the "horrific precedent set by the decision. If accommodating clamorous local interests over the statewide public interest is to become standard practice, what limits are there on future local demands to further violate the clear intent of Governor Baxter to maintain the park foremost as a wildlife sanctuary?" Other conservationists questioned the acquisition of new lands with limited park funds if only to make them just like other multiple use private and state lands.

Buzz was critical of environmental organizations after the votes. If they had mounted a vigorous campaign in favor of sanctuary designation, the outcome might have been different. He appreciated the confidence that environmentalists had in him to guide park affairs in the direction of greater wilderness protection, but he said he couldn't be left out on a limb almost by himself defending the wilderness-first perspective. It made him look like a radical and weakened his credibility in general.

The Authority set its own precedent in the West Branch lands issue. Never before had an Authority explicitly disregarded the full array of park experts and insiders. Never before had an Authority so clearly ignored broad public opinion. Never before had the Authority evidenced so little public accountability.

Chuck Gadzik sounded the alarm when he stated that he and Perry were looking anew at park issues—and that "fresh eyes can leave behind the baggage of the park from people who have been there a long time."

The Authority was attacked and praised in Maine newspapers and editorial columns. Those who disagreed with the votes concluded that the trustees had betrayed Percival Baxter's trust, while those on the other side felt that the trustees had made the right choice and that Lee Perry was a hero.

Perry wrote a note for the case files in defense of his vote. "I would like the minutes to reflect my statements that I had reviewed the Deeds of Trust, various plans provided to me by the Baxter Park staff, and minutes of previous meetings regarding this issue," he wrote. "I had also received letters and calls, a tape recording from Dave Priest, and Neil Rolde's book [on the Baxter family]. Upon review of the materials provided, I [concluded] that Governor Baxter would have made the same decision as we did under the circumstances."

▲ ▲ ▲ ▲ ▲

Anyone who knew Buzz well could guess that there would be another chapter in the West Branch case to right what he felt was wrong. Like a skillful parliamentarian, he knew how to change outcomes with a deft hand. The ticket was to convince the Authority that the Abol Bridge was so unsafe that it needed to be taken out within months, not years, thus stopping vehicle access.

The Authority had instructed Buzz to evaluate the Abol crossing and report back after ice-out in the spring. He set about making sure that the West Branch lands planning committee would recommend removing the Abol Stream culverts. Then Buzz led a site visit for the Authority and the Advisory Committee, pointing to safety and erosion problems and informing them that it would take capital to fix them. He had evidence of ATV and four-wheeler damage to the road, remains of illegal fires and litter, and emphasized that the park now had an uncontrolled access point. Buzz wanted the culverts pulled immediately. The trustees were not oblivious to the cleverness and import of Buzz's tactics.

At their May 8, 1997, meeting, Chuck Gadzik acknowledged that uncontrolled access was "a major concern and beg[ged] a revisit of [the January 13] decision." Perry agreed the park should have complete control of access, and he accepted that there were problems with the crossing and the roads. However, he thought it was premature to jump in and pull the culverts before a plan for the new lands was done. Drew Ketterer sided with Buzz.

Gadzik chided Buzz for putting the trustees in a corner, and Buzz called the assertion unfair. "You gave me . . . instructions, and I carried out those instructions," he said. Buzz complained that he had tried to communicate many times with Gadzik about the problems but received no response.

The question arose as to whether the Authority would reprimand Buzz in connection with the January 13, 1998, meeting. Gadzik said there was no intention to do that. "What Lee is saying as the newest member is that it's [hard] to walk into the absolute because all the issues haven't been sorted through. What we're looking for is a little more background, documentation. We need a broader description of your concerns."

Buzz reiterated that "the bridge is falling in. We need to fix it or get it out. Those are the options I see . . . it's time to take culverts out and move on to the long-term objectives." Ketterer complimented Buzz for doing "a great job . . . and you accurately understood what we wanted and did it. I think there are tough decisions. We're seeing the consequences of uncontrolled access. It's hard to manage the resource if we can't control the human element."

Gadzik said that respect for traditional uses was missing from the discussion. Perry wanted to see all the issues in context before they pulled the linchpin, and said, "I'm prepared to support [Ketterer's] position, but I don't feel good."

By the end of the meeting, the trustees capitulated and voted to stop motorized access, giving Buzz the victory he wanted. The Fin and Feather Club retaliated by informing Buzz that they would no longer participate in his annual public communications meetings and would deal directly with the Authority because they didn't trust him anymore. In a letter to the trustees, the club said that Buzz "deceives and manipulates the issues, and the people who take a sincere role and have a legitimate stake in how this park is administered, our public relations in dealing with Caverly are permanently damaged."

When Chuck Gadzik wrote Buzz's next annual evaluation in 1989, he commented on the collision of "alternative philosophies" around park issues and observed that "Buzz works hard to manage all of that constructively." Gadzik then offered his opinion that Buzz "occasionally forgets that other individuals, including the Authority members, can have different views yet the same dedication to the park." For the remainder of Buzz's tenure, all succeeding chairmen would comment on Buzz's difficulties keeping his objectivity, especially when his point of view was subjected to severe criticism.

▲ ▲ ▲ ▲ ▲

Kidney Pond Camps, West Gate, the West Branch lands debates, and other issues had stirred up people to such a pitched level that Buzz's opponents called for his retirement and threatened him physically. In an unprecedented move, he wrote a five-page perspective of his views on nine issues, from Kidney Pond Camps to his tenure, for the record and included it in his 1995 annual report.

On the subject of retirement, Buzz said he had "no desire to retire, for going to work today, I have the same enthusiasm for the challenges of the job that I experienced in my younger years." No matter who the director was, he or she had to be able to consider all matters, both controversial and non-controversial, and ask "is approval of a request necessary and in the best interest of Baxter State Park?"

As the result of upheaval over park matters, he said, "It has been suggested that my tenure . . . should expire. Beyond that, I was personally threatened on two occasions, and in addition, received an anonymous letter at my home post office box sixty-seven miles from Millinocket in an attempt to intimidate me physically, mentally, and professionally," he said. "Evidently some people have not learned that one can disagree without being disagreeable. Keep smiling!"

Bob Mott, manager of the Millinocket airport and a longtime friend, paid a visit to Buzz at the park office and urged Buzz to retire before he was driven off the road by an angry local. "Bob was so sincere," recalls Buzz. "He was honestly afraid someone would do harm to me. But I told him I was just not ready to retire."

Buzz's success in ending motorized access was important to him as keeping faith with Governor Baxter. He ultimately paid a big price in his relationship with Owen and Gadzik, and things would get harder between them in the days ahead.

▲ ▲ ▲ ▲ ▲

Buzz and George Smith's relationship was strained more, too, after the West Branch fight. As a neighbor of the park for five years, George Smith had come to the conclusion that Buzz's management goal was "inaccessible wilderness." However, Smith had to admit that restricted-access policies benefited him personally.

When Smith had first bought into the Camp Phoenix development, he could go from his back door in Mt. Vernon and arrive at his Phoenix cabin in three hours by traveling through the West Gate. When the West Gate closed, the trip took four hours because he had to drive the circuitous, long road north to the camp from Togue Pond— at no more than twenty miles per hour. "It was a terrible, terrible situation, and I was very upset that he closed West Gate," recalls Smith.

However, Smith began to notice the reduction in traffic in the north end. "My family could hike that [Tote Road] for hours and not see a vehicle," he remembers. To break up the travel time from home to camp, Smith's family started having a picnic and a hike along the way, relaxing more. "We liked it," he says. "It was a personal benefit."

Buzz's aggressive building removal initially angered Smith, too. After taking a camp out of McCarty Field and putting in lean-tos, the park gated the access road, and Smith had to walk in to fish Trout Brook. But the fishing improved so much that Smith again found himself supporting Buzz's action.

For every Buzz action that benefited Smith, there were two or more (usually access-related) that aggravated him. Buzz closed off the old Dwelley Road to bicycles, where Smith had ridden, hiked, and bird-watched. Smith thought that was an unnecessary restriction. When the Telos gate was eliminated, Buzz had a bulldozer create a vehicle barrier. It was so formidable that Smith couldn't ride his bicycle down the road to Thissell Pond anymore and had to bushwhack through swampy land to have a picnic there.

When the Wassataquoik Lake Trail was relocated to Center Mountain, it was twice as far to the lake and not a trail for children or older people, in Smith's opinion. On the old trail, there had been an open wetland and a beaver pond, and the Smith family had picnicked and fished there. The Camp Phoenix owners kept the old trail open for awhile in order to drive a ways in, but Buzz ordered them to stop. The road was soon impassable for vehicles. The Phoenix owners decided to have their own way with access up Strickland Mountain in back of the camps. They thinned the brush, flagged a trail to the top, and enjoy it as their own private mountain to this day.

Despite his differences with Buzz, Smith praised the park for cooperating with Phoenix owners to make it possible for them to have vehicle access to the camps and to carry out maintenance projects. Likewise, Buzz was glad to have owners at the facility who were interested in the park and mostly supportive of its mission.

▲ ▲ ▲ ▲ ▲

Since Buzz had been director, he had traveled farther and farther away from Maine for meetings and speaking engagements—to other New England states and down the East Coast, for visits with environmentalists and AT trail officials and gatherings with governmental agency officials. He traveled to the West of his cowboy heroes for the first time in the late 1990s.

The trip that meant the most was the 1997 venture to Montana, where he joined other wilderness managers at the Arthur Carhart National Wilderness Training Center in Huson, and then traveled with them on a three-day trip to the Bob Marshall Wilderness. Not only was it Buzz's first horse-pack trip, but it also was his inaugural camp-out at 6,000 feet and hike up to 7,000 feet. He was impressed with the "time out" for solitude the trips leaders insisted on to emphasize that particular wilderness value. He enjoyed the campfire chats with other wilderness managers at night, listening to them talk about challenges they faced in their respective parks and preserves.

Buzz recalls that he was "probably a real pain. I told them 'This is all great, but you should see our mountain in Maine.' I hammered on about Baxter Park all the time." Near the end of the meeting, the keynote speaker couldn't make it, and the participants voted on who among them would give the concluding talk. They picked Buzz. "Maybe they were a lot smarter than me, a lot more intellectual, but I planted a seed about what this little park in Maine was all about," he says. "I told them about Percival Baxter and my experiences and related many stories. I poured it on—without notes."

In 2000 he traveled to Golden, Colorado, to participate as a moderator at the National Mountain Conference, and he made a day trip into the Rockies.

*Buzz Caverly on a horse pack trip in the Bob Marshall Wilderness,*
*Montana, 1997*
BAXTER STATE PARK PHOTO ARCHIVES

Some might have expected Buzz could learn a lot from association with other wilderness leaders that might influence management at Baxter Park. He picked up some ideas to try—the use of firepans at remote backcountry sites and limiting motorized equipment in the park's sanctuary zone. Yet Buzz didn't see a need to change his management plan or goals for Baxter Park based on newer wilderness concepts. Baxter Park was one of a kind, and, as he always said, Governor Baxter's wishes were the driving force, not some outsider's.

Greg Kroll was the National Park Service representative at the Carhart Center in Montana when Buzz visited and was very impressed with the autonomy Buzz had in operating Baxter Park. "To me, Baxter Park was a fiefdom for Buzz," Kroll recalls. "His management style reminded me of Yellowstone in 1920. I thought it was great for Buzz." Buzz had told the story of using a pin in a gate to permit fishermen to get in and out of the park outside the normal hours. "I thought that kind of trust was such a luxury," says Kroll. "It was unbelievable to me they could still do that [in the late 1990s]."

▲ ▲ ▲ ▲ ▲

A milestone in Buzz's and Jan's careers occurred on January 31, 1998, when she retired as reservations supervisor. Jan had been on the park payroll for twenty-seven years and had served as a volunteer for nine years previously. She was ready for the full-time job of wife, mother, and grandmother, and she began traveling with Buzz virtually every time he was on the road.

Jan had always preferred a low profile, but Buzz wrote a public tribute to her that appeared in the *Katahdin Times*. Hailing her assistance to thousands of people in arranging for their vacations in the park, he also noted her important role in supporting search-and-rescue and evacuation efforts. Through the years, Jan was dutifully on call at all hours of the night when Buzz called to alert her he was on his way home with people who were cold, hungry, and needed shelter. "Whether it was a fully turkey dinner or hot apple pie, it was always ready when we arrived," Buzz wrote.

On March 31, 1998, Buzz celebrated his sixtieth birthday, and, with Jan now retired, he was hoping for less stress in their lives. However, the Caverly family was rocked by Tim Caverly's state park career coming to an abrupt and controversial end.

Tim was in his eighteenth year as manager of the Allagash Wilderness Waterway (AWW) and had been having his share of difficulties with supervisors and employees. In 1996, three female waterway staff went to Maine Bureau of Public Lands director Tom Morrison with allegations of sex discrimination. The charges, which Tim denied, didn't become public until 1998, when Kim Allen (the only full-time woman ranger in the Allagash) filed a complaint with the Maine Human Rights Commission.

That case was pending when, in April 1998, Tim spoke out strongly in favor of wilderness values during a public hearing on the proposed new Allagash management plan. His statement surprised his superiors and drew an official reprimand from Morrison. Over the next seventeen months, it became obvious that the agency was intent on forcing Tim out. He received eight reprimands and lost control of his staff, which began to take directives from the Bangor regional office. In June 1999 Tim was ordered to meet Morrison at Chamberlain Bridge, where he was handed a letter from conservation commissioner Ron Lovaglio telling Tim that he was terminated.

Tim contended that he was fired because he took a stand for greater protection of the Allagash waterway's remote character—effectively a statement in opposition to the bureau's position favoring increased motorized access. Morrison, however, asserted that Tim was fired for insubordination and failure to follow orders.

The Washington-based Public Employees for Environmental Responsibility (PEER) took up Tim's cause. Executive Director Jeff Ruch viewed Tim's situation as a classic case of bureaucratic harassment of an employee advocating for wilderness values that were "out of favor in some political circles." Tim filed a grievance with the state employee's union and won a settlement. He opened a Maine office for PEER and continued to live in Millinocket. He heard chatter in the local coffee shops to the effect "now we've gotten rid of one Caverly, we've got one more to go."

▲ ▲ ▲ ▲ ▲

As Buzz had provided personal assistance to AT thru-hiker Bill Irwin, he reached out to help Earl Shaffer when the seventy-nine-year-old trail legend made his third and last journey. It was a huge undertaking for Shaffer, and Buzz wanted to make sure he reached his goal.

Known as "The Crazy One," Shaffer had made the first documented thru-hike of the AT in 1948 in 124 days when he was twenty-nine years old. His second completion was accomplished in 1965 in ninety-nine days when he was forty-six, and Shaffer set a new milestone by starting out from Katahdin and hiking south. Buzz was the ranger at Katahdin Stream Campground at the time. But he didn't see Shaffer coming or going.

Shaffer's third thru-hike, in 1998, was a fiftieth-anniversary commemoration of his original hike. Always vigilant about the safety of late-season AT hikers, Buzz followed Shaffer's progress via telephone as Shaffer neared the park. As he had with Irwin, Buzz asked Shaffer if he would flip-flop and climb Katahdin early so he wouldn't be stopped by bad weather or the park's weather rules from reaching the summit. Shaffer reluctantly agreed to do so—no one could deny Buzz—and climbed the mountain on October 7, just days before his eightieth birthday.

Afterward, Buzz put Shaffer up in the administration camp at Togue Pond, and there were celebratory events at park headquarters and in Millinocket. Shaffer, a trail poet and author, died of cancer two and a half years after his much-publicized final thru-hike.

---

Primary Document Sources: BSPA Box 2 (2112-0718); BSP Annual Report, 1997; Austin Files.

Conversations with Buzz Caverly, Bucky Owen, Chuck Gadzik, Lee Perry, Andrew Ketterer, Cathy Johnson, George Smith, Darrell Morrell, Ray Campbell, Jym St. Pierre, John Neff, Paul Stern, Greg Kroll, Tim Caverly.

PART V: IRREVOCABLE PATHS

▲▲▲▲▲▲▲▲

CHAPTER 28

# COMPROMISES AND CONFLICTS

THE PENOBSCOT INDIAN NATION'S spiritual run to Baxter Park had grown tremendously since the early 1980s, and Buzz had allowed Katahdin Stream Campground to be used exclusively by the participants during the Labor Day weekend.

While nervous about the precedent and the tribe's desire for more concessions from the park, Buzz respected the run's mission and had worked cooperatively with tribal leaders. He approved reducing the camping rate for their use and allowed them to make advance reservations prior to the New Year's reservation opening for the general public.

It was the tribe's responsibility to keep track of the number of people who stayed in the park overnight, but they had fallen behind in reporting those numbers and in paying their bills.

In late 1998, tribal leaders asked the park for free camping, and to find a special site of their own. Buzz and the park use subcommittee began meeting with the Penobscots to see how to deal with the situation. Tribal spokesmen Barry Dana and Reuben "Butch" Phillips thought the tribe shouldn't have to pay camping fees for exercising their religious beliefs. They could afford to pay, so money wasn't the issue. Buzz opposed waiving the fees, saying the money was important to help maintain the campground. Tribal leaders had actually thought the park had already been exempting their fees until they discovered the Penobscot Health Center had been paying the bills—a special camping rate—from the park.

Finding a special site for a large group was a more difficult matter. There were now about 150 people participating in the run via canoe, bike, and foot—three times the capacity of Katahdin Stream Campground—and the Penobscots indicated they were interested in members of other tribes participating. The Authority had already stopped the Boy Scouts' High Adventure Program from having exclusive use of some sites on Matagamon and Webster Lakes on the grounds that it was inconsistent with the Deeds of Trust.

Buzz recognized the importance of doing all he could to help the tribe, but he explained to the Penobscots how the deeds restricted him to operating within certain parameters. Governor Baxter had made it clear that he didn't want additional campgrounds. However, Buzz had found "wiggle room" when Authority chairman Glenn Manuel wanted more campsites in the park, so he knew he had some leeway to help the tribe. He thought it might be possible to find an existing area that could be "somewhat improved" and allow the tribe to use it, provided it was not converted into a de facto campground. During the winter, Buzz and park staff drove around the park on snowmobiles to inspect several possible sites, and also made a flight over the area.

The old Ladd logging campsite on Rum Mountain, just below Katahdin, was initially thought to be a potential answer. But to handle the number of Indians involved in the marathon run, a road would have to be rebuilt to handle vehicle traffic, and that meant a big cost and other impacts. Abol Hill became another area of possibility.

The Native American issue became an example of how a politically minded entity like the Authority reacted to lingering, special interest pressures by the late 1990s. They didn't want to make a decision yet, so they tabled it and asked the staff to do more research.

The issue dragged on through the summer with sometimes tense meetings, as potential options evaporated. Governor Baxter's great-grandniece Connie Baxter Marlow entered the discussion. Marlow, a rights advocate for Native Americans, supported Abol Hill for a sacred fire and some tent sites where communion with Katahdin could occur. Socializing could be moved to a campground on private property, she proposed. Butch Phillips objected to separating the spiritual and social aspects of the marathon. The journey was a pilgrimage that involved suffering, "and pain and sacrifice are what take us back to our people who endured the hardships of this land," he told park leaders.

While Marlow and Buzz disagreed on how to settle the issues, he respected her efforts to find a resolution. "She was truly a peacemaker and a peace seeker, and from all my dealings with her I believe she was very, very dedicated to her cause," he recalls.

The Authority settled the fees issue in October 1999 by refusing to waive payment for camping. Park counsel Paul Stern outlined the constitutional and trust issues with the tribe's request to move the spiritual ceremonies to an undeveloped site. "I am unaware of any suggestions that [Governor Baxter] intended that there would be a special location for Indian ceremonies," he reported. Stern pointed to a 1960 letter saying that "no additional roads for automobiles be constructed . . . that no additional camps be erected." Constitutional law prohibited public funds from being used to promote or prohibit religious practices, he noted. At best, from a legal standpoint, Stern said the park could designate a camping site for all groups—religious, political, or secular.

The Authority directed Buzz to look at Lower Togue Pond for a group site, but then in December settled on continued use of Katahdin Stream on Labor Day weekend. Buzz and the trustees were in agreement, and he developed special accommodations guidelines that would apply to all groups equally. As it turned out, there was no competition for the Katahdin Stream site.

▲ ▲ ▲ ▲ ▲

As Buzz had found a way to stop motorized access to the West Branch lands, so did the Fin and Feather Club go looking for a means to upend him and get the decision reversed. They thought they had a "friendly" majority (Gadzik and Perry) on the Authority that would welcome their initiative. The most promising strategy was to employ the Americans with Disabilities Act (ADA).

Percival Baxter never addressed the particular needs of handicapped recreationists. Buzz thought that Baxter expected people would have different physical capacities and would need to tailor their use of the park to their particular limitations rather than demand that the park physically alter its wilderness character for them.

In the late 1990s, parks all over the country were struggling with recent changes in ADA that could potentially force alterations in wilderness areas to accommodate the handicapped and, in so doing, degrade the wilderness character of such parks and preserves.

In February 1998 Fin and Feather stalwart Vern Haines had notified the park that ADA required any entity that employed citizens and/or allowed the public to use its facilities to "make reasonable accommodations for citizens with disabilities." The club wanted some concessions but underscored a promise not to ask for something as outrageous as "an elevator to Katahdin peak." Instead, Haines said the club would settle for the existing roads in the West Branch lands township to be returned to "a safe and usable condition." Implicit in the club's position was that if the park didn't satisfy them, a lawsuit might follow.

In the past, handicapped-access issues were few and far between. The park attracted relatively few disabled visitors. Only one person—a Millinocket resident who wanted to drive past an old gated logging road to Rum Brook to fish—had gone to the Maine Human Rights Commission with a complaint of discrimination. That 1998 case had been dismissed.

In 1999 the Fin and Feather Club tried to get the legislature involved in handicapped-access issues in the park, and Gordon McCauslin, a member of the club, filed a disability rights complaint against the park with the National Park Service (NPS). McCauslin, who had a heart condition, alleged that elimination of vehicle access to the West Branch lands denied handicapped individuals equal opportunity to recreate on that parcel, and it triggered an NPS investigation.

Buzz took the new politics around ADA very seriously. Even before the Fin and Feather Club initiated actions, Buzz had begun improving handicapped access to toilets and other facilities at roadside. The NPS investigation, however, raised the ADA issue to a higher level—the specter of federal intrusion into park management. But while Buzz was willing to compromise to accommodate physically challenged visitors at additional roadside facilities, forget about paving trails or opening them to motorized vehicles.

Special National Park Service investigator Jack Andre visited the park in October 1999 to evaluate the situation. He found the park in violation of ADA with respect to designated parking and outhouse, cabin, and picnic table accessibility—all at roadside. Dianne Spriggs, NPS's equal opportunity program manager, asked Buzz to develop a compliance plan, and he went about it with the intent of working out a mutually agreeable solution.

Buzz was greatly relieved with NPS's findings because the concessions the park had to make did not undermine its integrity or mission. Spriggs concluded that the park could comply with ADA by "meeting accessibility requirements in developed intensive use areas and . . . leaving undeveloped natural areas in [their] primitive environment." Thus, she said there was "no requirement to allow the recently acquired undeveloped parcel of land to be developed or opened to motorized traffic while it remains in the natural preserve area."

Buzz hired Greg Kroll as a consultant to assist with the compliance plan. Kroll had been the NPS representative at the Carhart National

Wilderness Training Center in Montana when the two met in 1997. Buzz and the senior staff took Kroll on a tour of the park to see where handicapped access could be developed, and the trip was a fortuitous venture.

McCauslin had argued that those with disabilities needed to go to Katahdin Stream Falls so they could enjoy water slides. Kroll told Buzz that if there was another place in the park that provided the same opportunity roadside, building a hardened trail to Katahdin Falls could be avoided. Buzz was elated to show Kroll the roadside ledges at Ledge Falls and Kroll determined that these would meet the needs of the handicapped. On the issue of outhouse access, Kroll wanted to make sure disabled visitors could get into the structures year-round. All it took to overcome winter snow problems was changing hinges to make the doors open both in and out.

Some visitors viewed the larger handicapped-accessible toilets as changing the face of the park in a minor way. However others saw them as no more objectionable than the rest of the approximately 100 man-made structures scattered around the park.

▲ ▲ ▲ ▲ ▲

The ADA fight was a boldfaced retaliation against Buzz and the Authority for eliminating road access on the West Branch lands, and a challenge to the park's autonomy. While the NPS investigation was going on, the Fin and Feather Club carried out a second offensive—in the legislature.

Several bills were filed for the Fin and Feather Club by sympathetic lawmakers in hopes of restoring vehicle access to the West Branch, preventing the park from removing or closing any road, bridge, gate, or other structure in the park without lawmakers' prior approval, and intervening in park business in other ways. They were clear challenges to the Authority's legal power, but park leaders couldn't assume that the legislature would see things their way.

The Agriculture, Conservation, and Forestry Committee held hearings on several park-related bills. They weren't overly knowledgeable about the park, but it was a subject that grabbed their interest because of the mystique of Baxter. Buzz was an "enormously persuasive and engaging" spokesman for the park, and Eric Baxter was an eloquent representative of the family, according to house member Linda Rogers

McKee, the committee co-chair at the time. Buzz's appearances always "garnered support for the park," she says. "I honestly believe I saw people stop everything they were doing to listen to him."

Environmental groups—NRCM, Maine Audubon Society, and RESTORE—went to bat on the park's side, opposing the 1999 bills. The threat of legislative intervention evaporated by the end of the session, with all but one bill dying in the ACF committee. Lawmakers, remembers McKee, thought that the park had a mystique to it that they respected and didn't want to undermine.

▲ ▲ ▲ ▲ ▲

The attempts at legislative mischief in the 1990s and concern over the park's future without Buzz one day caused a group of longtime park supporters to form a Friends of Baxter Park organization in 1999. The intent was to create an independent watchdog group devoted solely to park issues and the protection of wilderness values.

Buzz could see the potential benefits of such an organization but wasn't altogether comfortable with it. He wouldn't be able to control the board of directors' agenda, and he was concerned that the Friends might actually work against him on certain issues.

He was right. He and the Friends didn't always see eye to eye, and he was slow to warm up to their involvement in park affairs. After his retirement, however, he would agree to serve as an honorary board member—but only if he could retain an independent voice if he opposed the position the Friends took on Authority actions.

▲ ▲ ▲ ▲ ▲

Although Percival Baxter had set up the park to be separate from the state parks system, the state still had its fingers in park business at the end of the 1990s. Buzz wanted the park to be freer of state connections and interference.

Under his watch, he had led several successful initiatives to get loose. First, he got the park out from under the Bureau of Purchases' control. Then he obtained exemption from the state law allowing concealed weapons to be carried; from having to furlough employees during state budget crunches; from having to pay a percentage of the park's income to the state to make up budget deficits; from the prohibition

against using state vehicles to commute; and from a proposed requirement to reserve 75 percent of campsites for Mainers. The highway
department, however, continued to have its hooks in the park by maintaining park roads.

A milestone was achieved in 1999 when the Authority approved
Buzz's proposal that the park take over control of its own roads. The
issues for Buzz and the trustees were not just park autonomy but the
character of the road system—and cutting ties with DOT would also
remove any possibility that the federal government could interfere
with park management through its funding link with DOT projects.

Buzz started the process of separating the park from DOT in 1998,
but he had had the matter on his to-do list for years. In 1943 the legislature began allocating money to the State Highway Commission for
park roads. The first year, the funding was $2,500, and it gradually
increased to $80,000 by the 1990s. DOT provided a two-person crew for
the summer and early fall to take care of four bridges, the forty-nine
miles of the Tote Road, and several shorter access roads to the campgrounds. Some of Buzz's enduring local critics repeatedly argued during land-use conflicts, saying that as long as the park was using
taxpayers' dollars, recreational uses couldn't be restricted—a claim that
peeved Buzz. With DOT out of the park, that threat of government
intervention and/or citizen suits disappeared.

When Buzz was a ranger, the road surfacing had been done by a
highway dump truck pulling a tow-behind grader. The equipment
was small enough to keep the roads narrow. There were frequent
turnouts to allow safe passage when meeting vehicles. In 1968 a
highway-sized power grader was put into use, and there was incremental widening so that two vehicles could pass each other with room
to spare most of the way.

Buzz felt that the road had lost the "wild forest" character of the
old tote road that was promised on a sign beyond Abol Pond. The sign
warned drivers that the road was narrow and winding, and the speed
limit was twenty miles per hour (except near campgrounds where it
decreases to fifteen miles per hour). The power grader, however,
was creating a more than adequate road system. With the widening,
vehicles speeded up, and there were not enough rangers to patrol for
speedsters.

To bolster his position on getting DOT out of the park, Buzz
referred to an inspection trip by Governor Baxter with then-forest

commissioner Al Nutting in the fall of 1957. Baxter had felt that the state highway crews were cutting too much brush and trees and making the Tote Road too wide. Baxter had come across a couple of men cutting a large birch tree below Abol Field, and it dropped across the road just as the governor's limousine came around the corner. Baxter wrote to highway commissioner David Stevens expressing his upset and opposition to further cutting. He wrote Stevens that the wilderness concept meant that "the roads should not be boulevards, only they should be reasonably safe."

The challenge to the park was paying maintenance costs for 62.5 miles of roads and replacing bridges and culverts without DOT's contribution. The 1999 road maintenance budget was $99,020. Park leaders were confident they could manage, and they set 2001 as the deadline for taking over the roads. Buzz directed his staff to take road measurements and examine old photographs in order to establish a historical road width and begin to gradually narrow the Tote Road back to its original size. The documentation, he hoped, would prevent future directors and Authorities from allowing the road to be widened again.

The only connection that remained between the park and the state was personnel. Employees were part of the state system and represented by five bargaining units. In the mid-1980s, Buzz had raised the question of whether employees wanted to be independent from the state, a move he thought could reduce the need for union entities to two. However employees feared that if they changed their situation, their bargaining position would be weakened and their pay and benefits would suffer. Consequently, Buzz felt he had to leave that issue alone, and that one cord between the park and state government continued.

▲ ▲ ▲ ▲ ▲

On a July 1999 picnic outing at Ledge Falls with Jan and their two granddaughters, Buzz had slipped on algae-covered rock and suffered a concussion. Six months later, he had surgery to repair two ruptured discs in his neck. He also had aggravating allergy problems; Jan's allergies were worse. Both of them had knee problems. At sixty-one, Buzz was seriously toying around with initiating retirement discussions with the Authority, although he was keeping that information to himself.

Besides the health issues, Buzz was more bogged down then ever with administrative responsibilities that kept him largely sedentary and behind a desk or in the car going to and from Augusta. Speaking engagements and meetings in and out of Maine also kept him away from the park.

His last climb up Katahdin had been in 1997 when he viewed Lester Kenway's trail stabilization work. He was worn out by the all-day hike and had trouble descending the iron bars below the Gateway on the Hunt Trail. But he was the first one in the party who got back to Katahdin Stream Campground because he was so exhausted he needed to get home and to his bed. In 1999 he didn't hike to Russell Pond or Chimney Pond during the summer—the first time in forty years that he'd missed Russell Pond.

On the last Katahdin trip, Buzz had enjoyed talking to hikers on the summit and thought it was important for the public to see the park director on top of the mountain. Although Helon Taylor had said that he didn't need to get into the field to see what was going on in the park, Buzz felt that while he was director he wanted to be physically able to see for himself what was going on—no matter where he had to go.

The park director wasn't required to retire by a certain age, since he served at the pleasure of the Authority. But Buzz's health was pushing him to come up with a plan about how to retire. "I was thinking I'd give the Authority a year's notice and recommend they create a temporary position for the person who would ultimately be the director," he says. "That seemed fair, with the number of years I've put in, and fair to the park to say I'd work with that individual and share whatever information I could."

Buzz didn't discuss his retirement thoughts with anyone on the Authority, and when Attorney General Steve Rowe became a trustee in 2001 and began to ask Buzz about his retirement plans, Buzz didn't want to discuss the subject. In any event, Buzz thought it would be up to him to decide exactly when and how he would depart.

▲ ▲ ▲ ▲ ▲

In 2000 Percival Baxter's ninety-nine-year-old niece, Mary Baxter White, made her last visit to the park, where she stayed in a lean-to at Katahdin Stream Campground. Her son and his wife, Rupert and Ruth White, accompanied her. Buzz joined the gathering every year to see how everyone was doing and to reminisce. While they talked, Mary Baxter White knitted clown dolls, and she gave one of them to Buzz.

White died in 2002, closing the chapter on her generation of Baxters. The only relatives remaining who had known Governor Baxter and were still connected to the park were Rupert White and his children, Michael (a member of the Advisory Committee), Stephen, and Rupert Jr.

▲ ▲ ▲ ▲ ▲

Chuck Gadzik was replaced in 1999 by Tom Doak, who joined Lee Perry and Andrew Ketterer. Doak had served on the Authority briefly in the early 1990s when John Cashwell was called up to serve in the Gulf War. Buzz had thought Doak was unusually interested in the park during his "acting" stint on the Authority, partly because Doak visited the park to see what the West Gate issue was all about. Buzz's warm relations with Doak and Ketterer gave him relief from the tensions with Lee Perry.

There was no way for Buzz to feel good about Perry, since Perry had made his intentions known to represent his sporting constituency while serving as a Baxter Park trustee. Matters large and small brought the two into conflict, starting with the West Branch lands.

Perry became Authority chairman in 2001, and an example of where he took on Buzz gratuitously was the park's annual report. Buzz felt "ownership" of the report that he had instituted in 1981, and Perry ordered him to shorten the document. In Perry's estimation, the report had grown too large, too expensive, and was of interest to only a small number of park aficionados. Buzz complied, gritting his teeth.

The 2001 and 2002 documents available to the public were reduced to under forty pages and were all business—no long opening or closing prose from Buzz. After Perry left the Authority in 2003, the reports returned to their previous comprehensive nature and size—an instance where the revolving door of trustees worked for Buzz.

Despite their differences, Perry followed all his Authority chair predecessors in rating Buzz an outstanding manager and complimenting him on running an efficient operation, surrounding himself with "talented professionals," and driving "for results and success." In the 2000–01 evaluation, Perry noted that Buzz tended "to lose his objectivity when subjected to criticism of his point of view," but added that Buzz was aware of his reaction and was committed to improving.

▲ ▲ ▲ ▲ ▲

In 2002, Perry's last year on the Authority, Wilder from Within brought Buzz and Perry into another go-round, and the proposal dogged Buzz for the rest of his career.

Wilder from Within had remained on the back burner ever since Buzz had introduced it seven years earlier. Steve Rowe, who had replaced Andrew Ketterer as attorney general in 2001, triggered the issue anew when he asked Buzz to give the Authority a "state of the park" report at a special workshop meeting at park headquarters.

Long before he had been elected attorney general, Rowe had been an avid Baxter camper, hiker, and volunteer, just the kind of park-knowledgeable Authority member with whom Buzz expected to bond. However, he wasn't so sure about Rowe because Rowe started asking him about his retirement plans—a question that Buzz felt was prohibited by a federal age discrimination act. Going into another round on Wilder from Within, Buzz was wary of both Rowe and Perry.

Seeing Buzz's Wilder from Within proposal on the agenda before the workshop, Perry asked Buzz to make sure that his thoughts on closing roads did not show up specifically on any regular Authority meeting agenda in the foreseeable future. Buzz was clear with Perry that the purpose of a discussion on Wilder from Within was to identify future possibilities to enhance the park's wilderness character.

At the March workshop, the staff made presentations on a variety of matters, such as the park budget, user trends, and new trails, and Buzz went over new policies and the park's most recent five-year management plan. He talked about park history, some of the controversies and the present status of those matters. He noted that when Helon Taylor retired, he left the park with recommendations for the future. While Buzz said he had no intention of retiring in the near future, he offered his Wilder from Within ideas hoping they would be beneficial to future park planners and managers.

He described each of his three key recommendations—eliminating a twelve-mile stretch of the Tote Road, ending the Roaring Brook Road at Windey Pitch to make the Roaring Brook Campground a walk-in site, and taking out the Kidney Pond Bridge to convert the Kidney Pond Campground to another walk-in area.

To accomplish Wilder from Within, Buzz advised the trustees, the "Authority's quality of determination must be above reproach and beyond political considerations, recognizing that [Percival] Baxter did not want to break faith with park visitors. He was determined that the park was for those who love nature and are willing to walk," Buzz added. "Although the park is accessible to facilities and trailheads roadside via vehicles, its potential for backcountry hiking, camping, and enjoying nature at peace is not limited in options."

Anticipating negative reactions from the Authority, Buzz emphasized that his proposal was "food for thought as we, the current generation, fulfill our responsibilities to those that follow in preserving and protecting Baxter State Park." The Authority did not engage in any substantive public discussion about the ideas, moving on to other matters.

However, as Buzz had outlined Wilder from Within, the trustees felt blindsided, just as their predecessors did in 1995 when they first heard about the ideas. Perry, Rowe, and Doak were wondering what in the world he was talking about and whether it was an actual plan that he had devised without involving them. In any event, they saw him as out of line *publicly* and moving into the policy arena that was their bailiwick.

A major difference between Buzz's 1995 and 2002 Wilder from Within initiatives is that the first was not presented at a public meeting of the Authority, although it was done publicly.

Despite newspaper and magazine articles on Wilder from Within from 1995, Perry, Rowe, and Doak responded as if the proposal was new and asserted that Buzz had put himself in a high-profile position of setting major park policy, or trying to do so. It raised the issue of deference again as to who was in the policy driver's seat. Doak wondered if Buzz thought Wilder from Within was a last chance to augment his park legacy.

On March 21 Buzz received an e-mail from Lee Perry confirming a telephone conversation between the two on the Wilder from Within road closures. Perry told Buzz that when he was asked about the issue, Buzz's "appropriate response" should be that the Authority was not considering any road closures at present and didn't expect to in the foreseeable future.

Buzz requested a meeting with all the trustees because he thought he was getting "mixed signals" about the Authority's position on issues. Buzz explained that road and access issues had long been in discussion but not on the Authority's agenda. The only reason it came up at the Authority meeting was as part of the State of the Park report. He noted that Percival Baxter spent considerable time thinking and talking about road access, and that Authorities had dealt with the matter in varying degrees, explaining "in my view, it is an issue that won't go away, for people feel strongly from both proponent and opponent perspectives."

Buzz mentioned that he would be addressing the Friends of Baxter Park annual meeting in April 2003, and that Wilder from Within was of interest to them. He also pointed to past news media attention to the subject. Other than "vocal reaction from a few of the locals," Buzz observed that the proposal was "well received by others in town, across our state, throughout the conservation community in New England, and across the country."

Perry informed Buzz that he had received a complaint about Wilder from Within from Ray Campbell of the Fin and Feather Club. "The reaction and subsequent domino effect of one person's phone call can be amazing," Buzz responded in an e-mail, adding "with all due respect, I suggest that actual public interest is likely to bring this issue up at any time, regardless of your desires to steer clear of the debate. I am not sure it will be a simple or responsible thing for me to avoid this issue; however, if the Authority, through its chair, is instructing me to ignore one of my task statements, then I certainly will comply. I do, however, feel there is an obligation to let people know why I am not talking about these issues."

Perry's second evaluation of Buzz followed the run-in with the Authority over Wilder from Within. "On the whole, you are doing an outstanding job of carrying out your duties," Perry wrote on the 2001–02 review. "Occasionally you initiate projects that would benefit from further discussion and policy involvement by the Authority," he said. Mentioning the April discussion between the trustees and Buzz, Perry called the session "constructive and appreciated. This sharing of expectations with you was in the spirit of insuring that we work in harmony as a team. . . . Your acceptance and open support of our position is appreciated."

At the Authority's October 17 meeting at Kidney Pond, the trustees voted to raise visitor fees, approve the budget for 2003, and hear how operations were going. Buzz mentioned that roads were in good condition, and the subject drew sharp criticism of road closures under Buzz by Fin and Feather Club leaders. After emotional exchanges, Buzz left the meeting in tears and walked down to the pond for some privacy.

Advisory Committee member Ed Dwyer followed him and wanted to know if anything was wrong. Buzz was taking prednisone for his allergies and blamed the medication for making him emotional. There was talk about Buzz's tears in the greater park community, and it led to rumors that Buzz had become too emotional to handle the demands of the director's job.

The truth was that Buzz had always shown his feelings—from tears to anger. His tears usually surfaced in situations that called up the sweep of park history that he had been part of and the long-term pressure to defend the park. While Buzz couldn't concede that it was a burden to try to meet what he felt were Percival Baxter's expectations, it looked overwhelming at times to outside observers.

Buzz's invitations to meetings and conferences of environmental organizations and wilderness managers gave him many chances to talk about Wilder from Within, and he took the opportunities. After a wilderness stewardship conference sponsored by the Association for the Protection of the Adirondacks in New York State in the fall of 2002, Dave Gibson congratulated Buzz for "deliver[ing] an important message for all of us concerned with Baxter Park and the future of the Maine woods. Your vision is remarkable and enduring. Your faithfulness and service to the legacy of Governor Baxter is inspiring and timeless."

Environmental organizations didn't lobby the Authority to support Wilder from Within because Buzz didn't seek the groups' support. They sensed any initiatives from them wouldn't be helpful and could even be counterproductive in the tense atmosphere of the times. Without exception, according to Jym St. Pierre, environmental groups tried to respond to support Buzz when he called on them. "Buzz always picked our fights and expected us to be there for him," said St. Pierre. It wasn't Buzz's style, however, to build support as an issue developed. He typically yelled crisis at the last minute.

▲ ▲ ▲ ▲ ▲

The election of Democratic Governor John Baldacci in November 2002 assured new appointees for Inland Fisheries and Wildlife and the Maine Forest Service. After so much difficulty with Perry, Buzz anxiously awaited the governor's nominations.

In early spring, Dan Martin, an Aroostook County commissioner and former legislator, was named head of IF&W, and Alec Giffen, a land-use consultant and former director of LURC, was tapped for the Maine Forest Service. When Buzz paid a courtesy call to Martin's office, he received an inkling of what was ahead.

Buzz remembers Martin asking him, "What's all this about Wilder from Within?" Buzz left the visit with the suspicion that Lee Perry had soured Martin on the proposal from the get-go. Martin told at least one park advisor that he intended to pick up where Lee Perry left off, leading to speculation among Buzz allies that Martin would not be a friend of Buzz's. Also, Giffen let it be known that he planned to carefully scrutinize park matters—a signal with an unknown meaning.

Being a good politician, Buzz sat back to wait to see how things would evolve with the Authority. With two new trustees, holdover Steve Rowe became chairman. Rowe's first evaluation of Buzz for August 2002 to August 2003 was "outstanding" in most performance categories. Rowe called Buzz "a unique individual . . . extremely honest, hardworking, and proud . . . an effective communicator . . . knows the park, its resources and needs better than any other living human being."

With regard to Buzz's management skills, Rowe wrote, "The 'proof is in the pudding.' The park is in top-notch condition, and the staff are also top-notch professionals." Buzz's senior management team was "very effective," Rowe said, and shared Buzz's passion and love for the park. He said the best qualified candidates were hired to fill (mostly seasonal positions) and that Buzz "smartly" hired a number of laid-off workers from the local paper mills. "All employees were well trained," Rowe said.

Rowe didn't agree with some peoples' opinion that Buzz was "thin-skinned" but could see he was personally affected by harsh attacks from critics. "I am impressed with [Buzz's] ability to maintain his professional composure and diplomatic demeanor during these times," Rowe wrote.

▲ ▲ ▲ ▲ ▲

At the July 22, 2002, meeting of the Advisory Committee, Buzz warned that a potential controversy might develop over his plan to remove two historic cabins on Daicey Pond cherished by visitors. There was an environmental issue, as well as structural problems, with Cabin 10. Part of the building sat over the water, and overnighters sometimes went out on the front step and urinated in the pond. The evidence of such habits, Buzz explained, was odor, and in winter, the snow around the steps was yellow. At Cabin 11, the biggest problem was deterioration (especially rotten sills) to the point the camp wasn't serviceable. Buzz wanted to remove both camps in the fall of 2003 and replace them with cabins set back a reasonable distance from the shore.

He preferred that the cabins be replaced by lean-tos in hopes of one day eliminating all cabins at Daicey. But socially and politically that would be a very hard sell, he acknowledged, and he could live with a compromise for awhile. As the cabins "attrition out, they should be replaced by lean-tos and tent sites," Buzz told the Advisory Committee. "I can't believe in [Baxter's] time he ever advocated that we move away from the lean-to and tent camping atmosphere. That's not to say there would not be a bunkhouse or an occasional cabin here and there, but certainly not the extent of what we inherited."

Advisory member John Loyd advised Buzz that if he intended to move toward eliminating all cabins at Daicey Pond, there had to be a detailed explanation and plan to defend such a proposal. It would invite a firestorm of opposition, Loyd predicted. He observed there still was no overall management plan for the park that dealt with the types of existing overnight accommodations. Loyd personally supported retaining some "crude cabins."

Buzz believed that Percival Baxter wanted the sporting-camp facilities the park inherited with land purchases phased out. But, Buzz said, Baxter was dealing with larger issues at the time and left it to managers to deal with accommodations. Over the last twenty-five years, Buzz had eliminated dozens of deteriorating or environmentally incompatible structures and had replaced some but not others. John Neff of MATC suggested researching what Baxter may have said or quotes that would lend support to the concept of phasing out cabins in favor of lean-tos. Wilderness lovers would support such a move, Neff said, but agreed with Loyd that it would raise a ruckus with others.

After the Advisory discussion, Buzz went through the cabins issue with the Authority, saying he wanted to make a public announcement after Labor Day 2004 that the cabins wouldn't be available for rent while they were being replaced. He expected to have the new cabins on line in early 2005.

The Authority didn't object to Buzz's plan at the time, but plenty of other people did, especially historic preservationists and those who had enjoyed vacationing for years in Cabins 10 and 11. A logbook in Cabin 10 revealed just how special a stay it was there because of the view. "Kelsey," who had vacationed at Daicey Pond for eleven years, wrote on July 23, 2002, "Whenever you go to bed, you take a look out [at Katahdin] and whenever you wake up you look at the beautiful sun hitting [the mountain] just right. Baxter is a great experience. Cherish it!"

Advocates of preserving the cabins quickly put pressure on the Authority to save them. The group Maine Preservation put the cabins on their 2004 list of Maine's Most Endangered Historic Properties, and Buzz's old nemesis, George Kerivan, readied for battle. "I am appalled at the wanton disregard for their one-of-a-kind place in Maine history," Kerivan wrote in an op-ed piece for the *Bangor Daily News*. "Because of his gross ineptitude and mismanagement in this matter, Caverly will not be a candidate for sainthood anytime soon." The Authority, Kerivan continued, "was negligent in not exercising more control over park affairs." He contended that there were craftsmen capable to restoring the early twentieth-century camps, even if the buildings were moved off the shore.

In his media interviews, Buzz reminded the public that historic preservation was not a goal of the park; rather, the mission was wilderness preservation. But since the cabins had been around for so many years, some people thought they would be there through their lifetimes and didn't want to give up the pleasure of staying in them, he acknowledged. Buzz felt that people didn't know how much the park's wild character had improved with the removal of dozens and dozens of obsolete and dilapidated structures.

The trustees resisted the outside political heat to retain the cabins, and Buzz felt enormous relief that the four of them had been able to agree and not do battle with each other.

▲ ▲ ▲ ▲ ▲

In the fall of 2002, Buzz achieved another goal he had wanted to accomplish ever since serving as a ranger at Katahdin Stream Campground in the mid-1960s—removal of the recreational dam.

The original barrier had been built around 1933. A large volume of sand washing downstream from the mountains collected at the dam and had to be removed periodically, and the DOT used a bulldozer to do the job. In 1968, during his first supervisory stint, Buzz determined that such a machine shouldn't be operating in the streambed, and had stopped it. Afterward, the sand had to be shoveled out by hand every so often, and sometimes it amounted to 1,000 pounds. His argument for removing the dam was safety and liability.

As with his old cabin at Russell Pond, Buzz was nostalgic about the Katahdin Stream dam, which created a pool in front of the ranger's camp. He had many memories about family times swimming and playing in the pool. The only other dam-created recreational pool in the park was at Abol Pond.

▲ ▲ ▲ ▲ ▲

During the summer of 2003, Buzz was hiking in the Russell Pond area with an old Massachusetts friend, Dave Gathman, whom he had met in 1960. In the afternoon, Gathman was tired, but Buzz was still going strong. Buzz left Gathman to continue hiking to Pogy Pond lean-to and then back to Russell Pond Campground. Before Buzz reached the campground, he became so tired and weak he almost had to lie down to sleep. At camp, he was "wasted," drank several glasses of water and one of juice. After that he felt better, but later his doctor confirmed that Buzz had Type II diabetes on top of his other physically limiting conditions.

▲ ▲ ▲ ▲ ▲

The crowds on Katahdin was only one factor that had forced Buzz to temper his romanticism about the park being a wilderness as defined in federal law. As long as he had been at the park, there had been exceptions to a strict wilderness interpretation—buildings, roads, generators, gas tanks, septic tanks, showers, flush toilets, and washing machines.

When he became director, Buzz dragged his feet on allowing more amenities, trying to keep the park as free of the trappings of civilization as possible. But as time went on, there was increased pressure to allow the spread of such comforts in the park for employees. For instance, with the park's unions advocating for the field crew, Buzz allowed a hot-water shower house to be built at Roaring Brook. Sometimes visitors were invited to use the facility.

Buzz's resistance to increased frills for employees in the field was part of his basic conservative philosophy that "less is more" and "the old ways worked well." He couldn't always stop them, but he was usually successful in postponing them. Those who disagreed with his stance viewed him more as a man whose time had passed, and Buzz contributed to that view when new technology knocked on the door.

The park's introduction to the tech age had come in the form of solar panels at district ranger Bob Howes' camp at Togue Pond in 1982. It took some convincing for Buzz to go along with the change, but he was persuaded by rangers that the panels weren't any more objectionable visually than the radio antennas. The beauty of solar panels is that they can keep radio batteries at the rangers' posts charged year-round. Otherwise, the batteries go dead in winter due to the cold. "I couldn't stay in the dark ages forever," Buzz acknowledges, adding that the solar power proved itself with search-and-rescue situations.

The microchip, however, was outside Buzz's universe. When computers came a'calling at headquarters, he didn't want them and didn't want to learn how to use one. He allowed only one at the beginning, for business manager Beth Gray Austin in 1990. Buzz's secretary, Roxie McLean, was eager to try out the computer, and he begrudgingly let her do correspondence on it for him. Austin received a replacement computer, and then the floodgate opened.

After computers were commonplace at headquarters, McLean ordered a program for Buzz in 1995 that would allow him to talk into a machine to do e-mail. However it didn't work well, and that was Buzz's first and last attempt at becoming computer friendly. "I was beyond my time when it came to computers," he admits. He dictated all of his Internet communications through his secretary. Buzz thought e-mailing was scary. "All those people going to meetings and exchanging information and opinions about confidential matters worried me," he says. In the early 2000s, laptop computers were being used by park staff in the SFMA and elsewhere in the field.

Cell phones arrived in the park with hikers and campers at the start of the 1990s. Park staff found out about their presence from callers who wanted to be rescued or change a reservation. Then rangers began to notice them being used by hikers on Katahdin, and Buzz put cell phones on the banned list of audio devices that included radios, televisions, and cassette players.

*Buzz at Wassataquoik Stream, 2004*
PHYLLIS AUSTIN PHOTO

But the prohibition didn't stop cell phones at the gate. After they became "personal devices" (and with multiple functions) by the end of the decade, they were tolerated in the park and their presence treated as an opportunity to educate owners on appropriate use in a wilderness setting.

Despite his philosophical position on cell phones, Buzz was the first on the park staff to get one installed in his vehicle. He quickly realized what a convenience it was. He could use driving time to return phone calls and didn't have to wait until he was back at the office. Cell phones for other key staff followed. Cell phones were kept at the two park entrances and at Chimney Pond and Russell Pond for search-and-rescue purposes.

Buzz's last stand against computerization was park reservations. Joe Averill, the Acadia National Park representative on the Baxter Advisory Committee, had raised the subject in 1984. Acadia had already moved to the new system using Ticketron, and it was a big success. Buzz was flat-out opposed, taking the position that although Baxter Park's manual system was laborious and getting more outdated, it worked well.

Buzz also defended the manual system for the personal contact it required between visitors and park staff. He felt that was a valuable public relations connection, and he didn't want to lose it. Another key factor in his opposition to computerizing reservations was that the system in place was one that Jan Caverly had spent many years putting together and managing. Out of support and respect for Jan, Buzz wanted to protect her system, at least until she retired—and that he did.

After Jan retired in 1999, the Advisory Committee moved forward on computerizing reservations and trying to equalize opportunities for people getting the sites they wanted. The outcome was a rolling reservation system that restricted the percentage of accommodations that could be made on opening day after New Year's, and people could not make reservations any time of year more than three months in advance.

It was a rare instance where Buzz and the Advisory Committee parted ways. He stood aside for the computerized rolling reservation system to be implemented in 2005, just months before he retired.

---

Primary Document Sources: BSPA Boxes 1, 2 (2112-0718); BSP Annual Report, 1999–2005; Caverly Files; Austin Files.

Conversations and communications: Jensen Bissell, Buzz Caverly, Tom Doak, Chris Drew, Ed Dwyer, Chuck Gadzik, Dave Gibson, Andrew Ketterer, George Kerivan, Greg Kroll, John Loyd, Connie Baxter Marlowe, Gordon McCauslin, Roxie McLean, Lee Perry, Linda Rogers McKee, Steve Rowe, Jym St. Pierre, Paul Stern, Rupert White.

▲▲▲▲▲▲▲▲

CHAPTER 29

# The Final Days

With the skirmish over removing the Daicey cabins settled, Buzz's priorities for 2005 were to start the process of replacing the last original building at the Daicey campground—the old ranger station—and relocating Nesowadnehunk Field Campground. Both projects had their opponents within and without the park, but the opposition didn't gain traction.

Nesowadnehunk Campground had been built in the mid-1950s, with lean-tos on a steep bank overlooking the stream. There were good reasons, in Buzz's judgment, to move the facilities. Log cribbing installed in the 1970s and 1980s to reduce bank erosion had rotted, and the campground was repeatedly beset with blowdowns from strong winds that gusted up the valley. The fifty-year-old former ranger camp had been struck by lightning twice and had tile flooring that contained asbestos.

Like the successful Kidney Pond Campground conversion, Neso-wadnehunk could be turned around too, Buzz decided. He thought campers would be happy to get out from under such a shady, buggy area and into a sunlit field with a breeze, beautiful views of surrounding mountains, and plenty of fresh blueberries for the picking in late summer.

There was another reason motivating Buzz: knowing that he was in his last years as director, he wanted to make sure that the old Nesowadnehunk gate would not be easily reopened for public access when he was gone. His plan to relocate the campground included taking out the bridge over the stream. The Authority accepted Buzz's recommendations and agreed with him that the relocation was a positive move.

There was also a new potential land acquisition in the wings in 2005—one that would greatly affect Buzz personally. As usual, he had to keep what he knew confidential. However the deal being discussed boosted his spirits, and he had faith that it wouldn't be a replay of the West Branch lands battle.

In 2003, the Trust for Public Land (TPL), had begun a joint effort with the Department of Conservation (DOC) to acquire J. D. Irving Ltd.'s 71,000 acres east of Baxter Park, including the Katahdin Lake area (Township 3 Range 8). The mission was to save the lands from development and give several thousand acres around the lake and bordering Baxter Park to the park. The Katahdin Lake area had special meaning: it was the missing piece of the puzzle that would complete Percival Baxter's initial vision for the park dating back to 1921.

Irving chose to sell its so-called East Branch lands to three other buyers who offered a higher price than the state. Gardner Land Company, a family-owned business based in Lincoln, bought the Katahdin Lake tract situated in T3R8 and planned to harvest the treasure-trove of mature and old-growth trees. Still intent on securing Katahdin Lake, TPL and DOC then took up purchase negotiations with Gardner.

▲ ▲ ▲ ▲ ▲

Talks with Gardner turned out to be prolonged and fell into the background for Buzz. Another matter took front and center for him early in 2005.

Buzz had heard rumblings from Chris Drew and Jean Hoekwater about Jensen Bissell's new project in the SFMA, and Bissell sat down with Buzz to explain his plans. Bissell had already extended the Wadleigh Mountain Road to come within a quarter-mile of the Tote Road, and he planned to carry out a harvest along the portion of the Tote Road called the Legal Mile. (This was the boundary between the SFMA and the sanctuary area of the park, although most park users were oblivious to the proximity.)

The project raised a red flag immediately with Buzz, who was concerned about the impact a logging operation would have on visitors expecting to encounter wilderness. But Bissell felt it was time to display the SFMA's "scientific forestry" practices along the Tote Road so the public could learn about and appreciate those management values. Buzz felt those values could be well displayed by the traditional access to the SFMA through the distant Telos/Coffeelos entrance—if visitors really wanted to observe timber harvesting.

Bissell asked if Buzz was directing him not to take the matter to the Authority at the March meeting. "I'm not telling you not to," Buzz remembers saying to Bissell. "I'm just telling you I'm concerned." Friends of Baxter Park's board of directors was concerned, too, and prepared to make its position known at the trustees' meeting.

Buzz had been a hands-on manager, and if something wasn't going in the right direction, he could grab the tiller and change course. But in this case, Buzz hadn't taken the time to see for himself how the Wadleigh Road had been extended toward the Tote Road. The first week in March, Buzz and Drew snowmobiled into the Matagamon/SFMA area for an inspection. Bissell met them in the SFMA but left the patrol before they reached the Wadleigh Road where it came closest to the Tote Road. When Buzz got off his snow machine and walked through the woods to see how close the Wadleigh Road really was to the Tote Road, he was shocked—and even more opposed to the harvest project.

Heretofore, Buzz's typical strategy had been to marshal the facts on an issue, talk it over with staff and the Advisory Committee, and work to reach consensus before going to the Authority for a decision. If there was a question at the last minute, he would ask the Authority to postpone taking up the issue until later. But Buzz didn't follow his own long-standing practice in dealing with Bissell's SFMA road plan.

On March 8, 2005, Bissell made his case to the Authority at a meeting at the Maine Forest Service's Bolton Hill facility in Augusta. The trustees were already familiar with Bissell's plan and ready to support it.

In his presentation, Bissell noted that active management of the SFMA had passed the twenty-five-year mark, and the operation was now a green-certified, sustainable forest. Access had been completed to the 24,200-acre timber base over eighty miles of roads (including spur roads). Timber harvesting had delivered a total of almost $3 million to the park operating account, provided steady employment for local people, and the SFMA's forest now had larger and more valuable standing trees than it did in 1980, Bissell reported. The estimated timber value had reached $14 million.

Bissell said it was time to demonstrate the exemplary forestry management and harvesting to "a larger and new audience"—park visitors traveling the Tote Road. Keeping it hidden from easy public view was not okay anymore, he suggested. The SFMA, Bissell reminded everyone, was important to Governor Baxter, who had specifically set the area aside from the wildlife sanctuary portion of the park to develop as a "showcase" for the best forest practices and "an inspiration to others."

Bissell further explained that harvesting would be limited to 1,100 feet of the Legal Mile, entirely within the SFMA. The plan called for removal of the forest overstory of ninety-year-old aspen, which would release spruce and pine undergrowth. To minimize the visual impact, Bissell planned to have a "transition buffer" along the road and to cut lighter in woods closest to the Tote Road. SFMA entrance signs and kiosks/signboards would be placed on the Tote Road to notify and educate the public about the SFMA mission and the harvesting operations.

Knowing that the trustees were about to give the plan their blessing, Buzz suddenly felt compelled to try to kill the plan on the spot. He felt an urgency to "speak up for wilderness," he remembers. Buzz had always felt great freedom in expressing himself before the Authority and bringing Percival Baxter into the discussion. It didn't occur to him to weigh the potential consequences before he stood up to speak his mind.

All eyes were on Buzz as he walked to the front of the room to face the group. "I'm having a tough time," he said, referring to Bissell's plan. When people enter the park, they are "looking for a wilderness experience, not a forest management experience." As the only person in the room who knew Percival Baxter personally, he felt he rightly reflected the donor's wishes to preserve the wilderness setting along the Tote Road. He recalled the "tug of war" between Baxter and the state highway department in the 1960s over excessive cutting of one tree and some roadside brush.

Buzz took responsibility for the situation reaching the point that he and Bissell were at odds. He acknowledged that he didn't have time to get into the park anymore as much as he would like. "Listen to this old ranger," Buzz pleaded with the Authority, and "provide a little mercy."

Bissell appeared taken aback by Buzz's public opposition, as did the Authority and the others witnessing the situation. Buzz had never put a staff member in such an openly embarrassing situation.

The trustees quickly progressed from surprise to anger at Buzz for not dealing with the disagreement in private or postponing open discussion of the issue. Steve Rowe expressed upset "at what I just saw," and Dan Martin lectured Buzz that the issue should have been "discussed, resolved, and ironed out" before the meeting. Alec Giffen

*Baxter Park Authority members (L to R) Alec Giffen and Dan Martin;*
*Governor John Baldacci, Baxter relative Clint Dyer, park naturalist*
*Jean Hoekwater, and Buzz at the 100th Anniversary commemoration of*
*Percival Baxter's first trip to the park, 2003*
BAXTER STATE PARK PHOTO ARCHIVES

backed Bissell's plan, declaring it would be "publicly beneficial" since most park visitors never get into the SFMA. Counsel Paul Stern advised that a legal interpretation of the project was unnecessary because it didn't violate the Deeds of Trust.

John Loyd, a former chairman of the Advisory Committee and on the board of Friends of Baxter Park, was the only one present to go to Buzz's aid. He agreed with Buzz that Bissell's project would force a harvesting operation on people who wanted to recreate in a wilderness environment. Loyd doubted that the sound of logging would be as unoffensive to visitors as Bissell predicted, and warned that the operation could be a "potential public relations problem" for the park. The letter sent to the Authority by Friends of Baxter Park before the meeting reiterated the points made by Loyd.

After Loyd's remarks, Bissell pointed out that since what he was proposing was a standard operation in keeping with the SFMA management plan and supported by the SFMA Advisory Committee, the project didn't need a formal vote by the Authority to go forward. Paul Stern agreed, adding that it was brought up at the meeting only because of the "sensitivity" of the matter.

Steve Rowe commented that if the project was inconsistent with the Deeds of Trust, the trustees would "speak up" about Bissell's plans. But they all agreed that they were not interested in pursing the matter further. The meeting was over and Buzz had lost.

The Authority was visibly ticked off. Numerous times they had heard Buzz invoke Percival Baxter and his relationship with the governor—a reference meant to convey, in the minds of some, that he knew more about the park than anyone. Was Buzz publicly defying the Authority with his opposition to the Authority's tacit approval of Bissell's plan? Had Buzz's behavior crossed a fatal line?

After the meeting ended, it was evident to Buzz that he had offended people. Some people didn't want to talk to him, so he and Jan quickly left Bolton Hill. As they drove home, Buzz realized he had made a mistake in not putting off discussion of the issue, and he regretted saying that he wasn't paying much attention to what was going on in the SFMA and the road development there. "My words were poorly chosen," he admitted later, explaining that what he meant to say was that he hadn't paid much attention to development of that road. "The day I got information it was there or going to be put there, I should have gotten on my snowshoes and sled and gone out there and looked at it," he reflected. "I was just so involved with other details and so dependent on Jensen as a forester to do the right thing. In Jensen's view, he was doing the right thing. To me it was not the right thing." Also, Buzz thought that when he brought up Percival Baxter's name, it added "a little fire" to the situation—that it was offensive to the Authority since they were the ones making the decision, not Buzz.

Buzz took a few vacation days, and when he returned to work he talked to Bissell. "Jensen was disappointed at what had happened and very upset," says Buzz. The two had disagreed before but had worked out their issues. Buzz had trusted Bissell completely, supported him on almost everything he wanted to do in the SMFA, and given him high praise for his achievements in the SFMA. Bissell told Buzz that Buzz was the one person he couldn't stay mad at, and the two left their meeting on good terms.

Steve Rowe's annual evaluation of Buzz, signed March 11, 2005, gave no hint that the relationship between Buzz and the Authority had been drastically affected. Buzz had continued to exceed performance expectations in five of six categories where the choice of ratings was "exceeded, met, or did not meet." The one that he "met" expectations in had to do with employees, and Rowe said "staff morale appeared to be high. . . . Director continued his efforts to create an environment in which all staff members felt that their opinions regarding park operations, activities, and policies were encouraged and valued. The director has clearly made improvements in this area. Park staff continued to impress all who dealt with them. Their professionalism, helpful attitudes, knowledge of the park and attention to duty was a testament to the director's leadership."

Buzz's rating was "outstanding" in nineteen of twenty-one categories where the choice was outstanding, satisfactory, or needs improvement. Rowe added that Buzz kept the Authority informed on important park issues and regularly sought the advice and direction of the chairman, continued to foster good interagency relationships with public agencies, and worked well with private land trusts and special interest groups. Buzz knew the park, its resources and needs, Rowe said, "better than any other living human being."

▲ ▲ ▲ ▲ ▲

In the days after the March 8 meeting, communications intensified between Buzz and the trustees. Buzz was not surprised to be ordered to report to Rowe's office in Augusta on April 15 for a reprimand for his March 8 conduct. He was braced for a difficult encounter. His recollection of the meeting was that the trustees had been blunt about how mad they were, accusing him of undermining their effectiveness as an Authority.

In contradiction of Buzz's performance evaluations for decades, Rowe, Martin, and Giffen said that Buzz was guilty of "gross mismanagement" and overstepping his rank. In the written reprimand they informed him that they no longer had confidence in him to lead the park, and that there had to be a management change. The Authority's abrupt action called into question how much they really knew about park goings-on in light of the glowing evaluations of Buzz in the past. Did they believe the performance reviews were true? How could he be guilty of such serious charges?

Buzz was stunned. Rowe took him into another room away from the other two trustees and asked him if he would be willing to hand over daily park operations to Bissell and focus exclusively on the state's effort to acquire the Katahdin Lake area. By now, things looked hopeful for the ultimate success of that enterprise. TPL and DOC had signed an option with Gardner to purchase the most valuable core of T3R8—more than 6,000 acres around Katahdin Lake that included the largest stand of old-growth hardwoods and spruce.

Gardner's price was $14 million, or $2,111 an acre—a figure that made it the most expensive of any north woods conservation project in Maine history and one that reflected the 649-acre lake's extraordinary development potential. Since neither the state nor the park could afford such a high cost, the parties decided to seek private funding. It would be the first acreage ever bought for the park with money other than Percival Baxter's assets. The fact that the Authority was willing to accept a privately funded parcel underscored the unique values of the property—the state's last unprotected stand of old growth, almost four miles of undeveloped lake shoreline, an outstanding trout fishery, and stunning views of Katahdin that had made the lake a magnet for famous landscape artists for more than 150 years.

As Rowe explained to Buzz, he would be the public face of the fundraising effort, and the job would necessitate his traveling to major East Coast cities to woo potential donors. Buzz would still retain the title of park director, but Jensen Bissell would be appointed deputy director and handle park operations.

Rowe's question was an affront to Buzz. Buzz knew immediately that he didn't want to give up his director's position to become a traveling fundraiser. After Buzz turned down the proposal, he recalled that Rowe said to him, "You would be doing me a favor—think about this." Buzz asked for the weekend to think things over, although he knew before he left Rowe's office that he wasn't going to accept the new arrangement no matter how much time he had to think about it.

Reacting with amazing practicality after such an emotionally charged confrontation with the Authority, he and Jan went quickly to the state retirement office. Buzz wanted to know what the financial impact would be of immediate retirement—if he chose that option—and he was relieved to find out it would be minimal.

The weekend was a roller coaster for Buzz and Jan. They stayed busy with projects around the house to deal with their increasing anxiety at the real possibility that his career in the park was coming to an abrupt end.

When Buzz met with the Authority again on April 18, he officially rejected their proposal. He signed the reprimand document but took issue with the charges against him. He wrote on the document that he disagreed that he had committed "gross mismanagement" or placed himself above the Authority. He said his statement against the SFMA project was "not premeditated" but was a spur-of-the-moment reaction.

The Authority then tightened the screws, informing Buzz that they were taking away his "appointing authority" so that he would no longer be able to hire and fire employees. Unbeknownst to Buzz at the time, they had decided to immediately carry out a management review of the park to solicit staff opinions on how Buzz had run things.

On April 28 Rowe wrote Laurel Shippee, the state's equal employment opportunity coordinator, and Denis Normandin, director of training and organizational development, thanking them for their willingness to oversee the management review. The Authority, Rowe said, wanted them to probe how the park's current organizational structure was functioning in terms of communication, collaboration, and the flow of information among staff and to the Authority, and look at the management of resources (including the SFMA), as well.

Rowe traveled to Millinocket on May 2 to notify Buzz of the management review and explain the whys and hows of the process to him and park staff. "We want you to know," Rowe said in the review announcement letter to Buzz, "that the Authority highly values your views and appreciates the work and dedication you have provided to Baxter State Park." Buzz had never heard of a management review, but the trustees told him it was a common practice in government and corporations.

The park rented a room at the Best Western motel across from park headquarters for Shippee and Normandin to conduct the interviews starting on May 9. About thirty-four people were interviewed, including Buzz. Most were park employees but some were former employees, at least one of them a public critic of Buzz's.

Interviewees filled out a five-page multiple-choice inquiry designed to evaluate their treatment by superiors and co-workers, the pros and cons of their jobs, and the weaknesses and strengths of park management. Some of the questions, for example, asked if they felt valued and appreciated, if there was open communication, and if there was a commonly held vision for the park.

On May 13, Buzz attended the spring meeting of the Authority in Millinocket, and Dan Martin continued to be short with him. Discussion on the problem of Tote Road washouts in spring raised a question of whether the culverts were too small to handle the flooding. Buzz took the opportunity once again to refer to what Percival Baxter would have wanted. Baxter had been very clear that the Tote Road was a wild forest passage, said Buzz, and to change the character of the road with major culvert work "would be a bit inconsistent" with Baxter's wishes. "I don't think anybody has suggested [major rebuilding], Buzz," retorted Dan Martin. He asked Buzz to have the staff review the issue and come up with a recommendation.[1]

After the Authority meeting, Buzz and Jan went to Russell Pond for several days to rest and take stock of things before Buzz was interviewed by Shippee and Normandin on May 24 for about two hours. Prior to the session, he had looked over the survey to see if the interview "was going to be a hatchet job." He wondered how others were answering the questions and evaluating his management.

On June 17 Buzz was called to Augusta to be informed by the Authority about the outcome of the management review. He was handed a three-page summary of immediate changes that would be made as the result of the management review findings.

▲ ▲ ▲ ▲ ▲

The document was a bombshell for Buzz. The Authority's invitation to employees to speak their mind unleashed a surge of pent-up animosity, accusations, and pettiness against Buzz that had built up over the years. He could hardly take it all in.

The survey responses contained a long list of park employee charges against management. Any names mentioned were blacked out in review documents available to the public, but it was easy to identify Buzz as the primary target.[2]

The most damning charges were: "autocratic/authoritarian leadership," "poor hiring practices and promotion opportunities," "micromanagement," "not enough training, and inadequate equipment." Year-round staff members said they felt unappreciated, and seasonal employees felt "defeated." They also expressed fear of retaliation and "blacklisting" if they ran afoul of Buzz in carrying out their duties.

In the area of hiring, employees felt that Buzz hired whom he wanted to and prevented career employees from moving up. Interviews were "a sham," employees alleged, and "geared to pre-select a person's skills." Another issue was communication—"up, down, and across the organization"—and between headquarters and the field. Communication was a "challenge," the staff asserted.

Employees claimed that communication with the Authority or Advisory members was "a no-no," and that Buzz had an "open door policy but not an open mind policy."

As Buzz read the review summary, there was no doubt in his mind that the Authority would use the findings to try to fire him if he didn't voluntarily retire.

A management review couldn't have failed to find a "smoking gun" for those determined to find one. Buzz had been in and out of power for more than thirty-seven years—decades of momentous change that saw literal shifts of eras in administration, management, and park use. Virtually no one in such a position over that time period could have had an unblemished record or pleased all employees.

Buzz couldn't help but see how history was repeating itself. In the 1970s, disgruntled employees (including Buzz) had signed petitions against Harry Kearney and Lee Tibbs. Kearney was outright fired, and Tibbs resigned. For those employees who had axes to grind, the management review was an invitation to vent years and years of dissatisfactions at their boss—and their best shot at "petitioning" to finally getting him out.

Given the limited career ladder for permanent employees, hiring and promotion were frustrating issues. For those who didn't move up the way they wanted, Buzz was an easy target to blame because he was the appointing authority. Buzz sometimes sat in on hiring interviews, but they were generally handled by a review board composed of administrative staff and year-round staff, the Advisory, and friends of the park.

After the interviews, Buzz was given the top three choices and made the appointments from those. Sometimes he chose the second or third choice, not the first. To Buzz, what mattered was who was the best candidate based on abilities, not who had the best qualifications. Those not chosen might believe that Buzz didn't like them, was retaliating against them, or had some other personal interest in keeping them in their place.

Before the March 8 meeting, the trustees were ready for Buzz to retire to give fresh leadership to the park. At sixty-six, Buzz wasn't old, but he was fatigued, and he had health problems. He had weathered so much and seemed not to have the energy for all the many repetitive problems of running Baxter Park. Other trustees in the late 1990s had also yearned for a new director, especially after clashing with Buzz over the West Branch lands. The trustees were trained professionals and/or scientists, and they wanted a savvy contemporary who valued all sides of an issue, listened carefully, and was more analytical than emotional.

With the management review in its back pocket, the Authority's plan to force Buzz out—cloaked as a way to address employee concerns—was to remove his decision-making power and leave him a figurehead. If he resisted, the trustees were going to assume the director's responsibilities "with respect to all employment actions, including appointments, promotions, merit pay increases, and disciplinary actions." Furthermore, the Authority said that prior to any employment changes, the director or his designee (in consultation with the business manager) would have to provide the Authority with a memorandum identifying the action contemplated and a detailed plan for accomplishing it. If the Authority didn't approve, the action couldn't be taken.

Business manager Betts Johnston was appointed to take over the Equal Employment Opportunity/Affirmative Action duties previously carried out by Buzz's secretary, Ada Angotti, and report directly to the Authority. The director and senior management team would meet at least once a week, with agendas developed partly from staff suggestions, and the agenda would have to be forwarded beforehand to the trustees and park counsel.

"While we support the practice of employees generally following the 'chain of command' in order to communicate issues or concerns related to their particular areas of responsibility, the director shall immediately create and support an environment where the senior management team and park staff feel free to engage in open communications with the director or members of the Authority on any such matters," the plan said.[3]

The Authority also required the director or senior management team not to retaliate "in any manner" against employees for directly communicating with Authority members, and to immediately begin to work on a delegation-of-authority plan for park staff to be presented to the Authority by September 1, 2005. Further, the plan said that Shippee and Normandin would be present at headquarters and in the park for an indefinite period to provide direction, support, and technical assistance in carrying out the directives of the plan and developing policies to address issues identified by the management review.

Lastly, the plan said that the director's failure to agree to the directives in the plan "will be cause for discipline, up to and including termination." Steve Rowe asked Buzz if he understood the gravity of the situation, and Buzz pounded the table, saying, "I get a lot more, Steve, than you think I get."

Besides losing his hiring and firing power, Buzz would have to clear every action with the Authority before proceeding, and he would have to hold weekly staff meetings to improve communications. He would have no authority over goings-on in the SFMA, and his plan to remove the old York camp at Daicey Pond was stopped in its tracks. (The camp had deteriorated to the point that it was no longer safe to sleep and cook in, according to Buzz, partly because it had been insulated with flammable orange mill paper. A new ranger's camp was in the budget, and that project was to continue. But the York camp—important to historic preservationists—would be kept as an office and thus would avoid the kind of political brouhaha that had occurred over taking down Cabins 10 and 11 in 2004.)

The bottom line in Buzz's mind was that he would have to do what Rowe told him and would not be allowed to have opinions or question Rowe. "Steve was going to be the director in reality," Buzz recalls. "I told them I couldn't be a team player under those circumstances." He said he knew he had made mistakes but stood by his long record of actions and accomplishments in the park.

Buzz thought that Dan Martin was surprised that he wouldn't fight the Authority. Buzz, however, wasn't interested in hiring an attorney to challenge the Authority's actions—despite urging from confidants to consider it. The few friends who were privy to the situation felt that the Authority had "manufactured just cause" and should be held accountable publicly. However, Buzz didn't want to put the park through a mess—possibly a scandal—over the Authority's action. "I was interested in moving forward," he says. "The only way I could do that was to retire. They agreed. The Authority didn't want a fight, either.

From that point on, everyone got nice."

Buzz picked June 30 as his departure date. He wanted time to provide a couple of promised park tours to senior citizens and to wrap up paperwork and correspondence. The Authority agreed to Buzz's request to take his park-purchased day pack, and he wanted to buy his 1999 snowmobile. The trustees offered to give him the pack and the sled and wanted to pay him a $15,000 severance. The paper Buzz signed accepting the severance payment required him to give up all potential legal claims against the state and not to disclose information about the settlement for eighteen months.4

Before he left his last meeting with the Authority, Buzz recommended Jensen Bissell to replace him as acting director. He considered Bissell his protégé in all respects, and he fully expected Bissell to be chosen as permanent park director. He felt that Bissell was "top-notch" and "extremely conscientious," and Buzz had full confidence in him personally and in the quality of work he had done in the SFMA and for the park in general. In fact, Buzz couldn't image that anyone could have accomplished more there than Bissell.

When it was all over, Buzz and Jan headed home in a state of disbelief that changed into distress and great upset. Jan called Advisory Committee chairman Gary Trask in Holden to ask if they could stop by his house. "We were both emotionally drained," remembers Buzz. "As mile after mile went by, it started to hit me what had happened. We needed to share things with a friend." When they sat down on Trask's porch, Buzz and Jan broke down and wept.

▲ ▲ ▲ ▲ ▲

Buzz's departure from the park had a remarkable similarity to Joe Dodge's separation from the AMC in the late 1950s and sheds light on the problem of working "beyond one's time." Dodge built the AMC hut system in the White Mountains National Forest and managed it in the 1920s, '30s, and '40s. Like the minimal field oversight of Baxter Park initially, so was there little management of Dodge's hut system from the club's Boston headquarters in the first years.

Like Buzz, Dodge was a larger-than-life personality. Besides running the hut system, he was the coordinator of search and rescue in the Whites and a founding member of the Mt. Washington Observatory. Like Buzz, Dodge was dynamic, strong-willed, and intimidating to those unsure of themselves. Both men inspired great loyalty from many who worked under them as employees or volunteers. Dodge's band of "hut men" included Bob Ohler and other young bucks, who later devoted their talents and energy to Baxter Park.

As the AMC's bureaucracy developed, Dodge didn't want to share decision-making with headquarters. Bitterness emerged toward Dodge from board members, dividing the club's leadership and the hut community. Like Buzz, Dodge resigned after being told that he really had no choice and that it was the best way to respect the organization and his own legacy. In both cases, the real reasons for their leaving were kept confidential.

The careers of Joe Dodge and Buzz lasted so long that, in the end, they became symbols of their eras—Dodge from the 1920s to the 1940s—and Buzz from the 1960s to the new millennium. But both remained in their jobs too long. The world had changed beyond what either of them could deal with comfortably. The AMC board and, later, the Baxter Authority, were ready for new blood and new perspectives.

Like the AMC board, the Authority didn't have to explain its actions or obtain outside approval. The Baxter Park snowmobile appeal case that went to the Maine Supreme Court left no doubt that the Authority had the power to do what it wanted.

▲ ▲ ▲ ▲ ▲

Back at park headquarters the following day, the staff was noticeably curious about what had happened, but Buzz shared the information that he was retiring just with his senior staff and his secretary. On the surface, it looked like Buzz was handling things well, but privately, he was devastated. At night when in Millinocket, he stole away from everyone to go to the place he loved the most—the park—and cry his heart out.

On June 20 Buzz wrote a confidential letter to the Authority. Despite some employees' concerns, Buzz said that if park records were "thoroughly reviewed," they would show that staff meetings with administrative staff were held and minutes recorded, interviews were conducted according to state guidelines, and that appointments by him had been made after "thorough examination."

"As has been often spoken by many, including our current chair several times, the proof is in the pudding—the park is in excellent physical shape," Buzz wrote. "Our staff is top-notch, and the park's future is secure due to productive operational management." In any organization with sixty-plus employees and another twenty volunteers, there is often dissatisfaction. However, overall my contact with employees and feedback from administrative staff have been positive. I do not retaliate or hold grudges, and I believe the management staff is just and fair."

He said the Authority's action was "over-reactive, but I am clear you are the Authority and your decisions are final. . . . The changes in the management system so that your director and any future director is a figurehead . . . I disagree with . . . therefore I am prepared to pursue retirement plans."

On June 21 Steve Rowe appeared at park headquarters for the formal announcement of Buzz's departure and Bissell's appointment as interim director while a nationwide search for a full-time replacement was carried out.

Attempting to cover up the real reason for Buzz's retirement, Rowe mentioned that Buzz had health problems, as did Buzz. Many people didn't buy the explanation because it didn't pass the straight-face test. After forty-five years in the park, Buzz was leaving abruptly in the middle of the summer season, had not indicated to anyone that he was considering retirement, and had not made preparations for a smooth leadership transition. It just didn't make sense to those who knew Buzz.

In a statement released on June 21 Buzz expressed deep gratitude for the extraordinary experiences of working for the park for so many years. "My job has been one of those that one gets up in the morning and looks forward to going to work. Baxter State Park is in excellent shape. The facilities we have are top-notch and appropriate for housing and maintaining staff with very few exceptions. Our finances are in great shape thanks to the efforts of the BSPA and their financial committee." The annual budgets he submitted to authorities had been adequate and conservative, he said. "We consistently operate within the black and in any given year have ended up with a surplus, thus avoiding the need to spend monies that were not necessary. But at the same time [we] preserve and protect park resources and provide extraordinary public services."

Buzz termed his personal relationships with authorities, advisory committees, volunteers, and staff over the years as "productive . . . and I am pleased the park has been well served. Only through the cooperation of all could this have been achieved," he said. "On day's end, June 30, 2005, I shall ride out of town. . . . I shall ride out of town knowing that the park is in good shape and in good hands, and for that I forever shall be grateful."

Helon Taylor had advised him that to be a good manager, he had to surround himself with good people and be committed to his mission. "I have truly done my best," he said. "I believe in the Deeds of Trust and have upheld and defended them to every extent that is possible, and I hope that I shall be remembered for that."

Three days before his departure, Buzz drove to Yarmouth to meet with Rupert White and Eric Baxter. He had alerted the family beforehand of his resignation. "We were flabbergasted and upset," says Eric Baxter, adding that Buzz was careful in what he told them because of the confidentiality document he had signed. Rupert White felt that the Authority's action was "mean-spirited," given how close Buzz was to initiating his own retirement.

Eric Baxter was concerned with the hiring process the Authority would use to replace Buzz and didn't want it to be done "in a vacuum. I feared if they drove Buzz out, they could hijack everything," he said. Baxter had been part of the interview committee when Buzz was hired as director in 1981, and he offered himself to the Authority again to help with Buzz's replacement. But the personnel law had changed, preventing outsiders from being part of the selection process.

On his final day, Buzz read to park employees in the field via a radio broadcast from headquarters. "Please, please always stay focused on Governor Percival P. Baxter's mission and enjoy your tenure," he counseled, "for it is a most noble and rewarding one. I will not return to the park in calendar year 2005 for there is a need for closure for Baxter State Park and yours truly and family. However, I will see you in future years. Happy trails. God bless, and oh, by the way, don't forget your ax."

There were tears and hugs from the staff on Buzz's departure day. He was the last to leave and switch off the lights, walking out gracefully to face life without a job for the first time since he was a teenager.

Buzz's retirement was front-page news in many Maine newspapers. There was an outpouring of support and appreciation for his service to the park. Steve Rowe released a statement declaring that "words cannot adequately describe the positive impact that Buzz Caverly has had on Baxter State Park. No human being has done more to protect that magnificent resource than Buzz Caverly. The people of Maine owe a great debt of gratitude to Buzz Caverly. His tireless devotion to duty and commitment to protect and preserve Baxter State Park are legend." In response to reporters' questions about his unexpected retirement, Buzz said he had health problems. Remarkably, no one in the news media probed further, or, if they heard rumors about Buzz's situation, they didn't follow up on them.

Like Joe Dodge, Buzz was terribly pained in the aftermath of leaving the park. Dodge had found it difficult to get reinvolved in hut matters with the Old Hutman's Association, but eventually became the chief impresario at their gatherings. Buzz worked hard to stay positive, and his spiritual faith was a big part of his getting through the retirement pretense.

He and Jan had always been churchgoers, but had attended various ones in different towns on a hit or miss basis. In 2003 they had decided to make a commitment to Cornerstone Baptist Church in Exeter. It was a country church with many members who were retired farmers. Buzz and Jan felt welcomed, happy with the friendly, outgoing, and service-oriented congregation. In 2005—before leaving the park—Buzz was baptized for the first time.

▲ ▲ ▲ ▲ ▲

The first week Buzz was home, the days seemed like vacation, as he finished work on his woodlot camp and attended to errands. On July 5 he woke up and told Jan he was ready to go back to work—at the park. "I remembered I needed to go back to take care of this or that," he says, "and then I realized I don't do that anymore."

Jan watched Buzz struggle through the transition. He was hardly able to sleep, paced the floor, and overate. He would get up in the middle of the night and watch television to try to get tired. If that didn't work, he went to the refrigerator. Despite his diabetes, he ate what he wanted—comfort foods and lots of sweets. "Putting the sugar to me was about the only way I could sleep because it would knock me out," he says. His sugar level and cholesterol counts went up to dangerous levels.

Another way he got through the nights was to go riding in his truck. It could be any time of the night when the urge would get to him, and he would get Jan up and drive down to Newport for a cup of coffee, or just ride the back roads.

Buzz expected that some of his good friends at the park would call to check on him, but there was silence. He couldn't help but take it personally, even though he knew that things must have been quite unsettled back at the office. "Gary Trask prepared me for this," Buzz recalls. "He told me, 'You can work for the park fifty years and all is great and wonderful, but when you leave, it's like a ripple in the water when you throw in a stone. The ripples disappear in a few minutes. This is going to happen to you.' It was heartbreaking," he says. "I didn't know if I was going to drive Jan crazy. I didn't know what I was going to do or where I was going to go. Life felt over."

Ironically, Cathy Caverly lost her job at Sugarloaf the same week that Buzz left the park. So Buzz decided to build her a small log house on the site where Herbert Nowitzsky's mobile home had sat. He bought a pre-fab shed to enlarge and revamp for Cathy's needs. But it had to have a foundation, and he ended up spending more on the building than his severance payment from the park. "I wore myself out physically and financially," he said.

▲ ▲ ▲ ▲ ▲

Buzz wasn't entirely divorced from the park in the summer. There were many aspects of the Katahdin Lake issue that had to be worked out, and Buzz met with members of the Baxter family and counsel Paul Stern to talk about how the property should be designated—sanctuary or multiple use. He advocated working out access and use before a deed was passed in order to avoid a West Branch lands-type of battle.

With concessions made to sportsmen in the West Branch and Togue Pond deals, Buzz was firm that Katahdin Lake *had* to be sanctuary—no motors, no hunting, and no trapping. If not sanctuary land, Buzz saw no use in acquiring it. Rupert White and Eric Baxter agreed.

The funding question was troublesome to all of them. DOC's commissioner Pat McGowan had raised the possibility of tapping into the park's major trust-fund principal, since the land-acquisition account had been nearly depleted by the previous two purchases. Buzz was staunchly against using trust principal because it could jeopardize the fund's security and would set a precedent.

The Authority met with Eric Baxter and White at Rowe's office in Portland in August to discuss the land designation issues and funding options. Steve Rowe asked Buzz to attend the meeting or be part of it via a conference call, but Buzz declined because he had already made his views clear. Baxter and White sided with Buzz on sanctuary designation, or nothing and on leaving the trust fund alone. Eric Baxter told the trustees the family wouldn't stand for raiding the trust fund, and, if they tried to, the family would fight it. Buzz and the family also opposed future historic preservation protection for Katahdin Lake Wilderness Camps, as they had for sporting camps at Daicey and Kidney Ponds. (The camps had been purchased in late 2003 by Charles FitzGerald.)

Throughout the summer, Steve Rowe called Buzz to try to plan a retirement party for him. Buzz was incredulous that Rowe would ask his cooperation in celebrating his departure from the park under the circumstances. Buzz felt it would be a charade, and he told Rowe he wasn't interested in a public party.

Gary Trask organized a private retirement party for him on September 10 at the River Driver's Restaurant in Millinocket. A number of Advisory members attended, along with Chris Drew, Jean Hoekwater, and Jensen Bissell.

A couple of weeks later, NRCM presented Buzz with a lifetime achievement award at its annual meeting. The council praised Buzz for a career being "the state's foremost advocate for defense of Governor Percival Baxter's vision for the park—a vision for an enduring wilderness of great beauty, tantalizing remoteness, and extraordinary ecological diversity." As defender of that vision, the council said, "Buzz stood as tall and was as rock-solid as Mt. Katahdin itself."

The ATC, at its thirty-fifth annual meeting, passed a resolution recognizing Buzz's "staunch support" of the AT community, especially the MATC. They expressed "appreciation to Buzz for his long years of service and friendship with the trail community" and wished him a "long and rewarding retirement."

Buzz finally gave in to Steve Rowe's insistence on a gathering that the public could attend. Governor Baldacci designated October 30 as "Buzz Caverly Day in Maine" and presided over a dinner at the University of Maine at Orono. Joining the trustees and staff in honoring Buzz were Baldacci, Congressman Mike Michaud, environmental and outdoor organization leaders, park fans, and friends. Despite Buzz's conflicted feelings about the trustees, he and Jan were overcome with emotion when the trustees announced they were changing the name of

*Governor John Baldacci and Buzz paddling on Daicey Pond, 2003*
BAXTER STATE PARK PHOTO ARCHIVES

Lookout Rock (the Caverly's "engagement" peak at Russell Pond) to Caverly Lookout and Round Pond to Caverly Pond. The Caverlys also were presented with a lifetime pass to the park and from several friends, framed photographs of special places in the park.

Baldacci and Rowe thanked Buzz, honoring his passion and leadership. Baldacci commended Buzz for never losing sight of his mission to protect and preserve the park. Steve Rowe acknowledged that Buzz's vision was "consistent with Governor Baxter's." Buzz, said Rowe, was "my hero in real life." Dan Martin told the audience that every time he drove by Katahdin to and from his home in Caribou, he would think of "my good friend, Buzz Caverly. It has been a pleasure and honor working with you." Alec Giffen said Buzz "has established his signature on the land."

Acting director Jensen Bissell told the gathering that Buzz's "greatest achievement may be his inspiration to his co-workers. Our passion, our zeal for this place, we got that from you, Buzz." The park staff's philosophy was shaped by Buzz, said Bissell. "You've done all you could do [to ensure its protection]."

A letter was read from Eric Baxter (away in Europe) on behalf of the Baxter family "You have carried the torch despite the storms and never altered the course," Baxter said. "For me, you are the most amazing example of a man with principle that I have ever met."

Buzz responded graciously that all the kudos were "humbling, overwhelming. I am particularly grateful to a couple of Authorities which allowed me to be promoted through the ranks. Already," he said, "I miss the park, I miss the responsibilities, I miss the people. Retirement, it's okay. It's the first time I've been unemployed since I was fifteen years old."

The closest he came to revealing how painful things were was a reference to not sleeping well. It was terribly hard for him to accept the accolades and gifts from the very ones who had caused him to leave the park—and on grounds that he felt were trumped up and wrong.

After the "Buzz Caverly Day" dinner, Buzz felt quite uncomfortable with the Authority's decision to name two sites in the park after him. "I thought it made me seem like a hypocrite, based on what I stood for about memorializing people in the park," he says. He discussed the situation with trustees, advisors, friends, and Paul Stern. Stern was able to get Buzz to accept the naming honor by convincing him that Percival Baxter surely would have approved.

Baxter had been almost 100 percent against memorials or markers in the park to people—even, himself, Buzz noted. Yet Baxter had turned around and honored Helon Taylor's name on a Katahdin trail and a pond off the Roaring Brook Road. Paul Stern pointed out to Buzz that Buzz had served much longer than his old supervisor and likely no one would ever again be park director for twenty-three years or have a forty-five-year career in the park. Buzz agreed to allow the sites named for him to stand.

In December 2005 Jensen Bissell was made permanent director of Baxter Park, and Bissell's former job was filled by Carol Redelsheimer, the park's first woman SFMA resource manager. Buzz warmly congratulated Bissell. He informed Bissell that he had recommended him to the Authority and noted that in past annual evaluations had suggested that Bissell "would be an excellent choice as the next director."

He cautioned Bissell to "avoid yielding to pressures social or political, and protect the integrity of the park and its resources above all other considerations." There were people with "personal agendas" who might try to influence Bissell on such issues as wilderness management, public use, research, "and overkill in trail maintenance and development," Buzz said, adding that new technology must also be "guarded against." Buzz singled out research for the most comment. "At Baxter, it's best, particularly in the sanctuary [area], that the resources be allowed to thrive and not be impacted by experimentation or study," he said.5

▲ ▲ ▲ ▲ ▲

In early 2006 the Katahdin Lake project came to a showdown in the legislature. Buzz and Jan, looking for "a little fun" during the winter and a way to keep in touch with park matters, decided to go to Augusta to hear lawmakers debate the bill. The Authority wasn't expecting Buzz to reappear. They thought he was gone and out of their hair. But they underestimated his resiliency and the Providence factor at work throughout Buzz's career.

The deal between the DOC and Gardner landed before lawmakers because it involved a land swap. Gardner didn't want cash for Katahdin Lake; instead, the company wanted timberlands to keep their logging and mill operations going. TPL, DOC, and Gardner had worked out an arrangement in which the state would sell 7,400 acres of public lots to TPL for $14 million and add another 14,000 acres of privately owned timberland. Then TPL would give the woodlands to Gardner in exchange for the Katahdin Lake land, which would become part of Baxter Park. The purchase landed in the lap of the legislature because state law required a two-thirds approval of lawmakers to dispose of any public lots.

The bill created a political firestorm, setting off vehement opposition in communities near the park and among organized sportsmen's groups. For them, the deal symbolized the continuing loss of age-old recreational freedoms and the traditional way of life in the north woods. The Sportsman's Alliance of Maine and the Maine Snowmobile Association worked hard to defeat the bill while it was before the Agriculture, Conservation, and Forestry Committee, and Al Cooper, former owner and still manager of FitzGerald's Katahdin Lake Wilderness Camps, joined them in the fight. Cooper became a formidable adversary because he claimed the historic sporting camp would suffer ruination if the land became part of Baxter Park. Cooper's situation and his standing in the sporting camp industry made him a very persuasive figure with the committee.

Buzz's mere presence at the hearings was significant. He was *the* iconic, living symbol of Baxter Park. Public opinion held Buzz in such high regard that TPL's Maine director, Sam Hodder, believed that if Buzz suddenly came out openly against the project too, it would fail. "We already had challenges because of the sanctuary provision land and with the high financial cost," he said. "Now we had the sportsmen threatening to derail the bill. Buzz was the keeper of the heart and soul of the park for forty years, and I felt if Buzz voiced concerns, then the Baxter family would be concerned and vocal, as well as park faithful, and all would be lost."

Hodder didn't have to worry. Buzz quickly recognized an extraordinary opportunity to play a key role in the success of the project. He made fifteen trips to Augusta in fourteen days to lobby legislators, and attended all but one of the many sessions of the ACF committee. He only spoke twice at the committee meetings, but his tireless presence was evidence of how important Buzz felt passage of the bill was. During the ensuing months, Buzz's relationship with the Authority improved as they developed a new working alliance. He was respectful of the trustees, giving no hint of resentment about the circumstances of his retirement. He worked well with everyone struggling to make the Katahdin Lake project come to fruition.

What eventually emerged from the highly pressured ACF committee was a compromise bill. It stipulated that Katahdin Lake and 4,119 surrounding acres that were part of Percival Baxter's earliest vision would be added to the park as sanctuary, but 2,572 acres to the north would be managed by DOC (for which the state would pay $2.5 million) and left open to traditional uses. The Authority agreed to negotiate a twenty-five-year lease to provide for continued operation of Katahdin Lake Wilderness Camps.

"Buzz made the bill fly," recalls Hodder. "He brought so much credibility to bear. There were people across the country who loved Baxter Park who trusted Buzz more than themselves. Buzz was the most influential spokesperson we could have had."

When the Maine Senate gave final approval to the bill one night at 10:00 P.M., Buzz and Jan were sitting at the back of the chamber, finally relieved and joyous. They had devoted hundreds of hours and traveled nearly 2,000 miles at their own expense to support passage of the bill. Ninety percent of the members of the house and senate voted in favor of the final proposal.

There was more discussion about tapping the Baxter Park trust funds to help with the acquisition, but the Baxter family was against raiding the endowment, as were other parties. Outside funding was the only answer, and agreeing to accept very large contributions seemed to be the last chapter in the long donations saga.

In April, at the TPL's request, Governor Baldacci appointed Buzz as honorary chairman of the fundraising campaign for the Katahdin Lake project. Throwing his full passion to the last hurdle, Buzz participated in countless strategy meetings, planning the fundraising effort, talking with potential donors, making phone calls, sending letters to newspapers, and even putting a message on his home answering machine soliciting donations from callers. He sent a letter and a brochure to 17,000 park visitors that brought in 1,000 donors. Buzz led twenty-two tours of the Katahdin Lake lands, starting in late April 2006.

Buzz saw his trip guide role as keeping him connected to the park and adding time toward his fifty-year commitment to the park. Since he knew the area so well, Buzz was full of entertaining stories, and he could put the acquisition in context because he knew Percival Baxter. With every group he led, when they neared the lake, he stopped and said, "You're about to enter the wow factor." Virtually every visitor let go a "wow" when he or she saw the lake and Katahdin's Knife Edge prominent in the background, Buzz says.

With so many other worthy conservation initiatives throughout the country needing donations, it was no small feat to raise $14 million for the Katahdin Lake purchase. A broad cross-section of people, organizations, and corporations donated to the cause—with dimes and million-dollar-plus contributions. The artists long inspired by the Katahdin landscape raised thousands of dollars by donating a dozen and a half of their paintings to a benefit auction.

With time running short to complete the fundraising, Providence again seemed at work through Buzz. One of the young college students Buzz that had befriended, Mike Boucher, came to the rescue. In 1985 Buzz had taken time with Boucher in the park to show him around, and Boucher was inspired by Buzz and the wilderness around him. They lost touch after that summer, but Boucher didn't forget Buzz or his Baxter Park experience. Boucher's path had led him to Islesboro, where he became friends with summer residents Frank Trautmann and cable television mogul John McCaw and worked for both of them. Boucher became a strategic player to help facilitate conversations and meetings among several parties to see how Trautmann could help TPL make its Katahdin Lake closing deadline. The project was in a momentary cash flow problem because several million dollars had been pledged over a period of time.

For a long time Trautmann had wanted to make a major contribution to Baxter Park, and when the Katahdin Lake project came along, it seemed the right time to sell his Islesboro property to put the campaign over the top financially. He donated his property to TPL, and in turn TPL sold it to John McCaw for $8 million and donated more than $3 million to the Katahdin Lake campaign.

With the funds secured, Buzz was one of the first to receive a phone call from Sam Hodder. "It was a wonderful, wonderful moment," Buzz says. "From that point on, my adrenaline was flying high, and I could hardly wait for the public announcement of the transfer of deeds." For those who loved Buzz, it was a thrilling comeback for him, and another confirmation of his uncanny ability to transcend his and others' imperfect actions.

Buzz was invited to join Governor Baldacci, DOC, the park Authority, and TPL officials at news conferences in Millinocket and Portland to celebrate the Katahdin Lake success. Besides lauding the new land purchase, Buzz had an important announcement of his own—a new private philanthropic trust to support Baxter Park operations. What Buzz wasn't free to say at the time was that veteran park volunteer Frank Trautmann was the trust fund donor. The worth of the fund was $1 million more than the value of Percival Baxter's original endowment in 1969.

The conservation opportunity that materialized unexpectedly for Frank and Margery Trautmann was a replay of that for many people of modest income who bought Maine coastal property when oceanfront could be purchased for little more than a song. The story of how those foresighted owners converted the accumulated value into significant land conservation acquisitions in recent years is already almost legend.

The Trautmanns had moved to Maine from Long Island, New York, in 1960 and purchased a fifty-eight-acre farm on Islesboro. Even though three sides of the property fronted on the ocean, the cost was an affordable $37,000.

The Trautmanns began to establish a friendship with Buzz and Jan in 2001, inviting them to Islesboro for a lobster dinner and a discussion about a park donation. An official offer of $500,000 was made to the

Authority in early 2003, but the Authority sat on the tender because it wasn't satisfied with a donation coming in the form of bonds.

Frustrated, Trautmann tried to approach J. D. Irving, Ltd., about buying the East Branch lands for the park but couldn't get to first base with the company. In 2006, with the death of his wife, he decided to move forward with establishing a trust fund.

After the Katahdin Lake acquisition was completed, Buzz threw himself into working with Trautmann on the details of how the trust would operate. It was clear from Trautmann that Buzz would have a leading role with the trust for as long as he wanted. Guided by the setup of the Baxter Park trust funds, Buzz helped determine the legal framework for the Trautmann trust. As Trautmann's advisor and confidant, Buzz was chosen to be a commissioner of the trust. Thus, he would be able to extend his involvement with the park and, through the trust's annual interest income, contribute financially to the preserve's continued well-being.

Again, Buzz's commitment to Baxter Park had come first. He kept the details of his departure from the park confidential from Trautmann because he rightly believed that if he had shared them, Trautmann would have turned his back on the park. After the land deal had been accomplished, Buzz discussed the events surrounding his retirement with Trautmann.

Because of Buzz's success in helping to secure Katahdin Lake, there was discussion by the Authority about a new role for Buzz with the park. The trustees were nervous about the potential for the old director to overshadow his successor. Consequently, the parties agreed that the way for Buzz to help at the time was to join the summer program and talk about the park's history, lead trail walks, and continue to provide more guided hikes into Katahdin Lake.

In April 2006 the TPL recognized Buzz's contribution to the success of the Katahdin Lake purchase by presenting him with the Annette and Kingsbury Brown Award as Volunteer of the Year. He received further kudos in May 2006 when the University of Maine at Machias presented him with an honorary doctor of science degree, recognizing his indefatigable efforts on behalf of the park, "[a] world-renowned natural treasure." L.L. Bean, Inc., honored Buzz in 2007 with the company's first Outdoor Hero Award, and TPL invited Buzz to join its advisory board of directors.

Upon learning of Buzz's retirement, Bill Meadows, president of The

Wilderness Society, wrote Buzz that he had left "an astonishing legacy" behind after forty-five years at the park. Meadows admitted he was "a little bit in awe of [one] who kept at it so successfully through thick and thin . . . through almost a half century of uncompromising service to the people of Maine and hundreds of thousands of Baxter visitors. . . . Your wisdom, tenacity, good humor in the face of adversity, and heartfelt love of the land are an inspiration to the entire conservation community."

He thanked Buzz for his "extraordinary contribution to the cause of wilderness." The phrase "forever wild" was not just a slogan to Buzz, Meadows observed, but rather "an ideal to be realized on the ground. You always took a stand against the incursion of structures and machinery into the landscapes that rightfully belonged to God's wildest creatures. We are a better nation for having such wonders in our backyard. Congratulations on a magnificent career. . . ."

---

1. BSPA Draft Minutes, May 13, 2005, meeting.
2. Baxter Park Management Review, May-June 2005, provided by the Attorney General's Office in response to a Freedom of Access Act request.
3. "Management Plan for Baxter State Park," memo to Buzz Caverly from the Baxter State Park Authority, June 17, 2005.
4. Exhibit A Release, June 21, 2005.
5. Letter from Buzz Caverly to Jensen Bissell, December 29, 2005.

Primary Document Sources: BSPA minutes, Box 2 (2112-0718); Caverly Files, Austin Files.

Conversations and communications: Eric Baxter, Mike Boucher, Buzz Caverly, Jan Caverly, Brendan Curran, Tom Deans, Chris Drew, Alec Giffen, Sam Hodder, John Loyd, Dan Martin, Gary Trask, Fred Stott, Roberta Orestes, Steve Rowe, Frank Trautmann.

▲▲▲▲▲▲▲▲

# Buzz Caverly 's Legacy

As Buzz's tenure showed, managing Baxter Park evolved into an incredibly complex and politically sensitive job. From the time he first ran the park in 1968 to the time he retired in 2005, the top management job changed dramatically in size and shape.

Buzz faced strong special interests, legal mandates, financial limits, conflicting user demands, politically driven Authorities, independent-minded employees, scrutiny by the news media, power plays by legislators, and his own unrelenting imperative to live up to Percival Baxter's trust. Buzz tenaciously met those challenges, leaving a famed legacy that will likely never be matched in longevity or passion.

His imprint is everywhere—the land, the mountains, the roads, the campgrounds, the trails, the flora and fauna, and the people who oversee the daily life of the place. With twenty-two years as a ranger and supervisor before he was appointed director, Buzz knew in his heart what he wanted to accomplish—defending and enhancing the park's wilderness character. His list of goals, whether increasing protection for wildlife or decreasing the amount of development inside the park, was framed and informed by his understanding of Percival Baxter's vision.

Although his controversial Wilder from Within proposal came to naught, Buzz retired knowing that a visitor to the park in 2005 was guaranteed a much more authentic experience of "forever wild" than he himself encountered when he became a ranger in the just-developing park of 1960. The once-plundered forest had recovered from its worst abuses and was moving toward the original undisturbed forest that Thoreau passed through in 1846 on his way to Katahdin. Vehicle access was limited, garbage dumps were gone, and buses and RVs were banned. Unessential buildings had been removed and facilities concentrated to minimize human impacts. Coyotes had returned on their own. The state-endangered American pipit, Roaring Brook mayfly, the northern bog lemming, and the Katahdin arctic butterfly were better protected. The park's innermost wilderness sanctum—the Klondike—remained trail-free and safe from all but intrepid bushwhackers. Scientific research was restricted to only those projects that would not harm the park's resources.

To Buzz's credit, his willingness to put forth the Wilder from Within concept refreshed the wilderness philosophy upon which the park was founded. The debate focused new attention on how large infrastructures in the park—roads, buildings, bridges—undermine wilderness character. It figured in post-Buzz decisions to decrease the number and size of crossings over bogs and streams and to build minimal shelters in the new Katahdin Lake parcel.

Buzz had joined the barebones field crew not long after graduating from high school. He had a lot of growing up to do. His was on-the-job training, trial and error. He had enough mettle and ambition to survive his early mistakes, and he benefited unquestionably from the wise guidance of Helon Taylor and the patience and confidence of numerous Authorities. By the time he became director, he had absorbed Taylor's teachings, healed from his bruises, and was determined to carrying out Baxter's wishes come hell or high water. To do so, Buzz had to change. Working to the edge of his capabilities, he transformed himself into a politically astute manager, inspirational leader, effective lobbyist, diplomat, media personality—and, yes, general.

Buzz's devotion to a singular path as Baxter's preeminent champion was known far and wide. His notoriety as "defender" gave him regional and national forums from which to invoke the words and deeds of Percival Baxter. The founders of national and other state wilderness parks might be lost in time, but not "Governor B" if Buzz had anything to do with it.

More importantly, he kept Percival Baxter *alive* for his staff, the Authority, the Advisory Committee, the public, and for future generations of park stewards. It was the best way he knew to educate and remind them of the former governor's great generosity and foresight, and it enriched peoples' appreciation for the land's history. A strong quote from Baxter or the Deeds of Trust was also an effective management strategy for Buzz in steering the park in the direction he believed Baxter wanted it to go—wilderness first!

Buzz was such a stellar figure that he was taken for granted by many, and the level of personal abuse and vicious attacks that he took in standing up for the park was little known by the public. He was incredibly cordial to his most severe critics. A weaker director or a director driven by a different set of goals could have exploited the contradictions in Percival Baxter's vision and the Deeds of Trust and thus altered the park significantly for the worse.

Buzz lived and breathed the park virtually twenty-four hours a day, seven days a week. By extension, so did Jan Caverly. Her unwavering support and constant companionship at home, in the office, and on the road sustained Buzz from sunup to sundown. Like Odysseus's Penelope, Jan was ever faithful and stayed the course.

No one during Buzz's era knew the park underfoot better than he did; even in his fifties, he was still quick enough to leave young rangers behind. A highly emotive man, he loved every square inch of the park and wore his feelings on his sleeve. The sanctuary—about 75 percent of the park—was sacred ground to him. He couldn't hide his hurt and pain when an Authority decision—most notably the West Branch lands use vote—went against his recommendation and, in his mind, stabbed the sanctuary in the heart. He was deeply saddened by the reality that not everyone cared about the park to the degree he did, and that no matter how hard he tried, he couldn't change everyone's point of view to match his, or, he believed, that of Percival Baxter.

Buzz's far-reaching reputation grew significantly from major controversies that largely arose out of land acquisitions or land uses—Kidney Pond, West Gate, the West Branch, Katahdin Lake. Those issues involved policymaking votes by the Authority, but the impetus for bringing them to the fore was Buzz. He, not the Authority members, was identified most in the public mind with the big battles because he was the park's enduring leader and spokesman. The trustees were rarely recognized by name with particular issues, if at all, and their short terms limited them as sources of inspiration for a wilderness concept that needed continuous reinforcement.

▲ ▲ ▲ ▲ ▲

Buzz exerted so much influence that it was often hard to tell where the trustees' power ended and the director's began. His job description gave him wide latitude in making decisions on his own, and he used it to its fullest—and then some. He felt he had no choice. He trusted himself to remain true to Percival Baxter, but he occasionally doubted or outright mistrusted Authority members who clearly were uninterested in the park or sacrificed park interests in favor of special interests.

Buzz was a bulldog on the most difficult political issues but also on the smallest operational concerns because every little thing mattered. Potential negative impacts of big decisions were easy to predict. However, Buzz knew instinctively that incremental damage could occur with careless field work, such as misplacing a path or using the wrong building materials, and he was persistent with staff to be ever mindful of how to do things by his definition of right. The park's Standard Operating Procedures manual, developed by Buzz, was his pride and joy. It covered all matters that park employees dealt with, from campground cleanliness to search-and-rescue protocol, and he expected them to know it cover to cover and follow it.

The public heard little about the park's financial condition during Buzz's years. There were sometimes ups and downs in income due to outside forces, but the budget was never in serious jeopardy. Buzz could always have used more money; unfunded needs, such as trails, were on the books year after year. However, thanks to Buzz's conservative spending, the prudent guidance of the Advisory Committee's investment subcommittee, and the Baxter trust advisors, the park was financially healthy throughout his tenure.

Buzz was praised and damned by park insiders and outsiders for his stubbornness and self-assured style, which could be overbearing. He appeared to not listen, or not listen well, and dismiss out of hand the opinions of others. But he saw himself as having an open mind—with a big "if"—*if* what was being proposed was good for Baxter Park, not just convenient for park visitors or influential interests.

Regardless of how Buzz's management was perceived, there were very few who could claim they knew more than Buzz about protecting and preserving the park for the long term. His forty-five years on the scene and at the helm was powerful validation of his institutional omniscience. After seven and a half years as a ranger, Buzz was elevated to the supervisor's position, and his management tenure incredibly spanned all or part of five decades. Validation of Buzz's job success was the annual evaluation kudos for exceptional management from every different Authority under which he served as director.

Chuck Gadzik, former member and chairman of the Authority in the late 1990s, acknowledges that trustees had differences with Buzz at times, but they had to do with his management style not his motivation. "There was never a question that Buzz's motivation was his passion for Baxter Park," says Gadzik.

▲ ▲ ▲ ▲ ▲

Maps of the park between 1982 and 2006 are physical evidence of Buzz's leadership. The park boundaries today include 7,483 more acres than when he arrived on the scene. Without his foresight and drive to bring the Togue Ponds and West Branch lands into park ownership, those purchases may never have occurred, and development could have occurred within feet of the park's main entrance. While the most recent acquisition, the Katahdin Lake parcel—occurred after Buzz had resigned from the park, he was the single most important person in the campaign, according to the leaders of that ambitious project. In that acrimonious debate, Buzz found a new role as outside park activist.

All three parcels added important and priceless resources to the park. The Togue Pond purchase allowed the park to keep new development from its main public entrance, preserve timeless scenic beauty, and restore the Class 1A pond shoreline. The West Branch lands added five miles of Penobscot riverfront to the park, and four miles of the AT along Nesowadnehunk Stream and Nesowadnehunk Falls. The Katahdin Lake parcel is a true icon of the Maine woods, and its purchase preserved the most important ecological and scenic land on the park's edge.

When Buzz was a ranger, all the lands around the park were commercial forest land owned primarily by large pulp and paper companies. He was very concerned about potential development of the outside ownerships and spoke out strongly for establishing a protective buffer zone around the park. Although "the B word" became a political hot potato that he had to drop, Buzz actually got most of what he wished for. Today, most of the buffer townships on the borders are in large conservation easements or owned outright by The Nature Conservancy, wilderness philanthropist Roxanne Quimby, and the Penobscot Indian Nation. While Buzz didn't have a direct hand in those acquisitions, it was the wilderness qualities of the park, which he amplified, that bred interest in saving those lands circling the preserve. A great landscape-scale wilderness region still has a chance to evolve, with Baxter at its core.

▲ ▲ ▲ ▲ ▲

Buzz will be remembered for his persistence in reducing the park's infrastructure and controlling access and visitors. The land that Percival Baxter purchased for the park was strewn with buildings (camps, woodsheds, privies) in all types of conditions. An estimated hundred man-made facilities were eliminated during Buzz's administration. For example, the conversion of Kidney Pond Campground was an early triumph for him, proving how the park experience for visitors could be better with fewer cabins that were primitive style instead of motel-like quarters.

Buzz was unwavering in following Percival Baxter's directive that no new campgrounds be built or expanded, and his position resulted in strict control on overnight visitor use. It was day use that created vexing problems for Buzz. the number of day users soared by the late 1980s, with most of them headed for Katahdin. Buzz used parking lot spaces to limit day use and relocated the main gate at Togue Pond for more effective oversight of traffic comings and goings. A decline in visitation then brought some relief from visitor pressures, giving park managers more time to figure out overuse solutions.

Many obsolete buildings and bridges were replaced over time, and Buzz insisted that whatever was constructed be made of wood—not concrete, steel, or metal. His rationale was that future park leaders should have a chance to reconsider, about every fifteen years, whether to keep or remove a particular structure—preserving the option of "wilder from within.'

Reducing the number of vehicle access points to the park was another hallmark of Buzz's tenure. For almost forty years, the evolving park was like a sieve, with entry and exit by vehicle at several different points, and by foot on bootleg trails. Buzz knew that the number of visitors couldn't be controlled without controlling access. He eliminated three gates, despite angry resistance from sportsmen. The last closure—West Gate—was the most politically difficult because by the time he proposed it in the early 1990s, park affairs had become more important to the public, especially to hunters and fishermen. Buzz deftly used budget impacts to support the closure, and he won. Having only two entrances—at Togue Pond and Matagamon—the last ten years of his career gave the park maximum control and oversight of people, assuring greater security all the way around.

Buzz judiciously recast the public perception of the park's major access road by renaming it. Originally called the Tote Road because it was a timber haul artery, the name was changed to the Perimeter Road in 1974. Twenty years and many visitor speeding cases later, Buzz brought back the historic name to remind the public that they were in the deep woods.

The road system was a complicated matter for Buzz because it involved a long-standing maintenance contract with the Department of Transportation. During the years DOT maintained the park roads, their large graders used incrementally widened the roads. By the late 1990s, the Tote Road was no longer primarily a one-lane road with turnouts. It was more a thoroughfare, and Buzz was sure that Percival Baxter hadn't wanted a "highway" through the park. He convinced the Authority to "fire" DOT and let the park do its own road work. That way, the road system could be returned to its more primitive condition as a wild forest road.

▲ ▲ ▲ ▲ ▲

Katahdin is an international magnet for hikers and climbers. To manage serious erosion and protect alpine vegetation, Buzz allowed intense concentration of trail crew effort on the mountain. Outstanding and innovative work was done to restore paths above tree line. But Buzz struggled ethically and philosophically with "disturbing" the mountain so much, and he halted alteration of Katahdin by rock removal and trail hardening.

The park's wildlife couldn't have had a better ally than Buzz. He defended predators such as coyotes, and he even went to bat for the tiny shrew. Governor Baxter was a well-known advocate of kindness to animals, and to Buzz, "sanctuary" meant safety for all the park's wildlife. He took the position that no living being in the park was expendable—no matter what the reason—a position some in the scientific research community felt was extreme.

Buzz's perseverance in protecting the Klondike—the purest wilderness in Baxter Park—could turn out to be one of his most important actions. Although included in hiking guidebooks, Buzz wouldn't lead anyone to the thickly forested, boggy tract, although he knew that some researchers with permits and bushwhackers explored the virtually undisturbed area. Buzz didn't even like to talk about the Klondike publicly. If the area received widespread attention, he felt it would be set upon by hikers and changed forever.

The Scientific Forest Management Area was well on its ways to becoming the inspiring example of reforestation and scientific harvesting practices that Percival Baxter envisioned. The credit due Buzz was in hiring the right forester to rectify the negligence and logging abuses committed in the SFMA in the 1980s. Buzz gave SFMA manager Jensen Bissell free rein to make the park proud. Bissell flowered, and so did the SFMA. Because private timberland owners operate to satisfy short-term profits, the SFMA could not be a model for them. However, professional foresters across the Northeast paid attention to the SFMA's display of sustainable management and harvesting practices. Through them, Percival Baxter's scientific forestry vision could influence their management of commercial lands in the future.

▲ ▲ ▲ ▲ ▲

From the 1960s on, Buzz was keen on cleaning up the park's dumps, toilets, and litter, and as director he achieved much in solving the human waste and garbage problems. The waste problem on Katahdin remains. Although Buzz facilitated the installation of a composting toilet at Katahdin Falls on the Hunt Trail to relieve some of the problem, much more needs to be done. He opposed the idea of an enclosed latrine facility downhill from the mountain summit or flying out wastes—the solution in the White Mountains. He viewed it as too costly and conflicting with the wilderness concept. Educating hikers on how they could minimize the problem personally while on the mountain was Buzz's baseline solution.

Following the death of ranger Ralph Heath in 1963, safety was never far from Buzz's mind, and he instituted rules—some thought outrageous—that reined in the freedom of hikers and climbers. Buzz justified the strong emphasis on safety because of the park's difficult, dangerous terrain and visitors' negligence in taking basic precautions. Safety measures didn't stop all park fatalities, but they did protect people from unnecessary risks, especially in bad weather. Equally, Buzz felt the rules helped protect his rangers from having to respond to extreme situations that threatened their own lives.

Buzz's accomplishments covered numerous other areas: limiting the intrusion of technology, such as banning cell phones; no amenities for campers; improvements in handicapped access; and achieving an agreement with Native Americans on spiritual ceremonies in the park.

When it came to hiring, Buzz had commendable instincts. His staff leaders were admired professionally. The knowledge and experience that Jensen Bissell, Chris Drew, Jean Hoekwater, Lester Kenway, and Buzz himself held—collectively almost 135 years—was a significant force in its own right, especially compared to the frequently changing Authority members who served an average of no more than eight years.

The intellectual capital and creativity of senior staff was indispensable to Buzz, providing strong support for his proposals and directives. Visitors from around the world were complimentary on how the park was run and how it looked. Buzz's management couldn't have been as successful without such a talented staff.

Like any family, the park staff disagreed and fought among themselves at times. But when all was sorted out (or not), they were a singular collective band of brothers and sisters. Buzz placed high value on the fact that together theirs was a park culture with a particular history that had unusually strong roots of use, service, and protection.

Besides the legends of directors and certain trustees that Buzz kept alive, he allowed the photo of LeRoy Dudley and Esther Hendrickson to hang on the wall of the Chimney Pond ranger camp and a list to remain up on the wall of the Russell Pond ranger camp with the names of everyone who had been the caretaker there. Those simple "artifacts" were reminders of the long line of rangers that had served before— reminders for everyone who saw them of the privilege it was to be part of the Baxter culture.

▲ ▲ ▲ ▲ ▲

Buzz's management style and the way he achieved his successes were subjects of much discussion publicly and privately. As a prominent public figure with unusual longevity, he was a lightning rod for all kinds of criticisms and second-guessing. Buzz spoke his mind because he felt the stakes were always so high. He had a personal ethic with regard to defending the park that he wouldn't compromise, even though it sometimes put him at odds with the Authority.

Buzz's sense of calling, instilled in him by Percival Baxter and Baxter's vision, resulted in his having such enthusiasm for the park that it was catching to those who were predisposed. Few could be in Buzz's presence for long without wanting to be a park defender too. His passion left him with little tolerance for trustees or anyone else uninterested in park affairs.

Buzz's standard of loyalty—to the park and Percival Baxter—was akin to fealty. He assessed new Authority members to figure out whether he or she would support the right way of doing things—the way he was sure Baxter wanted. If they didn't move into line with Buzz, he cooled toward them or wrote them off.

When the going got tough, one of Buzz's most effective tactics with the Authority or Advisory Committee to tip a decision his way was to bring up Percival Baxter—what the governor had said on the matter or likely would have done. Some Authority and Advisory Committee members, and others involved in park affairs, thought his method was presumptuous and manipulative. Yet because of his personal link with Baxter most people deferred to Buzz—the last director to hold that distinction. That factor alone gave him a potency that the Authority didn't have.

Overall, the trustees rarely overrode Buzz, but when they did it was usually on a proposal such as the West Branch lands use and the Kidney Pond bridge. It wasn't easy for short-termers to buck Buzz. He smartly had built a support system around him to further his agenda— the senior staff, the Baxter family, the Advisory Committee, and park counsel Paul Stern. The West Branch situation was a rare one in which the Authority put all of those other close interests in their place, reminding everyone that the trustees legally possessed the final trump card.

None of the Authorities for whom Buzz worked tried to change his management style, other than to occasionally make suggestions for improving employee morale or the like. The trustees' terms were too short to try to tackle a style makeover, according to Chuck Gadzik.

▲ ▲ ▲ ▲ ▲

Buzz's five "best friends" in helping him achieve his ends were money, deterioration, erosion, safety, and special personal attention. Like a magician, he pulled one from his hat of tricks to get the Authority or Advisory to agree with the direction he wanted to go. He called upon his staff to agree with him that one of those "problems," such as relocating the Nesowadnehunk Field Campground, needed immediate attention, and the Advisory would get to work to investigate and virtually always supported what Buzz wanted.

Eventually, Buzz's command-and-control style proved detrimental to maintaining a harmonious community of employees. Some of his oldest staff were aware of his foibles from his ranger days and judged him harshly after he became director. Mid-level employees who didn't like his second-guessing their work or didn't get the promotions they wanted resented Buzz, accused him of micromanagement, and said he was responsible for their career disappointments. Similarly, Buzz frustrated the AT trail community and other stakeholders with his arbitrary decision-making, such as on trail relocation and shelters. They thought he should have consulted them before he closed Katahdin's North Peak Trail to prevent increased use of the backcountry by IAT; before he relocated the AT around Daicey Pond to deal with run-ins between the thru-hikers and Daicey cabin users; and before he moved the AT lean-tos at Daicey from the field to a wooded roadside area nearer Katahdin Stream—the latter an especially terrible idea to some trail leaders.

In some instances, perhaps Buzz deserved the charges of living in a bygone era because of his "hold the line" style and resistance to modern park administration. However, from his perspective, the human contact with the park to make reservations was a tradition he felt worthy of extending as long as possible. When it was clear that the Internet was too important and powerful a tool to keep at bay, Buzz acquiesced.

He also showed he could compromise on trail work, modernizing the reservation system, accommodating physically challenged visitors, and Native American requests for special use. Yet it was an uncomfortable position for him. For instance, he personally relished hiking but as a manager viewed the trail network as too large and too demanding of financial investment. He was stingy with money and opposed creating new trails beyond 175 miles—a number he felt he had the resources to maintain reasonably well. New trails meant more access, and more access meant more people, and more people meant more impacts everywhere. It all added up in his mind to potential harm to the wilderness character of the park.

Despite his better judgment and under pressure from his rangers, the trail system expanded to 218 miles. He was glad when he had a good reason to close a trail segment because it meant allowing the resource to recover and saving funds for other purposes. An area of complaint against Buzz by outside trail leaders was that the focus on stabilizing Katahdin meant that other mountain peaks suffered from inattention and received less maintenance.

Another area of ongoing criticism was—and still is—the park's lack of alternative transportation for visitors. Then as now, vehicle traffic has been out of control, evidenced by speeding, accidents, and long lines of Katahdin-bound cars at the south gate in the early morning hours. The different Authorities didn't push Buzz for a solution. The park was left with traffic congestion, and rangers were turned into parking lot attendants at the height of the summer visitation.

▲ ▲ ▲ ▲ ▲

For friend and foe, understanding Buzz's legacy means understanding the reality of a park director's job. His responsibility was to hold the big picture, to keep his eye on how the whole enterprise was working and where it was going. Any person in such a position sometimes says one thing and does another behind the scenes because of everyday practicalities and internal politics. When critics found Buzz guilty of contradictory actions (no matter how small) they tried to tarnish his reputation with the incidents, charging that he had oscillating ethics, rather than seeing how relatively insignificant some of the matters were or recognizing the societal or political forces in play.

For example, Buzz was willing to ignore park rules to extend special privileges to certain groups and individuals, such as the Boy Scouts, which rankled detractors and some employees. He was regularly asked by Authority and Advisory members and their friends, state officials, and park regulars for special treatment, such as spur-of-the-moment reservations or a flight into the backcountry. He usually complied, as one-time Authority chairman Jim Tierney advised him to do to avoid trouble when Buzz became director. Perks might seem unfair, Tierney said, but they were just "the way things worked" politically.

The one matter that Buzz refused to budge on was scientific research; he wouldn't listen to anyone else's opinion because he felt so strongly that it was misdirected in the park. He had the power to reject any proposal, and his opposition resulted in limited proposals from the scientific community. As the primary objective of the park was preservation, he felt that researchers could find other "control" areas to do their research and that the scientific community should understand that the park couldn't be all things to all people.

▲ ▲ ▲ ▲ ▲

Former park trustee Bill Vail, who knew Buzz long and well, observed that he had never met anyone like Buzz, especially in public service, "who so narrowly focused on an ideal—a mission. He was so skilled at dealing with the Authority and the Advisory Committee that he was able to move that great big ship. We probably won't see that again. No one will ever have that depth of history with the park and that ability to manage things. He used his power wisely. It was never about Buzz, but always about the park."

The underlying details and commotion over how Buzz maneuvered "that great big ship" will be unimportant to history. He will be remembered for the sweep of his achievements, his guiding principles, and his guardianship of Percival Baxter's legacy.

In the minds of Buzz's many admirers across the country, he is a rare kind of wilderness hero. Clearly, the rigor and sheer force of his style helped to defend the park for decades against the unrelenting forces and egos pressing to undermine its management as a premier wild place unlike any other in New England—and, in some respects, the whole country.

Those who come after Buzz will be challenged by many problems and opportunities—how to deal with park use by commercial guides and outfitters, the size and maintenance demands of the trail network, evolving concepts of wilderness management, opportunities to further expand the park, and the impact of climate change. They would be wise to look to guidance from the past—the vision of Percival Baxter and the commitment of Buzz Caverly.

---

Conversations and communications: Philip Ahrens, Eric Baxter, Sue Bell, Jensen Bissell, John Cashwell, Steve Clark, Tom Doak, Charles FitzGerald, Chuck Gadzik, Alec Giffen, John Loyd, Jon Lund, Dan Martin, John Neff, Jym St. Pierre, Steve Rowe, Ken Spaulding, Paul Stern, Jim Tierney, Bill Vail.

APPENDIX I

# Park Statistics

Year Baxter State Park was created: 1931
Acreage of first park tract: 5,960
Acreage of the park when Percival Baxter died: 201,018
Acreage in 2008: 209,501
Ranking of park in U.S.: fourth largest
Acreage of the wildlife sanctuary: 156,874
Percentage of the park in the wildlife sanctuary: 74.8 percent
Acreage of SFMA: 29, 584
Percentage of the park in SFMA: 14.1 percent
Acreage open to hunting: 52,627 (all but 23,627 in the SFMA)
Percentage of the park open to hunting: 25.1 percent
Park budget in 1960: $39,000
Park budget in 2006/07: $3.1 million
First fee for camping: 10 cents, 1940
Commercial cutting rights extinguished: 1972
Greatest number of park visitors: 1973—99,051
Greatest number of vehicles: 1973—31,807
Number of visitors 2006: 58,416
Number of year-round employees in 1960: 2
Number of year-round employees in 2006: 22
Number of seasonal employees in 1960: 10
Number of seasonal employees in 2006: 37
Number of manmade structures: 100
Miles of main roads: 60
Miles of logging roads in SFMA: 70
Elimination of private leases: 1970
Year snowmobiles were allowed: 1969
Year snowmobiles were banned: 1976
Year snowmobile ban was lifted: 1981
Number of park snowmobiles: 15
Most serious forest fire: 1977
Native American sit-in: 1976

Purchase of Daicey Pond sporting camps: 1969, $45,000
Purchase of Kidney Pond sporting camps: 1968, $52,500
Purchase of Togue Pond lands: 1992, 495 acres, $200,000
Purchase of West Branch lands: 1997, 2,669 acres, $490,000
Purchase of Katahdin Lake lands: 2006,  4,119 acres, $11.5 million,
Miles of trails 1960: 150
Miles of trails 2008: 218
Miles of trails above tree line: 50
Most used Katahdin trail: Chimney Pond
Greatest number of hikers on Katahdin on one day: approximately 500
Most popular moose viewing spot: Sandy Stream Pond
Most popular fish: brook trout
Most remote place in the park: the Klondike
Endangered or threatened listed species: Katahdin arctic butterfly, American pipit,
Northern bog lemming, Roaring Brook mayfly
Number of loons: 33 (most of them on Magatamon Lake)
Number of hunters in SFMA in 1991: 391
Number of hunters in SFMA in 2006: 1,239


First supervisor: Hal Dyer, 1941–42; 1946–50
Supervisor Helon Taylor: 1950–67
Supervisor Harry Kearney: March 1969–May 1971
Director Lee Tibbs: March 1975–October 1981
Buzz Caverly: Supervisor, May 1968–March 1969
    Assistant supervisor, March 1969–June 1971
    Supervisor, June 1971–March 1975
    Assistant supervisor, March 1975–October 1981
    Acting director, October 1981–August 1982
    Director, August 1982–July 2005
Director Jensen Bissell: 2005–
Earliest caretaker: Roy Dudley, Chimney Pond, 1920–42
First park ranger: Dick Holmes, 1937
First chief ranger: Chris Drew, 1982
Longest serving ranger: Chris Drew, 36 years
First woman ranger: Esther Hendrickson
First woman law enforcement officer: Jody Tollett-Browning
First woman park naturalist: Jean Hoekwater
First woman SFMA forest manager: Carol Redelsheimer

Longest-serving Authority member: Austin Wilkins, 1958–72
Longest-serving Authority chairman: Austin Wilkins, 1958–71
Longest-serving Advisory Committee member: Bob Ohler, 1970–95

## APPENDIX II

# SOURCES

Ron Ahlquist
Philip Ahrens
Mel Allen
Tom Allen
Walter Anderson
Ada Angotti
Roger Auclair
Eric Baxter
Ed Beach
Sue Bell
Donat Bisque
Jensen Bissell
George Blackburn
Jerry Bley
Arlene Blum
Bill Bromley
Rufus Brown
Tom Butler
Dabney Caldwell
Ray Campbell
Mike Carpenter
Buzz Caverly
Jan Caverly
Cathy Caverly
Tammy Caverly
Tim Caverly
Steve Caverly
Tom Chase
John Cashwell
Steve Clark
Frank Clukey
Marjorie Cossaboom

Jerry Cossaboom
Bernard Crabtree
Bob Cummings
Brendan Curran
Barbara Downey Day
Ellie Damon
Ron Davis
Tom Deans
Carl Demrow
William Dimpff
Tom Doak
Warren Doyle
Chris Drew
Ed Dwyer
Clint Dyer
Anne Erickson
Jim Erwin
Ken Fink
Charles FitzGerald
Chuck Gadzik
Rob Gardiner
Jim Garland
Dave Getchell Sr.
Dave Gibson
Dan Glidden
Dave Goodrich
Clifford Goodall
Loren Goode
Leon Gorman
Bill Gormely
John Graham
Stuart Guay

Paul Haertel
Vern Haines
Greg Hamer
Jack Hauptmann
Esther Hendrickson
Chris Herter
Jean Hoekwater
Sam Hodder
J. T. Horn
Bob Howes
Al Howlett
Don Hudson
Bill Irwin
Linda Ives
Cathy Johnson
Paul Johnson
Leroy Jones
Harry Kearney
Harry Kennedy
Charlie Kenney
Lester Kenway
George Kerivan
Andrew Ketterer
Angus King
Joan King
Paul Knaut
Elmer Knowlton
Greg Kroll
Dick Leduc
John Loyd
Jon Lund
Virgil Lynch
Pete Madeira
Jay Madeira
Jim Mahony
Gordon Manuel
Connie Baxter Marlowe
Dan Martin
Barry McArthur

Mark McCollough
Phil McGlauflin
Pat McGowan
Linda Rogers McKee
Roxie McLean
Jon Milne
Keith Miller
Darrell Morrow
Gary Morse
Gordon Mott
Tom Mullen
John Neff
Warren Nelson
Steve Norris
Dave O'Toole
Roberta Orestes
Nina Osier
John Paterson
Lonnie Pingree
Ray Porter
Charlie Pray
David Priest
Robert Reynolds
Sarah Redfield
Frank Roberts
Wiggie Robinson
Nik Rogers
Neil Rolde
Steve Rowe
Rodney Sargent
Lee Schepps
Doug Scott
Doris Scott
Rick Scribner
Jack Sheltmire
Bill Silliker
George Smith
Michael Smith
Keith Smith

Dan Sosland
Ken Spaulding
Paul Stern
Bill Stern
Ken Stratton
Jym St. Pierre
Lance Tapley
Jane Thomas
Lee Tibbs
Rob Tice
Jodi Tollett-Browning
Ben Townsend
Gary Trask
Frank Trautmann
Hank Tyler

Bill Vail
John Walker
Dana Wallace
Laura Waterman
Howard Whitcomb
Rupert White
Ed Werler
Eric Wight
Rick Wilcox
Jeanette York
Gabe Williamson
Marcia Williamson
George Wuerthner
Ron Wyre

## SELECTED BIBLIOGRAPHY

The Baxter State Park Archives at the Maine State Archives in Augusta is the official repository of park files. Although incomplete, it is the primary documentary source for park history. Recent documents are housed at Baxter State Park headquarters in Millinocket and sent to the Archives periodically. Buzz Caverly retains personal files from his park years, and the author has extensive document copies gathered from reporting on park events from 1970 to 2005 and from research in state and park files. The Maine State Library holds the collections of Percival Baxter, and his personal correspondence was an important source for this book. All of these file collections were researched extensively for this book.

Buzz Caverly was an invaluable source in recounting his experiences between 1960 and 2005. His memory was prodigious, and he filled in many blanks in park history created by the loss and destruction of documents over the years.

## BOOKS

Anderson, Larry. *Benton MacKaye: Conservationist, Planner, and Creator of the Appalachian Trail.* Baltimore: The Johns Hopkins University Press, 2002.

Clark, Stephen. *Katahdin: A Guide to Baxter State Park and Katahdin.* Shapleigh, Maine: Clark Books, 2000.

Girvan, William R. *In Beyond Katahdin.* Self-published, 1982.

Gorman, Leon. *L. L. Bean: The Making of an American Icon.* Boston: Harvard Business School Publishing, 2006.

Hakola, John W. *Legacy of a Lifetime: The Story of Baxter State Park.* Camden, Maine: Wheelwright Books, 1981.

Neff, John. *Katahdin: An Historic Journey.* Boston: Appalachian Mountain Club, 2006.

Rolde, Neil. *The Baxters of Maine: Downeast Visionaries.* Gardiner, Maine: Tilbury House, Publishers, 1997.

Scee, Trudy. *In the Deeds We Trust: Baxter State Park 1970–1994.* Standish, Maine: Tower Publishing, 1999.

Waterman, Laura and Guy. *Forest and Crag: A History of Hiking, Trail Blazing, and Adventure in the Northeast Mountains.* Boston: Appalachian Mountain Club. 1989.
————. *Wilderness Ethics: Preserving the Ethics of Wildness.* Woodstock, Vermont: The Countryman Press, 1991.
Wilkins, Austin H., *Ten Million Acres of Timber: The Remarkable Story of Forest Protection in the Maine Forestry District (1909–1972).* Woolwich, Maine: TBW Books, 1978.
Whitcomb, Howard R. *Percival P. Baxter's Vision for Baxter State Park,* Vols. I–IV. Bangor, Maine: Friends of Baxter State Park, 2005.

JOURNALS, MAGAZINES AND NEWSPAPERS

Allen, Mel. "The Governor and the Ranger." *Yankee,* November 1988, pp. 100–07, 162–64, 166, 168–70, 172–75.
*Appalachia.* Journal of the Appalachian Mountain Club
*Bangor Daily News*
Kemsley, William Jr. "Three Decades of Protecting Our Nation's Trails." *American Hiker,* Fall, 2006.
*Maine Times*
*Portland Press Herald*
Smith, Edmund Ware. *Field & Stream,* April 1, 1959, pp. 65–67, 102, 123–37; April 1, 1962, pp. 35–37, 93–95, 165; December 1, 1965, pp. 10–11, 58–60.

## INDEX